THE WORKS OF JONATHAN EDWARDS

VOLUME 16

Harry S. Stout, General Editor

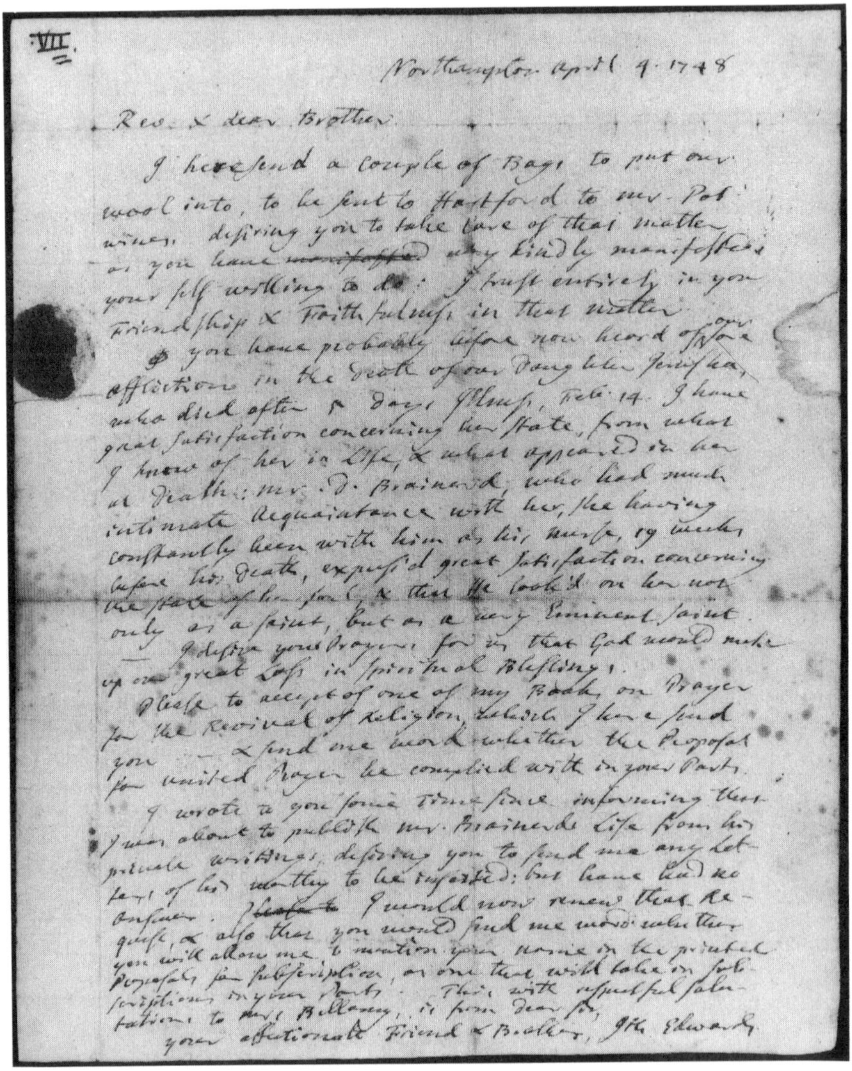

VII

Northampton April 4. 1748

Rev. & dear Brother

I here send a couple of Bags to put our wool into, to be sent to Hartford to Mr. Potwines, desiring you to take care of that matter as you have ~~manifested~~ very kindly manifested your self willing to do: I trust entirely in your Friendship & Faithfulness in that matter.

You have probably before now heard of our sore affliction in the Death of our Daughter Jerusha, who died after 5 days illness, Feb. 14. I have great satisfaction concerning her state, from what I knew of her in Life, & what appeared in her at Death: Mr. D. Brainerd, who had much intimate Acquaintance with her, she having constantly been with him as his nurse, 19 weeks before his Death, express'd great satisfaction concerning the state of her soul, & that he look'd on her not only as a saint, but as a very Eminent saint.

I desire your Prayers for us that God would make up our great Loss in spiritual Blessings.

Please to accept of one of my Books on Prayer for the Revival of Religion, which I here send you — & send me word whether the Proposal for united Prayer be complied with in your Parts.

I wrote to you some time since informing that I was about to publish Mr. Brainerds Life from his private writings, desiring you to send me any Letters of his writing to be inserted; but have had no Answer. ~~Please to~~ I would now renew that Request, & also that you would send me word whether you will allow me to mention your name in the printed Proposals for subscription, as one that will take in subscriptions in your Parts. This with respectful salutations to Mrs. Bellamy, is from dear Sir,

your affectionate Friend & Brother, Jon. Edwards

Jonathan Edwards' letter to Joseph Bellamy, April 4, 1748 (Letter No. 84), Beinecke Rare Book and Manuscript Library, Yale University. A typical though brief example of Edwards' correspondence, this letter discusses a business matter, the death of one of Edwards' daughters, the Concert of Prayer, and his effort to write a biography of David Brainerd.

JONATHAN EDWARDS

Letters and Personal Writings

EDITED BY
GEORGE S. CLAGHORN

PROFESSOR OF PHILOSOPHY
WEST CHESTER UNIVERSITY

New Haven and London

YALE UNIVERSITY PRESS, 1998

Funds for editing The Works of Jonathan Edwards
*have been provided by The Pew Charitable Trusts, The
Henry Luce Foundation, Inc., Lilly Endowment, Inc., and
The L. J. Skaggs and Mary C. Skaggs Foundation.*

*Published with assistance from The Exxon Education
Foundation.*

*Set in Baskerville type by The Composing Room of
Michigan, Inc., Grand Rapids, Michigan. Printed in the
United States of America by Vail-Ballou Press,
Binghamton, New York.*

Library of Congress Cataloging-in-Publication Data

Edwards, Jonathan, 1703–1758.
    [Selections. 1998]
    *Letters and personal writings / Jonathan Edwards ;
edited by George S. Claghorn.*
        *p.   cm. — (The works of Jonathan Edwards ;
v. 16)*
    *Includes bibliographical references and indexes.
    ISBN 0–300–07295-3 (cloth : alk. paper)
    1. Edwards, Jonathan, 1703–1758—
Correspondence. 2. Congregational churches—New
England—Clergy—Correspondence.
I. Claghorn, George S.   II. Title.   III. Series:
Edwards, Jonathan, 1703–1758.   Works.   1957 ;
v. 16.
BX7260.E3A4   1998
285.8'092—dc21
[B]   97–26557
                                                        CIP*

*A catalogue record for this book is available from the
British Library.*

*The paper in this book meets the guidelines for permanence
and durability of the Committee on Production Guidelines
for Book Longevity of the Council on Library Resources.*

10 9 8 7 6 5 4 3 2 1

PREVIOUSLY PUBLISHED

PAUL RAMSEY, ed., *Freedom of the Will*

JOHN E. SMITH, ed., *Religious Affections*

CLYDE A. HOLBROOK, ed., *Original Sin*

C. C. GOEN, ed., *The Great Awakening*

STEPHEN J. STEIN, ed., *Apocalyptic Writings*

WALLACE E. ANDERSON, ed., *Scientific and Philosophical Writings*

NORMAN PETTIT, ed., *The Life of David Brainerd*

PAUL RAMSEY, ed., *Ethical Writings*

JOHN F. WILSON, ed., *A History of the Work of Redemption*

WILSON H. KIMNACH, ed., *Sermons and Discourses, 1720–1723*

WALLACE E. ANDERSON AND MASON I. LOWANCE, eds.,
     Typological Writings

DAVID D. HALL, ed., *Ecclesiastical Writings*

THOMAS A. SCHAFER, ed., *The "Miscellanies," a–500*

KENNETH P. MINKEMA, ed., *Sermons and Discourses, 1723–1729*

STEPHEN J. STEIN, ed., *Notes on Scripture*

CONTENTS

Contents

ILLUSTRATIONS

ABBREVIATIONS

The following is a list of abbreviations for libraries and book titles frequently cited in this volume. Titles referred to by Edwards in the letters themselves have been cited in full (in the notes) at their first appearance and have been given short titles thereafter.

AAS | American Antiquarian Society, Worcester, Massachusetts.

Alderman Library | New England Company Letterbook, University of Virginia, Charlottesville, Virginia.

Alexander | Alexander, Archibald. *Biographical Sketches of the Founder, and Principal Alumni of the Log College.* Princeton, 1845; London, 1968 (*The Log College*).

ALS | Autograph letter, signed.

Baker Library | Dartmouth College, Hanover, New Hampshire.

Ballantine | "Journal of the Reverend John Ballantine, 1737–1774." Westfield Atheneum, Westfield, Massachusetts.

Beinecke Library | Beinecke Rare Book and Manuscript Library, Yale University, New Haven, Connecticut.

Bellamy | "Letters of and to Joseph Bellamy, 1739–1787." Transcribed by Richard Webster. PCUSADH.

BPL | Boston Public Library, Boston, Massachusetts.

BWNL | *Boston Weekly News-Letter.* Boston, 1704–1776.

Boyd and Taylor | Boyd, Julian P., and Robert J. Taylor, eds. *The Susquehannah Company.* Ithaca, N.Y., 1962–1971.

Burr | Karlsen, Carol F., and Laurie Crumpacker, eds. *The Journal of Esther Edwards Burr, 1754–1757.* New Haven, Connecticut, 1984.

CHS	Connecticut Historical Society, Hartford, Connecticut.
CL	Congregational Library, Boston, Massachusetts.
CMH	Robe, James, ed. *The Christian Monthly History.* Edinburgh, 1743–46.
CVHM	Connecticut Valley Historical Museum, Springfield, Massachusetts.
DEX	Dexter, Franklin B. *Biographical Sketches of the Graduates of Yale College, with Annals of the College History.* 6 vols. New York, 1885–1912.
Dexter, *History*	Dexter, Franklin B., ed. *Documentary History of Yale University, 1701–1745.* New Haven, Connecticut, 1916.
Dwight ed.	Dwight, Sereno E., ed. *The Works of President Edwards.* 10 vols. New York, 1830.
Faust and Johnson	Faust, Clarence H., and Thomas H. Johnson, eds. *Jonathan Edwards: Representative Selections.* New York, 1935.
Firestone Library	Princeton University, Princeton, New Jersey.
Forbes Library	Northampton, Massachusetts.
Hopkins	Hopkins, Samuel. *The Life and Character of the Late Reverend, Learned and Pious Mr. Jonathan Edwards.* Boston, 1765.
Houghton Library	Harvard University, Cambridge, Massachusetts.
HSF	Hartford Seminary Foundation, Hartford, Connecticut.
HSP	Historical Society of Pennsylvania, Philadelphia, Pennsylvania.
JMHR	*Journals of the Massachusetts House of Representatives.* 50 vols. Boston, 1919–1990.
Maclean	Maclean, John. *History of the College of New Jersey.* 2 vols. Philadelphia, 1877; New York, 1969.
MAR	Massachusetts State Archives, Columbia Point, Boston, Massachusetts.
MHS	Massachusetts Historical Society, Boston, Massachusetts.

NEQ	*New England Quarterly.* Boston, 1928–.
Noble	Noble, William B., H. F. C. Heagey, and Musetta E. McClellan. *A History of Faggs Manor United Presbyterian Church, 1730–1980.* Cochranville, Pennsylvania, 1980.
NYHS	New-York Historical Society, New York, New York.
NYPL	New York Public Library, New York, New York.
Parmenter	Parmenter, C. O. *History of Pelham, Massachusetts (1738–1898).* Amherst, Massachusetts, 1898.
Parsons	Parsons, Usher. *The Life of Sir William Pepperrell.* Boston, 1855; 1856.
PCUSADH	Presbyterian Church (U.S.A.) Department of History, Philadelphia, Pennsylvania.
Pilcher	Pilcher, George W., ed. *The Reverend Samuel Davies Abroad: The Diary of a Journey to England and Scotland, 1753–55.* Urbana, Illinois, 1967.
Pilcher, *SD*	Pilcher, George W. *Samuel Davies: Apostle of Dissent in Colonial Virginia.* Knoxville, Tennessee, 1971.
RIHS	Rhode Island Historical Society, Providence, Rhode Island.
SIB	Sibley, John L., et al. *Sibley's Harvard Graduates; Biographical Sketches of Those Who Attended Harvard College.* Cambridge, Massachusetts, 1873–.
Sprague	Sprague, William Buell. *Annals of the American Pulpit.* 9 vols. New York, 1859–69; 1969.
Sterling Library	Sterling Memorial Library, Manuscripts and Archives, Yale University, New Haven, Connecticut.
Stoughton	Stoughton, John A. *Windsor Farmes.* Hartford, Connecticut, 1883.
Trask Library	Franklin Trask Library, Andover Newton Theological School, Newton Centre, Massachusetts.
Trumbull	Trumbull, James Russell. *History of Northampton, Massachusetts, from Its Settlement in 1654.* 2 vols. Northampton, 1898–1902. (Vol. 3, "Genealogy," in typescript at Forbes Library.)

Webster	Webster, Richard. *A History of the Presbyterian Church in America.* Philadelphia, 1857.
Wellwood	Wellwood, Sir Henry Moncrieff. *Account of the Life and Writings of John Erskine, D.D.* Edinburgh, 1818.
Whitefield	Whitefield, George. *Journals.* 6 vols. London, 1770–72; rev. 1960.
Winslow	Winslow, Ola E. *Jonathan Edwards, 1703–1758.* New York, 1940.
Works	*The Works of Jonathan Edwards.* New Haven, Connecticut, 1957–
Wright	Wright, Wyllis E. *Colonel Ephraim Williams: A Documentary Life.* Pittsfield, Massachusetts, 1970.

NOTE TO THE READER

Preparation of the Text

The text of Jonathan Edwards is reproduced in this Edition as he wrote it in manuscript, or, if he published it himself, as it was printed in the first edition. In order to present this text to modern readers as practically readable, several technical adjustments have been made. Those which can be addressed categorically are as follows:

1. All spelling is regularized and conformed to that of *Webster's Third New International Dictionary,* a step that does not involve much more than removing the "u" from "colour" or "k" from "publick" since Edwards was a good speller, used relatively modern spelling, and generally avoided "y" contractions. His orthographic contractions and abbreviations, such as ampersands, "call'd," and "thems." are spelled out, though pronounced contractions, such as "han't" and "ben't," are retained.

2. There is no regular punctuation in most of Edwards' manuscripts and where it does exist, as in the earliest sermons, it tends to be highly erratic. Editors take into account Edwards' example in punctuation and related matters, but all punctuation is necessarily that of the editor, including paragraph divisions (especially in some notebooks such as the "Miscellanies") and the emphasizing devices of italics and capitalization. In reference to capitalization, it should be noted that pronouns referring to the deity are lower case except in passages where Edwards confusingly mixes "he's" referring to God and man: here capitalization of pronouns referring to the deity sorts out the references for the reader.

3. Numbered heads designate important structures of argument in Edwards' sermons, notebooks, and treatises. Numbering, including spelled-out numbers, has been regularized and corrected where necessary. Particularly in the manuscript sermon texts, numbering has been clarified by the use of systematic schemes of heads and subheads in accordance with eighteenth-century homiletical form, a practice

similar to modern analytical outline form. Thus the series of subordinated head number forms, 1, (1), *1*, a, (a), in the textual exegesis, and the series, I, *First,* 1, (1), *1*, a, (a), in Doctrine and Application divisions, make it possible to determine sermon head relationships at a glance.

4. Textual intervention to regularize Edwards' citation of Scripture includes the correction of erroneous citation, the regularizing of citation form (including the standardization of book abbreviations), and the completion of quotations which Edwards' textual markings indicate should be completed (as in preaching).

5. Omissions and lacunae in the manuscript text are filled by insertions in square brackets ([ ]); repeated phrases sometimes represented by Edwards with a long dash are inserted in curly brackets ({ }). In all cases of uncertain readings, annotation gives notice of the problem. Markings in the text designate whole word units even when only a few letters are at issue.

6. Minor slips of the pen or obvious typographical errors are corrected without annotation. Likewise, Edwards' corrections, deletions, and internal shifts of material are observed but not noted unless of substantive interest.

7. Quotations made by the editor from the Bible (AV) and other secondary sources are printed *verbatim ac literatim.* Edwards' quotations from such sources are often rather free but are not corrected and are not annotated as such unless significant omissions or distortions are involved.

The letters and personal writings present an array of editorial challenges. For information on such matters, please consult the note on the text at the conclusion of the introduction as well as the headnotes to each letter.

Acknowledgements

I am indebted to Harry S. Stout, our General Editor, who made this volume a reality, for his gifted leadership and outstanding contributions. The encouragement and guidance of Perry Miller has been an inspiring legacy at all times. I also greatly appreciate John E. Smith, who has been to me a stalwart over the years. Another unforgettable friend and essential benefactor is Paul Ramsey. With his remarkable editorial skills, Kenneth Minkema has provided helpful assistance, as have his able staff members, Ava Chamberlain and Douglas Sweeney. Throughout the preparation of this book, I have richly benefited from the encyclopedic learning, wise insights, and fine spirit of Thomas A. Schafer. Wilson Kimnach and Stephen J. Stein have likewise been most helpful in many ways. Susan Laity of Yale University Press expertly copyedited the manuscript.

Hosts of people in many libraries have given generous, cheerful assistance to the letters project. To one and all, I offer my deepest gratitude. Marjorie G. Wynne deserves special mention for support over and above the call of duty, from the beginning. Ellis O'Neal and Diana Yount merit accolades, as perfect hosts and masterful assistants. Elise Bernier-Feeley, Stanley Greenberg, Lawrence Wikander, Clifford K. Shipton, A. E. J. Hollander, James Ritchie, and Iain Brown comprise another strong cadre of expediters. Those who graciously presented copies of their works include Malcolm Freiberg, Leo Flaherty, Mrs. Robert Raymond, Alexander P. Clark, M. Halsey Thomas, Floyd Reinhart, M. X. Lesser, and William Kellaway. It is a pleasure to recognize, among those who "labored more abundantly," these student helpers: Jacquelyn Hahn, Harry Armstrong, Tara Hottenstein, Josephine Singer, Richard Graugh, and Sean M. Lucas. By tireless efforts, Lorrayne McGrath and AnnMarie Smith brought the manuscript from raw materials to finished product. Finally, I thank Shirley Haines Claghorn, for unstinting, whole-hearted assistance, all the way.

Many libraries, repositories, and individuals have contributed to this volume by providing permission to publish the texts that comprise it. The great majority of letters are housed at Andover Newton Theological School's Franklin Trask Library and Yale University's Beinecke Rare Book and Manuscript Library. Other holding institutions and individuals include: American Antiquarian Society, Worcester, Massachusetts; Boston Public Library, Rare Books and Manuscripts, Boston, Massachusetts; the Bostonian Society, Boston, Massachusetts; Congregational Library of the American Congregational Association, Boston, Massachusetts; Connecticut Historical Society, Hartford, Connecticut; Connecticut Valley Historical Museum, William Pynchon Memorial Building, Springfield, Massachusetts; Dartmouth College, Baker Library, Special Collections, Dartmouth, New Hampshire; Drew University, Rose Library, Madison, New Jersey; Edinburgh University Library, Special Collections, Edinburgh; Mr. John H. Edwards, Woodbridge, Connecticut; Edwards Church, Northampton, Massachusetts; Forbes Library, Northampton, Massachusetts; Mr. John F. Gately, Marlboro, Massachusetts; Hartford Seminary Foundation,

Case Memorial Library, Hartford, Connecticut; Harvard University, Houghton Library, Manuscript Department, Cambridge, Massachusetts; Haverford College, Magill Library, Special Collections, Haverford, Pennsylvania; Historical Society of Pennsylvania, Philadelphia, Pennsylvania; Lambeth Palace Library, London; Library of Congress, Washington, D.C.; Maine Historical Society, Portland, Maine; University of Manchester, John Rylands University Library, University of Manchester, Manchester; Commonwealth of Massachusetts, Massachusetts State Archives at Columbus Point, Boston, Massachusetts; Massachusetts Historical Society, Boston, Massachusetts; National Library of Scotland, Edinburgh; New-York Historical Society, New York, New York; New York Public Library, Rare Books and Manuscripts Division, Astor, Lenox and Tilden Foundations, New York, New York; Pierpont Morgan Library, New York, New York; Presbyterian Church (U.S.A.) Department of History, Philadelphia, Pennsylvania; Princeton University, Firestone Library, Rare Books and Special Collections, Scheide Library (with permission from Mr. William H. Scheide), and Seeley Mudd Library, Princeton, New Jersey; Rhode Island Historical Society, Providence, Rhode Island; and Yale University, Sterling Memorial Library, Manuscripts and Archives, New Haven, Connecticut.

Support for this volume and for the entire edition has been provided by the Pew Charitable Trusts, the Henry Luce Foundation, Inc., Lilly Endowment, Inc., and the L.J. Skaggs and Mary C. Skaggs Foundation. Sabbaticals and other assistance from West Chester University and Eastern College are gratefully acknowledged, as is a grant from the Penrose Fund of the American Philosophical Society.

LETTERS

INTRODUCTION

This volume assembles for the first time all the extant locatable letters by Jonathan Edwards, along with his major personal writings. The 236 letters published here were compiled during a search that spanned many years and several countries. Such letters as have been printed in previous editions were sometimes incomplete and inaccurately transcribed. This volume corrects the flaws of past editions by providing newly transcribed, edited, and annotated texts, making it an unprecedented resource for understanding Edwards, his times, and his personal connections. Furthermore, 116 of the texts presented below have never been published or have not been reprinted since Edwards' death. These include family letters, transatlantic communications, detailed accounts of Edwards' struggles with opponents at Stockbridge, and his only known statement on slavery. Together, they supply incomparable new information about Edwards' life and thought.

The letters and personal writings show the private, human Edwards, the man behind the treatises and sermons. Edwards emerges from these writings not as an austere and aloof scholar but as an alert observer, keenly interested in both local and worldwide events, and as an astute reader of persons and situations. The letters, in particular, reveal many aspects of Edwards' personal world. They range in mood from the aggressively argumentative to the gently comforting to the intellectually and spiritually searching.

Although Edwards is universally known for his profound thought and for perhaps the greatest preaching, or sermon compositions, in American history, little note has been taken of his letter writing. That this is an oversight of some importance is demonstrated by the following collection; moreover, it is an oversight Edwards himself might have objected to as showing neglect of what was in his time already a genre of intellectual and literary significance within the transatlantic literary community.

Letter-writing was necessary for those who lived far apart in an age before the conveniences of modern transportation and communications. In the eighteenth century, moreover, preoccupation with community and a new social interaction among hitherto exclusive groups created a confluence between the informal essay and personal communication that resulted in the medium designated epistolary. Edwards' contemporary Benjamin Franklin, perhaps the most astute exploiter of cultural trends in the history of American civilization, did not become a master of several epistolary forms for nothing. From the brilliant familial letters of Abigail Adams or the huge intellectual and political correspondence of Thomas Jefferson to Franklin's various forms of informal address, the American scene was alive with new modes of personal expression during the eighteenth century.

Like most early American cultural trends, the epistolary vogue began in Europe, particularly England, where during the seventeenth and early eighteenth centuries the familiar essay, established by the complementary sixteenth-century influences of Montaigne's *Essais* (1580) and Francis Bacon's *Essayes* (1597), evolved through periodical contributions, such as Jonathan Swift's Bickerstaff pamphlets, by skilled writers; it was perfected in Addison and Steele's *Tatler* and *Spectator*, periodical publications in which both entertaining informality and a personal voice that virtually defined a character gave immediacy to moral and political suasion. A new flexibility and nuanced expression entered the language of intellectual and social comment; likewise, the immediacy of direct personal expression became a conscious style—exemplified in the new trend for "epistolary" novels like those of Samuel Richardson and Tobias Smollett. Even poets chose the familiar letter as an appropriate vehicle for verse, as in Pope's "Epistle to Dr. Arbuthnot."

In New England's provincial culture, the epistolary mode may have received some reinforcement from the conversion narrative and other early reports that stressed the experience of an individual through personal narrative. Certainly some of Edwards' most striking compositions were delivered in the epistolary mode: his letter to Paul Dudley describing the flying spider (Oct. 21, 1723), his letter to Benjamin Colman detailing the Northampton awakenings (May 30, 1735), and his "Personal Narrative," which was probably part of a letter to Aaron Burr (Dec. 14, 1740). These documents demonstrate not only the appropriateness of the letter as a practical device but also Edwards' sense of the epistolary conventions of his day. Jonathan Edwards was neither an Abigail Adams nor a Benjamin Franklin as a letter writer, but he everywhere displays a keen sense of the epistolary conventions respecting subjective involvement, a carefully modulated acknowl-edgment of the reader, and a voice precisely adapted to the subject at hand.

Within this volume, Edwards is revealed engaged in all the issues he faced in life, and each letter is precisely adjusted to subject, recipient, and context. A number of these pieces are essays, some quite formal, but others are sinewy directives, terse reports, or paternal notes to loved ones. In all cases, there is a striking balance of precise detail and comprehensive focus. Perhaps most surprising is the political voice of Edwards as he strives to defend and improve the Stockbridge mission: in these letters he is not a *character*, in the manner of Franklin, but he modulates his voice wonderfully for different audiences and issues. An inhabitant of the epistolary culture of the eighteenth century, Ed-wards was comfortable and effective within the genre, and as aware of it *as* a genre as he was of the sermon or treatise. Today, by reading through the letters in sequence, one can witness a many-sided Ed-wards mediating the worlds of thought and action with remarkable grace and fluency.

Edwards' greatest means of expression was his pen. As he told the Trustees of the College of New Jersey in his letter of October 19, 1757, "So far as I myself am able to judge of what talents I have, for benefiting my fellow creatures by word, I think I can write better than I can speak." Seated in his study with quill in hand, he collabo-rated and contended with many of the brightest minds of his day, including educational, political, and military leaders. Although the extant record represents only a fraction of the letters he wrote, it amply confirms his power to attract and persuade. In addition, the letters record his dealings with ordinary people: family, neighbors, congregations, and fellow clergy. They also illustrate his relationships with disciples, such as Joseph Bellamy, who perpetuated his legacy. At the same time, Edwards' letters reveal his shortcomings and flaws, such as his self-righteousness and pride and his sometimes self-destructive adherence to duty.

The majority of Edwards' extant letters were written during the late 1740s and 1750s. Thus, they are perhaps most valuable in revealing his perspective on the final conflict with his Northampton congrega-tion, his participation in the transatlantic revivalistic network, and his ministry in frontier Stockbridge. Leading recipients include Bellamy, his student and confidant, who received twenty letters, and Thomas Foxcroft of Boston's First Church, Edwards' literary agent and editor, to whom Edwards wrote eighteen letters. Among foreign correspondents, Scottish minister John Erskine leads with eleven letters. Significantly, nearly half of the letters printed here were written while Edwards was at Stockbridge, providing a crucial source for the study not only of Edwards but also of missiology and Anglo-Indian relations.

Childhood, College, and Early Ministry

A scant eight letters predate Edwards' arrival at Northampton in 1726. Though few in number, they present pictures of Edwards at significant moments of his life. They include accounts of church and community activities and rare glimpses into his college life, and end with his first essay intended for publication, which was cast in the form of a letter.

Edwards' letter to his sister Mary, dated May 10, 1716—the earliest document by him known to have survived—quickly establishes the "pouring out of the Spirit of God" as a central theme in his life. At the time, Edwards' hometown of East Windsor, Connecticut, was experiencing one of the many awakenings it would see under his father, the Reverend Timothy Edwards. In his *Faithful Narrative* of 1737, Jonathan would recall that awakenings had been seen "four or five" previous times in "my honored father's parish, which has in times past been a place favored with occurrences of this nature above any on the western side of New England, excepting Northampton." Later in the century, Connecticut clergyman and historian Benjamin Trumbull wrote that "no minister in the colony had been favored with greater success" than Timothy Edwards.[1] Under his father's tutelage, Jonathan learned the importance of revivals as a mark of successful ministry.

Besides being a revivalist, Timothy was also a strong teacher. Assisted by his wife, Esther Stoddard Edwards, and their daughters, he prepared local boys for college. Such was the reputation the Edwards parsonage school achieved for excellence that matriculating students coming from there were rarely given entrance examinations. In a letter to his father of July 24, 1719, Jonathan related the "very short" and successful examination of Isaac Stiles (father of Ezra Stiles), a student of Timothy's.

The school for which Timothy prepared his students was Connecticut's Collegiate School, later Yale College, founded in 1701. When

---

1. *Works*, 4, 154; Benjamin Trumbull, *A Complete History of Connecticut, Civil and Ecclesiastical, from the Emigration of its First Planters, from England in the Year 1630, to the Year 1764; and to the Close of the Indian Wars* (2 vols. New Haven, 1818), 2, 140.

Jonathan entered in 1716, the towns of Saybrook, New Haven, and Wethersfield were vying to become the college's permanent location. Jonathan was sent to Wethersfield, not only because of its proximity but because his relative, Elisha Williams, was headmaster there. Jonathan acquitted himself well. In 1718, Timothy wrote to his daughter Mary that "your Brother Jonathan . . . hath a very Good name at Weathersfield, both as to his Carriage, and his Learning."[2]

In September 1718 the Connecticut General Assembly ordered all students to take up residence at the newly built college hall in New Haven, and in the following month Edwards moved there. However, doubts about the orthodoxy of tutor Samuel Johnson caused Edwards and many of his classmates to return to Wethersfield. As Edwards' letter of March 26, 1719, informs us, Johnson was removed in March by the Trustees, allowing for the disaffected students' re-admittance in June. In his letter of July 24 to his father, Edwards praised the new rector, Timothy Cutler. Under his "very good spirit of government," Edwards finished his baccalaureate studies in New Haven and was chosen to deliver the valedictory address at the 1720 commencement ceremonies.

Edwards started graduate studies in the fall of 1720, but trouble soon arose. His roommate and cousin Elisha Mix, a freshman, refused to assist Edwards in the college buttery, even though the task was a condition of his living with Edwards. Edwards drafted a report to Mix's father, Stephen, the minister of Wethersfield, asking that Elisha be brought into line. Upon learning of the situation, Timothy also sent a letter detailing his criticisms to Stephen. The two compositions share a spirit of admonition and plainspokenness that was to characterize Edwards' own letter-writing for the rest of his life.

Conditions at the college were apparently never entirely peaceful for Edwards. In early 1721 the undergraduates (Isaac Stiles among them) refused to eat any longer at the commons. The "cabal," Edwards informed his father, was "speedily quashed," but it was followed by increasingly mischievous behavior among the students. Edwards proudly reported to his father that he was "perfectly free of all their janglings." Yet his statement that there were "no *new* quarrels" between himself and the other students reveals previous friction.

From August 1722 until May 1723 Edwards ministered to a small Presbyterian church in New York City. For this period, Edwards' per-

---

2. Timothy Edwards to Mary Edwards, Jan. 27, 1717/18, Trask Library.

sonal writings, particularly his "Resolutions" and "Diary," as well as his sermons, are the best sources for following his activities. Only one important piece of correspondence from the period survives. In late 1722 the town of Bolton, Connecticut, very likely at the urging of Timothy Edwards, was trying to procure Jonathan as its pastor. During an earlier visit home, Edwards had met with representatives of the Bolton church and promised to consider their offer. On December 10, he wrote a letter to the Bolton church committee, in care of his father, which was amiable but noncommittal. In his own cover letter, Timothy put a more optimistic interpretation on his son's reply, saying that he saw nothing "discouraging" in it. Apparently, Timothy relished the idea of having his son settled in a town close at hand.

Edwards did minister at Bolton but not until after he had returned home in May 1723 and completed his master's degree in September. Now a fully qualified member of the intellectual elite, he sought ways to make his presence known. The first effort came through his father's connections. Judge Paul Dudley of Massachusetts, a classmate of Timothy's at Harvard College and a member of the Royal Society, collected scientific observations for the Society's *Philosophical Transactions.* Among his correspondents was Timothy, who sent a report, published in 1724, about a "pompion" (pumpkin) vine that produced a prodigious amount of fruit.[3] In response to Dudley's invitation to send more information, Timothy wrote to him on October 18, 1723, promising to do so. He also prompted Jonathan to write up his observations concerning insects. Thus the stage was set for the famous "Spider Letter," which scholars have pointed to both as an illustration of Edwards' powers as a scientist and for the imagery that he continued to use in sermons and other writings.

Awakenings and Aftermath

Nearly a decade passes before the letter record resumes, during which time Edwards succeeded to the pastorship of Northampton and oversaw an awakening in his church during 1734 and 1735. The juxtaposition in the surviving letters of Edwards' scientific reflections on spiders (1723) and his account to Benjamin Colman of the revival in Northampton (1735) well illustrates how in the intervening years pastoral and apologetical theology had come to take up an increasing proportion of Edwards' time. Over the next ten to twelve years, the

---

3. See *Works,* 6, 31–32.

range of Edwards' letter-writing increased dramatically to include a number of issues and correspondents. But revivalistic concerns remained central.

Edwards' letter of May 30, 1735, to Colman was the nucleus of one of the most significant writings of early American history, *A Faithful Narrative*. After an extract of Edwards' brief summary was published by Colman as an appendix to a collection of his uncle William Williams' sermons, Edwards was asked to write a fuller version, which was published in London. The letters of May 19, 1737, and May 2, 1738, to Colman mention, respectively, Isaac Watts and John Guyse's reception of the *Narrative* and the subsequent, corrected Boston edition. Eventually, the work was translated into several languages and served as an international manual for revivalism.[4]

Edwards' excitement over the *Faithful Narrative* was cut short by the controversy surrounding attempts to settle Robert Breck at Springfield in the latter half of 1735. For Edwards, Breck embodied the rise of Arminianism in Hampshire County that threatened further revivals—not to mention Calvinist orthodoxy. Contrary to Edwards' later claims that he was not involved in the affair, he co-signed a series of Hampshire Association communications from August 1735 supporting Breck's opposers within the Springfield church. Despite these measures, and despite Edwards' co-authorship of a printed defense of the Hampshire County ministers' opposition, Breck was ordained with the help of ministers from Boston and became an influential figure in Hampshire County religious life.[5]

In later years, Edwards pointed to the growth of Arminianism in western Massachusetts as a specific cause of the decline of the revival spirit. More generally, however, he felt that Arminianism was only a part of a general declension in religion. In the aftermath of the awakening of 1734–35, Edwards lamented how quickly his people, confident in their former conversion experiences, returned to their former sinfulness. When, on March 13, 1737, the gallery of the crowded Northampton meetinghouse crashed to the ground during the worship service with no loss of life, Edwards interpreted it as an instance of "divine preservation," by which God meant to warn the backsliding townspeople. In his description of the event to Colman on March 19, as well as in his letters of May 19, 1737, and May 27, 1738, Edwards

---

4. On the publication history of the *Faithful Narrative*, see *Works, 4*, 32–46.

5. For a description of the Breck affair, see *Works, 12*, 4–17; and for the text of *A Letter to the Author of the Pamphlet Called an Answer to the Hampshire Narrative*, see ibid., 93–163.

connects his church's and the colony's diminishing fortunes with an ebb in religion.

But a new star was on the horizon that promised to brighten the spiritual darkness over the Anglo-American world. Edwards' letter inviting George Whitefield to come to Northampton, dated February 12, 1740, marked an important milestone in Edwards' life, for it propelled him into the international world of evangelism in a way that publication of the *Faithful Narrative* had not. As his anticipation of Whitefield's arrival grew, so did his interest in revival news and his "hope that God is about to accomplish glorious things for his church." The letter of June 1, 1740, to Josiah Willard, Secretary of Massachusetts, for example, revealed Edwards' curiosity about revivals outside the colonies. Yet in the wake of the revival of 1734–35 he was plagued by self-doubts. The marked and seemingly irreversible drop in spirituality that he saw in churchmembers who had supposedly been converted made Edwards doubt his talent as a minister. As he confided to Eleazar Wheelock on October 9, 1740, he looked to the preaching of Whitefield "for good to my soul, and the souls of my people."

In the midst of revival concerns, Edwards was also caught up briefly in a mysterious controversy over slavery. Apparently, he came to the defense of a "pastor" (possibly Edwards himself) who was denounced by members of his congregation for owning slaves. Slave ownership was accepted in the Edwards households; Timothy and Jonathan saw slavery as part of the ordained order, and during their adult lives each owned at least one slave. In an unusual letter draft—the only known statement from Jonathan on the subject—he supports slave ownership under conformity to provincial law but opposes participation in the slave trade that deprived free Africans of their liberty. His position was apparently the result of millennial expectations that looked to the Christianization of all nations of the world. The slave trade, in his opinion, could only thwart the spread of the gospel.

Slavery, money, and other concerns were part of Edwards' day-to-day life, but his main focus was on furthering the revival spirit. As his published treatises reveal, Edwards was clearly intent on defending the revivals as "a work of the Spirit of God." However, his letters also reveal a vein of circumspection and wariness that may have resulted from his disappointments after the revival of 1734–35. Even in his optimistic report to Whitefield of December 14, 1740, Edwards was cautious not to give an unqualifiedly positive judgment on revival activity. The letter is filled with the words "seems" and "hope." Edwards was beginning to recognize the complexities behind the vast revival movement and to understand how carefully motive, profession, and behavior had to be examined before judgments could be made.

In spite of his cautious optimism, Edwards established himself as a social conservative when it came to judging some of the more radical consequences of the revivals. His letters to Moses Lyman of August 31, 1741, and May 10, 1742, demonstrate his belief that inappropriate religious behavior, among clergy as well as laity, must be discouraged. In the earlier letter, Edwards defends itinerancy, but only by qualified ministers who are invited to preach elsewhere and who do not neglect their own congregations. In the latter, Edwards admonished Lyman for preaching before "a public congregation," firmly arguing that only duly ordained ministers could take on that duty. Although his pastoral letter to Deborah Hatheway of June 3, 1741, sanctions the setting up of "religious meetings of young women by yourselves," the brunt of his advice pertains to the personal application of religious discourse. A sense of personal "unworthiness," furthermore, must regulate all public expression.

Although Edwards sought to restrain extremism and enthusiasm, his tactic was persuasion rather than coercion. The disciplinary course taken against the notorious itinerant James Davenport, for example, in which Edwards played a major role, led to Davenport's recantation and eventual resettlement in the ministry. In a remarkable letter to Elnathan Whitman, dated February 9, 1744, Edwards pleads for liberty of conscience in order to reclaim straying parishioners. When some members of Whitman's church absented themselves from Sunday worship in order to hear New Light preachers, Edwards counseled patience and understanding rather than harsh measures more suited to "contumacious offenders." Edwards frequently sympathized with New Light dissenters, as his role in the formation of the Separate Society in New Haven illustrates (letter to Stephen Williams, Aug. 27, 1744). Yet he regretted the measures dissenters often took, particularly when they involved creating schisms or joining other denominations (letters to Ebenezer Pemberton, Nov. 2, 1743, and Moses Lyman, Sept. 30, 1748).

Through letters, sermons, and published treatises, Edwards carefully constructed a sophisticated apologetic for the revivals, immersing himself in controversy and bringing upon himself the criticisms of

such Old Lights as Charles Chauncy. Another of his opponents was
Thomas Clap, Rector of Yale College. In 1745 Edwards became involved in a minor pamphlet exchange with Clap over Edwards' relationship with Whitefield, who by that time had been officially denounced by both Harvard College and the Connecticut legislature. In
a published account, Clap stated that Edwards had told him of Whitefield's intention to replace New England ministers with converted
leaders from Great Britain. In two published responses of his own
(Feb. 4 and May 20, 1745), Edwards denied telling Clap any such
thing.[6]

The exchange with Clap put Edwards in a delicate position. Always
mindful of the importance of defending and propagating revivals,
Edwards attempted to exonerate Whitefield while tactfully admitting
differences with him. There is no denying that Edwards admired
Whitefield's skill and power, but the relationship of the two men, by
Edwards' own admission, was merely cordial. Indeed, during Whitefield's first visit in 1740, Edwards had commented negatively, albeit in
private, on Whitefield's views concerning impulses, assurance, and
how to determine that someone has been converted. Following Whitefield's departure, Edwards had preached a lengthy series on the parable of the sower (Matt. 13), in which he had warned his congregation
not to be swept away by Whitefield's "eloquence" and "gesture."[7] In
short, a full examination of Edwards' letters in conjunction with his
sermons of the time reveals a different relationship than the affectionate one portrayed in Whitefield's *Journals*.

Edwards began his correspondence with ministers in Scotland in the
early 1740s. These new points of contact provided him with the opportunity to satisfy his curiosity about revivals abroad. The earliest such
letters on record were those to William McCulloch and James Robe of
May 12, 1743, which dwelt on the recent famous awakenings at Cambuslang and Kilsyth and requested further news of such occurrences
in Scotland.[8] Several years later, Edwards began his long-distance

---

6. On Whitefield's activities and reputation in the colonies, see especially Harry S. Stout,
The Divine Dramatist: George Whitefield and the Rise of Modern Evangelicalism (Grand Rapids,
1991). On the dispute between Clap and JE over Whitefield, see Letter Nos. 56 and 58, below,
and Louis Leonard Tucker, *Puritan Protagonist: President Thomas Clap of Yale College* (Chapel
Hill, Univ. of North Carolina Press, 1962), pp. 137–38, 142.

7. See JE's six-sermon series on Matt. 13:3–7, preached first in Nov. 1740, Beinecke
Library.

8. For an account of the Cambuslang revival, see Arthur Fawcett, *The Cambuslang Revival:
The Scottish Evangelical Revival of the Eighteenth Century* (London, 1971). On events in Kilsyth,
see the modern reprint of James Robe's narrative, *When the Wind Blows* (Glasgow, 1985).

friendship with John Erskine (see the letter of Aug. 31, 1748). Besides exchanging information on revivals, Edwards relied on his foreign connections for discussions of a constellation of issues relating to revivalism, including scriptural exegesis (letter to McCulloch, Mar. 5, 1744), responses to *Religious Affections* (letter to Thomas Gillespie, Sept. 4, 1747), prophecy (letter to McCulloch, Jan. 21, 1747), military conflicts with the French (letters to MacLaurin, Nov. 20, 1745, and to McCulloch, Sept. 23, 1747), and the establishment of a college in New Jersey (letter to Erskine, Oct. 14, 1748). Beginning in 1745, many letters to Scotland concerned Edwards' efforts to promote a Concert for Prayer, a task that involved holding days of united prayer for the advancement of religion.[9]

No letters by Edwards to his famous protégé David Brainerd have survived, but Brainerd is the topic of many letters to other correspondents, both in Scotland and New England. By the time he appears, however, Brainerd is nearing death. Edwards' letter to Joseph Bellamy of June 11, 1747, mentions Brainerd's traveling to Boston for his health in the company of Edwards' daughter Jerusha; the trip has been the basis for a supposed romance between the two. Other letters to local ministers tell of Brainerd's impending death and his funeral (letter to Stephen Williams, Oct. 9, 1747). Still others show Edwards' efforts to collect information about Brainerd for the publication of his *Life* (letter to John Brainerd, Dec. 14, 1747, and to Bellamy, Apr. 4, 1748).

Communion Controversy

Northampton's communion controversy might be said to have begun with the waning of religious fervor after New England's Great Awakening.[1] Edwards' correspondence from this period offers a fascinating glimpse into his frustration with declining piety and his attempts to counteract it. As early as December 12, 1743, in a letter to his colleague Thomas Prince that relays, among other things, the joyful news that Northampton has publicly renewed its covenant with God, Edwards confesses that the year before, he had noticed a distressing "abatement of the liveliness" of his congregation's "affections in religion." In March 1742, when Edwards had first proposed the covenant renewal, he encountered resistance from certain segments of his par-

9. On JE's involvement in the transatlantic Concert for Prayer, which culminated in the publication of his *Humble Attempt* (1748), see *Works*, 5, 29–48.
1. For a discussion of the communion controversy, see *Works, 12*, 1–90.

ish. Some people seem to have objected that Northampton already stood in sacred covenant with God and that a renewal of this relationship was "needless."[2] Although Edwards answered this objection from the pulpit, and Northampton's covenant was renewed, a nagging suspicion began to haunt him that his congregation was lapsing into spiritual declension, such as had been seen following the previous revival. By decade's end, Edwards would feel that his worst fears had been confirmed in spite of every effort on his part to sustain genuine piety.

Edwards' letter to Dorothy Danks Hannam of March 26, 1744, provides a little-known example of Edwards' concern for moral purity. Hannam appears to have been an important witness in Northampton's "bad book" affair, an event Samuel Hopkins once described as "the occasion of weakening Mr. Edwards' hands in the work of the ministry."[3] Having heard that several young men had acquired a midwives' manual and had used it to "make sport" of "women kind," Edwards responded by leading a public investigation into the affair and wound up alienating many of the families of those involved. In this, the sole surviving letter written by Edwards on the issue, he requests a narrative account detailing all that Hannam knew. He concludes with an earnest exhortation, advising that "in thus giving your . . . testimony I think you will do what [you] . . . are obliged to do as a Christian."

Edwards' ethical paternalism had been admired before the awakening of 1740–41, but his neighbors were finding it less attractive by the mid-1740s. Not only had the revivals helped to democratize the region's public moral discourse, but they occurred within a period of economic change within Northampton that engendered animosity toward society's elites. The town's leading families gained control of an increasing share of its civic power, and the common people lost the use of the public fields. This did not dispose them favorably toward an obtrusive religious leader who earned the highest clerical salary in western New England. During the "bad book" controversy, a brash young Timothy Root declared: "I won't worship a wig."[4] Not surprisingly, Edwards' salary and the way his family spent it became topics of special interest. As their pastor began to condemn Northampton's

2. See JE's MS sermon on Josh. 24:15–27 (Mar. 1742), Beinecke Library.

3. Hopkins, p. 55. On the bad book affair, see also Patricia J. Tracy, *Jonathan Edwards, Pastor: Religion and Society in Eighteenth-Century Northampton* (New York, Hill and Wang, 1980), pp. 160–64; and the documents included in John E. Smith, Harry S. Stout, and Kenneth P. Minkema, eds., *A Jonathan Edwards Reader* (New Haven, Yale Univ. Press, 1995), pp. 172–78.

4. See Smith, Stout, and Minkema, eds., *A Jonathan Edwards Reader*, p. 177.

post-awakening moral lapses, many parishioners decided that the Edwardses had become too "lavish" in their spending and gave their minister a difficult time in collecting his wages. The letters Edwards wrote to the town precinct in the winter of 1744–45 offer a unique perspective on these socioeconomic tensions. Defending himself and his family from allegations of extravagance, he asked the precinct to grant him a permanent, non-negotiable salary. The agreement then in place provided Edwards such support "as shall be suitable and well adapted to the honorable office of the gospel ministry." But it contained "nothing," complained Edwards, "that determines what that support is, nor is it said who shall be judge." It left the door open, in other words, for undue "meddling with a minister's affairs," and it also worried the minister with economic distractions. In return for a fixed wage, Edwards promised to remain contented with his salary and pledged never to ask for a raise.

Although by the late 1740s Edwards did receive a fixed income, his relations with the Northampton church did not improve. He continued to deplore the town's moral laxity and spiritual indolence but found himself increasingly unable to effect substantial change. In a well-known case of fornication (1747–48), the families of Elisha Hawley and Martha Root settled out of court, and Edwards failed to force a marriage.[5] And in a similar case, between Thomas Wait and Jemima Miller (reflected here for the first time in Edwards' letter to Robert Breck, Apr. 7, 1747), the defendant, Wait, appears to have gotten off without much punishment. (Although convicted by the Northampton church, Wait married another woman, Rachel Smith, only a year later.)[6]

Edwards' change of heart concerning the issue of Stoddardean sacramental measures was not unrelated to these practical moral problems. And though the controversy this change provoked has already received a fair share of scholarly attention,[7] the letters published here provide unprecedented access to the workings of Edwards' mind. The letters illuminate the proceedings of the seemingly endless local meet-

5. On the Hawley-Root case, consult Kathryn Kish Sklar, "Culture versus Economics: A Case of Fornication in Northampton in the 1740s," *Papers in Women's Studies* (University of Michigan), May 1978, 35–56; and Tracy, *Jonathan Edwards, Pastor,* pp. 164–66. JE's MSS on the case may be found in the "Memoranda on Cases of Discipline at Northampton" and in "Some Reasons briefly hinted at, why Those Rules . . . relating to the Obligation of a man to marry a virgin that He had humbled, ought to be esteemed . . . ," both at the Trask Library.

6. On the Wait-Miller case, see also Wait's letter to JE, Mar. 9, 1746, Beinecke Library.

7. See *Works, 12,* 52, n. 7.

ings held to haggle over the direction of his ministry. And they disclose
to us a pastor who was not above the petty wrangling that so often
characterizes such ecclesiastical disputes. As Edwards complained to
Joseph Bellamy on December 6, 1749: "There have been abundance
of meetings about our affairs since you was here: society meetings,
and church meetings, and meetings of committees; of committees of
the parish and committees of the church; conferences, debates, reports, and proposals drawn up, and replies and remonstrances." But
through it all the weary shepherd of Northampton stayed his course.
From the publication of his *Humble Inquiry* (1749), concerning the
qualifications for full communion (for an example of Edwards' desire
to communicate his convictions as firmly and effectively as possible in
this publication, see his letter to Thomas Foxcroft, May 24, 1749),
through his attempt to secure a ministerial council that could decide
his case with some measure of impartiality (note, for example, Edwards to the Northampton Church Committee, Dec. 5, 1749), to the
release in 1752 of *Misrepresentations Corrected* (see especially his letter to
the Northampton Church of June 1752), Edwards insisted on the
pivotal importance of his position. As he pleaded to his former flock in
the letter of 1752: "If you are not inclined to hearken to me, from any
remaining affection to one whose voice and counsels you once heard
with joy, and yielded to with great alacrity; yet let me desire you not to
refuse, as you would act the part of friends to yourselves and your dear
children."[8]

Although he was ultimately ejected in June 1750, Edwards did
prove an adroit church politician. As he demonstrated in correspondence to a wide variety of friends and colleagues (see, for example, his
letters from this period to his friend and literary agent, Thomas Foxcroft), he knew how to negotiate his way over rough ecclesiastical
terrain. Privately, he worked to mitigate the power and influence of his
enemies. And in more-public correspondence, he offered consistent
(and doggedly persistent) self-defense. Even after Edwards knew that
his dismissal was inevitable, he proved a tireless (and sometimes tire-
some) protector of his clerical reputation. In a telling letter to Foxcroft, written on May 24, 1749, Edwards expressed his desire to maintain the utmost propriety under duress:

8. For JE's own account of the communion controversy, see his "Narrative of Communion
Controversy," printed in *Works, 12*, 505–619.

I have many enemies abroad in the country, who hate me for my stingy principles, enthusiasm, rigid proceedings and that now are expecting full triumph over me. I need the prayers of my fathers and brethren who are friendly to me, that I may have wisdom given me by my great Master, and that I may be enabled to conduct with steady faithfulness to him, under all trials. . . . I seem as it were to be casting myself off from a precipice; and have no other way, but to go on, as it were blindfold, i.e. shutting my eyes to everything else but the evidences of the mind and will of God, and the path of duty; which I would observe with the utmost care.

After his dismissal, Edwards continued in "steady faithfulness" to his convictions and walked "the path of duty" all the way to the western New England frontier. A few of the letters printed below discuss his options for ministry elsewhere. Although each has been printed previously, their inclusion in this volume represents the first time they have appeared together since 1830. Edwards' letters to his Scottish friend, the Reverend John Erskine, written on July 5, 1750, and July 7, 1752, suggest that Edwards had employment options among Presbyterians in both Scotland and Virginia. And a letter to former neighbor Joseph Hawley (written on Nov. 18, 1754) gives Edwards' version of the proposal to install him at a second church in Northampton. Despite the attraction of more comfortable options, however, Edwards felt called to ministry in Stockbridge, and so it is to Stockbridge and its mission that we must turn.

Stockbridge

The fourth and largest division of Edwards' extant correspondence dates from his tenure as a frontier missionary and provides a wealth of largely untapped information on the troubled history of the Stockbridge mission. Given the recent scholarly and popular interest in Indian history, these letters should find an important place in the historiography of the period. Regarding Edwards, they confirm that he considered the Indians and their mission a high priority. Contrary to the received wisdom concerning Edwards' Stockbridge years, he did not view the mission as a retreat where he could hide away and write. Nor did he view the mission as a place of exile. As attested to in his letter to the missionary Eleazar Wheelock on July 13, 1744, and as confirmed by, among other things, his labor of love, the *Life of David*

Brainerd (1749), Edwards had long been a supporter of English missions to the Indians. Indeed, he and his Northampton church had supported the Stockbridge mission from its founding in the mid-1730s.[9] Even though Edwards came to differ from his grandfather Solomon Stoddard over the issue of admittance to the sacraments, he did not move away from his esteemed predecessor's deep concern for the evangelization of the region's native inhabitants. In fact, one might say that Edwards' move to the Stockbridge mission was actually an ironic fulfillment of a long-standing Stoddardean imperative.[1]

In a letter to Thomas Foxcroft written on November 21, 1749, Edwards provided a prescient confirmation of this imperative. Making what amounted to his strongest plea thus far on behalf of the unconverted Indians of Stockbridge, he wrote: "I wish that the Commissioners would now take care that there may be a man sent them of sound principles, and a pious character. There has been so much contributed towards an Indian school there, that if the affair may be under the care of a missionary of good character, there seems to be the best door for gradually propagating the gospel among the Indians that is opened at present." Though Edwards could not have known at the time that he would be the man selected, his correspondence suggests that, contrary to the views of many modern-day interpreters, Edwards' agreement to move to Stockbridge should not surprise us.

Edwards first journeyed to the Stockbridge mission in January 1751 and remained there until March of that year. On February 22, the town called him to settle permanently as its pastor. He could not accept immediately. A ministerial council (which eventually met in Northampton on May 16) had first to meet to advise him on the most fitting course of future service. Further, as is fleshed out a bit in letters written in April about this council, the minority group that had supported Edwards during his recent ecclesiastical ordeal was eager to retain him, and to form their own church in Northampton. Inasmuch as Edwards showed clear signs of uneasiness concerning the prospect of joining them, the ministerial council decided that he should accept the Stockbridge call. Edwards wasted no time in doing so, and by

---

9. Note also that, from 1743–47, JE had served as the only clerical member of a committee established to receive and disburse the funds given for the Stockbridge boarding school (the other members of this committee were Oliver Partridge, Eleazar Porter, John Stoddard, and Israel Williams). Samuel Hopkins (of Springfield), *Historical Memoirs, Relating to the Housatunnuk Indians* (Boston, 1753), p. 134.

1. See Solomon Stoddard, *Question Whether God is not Angry with the Country for doing so little towards the Conversion of the Indians* (Boston, 1723).

June 17 he had relocated and was ready to assume his duties. He was formally installed on August 8. His family moved to Stockbridge on October 18.[2]

The Stockbridge mission had been founded in 1736 by the Society for the Propagation of the Gospel in New England (created at the Puritans' Long Parliament of 1649). The New England Company, as it came to be called when it was reconstituted after the Restoration, was the oldest Protestant mission society in England. Its members collected and invested funds at home and entrusted the interest to colonial commissioners. These commissioners, in turn, hired the missionaries and paid their salaries. Before Edwards arrived, the New England Company's ministry in frontier Stockbridge was run by the Reverend John Sergeant and a schoolteacher, Timothy Woodbridge. Together, Sergeant and Woodbridge served a congregation of Indians and whites, made regular trips to upstate New York to minister to various Indian tribes there, sponsored a permanent Indian school, and developed a somewhat unstable boarding program for a select number of Indian boys. By 1749, when Sergeant died at the age of thirty-eight, there were 218 Indians living in Stockbridge. Of these, 129 had been baptized by Sergeant himself (Sergeant baptized 182 Indians in all), and 42 were communicant members of Stockbridge's Congregational church. There were 55 Indian scholars studying at Woodbridge's mission school and 12 young boys in the boarding program sponsored by the English philanthropist Isaac Hollis (nephew of the well-known Harvard benefactor Thomas Hollis).[3]

2. On the efforts of the minority group and the related events surrounding the May 1751 council, see Col. Timothy Dwight's draft (May 1751) of his reasons for resettling JE at Northampton, JE's "Vindication from the Church's Accusations," and JE's "Reflections on the remonstrance sent to Mr. Clark & Mr. Edwards," all in the Beinecke Library; three letters written by Timothy Dwight to Thomas Foxcroft (between Oct. 1750 and Dec. 1751) concerning the possibility of a second church, in the Dwight Family Papers, Sterling Library; a letter draft in JE's hand, Trask Library, f. 1751.14; Joseph Hawley's statement to the 1751 council in the Hawley Papers, NYPL; and Hopkins, pp. 65–66. The family move is recorded in Jonathan Judd, MS Diary, Oct. 15–16, 1751, Forbes Library; and in JE's MS Account Book, p. 62, Beinecke Library.

3. On the New England Company and its history, see William Kellaway, *The New England Company, 1649–1776: Missionary Society to the American Indians* (London, Longmans, 1961). On the Stockbridge mission, see also Hopkins, *Historical Memoirs;* Nathanael Appleton, *Gospel Ministers Must Be Fit for the Master's Use . . . Illustrated in a Sermon Preached at Deerfield, August 31, 1735, at the Ordination of Mr. John Sargent* (Boston, 1735); Sarah Cabot Sedgwick and Christina Sedgwick Marquand, *Stockbridge: 1739–1974* (Stockbridge, Berskhire Traveler Press, 1974); Jean Fitz Hankins, "Bringing the Good News: Protestant Missionaries to the Indians of New England and New York, 1700–1775" (Ph.D. diss., University of Con-

Unfortunately for Edwards, however, town life was dominated by the English. Of the dozen or so English families living in Stockbridge at this time, it was the Williamses, his arch-enemies, who up to that point had prevailed in civic affairs. Col. Ephraim Williams, Sr., who had acquired much of this land from manipulative and illegal dealings with the Indians, was the leading landholder in the region. His extended family included a number of local power brokers. Williams' daughter Abigail was the widow of the town's late pastor, John Sergeant, and Williams moderated the town meeting at which Edwards was called. The Williamses had originally attempted to settle first Elihu Spencer and then Ezra Stiles at the pulpit, before the town called the much more experienced Edwards. As the younger Ephraim explained in a letter written to Jonathan Ashley of Deerfield, Edwards seemed to his family to be a poor teacher and a "great bigot," who was unlikely, they thought (correctly), to learn the Indian languages. Aware of Edwards' sensitivity to his family's opposition, Ephriam confided, "I am sorry that a head so full of divinity should be so empty of politics."[4]

The Stockbridge Indians were Mahicans, "River Indians," as the English named them, or "Muh-he-ka-ne-ok" ("people of the flowing waters"), as they preferred to call themselves. An eastern Algonquian tribe, they are said to have descended from the Delaware Indians, and in the seventeenth century they ranged from Lake Champlain to the present Dutchess County, New York, extending into the western parts of Massachusetts and Connecticut as well. By the middle of the eighteenth century, however, they had dwindled in size and influence. With their numbers shrinking in New York, they moved their headquarters or "council fire" to Stockbridge and submitted to being "civilized" and "Christianized" at the mission. The first convert among the Stockbridge tribe was Ebenezer Poohpoonuk. Poohpoonuk was followed by Capt. Konkapot and Lieut. Umpachenee, tribal leaders who were granted commissions by the colonial militia. The spiritual exam-

necticut, 1993); and Rachel Wheeler, "Forgotten Conversations: The Indian-European Negotiation of Religion in the Eighteenth-Century Northeast" (Ph.D. diss., Yale University, forthcoming). Thanks to Rachel Wheeler for her help in assembling this history of the Stockbridge mission.

4. This letter is printed in Wright, pp. 61–62. On the Williams' exploitation of the Indians and their land, see also Lion G. Miles, "The Red Man Dispossessed: The Williams Family and the Alienation of Indian Land in Stockbridge, Massachusetts, 1736–1818," *NEQ* 67 (1994), 46–76. JE was hired by the Commissioners with the express understanding that he was to use an interpreter in preaching to the Indians (MAR, v. 32, 202).

ples of these men were followed by their families and many others, and before long, most of the Stockbridge Indians converted to the Christian faith.[5]

The Stockbridge mission was strongly favored by authorities back in Boston, not only for its ministry to the natives but for its military and commercial importance as well. In addition to its significance as an outpost during the French and Indian wars (as his letters show, Edwards, whose own house was used as a military garrison during the fighting, was well informed about the battles), the town of Stockbridge became important in boundary disputes with other English colonists as well. Massachusetts held territorial claims extending west beyond New York, but the New Yorkers' alliance with the powerful Mohawks rendered such claims moot. As the easternmost member of the Five Nations (later the Six Nations) of the Iroquois confederacy, the Mohawks influenced most Indian-English commerce that took place west of the Hudson River. Their leading trade partner, Sir William Johnson, was a nominal Anglican who, in the late 1740s, became sole Commissary for Indian Affairs in New York and in 1755 became Britain's first Superintendent of Indian Affairs. As one who enjoyed close personal, economic, and military ties with the Mohawks, and especially with the great Mohawk chief Hendrick, Johnson proved both an ally to the people of Massachusetts in their common opposition to the French and a competitor for Indian capital and Indian souls.

The Mahicans often lived in tension with their more powerful rivals to the west. But their Stockbridge mission remained attractive to the Mohawks as a center of English education. Massachusetts officials, Edwards included, tried to lure the Mohawks there (succeeding for a time with the help of Johnson himself), not only to preach to them the good news of the English Protestant gospel but also to form diplomatic ties that would strengthen the colony politically. As Edwards stressed to Thomas Hubbard, Speaker of the Massachusetts General Assembly, in August 1751, the Stockbridge mission provided the key to future relations with the Mohawks: "The only remaining means that divine providence hath left us to repair and secure these Indians in the British interest, is this very thing: viz. to our utmost, to

5. On the Stockbridge Indians, see Patrick Frazier, *The Mohicans of Stockbridge* (Lincoln, Neb., Univ. of Nebraska Press, 1992); Philip S. Colee, "The Housatonic-Stockbridge Indians: 1734–1749" (Ph.D. diss., University of New York, 1977); and Daniel Richard Mandell, "Behind the Frontier: Indian Communities in Eighteenth-Century Massachusetts" (Ph.D. diss., University of Virginia, 1993).

prosecute the design of instructing them thoroughly in the Protestant religion."[6]

As this letter to Hubbard indicates, despite Edwards' keen awareness of his mission's strategic political importance, he felt that its primary purpose was to nurture Indian souls. He deemed a rudimentary English education, moreover, as propaedeutic to this endeavor. His hope was to turn the mission into a regional center for the Indians' religious instruction, and he garnered support for this educational vision from both Johnson and the Stockbridge tribal leaders. (Aside from the Mahicans and the Mohawks, the mission would attract other tribes, like the Oneidas and Tuscaroras, as well.) Edwards' letters—particularly those written to Hollis (July 2, 1751), Sir William Pepperrell (Nov. 28, 1751), and Joseph Paice (Feb. 24, 1752)—provide the reader with an unparalleled view of his philosophy of Indian education. The most urgent need, Edwards believed, was to teach the Indians how to speak and read English. For him, even a rudimentary education required the reading of European works in a wide range of liberal arts and sciences; to translate them all from English into the relevant Indian languages would, in Edwards' view, simply take too long. Although he did make prejudicial comments about the "barbarous" quality of the Indian languages, he also spoke of the genius of the native people, and he did not view Indian education as a one-way street. As indicated by his decision to send his young son Jonathan, Jr., to New York with missionary colleague Gideon Hawley to develop his facility with Indian languages and gain firsthand experience of tribal customs, Edwards knew that the English had something to learn from Indian languages and cultures and believed that a genuine understanding of the curriculum would entail a bilingual appropriation of Western knowledge (see also the letter to Joseph Bellamy, June 1756).

Edwards' students worked the hardest at reading, writing, arithmetic, and singing. In contrast to the pedagogical methods to which many in Stockbridge had become accustomed, Edwards' practice rejected rote learning as conducive to mindless incantation. Instead, Edwards proposed a method of questions, answers, and lively discussion that was patterned after the leading grammar schools in Boston. English

6. Among several recent studies treating Johnson and his relation to the Mohawks, see the article by Timothy J. Shannon, "Dressing for Success on the Mohawk Frontier: Hendrick, William Johnson, and the Indian Fashion," *William and Mary Quarterly* 53 (1996), 13–42.

and Indian children studied together so they could learn from one another, and, when possible, the Indian children boarded with English families. Like Sergeant before him, Edwards deemed this an optimal method of socializing, or "civilizing," the Indians.

As many of Edwards' letters from the early 1750s attest, he also campaigned strongly for the Indian girls' school at the mission, though he opposed the manner in which its mistress, Abigail Williams Sergeant Dwight, controlled it. Shortly after Brig. Gen. Joseph Dwight moved to Stockbridge in 1752 as the general assembly's special agent to the Stockbridge mission, he married Abigail, who was Ephraim Williams' daughter, widow of Edwards' predecessor, and mother of three small children. She was soon offered a position as the new mistress of the Indian girls' school, to be run on her husband's land and financed by the New England Company. She was allocated enough money to buy food and clothing for ten girls a year and was paid an additional £30 a year in salary. Before his marriage, Joseph Dwight had been an admirer and supporter of Edwards', but his relations with the Williamses soon changed him. Before long, he was siding with his new kinfolk in opposing Edwards' ministry, and Edwards was becoming Abigail Dwight's most trenchant critic. Edwards had been frustrated since his coming by the ineptitude of Capt. Martin Kellogg, the man hired in 1748 to run the boys' boarding school. When he learned that the girls' school was to be run by another ill-trained local, his disappointment with the mission could no longer be contained. Firing off letter after letter to members of the New England Company, the general assembly, and British sponsors, he fought hard for complete control of both the mission and its schools.

Edwards' struggle was no easy task, as the Williams clan did all it could to thwart him. In addition to the ploys of the immediate Ephraim Williams family, other Williamses became active opponents of Edwards as well. Ephraim's cousins, Col. Israel Williams (who commanded the English militia on the western New England frontier), Rev. Solomon Williams (who wrote *The True State of the Question* in response to Edwards' *Humble Inquiry*), and Col. Elisha Williams (Edwards' tutor at Yale, who had become a New England Company commissioner and who was heavily involved in Connecticut politics), each actively opposed Edwards in both Northampton and Stockbridge. Joseph Dwight went so far as to present a negative report on Edwards to the Massachusetts House in November 1752, and Elisha Williams sent a copy of this report to the board of the New England Company back in London.[7]

But despite such powerful opposition, Edwards enjoyed a great deal of public support in Stockbridge itself, among the commissioners back in Boston, and throughout the colonial leadership at large. Among the Boston clergy, Thomas Prince and Thomas Foxcroft proved faithful defenders; and the city's Old South Church proved a bastion for such highly-placed followers as Speaker Hubbard, provincial secretaries Josiah Willard and Andrew Oliver (who succeeded Hubbard), and Lieut. Gov. Spencer Phips. Jonathan Belcher, the governor first of Massachusetts and then of New Jersey and a long-time leader of the New England Company's commissioners, also remained a faithful supporter of Edwards'.

After two years of internecine struggle, the mission's fate was finally decided in February 1754 by a decision from the English donor, Isaac Hollis. As the mission's single leading patron and as one well-versed in Edwards' view of its affairs (see Edwards' letters to Hollis written in the summer of 1751 and on July 17, 1752), Hollis determined that Edwards should be in sole charge of the Stockbridge schools. Unfortunately for the work of the mission, however, Hollis' decision came too late. The boys' schoolhouse had burned down (mysteriously) in February 1753, and another contingent of Mohawks had left in disgust in December of that year. Indeed, Edwards' victory proved Pyrrhic. In the end, English in-fighting over the direction the mission should take undermined Edwards' goal of building it into a major center of religious education—his progressive plans were never allowed to bear much fruit.

No introduction to the Stockbridge letters would be complete without some mention of their relation to the publication of Edwards' major treatises. Not surprisingly, beyond the information these letters contain about the mission, they enhance our knowledge of Edwards' scholarly pursuits. Perhaps the most surprising thing the letters reveal about his academic endeavors in general is the way his work was aided by friends and colleagues who served as agents and promoters. Many of Edwards' letters to his well-placed friend Rev. Thomas Foxcroft of Boston pertain to the preparation of Edwards' treatises—especially *Freedom of the Will*—for public consumption (see, for example, the

---

7. Dwight ed., *1*, 519–20; and Jasper Mauduit to Elisha Williams, Apr. 11, 1753, Alderman Library, p. 273.

letters of Apr. 13, 1753, May 24, 1753, Feb. 5, 1754, Mar. 6, 1754, Dec. 20, 1754). And much of his Scottish correspondence (often conveyed by Foxcroft), such as his letters to the Rev. John Erskine, include a discussion of his influence overseas (see especially the letters of July 25 and Aug. 3, 1757).

Thus, to insist that Edwards was actively involved in the mundane affairs of the Stockbridge mission is not to deny the usual view of his life there; it is only to suggest that, as happened in every other period of his life, Edwards' scholarship emerged from a rich and often tumultuous context of social experience.

Princeton

In the midst of continual concerns about the Indian missions and Indian wars, Edwards received an invitation to succeed his late son-in-law, Rev. Aaron Burr, as the president of the College of New Jersey. Although Edwards expressed surprise, the invitation was logical, not only because of his family connection with Burr but also because he had supported the founding of the college, was well known to the Trustees, and had sent one of his sons there. Edwards' letter to the Trustees, dated October 19, 1757, ranks as one of the most illuminating in his corpus. It tells us much about Edwards as a person, about his own estimation of his abilities and temperament, and about the projects he was working on to fulfill his life of study and reflection. Despite the doubts expressed in the letter, however, the Trustees urged him to accept the post.

The letters immediately following relate to Edwards' efforts to arrange a council that would release him from his duties at Stockbridge and give him permission to go to Princeton. Writing to Esther Edwards Burr on November 20, 1757, he worried about what influence Stockbridge's deacon and schoolteacher Timothy Woodbridge might exert to prevent his departure; and the letters to Mark Leavenworth and Joseph Bellamy (Nov. 21 and Dec. 1, 1757, respectively) betray his anxiety over assembling the council. Yet however much he may have expressed reservations, Edwards was excited at the prospect of becoming a college president. This may explain why, even before the council, he tried to sell some of his land in Massachusetts (see the letter to Nathaniel Dwight, Dec. 5, 1757).

As Edwards' letter to Gideon Hawley of January 14, 1758, relates, the council finally met and determined that his "call was clear to go."

Edwards reportedly wept on hearing the decision, which meant having to uproot his large family once more. He departed by himself in January and began his duties by preaching weekly in the college chapel and distributing questions to the undergraduates.

In Princeton, Edwards carried forward the scientific spirit of the "Spider Letter" to the end. When confronted by a smallpox epidemic, he willingly underwent inoculation, which was still a new and controversial procedure. Unfortunately, after an initially encouraging reaction, Edwards contracted a "secondary fever." Following a short illness, he died, on March 22, 1758. The attending physician, William Shippen, wrote to Sarah Pierpont Edwards: "Never did any Person expire with more perfect freedom from pain, not so much as one distorted hair but in ye most proper sense of the Words, he really fell asleep—for Death had certainly lost its Sting, as to him."[8]

Note on the Texts

Editing the letters presents one of the greatest challenges within the scope of the Edwards Edition, not only because of the sheer number of texts but because of the variety of formats in which they have survived and the often difficult task of deciphering Edwards' handwriting—particularly in drafts. Wherever possible, the texts presented here are based on Edwards' own final manuscript or on printed versions of letters that were published while Edwards was still alive. At times, however, I have had to rely on rough and fragmentary drafts, on published excerpts of letters for which no corresponding manuscript survives, or on later copies (both published and unpublished) made by others of long-lost letters. Where the original manuscripts are available but contain indecipherable passages, posthumously transcribed or published letters have been used to verify questionable readings. The headnotes point the reader to alternative texts and discuss textual issues relevant to each letter.

The letters contain a rich store of references to individuals, groups, events, books, and other letters, both sent and received. A biographical glossary at the back of the volume (Appendix A) provides information about persons mentioned in the letters. For ease of reference, Indian names have been regularized and place names modernized. The indication of place of origin and date of each letter has been

---

8. William Shippen to Sarah Pierpont Edwards, Mar. 22, 1758, Trask Library.

expanded and placed at the beginning of the letter. Whenever feasible, events and books are identified in the notes. Some letters, especially those cut up by Edwards for the construction of sermon booklets, are far too fragmentary and brief for coherent presentation. These are listed in Appendix B. Finally, a list of those letters received by Edwards whose locations are known may be found in Appendix C.

1. TO MARY EDWARDS

This is Jonathan Edwards' earliest extant autograph letter. It was composed when he was twelve years old and in the last year of instruction under his father, Rev. Timothy Edwards, at East Windsor, Connecticut. The recipient was his sister Mary, who was two years his senior. By reporting on matters of religion first, Edwards, even at that early age, expresses the central theme of his life.

(Trask Library, ALS, one folio leaf, addressed on verso to Mary Edwards at the house of Samuel Partridge at Hadley. Published in Dwight ed., *1*, 21–22; Winslow, pp. 48–50.)

* * *

Windsor, May 10, 1716

Dear Sister,

Through the wonderful mercy and goodness of God there hath in this place been a very remarkable stirring and pouring out of the Spirit of God, and likewise now is, but I think I have reason to think it is in some measure diminished, but I hope not much. About thirteen have been joined to the church in an estate of full communion.

These are those which by inquiry I find you have not heard of that have joined to the church, viz. John Huntington, Sarah Loomis, the daughter of Thomas Loomis, and Esther Ellsworth. And there are five that are propounded which are not added to the church, namely, John Loomis, John Rockwell's wife, Sergt. Thomas Ellsworth's wife, Isaac Bissel's wife, and Mary Osborn.

I think there comes commonly a-Mondays above thirty persons to speak with father about the condition of their souls.

It is a time of general health here in this place. There has five persons died in this place since you have been gone, viz. old Goodwife Rockwell, old Goodwife Grant, and Benjamin Bancroft, who was drowned in a boat many rods from shore, wherein were four young women and many others of the other sex, which were very remarkably saved, and the two others which died I suppose you have heard of. Margaret Peck of the New Town, who was once Margaret Stiles, hath lost a sucking babe, who died very suddenly and was buried in this place.

Abigail, Hannah, and Lucy have had the chicken pox and are recovered, but Jerusha[1] has it now but is almost well. I myself sometimes am much troubled with the toothache, but these two or three last days I have not been troubled with it but very little. As far as I know the whole family is well, except Jerusha. Sister, I am glad to hear of your welfare so often as I do. I should be glad to hear from you by a letter and therein how it is with you as to your crookedness.

Your loving brother,
Jonathan Edwards.

Father and mother remember their love unto you. Likewise do all my sisters and Mercy and Tim.[2]

2. TO MARY EDWARDS

From Yale's founding in 1701, and for almost two decades thereafter, struggles took place over its permanent location. When a majority of trustees finally agreed on New Haven, the Hartford trustees, undeterred, proceeded to create their own school at Wethersfield, under the direction of Elisha Williams.

Jonathan Edwards started college at New Haven in October 1716, but went to Wethersfield after a few weeks. He remained there until the last week of November 1718, when the students were transferred to New Haven. By early January 1719, however, Edwards and his friends were back in Wethersfield, citing dissatisfaction with tutor Samuel Johnson. Edwards and his classmates were then shuttled back and forth as pawns in a political chess game.[1]

The following letter was written shortly after the removal of Johnson as tutor and appointment of Rev. Timothy Cutler as rector. These actions cleared the way for the return of the Wethersfield students, Edwards among them, to New Haven, in June 1719. Jonathan's father, Timothy, had been pleased with the "good name" his son had made for himself at Wethersfield, "both as to his carriage and his learning."[2] A solid foundation was being established for future achievement.

1. Sisters of Jonathan Edwards.
2. Mercy Brooks and Timothy Demming were servants of JE's father.
1. Brooks Mather Kelley, *Yale: A History* (New Haven, Yale Univ. Press, 1974), pp. 9, 21–31; Dexter, *History*, pp. 20–191; Edwin Oviatt, *The Beginnings of Yale, 1701–1726* (New Haven, Yale Univ. Press, 1916), pp. 304–43, 360–75; and Richard Warch, *School of the Prophets: Yale College, 1701–1740* (New Haven, Yale Univ. Press, 1973), pp. 72–95.
2. Timothy Edwards to Mary Edwards, Jan. 27, 1717/18, Trask Library.

(Trask Library, ALS, addressed on verso to Mary Edwards at Northampton. Published in Dwight ed., *1*, 29–30.)

* * *

Wethersfield, March 26, 1719

Dear Sister,

Of all the many sisters I have, I think I never had one so long out of my hearing as yourself, inasmuch as I cannot remember that I ever heard one tittle from you from the time you last went up the country until the last week by Sir [Daniel] Buck, who then came from thence, whom I rejoiced to see because I fully expected to receive a letter from you by him. But being disappointed (and that not a little), I was willing to make that, which I hoped would be an opportunity of receiving, the same of sending. For I thought it was pity that there should not be the least correspondence between us, or communication from one to another, [when] no farther distant.

Hoping that this may be a means of exciting the same in yourself, and so having more charity for you than to think that I am quite out of [your] mind, that you are not at all concerned for me, [I] think it fit that I should give you an account of something of my condition relating to the school. I suppose you are fully acquainted with our coming away from New Haven and the circumstances thereof, since which time we have been in a more prosperous condition (as I think) than ever. But the Council and Trustees, having lately had a meeting at New Haven concerning it, they have removed that which was the cause of our coming away, viz. Mr. [Samuel] Johnson, from the place of a tutor, and have put in Mr. [Timothy] Cutler, pastor of Canterbury, president, who (as we hear) intends very speedily to be resident at Yale College, so that all the scholars belonging to our school expect to return there, as soon as our vacancy after the election is over. I am,

> Your loving brother in good health,
> Jonathan Edwards.

P.S. Please to give my duty to grandfather [Solomon Stoddard], grandmother [Esther Stoddard], uncle Major [John Stoddard], and aunt Rebecca [Hawley].

3. TO THE REVEREND TIMOTHY EDWARDS

In his letter of June 30, 1719,[1] Rector (President) Cutler congratulated Timothy Edwards on the academic progress of his son. He also expressed appreciation for the elder Edwards' support:

> I can assure you, Sir, your and the ministers' of your parts good affection to me in this affair is no small inducement to me, and if I am prevailed on thereby, it shall be a strong motive to me to improve my poor abilities in the service of such hopeful youths as are with us. They may suffer much from my weakness, but they shall not from my neglect.

With respect to Isaac Stiles, the young man sent to him by Timothy, Cutler vacillated in his report:

> I find him, Sir, to have made advances but small in learning, but I look upon them considerable with respect to the time he hath had, and disadvantages he hath lyen under; and look upon his natural parts as not mean. And though I think we may be too lax in admission, yet I know not but that all things considered he ought to be encouraged.

He went on to say that he had asked trustee Samuel Andrew's opinion of the candidate. When Andrew made no objection, Cutler put Stiles under the instruction of tutor Daniel Brown until commencement, when the verdict of the trustees would be sought. Cutler intimated that the verdict should be favorable, but the whole statement was clouded with ambiguity. To clarify the matter, Timothy evidently asked his son to investigate the facts. This letter is Jonathan's report.

(Trask Library, ALS, one folio leaf.)

* * *

New Haven, July 24, 1719

Ever Honored Sir,

I received (with two books) a letter from yourself bearing the date of July 7th, and therein I received with the greatest gratitude your most wholesome advice and counsel, and I hope I shall, God helping of me, use my utmost endeavors to put the same in practice. I am sensible of the preciousness of my time and am resolved it shall not be through any neglect of mine, if it slips without the greatest advantage.

1. Trask Library, ALS, one quarto leaf.

I take very great content under my present tuition as all the rest of the scholars seem to do under theirs. Mr. [Timothy] Cutler is extraordinary courteous to us, has a very good spirit of government, keeps the school in excellent order, seems to increase in learning, and is loved and feared by all that are under him, and when he is spoken of in the school or town he generally has the title of "President." The scholars all live in very good peace with the people of the town, and there is not a word said about our former carryings-on, except now and then by aunt [Elizabeth Davenport] Mather.

I have diligently searched into the circumstances of [Isaac] Stiles' examination, which was very short, and as far as I can understand was to no other disadvantage than that he was examined in Tully's *Orations*,[2] in which although he had never construed before he came to New Haven, yet he committed no error in that, nor in any other book, whether Latin, Greek, or Hebrew, except Virgil, wherein he could not tell the *præteritum* of *requiesco*. He is very well treated among the scholars, and accepted in the College as a member of it by everybody, and also as a freshman; neither (as I think) is he inferior as to learning to any of his classmates.

I have inquired of Mr. Cutler what books we should have need of the next year. He answered he would have me get against that time Alsted's *Geometry,* and Gassendi's *Astronomy;* with which I would entreat you to get a pair of dividers or mathematician's compasses, and a scale, which are absolutely necessary in order to learning mathematics; and also the *Art of Thinking*,[3] which I am persuaded would be no less profitable than the other necessary to me, who am

Your most dutiful son,
Jonathan Edwards.

Please to give my duty to my honored mother. Love to my sisters and Mercy.

P.S. What we give a week for our board is £0 5*s* 0*d*.

2. Marcus Tullius Cicero, *Orationes* (3 vols. Amsterdam, 1695–99), is the most likely edition available.

3. Johann Heinrich Alsted's *Encyclopedia Scientiarum Omnium* (Herborn, 1628), is a likely source of his geometry; Pierre Gassendi, *Institutio Astronomica* (London, 1653); and Antoine Arnauld, *The Art of Thinking*, ed. John Ozell (London, 1717). The Beinecke Library holds a copy of Arnauld containing JE's signature.

4. TO ELISHA MIX

Edwards' cousin and roommate Elisha Mix was probably returning home to Wethersfield for a visit. Jonathan was trying to get Mix to take a horse to his father, Timothy, at East Windsor, only ten miles beyond. If Edwards sent the letter printed after this one to Stephen Mix by his son Elisha, Stephen would be given an opportunity to talk to Elisha about his college duties, and Elisha's uncle Timothy would also have had the chance to make inquiries, which proved to be the case. So the horse delivery served a triple purpose.

(Trask Library, ALS, written on top one-fifth of folio leaf.)

* * *

New Haven, November 1, 1720

Sir,

I have [. . .][1] father's horse and not having an opportunity to send him directly [home],[2] have ordered him to be left at your house. And I entreat you that you would take some care speedily to convey him to my father's house. He has lyen here a month already, upon charge, for want of an opportunity to send him up. And if you don't quickly light of somebody going up by whom you may send him, I entreat you to hire somebody on purpose, and I make no doubt but my father will fully satisfy you therefor; and in so doing (and in giving my duty to my grandmother [Esther Warham Mather Stoddard], and service to my aunt Hannah [Stoddard Williams] and uncle [William Williams]) you will very much oblige your

Humble servant and respectful cousin,
Jonathan Edwards.

5. TO THE REVEREND STEPHEN MIX

The Reverend Stephen Mix was minister of the First Church, Wethersfield, the town where young Edwards had studied for almost three years. In addition, Mix was his uncle, the husband of Mary Stoddard (the older sister of Edwards' mother). They were the parents of Edwards' roommate, Elisha Mix. The rooming together of the two cousins was promoted in the first place by Elisha's father. Unfortunately, the arrangement, instead of being compatible and mutually beneficial, was not working. Jonathan was two years older, academically serious, and aware of his seniority. In contrast, Elisha was more

1. MS damage.
2. Idem.

carefree and nonchalant about his cousin's expectations. After this report, Elisha measured up to his responsibilities and harmony was restored.[1]

This letter draft reveals Edwards' tenacity and early skill in correspondence, a facility that would increase during the succeeding years.

(Trask Library, signed draft, written on the same folio leaf as the preceding letter; irregular at top.)

* * *

[c. November 1, 1720]

Ever Honored,

To my great surprisal I find my cousin Elisha [Mix] to be discontented in his dwelling with me. I have inquired of him strictly what is the reason of it. It cannot be because I hinder him from his studies, but as far as I can judge from his own words, it's because I hinder him from a superabundance of that which he loves much better.

I first discovered his discontentedness by his refusing to answer once when I called him, I judging it to be at unseasonable hours after he came home. I desiring of him whether or not he heard me call him, he answered yes. I again asked him what was the reason he did not come. He answered with some earnestness that he did [not] love to be called from play to draw cider. I was astonished at his answer, and it is the first instance I have known of a freshman's absolutely refusing his senior, whether graduate or undergraduate. Neither did I expect so suddenly to meet with this from him, with whom I promised myself so tranquil and peaceful a winter. I am loath to make any stir about it in the college, neither have I as yet made it known to any living soul, being that he is my cousin and the son of an uncle whom I so much respect, though he yet strongly persists in what I take to be his fault.

I thought it very expedient to write to you about it (and my writing is also what my cousin has consented to upon my telling of him that I designed it), inasmuch as, as long as he that lives with me is uneasy and cannot be easy, and inasmuch as he has declared he had rather live at another place than with me if he must draw cider; the strength of which reason I can in nowise conceive, for I am fully satisfied that the burthen of his freshmanship *cæteris paribus* is no greater than of other freshmen, notwithstanding his living with me, and considering that he is sent of other errands much less therefor, and I have done what I

1. Timothy Edwards wrote a spirited appeal to Stephen Mix for the exercise of paternal authority to redress the situation. ALS fragment, Trask Library.

could that he might be considered on that head, and besides if he were not he draws not at most above ten pots of cider a day, and that right out of a cellar that is right under our room.

I had rather have my cousin to be my chambermate than anybody, if he would but demean 'im becomingly and be contented. But while that he is otherwise living with me, I cannot but be in pain, so I ascertain you that it is not without reluctance that I have [been] forced to relate anything that may be blameworthy in your son. But since I am, I humbly request a speedy answer from you. In so doing, and in giving my duty to my aunt [Mary Stoddard Mix] and humble service to my cousin,[2] you will exceedingly engage, Sir,

Your most humble servant and dutiful nephew,
Jonathan Edwards.

I entreat you to free me of my obligations to keep 'Lisha study since it is impracticable and since therefore I daily find my [efforts][3] on that account are vain.

6. TO THE REVEREND TIMOTHY EDWARDS

Halfway through his first year of graduate studies, Jonathan Edwards wrote to his father concerning recent events at Yale. First came the dining hall rebellion. College fare does not always live up to student expectations but in this case, dissatisfaction erupted into a full-scale boycott. Rector Cutler lost no time in summoning powerful trustees to advise on the matter. The rector was a commanding presence by himself; when joined by the others, he became even more awe-inspiring.[1] The mutineers promptly capitulated.

Edwards' other concern was student exuberance. Down through history, outbursts of student rowdiness had occurred. Campuses had not been exempt from boisterous activity; games in hallways, gangs on the streets at night, the throwing of stones, breaking of windows, firing of guns, pouring of water on passers-by, ringing of bells, and "horrible shoutings and unwonted songs"— and worse—were part of the tradition.[2] Elsewhere, these excesses might seem commonplace; but to Edwards, they did not belong in a citadel of faith.

---

2. Identity uncertain. The cousin referred to is most likely Elisha himself, but may also be one of Elisha's five siblings (Sarah, Mary, Rebecca, Esther, or Christian).

3. MS damage.

1. DEX, *1*, 272.

2. Hastings Rashdall, *The Universities of Europe in the Middle Ages* (3 vols. Oxford, Clarendon Press, 1936), *3*, 426–33; Samuel E. Morison, *Harvard College in the Seventeenth Century* (2 vols. Cambridge, Mass., Harvard Univ. Press, 1936), *1*, 118–21; Dexter, *History*, p. 246.

(Trask Library, ALS, one folio leaf, addressed on verso to the Reverend Timothy Edwards at East Windsor.)

* * *

Yale College, March 1, 1720/1

Honored Sir,

It was not with a little joy and satisfaction that I received your letter of the 21st of February by Mr. Grant, and with a great deal of thankfulness from the bottom of my heart for your wholesome advice and counsel, and the abundance of father-like tenderness therein expressed.

As concerning the complaint of the scholars about their commons, the manner of it I believe was no less surprising to me than to you. It was on this wise: every undergraduate, one and all that had anything to do with College commons, all on a sudden, before Mr. [Timothy] Cutler or (I believe) anybody knew that they were discontented, entered into a bond of 15*s* never to have any more commons of the steward, whereupon they all forewarned him never to provide more for them, telling him if he did they would not pay him for it. Mr. [Daniel] Browne, notwithstanding, ordered commons to be provided, and set upon the table as it used to be, and accordingly it was, but there was nobody to eat it. Mr. Cutler, as soon as he was apprised of this cabal, sent on the same day for Mr. [Samuel] Andrew and Mr. [Samuel] Russel, who came on the next, and with the rector ordered all to appear before them; where the rector manifested himself exceedingly vexed and displeased at the act, which so affrighted the scholars that they unanimously agreed to come into commons again. I believe the scholars that were in this agreement have so lost Mr. Cutler's favor that they scarce ever will regain it. [Isaac] Stiles (to my grief and I believe much more to his) was one that set his hand to this bond; he did it by the strong instigations of others who persuaded him to it; neither had he a minute's time to consider before his hand was down. As soon as I understood him to be one of them, I told him that I thought he had done exceeding unadvisedly, and told him also what I thought the ill consequences of it would be, and quickly made him sorry that he did not take advice in the matter. I am apt to think that this thing will be the greatest obstacle of any to Stiles' being butler. I must needs say for my own part, that although the commons at sometimes have not been sufficient as to quality, yet I think there has been very little occasion for such an insurrection as this.

Although these disturbances were so speedily quashed, yet they are succeeded by much worse, and greater, and I believe greater than ever were in the College before. They are occasioned by the discovery of some monstrous impieties, and acts of immorality lately committed in the College, particularly stealing of hens, geese, turkeys, pigs, meat, wood, etc., unseasonable night-walking, breaking people's windows, playing at cards, cursing, swearing, and damning, and using all manner of ill language, which never were at such a pitch in the College as they now are. The Rector has called a meeting of the Trustees on this occasion, they are expected here today, 'tis thought the upshot will be the expulsion of some, and the public admonition of others.

Through the goodness of God I am perfectly free of all their janglings. My condition at the College at present is every way comfortable: I live in very good amity and agreement with my chambermate. There has no new quarrels broke out betwixt me and any of the scholars, though they still persist in their former combination; but I am not without hopes that it will be abolished by this meeting of the Trustees.

I have not as yet wrote to uncle [Stephen] Mix, because I heard he was coming down. But he delaying his coming I shall do it speedily. I am at present in perfect health, and it is a time of health throughout the College and town. I am about taking the remainder of my *lignum vitæ*. I am much reformed with respect to visiting of friends, and intend to do more at it for the future than in time past. I think I shall not have occasion for the coat you mentioned in your letter till I come home. I received a letter from my sister Mary the week before last, and have heard of her welfare this week by a man that came directly from thence. I pray you in your next letter to send me your advice whether or no I had best come home in May, or tarry till June.

Please to give my humble duty to my mother, hearty love to sisters and Mercy [Brooks], and still to be mindful before the throne of grace of me, who am, honored Sir,

Your most dutiful son,
Jonathan Edwards.

Stiles presents his duty to yourself with my mother, and service to my sisters.

7. TO MARY EDWARDS

In this letter, written during Edwards' second year of graduate studies, he reiterates affection for his sister Mary. The College is quiet. Edwards is interested in news of the family. No hint is given of the "uneasy thoughts" that he was experiencing about the state of his soul.[1] His life-changing religious experience, which he later described in his "Personal Narrative," had occurred in the spring of 1721.

(Trask Library, ALS, one folio leaf.)

* * *

Yale College, December 12, 1721

Dear Sister,

I at length have obtained the wished-for opportunity of sending a letter to you, though disappointed of the much more desired one of receiving one from you. 'Tis really a thousand pities that the great remove and distance of place which we are at from each other, should cause anything that should appear as if we were at as great a distance in all other respects, whereas we are no further distant than the bounds of the same family will let us be, and tied by the near relation of brother and sister. I'll tell you, my sister, the consideration of this much affects me. I heartily wish it may be otherwise and promise that I will do my part for the future to make it otherwise. I assure you the distance of place does not detract at all from my affections to you. And I hope that which remains in you to me will prompt you to do your part also, and to send me a letter by the first opportunity and therein an account of your state in the family, whether comfortable or otherwise particularly with [respect to your crookedness].[2] And I should be glad of particular information concerning cousin Solomon [Williams], whether he is like to settle or no, and anything else remarkable that occurs in your parts. I have nothing to inform you of from hence but health, peace, and quiet, and that I am got settled in the buttery for another year and all things hitherto proceed prosperously.

There is one of the scholars lies under suspension for some atrocious crimes. The fellow is that noted [Ebenezer] Gould who I suppose you have heard of, for I conclude that he is known all over your county. I have nothing else whereby I may produce this letter to a suitable

---

1. Hopkins, quoting JE's "Personal Narrative," pp. 24–26.
2. MS damage; supplied text based on JE's letter to Mary Edwards, May 10, 1716.

length, but my duty to be presented to my grandparents [Solomon and
Esther Stoddard], uncle and aunt [William and Christian Stoddard
Williams], and humble service to cousin Solomon [and to] tell you that
I am [. . .]

Jonathan Edwards.[3]

8. TO THE COMMITTEE OF BOLTON, CONNECTICUT

The people of Bolton, Connecticut, wanted Jonathan Edwards as their
minister. He had promised to consider the offer before he left Bolton for New
York in August 1722. Now, in fulfillment of that promise, he gave his answer:
he would probably not remain as pastor in the city but return home in the
spring. Whether the congregation waited for him was up to them. His father
evidently wanted to keep the opportunity open and wrote in his forwarding
note that he saw nothing in Jonathan's letter to discourage them.[1]

After Edwards returned home, on May 27, 1723, the Bolton town meeting
formally voted to call him as minister and confirmed this by salary votes on
October 10 and 28 and November 4. Edwards signed the town book, accepting the pastorate, on November 11.[2] Thomas Schafer has demonstrated that
Edwards served in Bolton as minister, with occasional sidetrips, until he began
work as a tutor at Yale in June 1724.[3]

(CHS, ms. 71914, ALS, one folio leaf; heading, in the hand of Timothy
Edwards, to the Gentlemen of the Committee for the Town of Bolton; addressed on verso to Mr. Nathaniel Loomis in Bolton. Published in Stoughton,
pp. 84–85.)

*   *   *

New York, December 10, 1722

Gentlemen,

According to my promise I here send you the most plenary and
satisfactory answer that I can from the best observations and most
mature deliberations I have been able to make since my return to New
York. I have not been able to come to a full determination whether to

3. The leaf is torn at the bottom, but the top of the signature is visible.
1. Timothy Edwards to the Gentlemen of the Committee in the Town of Bolton, Jan. 16,
1722/23, letter printed in Stoughton, pp. 83–84. Bolton was about twelve miles southeast of
East Windsor.
2. Stoughton, pp. 81–82.
3. *Works, 13,* 13–14, 80–82. Schafer has corrected Dwight's notion (*1*, 95) that JE spent
the winter and spring, 1723–24, at New Haven in study. See also Dexter, *History,* p. 254;
Hopkins, p. 20.

leave [New] York in a short time or no, but I think for the present, considering the circumstances of the society, and my father's inclinations to the contrary, it seems most probable that I shall not settle here, but am ready to think I shall leave them in the spring. I believe I shall not return into New England till that time. Whether you will wait with expectation of me so long a time is entirely with you and as you think fit. I think it would be unreasonable in me to desire or expect it of you, especially considering that it is not absolutely certain that I shall leave [New] York then.

This is all the resolution, gentlemen, that I can possibly give you at this time. I assure you I have a great esteem of, and affection to, the people of your town so far as I am acquainted with them, and should count it a smile of providence upon me if ever I should be settled amongst such a people as your Society seems at present to me to be. I heartily wish for your prosperity in all things, especially upon spiritual accounts, that God would give you an able, faithful, pious, and successful pastor that may be a great instrument of the advancement of God's glory and the eternal interests of souls among you.

I am your hearty friend and humble servant,
Jonathan Edwards.

9. TO JUDGE PAUL DUDLEY

The "Spider Letter" is one of the best known of Edwards' writings. Though no longer believed to have been written when Edwards was aged twelve or younger, as Sereno Dwight surmised, the letter nevertheless exhibits Edwards' keen interest in nature and natural laws. For years, starting as a boy, Edwards had observed spiders, analyzed his findings, and systematically recorded them. While endeavoring to explain spider behavior within the framework of modern science, he sought the "why" as well as the "how." Here, in a truly Augustinian-Franciscan fashion, and in the manner of St. Bonaventure's *Mind's Journey to God,* Edwards finds the handiwork of the Creator in the least of his creatures.

His father, no doubt, encouraged Jonathan's activity from the outset, as well as the preparation of this report, which was in all likelihood sent to Judge Paul Dudley, Timothy's friend and college classmate and Fellow of the Royal Society in London.

(NYHS, Misc. Mss., ALS, one full sheet of foolscap; Trask Library, AL draft, in two parts: one folio leaf, irregular, on a letter cover, addressed to Jonathan Edwards at Windsor; and one folio leaf. Published in Dwight ed., *1,*

22–28; Egbert C. Smyth, "The Flying Spider," *Andover Review* 17 [Jan. 1890], 1–19; *Works, 6,* 163–69. For Timothy Edwards and Paul Dudley, see Timothy's ms. letter to Dudley, Oct. 18, 1723, HSP, Dreer Collection, American Clergy. For the wider implications of the letter, and of Edwards' interest in science, see *Works, 6,* 38–42.)

* * *

Windsor, October 31, 1723

Sir:

In the postscript of your letter to my father you manifest a willingness to receive anything else that he has observed in nature worthy of remark; that which is the subject of the following lines by him was thought to be such: he has laid it upon me to write the account, I having had advantage to make more full observations. If you think, Sir, that they are not worthy the taking notice of, with greatness and goodness overlook and conceal. They are some things that I have happily seen of the wondrous and curious works of the spider. Although everything pertaining to this insect is admirable, yet there are some phenomena relating to them more particularly wonderful.

Everybody that is used to the country knows of their marching in the air from one tree to another, sometimes at the distance of five or six rods, though they are wholly destitute of wings: nor can one go out in a dewy morning at the latter end of August and beginning of September but he shall see multitudes of webs reaching from one tree and shrub to another; which webs are commonly thought to be made in the night because they appear only in the morning by reason of the dew that hangs on them, whereas they never work in the night, they love to lie still when the air is dark and moist; but these webs may be seen well enough in the daytime by an observing eye, by their reflection of the sunbeams; especially late in the afternoon may those webs that are between the eye, and that part of the horizon that is under the sun, be seen very plainly, being advantageously posited to reflect the rays, and the spiders themselves may be very often seen traveling in the air from one stage to another amongst the trees in a very unaccountable manner.

But, Sir, I have often seen that which is yet more astonishing. In a very calm serene day in the forementioned time of year, standing at some distance behind the end of an house or some other opaque body, so as just to hide the disk of the sun and keep off his dazzling rays, and looking along close by the side of it, I have seen vast multitudes of little shining webs and glistening strings, brightly reflecting the sunbeams, and some of them of a great length, and at such a height that one would think that they were tacked to the vault of the heavens, and would be burnt like tow in the sun, making a very pleasing as well as surprising appearance. It is wonderful at what a distance these webs may plainly be seen in such a position to the sunbeams, which are so fine that they cannot be seen in another position, though held near to the eye; some that are at a great distance appear (it cannot be otherwise) several thousands of times as big as they ought: they doubtless appear under as great an angle as a body of a foot diameter ought to do at such a distance; so greatly doth coruscation increase the apparent bigness of bodies at a distance, as is observed of the fixed stars. But that which is most astonishing is that very often there appears at the end of these webs, spiders sailing in the air with them, doubtless with abun-

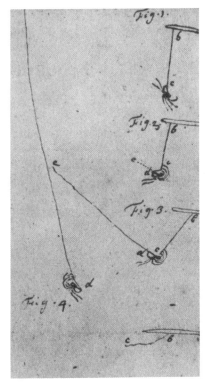

dance of pleasure, though not with so much as I have beheld them and showed them to others. And since I have seen these things I have been very conversant with spiders. Resolving if possible to find out the mysteries of these their amazing works, and pursuing my observations, I discovered one wonder after another till I have been so happy as very frequently to see their whole manner of working; which is thus:

When a spider would go from one tree or branch to another, or would recreate himself by sailing or floating in the air, he first lets himself down a little way from the twig he stands on by a web, as [in] fig. 1; and then taking hold of it by his forefeet as in fig. 2, and then separates or loosens the part of the web *cd* from the part *bc* by which he hangs; which part of the web *cd*, being thus loosened, will by the motion of the air be carried out towards *e*, which will by the sufferance of the spider be drawn [out] of his tail with infinite ease by the moving air, to what length the spider pleases, as [in] fig. 3. And if the further end of the web *de*, as it is running out and moving to and fro, happens to catch by a shrub or the branch of a tree, the spider immediately feels it and fixes the hither end of it, *d*, to the web *bc*, and goes over as by a bridge by the web *de*. Every particular of this, Sir, my eyes have innumerable times made me sure of, saving that I never could distinctly see how they separated the part of the web *cd* (fig. 2) from the part *bc*, whether it be done by biting of it off or how, because so small a piece of so fine a web is altogether imperceptible amongst the spider's legs, and because the spider is so very quick and dexterous in doing of it all. But I have seen that it is done, though I have not seen how they do it. For this, Sir, I can see that the web *bc* (fig. 3) is separated, and not joined to the spider's tail, while the web *de* is drawing out.

Now, Sir, it is certain that these webs, when they first come from the spider, are so rare a substance that they are lighter than the air, because they will immediately ascend in a calm air, and never descend except driven by a wind; and 'tis as certain that what swims and ascends in the air is lighter than the air, as that what ascends and swims in water is lighter than that. So that if we should suppose any such time wherein the air is perfectly calm, this web is so easily drawn out of the spider's tail, that barely the levity of it is sufficient to carry it out to any length. But at least its levity, or ascending inclination, together with so much motion as the air is never without, will well suffice for this. Wherefore, if it be so that the end of the web *de* (fig. 3) catches by no tree nor other body till it be drawn out so long that its levity shall be so great as to be more than equal to the gravity of the spider, or so that the web and the spider taken together shall be lighter than such a quantity of air as takes up equal space, then according to the universally acknowledged laws of nature the web and the spider together will ascend and not descend in the air. As when a man [is] at the bottom of the water, if he has hold of a piece of timber so great that the wood's tendency upwards is greater than the man's tendency downwards, he together with the wood will ascend to the surface of the water. Therefore, when the spider perceives that the web *de* is long enough to bear him up by its ascending force (which force the spider feels by its drawing of him towards *e*), he lets go his hold of the web *bc* (fig. 4) and, holding by the web *de*, ascends and floats in the air with it. If there be not web more than enough just to equal with its levity the gravity of the spider, the spider together with the web will hang *in equilibrio*, neither ascending nor descending, otherwise than as the air moves; but if there be so much web that its ascending tendency, or rather the buoying force of the air upon it, shall be greater than the descending tendency of the spider, they will ascend till the air is so thin, till they together are just of an equal weight with so much air. But if the web be so short as not to counterpoise the weight of the spider, the web and spider will fall till they come to the ground.

And this very way, Sir, I have multitudes of times seen spiders mount away into the air with a vast train of this silver web before them from a stick in mine hand; for if the spider be disturbed upon the stick by shaking of [it] he will presently in this manner leave it. Their way of working may very distinctly be seen if they are held up in the sun, in a calm day, against a dark door or anything that is black.

And this, Sir, is the way of spiders' working. This is the way of their going from one thing to another at a distance, and this is the way of their flying in the air. And although I can say I am certain of it, I don't desire that the truth of it should be received upon my word, though I could bring others to testify to it to whom I have shown it, and who have looked on with admiration: but everyone's eyes who will take the pains to observe will make them equally sure of it; only those who would make experiment must take notice that it is not every sort of spider that is a flying spider, for those spiders that keep in houses are a quite different sort, as also those that keep in the ground, and those [that] keep in swamps upon the ground amongst the bogs, and those that keep in hollow trees and rotten logs; but those spiders that keep on branches of trees and shrubs are the flying spiders. They delight most in walnut trees, and are that sort of spiders that make those curious, network, polygonal webs that are so frequently to be seen in the latter end of the year. There are more of this sort of spider by far than of any other.

Corol. 1. Hence the wisdom of the Creator in providing of the spider with that wonderful liquor with which their bottle tail is filled, that may so easily be drawn out so exceeding fine, and being in this way exposed to the air will so immediately convert to a dry substance that shall be so very rare as to be lighter than the air, and will so excellently serve to all their purposes.

Corol. 2. Hence the exuberant goodness of the Creator, who hath not only provided for all the necessities, but also for the pleasure and recreation of all sorts of creatures, even the insects.

But yet, Sir, I am assured that the chief end of this faculty that is given them is not their recreation but their destruction, because their destruction is unavoidably the constant effect of it; and we find nothing that is the continual effect of nature but what is the end of the means by which it is brought to pass; but it is impossible but that the greatest part of the spiders upon the land should every year be swept into the ocean. For these spiders never fly except the weather be fair and the atmosphere dry, but the atmosphere is never clear and dry, neither in this nor any other continent, only when the wind blows from the midland parts, and consequently towards the sea, as here in New England, the fair weather is only when the wind is westerly, the land being on that side and the ocean on the easterly. I scarcely ever have seen any of these spiders flying but when they have been hastening directly towards the sea. And the time of their flying being so long, even from about the middle of August, every sunshiny day till about the end of October (though their chief time, as was observed before, is the latter end of August and beginning of September). And they, never flying from the sea but always towards it, must get there at last. And it seems unreasonable to think that they have sense to stop themselves when they come near the sea, for then we should [see] hundreds of times more spiders on the seashore than anywhere else. When they are once carried over the water, their webs grow damp and moist and lose their levity and their wings fail them, and let them down into the water.

   The same also holds true of other sorts of flying insects, for at those times that I have viewed the spiders with their webs in the air there has also appeared vast multitudes of flies at a great height, and all flying the same way with the spiders and webs, direct to the ocean. And even such as butterflies, millers, and moths, which keep in the grass at this time of year, I have seen vastly higher than the tops of the highest trees, all going the same way. These I have seen towards evening, right overhead, and without a screen to defend my eye from the sunbeams, which I used to think were seeking a warmer climate. The reason of their flying at that time of year, I take to be because the ground and trees and grass, the places of their residence in summer, begin to be chill and uncomfortable. Therefore when the sun shines pretty warm they leave them, and mount up into the air and expand their wings to the sun, and flying for nothing but their own ease and comfort, they suffer themselves to go that way that they can go with the greatest ease, and so where the wind pleases; and it being warmth they fly for, they never fly against the wind nor sidewise to it, they find that cold and laborious; they therefore seem to use their wings but just so much as to bear them up, and suffer themselves to go with the wind. So that it must necessarily be that almost all aerial insects, and spiders which live upon them and are made up of them, are at the end of the year swept away into the sea and buried in the ocean, and leave nothing behind them but their eggs for a new stock the next year.

Corol. 1. Hence [there] is reason to admire at the wisdom of the Creator, and to be convinced that it is exercised about such little things in this wonderful contrivance of annually carrying off and burying the corruption and nauseousness of the air, of which flying insects are little collections, in the bottom of the ocean where it will do no harm; and especially the strange way of bringing this about in spiders, which are collections of these collections, their food being flying insects, flies being the poison of the air, and spiders are the poison of flies collected together. And what great inconveniences should we labor under if it were not so, for spiders and flies are such exceedingly multiplying creatures, that if they only slept or lay benumbed in winter, and were raised again in the spring, which is commonly thought, it would not be many years before we should be plagued with as vast numbers as Egypt was. And if they died ultimately in winter, they by the renewed heat of the sun would presently again be dissipated into those nauseous vapors of which they are made up, and so would be of no use or benefit, in that in which now they are so very serviceable and which is the chief end of their creation.

Corol. 2. The wisdom of the Creator is also admirable in so nicely and mathematically adjusting their plastic nature, that notwithstanding their destruction by this means and the multitudes that are eaten by birds, that they do not decrease and so by little and little come to nothing; and in so adjusting their destruction to their multiplication they do neither increase, but taking one year with another, there is always an equal number of them.

These, Sir, are the observations I have had opportunity to make on the wonders that are to be seen in the most despicable of animals. Although these things appear for the main very certain to me, yet, Sir, I submit it all to your better judgment, and deeper insight. I humbly beg to be pardoned for running the venture, though an utter stranger, of troubling you with so prolix an account of that which I am altogether uncertain whether you will esteem worthy of the time and pains of reading. Pardon me if I thought it might at least give you occasion to make better observations on these wondrous animals, that should be

worthy of communicating to the learned world, from whose glistening
webs so much of the wisdom of the Creator shines. Pardon, Sir,

Your most obedient humble servant,
Jonathan Edwards.

10. TO THE REVEREND BENJAMIN COLMAN

This letter is a key document of the period that came to be known as the
Great Awakening. It precipitated the waves of religious fervor that swept the
American colonies during the next twenty-five years, and had repercussions
far beyond.

Benjamin Colman, the distinguished influential Boston minister who was
the recipient of the letter, immediately requested of Edwards a more detailed
version of the awakening of 1734 and 1735 described in it. As a result, Edwards wrote a larger letter that was abridged by Colman and first published in
Boston in 1736 under Colman's supervision as an appendix to two sermons of
William Williams.[1] On publication, Colman sent copies of the extract to Isaac
Watts and John Guyse, friends in London, who were greatly impressed by it.
They at once asked for the full text, as well as for permission to edit and print
it. These were given, and *Faithful Narrative* issued from the London press in
1737.[2]

Many other books on the subject had appeared before, but this one caught
on like wildfire, igniting flames of revival in England, Scotland, and America.
It encouraged intense interest in conversion experiences, prepared the way
for George Whitefield's historic tours, and initiated a broad range of ministerial activity.

(Trask Library, AL writer's copy, four folio leaves, notation on verso in

---

1. *The Duty and Interest of a People, among Whom Religion Has been Planted, to Continue Stedfast
and Sincere in the Profession and Practice of It, from Generation to Generation. With Directions for
Such as Are Concerned to Obtain True Repentance and Conversion to God* (Boston, 1736).

2. *A Faithful Narrative of the Surprizing Work of God in the Conversion of Many Hundred Souls in
Northampton, and the Neighbouring Towns and Villages of New-Hampshire in New-England* (London, 1737).

Watts was a long-time correspondent of Benjamin Colman, as attested by his letters to
Colman, from 1723 to 1741, in the Watts Collection of the MHS. Colman's letter to Watts is
quoted in Thomas Milner, *The Life, Times, and Correspondence of the Rev. Isaac Watts, D. D.*
(London, 1834), pp. 553–54. The response of Watts and Guyse is given in Watts' letter dated
Feb. 28, 1737, quoted in *PMHS*, ser. 2, IX (1894–95), 353. For JE's permission for Watts and
Guyse to edit, see his letter to Colman of May 19, 1737 (No. 16), below. His later caveat
concerning their alterations and mistakes, written in a copy of the first edition JE presented
to Yale, is quoted in *Works, 4*, 38.

Edwards' hand, "My Letter to a Brother May 30–35"; Trask Library, Dwight ms. transcript. Published in Faust and Johnson, pp. 73–84; *Works, 4,* 99–110.)

* * *

Northampton, May 30, 1735

Dear Sir,

In answer to your desire, I here send you a particular account of the present extraordinary circumstances of this town, and the neighboring towns with respect to religion. I have observed that the town for this several years have gradually been reforming; there has appeared less and less of a party spirit, and a contentious disposition, which before had prevailed for many years between two parties in the town. The young people also have been reforming more and more; they by degrees left off their frolicking, and have been observably more decent in their attendance on the public worship. The winter before last there appeared a strange flexibleness in the young people of the town, and an unusual disposition to hearken to counsel, on this occasion. It had been their manner of a long time, and for ought I know, always, to make sabbath-day nights and lecture days to be especially times of diversion and company-keeping. I then preached a sermon on the sabbath before the lecture, to show them the unsuitableness and inconvenience of the practice, and to persuade them to reform it; and urged it on heads of families that it should be a thing agreed among them to govern their families, and keep them in at those times. And there happened to be at my house the evening after, men that belonged to the several parts of the town, to whom I moved that they should desire the heads of families, in my name, to meet together in their several neighborhoods, that they might know each others' minds, and agree every one to restrain his family; which was done, and my motion complied with throughout the town. But the parents found little or no occasion for the exercise of government in the case; for the young people declared themselves convinced by what they had heard, and willing of themselves to comply with the counsel given them; and I suppose it was almost universally complied with thenceforward.

After this there began to be a remarkable religious concern among some farm houses at a place called Pascommuck, and five or six that I hoped were savingly wrought upon there. And in April [1734] there was a very sudden and awful death of a young man in town, in the very bloom of his youth, who was violently seized with a pleurisy and taken immediately out of his head, and died in two days; which much affected many young people in the town. This was followed with another death of a young married woman, who was in great distress in the beginning of her illness, but was hopefully converted before her death; so that she died full of comfort, and in a most earnest and moving manner, warning and counseling others, which I believe much contributed to the solemnizing of the spirits of the young people in the town; and there began evidently to appear more of a religious concern upon people's minds. In the fall of the year I moved to the young people that they should set up religious meetings, on evenings after lectures, which they complied with; this was followed with the death of an elderly person in the town, which was attended with very unusual circumstances, which much affected many people. About that time began the great noise that there was in this part of the country about Arminianism, which seemed strangely to be overruled for the promoting of religion. People seemed to be put by it upon inquiring, with concern and engagedness of mind, what was the way of salvation, and what were the terms of our acceptance with God; and what was said publicly on that occasion, however found fault with by many elsewhere, and ridiculed by some, was most evidently attended with a very remarkable blessing of heaven, to the souls of people in this town, to the giving of them an universal satisfaction with respect to the thing in question, and engaging their minds the more earnestly to seek salvation in the way that had been made evident to them.

And then a concern about the great things of religion began, about the latter end of December and the beginning of January [1735], to prevail abundantly in the town, till in a very little time it became universal throughout the town, among old and young, and from the highest to the lowest. All seemed to be seized with a deep concern about their eternal salvation; all the talk in all companies, and upon occasions was upon the things of religion, and no other talk was anywhere relished; and scarcely a single person in the whole town was left unconcerned about the great things of the eternal world. Those that were wont to be the vainest and loosest persons in town, seemed in general to be seized with strong convictions. Those that were most disposed to contemn vital and experimental religion, and those that had the greatest conceit of their own reason, the highest families in the town, and the oldest persons in the town, and many little children were affected remarkably; no one family that I know of, and scarcely a person, has been exempt. And the Spirit of God went on in his saving influences, to the appearance of all human reason and charity, in a truly wonderful and astonishing manner. The news of it filled the neighboring towns with talk, and there were many in them that scoffed and made a ridicule of the religion that appeared in Northampton. But it was observable that it was very frequent and common that those of other towns that came into the town, and observed how it was here, were greatly affected, and went home with wounded spirits, and were never more able to shake off the impression that it made upon them, till at length there began to appear a general concern in several of the towns in the county.

In the month of March the people in New Hadley seemed to be seized with a deep concern about their salvation, all as it were at once, which has continued in a very great degree ever since. About the same time there began to appear the like concern in the west part of Suffield, which has since spread into all parts of the town. It next began to appear at Sunderland, and soon became universal, and to a very great degree. About the same time it began to appear in part of Deerfield, called Green River, and since has filled the town. It began to appear also at a part of Hatfield, and after that the whole town in the second week in April seemed to be seized at once, and there is a great and general concern there. And there gradually got in a considerable degree of the same concern into Hadley Old Society, and Mr. [Samuel] Hopkins' parish in [West] Springfield, but it is nothing near so great as in many other places. The next place that we heard of was Northfield, where the concern is very great and general. We have heard that there is a considerable degree of it at Longmeadow, and there is something of it in Old Springfield in some parts of the Society. About three weeks ago the town of Enfield were struck down as it were at once, the worst persons in the town seemed to be suddenly seized with a great degree of concern about their souls, as I have been informed. And about the same time, Mr. [Nehemiah] Bull of Westfield [said] that there began to be a great alteration there, and that there had been more done in one week before that time that I spoke with him than had been done in seven years before. The people of Westfield have till now above all other places, made a scoff and derision of this concern at Northampton.

There has been a great concern of a like nature at Windsor, on the west side of the [Connecticut] River, which began about the same time that it began to be general here at Northampton; and my father has told me that there is an hopeful beginning on the east side in his society. Mr. [Joseph] Noyes writes me word that there is a considerable revival of religion at New Haven; and I have been credibly informed that there is something of it at Guilford and Lyme, as there also is at Coventry, Bolton and a Society in Lebanon called The Crank. I yesterday saw Mr. [Thomas] White of Bolton, and also last night saw a young man that belongs to Coventry, who gave me a very remarkable account of that town, of the manner in which the rude debauched young people there were suddenly seized with a concern about their souls.

As to the nature of persons' experiences, and the influences of that spirit that there is amongst us, persons when seized with concern are brought to forsake their vices, and ill practices; the looser sort are brought to forsake and to dread their former extravagances. Persons are soon brought to have done with their old quarrels; contention and intermeddling with other men's matters seems to be dead amongst us. I believe [that] there never was so much done at confessing of faults to each other, and making up differences, as there has lately been. Where that concern comes it immediately puts an end to differences between ministers and people: there was a considerable uneasiness at New Hadley between some of the people and their minister, but when this concern came amongst them it immediately put an end to it, and the people are now universally united to their minister. There was an exceeding alienation at Sunderland, between the minister and many of the people; but when this concern came amongst them it all vanished at once, and the people are universally united in hearty affection to their minister. There were some men at Deerfield, of turbulent spirits, that kept up an uneasiness there with Mr. [Jonathan] Ashley; but one of the chief of them has lately been influenced, fully and freely, to confess his fault to him, and is become his hearty friend.

People are brought off from inordinate engagedness after the world, and have been ready to run into the other extreme of too much neglecting their worldly business and to mind nothing but religion. Those that are under convictions are put upon it earnestly to inquire what they shall do to be saved, and diligently to use appointed means of grace, and apply themselves to all known duty. And those that obtain hope themselves, and the charity of others concerning their good estate, generally seem to be brought to a great sense of their own exceeding misery in a natural condition, and their utter helplessness, and insufficiency for themselves, and their exceeding wickedness and guiltiness in the sight of God; it seldom fails but that each one seems to think himself worse than anybody else, and they are brought to see that they deserve no mercy of God, that all their prayers and pains are exceeding worthless and polluted, and that God, notwithstanding all that they have done, or can do, may justly execute his eternal wrath upon them, and they seem to be brought to a lively sense of the excellency of Jesus Christ and his sufficiency and willingness to save sinners, and to be much weaned in their affections from the world, and to have their hearts filled with love to God and Christ, and a disposition to lie in the dust before him. They seem to have given them a lively conviction of the truth of the gospel, and the divine authority of the holy Scriptures; though they can't have the exercise of this at all times alike, nor indeed of any other grace. They seem to be brought to abhor themselves for the sins of their past life, and to long to be holy, and to live holily, and to God's glory; but at the same time complain that they can do nothing, [for] they are poor impotent creatures, utterly insufficient to glorify their Creator and Redeemer. They commonly seem to be much more sensible of their own wickedness after their conversion than before, so that they are often humbled by it; it seems to them that they are really become more wicked, when at the same time they are evidently full of a gracious spirit. Their remaining sin seems to be their very great burthen, and many of them seem to long after heaven, that there they may be rid of sin. They generally seem to be united in dear love and affection one to another, and to have a love to all mankind. I never saw the Christian spirit in love to enemies so exemplified in all my life as I have seen it within this half year. They commonly express a great concern for others' salvation; some say that they think they are far more concerned for others' conversion, after they themselves have been converted, than ever they were for their own; several have thought (though perhaps they might be deceived in it) that they could freely die for the salvation of any soul, of the meanest of mankind, of any Indian in the woods.

This town never was so full of love, nor so full of joy, nor so full of distress as it has lately been. Some persons have had those longing desires after Jesus Christ, that have been to that degree as to take away their strength, and very much to weaken them, and make them faint. Many have been even overcome with a sense of the dying love of Christ, so that the frame of the body has been ready to fail under it; there was once three pious young persons in this town talking together of the dying love of Christ, till they all fainted away; though 'tis probable the fainting of the two latter was much promoted by the fainting of the first. Many express a sense of the glory of the divine perfections, and of the excellency and fullness of Jesus Christ, and of their own littleness and unworthiness, in a manner truly wonderful and almost unparalleled; and so likewise of the excellency and wonderfulness of the way of salvation by Jesus Christ. Their esteem of the holy Scriptures is exceedingly increased. Many of them say the Bible seems to be a new book to them, as though they never read it before. There have been some instances of persons that by only an accidental sight of the Bible, have been as much moved, it seemed to me, as a lover by the sight of his sweetheart. The preaching of the Word is greatly prized by them; they say they never heard preaching before: and so are God's sabbaths, and ordinances, and opportunities of public worship. The sabbath is longed for before it comes; some by only hearing the bell ring on some occasion in the week time, have been greatly moved, because it has put them in mind of its ringing to call the people together to worship God. But no part of public worship has commonly [had] such an effect on them as singing God's praises. They have a greater respect to ministers than they used to have; there is scarcely a minister preaches here but gets their esteem and affection.

The experiences of some persons lately amongst [us] have been beyond almost all that ever I heard or read of. There is a pious woman in this town that is a very modest bashful person, that was moved by what she heard of the experiences of others earnestly to seek to God to give her more clear manifestations of himself, and evidences of her own good estate, and God answered her request, and gradually gave her more and more of a sense of his glory and love, which she had with intermissions for several days, till one morning the week before last she had it to a more than ordinary degree, and it prevailed more and more till towards the middle of the day, till her nature began to sink under it, as she was alone in the house; but then came somebody into the house, and found her in an unusual, extraordinary frame. She expressed what she saw and felt to him; it came to that at last that they raised the neighbors, they being afraid she would die; I went up to see her and found her perfectly sober and in the exercise of her reason, but having her nature seemingly overborne and sinking, and when she could speak expressing in a manner that can't be described the sense she had of the glory of God, and particularly of such and such perfections, and her own unworthiness, her longing to lie in the dust, sometimes her longing to go to be with Christ, and crying out of the excellency of Christ, and the wonderfulness of his dying love; and so she continued for hours together, though not always in the same degree. At some times she was able to discourse to those about her; but it seemed to me if God had manifested a little more of himself to her, she would immediately have sunk and her frame dissolved under it. She has since been at my house, and continues as full as she can hold, but looks on herself not as an eminent saint, but as the worst of all, and unworthy to go to speak with a minister; but yet now beyond any great doubt of her good estate.

There are two persons that belong to other towns that have had such a sense of God's exceeding greatness and majesty, that they were as it were swallowed up; they both of them told me to that purpose that, if in the time of it, they had had the least fear that they were not at peace with that great God, they should immediately have died. But there is a very vast variety of degrees of spiritual discoveries, that are made to those that we hope are godly, as there is also in the steps and method of the Spirit's operation in convincing and converting sinners, and the length of time that persons are under conviction before they have comfort.

There is an alteration made in the town in a few months that strangers can scarcely conceive of; our church I believe was the largest in New England before, but persons lately have thronged in, so that there are very few adult persons left out. There have been a great multitude hopefully converted; too many, I find, for me to declare abroad with credit to my judgment. The town seems to be full of the presence of God; our young people when they get together instead of frolicking as they used to do are altogether on pious subjects; 'tis so at weddings and on all occasions. The children in this and the neighboring towns have been greatly affected and influenced by the Spirit of God, and many of them hopefully changed; the youngest in this town is between nine and ten years of age. Some of them seem to be full of love to Christ and have expressed great longings after him and willingness to die, and leave father and mother and all things in the world to go to him, together with a great sense of their unworthiness and admiration at the free grace of God towards them. And there have been many old people, many above fifty and several near seventy, that seem to be wonderfully changed and hopefully newborn. The good people that have been formerly converted in the town have many of them been wonderfully enlivened and increased.

This work seems to be upon every account an extraordinary dispensation of providence. 'Tis extraordinary upon the account of universality of it, its affecting all sorts, high and low, rich and poor, wise and unwise, old and young, vicious and moral; 'tis very extraordinary as to the numbers that are hopefully savingly wrought upon, and particularly the number of aged persons and children and loose livers; and also on the account of the quickness of the work of the Spirit in them, for many seem to have been suddenly taken from a loose way of living, and to be so changed as to become truly holy, spiritual, heavenly persons; 'tis extraordinary as to the degrees of gracious communications, and the abundant measures in which the Spirit of God has been poured out on many persons; 'tis extraordinary as to the extent of it, God's Spirit being so remarkably poured out on so many towns at once, and its making such swift progress from place to place. The extraordinariness of the thing has been, I believe, one principal cause that people abroad have suspected it.

There have been, as I have heard, many odd and strange stories that have been carried about the country of this affair, which it is a wonder some wise men should be so ready to believe. Some indeed under great terrors of conscience have had impressions on their imaginations; and also under the power of spiritual discoveries, they have had livelily impressed ideas of Christ shedding his blood for sinners, his blood running from his veins, and of Christ in his glory in heaven and such like things, but they are always taught and have been several times taught in public not to lay the weight of their hopes on such things and many have nothing of any such imaginations. There have been several persons that have had their natures overborne under strong convictions, have trembled, and han't been able to stand, they have had such a sense of divine wrath; but there are no new doctrines embraced, but people have been abundantly established in those that we account orthodox; there is no new way of worship affected. There is no oddity of behavior prevails; people are no more superstitious about their clothes, or anything else than they used to be. Indeed, there is a great deal of talk when they are together of one another's experiences, and indeed no other is to be expected in a town where the concern of the soul is so universally the concern, and that to so great a degree. And doubtless some persons under the strength of impressions that are made on their minds and under the power of strong affections, are guilty of imprudences; their zeal may need to be regulated by more prudence, and they may need a guide to their assistance; as of old when the Church of Corinth had the extraordinary gifts of the Spirit, they needed to be told by the Apostle that the spirit of the prophets were subject to the prophets, and that their gifts were to be exercised with prudence, because God was not the author of confusion but of peace [I Cor. 14:32–33]. There is no unlovely oddity in people's temper prevailing with this work, but on the contrary the face of things is much changed as to the appearance of a meek, humble, amiable behavior. Indeed, the devil has not been idle, but his hand has evidently appeared in several instances endeavoring to mimic the work of the Spirit of God and to cast a slur upon it, and no wonder. And there has hereby appeared the need of the watchful eye of skillful guides, and of wisdom from above to direct them.

There lately came up hither a couple of ministers from Connecticut, viz. Mr. [Hezekiah] Lord of [North] Preston, and Mr. [John] Owen of Groton, who had heard of the extraordinary circumstances of this and the neighboring towns, who had heard the affair well represented by some, and also had heard many reports greatly to its disadvantage, who came on purpose to see and satisfy themselves; and that they might thoroughly acquaint themselves, went about and spent [the] good part of a day in hearing the accounts of many of our new converts, and examining of them, which was greatly to their satisfaction; and they took particular notice, among other things, of the modesty with which persons gave account of themselves, and said that the one-half was not told them, and could not be told them; and that if they renounced these persons' experiences they must renounce Christianity itself. And Mr. Owen said particularly as to their impressions on their imaginations, they were quite different from what had been represented, and that they were no more than might naturally be expected in such cases.

Thus, Sir, I have given you a particular account of this affair which Satan has so much misrepresented in the country. This is a true account of the matter as far as I have opportunity to know, and I suppose I am under greater advantages to know than any person living. Having been thus long in the account, I forbear to make reflections, or to guess what God is about to do; I leave this to you, and shall only say, as I desire always to say from my heart, "To God be all the glory, whose work alone it is." And let him have an interest in your prayers, who so much needs divine help at this day, and is your affectionate brother,

And humble servant,
Jonathan Edwards.

Northampton, June 3, 1735

Since I wrote the foregoing letter, there has happened a thing of a very awful nature in the town. My Uncle [Joseph] Hawley, the last sabbath-day morning [June 1], laid violent hands on himself, and put an end to his life, by cutting his own throat. He had been for a considerable time greatly concerned about the condition of his soul; till, by the ordering of a sovereign providence he was suffered to fall into [a] deep melancholy, a distemper that the family are very prone to; he was much overpowered by it; the devil took the advantage and drove him into despairing thoughts. He was kept very much awake a-nights, so that he had but very little sleep for two months, till he seemed not to have his faculties in his own power. He was in a great measure past a capacity of receiving advice, or being reasoned with. The coroner's inquest judged him delirious. Satan seems to be in a great rage, at this extraordinary breaking forth of the work of God. I hope it is because he knows that he has but a short time. Doubtless he had a great reach, in this violent attack of his against the whole affair. We have appointed a day of fasting in the town this week, by reason of this and other appearances of Satan's rage amongst us against poor souls. I yesterday saw a woman that belongs to Durham [Connecticut], who says there is a considerable revival of religion there.

I am yours, etc.,
Jonathan Edwards.

11. TO COL. JOHN PYNCHON ET AL.

Robert Breck, the young master of arts from Harvard, began preaching for the First Church of Springfield, Massachusetts, on May 26, 1734. On August 7, the parish called him as minister. Rumors began to fly about his doctrine and conduct, to such an extent that the Hampshire Association refused to proceed with ordination until Thomas Clap had attested to his orthodox character. This was a blow to Breck, who earlier had been forced to leave the Scotland Parish (Second Church of Windham, Connecticut) because of Clap's opposition. Consequently, on October 12 he declined the Springfield call.[1]

The church, persisting in its desire to have Breck as pastor, appointed a committee on March 18, 1735, to meet with the association and consider its objections. William Pynchon wrote a letter to the association, and Breck him-

1. SIB, *8*, 661–64; CVHM, Parish Records, First Church, Springfield, Mass., 1734, pp. 1, 3.

self submitted a defense, but the association's request for a meeting to discuss allegations went unanswered.[2]

Impatient at the delay, the church repeated the call to Breck on April 4. He accepted on July 28, and battle was joined.[3] Most of the association ministers were arrayed against Breck, who was supported by a majority of the Springfield church. Closely watching the fray from a distance were his old nemesis, Thomas Clap, on one side, and some well-connected Boston ministers on the other. This letter is the opening volley.

(CVHM, ALS, written by Samuel Hopkins and signed by Edwards and his colleagues on behalf of the Association, one folio leaf, addressed on verso to Col. John Pynchon and others at Springfield.)

* * *

Hatfield, August 7, 1735

Gentlemen,

We have received yours, considered the contents, and in answer we say: We are sorry to find so little regard is shown to the advice we offered to the town of Springfield, respecting their settlement of Mr. [Robert] Breck. We think we have acted in faithfulness to the parish, and in tenderness to him, being not only willing, but desirous, of his improvement in public service, so it may be consistent with the honor of God, and of the gospel ministry. We were and still are of opinion that it was the first step that ought to have been taken, that the matters objected against him should have been duly inquired into by a committee of our Association, and upon his declining that, it hath been proposed to him to have it heard before the whole Association; which, being refused, we judge it proper for you to inform yourselves as to the truth of the things objected against him, that you may the better judge whether, in faithfulness to your souls and to the souls of your children, you may submit to his settlement with you, and to lay the matter before

2. Parish Records, First Church, Springfield, Mass., 1735, CVHM, p. 5; and Breck Controversy Collection, CVHM (hereafter BCC), MS letters: Breck to the Hampshire Association, copy by Peter Reynolds, April 1735, and William Pynchon to the Association, Apr. 8, 1735.

When the Association met on Apr. 8, 1735 at the Second Parish of Springfield (later West Springfield), the members discussed the Breck case. JE was in attendance. See the Hampshire Association of Ministers Records, 1731–47, Forbes Library.

3. Parish Records, First Church, Springfield, Mass., 1735, pp. 7, 9; for Breck's acceptance, see the MS copy by Thomas Stebbins, clerk, BCC.

the next Association, the beginning of October (unless this case shall require that it be convened sooner). We esteem them to be the only proper judges of the case, but if your neighbors drive on an ordination speedily, we judge it to be your duty, to enter your dissent and give your reasons for so doing, and support them by all the evidence you can obtain in the case.

That peace and truth may flourish amongst you and your neighbors, is the hearty desire of

> Your friends and servants,
> William Williams
> Stephen Williams
> Samuel Hopkins
> Jonathan Edwards.

12. TO CAPT. WILLIAM PYNCHON, JR.

This letter, written at the same time as the preceding, to another Springfield leader opposed to Breck, gives guidance as to strategy and timing. The ministers requested that a council meet on the charges in advance of the ordination. Following Edwards' advice, the dissenters repeated their wish that there be an association meeting, but their request was denied.[1]

(CVHM, ALS, probably written by Nehemiah Bull but signed by Edwards and others, one quarto leaf, addressed on verso to Capt. William Pynchon, Jr., at Springfield. Ms. postscript in Edwards' hand.)

* * *

Hatfield, August 14, 1735

Sir,

We have considered the application made by a number of you to us, that we would use our endeavors, etc. We are ready to do any service that is proper for us to do in the case, but if you expect that the ministers of the county should do anything for you, we apprehend that it is proper and most likely to be serviceable, if your company

1. See MS pledge of twenty-three members, headed by William Pynchon, Jr., to share any legal expenses required, Aug. 8, 1735; writer's copy of letter from persons dissatisfied with Breck (signed by initials, with William Pynchon, Jr.'s first) to Reverend Sirs (Association ministers), Aug. 16, 1735; Springfield dissenters (twenty-two signatures) to Hampshire Association, Aug. 15, 1735; and unsigned letter to Rev. William Williams, Sept. 10, 1735; all in BCC.

should call the Association together to Springfield and send for Mr. [Daniel] Kirtland, [Thomas] Clap, and such others as they shall think needful to bring with 'em to be present at the meeting of the Association, some suitable time before the intended ordination comes on. And if you should, by a letter subscribed by your whole number to the moderator of the Association, call the Association together, care shall be taken to inform Mr. [Robert] Breck and desire his appearance.

We think it proper that your party should show the letter we send 'em to Mr. Breck and his adherents, and let 'em know your design of calling the Association, etc. And if they please to join two or three unexceptionable gentlemen to the Association, we have nothing against it. Please to keep this letter wholly with yourself.

Your hearty friends,
William Williams
Samuel Hopkins
Jonathan Edwards
Nehemiah Bull.

P.S. By what we understand by Mr. [William] Rand and Mr. [Grindall] Rawson, we think it probable that the ordination is intended either on the first or second week in September, and most probably on the first; and, therefore, what is done must be done with all possible speed; the Association at furthest must be called on Tuesday, the first week in September.

13. TO COL. JOHN PYNCHON

In August 1735, the Hampshire Association of ministers was seeing its recommendations ignored and its authority flouted. Determined to install Breck as pastor, the main body of First Church, Springfield, moved rapidly to summon an advisory council that would include Boston ministers. At the same time, some church leaders, backed by a quarter of the members, made feverish efforts to block the ordination, or at least to have an open hearing under the auspices of the association. This letter shows the encouragement the ministers, under their leader, Rev. William Williams, gave to the opposition.

(CVHM, ALS, not in Edwards' hand but signed by him and others, one folio leaf, addressed on verso to Col. John Pynchon, at Springfield.)

* * *

Hatfield, August 14, 1735

Gentlemen,

We have received yours and the enclosed copy of your declaration to Mr. [Robert] Breck, which we look upon to be very reasonable and just, and which in concern for the honor of God and the ministry ought to be done; and we account it preposterous for the church of Springfield to call him, or for him to accept a call to the ministry, before the matters objected against him had been duly inquired into and he had obtained a due vindication, and to proceed as the church and Mr. Breck have done and we hear are about to do seems to be, after vows to make inquiry; and we cannot but testify against it as an irregular and disorderly proceeding, and we cannot in conscience concur to such an ordination, and must say that Mr. Breck's conduct in this affair is very surprising to us. We are free to declare before God and the world that, according to our best judgment in all the advice we have given in the affair, we have acted in faithfulness to Springfield and from no prejudice against Mr. Breck.

And we think we have reason to resent the reflections that have been cast upon us as persons prepossessed and prejudiced, etc., but are willing to bind it as a crown to us, knowing in whose cause we suffer it. We can hardly think any number of ministers will be found to serve the scheme of Springfield and Mr. Breck and impose a pastor upon our Association without our consent. But if they desire some other ministers to be joined with us in hearing the cause, and Mr. [Thomas] Clap and others be duly notified some convenient time before an ordination be concluded on, it is what we have been willing to concur with.

We subscribe, your loving friends, wishing the peace of your parish and the prosperity of religion among you.

William Williams
Samuel Hopkins
Jonathan Edwards
Nehemiah Bull.

14. TO CAPT. WILLIAM PYNCHON, JR.

Edwards continued to take an active part in the association's committee on the Breck situation. This letter is his last before departing on an extended trip to New York for his health. In it he repeats the association's offer to meet with Breck and the church to consider objections, a proposal that was never accepted.

(CVHM, ALS, two-thirds of one folio leaf, addressed on verso to William Pynchon, Jr., Esq., at Springfield, to be communicated [to the church].)

* * *

Hatfield, August 26, 1735

Gentlemen,

We received your information as to the day appointed by your church for the ordination of Mr. [Robert] Breck. We before signified our willingness, if you desired it, that our Association should be convened, and that your neighbors, if they desire it, should join two or three meet persons to hear Mr. [Thomas] Clap's and others' objections against Mr. Breck. We wait to know your desire and your neighbors'; and that we may know when Mr. Clap's, etc., coming may be expected, and whether tomorrow three weeks may be proper for it, unless, instead of having the Association of the ministers called together, you choose jointly to have a council of the churches convened at that time, or at least a week before ordination, to whom the affair may be submitted for determination. Having, we hope, nothing else in our view but the honor of God and the ministry, and your peace and edification, we are

> Your brethren and friends,
> William Williams
> Jonathan Edwards
> Nehemiah Bull.

15. TO THE REVEREND SAMUEL HOPKINS (OF SPRINGFIELD)

When Edwards returned from New York, he resumed his leading role in the Breck matter. During his absence, the struggle had escalated, with the arrest of Breck for preaching heresy and consequent appeal of the church to the Massachusetts House of Representatives. In the effort to win public support, the association hurried to publish its side of the case. As this letter shows, Edwards actively gathered statements to win subscribers. The finished product, co-written by Edwards and his brother-in-law Samuel Hopkins, appeared in Boston in early 1736, too late to prevent the association's legislative defeat. Breck was ordained in January.[1]

1. For the Association apologetic, see *A Narrative of the Proceedings of Those Ministers of the*

(Beinecke Library, ALS, shorn fragment. Place and date are probable.)

* * *

[Northampton, c. November 1735]

Rev. and Dear Sir,

I would desire you to send me by the bearer the testimonies against Mr. [Robert] Breck, all of them, if you have them by you. I have desired that some of our people might meet at my house on Wednesday night, that I may give them a particular account of the affair, in order to their subscribing to print our narrative and defense. And I should be glad then to show them the testimonies.

I desire you would also send me an account how much Springfield people have subscribed, and whether or no you sent any order to Capt. [William] Pynchon, [Jr.,] what number should be printed. And if you have not, I wish you would do it by the first opportunity. I should think that a thousand should be printed at least, and don't be afraid lest we should not get money enough. My wife prays that her cloth may be sent if done. I am, Sir, your affectionate brother [and][2]

Humble servant,
Jonathan Edwards.

16. TO THE REVEREND BENJAMIN COLMAN[1]

The old meetinghouse of the First Church, Northampton, was packed with worshipers on Sunday morning, March 13, 1737. Edwards had just "laid

---

County of Hampshire, &c. That have Disapproved of the late Measures Taken in Order to the Settlement of Mr. Robert Breck (Boston, 1736). The book generated much discussion, both before and after publication. See Samuel Kneeland to Stephen Williams, Jan. 15, 1735/6, HSP; and note the controversy that arose subsequent to publication, discussed in *Works, 12*, 4–17. This controversy culminated in a defense, written by JE, of the Association's original apologetic, *A Letter to the Author of the Pamphlet Called An Answer to the Hampshire Narrative* (Boston, 1737), in ibid., 91–163. See also, in the CVHM: Stephen Williams to Capt. William Pynchon, Jr., Dec. 20, 1735, which speaks of the Association's original work being collaborative and in which Williams seeks the approval of Benjamin Colman and William Williams of Weston before publication; Samuel Hopkins to William Pynchon, Esq., Dec. 20, 1735, with which the MS of the original apologetic was forwarded and in which Hopkins reveals that he wrote the first part, JE the last; the Appeal of the church to the House of Representatives, Oct. 31, 1735; and the resolution of the House, Dec. 9, 1735, that it will hear the case.

2. MS damage, word missing.
1. The most probable recipient.

down his doctrines" for the text "Behold, ye despisers, and wonder, and perish." He recounts here what happened next.[2]

(Published in *The Boston Gazette,* Mar. 28–Apr. 4, 1737. Excerpted in Dwight ed., *1,* 139–40. The text is in all likelihood only an extract of the original, no longer extant.)

* * *

Northampton, March 19, 1736/7

We in this town were, the last Lord's day (March 13th), the spectators, and many of us the subjects, of one of the most amazing instances of divine preservation, that perhaps was ever known in the land. Our meeting house is old and decayed, so that we have been for some time building a new one, which is yet unfinished. It has been observed of late, that the house that we have hitherto met in, has gradually spread at the bottom; the sills and walls giving way, especially in the foreside, by reason of the weight of timber at top pressing on the braces that are inserted into the posts and beams of the house. It has so done more than ordinarily this spring, which seems to have been occasioned by the heaving of the ground by the extreme frosts of the winter past, and its now settling again on that side which is next the sun, by the spring thaws. By this means, the underpinning has been considerably disordered, which people were not sensible of, till the ends of the joists, which bore up the front gallery, were drawn off from the girts on which they rested, by the walls giving way. So that in the midst of the public exercise in the forenoon, soon after the beginning of sermon, the whole gallery—full of people, with all the seats and timbers, suddenly and without any warning—sunk, and fell down, with the most amazing noise, upon the heads of those that sat under, to the astonishment of the congregation. The house was filled with dolorous shrieking and crying; and nothing else was expected than to find many people dead, or dashed to pieces.

The gallery, in falling, seemed to break and sink first in the middle; so that those that were upon it were thrown together in heaps before the front door. But the whole was so sudden, that many of those who fell, knew nothing what it was, at the time, that had befallen them. Others in the congregation thought it had been an amazing clap of

2. The second meeting house, in use for seventy-six years, was in decrepit condition, taxed beyond capacity by the large congregation. More than 300 new members had been added during the revival only a short time before. The new, third meeting house, then being built, was not ready for use until Jan. 1738. Trumbull, 2, 75–77.

thunder. The falling gallery seemed to be broken all to pieces before it got down; so that some who fell with it, as well as those that were under, were buried in the ruins; and were found pressed under heavy loads of timber, and could do nothing to help themselves.

But so mysteriously and wonderfully did it come to pass, that every life was preserved; and though many were greatly bruised, and their flesh torn, yet there is not, as I can understand, one bone broken, or so much as put out of joint, among them all. Some, who were thought to be almost dead at first, are greatly recovered; and but one young woman seems yet to remain in dangerous circumstances, by an inward hurt in her breast: but of late there appears more hope of her recovery.

None can give an account, or conceive, by what means people's lives and limbs should be thus preserved, when so great a multitude were thus eminently exposed. It looked as though it was impossible but that great numbers must instantly be crushed to death or dashed in pieces. It seems unreasonable to ascribe it to any thing else but the care of providence, in disposing the motions of every piece of timber, and the precise place of safety where every one should sit and fall, when none were in any capacity to care for their own preservation. The preservation seems to be most wonderful with respect to the women and children in the middle alley, under the gallery, where it came down first and with greatest force, and where there was nothing to break the force of the falling weight.

Such an event, may be a sufficient argument of a divine providence over the lives of men. We thought ourselves called on to set apart a day to be spent in the solemn worship of God, to humble ourselves under such a rebuke of God upon us, in the time of public service in his house, by so dangerous and surprising an accident; and to praise his name for so wonderful, and as it were miraculous, a preservation. The last Wednesday was kept by us to that end; and a mercy, in which the hand of God is so remarkably evident, may be well worthy to affect the hearts of all who hear it.

[Jonathan Edwards.]

17. TO THE REVEREND BENJAMIN COLMAN

In 1737 Edwards was already experiencing a letdown from the euphoric heights of the revival. Even the good news of *Faithful Narrative*'s favorable impact abroad failed to lift his spirits in the face of spiritual declension at home. His parishioners were drifting back into their old ways. Edwards is circumspect in this letter to his Boston sponsor, not mentioning qualms he harbors about editorial changes in the London edition of *Faithful Narrative*.[1]

(MHS, Benjamin Colman Papers, ALS, three octavo leaves.)

* * *

Northampton, May 19, 1737

Rev. and Honored Sir,

I humbly thank you for such respect put upon me by you in so large a letter, and those kind and acceptable presents you sent me, which is much more than I deserve or could expect. It is refreshing to hear of the notice that God's servants abroad take of the great things God has done for us; it, as it were, renews the joy of those mercies; but yet at the same time it is a great damp to that joy to consider how we decline, and what decays that lively spirit in religion suffers amongst us, while others are rejoicing and praising God for us.

The work that went on so swiftly and wonderfully while God appeared in mighty and irresistible power to carry it on, has seemed to be very much at a stop in these towns for a long time, and we are sensibly by little and little, more and more declining. And though some that were wrought upon in the time of this great work of God have lately been favored with blessed tokens of God's presence in their souls, enlivening and comforting them, yet there is an evident appearance of a general languishing of persons' lively affections and engagedness of heart in religion, which appears not so much by a return to ways of lewdness and sensuality, among young or old, as by an over-carefulness about, and eagerness after the possessions of this life, and undue heats of spirit among persons of different judgments in public affairs. Contention and a party spirit has been the old iniquity of this town; and as God's Spirit has been more and more withdrawn, so this spirit has of late manifestly revived: not that the generality of the people have been affected with it; there are many that seem sincerely to lament such an appearance of declension; and contention has not been in any wise at the height that it has sometimes formerly been; but yet I am ashamed, and ready to blush, to speak or think of such an appearance of strife, and division of the people into parties as there

1. For further information on these editorial changes, see *Works*, *4*, 36–45. A corrected text of the *Faithful Narrative* may be found in ibid., 144–211.

has been, after such great and wonderful things as God has wrought
for us, which others afar off are rejoicing in, and praising God for, and
expecting (as justly they may) to hear better things of us: but I would
by no means represent us better than we are.

Many in the town seemed to be greatly affected with the late marvelous preservation of so many of us, when so exceedingly exposed to
immediate death (and no life is yet lost, and all are restored to health
and soundness but one very pious young woman, who has been held
down ever since with exceeding inward bruises and ulcers, but seems
very slowly to mend), and some seem to be affected still; but yet it has
had in no wise the effect that ten times less things were wont to have
two or three years ago. God is pleased to let us see how entirely and
immediately the great work lately wrought was his, by withdrawing,
and letting us see how little we can do, and how little effect great things
have without him.

I would pray, honored Sir, if the hearing such things don't dishearten you, that you would earnestly pray for us, that God would not
leave us, but as it has been his good pleasure to do such great things for
us, notwithstanding our unworthiness, for his own name's sake, so that
he would not forsake the work of his own hands, but magnify the same
infinite grace by returning to us, and renewing of us after our ingratitude: if God leaves us to ourselves we shall greatly dishonor religion
and sadly wound and dishonor ourselves. I am sensible I have reason
to lie down in the dust in my own infirmities and unworthiness: God
shows me that whatever he has done here among the people under my
ministry, that yet I am nothing, and can do nothing: I desire your
prayers that I may be more sensible of it, and that God would grant me
his presence and assistance, and *again* grant me success. There seems
to be a spirit of strife prevailing in most of the neighboring towns, at
the same time that God is frowning upon us in our temporal interests:
we in this town indeed have been remarkably preserved from the *throat
distemper,* which has been so terrible in multitudes of towns in the land;
but we have been distressed by the backwardness of the spring; though
not as they have been in many other places in the country, where
multitudes of cattle have died of hunger and cold. The severity of the
past winter has (I suppose) killed more than half of the winter grain
that was sown in this county, and by what I can hear, no less in other
parts of the country: and it now begins to be a time of drought with us.
A dark cloud seems to hang over the land in general, by our being
pursued by one judgment after another, and, which is darkest of all, by

Isaac Watts, anonymous, undated, Dr. Williams' Library, London

our being left, at the same time, to such a degree, to the vile corruptions of our own hearts, and particularly a spirit of contention, disorder, and tumult, in our capital town, and many other places. What seems to be for us to do, is to "wait upon God in our straits and difficulties," according to one of the sermons you kindly sent me, which seems to be very seasonable not only for the present circumstances of *Boston,* but of the country in general.

You mention, Sir, my being displeased at the liberty taken in the extract at the end of my uncle [William] Williams' sermons:[2] certainly somebody has misrepresented the matter to you; I always looked upon it an honor too great for me, for you to be at the trouble to draw an extract of my letter to publish to the world, and that it should be annexed to my honored uncle Williams' sermons: and my main objection against it was that my uncle *Williams* himself never approved of its being put into his book. With regard to the *letter* itself that I wrote, which you have sent to Dr. [Isaac] *Watts,* and Dr. [John] *Guyse,* I will-

2. The reference is to JE's letter to Colman, Nov. 6, 1736, published eventually as the *Faithful Narrative,* but which was first abridged and appended to Williams' *The Duty and Interest of a People.* See *Works, 4,* 32–46.

ingly submit it to their correction, if they think fit to publish it after they come to see it: I am sensible there are some things in it that would not be best to publish in *England*.

I humbly thank you for the honor you have done me in the notice you have taken of that *letter* in one respect or another. I desire, honored Sir, that among the many [things] that you have to bear on your mind, and to bring before the mercy seat in your prayers, you would not forget

> Your most humble, and most obliged son and servant,
> Jonathan Edwards.

18. TO JACOB WENDELL

Jonathan Edwards' love of books was evident throughout his lifetime. He constantly sought, recommended, and lent them. In the next two letters he enlists the aid of a Boston merchant to secure several works.

(Beinecke Library, ALS, one half-sheet.)

* * *

Northampton, August 8, 1737

May It Please Your Honor,

I made so bold with you some time since as to request of you that you would send to England for Chambers' *Cyclopedia*[1] for me, being encouraged thereto by your generosities to the Hampshire ministers. I want very much to know whether you have seen cause to comply with my request, that I may order my business accordingly. If you have sent for them and I may expect their arrival before winter, I would entreat you to send me word by the bearer. Herein you will oblige him who is with the rest of the ministers of this county already, Sir,

> Your obliged, humble servant,
> Jonathan Edwards.

---

1. Ephraim Chambers, *Cyclopedia; or an Universal Dictionary of Arts and Sciences* (London, 1728).

19. TO JACOB WENDELL

(MHS, Wendell Family Papers, ALS, one quarto leaf.)

* * *

Springfield, August 23, 1737

May it please Your Honor,

I sent lately by Mr. [John] Worthington of Springfield, and desired him to inquire of you whether I was like to have those books, that I was so bold with you as to desire you to send for. I am now come down from Northampton to Springfield to see what return Mr. Worthington brings, who informs me that you design to convey to me a set that you have had by you for some time. I am very glad of it, and very thankful to you: I acknowledge it as another instance of that generosity that the ministers of Hampshire have experienced in so many instances.

I send this by Mr. Bliss to inform of a good opportunity to convey them: he is about to send some things of his own by water. And I have desired him to take those books and put them amongst his things, and to take good care to have 'em conveyed. I desire that you would send me an account of the price of the books and I will endeavor to send you the money. I am, honored Sir,

Your most obliged, humble servant,
Jonathan Edwards.

20. DRAFT LETTER ON SLAVERY

Though fragmentary and frustratingly cryptic at points, this document is extremely valuable because it is the only known instance of Edwards speaking explicitly on the issue of slavery and, more specifically, on the enslavement of Africans in the American colonies.[1] Edwards defends the purchase and ownership of slaves provided they fall under the legal definition of a slave, are treated humanely according to law, and are Christianized. He condemns as hypocritical those who denounce slave owning while benefiting from goods produced or imported as a result of the slave trade. Adopting an unusual position, he opposes the extension of the slave trade, that is, enslaving free Africans. He bases his argument on passages taken primarily from the Old

1. For a fuller discussion of the issue and a transcription of the manuscript, see Kenneth P. Minkema, "Jonathan Edwards on Slavery and the Slave Trade," *William and Mary Quarterly* LIV (Oct. 1997), 823–34.

Testament regarding God's allowing the Israelites to buy slaves, and, to a lesser
extent, on passages in the New Testament.

Whereas defenders of the slave trade pointed to it as a means of spreading
the gospel, Edwards foresees the opposite effect. The chances that prophecies
concerning the spread of the gospel to every nation of the world will come
true are diminished, he feels, as a result of the resentment caused by European incursions into Africa.

Edwards' position represented a step toward the immediatism of his New
Divinity disciples. Samuel Hopkins and Jonathan Edwards, Jr., would build
on and extend Edwards' views to advocate the complete abolition of slavery
and a plan of colonization to evangelize Africa.

(Trask Library, letter draft, fragment, two leaves. The text presented here
reflects the incomplete manner in which Edwards sketched out his points for
full elaboration later.)

* * *

[Northampton, c. 1738]

If they ben't partakers of the slaves, they are of their slavery, wherein
the injustice, if there be any, consists. Their slavery mainly consists in
that slavish cruel labor they are put to.

They are partakers of a far more cruel slavery than that which they
object against in those that have slaves here.[2]

That which is almost altogether by their slavery [. . .]

How ill does it suit for a man to cry out of another for taking money
that is stolen, and then taking it of him in that wherein the injustice
consists.

If the slaves are unjustly theirs, then their slavery is unjustly theirs,
and this they are partakers of.

All the difference there can be, is that they are not so immediate
partakers, that it is a step farther off.

No more are we so immediate partakers.

Their argument, if it carries anything, implies that we ought not to
be partakers, neither immediately nor remotely. We ought not to be
partakers at all. If they don't mean so, but only mean by so many steps,
they would do well to fix the number of steps.

And besides, they don't know but that they are partakers as immediately as we. They may have their slaves at next step.

2. JE deleted: "They are partakers of that which is undoubtedly cruel."

Either let them answer them, or let 'em own the matter is well proved, and not go on pretending that those arguments are of no force which they can't or at least don't see cause to answer, only to make disturbances and raise uneasiness among people against their minister, to the great wounding of religion. If they do it, and yet don't answer.

Reproaching their pastor as though he lived in notorous iniquity and indulgence of his lusts—a sin that has no more to be said for it than robbery in the highway—and that which he was not able to vindicate, and had nothing to say for, worth the mentioning. The pastor of the church that has thus been reproached may well insist upon it that his reasons, every one of them, be answered, or otherwise that they be silent for the future. And not only [so], but confess that they were too sudden and rash in casting such reproaches on their pastor, to the great wounding of religion.

Let them also fully and thoroughly vindicate themselves and their own practice in partaking of negroes' slavery, or confess that there is no hurt in partaking in it, or else let 'em cease to partake in it for the future, one of the three. For if they still continue to cry out against those who keep negro slaves as partakers of injustice in making them slaves, and continue still themselves notwithstanding to be partakers of their slavery, let 'em own that their objections are not conscientious, but merely to make difficulty and trouble for their neighbors. Whether or no other nations have any power or business to disfranchise all the nations of Africa. And if they should, whether or no this would not be a greater encroachment on their liberties than even the opposers of this trade themselves do suppose this trade, making those slaves which they offer to sale.

It would have a much greater tendency to sin, to have liberty to disfranchise whole nations.

And let the answers be in writing, that everybody that is so disposed may see what they be, and know whether there be just cause for their boasts when they go about and say the pastor of the church could not answer 'em, could say nothing that was worth a-saying. 'Tis an easy thing for a man thus to boast of his victory in a dispute that nobody heard but him, and so is not able to contradict him.

If men are such notable disputants, and have such invincible reasons to offer, and are so able to baffle their minister, let it appear that they are so by their great arguments being written down, to be read by all.

Don't let some things only be answered and others slipped over in silence.

The practice that prevails in the world of eating and drinking tends to sin, and a world of iniquity is the consequence of it, but we are not therefore to abstain from sin.

And if he should compel him to make a number to sell, will any say that he came honestly by them, or that they were honestly his?

If[3] God's observing and giving leave for a thing prove that it is not unreasonable in its own nature.

God might, by a special interpretation, execute punishment on a people and make men the executioners. But to make it an established rule in all cases so to treat all mankind, and that after they were become his own people, is a monstrous supposition, if it be in itself unreasonable. All God's rules that respect treatment of men and war have moral equity in them, otherwise why is it said, "All this law" which is so righteous as "I set before you" [Deut. 4:8]? A special precept for a particular act is not a rule.

To give leave for a special punishment of the injuriousness of the Egyptians to borrow is quite a different thing from establishing it as a rule that his people might borrow and not pay in all ages.[4]

3. JE drew a vertical line through the next four paragraphs.
4. See Deut. 15:6.

Nothing in itself unlawful. 'Tis unlawful for a man to speak ill of God. 'Tis unlawful for a man to sell those things. They are in their own nature unlawful to be the subject of commerce.

Woe pronounced against him that uses his neighbor's work without wages. This makes the Scripture contradict itself.

All mankind were their neighbors then. Especially all of the same religion. Christ reproves the corrupt interpretation of the Pharisees, who thought otherwise.

Neighbor. By this there is no rule that respects the treatment of any of mankind in the moral law, but only the children of Israel.

Hence it was not against any command of the moral law for the Jews to commit adultery with the wives of men of other nations, or to steal from them, or to bear false witness against them. 'Tis said, "Thou shalt not bear false witness against thy neighbor" [Ex. 20:16].

With respect to the glorious times, it does not follow, because things shall be settled in peace. Here is another admirable [. . .][5]

Lay down this: If it were once lawful, but now unlawful, and not made unlawful by any new positive law that was not in force then when it was lawful, then it must be because 'tis unreasonable in its own nature. But if it be unreasonable in its own nature [. . .].

He says we must know in order to any injury to a man. Then we must know in order to killing a man in war, for there is a personal injury.

I say its not being forbidden under such circumstances, expressly allowed before, and so great a crime in it and so general in the world, is a good argument, because 'tis not conceivable that [. . .]. No other sin generally prevalent that is not expressly mentioned and strictly forbidden. The Apostle speaks of God's winking at some things that were early[6] was of old, in those times of darkness, which intimates that [God] don't wink at such things now under the gospel. But this would be to wink at it in the highest degree conceivable.

There[7] is no action without circumstance. But circumstances are included in the very word. Killing a man is not in itself unlawful, but murder is in itself unlawful. So taking away from our neighbor is not in itself unlawful, in itself reasonable or unreasonable.

I answer, [1.] no more of a contradiction than it is that an inanimate commodity may be justly taken out of the hands of the right owner and yet justly kept out of his hands.

5. "Here is another admirable" is conjectural for an interlineation squeezed in below line.
6. I.e. early in time, in the days of idolatry before the gospel. See Acts 17:30.
7. JE drew a vertical line through this paragraph.

2.[8] It supposes that God gave a law that did tend greatly to encourage iniquity in all the nations round about Canaan by his own pleasure.[9] So that instead of their being a light in the earth, a blessing in the midst, it was dangerous for other nations to live near God's people, which would be a blasphemous way of talking.

The[1] law supposes that they were theirs of whom they bought them, by directing them to buy who were not under laws peculiar to the Jews, and which way came they by them. Otherwise, why did God direct them buy? Why did he not direct them to buy the service of the persons themselves?

It is less supposeable a great deal, than if God had given 'em leave to go and take others at all times. But to buy a thing is to come by [it] in a way of valuable consideration, in a way of commutative justice, and supposes that person possessed.

To give liberty to take those that were *sui juris* what they pleased, is to put 'em into a state of war with all nations.

This supposition, that God gave such a law for a standing rule to his people for a great many ages, is a great reflection on the wisdom, holiness and goodness of God and ought to be abominable to all Christians.

[Jonathan Edwards.]

21. TO THE REVEREND BENJAMIN COLMAN

The *Faithful Narrative* attracted widespread interest in England, Scotland, and elsewhere. A corrected American edition, referred to here, was published later in 1738.

(MHS, Stoddard Family Papers, ALS, one folio leaf.)

*   *   *

Northampton, May 2, 1738

Rev. and Honored Sir,

My wife, being called to Boston on business that we need to have done for our family, that she is much better able to do than I, waits upon you with this, to pay her and my duty to you; I request your blessing and prayers for her. We greatly condole the great sorrows God, in his holy providence, is pleased to bring upon you in your age,

8. JE drew a vertical line through this paragraph.
9. Here JE interlineated the cue, "4. Particular 1. P. 2^d sheet." The sheet is not extant.
1. JE drew a vertical line through the remaining part of the draft.

which we have heard do still continue, and have, not very long since, been attended with peculiar aggravations: we hope that the more outward comforts fail, the more abundantly will the fountain of good be with you.

Mr. [Daniel] *Henchman* some time since informed me that he, and Mr. [Samuel] *Kneeland* had determined to reprint my letter to you, whether they determined it with your *leave* I don't know; I wrote to him by no means to do it without your advice. I hope, Sir, you have let them know your thoughts concerning it.

It has lately been somewhat of a dying time amongst us: and the last week Mr. [Asa] *Wright,* the man that waited on you with my last letter, and brought your return (for which I humbly thank you), had a child killed outright, by a cart's running over him. Religion remains much in the same state amongst us that it has lately been; it is not as it was with us three years ago, nor yet is it as it was before that time of great blessing, and I hope never will be. I desire your prayers for the presence of God with us all, and particularly with him who is, honored Sir,

Your most obedient and obliged son and servant,
Jonathan Edwards.

22. TO THE REVEREND BENJAMIN COLMAN

Edwards here expresses gratitude for the generous welcome Dr. Colman gave his wife in Boston. Reciprocating Colman's news about the favorable reception of Edwards' *Faithful Narrative* by churches in Maine, he includes a report on ten ministers in the Connecticut Valley. Through such letters as this, as well as personal visits, ministers kept in touch with their colleagues' activities.

(Firestone Library, Scheide Library, ALS, one folio leaf.)

*   *   *

Northampton, May 27, 1738

Rev. and Honored Sir,

I return humble thanks for the great civility, and very kind and condescending treatment, which my wife received from yourself and Madam when she was in Boston, and your generous presents sent me by her, together with your letter, in which I am sorry to read that you have no prospect but of the bitter continuance of your great and uncommon affliction, but rejoice that you are so supported under it that it don't wholly sink you but you are enabled still to go on in God's strength in the service of God and his people, and in eminent usefulness to your own congregation and to the land.

I desire to bless God for such a reception of the *Narrative* of the work of God in this county, by Mr. [Samuel] Moody, and the two congregations of York and Berwick, and for the good and lasting impressions on some occasioned by the reading of it, which he mentions. What you inform of Mr. Gibbs of Hackney looks very sorrowful,[1] as many other things do respecting the present state of religion in England, which would be enough to sink the friends of Zion, were it not that God is wont often to appear wonderfully for her, at such times as when enemies have almost swallowed her up.

I am in a poor state of health, and desire of you, honored Sir, your prayers to God that, if it may consist with his will, he would strengthen and renew me in both body and soul, that I may be enabled to go on in, and perform to his acceptance and his people's profit, the great work of the gospel ministry, to which he has called me. I desire to be thankful to God that I am not yet so ill as to be taken off from my work, as I heretofore have been, for a time, once and again, and as many other ministers in the land have been this spring, especially in Connecticut, as particularly Mr. [Stephen] Mix of Wethersfield, Mr. [Thomas] Hawley of Ridgefield, Mr. [Daniel] Chapman of part of Fairfield, Mr. [Elisha] Kent of Newtown, Mr. [Daniel] Humphreys of Derby, Mr. [Judah] Lewis of part of Colchester, Mr. [Chileab] Brainerd of part of Glastonbury, all which have of late been disabled from going on with the ministry by illness, besides Mr. [Nathaniel] Appleton of Cambridge, and Mr. [Stephen] Williams of Longmeadow, in this province; and Mr. [William] Williams of Hatfield, though he still goes on with his work, yet considerably fails in his health this spring, so that he has desired his people to seek an assistant, which they are doing. These things, after the death of Judge [Edmund] Quincy, together with the threatening aspect of things with respect to the line between the Massachusetts and New Hampshire, and the affair now depending in Connecticut, before the King's Court of Commission there, and the injurious, oppressive designs of the Church of England against us, all serve to thicken and darken the cloud that hangs over the land.[2]

1. Not further identified.
2. *The Boston Gazette* for Nov. 27–Dec. 4, 1738, reported that John Tomlinson, Agent for the House of Representatives of New Hampshire, had written a memorial to the King complaining of "Encroachments" by the Governor and General Assembly of Massachusetts

My wife gives her humble duty, and renewed thanks to you and Madam, which I desire may be accepted with my own and that you would remember us both before the throne of grace. I am, honored Sir,

Your most humble and obliged son and servant,

Jonathan Edwards.

23. TO THE REVEREND GEORGE WHITEFIELD

George Whitefield was one of the most compelling preachers in the history of Christianity. Over a span of thirty-two years, beginning in 1738, his oratorical skills and fervent spirit rekindled the fires of revival from Georgia to Maine. Wherever he went, he drew congregations by the hundreds and thousands. Wholesale conversions followed, lives were transformed, and a lasting impact was made on the character of American people. In this letter, Edwards, the father of the Great Awakening, invites its most eloquent spokesman to Northampton, the place where it all began.[1]

(John Rylands Univ. Library, ALS, two folio leaves. Published in Henry Abelove, "Jonathan Edwards' Letter of Invitation to George Whitefield," *William and Mary Quarterly*, ser. 3, 29 [1972], 487–89.)

*   *   *

---

in "their Proceedings respecting the Settlements of the Boundaries between the *Massachusetts* Province and *New Hampshire*." The case was eventually decided in favor of New Hampshire.

The "affair" before "the King's Court of Commissioners" involved another boundary dispute, this time between Connecticut and Rhode Island. On May 24, 1738, representatives from the two colonies as well as from New York convened at Norwich to settle the issue. *Public Records of the Colony of Connecticut* (Hartford, 1852), 7, 156, 164, 178; *8*, 151, 294, 489. Christopher Collier of the University of Connecticut kindly provided this reference.

The 1730s saw increased activity by Church of England missionaries in New England. Such was the resentment amongst New England Congregationalists that when in 1738 an Anglican missionary attempted to build a church on the New Haven green next to Yale College, he was threatened with death by students. Also, new laws sanctioned tax exemptions for Church of England members, Quakers, and Baptists. In May 1738, the Connecticut General Assembly received petitions for equal privileges from Fairfield, Greenwich, Groton, and Hebron. See Robert J. Taylor, *Colonial Connecticut: A History* (Millwood, N.Y., KTO Press, 1979), pp. 128–29; Connecticut Archives, First Series, Ecclesiastical Affairs, 1658–1789, Connecticut State Library.

1. Whitefield accepted the welcome extended in this letter and made his initial visit to Northampton from Friday, Oct. 17, until Sunday, Oct. 20, 1740. He spoke four times publicly and twice to small groups in the Edwards home. The visit is recorded in Daniel Rogers' MS Diary, NYHS; in JE's letter of Dec. 14, 1740 (No. 29), below; and in Whitefield, pp. 475–79.

Northampton in New England, February 12, 1739/40

Sir,

My request to you is that, in your intended journey through New England the next summer, you would be pleased to visit Northampton. I hope it is not wholly from curiosity that I desire to see and hear you in this place; but I apprehend, from what I have heard, that you are one that has the blessing of heaven attending you wherever you go; and I have a great desire, if it may be the will of God, that such a blessing as attends your person and labors may descend on this town, and may enter mine own house, and that I may receive it in my own soul.

Indeed I am fearful whether you will not be disappointed in New England, and will have less success here than in other places: we who have dwelt in a land that has been distinguished with light, and have long enjoyed the gospel, and have been glutted with it, and have despised it, are I fear more hardened than most of those places where you have preached hitherto. But yet I hope in that power and mercy of God that has appeared so triumphant in the success of your labors in other places, that he will send a blessing with you even to us, though we are unworthy of it. I hope, if God preserves my life, to see something of that salvation of God in New England which he has now begun, in a benighted, wicked, and miserable world and age and in the most guilty of all nations.

It has been with refreshment of soul that I have heard of one raised up in the Church of England to revive the mysterious, spiritual, despised, and exploded doctrines of the gospel, and full of a spirit of zeal for the promotion of real vital piety, whose labors have been attended with such success. Blessed be God that hath done it! who is with you, and helps you, and makes the weapons of your warfare mighty. We see that God is faithful, and never will forget the promises that he has made to his church; and that he will not suffer the smoking flax to be quenched, even when the floods seem to be overwhelming it; but will revive the flame again, even in the darkest times. I hope this is the dawning of a day of God's mighty power and glorious grace to the world of mankind. May you go on, reverend Sir! and may God be with you more and more abundantly, that the work of God may be carried on by a blessing on your labors still, with that swift progress that it has been hitherto, and rise to a greater height, and extend further and further, with an irresistible power bearing down all opposition! and may the gates of hell never be able to prevail against you! and may God send forth more laborers into his harvest of a like spirit, until the kingdom of Satan shall shake, and his proud empire fall throughout the earth and the kingdom of Christ, that glorious kingdom of light, holiness, peace and love, shall be established from one end of the earth unto the other!

Give my love to Mr. [William] Seward:[2] I hope to see him here with you. I believe I may venture to say that what has been heard of your labors and success has not been taken notice of more in any place in New England than here, or received with fuller credit. I hope therefore if we have opportunity, we shall hear you with greater attention. The way from New York to Boston through Northampton is but little further than the nearest that is; and I think leads through as populous a part of the country as any. I desire that you and Mr. Seward would come directly to my house. I shall account it a great favor and smile of providence to have opportunity to entertain such guests under my roof, and to have some acquaintance with such persons.

I fear it is too much for me to desire a particular remembrance in your prayers, when I consider how many thousands do doubtless desire it, who can't all be particularly mentioned; and I am far from thinking myself worthy to be distinguished. But pray, Sir, let your heart be lifted up to God for me among others, that God would bestow much of that blessed Spirit on me that he has bestowed on you, and make me also an instrument of his glory. I am, reverend Sir,

Unworthy to be called your fellow laborer,
Jonathan Edwards.

24. TO THE REVEREND ISAAC CHAUNCY

The Reverend Isaac Chauncy, minister at Hadley, Massachusetts, sided with Robert Breck during the ordination controversy of 1735, and he participated in Breck's ordination council. He was so disaffected by those events that he never attended another meeting of the Hampshire Association. As this letter reveals, however, he maintained his ministerial relationships with association members.

2. William Seward accompanied the evangelist on tours and served as administrative assistant. He never got to Northampton because of his unexpected death in London, not long after he was dispatched, in April 1740, to raise funds for a school for African Americans in Philadelphia. "George Whitefield," *Dictionary of National Biography* (22 vols. London, 1908–09), 21, 85–92.

(Beinecke Library, two duodecimo double leaves, in sermons on Heb. 12:22–24 [3] and Titus 2:14.)

* * *

Northampton, February 18, 1739/40

Rev. and Honored Sir,

I fully intended to come to Hadley the next Wednesday, and to have assisted in keeping the fast, as I have been desired, provided it had been safe passing the river. But I have since heard that the measles is in the town, which is a distemper that I am unwilling to expose myself to, both as I am loath to have it myself, so infirm as I am, if I can avoid it, and also as I would be unwilling to bring it into my numerous family, especially under my wife's present circumstances.[1] And having heard that it is a distemper that is often given in persons' breath, to great numbers at meeting, before the persons that give it are taken ill themselves, I think myself in prudence and duty, not called to expose myself.

Wishing you God's smiles and blessing in that important affair that your people now are seeking direction about;[2] and that they may be so directed in their choice as may be much for your comfort, I remain, honored Sir,

Your son and servant,
Jonathan Edwards.

My wife joins with me in presenting our service and duty to you and Mrs. Chauncy.

25. TO SEC. JOSIAH WILLARD

Josiah Willard, Secretary of the Province, was an influential leader in eighteenth-century Massachusetts. His evangelical sympathies, wide contacts, and awareness of world events, made him a logical person to answer Edwards' inquiries about revivals in distant places. The friendship between these two men ripened over the years. In the following decade, Willard would prove to be a staunch, loyal advocate in Edwards' time of need.

(MAR, vol. 53, pp. 65–66, ALS, two folio leaves.)

* * *

1. She was pregnant with daughter, Susannah Edwards, b. June 20, 1740.
2. This refers to calling a colleague pastor for the aged, ailing Chauncy. Chester Williams was chosen.

Northampton, June 1, 1740

Honored Sir,

Such has been your kindness and condescension to me and my wife, both formerly and lately, that I thought myself obliged to acknowledge it in a letter; and am encouraged by it to [be] further in debt to Your Honor, by asking new favors.

From what we hear of the Reverend Mr. [George] Whitefield, his great labors and success, together with other things in providence and the present circumstances of the world, taken with what is foretold in the Scriptures, I cannot but hope that God is about to accomplish glorious things for his church, which makes me the more desirous of knowing as fully as may be the present state of religion in the world. Mr. Whitefield has been so kind as to send me his *Journals*,[1] which give me a considerable idea of the hopeful state of reviving religion in England. But what I desire of you, honored Sir, if you have leisure for it, and it ben't too great a burden for me to desire you to take upon you, is to give me information concerning some things I have heard something of in other parts of the world.

I have some time since heard something of a revival of religion in the King of Prussia's dominions; and there have been some hints of something of that nature in some public prints. If Your Honor has any particular account of that affair, I should be glad [to] know something particularly of it; and also what are the latest accounts of the progress of that affair at Halle in Saxony, begun by the famous Dr. [August Hermann] Francke. I have seen nothing since the account we had of Dr. Francke's life, published by Mr. Samuel Mather in Boston. I exceedingly want to know how things have been since Mr. [Robert] Millar in his *History of the Propagation of Christianity* gives an account of a glorious beginning made in the East Indies by some Danish missionaries; but I have heard nothing since that book was published, which was about nine years ago. He also mentions some things that appeared very hopeful in Moscovy.[2]

Knowing, honored Sir, how much your heart is upon the flourishing

1. See the list of frequently cited titles, above.
2. The paragraph begins with a reference to a revival in Halberstadt, Prussia in 1739 and to the evangelical, charitable, and publishing center established by August Hermann Francke in Halle, Brandenburg-Prussia. The titles are Samuel Mather, *Vita B. August Hermann Francke. . . . Cui adjecta est, narratio rerum memorabilum in ecclesii Evangelicis per Germaniam, etc.* (Boston, 1733); and Robert Millar, *History of the Propagation of Christianity and the Overthrow of Paganism* (London, 1723; 3rd ed., 1731).

of religion, and the advancement of Christ's kingdom, I thought you a person likely to inform yourself concerning things of this nature, and also the more ready to inform others; otherwise, I should not have written to you such a request.

When I thought of writing, I was some time at a loss whether I should not be too bold to put you to so much trouble; but what I have seen and found of your candid and condescending spirit encouraged me to hope that you would at least pardon me. If Your Honor can give me particular information concerning these things, I hope it will be of use not only to me, but to neighboring ministers and many others. My wife joins with me in giving her duty to Your Honor and your Lady. I am, honored Sir,

> Your humble and obliged servant,
> Jonathan Edwards.

26. TO THE REVEREND ELEAZAR WHEELOCK

In this letter, Edwards acts in an official capacity. As representative of the Northampton church, he recommends a former parishioner for full membership in the church at Lebanon Crank, Connecticut. Such a message was "to be communicated," or read to the assembled church.

(Edinburgh University Library, ms. La.II.259, ALS, one duodecimo double leaf.)

* * *

Northampton, July 14, 1740

To the Reverend Mr. Eleazar Wheelock, Pastor of a Church of Christ in Lebanon, to be Communicated.
Rev. and Beloved,

These may certify you that Eunice Lee, formerly Searle, has been admitted as a member of this church in full communion, and so remained, without offense, during her abode here. And being by divine providence removed hence to dwell with you, I can freely recommend her to a reception in like standing with you. Praying that grace, mercy, and peace may be multiplied to you, and asking an interest in your prayers for me and God's church and people here, I am your unworthy friend, fellow laborer, and servant in Christ,

Jonathan Edwards, Pastor of the Church of Christ in Northampton

27. TO THE REVEREND ELEAZAR WHEELOCK

The Reverend Eleazar Wheelock, energetic young minister of Lebanon Crank, Connecticut, had felt the spirit of revival among his own people. After his encounter with George Whitefield at Wethersfield, on October 22, 1740, he would redouble his itinerant activity. In this letter, Edwards expresses appreciation to Wheelock, and reminds him of the Grand Itinerant's imminent arrival.[1]

Edwards also refers to his "aged father," Timothy Edwards, pastor of East Windsor, who was in the midst of a prolonged controversy with his congregation. A couple who had married without their parents' permission wished to baptise their children, but Timothy refused. The argument divided the church, causing Timothy to suspend communion from 1739 to 1741.[2]

(Forbes Library, ALS, one folio leaf.)

* * *

Northampton, October 9, 1740

Rev. and Dear Sir,

I congratulate you, and would bless God for that success which he has lately given to your labors which you mention, and for the many joyful things we have lately heard concerning the city of our God. I think that those that make mention of the Lord should now be awakened and encouraged to call upon God, and not keep silence, nor give him any rest, till he establish and till he make Jerusalem a praise in the earth. And particularly should be earnest with God that he would still uphold, and succeed the Reverend Mr. [George] Whitefield, the instrument that it has pleased him to improve to do such great things for the honor of his name, and at all times so to guide and direct him under his extraordinary circumstances, that Satan may not get any advantage of him.

I thank you for your concern for my aged father under his troubles, and the pains you have occasionally taken with some of his people on his behalf. And also for your kind wishes for me, and for the success of my ministry. We need the prayers of all that are favored with God's presence and the lively influences of his Spirit. It is a sorrowfully dull and dead time with us. The temporal affairs of this town are, and have

1. DEX, *1*, 493–94; "Wheelock, Eleazar," *Dictionary of American Biography*, 20, 58–59; Sprague, *1*, 397–99; Whitefield, p. 479.
2. Stoughton, pp. 73–75.

been for some years, most unhappily situated to be a snare to us, and I know not where to look for help but to God.

O dear Sir! earnestly pray for us. And I desire that now while God smiles upon you, and it is a day of his special favor towards you, that you would pray earnestly for me that I may be filled with the divine Spirit, and that God would improve me though utterly unworthy as an instrument of glory to his name, and of good to the souls of men, and particularly that he would bless Mr. Whitefield's coming here for good to my soul, and the souls of my people. That God would more and more bless and succeed you, and make you more and more a burning and shining light, is the sincere desire and prayer of

> Your unworthy brother and fellow laborer,
> Jonathan Edwards.

P.S. Mine and my wife's love to cousin Wheelock.[3]

28. TO JAMES PIERPONT

Edwards customarily attended the Yale commencement each year during the 1730s and early 1740s. At these times, he and his family would stay with his brother-in-law James Pierpont. Pierpont is almost certainly the recipient, therefore, and September 1740 a likely date.

(Beinecke Library, in Sermon on Matt. 7:13–14, Jan. 1740/1, ALS, two duodecimo leaves, shorn at bottom.)

* * *

[September 1740]

Dear Brother,

Being in haste, I shall only say that if providence allows, and there be any tolerable traveling, my wife and I intend to set out for New Haven the next week. I have sent word of it already to Mr. [William] Russell. If the weather should be extremely stormy, or if anything else unexpectedly should hinder our coming then, we shall come as soon as we can, which with love to you and sister, and prayers to God that he would fill up the great vacancy that he has lately made in your house with his own

---

3. The identity of "cousin Wheelock" cannot be ascertained, though it could have been one of Eleazar's five siblings. Possibly JE considered the Wheelocks as distant relatives through the Huntington family. Eleazar's mother was Ruth Huntington of Norwich, and JE's sister Elizabeth had married Jabez Huntington of Windham.

presence,[1] and that that awful dispensation may be sanctified to us all, is from your

Loving brother,
Jonathan Edwards.

29. TO THE REVEREND GEORGE WHITEFIELD

The revival at Northampton reached its peak in 1740 and 1741, in the aftermath of Whitefield's visit. Here an exultant Edwards reports the early, beneficial effects.

(Published in *The Weekly History*, no. 9 [London, 1741], [1], 2.)

* * *

Northampton, December 14, 1740

Rev. and Dear Sir,

I have joyful tidings to send you concerning the state of religion in this place. It has been gradually reviving and prevailing more and more, ever since you was here. Religion is become abundantly more the subject of conversation; other things that seemed to impede it, are for the present laid aside. I have reason to think that a considerable number of our young people, some of them children, have already been savingly brought home to Christ. I hope salvation has come to this house since you was in it, with respect to one, if not more, of my children. The Spirit of God seems to be at work with others of the family. That blessed work seems now to be going on in this place, especially amongst those that are young.

And as God seems to have succeeded your labors amongst us, and prayers for us, I desire your fervent prayers for us may yet be continued, that God would not be to us as a wayfaring man, that turns aside to tarry but for a night, but that he would more and more pour out his Spirit upon us, and no more depart from us; and for me in particular, that I may be filled with his Spirit, and may become fervent, as a flame of fire in my work, and may be abundantly succeeded, and that it would please God, however unworthy I am, to improve me as an instrument of his glory, and advancing the kingdom of Christ.

[Jonathan Edwards.]

1. The "great vacancy" in the Pierpont house was the death of the late James Pierpont, Sr.'s third wife, and James, Jr.'s mother, Mary Willett Hooker, on Nov. 1, 1740. Donald L. Jacobus, *Families of Ancient New Haven* (8 vols. Rome, New York, 1927), *4*, 1441.

30. TO THE REVEREND BENJAMIN COLMAN

Colman and Edwards had long held each other in high esteem. Here Edwards, in the midst of the revival following Whitefield's visit, reports spiritual victories at home and seeks news of others from Boston.

(MHS, Benjamin Colman Papers, ALS, two quarto leaves, addressed on second verso to the Reverend Dr. Benjamin Colman in Boston.)

* * *

Northampton, March 9, 1740/41

Rev. and Honored Sir,

I humbly thank you for your kindness by Mr. [Noah] Clark in those books you sent me by him, and for all former instances of kindness and condescension to me and my wife. I thank you in particular for the joyful information you are at the trouble to give me in your letter, of the glorious work of God begun at Boston, Charlestown, and Cambridge. I hope it will not only be entertaining but very profitable to many. I read the account you give to our congregation, who seemed sensibly affected with it; and upon it I appointed a lecture to improve it in a sermon. I have lately been credibly informed of a work of God's Spirit wonderfully breaking forth at Hartford in Connecticut. There is considerable degree of it now in this place, chiefly among children, or those who were so in the time of the great work six years ago.

This winter has been a time of the most remarkable and visible blessing of heaven upon my family that ever was; all our children that are capable of religious reflections have been under remarkable impressions, and I can't but think that salvation is come into my house, in several instances. I hope that my four eldest children (the youngest of them between six and seven years of age) have been savingly wrought upon, the eldest some years ago.[1] I desire your thanksgivings to God for the answer of your desires and prayers for us, and the continuance of your prayers for us, and also that God would continue to carry on his work in this town. There is I believe at Deerfield a greater concern than here, and something of it seems to be beginning in some other of the neighboring towns.

I hope, honored Sir (though I know your hands are very full), if there should still come to pass things more remarkable and glorious

---

1. Sarah, Jerusha, Esther, and Mary Edwards.

things, concerning the city of our God in your parts, that you won't be unwilling to send me some information of it. I desire it that I may improve such information to quicken and stir up God's people here and in the neighboring towns. Boston is the head town of the whole land, and Cambridge the chief school of learning. Tidings, therefore, of this nature from these places will have the greater tendency to influence other parts of the country. It is indeed a thing of a most favorable and promising aspect that these places are fired with so happy an impression; they are in New England as the vitals are in the body, and as when they are sick the whole body is diseased, so when health is renewed in them it will tend to diffuse an healthful influence throughout the body.

That God may strengthen you, honored Sir, in your age, and more and more refresh your heart, and cause you to bring forth abundant fruit in old age, and to see much of the salvation of God before you depart, is the hearty prayer

Of your dutiful son and servant,
Jonathan Edwards.

P.S. My wife gives her humble duty to you.

31. TO THE REVEREND ELEAZAR WHEELOCK

At the time this letter was written, Rev. Timothy Edwards had been at odds with his parishioners for three years, barring them from communion. In this stalemate, Jonathan's solution was to have two young revivalists come in with their fresh, enthusiastic approach. The plan proved successful, and harmony was restored.[1]

(Baker Library, Frederick Chase Coll., ms. 741351, AL, one folio leaf fragment, torn at bottom.)

* * *

Northampton, June 9, 1741

Rev. and Dear Sir,

The special occasion of my now writing to you is a desire I have of two things. One is that you and your brother [Benjamin] Pomeroy would go to Scantic,[2] my father's parish, and preach there as often as the people will be willing to hear you, and continue so doing as long as

1. Stoughton, pp. 73–74.
2. Another name for East Windsor.

the concerns of your own parishes will allow of your being absent. You know the wretched circumstances of that society; and if ever they are healed, I believe it must be by a reviving and prevailing of true religion amongst them. By all that I can understand they are wholly dead, in this extraordinary day of God's gracious visitation. The minds of people there will be more open to your preaching than to my father's, against whom they have such a personal prejudice. You have lately been so remarkably blessed elsewhere, that I can't but hope you would have success there also. I have written to my father to inform him that I have desired this of you.

Another thing that I desire of you is that you would come up hither and help us, both you and Mr. Pomeroy. There has been a reviving of religion amongst us of late; but your labors have been much more remarkably blessed than mine. Other ministers I have heard have [. . .] but here I engage you shall [. . .] with the like [. . .]

[Jonathan Edwards.]

32. TO DEBORAH HATHEWAY

The town of Suffield, Massachusetts,[1] had experienced revivals in 1734 and, later, as a result of Whitefield's visit in 1740 and a visit from Edwards in early 1741, before the famous preaching of *Sinners*.[2] So it was natural for Deborah Hatheway, an eighteen-year-old convert who was without a pastor,[3] to turn to a known, trusted adviser for counsel. Responding to her inquiry, Edwards wrote this guide for a young Christian, with emphasis upon attitude and behavior.

Conspicuously absent from this letter are minatory rhetoric and theological complexities. Instead, a serene tone pervades. Lay exhortation is permitted on a private level; initiative and responsibility are stressed, as long as they accompany absolute reliance on direct divine assistance. In this, Edwards echoes the Shema, Psalms, and New Testament.

(The location of the original ms. is unknown. In addition to early printed copies, there is a ms. copy in an unknown hand, probably eighteenth century, in the Beinecke Library, which is followed here; and a Dwight ms. copy in the Trask Library. The letter, often reprinted, has become a classic of Christian

1. Suffield was not part of Connecticut until May 1749. Conn. *Register and Manual* (1962), p. 452.

2. Whitefield, p. 478; Stephen Williams, Diary for Apr. 14, 1741, Storrs Library, Longmeadow, Mass.; JE, Sermon on Luke 19:41 (1741), Beinecke Library.

3. Rev. Ebenezer Devotion, a promoter of the revivals, died Apr. 11, 1741. His successor, Rev. Ebenezer Gay, was not called until Nov. 5, 1741.

devotion. Publication began in 1807 under the title *Advice to Young Converts;* beginning in 1827, the letter was widely distributed by the American Tract Society. By 1875, at least 328,000 copies had been issued. See Thomas H. Johnson, *The Printed Writings of Jonathan Edwards, 1703–1758, A Bibliography* [Princeton, 1940], pp. 99–101.)

* * *

Northampton, June 3, 1741

Dear Child,

As you desired me to send you in writing some directions, how to conduct yourself in your Christian course, I would now answer your request. The sweet remembrance of the great things I have lately seen at Suffield, and the dear affections for those persons I have there conversed with, that give good evidences of a saving work of God upon their hearts, inclines me to do anything that lies in my power, to contribute to the spiritual joy and prosperity of God's people there. And what I write to you, I would also say to other young women there, that are your friends and companions and the children of God; and therefore desire you would communicate it to them as you have opportunity.

1. I would advise you to keep up as great a strife and earnestness in religion in all parts of it, as you would do if you knew yourself to be in a state of nature and was seeking conversion. We advise persons under convictions to be earnest and violent for the kingdom of heaven, but when they have attained to conversion they ought not to be the less watchful, laborious and earnest in the whole work of religion, but the more; for they are under infinitely greater obligations. For want of this, many persons in a few months after their conversion have begun to lose the sweet and lively sense of spiritual things, and to grow cold and flat and dark, and have pierced themselves through with many sorrows, whereas if they had done as the Apostle did, Phil. 3:12–14, their path would have been as the shining light, that shines more and more unto the perfect day.

2. Don't leave off seeking, striving and praying for the very same things that we exhort unconverted persons to strive for, and a degree of which you have had in conversion. Thus pray that your eyes may be opened, that you may receive your sight, that you may know your self, and be brought to God's foot, and that you may see the glory of God

and Christ and may be raised from the dead, and have the love of Christ shed abroad in your heart; for those that have most of these things, had need still to pray for them; for there is so much blindness and hardness and pride and death remaining, that they still need to have that work of God wrought upon them, further to enlighten and enliven them; that shall be a bringing out of darkness into God's marvelous light, and a kind of new conversion and resurrection from the dead. There are very few requests that are proper for a natural person, but that in some sense are proper for the godly.

3. When you hear sermons hear 'em for yourself: though what is spoken in them may be more especially directed to the unconverted, or to those that in other respects are in different circumstances from yourself. Yet let the chief intent of your mind be to consider with yourself, in what respects is this that I hear spoken, applicable to me, and what improvement ought I to make of this for my own soul's good?

4. Though God has forgiven and forgotten your past sins, yet don't forget 'em yourself: often remember what a wretched bond slave you was in the land of Egypt. Often bring to mind your particular acts of sin before conversion, as the blessed apostle Paul is often mentioning his old blaspheming, persecuting and injuriousness, to the renewed humbling of his heart and acknowledging that he was the least of the apostles, and not worthy to be called an apostle, and the least of all saints, and the chief of sinners. And be often in confessing your old sins to God, and let that text be often in your mind, Ezek. 16:63, "That thou mayest remember and be confounded, and never open thy mouth any more because of thy shame, when I am pacified toward thee for all that thou hast done, saith the Lord God."

5. Remember that you have more cause, on some accounts a thousand times, to lament and humble yourself for sins that have been since conversion than before, because of the infinitely greater obligations that are upon you to live to God. And look upon the faithfulness of Christ in unchangeably continuing his loving favor, and the unspeakable and saving fruits of his everlasting love, notwithstanding all your great unworthiness since your conversion, to be as great or wonderful, as his grace in converting you.

6. Be always greatly abased for your remaining sin, and never think that you lie low enough for it, but yet don't be at all discouraged or disheartened by it; for though we are exceeding sinful, yet we have an advocate with the Father, Jesus Christ the righteous, the preciousness of whose blood, and the merit of whose righteousness and the great-

ness of whose love and faithfulness does infinitely overtop the highest mountains of our sins.

7. When you engage in the duty of prayer, or come to the sacrament of the Lord's Supper, or attend any other duty of divine worship, come to Christ as Mary Magdalene did, Luke 7:37–38. Come and cast yourself down at his feet and kiss 'em, and pour forth upon him the sweet perfumed ointment of divine love, out of a pure and broken heart, as she poured her precious ointment out of her pure, alabaster, broken box.

8. Remember that pride is the worst viper that is in the heart, the greatest disturber of the soul's peace and sweet communion with Christ; it was the first sin that ever was, and lies lowest in the foundation of Satan's whole building, and is the most difficultly rooted out, and is the most hidden, secret and deceitful of all lusts, and often creeps in, insensibly, into the midst of religion and sometimes under the disguise of humility.

9. That you may pass a good judgment of the frames you are in, always look upon those the best discourses and the best comforts that have most of these two effects, viz. those that make you least, lowest, and most like a little child; and secondly, those that do most engage and fix your heart in a full and firm disposition to deny yourself for God, and to spend and be spent for him.

10. If at any time you fall into doubts about the state of your soul under darkness and dull frames of mind, 'tis proper to look over past experiences, but yet don't consume too much of your time and strength in poring and puzzling thoughts about old experiences, that in dull frames appear dim and are very much out of sight, at least as to that which is the cream and life and sweetness of them: but rather apply yourself with all your might, to do an earnest pursuit after renewed experiences, new light, and new, lively acts of faith and love. One new discovery of the glory of Christ's face, and the fountain of his sweet grace and love will do more towards scattering clouds of darkness and doubting in one minute, than examining old experiences by the best mark that can be given, a whole year.

11. When the exercise of grace is at a low ebb, and corruption prevails, and by that means fear prevails, don't desire to have fear cast out any other way, than by the reviving and prevailing of love, for 'tis not agreeable to the method of God's wise dispensations that it should be cast out any other way; for when love is asleep, the saints need fear to restrain them from sin and therefore it is so ordered that at such times

fear comes upon them, and that more or less as love sinks. But when love is in lively exercise, persons don't need fear, and the prevailing of love in the heart, naturally tends to cast out fear, as darkness in a room vanishes away as you let more and more of the perfect beams of the sun into it, I John 4:18.

12. You ought to be much in exhorting and counseling and warning others, especially at such a day as this, Heb. 10:25. And I would advise you especially, to be much in exhorting children and young women your equals; and when you exhort others that are men, I would advise that you take opportunities for it, chiefly when you are alone with them, or when only young persons are present. See I Tim. 2:9, 11–12.

13. When you counsel and warn others, do it earnestly, affectionately and thoroughly. And when you are speaking to your equals, let your warnings be intermixed with expressions of your sense of your own unworthiness, and of the sovereign grace that makes you differ; and if you can with a good conscience, say how that you in yourself are more unworthy than they.

14. If you would set up religious meetings of young women by yourselves, to be attended once in a while, besides the other meetings that you attend, I should think it would be very proper and profitable.

15. Under special difficulties, or when in great need of or great longings after any particular mercies for your self or others, set apart a day of secret fasting and prayer alone; and let the day be spent not only in petitions for the mercies you desired, but in searching your heart, and looking over your past life, and confessing your sins before God not as is wont to be done in public prayer, but by a very particular rehearsal before God, of the sins of your past life from your childhood hitherto, before and after conversion, with particular circumstances and aggravations, also very particularly and fully as possible, spreading all the abominations of your heart before him.

16. Don't let the adversaries of religion have it to say, that these converts don't carry themselves any better than others. See Matt. 5:47, "What do ye more than others"; how holily should the children of God, and the redeemed and the beloved of the Son of God behave themselves? Therefore walk as a child of the light and of the day and adorn the doctrine of God your Savior; and particularly be much in those things, that may especially be called Christian virtues, and make you like the Lamb of God; be meek and lowly of heart and full of a pure, heavenly and humble love to all; and abound in deeds of love to others,

and self-denial for others, and let there be in you a disposition to account others better than yourself.

17. Don't talk of things of religion and matters of experience with an air of lightness and laughter, which is too much the manner in many places.

18. In all your course, walk with God and follow Christ as a little, poor, helpless child, taking hold of Christ's hand, keeping your eye on the mark of the wounds on his hands and side, whence came the blood that cleanses you from sin and hiding your nakedness under the skirt of the white shining robe of his righteousness.

19. Pray much for the church of God and especially that he would carry on his glorious work that he has now begun; and be much in prayer for the ministers of Christ, and particularly I would beg a special interest in your prayers, and the prayers of your Christian companions, both when you are alone and when you are together, for your affectionate friend, that rejoices over you, and desires to be your servant,

In Jesus Christ,
Jonathan Edwards.

33. TO SARAH EDWARDS

Edwards' oldest daughter, Sarah, who was twelve years old when this letter was written, was visiting her uncle and aunt, William and Abigail Edwards Metcalf, in Lebanon, Connecticut. Her father, in familiar fashion, begins with a reminder that religious commitment is the only worthy basis for life. At the time Edwards wrote this letter, Sarah's body may have appeared "very weak and infirm," but it carried her to seventy-six years of age, into the next century.

(Yale, Jonathan Edwards College, ALS, one folio leaf, addressed on verso to Sarah Edwards in Lebanon.)

* * *

Northampton, June 25, 1741

Dear Child,

Your mother has received two letters from you since you went away. We rejoice to hear of your welfare, and of the flourishing of religion in Lebanon. I hope you will well improve the great advantage God is thereby putting into your hands for the good of your own soul. You have a very weak and infirm body, and I am afraid are always like to have; and it may be are not to be long-lived; and while you do live, are not like to enjoy so much of the comforts of this life as others do by reason of your want of health; and therefore if you have no better portion, will be miserable indeed. But if your soul prospers you will be an happy blessed person, whatever becomes of your body. I wish you much of the presence of Christ and communion with him, and that you might live so as to give him honor in the place where you are by an amiable behavior towards all.

Your mother would have you work your shoes if you can, and she would be glad if your aunt [Abigail Edwards Metcalf] would set you to work something of hers, though you do but little in a day. She would have you send word by Mr. [Eleazar] Wheelock, who I suppose will come up the next week or the week after, whether you are well enough to make lace. If you are, she will send you a lace and bobbins.

The flourishing of religion in this town, and in these parts of the country, has rather increased since you went away. Your mother joins with me in giving her love to you, and to your uncle [William Metcalf] and aunt. Your sisters give their love to you, and their duty to them. The whole family is glad when we hear from you. Recommending you to the continual care and mercy of heaven, I remain,

Your loving father,
Jonathan Edwards.

34. TO DEACON MOSES LYMAN

When Edwards wrote this letter, New England was still being shaken by revivals. Although he disagreed with extremists like James Davenport, with his boisterous spirit, emotional extremism, and vituperative attacks, Edwards was not about to disown the movement he had done so much to foster. From this brief reply to a former resident of Northampton who had moved to Goshen, Connecticut, in 1739, Edwards would expand and refine his views over the next five years, beginning with *Distinguishing Marks*, preached the next month at Yale College, and continuing through *Some Thoughts* and *Religious Affections*. As an advocate of Whitefield's, Edwards was obligated to uphold the principle of itinerancy, but it was doomed to be restricted by act of the Connecticut legislature in May 1742.[1]

1. DEX, *1*, 447–48.

(Trask Library, ALS, one folio leaf. No address by Edwards, but a cata-
loguer has penciled in that the recipient was Lyman.)

* * *

Northampton, August 31, 1741

Dear Friend,

In my prodigious fullness of business and great infirmity of body, I
have time to write but very briefly concerning those things you mention. Concerning the great stir that is in the land, and those extraordinary circumstances and events that it is attended with, such as persons
crying out, and being set into great agonies, with a sense of sin and
wrath, and having their strength taken away, and their minds extraordinarily transported with light, love and comfort, I have been abundantly amongst such things, and have had great opportunity to observe them, here and elsewhere, in their beginning, progress, issue
and consequences, and however there may be some mixtures of natural affection, and sometimes of temptation, and some imprudences
and irregularities, as there always was, and always will be in this imper-
fect state; yet as to the work in general, and the main of what is to be
observed in these extraordinary things, they have all the clear and
incontestable evidences of a true divine work. If this ben't the work of
God, I have all my religion to learn over again, and know not what use
to make of the Bible.

As to any absolute promises made to natural men, the matter is
exceeding plain. God makes no promises of any future eternal good to
fallen man in any other covenant but the covenant of grace; but how
can they have any interest in the promises of the covenant of grace,
that have no interest in the Mediator of that covenant, and never have
performed the condition of that covenant, which is faith in the Mediator? The Scripture is ignorant of any other way of coming to a title to
any promises of God, but only laying hold of the promises by faith,
which surely men that have no faith don't do.

As to the ministers that go about the country to preach, I believe
most of the clamor that is made against them must needs be from some
other principle than a regard to the interest of religion; because I
observe now there is vastly a greater outcry against ministers riding
about to preach the gospel, than used to be heretofore when ministers
rode about on the business of a physician, though that be so much
more alien from their proper work and though they were gone from

their own people five times as much. But I observe that nowadays, no irregularities are so much cried out against as exceeding in religion. As to ministers that ride about the country, I can't say how the case is circumstanced with all of 'em; but I believe they are exceedingly misrepresented. Mr. [Benjamin] Pomeroy and Mr. [Eleazar] Wheelock have been cried out of as much as most; and by particular opportunity I have had to know how it has been with them: they scarcely ever are absent from their people on the sabbath, and are very careful not to leave them destitute, and are not wont to go abroad but only where they are invited, and not to go into other ministers' pulpits without their consent, and rarely without being desired of them, and at the same time are more abundant in labors among their own people than ever.

I rejoice to hear of the flourishing of the work of God in your parts: I hope God will cause it to prevail against all opposition. Let us look to God to plead his own cause, and to get to himself the victory. Seek to him to direct you and give you wisdom, humility and zeal. I desire your prayers for me.

I am your sincere and entire friend,
Jonathan Edwards.
P.S. The Reverend Mr. [William] Williams of Hatfield died this morning.

35. TO THE REVEREND JOSEPH BELLAMY

Edwards spent a great deal of time in the saddle during 1742. He was in demand at churches far and wide.[1] This letter focuses on distant revival successes, but he later recalls, in a retrospective letter of December 12, 1743, that renewal was also having an impact on Northampton at this time.

(Firestone Library, Jonathan Edwards Collection, ALS, two quarto leaves, addressed on verso to Joseph Bellamy at Bethlehem.)

* * *

Northampton, January 21, 1741/2

Rev. and Dear Sir,

I received yours of January 11, for which I thank you. Religion in this and the neighboring towns has now of late been on the decaying

---

1. JE was on an extensive preaching tour in November and December 1741, and then left for Leicester, Mass., on Jan. 27, 1742, for another two weeks, visiting Marlborough and Sutton, Mass. Subsequently, he traveled to New Haven, Conn.; Longmeadow (twice); Hopkinton; and made a return visit to Westborough, Mass.

hand. I desire your prayers that God would quicken and revive us again, and particularly that he would greatly humble, and pardon, and quicken me; and fill me with his own fullness; and, if it may consist with his will, improve me as an instrument to revive his work. There has been the year past the most wonderful work amongst children here, by far, that ever was: God has seemed almost wholly to take a new generation, that are come on since the late great work seven years ago.

Neither earth or hell can hinder his work that is going on in the country. Christ gloriously triumphs at this day. You have probably before now heard of the great and wonderful things that have lately been wrought at Portsmouth, the chief town in New Hampshire government. There are also lately appearing great things at Ipswich, and Newbury, the two biggest towns in this province, except Boston, and several other towns beyond Boston, and some towns nearer. By what I can understand, the work of God is greater at this day in the land, than it has been at any time. O! what cause have we, with exulting hearts, to agree to give glory to him who thus rides forth in the chariots of his salvation, conquering and to conquer, and earnestly to pray that now the Sun of Righteousness would come forth like a bridegroom, rejoicing as a giant to run his race, from one end of the heaven to the other, that nothing may be hid from the light and heat thereof.

'Tis not probable that I shall be able to attend your meeting at Guilford; I have lately been so much gone from my people, and don't know but I must be obliged to leave 'em again next week about a fortnight, being called to Leicester, a town about halfway to Boston, where a great work has lately broke out, and probably soon after that to another place, and having at this time some extraordinary affairs to attend at home.[2] I pray that Christ our good shepherd will be with you and direct you and greatly strengthen and bless you.

Dear Sir, I have none of those books you speak of to sell. I have only a few that I intend to send to some of my friends. I have already sent you one of my New Haven sermons[3] by Mr. [Moses] Lyman of Goshen, nevertheless I have herewith sent another, that I desire you would give to Mr. [Jedidiah] Mills, if he has none, but if he has dispose of it where you think it will do most good. I have sent one of those sermons I

2. Beginning on Jan. 19, 1742, Sarah Pierpont Edwards experienced a prolonged and unusually intense religious episode, as recounted in her narrative (Dwight ed., *1*, 171–86). Without naming her, JE cited his wife's experiences in *Some Thoughts*, published later that year (*Works, 4*, 331–41).

3. *Distinguishing Marks.*

preached at Enfield,[4] as to the other I have but one of 'em in the world. I am, dear Sir, your affectionate and unworthy

> Brother and fellow-laborer,
> Jonathan Edwards.

36. TO THE REVEREND STEPHEN WILLIAMS

This note to the Reverend Stephen Williams represents Edwards' attempt to rally orthodox ministers to make a strong showing at Timothy Woodbridge's ordination at South Hadley, thus possibly adding another recruit to their cause. Timothy Woodbridge was succeeding William Williams, Edwards' uncle and good friend, who had died on August 31, 1741. The wounds of the Breck case had demonstrably not healed six years later, when Edwards and his ministerial allies absented themselves from John Ballantine's ordination at Westfield, on June 17, 1741, because of Breck's presence there.[1]

(Sterling Library, Manuscripts and Archives, Wetmore Family Papers, ALS, one quarto leaf, addressed on verso to the Reverend Stephen Williams in Longmeadow.)

* * *

South Hadley, March 4, 1741/2

Rev. Sir,

The people here are concerned for fear you will not be present the next week, at the installment of Mr. [Timothy] Woodbridge; and that by one and another's failing, the whole affair will drop through, or at least that there will be so few to assist as not to be sufficient to put a good face upon the affair in the eyes of the country. Reverend Sir, I would beseech you not to fail, if you can possibly come: it seems to me that charity to a poor, distressed people, as well as a regard to the interest of religion, requires your being present. I should be exceeding sorry, if but a very small number of ministers should be present. Hoping to see you here next week, I am, Sir,

> Your humble servant,
> Jonathan Edwards.

4. *Sinners in the Hands of an Angry God.*
1. If indeed JE expected friendship from Woodbridge, he would be disappointed; as a member of the 1750 Northampton council, he voted for JE's dismissal. SIB, *9*, 468–69; DEX, *1*, 469.

37. TO CONSTABLE JONATHAN BURT

Edwards used his salary in the way we now draw on a checking account. For small debts, he would simply ask the paymaster to remit the amount against his remuneration. The example given here is typical. Similar requests, located in letters incorporated in manuscript sermons, include:

Sermon and Date	Request Date	Payer and Payee	Amount
John 7:18 (3/1745)	5/7/42	Preserved Bartlett to Ebenezer Clark	£9
Eph. 4:15 f. (5/1743)	4/21/1743	Jonathan Burt to Lt. Moses Lyman	£7, 14s
Ps. 78:57 (6/1743)	5/13/1743	Samuel Allyn to same	£1, 9s
Rom. 1:20 (6/1743)	5/15/1743	Samuel Allyn to Joseph Allyn	£3, 15s

(All of the above, including the present letter, are at the Beinecke Library and are ALS.)

* * *

Northampton, March 10, 1741/2

To Jonathan Burt, Constable:

Please to pay Preserved Bartlett the sum of two pounds and eight shillings and six pence. And this note returned by you to me shall be accepted of you as so much of my salary.

Jonathan Edwards.

38. TO DEACON MOSES LYMAN

Lay exhortation was a lively topic of discussion around New England in the 1740s.[1] Although the clergy in general opposed it, fearing further encroachments on their position and prerogatives, revival defenders welcomed the sharing of experiences by new converts. Edwards here balances these concerns. To avoid anarchy, he supports the ministerial view; not to quench newfound enthusiasm, he encourages member participation on a personal, private basis.

Moses Lyman of Northampton had moved to Goshen, Connecticut, in 1739. The church there was racked by tensions between New Light parishio-

1. See Rev. William Russell's letter of May 6, 1742, soliciting JE's thoughts on this subject (Beinecke Library, in Sermon on Matt. 7:15, Jan. 1742/3).

ners and the Old Light minister, Rev. Stephen Heaton. To his former parishioner, caught in a troubled situation, Edwards offers friendly, firm counsel.

(Collection of John H. Edwards, Woodbridge, Conn., ALS, two quarto
leaves. Published in *The Spirit of the Pilgrims* 6 [1833], 545–46; Samuel Miller,
Jonathan Edwards [Boston, 1837], pp. 71–73; and *Bibliotheca Sacra* 28 [1871],
95–97. On Lyman, see Trumbull, *3, 2,* 294, 296; and on Heaton, DEX, *1,*
480–82, and *Works, 12,* 595.)

*   *   *

Northampton, May 10, 1742

My Dear Friend,

I am fully satisfied by the account your father has given me, that you
have lately gone out of the way of your duty, and done that which did
not belong to you, in exhorting a public congregation. I know you to be
a person of good judgment and discretion, and, therefore, can, with
the greater confidence put it to you to consider with yourself what you
would reasonably judge would be the consequence, if I and all other
ministers would approve and publicly justify such things as laymen's
taking it upon them to exhort after this manner? If one may, why
mayn't another? And if there be no certain limits or bounds, but everyone that inclines, may have liberty, alas, what should we soon come to?
If God had not seen it necessary that such things should have certain
limits and bounds, he never would have appointed a certain particular
order of men to that work and office, to be set apart to it, in so solemn a
manner, in the name of God. The head of the church is wiser than we,
and knew how to regulate things in his church.

'Tis no argument that such things are right, that they do a great deal
of good for the present, and within a narrow sphere; when at the same
time, if we look on them in the utmost extent of their consequences,
and in their long view of events, they do ten times as much hurt as
good. Appearing events are not our rule, but the law and testimony.
We ought to be vigilant and circumspect, and look on every side, and,
as far as we can, to the further end of things. God may, if he pleases in
his sovereign providence, turn that which is very wrong to do a great
deal of good for the present; for he does what he pleases. I hope you
will consider the matter, and for the future avoid doing thus. You
ought to do what you can by private, brotherly, humble admonitions
and counsels; but 'tis too much for you to exhort public congregations,
or solemnly to set yourself by set speech to counsel a room full of

people, unless it be children, or those that are much your inferior or to speak to any in an authoritative way. Such things have done a vast deal of mischief in the country, and have hindered the work of God exceedingly. Mr. [Gilbert] Tennent has lately wrote a letter to one of the ministers of New England earnestly to dissuade from such things.[2] Your temptations are exceeding great; you had need to have the prudence and humility of ten men. If you are kept humble and prudent you may be a great blessing on that part of the land; otherwise you may do as much hurt in a few weeks as you can do good in seven years. You might be under great advantage by your prudence to prevent those irregularities and disorders in your parts that prevails, and greatly hinder the work of God in other parts of the country; but by such things as these you will weaken your own hands, and fill the country with nothing but vain and fruitless and pernicious disputes. Persons when very full of a great sense of things are greatly exposed; for then they long to do something, and to do something extraordinary; and then is the devil's time to run them upon their heads if they ben't extraordinary circumspect and self diffident. I hope these lines will be taken in good part from

Your assured friend,
Jonathan Edwards.

P.S. Give my love to your dear wife. I long to see you both, whom I love as a couple of the dear children of God, united as I trust in happy bands.

39. TO SARAH PIERPONT EDWARDS

Edwards informs his wife that his return to Northampton will be delayed because the church of New London, Connecticut, devastated by revival excesses spurred on by James Davenport, needs emergency assistance. A few days later, Edwards led a council of ministers there to restore order and persuade Davenport of his errors.[1]

(Beinecke Library, ALS, in Sermon on Eph. 4:15 [May 1743], two duodecimo double leaves. Published in *PMHS*, ser. 2, XV [1901–02], 8–9. This is in acknowledgment of Sarah's brief note of Mar. 17, 1743, Beinecke Library.)

* * *

2. *BWNL*, Apr. 2–15, 1742, pp. 1–2.
1. S. LeRoy Blake, *The Later History of the First Church of Christ, New London, Conn.* (New London, Press of the Day Pub., 1900), pp. 99–136.

Mrs. Jonathan Edwards
(Sarah Pierpont
Edwards), by Joseph
Badger, undated, Yale
University Art Gallery,
bequest of Eugene
Phelps Edwards

Lebanon, at Mr. [William] Metcalf's, March 25, 1743

Dear Spouse,

I received this morning by Mr. [John] Potwine the short letter you sent me, with the books, papers, etc., for which I thank you. By this I would inform you that I have been considerably amiss since I came from home; riding in such tempestuous weather increased my cold, and almost overcame me. But am now a little better. I failed of seeing Mr. [Eleazar] Wheelock as I came down, and so had no opportunity to agree with him about the alteration of the time of my absence from home, but intended notwithstanding to have gone home next week. But many ministers have been urging me to go to New London, but I refused unless a number of them would go with me. And last night Mr. [Joseph] Meacham, Mr. [Solomon] Williams, and Mr. [Benjamin] Pomeroy agreed to go down with me the next week, to endeavor to reclaim the people there from their errors. So that I believe I shall not be at home till the week after next. Give my love to my children and Mr. Wheelock. Brother and sister [Abigail Edwards] Metcalf give their love to you and the children. Remember me in your prayers. I am, my dearest companion,

> Your affectionate consort,
> Jonathan Edwards.

40. TO THE REVEREND WILLIAM McCULLOCH

Edwards' friendship with Scottish ministers was of major and enduring value. This letter and one written to James Robe the same day are the earliest recorded communications to the ministers. The glory days of revival were past for Edwards. His interest in the movement remained keen, but after face-to-face encounters with extremists he took a decidedly more cautious, realistic attitude toward the idea.

In this letter, Edwards expresses elation at news of the Cambuslang revival, said to have originated in McCulloch's parish near Glasgow. By contrast, he considers the American awakening flawed: talk without action, polarization, and emotion for its own sake. The root cause for the problems, he confesses, is lack of ministerial leadership.

(Trask Library, ALS, three quarto leaves, addressed on verso of third leaf to the Reverend William McCulloch at Cambuslang, near Glasgow, Scotland. Published in Dwight ed., *1*, 196–98; and in *Works, 4*, 539–41.)

* * *

> Northampton, May 12, 1743

Rev. and Dear Sir,

Mr. [John] MacLaurin of Glasgow, in a letter he has lately sent me, informs me of your proposing to write a letter to me, and being prevented by the failing of the expected opportunity: I thank you, reverend Sir, that you had such a thing in your heart. We were informed the last year by the printed, and well-attested narrative, of the glorious work of God in your parish, which we have since understood has spread into many other towns and parishes in that part of Scotland. Especially are we informed of this by Mr. [James] Robe's *Narrative;*[1] and I perceive by some papers of the *Weekly History,* sent me by Mr. MacLaurin of Glasgow, that the work has continued to make glorious progress at Cambuslang, even till it has prevailed to a wonderful degree indeed. God has highly favored and honored you, dear Sir, which

1. James Robe, *A Short Narrative of the Extraordinary Work at Cambuslang* (Boston, 1742). See Fawcett, *The Cambuslang Revival.*

may justly render your name precious to all that love our Lord Jesus Christ.

We live in a day wherein God is doing marvelous things; in that respect we are distinguished from former generations. God has wrought great things in New England, which, though exceeding glorious, have all along been attended with some threatening clouds; which from the beginning caused me to apprehend some great stop or check to be put to the work, before it should be begun and carried on in its genuine purity and beauty, to subdue all before it, and to prevail with an irresistible and continual progress and triumph; and it is come to pass according to my apprehensions. But yet I cannot think otherwise, than that what has now been doing, is the forerunner of something vastly greater, more pure, and more extensive. I can't think that God has come down from heaven, and done such great things before our eyes, and gone so much beside and beyond his usual way of working, and wrought so wonderfully, and that he has gone away with a design to leave things thus. "Who hath heard such a thing? Who hath seen such things?" And will God, when he has wrought so unusually, and made the earth "to bring forth in one day, [. . .] bring to the birth and not cause to bring forth?" And shall he "cause to bring forth and shut the womb?" (Is. 66:8–9). I live upon the brink of the grave, in great infirmity of body, and nothing is more uncertain than whether I shall live to see it: but I believe God will revive his work again before long, and that it will not wholly cease till it has subdued the whole earth.

But God is now going and returning to his place, till we acknowledge our offense, and, I hope, to humble his church in New England, and purify it, and so fit it for yet greater comfort, that he designs in due time to bestow upon it. God may deal with his church, as he deals with a particular saint; commonly after his first comfort, the clouds return, and there [is] a season of remarkable darkness, and hidings of God's face, and buffetings of Satan; but all to fit for greater mercy; and as it was with Christ himself, who presently after the heavens were opened over his head, and the Spirit was poured out upon him, and God wonderfully testified his love to him, was driven into the wilderness to be tempted of the devil forty days [Matt. 3:16–4:1]. I hope God will show us our errors, and teach us wisdom by his present withdrawings. Now in the day of adversity we have time and cause to consider, and begin now to have opportunity to see the consequences of our conduct.

I wish that God's ministers and people everywhere would take warning by our errors, and the calamities that are the issue of them. I have mentioned several things in my letters to Mr. MacLaurin and Mr. Robe; another I might have mentioned, that most evidently proves of ill consequence, i.e. we have run from one extreme to another, with respect to talking of experiences; that whereas formerly there was too great a reservedness in that matter, of late many have gone to an unbounded openness, frequency, and constancy in talking of their experiences, declaring almost everything that passes between God and their own souls, everywhere and before everybody. Among other ill consequences of such a practice this is one, that religion runs all into that channel; and religion is placed very much in it, so that the strength of it seems to be spent in it; that other duties that are of vastly greater importance, have been looked upon light in comparison of this, so that other parts of religion have [been] really much injured thereby; as when we see a tree excessively full of leaves, we find so much less fruit; and when a cloud arises with an excessive degree of wind, we have the less rain.

How much, dear Sir, does God's church at such a day need the constant, gracious care and guidance of our Good Shepherd! And especially we that are ministers.

I should be glad, dear Sir, of a remembrance in your prayers, and also of your help, by information and instructions, by what you find in your experience in Scotland. I believe it to be the duty of one part of the church of God thus to help another. I am, dear Sir, your affectionate

Brother and servant in Jesus Christ,
Jonathan Edwards.

41. TO THE REVEREND JAMES ROBE

The 1740 revival at Kilsyth, Scotland, offered striking similarities to the one in Northampton in 1735. Robe ever published his own *Faithful Narrative,* serialized in part in Thomas Prince, Jr.'s *Christian History* (Boston, 1743–44). Here Edwards initiates correspondence with his overseas counterpart, praising progress there and lamenting decline at home. After a litany of errors made, he recommends the signs to be sought of positive spiritual life.

(Published in *CMH* 2 [1745], 127–30; and in *Works, 4,* 535–38.)

* * *

Northampton, May 12, 1743

Rev. and Dear Sir,

Last week I was surprised with the unexpected favor of your letter, with one from Mr. [John] MacLaurin. It may well make me blush at the consideration of my vileness, to receive such undeserved testimonies of respect from servants of the Lord, at so great a distance, and that have been so highly favored and honored of God as you have been. Pleasant and joyful are the accounts which we have lately had from Scotland, concerning the kingdom of our God there, for which we and the world are specially indebted to you, who have honored your dear Lord, and refreshed and served his church, by the accounts you have published in your *Narrative* and *Journals* of the work of God in Kilsyth and other parts in the west of Scotland.[1] Future generations will own themselves indebted to you for those accounts. I congratulate you, dear Sir, on the advantages God has put you under to favor the church of God with a narrative of his glorious works, by having made you the instrument of so much of them, and giving you such glorious success in your own congregation. The accounts which we have received from you are, on some accounts, more pleasant and agreeable than what we have had to send to you: the work of God with you has been less mixed with error and extravagance; you have taken a more wise and prudent care to prevent things of that nature, or to suppress them as soon as they have appeared; and ministers that have been the principal pro-moters of the work, have seemed to be more happily united in their sentiments, and so under greater advantage to assist one another, and to act as co-workers and fellow-helpers.

You have heard great things from New England of late, which, I doubt not, have refreshed and rejoiced your hearts; and indeed, great and wonderful have the things been in which God has passed before us. But now we have not such joyful news to send you; the clouds have lately thickened, and our hemisphere is now much darkened with them. There is a great decay of the work of God amongst us, especially as to the awakening and converting influence of the Spirit of God; and the prejudices there are, in a great part of the country, are riveted and inveterate. The people are divided into two parties, those that favor the work and those that are against it, and the distinction has long been growing more and more visible, and the distance greater, till

1. James Robe et al., *Narratives of the Extraordinary Work of the Spirit of God, at Cambuslang, at Kilsyth, etc. Begun in 1742* (Glasgow, rep. 1790).

there is at length raised a wall between them up to heaven; so that one party is very much out of the reach of all influence of the other. This is very much owing to imprudent management in the friends of the work, and a corrupt mixture which Satan has found means to introduce, and our manifold sinful errors, by which we have grieved and quenched the Spirit of God.

It can scarcely be conceived of what consequence it is, to the continuance and propagation of a revival of religion, that the utmost care be used to prevent error and disorder among those that appear to be the subjects of such a work; and also, that all imaginable care be taken by ministers in conducting souls under the work; and particularly that there be the greatest caution used in comforting and establishing persons, as being safe and past danger of hell. Many among us have been ready to think, that all high raptures are divine; but experience plainly shows, that it is not the degree of rapture and ecstasy (although it should be to the third heavens), but the nature and kind that must determine us in their favor. It would have been better for us, if all ministers here had taken care diligently to distinguish such joys and raised affections, as were attended with deep humiliation, brokenness of heart, poverty of spirit, mourning for sin, solemnity of spirit, a trembling reverence towards God, tenderness of spirit, self-jealousy and fear, and great engagedness of heart, after holiness of life, and a readiness to esteem others better than themselves; and that sort of humility that is not a noisy showy humility, but rather this, which disposes to walk softly, and speak trembling; and if we had encouraged no discoveries or joys, but such as manifestly wrought this way, it would have been well for us.

And I am persuaded we shall generally be sensible, before long, that we run too fast, when we endeavor by our positive determinations to banish all fears of damnation from the minds of men, though they may be true saints, if they are not such as are eminently humble and mortified, and (what the Apostle calls) "rooted and grounded in love" [Eph. 3:17]. It seems to be running before the Spirit of God. God by his Spirit does not give assurance any other way, than by advancing these things in the soul. He does not wholly cast out fear, the legal principle, but by advancing and filling the soul full of love, the evangelical principle. When love is low in the true saints, they need the fear of hell to deter them from sin, and engage them to exactness in their walk, and stir them up to seek heaven; but when love is high, and the soul full of it, we don't need fear. And therefore, a wise God has so ordered it that love and fear should rise and fall like the scales of a balance, when one rises, the other falls, as there is need; or as light and darkness take place of each other in a room, as light decays, darkness comes in, and as light increases and fills the room, darkness is cast out; so love, or the spirit of adoption, casts out fear, the spirit of bondage. And experience convinces me, that even in the brightest and most promising appearances of new converts, it would have been better for us to have encouraged them only as it were conditionally, after the example of the Apostle, Heb. 3:5. "Whose house are we, if we hold fast the confidence, and the rejoicing of the hope firm unto the end"; and v. 14, "For we are made partakers of Christ, if we hold the beginning of our confidence steadfast unto the end." And after the example of Christ, Rev. 2:10, "Be thou faithful unto death, and I will give thee a crown of life." So Luke 21:34, 36, and in many other places.

'Tis probable that one reason why God has suffered us to err, is to teach us wisdom, by experience of the ill consequence of our errors. What you relate of the opposition of the seceding ministers is very surprising; especially of the two Erskines, whose writings, especially Mr. Ralph Erskine's *Gospel Sonnets*,[2] have been in great repute among God's people here: but this is a day of wonders of various kinds. I have reason to admire divine condescension in making any use of anything I have written for the defense of the work of God in Scotland.

As to what you propose concerning my writing a narrative, etc., I am not conveniently situated for it, living in an extreme part of the land, and an hundred miles from the press, as well as on many other accounts unfit for it. But Mr. [Thomas] Prince of Boston, who is every way fit, and under good advantages for it, has already undertaken it, and I suppose, will prosecute the undertaking, so far as it shall be thought for God's glory.

I hope, dear Sir, you'll remember me in your prayers. Never was I so sensible in any measure, how vain a creature man is; what a leaf driven of the wind, what dry stubble, what poor dust, a bubble, a shadow, a nothing, and more vain than nothing; and what a vain, and vile helpless creature I am, and how much I need God's help in everything as of late. Dear Sir, don't forget New England; and don't forget your affectionate and obliged brother and servant,

And unworthy fellow-laborer,
Jonathan Edwards.

2. Ebenezer and Ralph Erskine, who were among the leaders of the Seceders. Ralph Erskine's *Gospel Sonnets* (2nd ed., Edinburgh, 1726) was a favorite in the colonies.

42. TO THE ASSEMBLY OF PASTORS OF CHURCHES IN NEW ENGLAND

The convention of clergy in Boston on July 7 and 8, 1743, was a notable event in the history of the revival movement in colonial New England. Here Edwards and his colleagues from Hampshire County join the chorus of affirmation.

(Published in *The Testimony and Advice of an Assembly of Pastors of Churches in New-England* (Boston, 1743); *The Christian History*, no. 22 [Aug. 6, 1743], 178–80. Reprinted in *CMH* 3 [1744], 32–34; and *Works, 4*, 542–43.

* * *

County of Hampshire, June 30, 1743

Rev. and Honored Sirs,

Whereas an advertisement hath lately been published, wherein it is signified, that it is the desire of a number of ministers that there should be a meeting of all such ministers in this province as are persuaded that there has of late been a happy revival of religion in the land, at Boston, the day after [Harvard's] commencement, to give a joint testimony to the late glorious work of God's grace, and to consult what should be done to promote this work, and to suppress those things that bring a reproach upon it and hinder it; and in the same advertisement it is desired that if any such ministers are not able to be present at this interview, they would not fail to send their testimony and thoughts in writing: we whose names are subscribed to this, living at a great distance, and our circumstances not well allowing us to go so great a journey at the time proposed, would hereby signify, that according to what understanding we have of the nature of Christianity, and the observation we have had opportunity to make, we judge that there has been within the last two years and an half, a blessed outpouring of the Spirit of God in this county in awakening and converting sinners, and in enlightening, quickening and building up saints in faith, holiness and comfort; which has been attended in great numbers with an abiding alteration and reformation of disposition and behavior. And particularly we would hereby declare to the glory of God's grace, that we judge that there has been a happy revival of religion in the congregations that have been committed to our pastoral care, and that there are many in them that, by abiding manifestations of a serious, religious and humble spirit, and a conscientious care and watchfulness in their behavior towards God and man, give all grounds of charity towards them, as having been sincere in the profession they have made. And however there has been, especially in some places, a mixture of enthusiasm and false religion, and some have run into great errors in their conduct, and some have fallen away, and there is a declension in others that is to be lamented; yet we think the effect has been such, and still continues to be such, as leaves no room reasonably to doubt of God's having been wonderfully in the midst of us, and such as has laid us under great obligations forever to admire and extol the riches of his grace in doing such great things for us.

Thus, reverend Sirs, begging of him that he would be with you in your meeting, and guide you in your thoughts and conclusions with respect to these things, and direct you to that which may be for his glory and the prosperity of Zion, and desiring your prayers to God for us, and the flocks committed to our care, we remain, honored and dear Sirs, your brethren and fellow servants in the gospel ministry,

Stephen Williams, pastor of a church in Springfield.
Peter Reynolds, pastor of the church in Enfield.
Jonathan Edwards, pastor of the church in Northampton.
Samuel Allis, pastor of the church in Somers.
John Woodbridge, pastor of the Second Church in Hadley.
David Parsons, Jr., pastor of the Third Church in Hadley.
Edward Billing, pastor of the church in Cold Spring.

43. TO THE REVEREND JONATHAN ASHLEY

(Beinecke Library, Sermon on Rev. 14:15, Jan. 1743/4; and Trask Library, Sermon on Is. 65:17–18, n.d. [probably early 1744]. The ms. is torn into three parts: one part, right hand margin missing, top shorn; remaining sections each two duodecimo leaves; addressed on verso to the Reverend Mr. Jonathan Ashley in Deerfield.)

* * *

[Northampton, Fall 1743]

Rev. Sir,

By this [I would] signify to you that it happens that I shall not be in necessity of more than forty bushels of wheat. Some that were indebted to me, of whom I expected money, chose [to] pay me in wheat; and I, because I thought I should not easily get the money, have accepted the wheat.

If I remember right, you told me you had laid in some forty bushels with one man, and ten with [another]. Forty being as much as can well be brought at a load, I should choose to take only the forty bushels, if it be no inconvenience to the other man that was agreed with the ten. If there be any inconvenience [to] it, I shall make no difficulty, but will take the whole fifty bushels as has been agreed. And should be glad if what [wheat] I am to have may be brought as soon as [can] be, for we shall soon need it to use in [the] family. I would desire you to be so kind [as] to speak to the men about it; which, with acknowledgment of your kindness in your [help in] this matter, is from

Your brother and servant,
Jonathan Edwards.

44. TO THE REVEREND EBENEZER PEMBERTON

Some awakened parishioners of the Milford, Connecticut, church were chafing under the leadership of their Old Light minister. For affiliation and preaching assistance, they applied to like-minded New York Presbyterians, who in turn sought the advice of Edwards. Here he is sympathetic; although unwilling to sanction schism, he is disturbed by the repression of new converts. He concludes that those nearer the situation should decide the course of action to be taken.

(Sterling Library, Manuscripts and Archives, Strong Family Papers, copy of ALS, probably in the hand of Ephraim Strong, a leader of the Milford Separatist movement, two quarto leaves. On Milford, see C. C. Goen, *Revivalism and Separatism in New England, 1740–1800* [New Haven, 1962; rep. New York, 1969], pp. 59–6l, 205, 215; and DEX, *1*, 742–43.)

* * *

Northampton, December 2, 1743

Rev. and Dear Sir,

From what I have heard from time to time from various sorts of persons, I can have no doubt in my own mind, but that the people at Milford that have separated from Mr. [Samuel] Whittelsey are a poor, oppressed people. I confess I have had no proper hearing of both parties face to face and should not be so free in giving my opinion without it, were it not that the circumstances of the land and the times are such, that there is no such thing as any proper hearing and trial of such cases to be expected. Persons and societies that have the most righteous cause, and are most cruelly oppressed year to year, may earnestly desire and seek a fair trial before proper judges; and never obtain it or have any prospect of it. In such a state of things, I therefore believe it to be necessary in many cases for persons to [be] using all proper cautions, to form a judgment and act upon it from the best information they can obtain.

Whether this people have taken a proper course for their relief in their extremity, I am not able at present to determine; particularly in taking the oath they have done and putting themselves under the law of a presbytery at such a distance. I leave those things to the judgment of those that are wiser and know more of the matter. And also whether it be proper for them now to change the presbytery they are subject to; or whether there be any probability of its answering their end or of their having any relief by it: I must leave this with them and you who, I believe, are much better able to determine. But in this I am fully of Mr. [Solomon] Williams of Lebanon's mind, that their not being set off regularly (as it is called), according to the method of the ecclesiastical constitution of that government, is no just bar in the way of their being acknowledged and received by you or any other Christians or ministers or Christian societies or consistories. You are doubtless so well acquainted with [the] late and present state of that colony, that it may be safely left with you to judge, whether it be reasonable that all those in that government that have visibly been the subjects or favorers of the late glorious work of God should in all their religious affairs be held indispensably bound to be subject to what is there called order, viz. in the conduct of themselves in affairs of conscience and their eternal salvation.

Fine, their treatment of one another, to submit evermore to the judgment and decisions of the major part of the ministers and people within the limits of their consociations, or of the whole government taken together: this would be for these people to yield up themselves in matters of infinite consequences into the hands of those who are evidently, in the face of the world, their embittered enemies that seek by all means to crush them, right or wrong, even to that degree of prejudice and spirit that appears to me a sort of madness. It is manifest that there [are] many in that government under the most terrible oppression both from civil and ecclesiastical authority, and [I] think no impartial person can doubt but that it must be the duty of all friends to religion and to mankind in other colonies, whether particular persons or consistories, [to] be approved for them, and to help them as they have opportunity in the use of any proper means; not at all the less for

Connecticut private law or their sacred constitution, but as to the particular course that should be taken for the relief of this poor people at Milford, or unless that your presbytery can afford them any relief in the pursuit of any proper measures, I must leave to those that are under better advantages to judge than I am.

Present my humble service to Mrs. Pemberton and Messrs. [William] Smith, Noble and [Nathaniel] Hazard, father and son, and my love and service to the other ministers in your presbytery. And remember in your prayers, dear Sir,

> Your affectionate brother and humble servant,
> Jonathan Edwards.

45. TO THE REVEREND THOMAS PRINCE

Publicly, at least, Edwards is still riding the wave of excitement from the 1740–41 revival. He recounts Whitefield's visit, describes its aftereffects, and betrays a growing uneasiness with emotional excess. He sets great store by Northampton's covenant renewal, the text of which is included, as a means to continue the awakening spirit.

(Published, most likely as an excerpt, in Prince, *Christian History* 1 [1743], 367–81; *CMH* 4 [1745], 101–14; Dwight ed., *1*, 160–70; and *Works, 4*, 544–60.)

*   *   *

Northampton, December 12, 1743

[Rev. and Dear Sir,]

Ever since the great work of God that was wrought here about nine years ago, there has been a great abiding alteration in this town in many respects. There has been vastly more religion kept up in the town, among all sorts of persons, in religious exercises and in common conversation, than used to be before: there has remained a more general seriousness and decency in attending the public worship; there has been a very great alteration among the youth of the town, with respect to reveling, frolicking, profane and unclean conversation, and lewd songs; instances of fornication have been very rare; there has also been a great alteration amongst both old and young with respect to tavern-haunting. I suppose the town has been in no measure so free of vice in these respects, for any long time together, for this sixty years, as it has been this nine years past. There has also been an evident alteration with respect to a charitable spirit to the poor (though I think with regard to this, we in this town, as the land in general, come far short of gospel rules). And though after that great work nine years ago there has been a very lamentable decay of religious affections, and the engagedness of people's spirit in religion, yet many societies for prayer and social religion were all along kept up, and there were some few instances of awakening and deep concern about the things of another world, even in the most dead time.

In the year 1740 in the spring, before Mr. [George] Whitefield came to this town, there was a visible alteration: there was more seriousness and religious conversation, especially among young people. Those things that were of ill tendency among them were more forborne; and it was a more frequent thing for persons to visit their minister upon soul accounts, and in some particular persons there appeared a great alteration about that time. And thus it continued till Mr. Whitefield came to town, which was about the middle of October following: he preached here four sermons in the meetinghouse (besides a private lecture at my house), one on Friday, another on Saturday, and two upon the sabbath. The congregation was extraordinarily melted by every sermon; almost the whole assembly being in tears for a great part of sermon time. Mr. Whitefield's sermons were suitable to the circumstances of the town; containing just reproofs of our backslidings, and in a most moving and affecting manner, making use of our great profession and great mercies as arguments with us to return to God, from whom we had departed. Immediately after this the minds of the people in general appeared more engaged in religion, showing a greater forwardness to make religion the subject of their conversation, and to meet frequently together for religious purposes, and to embrace all opportunities to hear the Word preached. The revival at first appeared chiefly among professors, and those that had entertained the hope that they were in a state of grace, to whom Mr. Whitefield chiefly addressed himself, but in a very short time there appeared an awakening and deep concern among some young persons that looked upon themselves as in a Christless state; and there were some hopeful appearances of conversion; and some professors were greatly revived. In about a month or six weeks there was a great alteration in the town, both as to the revivals of professors, and awakenings of others. By the middle of December a very considerable work of God appeared among those that were very young, and the revival of religion continued to increase; so that in the spring, an engagedness of spirit about things of religion was become very general amongst young people and children, and religious subjects almost wholly took up their conversation when they were together.

In the month of May 1741, a sermon was preached to a company at a private house. Near the conclusion of the exercise one or two persons that were professors were so greatly affected with a sense of the greatness and glory of divine things, and the infinite importance of the things of eternity, that they were not able to conceal it; the affection of their minds overcoming their strength, and having a very visible effect on their bodies. When the exercise was over, the young people that were present removed into the other room for religious conference; and particularly that they might have opportunity to inquire of those that were thus affected what apprehensions they had; and what things they were that thus deeply impressed their minds: and there soon appeared a very great effect of their conversation; the affection was quickly propagated through the room: many of the young people and children that were professors appeared to be overcome with a sense of the greatness and glory of divine things, and with admiration, love, joy and praise, and compassion to others that looked upon themselves as in a state of nature; and many others at the same time were overcome with distress about their sinful and miserable state and condition; so that the whole room was full of nothing but outcries, faintings and such like. Others soon heard of it, in several parts of the town, and came to them; and what they saw and heard there was greatly affecting to them; so that many of them were overpowered in like manner: and it continued thus for some hours; the time being spent in prayer, singing, counseling and conferring. There seemed to be a consequent happy effect of that meeting to several particular persons, and in the state of religion in the town in general.

After this were meetings from time to time attended with like appearances. But a little after it, at the conclusion of the public exercise on the sabbath, I appointed the children that were under sixteen years of age to go from the meetinghouse to a neighbor house; that I there might further enforce what they had heard in public, and might give in some counsels proper for their age. The children were there very generally and greatly affected with the warnings and counsels that were given them, and many exceedingly overcome; and the room was filled with cries: and when they were dismissed, they, almost all of them, went home crying aloud through the streets, to all parts of the town. The like appearances attended several such meetings of children that were appointed. But their affections appeared by what followed to be of a very different nature: in many they appeared to be indeed but childish affections; and in a day or two would leave 'em as they were before: others were deeply impressed; their convictions took fast hold of them, and abode by them: and there were some that from one meeting to another seemed extraordinarily affected for some time, to but little purpose, their affections presently vanishing from time to time; but yet afterwards were seized with abiding convictions, and their affections became durable.

About the middle of the summer, I called together the young people that were communicants, from sixteen to twenty-six years of age to my house; which proved to be a most happy meeting: many seemed to be very greatly and most agreeably affected with those views which excited humility, self-condemnation, self-abhorrence, love and joy: many fainted under these affections. We had several meetings that summer of young people attended with like appearances. It was about that time that there first began to be cryings out in the meetinghouse; which several times occasioned many of the congregation to stay in the house after the public exercise was over, to confer with those who seemed to be overcome with religious convictions and affections; which was found to tend much to the propagation of their impressions, with lasting effect upon many; conference being at these times commonly joined with prayer and singing. In the summer and fall the children in various parts of the town had religious meetings by themselves for prayer, sometimes joined with fasting; wherein many of them seemed to be greatly and properly affected, and I hope some of them [were] savingly wrought upon.

The months of August and September [1741] were the most remarkable of any this year, for appearances of conviction and conversion of sinners, and great revivings, quickenings, and comforts of professors, and for extraordinary external effects of these things. It was a very frequent thing to see an house full of outcries, faintings, convulsions and such like, both with distress, and also with admiration and joy. It was not the manner here to hold meetings all night, as in some places, nor was it common to continue 'em till very late in the night: but it was pretty often, so that there were some that were so affected, and their bodies so overcome, that they could not go home, but were obliged to stay all night at the house where they were. There was no difference that I know of here, with regard to these extraordinary effects, in meetings in the night and in the daytime: the meetings in which these effects appeared in the evening, being commonly begun, and their extraordinary effects, in the day, and continued in the evening; and some meetings have been very remarkable for such extraordinary effects that were both begun and finished in the daytime.

There was an appearance of a glorious progress of the work of God upon the hearts of sinners in conviction and conversion this summer and fall; and great numbers, I think we have reason to hope, were brought savingly home to Christ. But this was remarkable: the work of God in his influences of this nature seemed to be almost wholly upon a new generation; those that were not come to years of discretion in that wonderful season nine years ago, children, or those that were then children: others that had enjoyed that former glorious opportunity without any appearance of saving benefit, seemed now to be almost wholly passed over and let alone. But now we had the most wonderful work among children that ever was in Northampton. The former great outpouring of the Spirit was remarkable for influences upon the minds of children, beyond all that had ever been before; but this far exceeded that. Indeed as to influences on the minds of professors, this work was by no means confined to a new generation: many of all ages partook of it; but yet, in this respect it was more general on those that were of the younger sort. Many that had formerly been wrought upon, that in the times of our declension had fallen into decays, and had in a great measure left God, and gone after the world, now passed under a very remarkable new work of the Spirit of God, as if they had been the subjects of a second conversion. They were first led into the wilderness, and had a work of conviction, having much greater convictions of the sin of both nature and practice than ever before (though with some new circumstances, and something new in the kind of conviction); in some with great distress, beyond what they had felt before their first conversion. Under these convictions they were excited to strive for salvation, and the kingdom of heaven suffered violence from some of them in a far more remarkable manner than before: and after great convictions and humblings, and agonizings with God, they had Christ discovered to them anew as an all-sufficient Savior; and in the glories of his grace, and in a far more clear manner than before, and with greater humility, self-emptiness and brokenness of heart, and a purer and higher joy, and greater desires after holiness of life, but with greater self-diffidence, and distrust of their treacherous hearts.

One circumstance wherein this work differed from that which had been in the town five or six years before, was that conversions were frequently wrought more sensibly and visibly; the impressions stronger, and more manifest by external effects of them; and the progress of the Spirit of God in conviction, from step to step, more apparent; and the transition from one state to another more sensible and plain; so that it might, in many instances, be as it were seen by bystanders. The preceding season had been very remarkable on this account beyond what had been before; but this [was] more remarkable than that. And in this season these apparent or visible conversions (if I may so call them) were more frequently in the presence of others, at religious meetings, where the appearances of what was wrought on the heart fell under public observation.

After September 1741, there seemed to be some abatement of the extraordinary appearances that had been; but yet they did not wholly cease, but there was something of them from time to time all winter.

About the beginning of February 1741/2, Mr. [Samuel] Buell came to this town, I being then absent from home, and continued so till about a fortnight after. Mr. Buell preached from day to day, almost every day, in the meetinghouse (I having left to him the free liberty of my pulpit, hearing of his designed visit before I went from home) and spent almost the whole time in religious exercises with the people, either in public or private, the people continually thronging him. When he first came, there came with him a number of the zealous people from Suffield, who continued here for some time. There were very extraordinary effects of Mr. Buell's labors; the people were exceedingly moved, crying out in great numbers in the meetinghouse, and great part of the congregation commonly staying in the house of God for hours after the public service, many of them in uncommon circumstances. Many also were exceedingly moved in private meetings, where Mr. Buell was: and almost the whole town seemed to be in a great and continual commotion, day and night; and there was indeed a very great revival of religion. But it was principally among professors; the appearances of a work of conversion were in no measure equal to what had been the summer before. When I came home I found the town in very extraordinary circumstances, such in some respects as I never saw it in before. Mr. Buell continued here a fortnight or three weeks after I returned: there being still great appearances attending his labors; many in their religious affections being raised far beyond what they ever had been before: and there were some instances of persons lying in a sort of trance, remaining for perhaps a whole twenty-four hours motionless, and with their senses locked up; but in the meantime under strong imaginations, as though they went to heaven, and had there a vision of glorious and delightful objects. But when the people were raised to this height, Satan took the advantage, and his interposition in many instances soon became very apparent: and a great deal of caution and pains were found necessary to keep the people, many of them, from running wild.

In the month of March I led the people into a solemn public renewal of their covenant with God. To that end I made a draft of a covenant, and first proposed it to some of the principal men in the church; then proposed it to the people in their several religious societies, in various parts of the town; and then proposed it to the whole congregation in public; and then deposited a copy of it in the hands of each of our four deacons, that all that desired it might resort to them, and have opportunity to view and consider it. Then the people in general that were above fourteen years of age first subscribed the covenant with their hands, and then on a day of fasting and prayer, all together presented themselves before the Lord in his house, and stood up, and solemnly manifested their consent to it, as their vow to God. The covenant was as follows:

> *A Copy of a Covenant Entered into and Subscribed by the People of God at Northampton, and Owned Before God in His House As their Vow to the Lord, and Made a Solemn Act of Public Worship, by the Congregation in General That Were Above Fourteen Years of Age, on a Day of Fasting and Prayer for the Continuance and Increase of the Gracious Presence of God in That Place, March 16, 1741/2.*

Acknowledging God's great goodness to us, a sinful, unworthy people, in the blessed manifestations and fruits of his gracious presence in this town, both formerly and lately, and particularly in the very late spiritual revival; and adoring the glorious majesty, power, and grace of God, manifested in the present wonderful outpouring of his Spirit in many parts of this land, and in this place; and lamenting our past backslidings and ungrateful departings from God; and humbly begging of God that he would not mark our iniquities, but for Christ's sake come over the mountains of our sins, and visit us with his salvation, and continue the tokens of his presence with us, and yet more gloriously pour out his blessed Spirit upon us, and make us all partakers of the divine blessings he is, at this day, bestowing here and in many parts of this land; we do this day present ourselves before the Lord, to renounce our evil ways, and put away our abominations from before

God's eyes, and with one accord to renew our engagements to seek and serve God: and particularly do now solemnly promise and vow to the Lord as follows:

In all our conversation, concerns, and dealings with our neighbor, we will have a strict regard to rules of honesty, justice, and uprightness; that we don't overreach or defraud our neighbor in any matter, and either willfully or through want of care, injure him in any of his honest possessions or rights; and in all our communication, will have a tender respect, not only to our own interest, but also to the interest of our neighbor; and will carefully endeavor in everything to do to others as we should expect, or think reasonable, that they should do to us, if we were in their case and they in ours.

And particularly we will endeavor to render to everyone his due; and will take heed to ourselves, that we don't wrong our neighbor, and give them a just cause of offense, by willfully or negligently forbearing to pay our honest debts.

And wherein any of us, upon strict examination of our past behavior, may be conscious to ourselves that we have by any means wronged any of our neighbors in their outward estate; we will not rest till we have made that restitution, or given that satisfaction, which the rules of moral equity require: or if we are, on a strict and impartial search, conscious to ourselves that we have in any other respect considerably injured our neighbor; we will truly endeavor to do that which we, in our consciences, suppose Christian rules require, in order to a reparation of the injury and removing the offense given thereby.

And furthermore we promise that we will not allow ourselves in backbiting; and that we will take great heed to ourselves to avoid all violations of those Christian rules, Titus 3:2, "Speak evil of no man"; Jas. 4:11, "Speak not evil one of another, brethren"; and II Cor. 12:20, "Lest there be [. . .] strifes, backbitings, whisperings": and that we will not only not slander our neighbor, but also will not, to feed a spirit of bitterness, ill will, or secret grudge against our neighbor, insist on his real faults needlessly, and when not called to it; or from such a spirit speak of his failings and blemishes with ridicule, or an air of contempt.

And we promise that we will be very careful to avoid doing anything to our neighbor from a spirit of revenge. And that we will take great care that we do not, for private interest, or our own honor, or to maintain ourselves against those of a contrary party, or to get our wills, or to promote any design in opposition to others, do those things which we, on the most impartial consideration we are capable of, can think in our consciences will tend to wound religion and the interest of Christ's kingdom.

And particularly that so far as any of us, by divine providence, have any special influence upon others, to lead them in the management of public affairs; we will not make our own worldly gain, or honor, or interest in the affections of others, or getting the better of any of a contrary party, that are in any respect our competitors, or the bringing or keeping them down, our governing aim, to the prejudice of the interest of religion and the honor of Christ.

And in the management of any public affair wherein there is a difference of opinions, concerning any outward possessions, privileges, rights or properties: we will not wittingly violate justice for private interest; and with the greatest strictness and watchfulness, will avoid all unchristian bitterness, vehemence, and heat of spirit; yea, though we should think ourselves injured by a contrary party: and in the time of the management of such affairs, will especially watch over ourselves, our spirits, and our tongues, to avoid all unchristian inveighings, reproachings, bitter reflectings, judging and ridiculing others, either in public meetings, or in private conversation, either to men's faces, or behind their backs; but will greatly endeavor, so far as we are concerned, that all should be managed with Christian humility, gentleness, quietness and love.

And furthermore, we promise that we will not tolerate the exercise of enmity and ill will, or revenge in our hearts, against any of our neighbors; and we will often be strictly searching and examining our hearts with respect to that matter.

And if any of us find that we have an old secret grudge against any of our neighbors, we will not gratify it, but cross it, and endeavor to our utmost to root it out, crying to God for his help; and that we will make it our true and faithful endeavor, in our places, that a party spirit may not be kept up amongst us, but that it may utterly cease; that for the future we may all be one, united in undisturbed peace and unfeigned love.

And those of us that are in youth do promise never to allow ourselves in any youthful diversions and pastimes, in meetings or companies of young people, that we in our consciences, upon sober consideration, judge not well to consist with, or would sinfully tend to hinder the devoutest, and most engaged spirit in religion; or indispose the mind for that devout and profitable attendance on the duties of the closet, which is most agreeable to God's will, or that we in our most impartial judgment, can think tends to rob God of that honor which he expects, by our orderly, serious attendance on family worship.

And furthermore we promise that we will strictly avoid all freedoms and familiarities in company, so tending either to stir up or gratify a lust of lasciviousness, that we cannot in our consciences think will be approved by the infinitely pure and holy eye of God; or that we can think on serious and impartial consideration, we should be afraid to practice, if we expected in a few hours to appear before that holy God, to give an account of ourselves to him, as fearing they would be condemned by him as unlawful and impure.

We also promise, with great watchfulness, to perform relative duties, required by Christian rules, in the families we belong to; as we stand related respectively, towards parents and children, husbands and wives, brothers and sisters, masters or mistresses and servants.

And we now appear before God, depending on divine grace and assistance, solemnly to devote our whole lives to be laboriously spent in the business of religion: ever making it our greatest business, without backsliding from such a way of living; not hearkening to the solicitations of our sloth and other corrupt inclinations, or the temptations of the world, that tend to draw us off from it; and particularly, that we will not abuse an hope, or opinion that any of us may have of our being interested in Christ, to indulge ourselves in sloth, or the more easily to yield to the solicitations of any sinful inclinations; but will run with perseverance the race that is set before us [Heb. 12:1], and work out our own salvation with fear and trembling [Phil. 2:12].

And because we are sensible that the keeping [of] these solemn vows may hereafter, in many cases, be very contrary to our corrupt inclinations and carnal interests; we do now therefore appear before God, to make a surrender of all to him, and to make a sacrifice of every carnal inclination and interest to the great business of religion, and the interest of our souls.

And being sensible of our own weakness, and the deceitfulness of our own hearts, and our proneness to forget our most solemn vows and lose our resolutions; we promise to be often strictly examining ourselves by these promises, especially before the sacrament of the Lord's Supper; and beg of God that he would, for Christ's sake, keep us from wickedly dissembling in these our solemn vows; and that he who searches our hearts [Rom. 8:27] and ponders the path of our feet [Prov. 4:26] would from time to time help us in trying ourselves by this covenant, and help us to keep covenant with him, and not leave us to our own foolish, wicked and treacherous hearts.

In the beginning of the summer, 1742, there seemed to be some abatement of the liveliness of people's affections in religion: but yet many were often in a great height of them. And in the fall and winter following there were at times extraordinary appearances. But in the general people's engagedness in religion and the liveliness of their affections have been on the decline: and some of the young people especially have shamefully lost their liveliness and vigor in religion, and much of the seriousness and solemnity of their spirits. But there are many that walk as becometh saints [Eph. 5:2–3]; and to this day, there are a considerable number in the town that seem to be near to God, and maintain much of the life of religion, and enjoy many of the sensible tokens and fruits of his gracious presence.

With respect to the late season of revival of religion amongst us, for three or four years past; it has been observable that in the former part of it, in the years 1740 and 1741, the work seemed to be much more pure, having less of a corrupt mixture, than in the former great outpouring of the Spirit in 1735 and 1736. Persons seemed to be sensible of their former errors, and had learnt more of their own hearts, and experience had taught them more of the tendency and consequences of things: they were now better guarded, and their affections were not only greater, but attended with greater solemnity, and greater humility and self-distrust, and greater engagedness after holy living and perseverance; and there were fewer errors in conduct. But in the latter part of it, in the year 1742, it was otherwise. The work continued more pure till we were infected from abroad: our people hearing, and some of them seeing the work in other places, where there was a greater visible commotion than here, and the outward appearances were more extraordinary; were ready to think that the work in those places far excelled what was amongst us; and their eyes were dazzled with the high profession and great show that some made who came hither from other places.

That those people went so far beyond them in raptures and violent emotions of the affections, and a vehement zeal, and what they called boldness for Christ; our people were ready to think was owing to their far greater attainments in grace, and intimacy with heaven: they looked little in their own eyes in comparison of them, and were ready to submit themselves to 'em, and yield themselves up to their conduct, taking it for granted that everything was right that they said and did. These things had a strange influence on the people, and gave many of them a deep and unhappy tincture, that it was a hard and long labor to deliver 'em from, and which some of them are not fully delivered from to this day.

The effects and consequences of things amongst us plainly shows the following things, viz. that the degree of grace is by no means to be judged of by the degree of joy, or the degree of zeal; and that indeed we can't at all determine by these things, who are gracious and who are not; and that it is not the degree of religious affections, but the nature of them that is chiefly to be looked at. Some that have had very great raptures of joy, and have been extraordinarily filled (as the vulgar phrase is) and have had their bodies overcome, and that very often, have manifested far less of the temper of Christians, in their conduct since, than some others that have been still, and have made no great outward show. But then again there are many others, that have had extraordinary joys and emotions of mind, with frequent great effects on their bodies, that behave themselves steadfastly as humble, amiable, eminent Christians.

'Tis evident that there may be great religious affections, that may in show and appearance imitate gracious affections, and have the same effects on their bodies, but are far from having the same effect in the temper of their minds, and course of their lives. And likewise there is nothing more manifest by what appears amongst us, than that the goodness of [a] person's state is not chiefly to be judged of by any exactness of steps, and method of experiences, in what is supposed to be the first conversion; but that we must judge more by the spirit that breathes, the effect wrought on the temper of the soul, in the time of the work, and remaining afterwards. Though there have been very few instances among professors amongst us, of what is ordinarily called scandalous sin, known to me; yet the temper that some of them show, and the behavior they have been of, together with some things in the kind and circumstances of their experiences, make me much afraid lest there be a considerable number that have woefully deceived themselves. Though on the other hand, there is a great number whose temper and conversation is such as justly confirms the charity of others towards them; and not a few in whose disposition and walk, there are amiable appearances of eminent grace. And notwithstanding all the corrupt mixtures that have been in the late work here; there are not only many blessed fruits of it in particular persons, that yet remain, but some good effects of it upon the town in general. A party spirit has more ceased: I suppose there has been less appearance these three or four years past, of that division of the town into two parties, that has long been our bane, than has been these thirty years; and the people have apparently had much more caution, and a greater guard on their spirit and their tongues, to avoid contention and unchristian heats, in town meetings and on other occasions. And 'tis a thing greatly to be rejoiced in, that the people very lately have come to an agreement and final issue, with respect to their grand controversy relating to their common lands; which has been above any other particular thing, a source of mutual prejudices, jealousies, and debates, for fifteen or sixteen years past. The people are also generally of late in some respects considerably altered and meliorated in their notions of religion: particularly they seem to be much more sensible of the danger of resting in old experiences, or what they were subjects of at their supposed first conversion; and to be more fully convinced of the necessity of forgetting the things that are behind, and pressing forward [Phil. 3:13–14], and maintaining earnest labor, watchfulness and prayerfulness as long as they live.

[Jonathan Edwards.]

46. TO THE REVEREND ELNATHAN WHITMAN

This letter is a plea for charity and freedom of conscience. It is the only known letter from Edwards to his first cousin, Rev. Elnathan Whitman, minister of the Second Church of Christ, Hartford, Connecticut. The Northampton pastor is aware of the danger of divisiveness but warns against being judgmental and precipitous. The confusion of the times, the apostolic example, and a recognition of human frailty all call for patience.

(Trask Library, AL, writer's copy, four quarto leaves. Published in Dwight ed., *1*, 204–09; Edwin P. Parker, *History of the Second Church of Christ in Hartford* [Hartford, 1892], pp. 111–48.)

* * *

Northampton, February 9, 1743/4

Rev. and Dear Sir,

Mr. [John] Potwine was here this week, and among other things that were the subjects of our conversation, he gave me some account of the circumstances of a number of persons that had absented themselves from your meeting and had attended the public worship at Windsor, and desired my sentiments. I told him I should give no judgment of their particular case because I was not under a capacity of knowing it, but gave him my thoughts of some things in general, and on further reflecting on the matter am come to a determination to express the same sentiments that I signified to him, in a letter to you. I think not from any inclination to meddle with other folks' business, nor from any disposition to justify those pernicious principles tending to promote and foment censoriousness and division that have prevailed in many parts of the land of late, which I have ever borne a testimony against. But as it has been a time wherein the state of things has been very extraordinary, attended in some respects with general confusion; and the remedying the mischiefs that have been, being an affair of general concern; and the proper methods to be taken in order to it, being that about which there is a great diversity of sentiments: I thought it might not be amiss for me in general to express my thoughts to you as a friend and relation, leaving it with you to make what use of them and lay what weight to them you see best.

As to differences among professing Christians of opinion and practice about things that appertain to religion and the worship of God, I am ready to think that you and I are agreed as to the general principles of liberty of conscience; and that men's using coercive methods with their neighbors to oblige them to a conformity to their sentiments or way, is in nothing so unreasonable as in the worship of God, because that is a business wherein each person acts for himself with his Creator and supreme judge, as one concerned for his own acceptance with him, on which depends his own and not his neighbor's eternal happiness and salvation from everlasting ruin. And it is an affair wherein each man is infinitely more concerned with his Creator than he is with his neighbors. And so I suppose it will be allowed that each man ought to be left to his own conscience, in what he judges will be most acceptable to God, or what he supposes is the will of God, as to the kind or manner or means of worship, or the society of worshippers he should join with in worship. Not but that a great abuse may be made of this doctrine of liberty of conscience in the worship of God. I know that many are ready to justify everything in their own conduct from this doctrine, and I don't suppose that men's pretense of conscience is always to be regarded when made use of to justify their changing the society of worshippers they join with, or the means of their worship, or indeed the kind and manner of their worship. Men may make this pretense sometimes with such circumstances, that they may be worthy of no credit in what they pretend. It may be so manifest from the nature and circumstances of the case and their own manner of behavior, that it is not conscience, but petulancy and malice and willfulness and carnal vices that influence them. And, therefore, it seems to me evident that when such pleas are made, those that are especially concerned with them, as persons peculiarly obliged to take care of their souls, have no other way to do but to consider the nature and circumstances of the case, and from thence to judge whether the case be such as will admit of such a plea; or whether the nature of things will admit of such a supposition, that the men act conscientiously in what they do, considering all things that appertain to the case. And in this I conceive many things are to be considered and laid together: as the nature of that thing that is the subject of controversy, or wherein they differ from others or have changed their own practice; the degree in which it is disputable and how it may be supposed liable to diversity of opinions one way or the other, as to its agreeableness to the Word of God, and as to the importance of it with regard to men's salvation or soul's good; the degree of knowledge or ignorance of the persons; the advantages they have had for information, or the disadvantages they have been under, and what has been in their circumstances that might mislead their judgment; the principles that have been instilled into them; the instructions they have had from those that they have had an high opinion of for wisdom and piety, that might misguide the judgment of persons of real honesty and sincerity and tender conscience; the example of others; the diversities of opinions among ministers; the general state of things in the land; the character of the persons themselves and the manner of their behavior in the particular affair in debate.

Now, Sir, I imagine with regard to those persons that have gone from you to Windsor, that however you look upon their behavior herein as very disorderly, yet if you suppose (the case being considered with all its circumstances) that there was any room for charity that it might be through infirmity, ignorance, and mistakes of judgment, so that they might be truly conscientious in it, i.e. might really believe it to be their duty and what God required of 'em to do as they have done: you would by no means think that they ought to be proceeded with in the use of such means as are proper to be used with contumacious offenders, or those that are stubborn and obstinate in scandalous vice or willful wickedness; or that you would think it proper to proceed with persons, towards whom there is this room left for charity; that possibly they may be honest and truly conscientious, acting as persons afraid to offend God, so as to cut them off from the congregation of the Lord, and cast 'em forth into the visible kingdom of Satan, to be as harlots and publicans.

Now, Sir, I would pray that it may be considered, whether it can positively be determined, when all things are considered with respect to those persons that have absented themselves from your assembly, that it could not be in their case that that might really be their judgment, that it was their duty so to do, and that God required it of them, and that they should greatly expose the welfare of their own souls in attending no other public worship, but that in your congregation. I suppose those persons are not much versed in casuistical divinity. They are of the common people, whose judgment in all nations and ages are exceeding easily led and swayed. They are not very capable of viewing things in the extent of their consequences and of estimating things in their true weight and importance. And you know, dear Sir, the state that things have been in the country. You know what opinions have lately prevailed and have been maintained and propagated by those that have been lifted up to heaven in their reputation for piety and great knowledge in divine matters, with a great part of the people of New England. I don't pretend to know what has influenced these people in particular; but I think under these circumstances it would be no strange thing, if great numbers of the common people in the country that are really conscientious and concerned to be accepted with God and to take the best course for their soul's good, should really think in their hearts that God requires 'em to attend the ministry of these that are called New Light ministers; and that it would be dangerous to their souls and what God approved not of, ordinarily to attend the ministry of others. Yea, I should think it strange if it were otherwise.

It ought to be considered how public controversy and a great and general cry in matters of religion strongly influences the minds of multitudes of the common people, how it blinds their minds and wonderfully misleads their judgment. And Christian rules and the example of the apostles most certainly require that great allowances be made in such cases. And particularly the example of the apostle Paul with regard to great numbers of professing Christians in the Church of Corinth who, in a time of great and general confusion in that church, through the evil instruction of teachers that they admired that misled and blinded their judgment, ran into many and great disorders in their worship and woeful schisms and divisions among themselves, and particularly with regard to ministers and with regard to the apostle Paul himself, whom many of them seem for a time to have forsaken to follow others that set up themselves in opposition to him; though, as he says, he had been their father, who had begotten them through the gospel. Yet with how much gentleness does the Apostle treat them, still acknowledging them as brethren. And though he required church censures to be used with regard to the incestuous persons, yet there is no shadow of the Apostle taking any such course with those that had been misled by those false teachers or with any that had been guilty of these disorders except the false teachers themselves. But as soon as they are brought off from following these false apostles any longer, he embraces 'em without further ado with all the love and tenderness of a father; burying all their censoriousness and schisms and disorders at the Lord's Supper—and ill treatment of him, the extraordinary messenger of Christ to them. And indeed, the Apostle never so much as gave any direction for the suspension of any one member from the Lord's Supper on account of these disorders or from any other part of the public worship of God; but instead of that, gives 'em directions how they shall go on better to attend the Lord's Supper and other parts of worship. And he himself, without suspension or interruption, goes on to call and treat them as beloved brethren, Christians, sanctified in Christ Jesus, called to be saints, and praises God on their behalf for the grace that is given them by Christ Jesus; and often and abundantly expresses his charity towards them in innumerable expressions that I might mention. And nothing is more apparent than that he don't treat them as those with respect to whom there lies a bar in the way of others' treating them with the charity that belongs to saints and good and honest members of the Christian church, till the bar be removed by a church process. And, indeed, the insisting on a church process with every member that has behaved himself disorderly, in a such like state of general confusion, is not a way to build up the church of God (which is the end of church discipline), but to pull it down. It will not be the way to cure a diseased member, but to bring a disease on the whole body.

I am not alone in these sentiments, but I have reason to think that Col. [John] Stoddard, from the conversation I have had with him, is in the like way of thinking.

There came hither the last fall a couple of Scotsmen belonging to the church at New Haven, that had been members of Mr. [Joseph] Noyes' church, but had left it and had incorporated with the separate church and entered into covenant with them when that church was embodied. This was looked upon as a crime that ought not to be passed over by Mr. Noyes and the Rector [Thomas Clap]. They manifested themselves willing to return to Mr. Noyes' meeting, but a particular confession was required of 'em in the meeting house. Accordingly, each of 'em had offered a confession, but it was not thought sufficient; but it was required of them that they should add some things that they thought hard of; and they consulting me about it, I acquainted Colonel Stoddard with the affair and desired his thoughts. He said he looked upon it unreasonable to require any confession at all; and that considering the general state of confusion that there had been, and the instructions and examples these young men had had, it might well be looked upon enough that they now alter their practice, and return again to Mr. Noyes' meeting. Not that you are obliged to think as Colonel Stoddard does, yet I think, considering his character and relation, his judgment may well be of so much weight as to engage you the more to attend to and weigh the reasons he gives.

The objections that these persons may have had against ordinarily attending your meeting may perhaps be very trivial; but yet I apprehend that through infirmities the case may be so with truly honest and conscientious Christians, that trivial things may have great weight in their conscience so as to have fast hold of them till they are better enlightened, as in the former time in the country it was with respect to controversy between Presbyterians and Congregationalists. It was, as I have heard, in those days real matter of question with some whether a Presbyterian, living and dying so, could be saved. Some Irish Presbyterians that have lived with us have desired baptism for their children that yet lived in neglect of the ordinances of the Lord's Supper, because of a difference on some trivial circumstances of the administration from the method of the Church of Scotland. This matter being discoursed of, it was thought by Colonel Stoddard in particular that their neglect ought to [be] borne with and they ought to be looked upon as Christians and their children received to baptism; because however trivial the foundations of their scruples were, yet through ignorance they might be honest and conscientious in them.

As to the church covenant that these persons have entered into, wherein they have obliged themselves ordinarily to join in the worship of that church, I suppose none interpret the promises of the church covenant in such a sense as to exclude all reserves of liberty in case of an alteration of the judgment in the affairs of conscience and religion in one respect or another. As if a person, after incorporating with a Congregational church, should become a conscientious Church [of England] man, or Anabaptist, or should by any change of judgment come to think the means or manner of worship unlawful; and so in other respects that might be mentioned.

And if it be so that these persons in some of their talk and behavior have manifested a contentious, forward spirit at the time of their withdrawing from your church, I confess this gives greater ground of suspicion of the sincerity [of] their profession of conscience—yet as to this, I humbly conceive allowances must be made. It must be considered that it is possible that persons, in an affair of this nature, in the thing itself may be conscientious, and yet in the course of the management of it may be guilty of very corrupt mixtures of passion and many evil dispositions, as indeed is commonly the case with men in long controversies of whatever nature, and even with conscientious men. And therefore it appears to me that if persons in such a case are not obstinate in what is amiss in them in this respect and don't stand to justify their forwardness and unchristian speeches, they notwithstanding may deserve credit when they profess themselves conscientious in the affair in general.

Thus, dear Sir, I have freely signified to you some of my thoughts with regard to some of the concerns of the difficult day which prove a trouble to you, not with any aim at controlling you. I am sensible that you and not I are the pastor of the Second Church of Hartford. I only desire you would impartially consider the reasons I have offered. Begging of Christ, our common Lord, that he would direct you in your thought and practice to that which will be acceptable in his sight, I am,

[Jonathan Edwards.]

47. TO THE REVEREND WILLIAM McCULLOCH

Edwards does not hesitate to catalog the lapses of those who earlier claimed revival benefits and to repudiate any claim that the millennium has begun. Not only should a cooling of ardor be expected, he writes, but the church should prepare for persecutions, even defeats, before its final triumph. Ultimately, God will usher in his perfect rule. Edwards sketches here the prophetic themes expanded in "Notes on the Apocalypse" and *Humble Attempt.*

(Trask Library, ALS, six quarto leaves, infolded quire. Published in Dwight ed., *1*, 211–19; and abridged in *Works, 4,* 558–60. For a fuller discussion of the themes in this letter, particularly the interpretations of Rev. 11, see *Works, 5.*)

* * *

Northampton, March 5, 1743/4

Rev. and Dear Sir,

I return you thanks for your most obliging, entertaining, and instructive letter, dated August 13, 1743, which I received about the latter end of October. My answering—which has been unhappily delayed, by reason of my distance from Boston, and not being able to find any opportunity to send thither till the ship was gone that brought your letter, which I much regretted—my delaying to answer has been far from arising from any indifference with respect to this correspondence by which, I am sensible, I am highly honored and privileged.

'Tis probable that you have been informed by other correspondents before now what the present state of things in New England is. It is indeed on many accounts very melancholy. There is a vast alteration within this two years; for about so long, I think it is, since the Spirit of God began to withdraw, and this great work has been on the decline. Great numbers in the land about two years ago were raised to an exceeding great height, in joy and elevations of mind. And through want of watchfulness and sensibleness of the danger and temptation that there is in such circumstances, many were greatly exposed. And the devil taking the advantage, multitudes were soon, and to themselves insensibly, led far away from God and their duty. God was provoked that he was not sanctified in this height of advancement, as he ought to have been. He saw our spiritual pride and self-confidence, and the polluted flames that arose of intemperate, unhallowed zeal; and he soon in a great measure withdrew from us. And the consequence has been that "the enemy has come in like a flood," in various respects, until the deluge has overwhelmed the whole land. There had from the beginning been a great mixture, especially in some places, of false experiences, and false religion with true; but from about this time, the mixture became much greater, many were led away with sad delusions. And this opened the door for "the enemy to come in like a flood" in another respect: it gave great advantage to the enemies and opposers of this work, furnished them with weapons, and gave 'em new courage, and has laid the friends of the work under such disadvantages that nothing that they could do would avail anything to withstand their violence. And now it is come to that, that the work is put to a stop everywhere, and it is the day of the enemy's triumph; but I believe also a day of God's people's humiliation, which will be better to 'em in the end than their elevations and raptures. The time has been amongst us "when the sower went forth to sow," and we have seen the spring, wherein the seed sprang up in different sorts of ground, appearing then fair and flourishing; but this spring is past, and we now see the summer, wherein the sun is up with a burning heat, that tries the sorts of ground. And now appears the difference: the seed in stony ground, where there was only a thin layer of earth on a rock, whithers away, the moisture being dried out; and the hidden seeds and roots of thorns, in unsubdued ground, now springs up and chokes the seed of the Word. Many high professors are fallen, some into gross immoralities; some into the opinions of sectaries; some into a rooted, spiritual pride, enthusiasm, and an incorrigible wildness of behavior; some into a cold, carnal frame of mind, showing a great indifference to things of religion. But there are many—and I hope those the greater part of those that were professed converts—appear hitherto like the good ground. And notwithstanding the thick and dark clouds that so soon follow that blessed sunshine that we have had, yet I cannot but steadfastly maintain an hope and persuasion that God will revive his work, and that what has been so great and very extraordinary is a forerunner of a yet more glorious and extensive work.

It has been slanderously reported and printed concerning me, that I have often said that the millennium was already begun, and that it began at Northampton. A doctor of divinity in New England,[1] has ventured to publish this report to the world from a single person, who is concealed and kept behind the curtain; but the report is very diverse from what I have ever said. Indeed, I have often said, as I say now, that

1. I.e. Charles Chauncy in *Seasonable Thoughts on the State of Religion in New England* (Boston, 1743), pp. 372–73.

I looked upon the late wonderful revivals of religion as forerunners of those glorious times so often prophesied of in the Scripture, and that this was the first dawning of that light, and beginning of that work which in the progress and issue of it would at last bring on the church's latter-day glory. But there are many that know that I have from time to time added, that there would probably be many sore conflicts and terrible convulsions, and many changes, revivings and intermissions, and returns of dark clouds, and threatening appearances, before this work shall have subdued the world, and Christ's kingdom shall be everywhere established and settled in peace, which will be the beginning of the millennium, or day of the church's peace, rejoicing and triumph on earth, so often spoken of.

I was much entertained and delighted, dear Sir, with your thoughts on that text in Is. 59:19, which you signify in your letter: and so have many others been to whom I have communicated them. And as to what you say of some dreadful stroke or trial yet abiding, before the happy days of the promised peace and prosperity of the church, I so far agree with you, that I believe that before the church of God shall have obtained the conquest, and the visible kingdom of Satan on earth shall receive its overthrow, and Christ's kingdom of grace be everywhere established on its ruins, there shall be a great and mighty struggle between the kingdom of Christ and the kingdom of Satan, attended with the greatest and most extensive convulsions and commotions that ever were upon the face of the earth, wherein doubtless many particular Christians will suffer, and perhaps some parts of the church. But that the enemies of the church of God should ever gain such advantages against her any more, as they have done in times past, that the victory should ever any more be on their side, or that it shall ever be given to the Beast again to make war with the saints, and to prevail against them, and overcome them (as in Rev. 13:7 and 11:7; and Dan. 7:21) to such a degree as has been heretofore, is otherwise than I hope—though in this I would be far from setting up my own judgment, in opposition to others who are more skilled in the prophecies of the Scripture than I am.

I think that what has mainly induced many divines to be of that opinion is what is said in Rev. 11 concerning the slaying of the witnesses, vv. 7–8, "And when they shall have finished their testimony, the Beast that ascendeth out of the bottomless pit, shall make war against them, and shall overcome them, and kill them; and their dead bodies shall lie in the street of the great city, which spiritually is called Sodom and Egypt, where also our Lord was crucified." The event here spoken of seems evidently to be that wherein the enemies of the church gain the greatest advantage against her that ever they have, and have the greatest conquest of her that ever they obtain, and bring the church nearest to a total extinction. For a long time the church is very small, represented by two witnesses, and they had been long in a very low state, prophesying in sackcloth; but now they are dead, and their enemies triumph over them as having gotten a complete victory, and look upon it that they are now past all possibility of recovery, there being less prospect of the church's restoration than ever there was before.

But are we to expect this, dear Sir, that Satan will ever find means to bring things to that pass, that after all the increase of light that has been in the world since the Reformation, there shall be a return of a more dark time than in the depth of the darkness of popery, before the Reformation, when the church of God shall be nearer to a total extinction, and have less of visibility; all true religion and light more blotted out of the memories of mankind; Satan's kingdom of darkness more firmly established; all monuments of true religion more abolished; and that the state of the world should be such, that it should appear farther from any hope of a revival of true religion than ever it has done? Is this conceivable, or possible, as the state of things now is all over the world, even among papists themselves, without a miracle, a greater than any power short of divine can effect, without a long tract of time gradually to bring it to pass, to introduce the grossest ignorance and extinguish all memory and monuments of truth? Which was the case in that great extinction of true religion that was before the Reformation. And besides, if we suppose this war of the Beast, that ascends out of the bottomless pit, with the witnesses, wherein he overcomes them and kills them, to be that last war which the church shall have with the Beast, that great and mighty conflict that shall be just before the final overthrow of Antichrist, that we read of in the 16th chapter, 13th and following verses, and in the 19th chapter; how shall we make them consist together? In the 11th chapter, the church conflicts in sorrow, clothed in sackcloth and in blood; in the 19th chapter, the saints are not represented as fighting in sorrow and blood, though the battle be exceeding great, but in strength, glory, and triumph. Their captain goes forth to this battle in great pomp and magnificence, on a white horse, and on his head many crowns, and on his vesture and on his thigh a name written, "KING OF KINGS, AND LORD OF LORDS"; and the saints follow him not in sackcloth, but coming forth on white horses, clothed in fine linen, clean and white, the raiment of triumph, the same raiment that the saints appear in (Rev. 7:14) when they appear with palms in their hands, after they had washed their robes, that had been stained with their own blood, and made them white in the blood of the Lamb. In the conflict spoken of (ch. 11) the Beast makes war with the witnesses, and overcomes them, and kills them; the same is foretold, Dan. 7:21 and Rev. 13:7. But in that last great battle, just before the fall of Antichrist, we find the reverse of this; the church shall obtain a glorious victory over the Beast, and the Beast is taken and cast into the lake of fire. Rev. 17:14, "These shall make war with the Lamb; and the Lamb shall overcome them; for he is Lord of Lords, and King of Kings: and they that are with him are called, and chosen, and faithful," compared with ch. 19:6 to the end, and ch. 16:16–17. In that conflict (ch. 11) the Beast has war with the witnesses, and kills them, and their dead bodies lie unburied, as if it were to be "meat for the beasts of the earth and fowls of heaven"; but in that last conflict, Christ and his church shall slay their enemies, and give their dead bodies to be "meat for the beasts of the earth and fowls of heaven" (ch. 19:17, etc.).

There is no manner of appearance in the descriptions that are given of that last great battle, of any great advantages gained in it against the church, before the enemy is overcome; but all appearance of the contrary. The descriptions in the 16th and 19th chapters of Revelation will by no means allow of such an advantage as that, [of] the overcoming and slaying the church or people of God, and their lying for some time unburied, that their dead bodies may be for their enemies to abuse and trample on, and make sport with. In the 16th chapter, we have an account of their being gathered together into the place called "Armageddon"; and then the first thing we hear of after that, is the pouring out of the seventh vial of God's wrath, "and a voice saying, 'It is done.'" And so in the 19th chapter [v. 19] we read of "the Beast, and the kings of the earth, and their armies, being gathered together, to make war against him that sat on the horse, and against his army." And then the next thing we hear of, is the "Beast's being taken," etc. The event of the conflict of the Beast with the church (Rev. 11:9–10) is the triumph of the church's enemies, when "they of the people, and kindreds, and tongues, and nations," and "they that dwell on the earth," shall see the dead bodies of the saints lying in the streets, and "shall rejoice over them, and make merry, and send gifts one to another." But the event of that great and last battle before the fall of Antichrist is quite the reverse of this, even the church's triumphing over their enemies, as being utterly destroyed. Those events that are consequent on the issue of the war with the witnesses (ch. 11) do in no wise answer to those that are represented as *consequent* on that last conflict of Antichrist with the church. 'Tis said that when the "witnesses ascended into heaven," the same hour there was a great earthquake, and the tenth part of the city fell, and in the earthquake were slain of men seven thousand" [Rev. 11:13]. But this don't seem at all to answer what is described, ch. 16:19, "The great city was divided into three parts, and the cities of the nations fell; and great Babylon came in remembrance before God, to give her the cup of the wine of the fierceness of his wrath; and every island fled away, and the mountains were not found." And it had been said before, "there was a great earthquake, such as was not since men were upon the earth, so mighty an earthquake, and so great" [Rev. 16:18]. And in the 19th chapter, instead of slaying seven thousand men, it seems as if there was a general slaughter of all the enemies of the church through the world.

And besides, if we read this 11th chapter through, we shall see that the falling of the tenth part of the city and the rising of the witnesses, and their standing on their feet, and ascending into heaven, are represented there as entirely distinct from the accomplishment of the church's glory after the fall of Antichrist, and God's judging and destroying the enemies of the church. The judgments here spoken of as executed on God's enemies are under another woe, and the benefits bestowed on the church are under another trumpet; for immediately after the account of the rising and ascending of the witnesses, and its consequences, follow these words, vv. 14–15: "The second woe is past, and behold the third woe cometh quickly: and the seventh angel sounded, and there were great voices in heaven, saying, 'The kingdoms of this world are become the kingdoms of our Lord and of his Christ, and he shall reign forever and ever.'" And then in the following verses we have an account of the praises sung to God on that occasion; and in the last verse we have a brief hint of that same great earthquake, and the great hail, and those thunders and lightnings and voices, that we have an account of in the latter part of the 16th chapter: so that the earthquake mentioned in the last verse of ch. 11 seems to be the great earthquake that attends the last great conflict of the church and her enemies, rather than that mentioned, v. 13.

The grand objection against all this is that it is said, that the "witnesses should prophesy 1,260 days, clothed in sackcloth; and when they have finished their testimony, the Beast should make war against them, and kill them," etc.; and that it seems manifest that after this they are no longer in sackcloth; for henceforward they are in an exalted state in heaven: and that, therefore, seeing the time of their wearing sackcloth is a 1,260 days, i.e. during the time of the continuance of Antichrist, hence their being slain, and their rising again must be at the conclusion of this period, at the end of Antichrist's reign.

In answer to which I would say, with submission to better judgments, that I humbly conceive that we can justly infer no more from this prophecy than this, viz. the 1,260 days is the proper time (as it were) of the church's trouble and bondage, as being clothed in sackcloth, because it is the appointed time of the reign of Antichrist; but this don't hinder but that God, out of great compassion to his church, should in some respect shorten the days, and grant that his church should in some measure anticipate the appointed great deliverance that should be at the end of these days, as he has in fact done in the Reformation, whereby his church has had a great degree of restoration granted her from the darkness, power, and dominion of Antichrist before her proper time of restoration, which is at the end of the 1,260 days. And so the church, through the compassions of her Father and Redeemer, anticipates her deliverance from her sorrows; and has in some respects an end put to her testifying in sackcloth, as many parts of the church are henceforward brought out from under the dominion of the Antichristian powers, into a state of liberty; though in other respects the church may be said still to continue in her sackcloth, and in the wilderness (as ch. 12:14), till the end of the days. And as to the witnesses standing on their feet, and ascending into heaven, I would propose that it may be considered whether any more can be understood by it, than the Protestant church's being now (at least as to many parts of it) able to stand on her own legs, and in her own defense, and being raised to such a state, that she henceforward is out of the reach of the Romish powers, that, let them do what they will, they shall never any more be able to get the church under their power, as they had before: as oftentimes in Scriptures, God's people's dwelling in safety, out of the reach of their enemies, is represented by their dwelling on high, or being set on high (Ps. 59:1; Is. 33:16; Ps. 69:29, 91:14, and 107:41; Prov. 29:25); and as the children of Israel, when brought out of Egypt, were said to be carried on eagle's wings, that is lofty in its flight, flies away towards heaven, where none of her enemies can reach her.

I might here observe that we have other instances of God's shortening the days of his church's captivity and bondage, either at the beginning or latter end, in some measure parallel with this. Thus the proper time of the bondage of the posterity of Abraham in a strange land was 400 years (Gen. 15:13), but yet God in mercy delayed their bondage, whereby the time was much shortened at the beginning. So the time wherein it was foretold that the "whole land of Israel should be a desolation, and an astonishment," and the land should enjoy her sabbaths [II Chron. 36:21], was seventy years (Jer. 25:11–12), and these seventy years are dated in II Chron. 36:20–21 from Zedekiah's captivity; and yet from that captivity, to Cyrus' decree, was but about fifty-two years—though it was indeed about seventy years before the temple was finished. So the proper time of the oppression of Antiochus Epiphanes, wherein "both the sanctuary, and the host should be trodden under foot by him, was two thousand and three hundred days" (Dan. 8:13–14). And yet God gave Israel a degree of deliverance by the Maccabees, and they were holpen with a little help and the host ceased to be trodden under foot before that time was expired (Dan. 11:32, 34).

But in these things, dear Sir, I am by no means dogmatical. I do but humbly offer my thoughts on what you suggested in your letter, submitting them to your censure. 'Tis pity that we should expect such a terrible devastation of the church, before her last and most glorious deliverance, if there be no such thing to be expected. It may be a temptation to some of the people of God the less earnestly to wish and pray for the near approach of the church's glorious day, and the less to rejoice in the signs of its approach.

But let us go on what scheme we will, it is most apparent by the Scriptures that there are mighty strugglings to be expected between the church of God and her enemies, before her great victory; and there may be many lesser strugglings before that last and greatest and universal conflict. Experience seems to show that the church of God, according to God's method of dealing with her, needs a great deal gradually to prepare her for that prosperity and glory that he has promised her on earth, as the growth of the earth after winter needs gradually to be prepared for the summer heat. I have known instances, wherein, by the heat's coming on suddenly in the spring without intermissions of cold to check the growth, the branches, many of them, by a too hasty growth have afterwards died. And perhaps God may bring on a spiritual spring as he does the natural, with now and then a pleasant sun-shiny season, and then an interruption by clouds and stormy winds, till at length the sun, by more and more approaching and the light increasing, the strength of the winter is broken. We are extremely apt to get out of the right way. A very great increase of comfort that is sudden, without time and experience, in many instances has appeared to wound the soul, in some respects, though it seems to profit it in others. Sometimes, at the same time that the soul seems wonderfully delivered from those lusts that are more carnal and earthly, there is an insensible increase of those that are more spiritual, as God told the children of Israel that he would put out the former inhabitants of the land of Canaan by little and little, and would not consume 'em at once, lest the beasts of the field should increase upon them. We need much experience to teach us the innumerable ways that we are liable to err, and to show us the evil and pernicious consequences of those errors. If it should please God before many years to grant another great revival of religion in New England, we should perhaps be much upon our guard against such errors as we have run into, and which have undone us this time, but yet might run insensibly into other errors that now we think not of.

You inquire of me, Reverend Sir, whether I reject all those for counterfeits that speak of visions and trances. I am far from doing of it: I am, and always have been, in that matter of the same opinion that Mr. [James] Robe expresses in some of those pamphlets Mr. [John] Mac-Laurin sent me, that persons are neither to be rejected, nor approved on such a foundation. I have expressed the same thing in my discourse on the marks of a work of the true Spirit,[2] and han't changed my mind.

I am afraid, dear Sir, that I have been too bold with you in being so lengthy and tedious, and been too impertinent and forward to express my opinion upon this and that; but I consider myself as writing to a candid Christian friend and brother, with whom I may be free and bold, and from whom I may promise myself excuse and forgiveness. Dear brother, asking your earnest prayers for me and for New England, I am your affectionate brother and engaged friend and servant,

Jonathan Edwards.

2. *Distinguishing Marks*, in *Works, 4*, 236–38.

48. TO DOROTHY DANKS HANNAM

Samuel Hopkins singled out the "bad book" episode as the beginning of the chain of events that led to Edwards' dismissal from Northampton.[1] A group of young men had acquired an illustrated midwives' manual, which became the basis for unwelcome comments from them to young women of the parish. To Edwards, who had publicly praised the high moral standards of his church's young people, such conduct was scandalous and humiliating. The matter was eventually settled, but resentment smoldered until it grew into the conflagration of 1750. This letter, part of Edwards' efforts to gather evidence against the culprits, is the only known communication relating to the incident.

(Beinecke Library, ALS, in Sermon on Mic. 5:7–8, one quarto leaf, shorn on right side.)

* * *

Northampton, March 26, [1744]

To Eleazar Hannam's Wife:

It has been testified by one before [the] church, that she was once at the [widow] [Elizabeth] Macklin's house, where were Oliver Warner and Medad Lyman reading in [a book] about womenkind, that which was [very] unclean to be read; and that they [made] sport of what they read before some womenkind; and that Thankful Parsons [and] you were there. This therefore is [to] desire you, as you are a member of the Christian church, and would maintain communion of churches, whereby they [are] obliged to assist one another as occasion [arises], to send an exact and full testimony [of all] that you know relating to this matter particularly as near as you can, how [unclean] it was; which of these two young [men] read in the book, whether one or [another] of them; what this book was about, whether it was about womenkind, [whether] it was about women's having children; whether they seemed to make sport [and] diversion of what was read; whether [they] took occasion from it to run upon the [girls]; and the like. In thus giving your testimony, I think you will do what [you] are obliged to do as a Christian.

Jonathan Edwards.

1. See Hopkins, pp. 53–55; Tracy, *Jonathan Edwards, Pastor*, pp. 160–64, 256–57; and Thomas H. Johnson, "Jonathan Edwards and the Young Folks' Bible," *NEQ* 5 (1932), 37–54.

49. TO THE REVEREND BENJAMIN COLMAN

Edwards took an active interest in music, particularly because singing, then as now, often went hand in hand with revivalism. Here, he finds unbelievable a report claiming that Colman had recommended that Watts' hymns not be sung, for Watts was both Colman's friendly correspondent and a sponsor of the publication of the *Faithful Narrative* in London.

(Published in *PMHS*, ser. 2, X [1895–96], 429, from the papers of Benjamin Colman of the Brattle Street Church, Boston.)

* * *

Northampton, May 22, 1744

Rev. and Honored Sir,

It has been our manner in this congregation, for more than two years past, in the summer time, when we sing three times upon the sabbath, to sing an hymn, or part of a hymn of Dr. [Isaac] Watts', the last time, viz.: at the conclusion of the afternoon exercise. I introduced it principally because I saw in the people a very general inclination to it. Indeed, I was not properly he that introduced it: they began it in my absence on a journey; and seemed to be greatly pleased with it; and sang nothing else, and neglected the Psalms wholly. When I came home I disliked not their making some use of the hymns, but did not like their setting aside the Psalms; and therefore used them principally, only in the manner that I have spoken of, and thus we continued to use them: which at first I suppose, was to universal satisfaction.

And [so] it continued to be till very lately, excepting one man, one Mr. Root; he after a little while manifesting a disgust, not by coming to me to say anything [to] me, but by turning his back on that part of public worship from time to time, and [going] out of the meeting-house. There was no appearance of dislike in any other person that I know of, till lately I have heard some other persons have appeared not well pleased: which I suppose principally arises from what Mr. Root says you said to him concerning our singing those hymns, more than a twelvemonth ago, and a message that he says you desired him to deliver to me (though he never delivered it, or informed me of it till yesterday). He says that he went to you on purpose to talk with you on the affair, and that you charged him with this message to me, once and again, "Tell Mr. Edwards from me, that I desire that he would by no means sing Dr. Watts' Hymns." This message which Mr. Root has spoken much of to others, though he did not deliver it to me, has I believe made some difficulty.

And because I was ready to think there was some mistake, and it is pity that trouble should arise among us from nothing, I thought it would be best to write to you, that I might know the certainty. Therefore I would pray you, honored Sir, to inform me whether Mr. Root did not mistake you, by writing briefly to me concerning this matter. Herein, honored Sir, you will much oblige

Your already greatly obliged son and servant,
Jonathan Edwards.

50. TO THE REVEREND ELEAZAR WHEELOCK

The Reverend James Davenport, one of the most outrageous itinerants, had been pronounced mentally ill in 1742 by authorities in both Hartford and Boston. Edwards had firsthand experience of Davenport's excesses during his New London visit of 1743, when Davenport induced people to consign idolatrous apparel and heretical books to the flames. Edwards greets news of Davenport's returning sanity with relief, as do others.[1] On the question of whether he will attend a convention of clergy in New Haven, Edwards explains that he is fully occupied at home. Finally, the Northampton church, heavily committed to the Stockbridge Indians at this time, is unable to help support Wheelock's Indian student.

(HSP, ALS, two folio leaves, addressed on second verso to the Reverend Eleazar Wheelock, pastor of a church in Lebanon.)

*   *   *

Northampton, July 13, 1744

Dear Brother,

Mr. [James] Davenport is truly very much altered; I am affected to see the happy alteration and change in him; he is quite another man. It has been moving to me to see the grace of God in so subduing, humbling, and enlightening him. He really shows an excellent spirit, much to the honor and glory of God; and I believe he is now much fuller of the Spirit of God than he was in years past, when he seemed to have such a constant series of high elevations and raptures. I think he is now fully satisfied in his duty in making a public, humble, and suitable recantation and confession of his great errors, that have been of such extensive and extremely hurtful consequence to the interest of religion. I cannot but believe that, notwithstanding all the insults which his humble retractations may be the occasions of among a generation

---

1. On Davenport, see DEX, *1*, 448–49; Prince, *Christian History* 2 (1744), 236–41.

of vipers, that yet they will be of great service to religion, and will open the door for his being now truly very serviceable by his preaching, in many places in New England, and especially there where he has done most hurt.

As to the proposed convention at [Yale's] commencement, I don't know what particular views Mr. [Samuel] Cooke may have, but my prevailing thoughts are that unless he or somebody else has some projection to propose, that may probably be of some great public benefit, the meeting and consulting of those that are called the New Light ministers from all parts, or making any great ado, will only serve to raise, or at least continue the spirit of that government. However, I believe it will be difficult for me to be there.

As to the Indian which you are instructing, such are the present circumstances of our people, that I have not courage to set forward any collection for him among them. They have been moved to many contributions of late, and they have now one in consideration for the promoting a free boarding school for the Indians at Housatonic, which it is supposed will cost at the beginning at least £3,000. And it is a time of the greatest scarcity of money among them, and they have of late been in the most unhappy frame that I have known them ever to be in. Please to give my love to Mrs. Wheelock. I am, dear Sir,

> Your affectionate brother and servant,
> Jonathan Edwards.

51. TO THE REVEREND THOMAS PRINCE

The high esteem in which Edwards and Prince held each other was matched by the mutual affection of their families. Hence the death of Prince's daughter, Deborah Prince, in Boston, was keenly felt at the Northampton parsonage.

(Published in *Biblical Review and Congregational Magazine* 1 [1846], 223–24. Deborah Prince's death was reported in the *Boston Gazette*, July 24, 1744, p. 3; and in Prince, *Christian History* 2 [1744], 208.)

* * *

Northampton, July 27, 1744

Rev. and Honored Sir,

We had some time ago heard of your daughter's dangerous illness, which my daughter in Boston informed us from time to time of the prevalence and increase of; and we have lately heard the sorrowful tidings of her death, which we have received with hearty condolence with you in your affliction; which must needs be great, but yet, by what we have heard, is attended with great ground of comfort and cause of thankfulness to God. We have heard of very hopeful evidences that she gave in her lifetime of a saving interest in Christ, which puts out of the reach of all the ill consequences of death, or any hurt that death can do, those that are the subjects of such an infinite privilege; and not only so, but makes death their great gain.

And how unspeakable, dear Sir, must the support and consolation needs be to surviving friends, in the case of the death of dear relatives, to have ground to think of them as being now in glory, in a state of eternal rest and perfect blessedness, having all tears wiped away from their eyes, and sorrow and sighing forever banished! And surely when we mourn for the death of such friends, our mourning should be moderate, for that which they rejoice at; and if we may mourn, our mourning may well be mingled with rejoicing. As we hope we belong to the same society with the blessed in heaven, and have our conversation and citizenship with them, it becomes us to partake with them in their joys, and rejoice with them, especially those of them that were our nearest and dearest friends on earth; and surely we should not sink in mourning and tears while they sing and rejoice with exceeding, inconceivable, and eternal joy. But yet, such is our infirmity, so dark are our minds, and so little do we see beyond the grave, that we need much divine assistance and support to do as becomes Christians under our trials. And we have, therefore, to wonder that God has made such glorious provision in Christ Jesus for the support and comfort of all that trust in him under all afflictions, and that he has given us so many great and precious promises, sealed with his blood, and confirmed with his oath, that we might, in every case, have strong consolation. We live in a vale of tears, a world of sorrow. Oh, that all that we meet with here may cause us to live more as pilgrims and strangers on the earth, and to be followers of them who through faith and patience inherit the promises!

Remember me, honored Sir, to your mournful spouse and dear surviving children, as one of their friends that heartily sympathizes with them. That God may abundantly support both you and them, and make up the great loss to you in himself, and grant that you may at last have a joyful meeting with your dear departed relative in immortal glory, is the prayer of, dear Sir, your friend and servant,

In Christian love and affectionate sympathy,
Jonathan Edwards.

P.S. My wife joins with me in sympathy and condolence with you and your family under this heavy affliction.

52. TO THE REVEREND STEPHEN WILLIAMS

Edwards wished to attend the council at New Haven regarding the Separate Society there, as well as convene a preliminary conference about it, but he was preparing for the ordination of the Reverend Robert Abercrombie on August 30. His sermon on that occasion was published in 1744 as *The True Excellency of a Minister of the Gospel.*

(HSP, ALS, one oversize quarto leaf, addressed on verso to the Reverend Stephen Williams at Longmeadow. See also Parmenter, p. 300.)

* * *

Northampton, August 27, 1744

Rev. Sir,

I conclude that you and Mr. [Peter] Reynolds have each of you lately received a letter, to be communicated to your churches, from the Separate Society at New Haven, desiring your presence and assistance at a council there the day after commencement; to which council the churches of Northampton and Hatfield are also called. Were it not that the ordination at Pelham is this week (where I must be), and our public lecture the next week, I should determine to ride down to confer with you on this affair; but it being so that these things prevent my coming to you, I would propose to you that you and Mr. Reynolds should come to Mr. [Robert] Abercrombie's ordination on Thursday this week, that we may have some opportunity to confer together on this affair, together with Mr. [Timothy] Woodbridge; or if you can't come to the ordination, I would propose that you should come to my lecture the next week.

I have conferred with Col. [John] Stoddard on the affair, and he seems to think that 'tis our duty to go.

I desire that you would communicate my proposal of a conference to Mr. Reynolds. Herein you will oblige, Sir,

Your humble servant,
Jonathan Edwards.

53. TO GENTLEMEN

Edwards answers critics regarding his supposed financial extravagance. The proper recipients of this letter would have been a committee of the Precinct.

(Beinecke Library, AL draft, fragment, two duodecimo leaves.)

* * *

[Northampton, November 1744]

Gentlemen,

Soon after the town had voted me my salary for the year past, I heard by many of a great deal of uneasiness at the addition of fifty pounds that was made, which occasioned many jealousies expressed of me and my family, as though we were lavish of what we received and of a craving disposition and abused the town's freeness in their allowances they had made. And I perceived that much fault was found by some persons with our manner of spending, with the clothes that we wore and the like, from which, together with some mistakes of matters of fact, there manifestly appeared a considerable degree of disgust in many. And so much was said that made me suspect whether the town did not repent what had been voted and begrutched the addition that had been made, whether we needed the addition or no. Yet I would pray those persons that have from hence taken occasion to reflect upon me, to consider whether or no it be not hard that I should suffer so much for what the town have done of their own accord. Since there has been so much uneasiness and some misunderstandings with respect to our manner of spending, I will yield to give the town an account of some of those things concerning which, I have understood, some of the uneasiness has been: all that ever has in any respect, from our outward expenses, been laid up for my children of all that ever I have received of the town for this twelve years past.[1] The last of this was paid [. . .][2] the next June and it was saved with a great deal of saving and that time we never [. . .][3]

[Jonathan Edwards.]

54. TO THE FIRST PRECINCT, NORTHAMPTON

Weary of the annual struggle for an adequate salary, Edwards here proposes that a fixed amount be set. In return, he promises never to ask for a raise. The arrangement was agreed upon, but not until three years later.

(NYPL, Hawley Papers, ALS, one folio leaf. Other documents related to Edwards' salary are held in the Beinecke Library. See also the letter of Mar. 4, 1745 [No. 57], below.)

* * *

1. JE continues by writing "all that has been," but does not finish the thought.
2. MS damage.
3. The rest of the MS is missing, only the tops of a few words appearing.

Northampton, November 8, 1744

Dear Brethren,

What I have to propose to you is not from any uneasiness with my maintenance, or any fault I find with the salary you have given me from year to year; but from a desire that I have, not only of my own, but also of the town's, comfort and benefit hereafter.

The thing that I would propose is that, instead of determining what my salary shall be from year to year, you would settle a certain salary upon me; and to that end appoint another Precinct meeting, and now choose a committee to confer with me and prepare things for that meeting. If you think it best that some salary should be settled, I look upon it very likely that there will be no great difficulty in our agreeing upon the sum, from the reasonable and Christian disposition you have manifested heretofore with respect to my maintenance; together with my own consciousness to myself of my not reaching or aiming at great things, or any more than will put me in a tolerable capacity of attending my work as it ought to be attended.

I have a growing family; and if God preserves our lives, as he, by distinguishing mercy, has done hitherto, the charge of my family is likely to grow, not only by the increase of it, but by the increase of my family's acquaintance, whereby my house will probably become still more a place of resort, as it has been more and more so for many years past. There may also perhaps be extraordinary charge hereafter arising, by bringing up a son to learning, or by settling of my children in the world. And the many and great alterations that may arise in my family's circumstances, if things remain as they are (there being no certain agreement between me and my people, with respect to my yearly income from them), will naturally open a door for difficulty, that may be much to the interruption both of mine and the people's quietness and comfort, and to the hindrance of the flourishing of virtue and religion amongst us. I think there needs no great capacity of discerning, to foresee this. If we can now agree upon a certain salary (as I think it probable we may, if you think it best to settle a salary), I shall never expect any greater salary from you, and promise never to complain that I have no more. And how large and chargeable soever my family may become, and whatever charge I may be called to in entertaining strangers, bringing up, or settling children, etc., you will have no further trouble or concern about it. The affair of your minister's support, and the consideration of his family's circumstances, won't come over every year, to exercise your minds, and to occasion various opinions and speeches, and to be a constant temptation to persons to look into the way in which the minister spends his money; all occasion for such difficulties will be cut off: which must needs be greatly for the comfort and benefit of the public Society.

I have no aim at leading you into any snare. 'Tis possible that through prevailing weakness and a broken constitution, I may hereafter be disabled from following the work of the ministry. I am, therefore, willing it should be inserted as one clause of the agreement that shall be made that, this new agreement shall be of no force any longer than while I am able to carry on the work of the ministry, without the people's being obliged to maintain an assistant or successor in the pulpit.

In the agreement that is now subsisting between me and the people, the people have obliged themselves, in a general clause, to make my support [such] as shall be suitable and well adapted to the honorable office of the gospel ministry; but there is nothing in that agreement that determines what that support is, nor is it said who shall be judge. And while things remain thus, there is a door left continually open for difficulty and difference. It can't be expected in so large a society as this is, but that, under these circumstances, there will be some that will be unsuitably meddling with a minister's affairs; and it may be a temptation even to rational, good sort of men, to look more into a minister's affairs, and his way of spending his money than is convenient; and it may also in several respects be a temptation to a minister. If it may be, it must needs be best to cut off such temptations.

I hope that what I propose will not appear to any a frightful thing; it being no more than what is generally done throughout New England in the settlement of a minister, and has been from the first foundation of the country. But, however, I don't pretend to oblige you to it, but only to request it of you; which I earnestly do, not only because I aim at my own comfort, but your peace; which is a thing that I have ever greatly desired and delighted in.

If this which I now request of you be done, I hope it may be a means of establishing an happy agreement and peace between me and you; that henceforward we may walk together in Christian harmony and love, engaged with one heart and soul to seek and serve the Lord, all traveling the same road, towards the heavenly Canaan, without falling out by the way.

I am, dear brethren, your affectionate pastor, being myself, with what I have, devoted to your service for Jesus' sake,

Jonathan Edwards.

55. TO THE REVEREND STEPHEN WILLIAMS

This letter is an appeal for fairness and justice. Edwards, from long association with West Suffield, sympathized with its New Light spirit. The town's candidate for the pulpit, Amos Munson, a pro-revivalist graduate of Yale and an original member of the New Haven Separate Church, was controversial. Old Lights within the church and local ministerial association charged him with heretical preaching and causing church disorder. Edwards feels that Munson should be given an opportunity to defend himself. Above all, he should be considered on his own merits.

(HSP, ALS, one quarto leaf, folded, addressed on verso to the Reverend Stephen Williams at Longmeadow.)

* * *

Northampton, January 1, 1744/5

Rev. Sir,

'Tis not because I think it proper for me to direct you or dictate to you, that I now write to you, to signify to you something of my thoughts respecting Mr. [Amos] Munson; but it is to gratify the urgent desires of Dr. [John] Nelson.

Whether Mr. Munson be a person of suitable qualifications for West Suffield, I will not determine. But would suggest, whether or no (let that matter be as it will) if he, and the people, do agree in proceeding in order to his settlement there, the ministers in that neighborhood can avoid saying or doing something. And seeing Mr. [Samuel] Whittelsey, [Sr.,] has written to Mr. [Samuel] Hopkins [of West Springfield], that he lies under censure by the Consociation there, for disorders; and that when he lately appeared before the Committee of the Association, he refused to make such satisfaction, as they thought necessary; whether it would not be proper for the ministers neighboring to West Suffield, to write to some of those gentlemen, and desire of them a particular account of Mr. Munson's offense, and of the pretended satisfaction that he has made.

However unfit Mr. Munson may be for the place where he is, yet I humbly conceive that there ought to be fair dealing with him; and he may, if he be unfit, be advised not to settle at Suffield, and the people advised not to settle him. But to expect that all the Christians through the world, should look upon themselves obliged to treat one as a heathen and publican, that has been devoted from his childhood to the work of the ministry by his parents and brought up for it with great expense, only because a particular body of men, in a certain neighborhood, famed for extraordinary warmth and engagedness of spirit in a public religious controversy, wherein the whole land have been so divided, do condemn him, being of the other side of the question; and refuse to give any that inquire any particular reasons why or wherefore; seems to me not to be fair treatment of him; but to be an opposing of him, and an attributing a very exorbitant despotic power unto them. Especially seeing it is notoriously known that many things are esteemed very scandalous by that sort of men, and worthy the severest censures, that by many others, that are men of calm tempers, and solid wisdom and piety, are looked upon as no censurable evils at all.

Sir, I hope you will excuse my seeming to take so much upon me. This with my sincere regards to your family is from, reverend Sir,

Your humble servant,
Jonathan Edwards.

56. TO A FRIEND

Rector Thomas Clap of Yale delivered a thunderbolt at the 1744 Harvard commencement when he charged that Jonathan Edwards had confided to him that George Whitefield intended to replace New England ministers with evangelicals from England, Scotland, and Ireland. To Edwards, the allegation was as absurd as it was shocking. Nevertheless, he moved immediately to vindicate himself and Whitefield. When quiet correspondence produced no positive result, he decided to go public. A pamphlet battle ensued. Clap was the first to rush into print,[1] but this open letter of Edwards' followed shortly afterward.

(Published in Edwards, *Copies of Two Letters Cited by The Reverend Mr. Clap* [Boston, 1745]. See also Edwards to Clap, May 20, 1745 [No. 58], below.)

* * *

Northampton, February 4, 1744/5

Sir,

I have lately had a sight of a printed letter from the Reverend Mr. [Thomas] Clap, Rector of the College at New Haven, to his friend in Boston, concerning what he has declared that he heard me say, that Mr. [George] Whitefield told me, of a design he had, of turning out the

---

1. Thomas Clap, *A Letter from the Rev. Mr. Thomas Clap . . . to a Friend in Boston* (Boston, 1745).

generality of the ministers in the country, etc., wherein he cites two letters that I sent him about that affair. The representation he makes of what I said in those letters, make it necessary, in my opinion, that those letters should be published at large. I therefore here send you a copy of each of them; and would pray you to publish them as soon as may be.

The letters are as follows:

A copy of the first letter cited by the Reverend Mr. Clap:

Northampton, October 18, 1744

Rev. Sir,

I have often heard that you, when you was down at Boston and Cambridge the summer past, did before many persons, declare that you heard me say, that Mr. Whitefield told me, that he had a design of turning out of their places, the greater part of the ministers in New England, and of supplying their pulpits with ministers from Great Britain and Ireland. Particularly Mr. [Ebenezer] Williams of Pomfret told me that he was there, and heard you say it: but only instead of Great Britain and Ireland, says, that you said to him, Scotland and Ireland. And says that he could scarcely believe it: and therefore was particular in inquiring of you, taking care that he might not misunderstand you, and you asserted to him more than once.

I was exceedingly astonished to hear it; not only because that I knew that I never had said it to you, nor to any mortal, as well as it is possible for me to know a negative, or to know that I had not said anything whatsoever that could be mentioned; but also, because when I first heard this report, the thought of Mr. Whitefield's saying any such thing, was perfectly new to me. Indeed I heard Mr. Whitefield say that he had thoughts of bringing over a number of young men from England, into the Jerseys and Pennsylvania, to be ordained by the Tennents [William and sons]; but said not one word of any design of their supplying the pulpits of other ministers (made vacant by their being turned out) either there, or in New England. I have also on some occasions mentioned it as my opinion, that Mr. Whitefield was formerly in the opinion and scheme of people's forsaking unconverted ministers, which possibly you might hear of from others; for I have no remembrance of my ever having any conversation with you about things of this nature; and think it on some accounts very unlikely that I should; I have had but very little opportunity of conversation with you, as you know, since Mr. Whitefield has been in the country; and I have always known that your thoughts of Mr. Whitefield, and the late work, were generally supposed to be diverse from mine, and less favorable: it is much more unlikely on that account, that I should enter into conversation with you, tending to confirm prejudices against Mr. Whitefield. But however, this I declare, that I have no manner of remembrance that I ever heard Mr. Whitefield express, or hint any design he had of turning out the greater part of the ministers of New England, or any part of them, and introducing others into their places, from Great Britain and Ireland, or any other place, or anything like it; nor have I any imagination that I ever heard Mr. Whitefield say anything of this nature, any more than that I heard him say he had a design of dethroning the great Turk, and introducing a new sultan to sit upon his throne: and I have equal reason to be confident that I never represented, that Mr. Whitefield said the former, as I have, that I never represented that he said the latter.

If I have ever reported any such thing to you, who are at so great a distance from me, and with whom I have had so little conversation; it is exceeding likely that I have told others the same: but I challenge the whole world besides you, to say that they ever heard me say any such thing. Therefore, I desire you to do me and Mr. Whitefield the justice, as publicly to correct your mistake in this, which you have publicly declared; which I perceive has been very much taken notice of, and has been much the subject of talk. I can't but think, that when you come to consider of the matter, you will soon be sensible that you have been greatly mistaken; and have by some means or other, strangely confounded things in your mind; and that justice and integrity will constrain you speedily to declare your mistake to the world. In expectation of this I remain, Sir,

Your humble servant,
Jonathan Edwards.

A copy of the second letter cited by Mr. Clap.

Northampton, October 29, 1744

Rev. Sir,

The relation you give in your letter of October 12, of the conversation that passed between us as we rode together through Leicester, the last May was twelvemonth, is one of the most amazing things to me that ever I met with in my life. I don't remember our having any conversation about Mr. Whitefield: but that might be, and I might forget it. But if I told such a story about Mr. Whitefield, and what passed between him and me, with so many particulars and circumstances (which must have been altogether of mine own invention, without the least foundation in truth) I don't believe I should have forgot it. I have sometimes said to others (as I informed you, in my late letter to you), that I supposed that Mr. Whitefield was formerly of the opinion, that unconverted ministers ought not to continue in the ministry: and I do suppose he endeavored to propagate this opinion, and a practice agreeable to it. But all that ever I have said about it, has been only as expressing my opinion; and not any declared design of Mr. Whitefield.

You are express in it, that I said that Mr. Whitefield not only spake to me of bringing over ministers from England, but also from Scotland and Ireland: which is peculiarly wonderful to me. For I not only never heard Mr. Whitefield say anything of bringing ministers into America from those countries last mentioned, and from neither of the countries, into New England, but I had never heard, at that time when Mr. Whitefield was here, of his having any followers in those countries; and I suppose he had none. The wonderful work that has been in Scotland has been all since, and Mr. Whitefield's design of going to Scotland was, I suppose, formed afterwards. Some things that he told me of his designs, seemed inconsistent with his having formed the design then. But the most amazing of all is, that Ireland should be mentioned as one of the countries from whence Mr. Whitefield would supply New England with ministers. If I had ever heard any such thing from Mr. Whitefield, doubtless I should have remembered it; for I should have looked upon it very strange; having never heard of anything like a revival of religion, of late in Ireland; or any interest that Mr. Whitefield had there; or any expectations he had from thence. I don't know that Mr. Whitefield ever so much as mentioned the name of that land to me.

You say that I told you, "That I took all opportunities to talk with Mr. Whitefield alone about this matter. But when Mr. Whitefield saw that I did not approve of his design in that matter, he did not seem to choose to say anything about it; he would either turn off the discourse upon something else, or go out of the room." This account is amazing to me. It is all of it perfectly new to me. Nor can I conceive what any imagination, that ever I said any such things, should arise from. I indeed have told several persons, that I once purposely took an opportunity to talk with Mr. Whitefield alone about impulses, and have mentioned many particulars of our conference together on that head: that I told him some reasons I had to think he gave too great heed to such things; and have told what manner of replies he made; and what reasons I offered against such things. And I also said that Mr. Whitefield did not seem to be offended with me, but yet did not seem to be inclined to have a great deal of discourse about it. And that in the time of it he did not appear to be convinced by anything I said. I have also said that I at that time talked with Mr. [Jonathan] Barber (who came to my house with Mr. Whitefield) about some of his impulses; dealing plainly with him; whereby he seemed to be displeased, and replied with earnestness and zeal. It is also true (though I don't know that ever I spake of it before) that I thought Mr. Whitefield liked me not so well, for my opposing these things: and though he treated me with great kindness, yet he never made so much of an intimate of me, as of some others.

It is also true, that I once talked with Mr. Whitefield (though not alone) about judging other persons to be unconverted. But that I took all opportunities to talk with him, about a design of his, of turning out the generality of the ministers of New England, or any ministers; or that I took any one opportunity to talk with him about it; or that I ever said a word to him, or he to me, either alone, or with others, about any such design; or that I took many opportunities to talk with him about any of his errors (as your expression seems to imply), or that he ever went out of the room when I was talking with him about any of his errors, so putting an end to, or avoiding the discourse; or that he ever turned off such discourse to anything else; *I say these things are not true*. And if I ever told you any such things as these when we were riding through Leicester, or at any other time, I was beside myself and knew nothing what I said; or else I am beside myself now, and have had some strange supernatural change passed upon me, so obliterating my own ideas, and all memory of most remarkable things that formerly I knew, and remembered for a long time, so as to give a particular account of 'em to you; that they are to me as if they never had been. I do solemnly declare in the fear of God, that I han't the least trace or footstep of any one of these things in my memory, either as true in fact, or spoken by me.

And, dear Sir, if these remarkable things are true, is it not strange that I should keep these great secrets shut up in my own breast, from all mankind, to reveal 'em to you only; that when I knew such remarkable things of one so famous as Mr. Whitefield, and so much the subject of conversation through New England, I should make you, above all the world, my confidant, to declare them so freely to you, after I had kept them secret for two or three years. If I had mentioned such remarkable things to any other, it could not but be much taken notice of by them, and it would doubtless have been talked of by somebody else besides you. These things are all new to my nearest friends; they never heard of any of them, till they heard of them as coming from you. And I am willing that all my acquaintance, and those that I have been most conversant with, ministers or others, in this town or elsewhere, should be inquired of, whether they ever heard me report any such thing. I have most diligently searched my memory as to what passed between Mr. Whitefield and me, to find out what there was that I could say about it, from whence it should be possible for you so to conceive of things. And I cannot conceive what it should be. Whether you have heard some report from somebody else, that in length of time is become insensibly blended with something that I might say, and you might misapprehend, I cannot tell; if you diligently inquire, you will be most likely to find out. But certainly there has been some strange and wonderful misapprehension and confusion arisen in your mind, by some means or other, that caused you so confidently, publicly and plentifully to report these things of me. I beg of you thoroughly to consider it; and insist upon it, as what justice to others' characters does greatly require from you, publicly to correct these gross mistakes.

I am, Sir, your humble servant,
Jonathan Edwards.
Northampton, Nov. 3, 1744

P.S.

Rev. Sir,

I just now received your letter of October 28, and would only say, that I don't say it was not possible for you to mistake anything I might say to you, about Mr. Whitefield, going to Boston; so as now to think that I said as you have represented. I do suppose that it arises from some strange mistake, that you have reported as you have. Though as I said, I remember no conversation about Mr. Whitefield at that time (though I remember considerable of other conversation, as about my book, and about Connecticut laws), yet it's possible I might say to you, that I believed Mr. Whitefield did aim at people's forsaking unconverted ministers, and to endeavor that there should be a supply of converted ministers, as far as in him lay; or something to that purpose. In the same discourse it's possible I might mention what Mr. Whitefield told me of his design of bringing over a number of young men from England, to be ordained by the Tennents, in the Jerseys; and might say that I thought I dealt more plainly with Mr. Whitefield about his errors, than any other minister; and that when I talked with him about impulses, he did not seem to like to have much discourse about it. And how far you might mistake any such things, I might say, I do not determine; but certain I am, that by some means or other, you have labored under an exceeding great mistake.

I am yours, etc.,
Jonathan Edwards.

These, Sir, are the letters that Mr. Clap mentions and cites, in what he has lately published about this affair. These are some of the letters that have passed between us (and those of 'em which he cites as most to his purpose), considering which, he tells the world, that it was very unexpected to him, to hear that I should write a letter to Boston, to be printed, wherein there is a denial of some things which he had reported: insinuating to the world, that in these letters, I had in effect owned all. Whereas it appears that I have owned no part of his report, but have most solemnly denied every article of it. These are the individual letters, of which he says expressly, that in these letters, though I have not used exactly the same terms with him, yet I have used a variety of those which are equally full and strong; and if we still differ, it is only about some particular terms, and inconsiderable circumstantials, which are not worthy of any dispute. These are the letters in which Mr. Clap plainly insinuates, that I in a manner had conceded to all that he had reported, by sundry fair and ingenuous concessions to him, as he expresses himself; slightly adding these words, "Indeed Mr. Edwards seems not willing to allow that he mentioned Ireland; because he never heard of any interest Mr. Whitefield had there," etc., just as though this was almost the only circumstance wherein he and I differed; and as though I scarcely denied that; though (as he says) I seemed not willing to allow it; because I never heard of any interest Mr. Whitefield had there.

Now, dear Sir, you have opportunity to compare these letters with what he has published to the world about them. And I am willing to leave it with you, and every one that pleases, to judge how full his paper is of artifices, entirely to mislead the minds of his readers, as to their conception of the whole import and drift of these letters; not only in what has been mentioned, but in his manner of introducing and intermingling broken scraps of these letters, and his manner of joining together distant sentences, and broken pieces of sentences (that have no connection in the letters themselves), as though they were a continued discourse, and his manner of descanting on them. I am willing that every reader, who has read his paper, should judge for himself, whether in reading it his own mind was not led to conceive of these letters, as things extremely diverse from what he finds them to be. Doubtless Mr. Clap trusted to it, that I had kept no copies of my letters; otherwise he would never have so exceedingly exposed himself. I am willing that you and others should judge for themselves, how far, one whose conscience will not restrain him from making such representations of letters written, that he may destroy others characters, and render 'em odious to the world, is capable of unfair dealing in representing private conversation; where there are no witnesses, or written words, that can be produced to confute him. And who can be safe in human society, if such liberties are taken, in order to ruin their fellow-creatures and brethren, by gentlemen from whom so different things might be expected? If it had been true, that I had said just as Mr. Clap has reported, yet how vehemently has that practice been cried out of, by gentlemen on that side of the controversies of the present day, of publicly making use of private conversation, and the report of single persons, to destroy the characters of others? And especially how ill does this become Rector Clap, after he knows that that single person that he says thus reported to him, does so strongly and solemnly deny it, entreating of him therefore to forbear? What a treatment is this of Christian brethren!

This, dear Sir, is a specimen of the manner and spirit, in which the controversies of the present day are carried on against Mr. Whitefield, by many persons (for I am far from thus charging all his opposers), the persons frequently hiding themselves, and concealing their names. And though I think it but to little purpose, to carry on a controversy with these persons from the press, unless when forced to it by gross slanders; yet I can't but say on this occasion, that it seems to me worthy greatly to be lamented, by all true lovers of the Christian religion, which consists so much in love and forgiveness, that Mr. Whitefield should be pursued with so much violence, and appearance of inveterate opposition, and indefatigable endeavors to blacken him to the utmost; and with such artifices, as it would be mean to use, with respect to the basest miscreant; and that for former errors, which are not at all to be wondered at, considering his youth, and the circumstances of his education, etc.; when there seems to be so little appearance of obstinacy and incorrigibleness in him, and so much of the contrary; and when so little can be found, by his most watchful enemies, now, to blame him for. I think this is a proper occasion, for the meek followers of the Lamb of God, to lie low before God, and lament the corruption of human nature, and the sin and shame of their dear country, and cry humbly to Christ, that he would ride forth prosperously, because of truth, meekness, and righteousness.

And with respect to the affair that is the subject of the preceding letters, doubtless so great a contradiction between Mr. Clap and me, in such a state of things as the country is now in, and relating to a person, concerning whom the country is so much divided in their sentiments, with spirits so deeply, and contrarily engaged, will cause a variety of reflections and censures; and every one will say as he is disposed. However, I think myself now called openly to make this DECLARATION: That ever Mr. Whitefield said anything to me, or I to him, of any design of his of turning out the bigger part of the ministers of New England, or any ministers in New England, or anywhere else, or ever so much as hinted, either he or any of his company, anything of that nature; or of his bringing over any minister, or candidate for the ministry, from Scotland or Ireland, into any part of America, or from any one country in Europe, into New England; or that I ever reported any such thing to Mr. Clap, or any other person; or that ever any thought of Mr. Whitefield's saying, or hinting, anything like either of these things, ever entered into my heart, till I heard 'em as coming from Mr. Clap; or that Mr. Whitefield ever intimated to me, any design of his going to Scotland, or making any interest there; or that he ever mentioned the name of Ireland in my hearing—I say that [if] any of these things ever were, I have no remembrance. God is my witness who searches my heart, and will bring to light the hidden things of darkness, and make manifest the counsels of the heart. And whether it be probable that I should wholly forget all these things, if they indeed had been—especially those remarkable, great things, that Mr. Clap has reported that I said, after I had well-remembered them for two years and an half, so as to give him a distinct account of them—I leave others to judge. And whether I have a conscience sufficient to restrain me from lying with this solemnity or no; yet, I must also leave it to others to judge, whether it be likely that when I had so grand a secret committed to me, of a scheme to bring about so great a revolution, as the turning out most of the ministers in the country, and bringing over four or five hundred from Europe, to settle in their places, I should carefully keep it secret from every mortal for two or three years, and declare it freely to Mr. Clap, and never to any other person before or since. For I now publicly challenge the whole world besides Mr. Clap to declare, if they ever heard me report any such thing.

Mr. Clap says, he and I well agreed to condemn many errors, etc.: that might be; for all the land knows that I ever condemned many errors. But there was little in our conversation, in the journey Mr. Clap speaks of, to draw me to such a confidence in him, as to choose him above all the world, to reveal my greatest secrets to: for he immediately fell upon me, as he knows, as soon as ever we began to ride the road together, about some passages in my book, concerning the revival of religion, greatly blaming me, earnestly disputing, I suppose, for hours together. After this we had another dispute about Connecticut laws. And these disputes were about the same part of the journey, in which he says I told him this about Mr. Whitefield.

Thus, dear Sir, I have endeavored to set forth this matter as it is. Public controversy from the press, and especially public contradiction, is not, for its own sake, desirable, but much otherwise; and is what I have a great aversion to. But Mr. Clap has been pleased to carry things to that length, that I think has rendered it my indispensable duty, publicly to contradict him. I therefore desire that you would publish what I now send you, as soon as may be; herein you will oblige, Sir,

Your affectionate friend and humble servant,
Jonathan Edwards.

57. TO THE FIRST PRECINCT, NORTHAMPTON

The Precinct Committee met with Edwards about his salary proposal but refused to agree to a fixed salary until he named the approximate figure expected. For his part, Edwards considered it futile to fix an amount if they did not accept the idea.

(Edwards Church, Northampton, Mass., ALS, one quarto leaf. Published in

The Daily Hampshire Gazette, Oct. 1, 1903. See also Edwards' letter of Nov. 8, 1744 [No. 54], above.)

* * *

Northampton, March 4, 1744/5

Dear Brethren,

A difficulty having arisen in the minds of some of the Committee, chosen to treat with me concerning the settlement of my salary; which difficulty, the greater part of them think, it is very needful that the Precinct should have a particular consideration of, before they determine to settle any salary agreeable to my proposal; it would therefore be improper for me to propose any particular sum, till that matter has been considered, and till it has been determined whether you are willing to settle a salary upon me, agreeable to my desire, provided that any sum could be agreed upon. Therefore, I desire that that matter may be first determined. And I desire it of you, particularly and impartially to reconsider the reasons that I have already mentioned, why the salary should be settled before you determine to deny this request.

I am your affectionate pastor and servant for Jesus' sake,
Jonathan Edwards.

58. TO THE REVEREND THOMAS CLAP

This second public letter of Edwards' on the Whitefield controversy came swiftly on the heels of Rector Clap's rejoinder of April 1, 1745. It is the last word in the series.

(Published as *An Expostulary Letter from the Reverend Mr. Edwards* [Boston, 1745]. For Edwards' first response, see the letter of Feb. 4, 1745 [No. 56], above.)

* * *

Northampton, May 20, 1745

Rev. Sir,

I have seen the pamphlet you lately published, in form of a letter to me,[1] relating to the controversy that has been between us, about what you have reported that I told you, concerning Mr. [George] White-

1. Thomas Clap, *A Letter from the Rev. Mr. Thomas Clap . . . to the Rev. Mr. Edwards* (Boston, 1745).

field, viz. that "He told me he designed to turn the generality of ministers in the country out of their places, and bring over ministers from England, Scotland, and Ireland, and place them in their room."

And concerning this letter of yours, which is your pretended answer to what I have published about that matter, in answer to your printed *Letter to a Friend in Boston*,[2] wherein you asserted that I had in two private letters to you, in effect, in very full and strong terms owned the whole matter to you that you had reported. I say, concerning this letter of yours, I would observe that you don't deny the genuineness of the copies of my letters that I have published; nor do you produce any attestations of what you have reported of me, which you say was in a journey to Boston, in May 1743. Although there were many persons in company with us in that journey, at the time you speak of, viz. the Reverend Mr. [Robert] Breck of Springfield, and the Reverend Mr. [Ebenezer] Gay of Suffield and his wife [Hannah Angier Gay], and Mrs. [Mary Hanes] Clap, your own lady (who, I am confident, was not wont to be at so great a distance from you as to be out of hearing of conversation), and your son-in-law [David Wooster] that waited on you, and one with me on the same horse, viz. my eldest daughter [Sarah], at the very time when you say I told you this remarkable story, who has lived at New Haven all the time of this controversy between us, and most of the time at Mr. [Joseph] Noyes' house, where you are very conversant, and she was often in your way; and not only so, but she was very conversant at your own house, with your daughters; and if you had seen cause to have inquired of her, would have informed you, that she well-remembered other conversation that we had in that journey, particularly the long dispute we had about some things you found fault with in my book, concerning the late revival of religion; but that she remembered not a word said about Mr. Whitefield in that journey. Nor did you in your letter produce one person that you have found anywhere, who ever heard me say any such thing as you have reported, or anything like it at any time; though I have publicly declared that I was willing all my acquaintance, and those that I have been most conversant with, ministers or others, in this town and elsewhere, should be inquired of; and have openly challenged the whole world, besides you, to declare if they ever heard me report any such thing. But all the world besides you are wholly silent, though there are many hundreds to whom it is every way more likely I should reveal such a secret, than to you, if I had it to reveal.

2. Clap, *A Letter from the Rev. Mr. Thomas Clap . . . to a Friend in Boston.*

Nor is anybody produced in your letter that says he heard you speak of my saying this to you, soon after the time you say I said it; though in your first letter you say, you took good notice of my words, and laid them up in your mind, and soon related them to others; so that by your own account, you was under no restraint or difficulty as to speaking of this grand secret I revealed to you. But however, it is something re-markable, that you was then in a journey to Boston and Cambridge, at that time when you say I told you this, and was in those parts at the time of the election, and convention of ministers; and yet it seems you was wholly silent about it then, nothing was said or heard about it in Boston or Cambridge; though one would think, if I had indeed de-clared so extraordinary a thing to you, it would upon every account have been most likely that you should speak of it then, when we must suppose your mind was most affected with it, and your heart fullest of it, having but just received it from my mouth; and then the country was fuller of talk about Mr. Whitefield, his coming, and the remarkable consequences of it were more recent and fresh in memory: yet not a word is heard of it in those parts that year. But when you go to Boston the year following, even the last summer, more than a twelvemonth after, then you are prepared to tell the story, and tell it abundantly in Cambridge and Boston, and surprise ministers and others with the remarkable report; and those parts, and the country in general, are quickly filled with it.

The title page of your first printed letter, dated last December, speaks of the report, as what you declared when in Boston last, which was the last summer; though the time when we were going to Boston together, when you say I told you the story, was the year before. And it is public, and apparent, that the report was new in those parts then; every one spake of it, as well as you yourself, as coming from you when you was in Boston last summer.

And though it be true, that I had a suspicion of Mr. Whitefield's aiming at people's forsaking unconverted ministers; and so it was not wholly impossible that I should mention it to you, going to Boston; and therefore I can't absolutely deny that, and have hitherto strained my charity towards you to the utmost, with respect to that matter (though as I often said before, I had no remembrance of it); yet the more I think of it, the more improbable it appears to me that I should. My daughter, that was with me at the particular time you fix upon, re-members nothing of it; and besides there is that in particular, that makes it very unlikely that I should say anything to you at that time, of so much as that suspicion, viz. that presently after Mr. Whitefield went from these parts, being in conversation with the Reverend Mr. [Samuel] Hopkins of Springfield, even the next day after we parted with Mr. Whitefield at Windsor, Mr. Hopkins being my brother-in-law, and then appearing friendly to Mr. Whitefield, I mentioned that suspicion to him (which is the only time that I know of that I ever mentioned it to anybody, any otherwise than on its being reported from him, I might give an account what I said to him). I gave him several reasons of my suspicion, but that Mr. Whitefield had told me any such thing, was not among these reasons. After this, before our forementioned journey to Boston, I heard that Mr. Hopkins had reported it to others, and that the report was carried to New Haven to you and others there, and much taken notice of by you; which gave me no small uneasiness: I was not a little concerned that what I had thus said privately to my brother Hopkins, should be thus carried abroad, and especially that it should be handed to you. Now after this, it is not very likely that I should go, and more fully declare the same thing to you myself; and especially that I should tell you much more than that; and that, which if it was true, I closely concealed from my brother Hopkins. Some of the ministers of this county, that have lately signed a testimony against Mr. Whitefield, had before heard Mr. Hopkins relate what I told him of my suspicion, with the reasons I gave him; and since this controversy between you and me, have declared freely that it is a convincing argument with them, that I never told you, that Mr. Whitefield informed me that he had any such design as you mention, because it is to them inconceivable, that I should signify my suspicion to Mr. Hopkins, and gather up these and those arguments to confirm it, without saying anything to him, as if Mr. Whitefield had told me, that it was his design, when it was so indeed, and though I afterwards freely declared it to you.

And now I have mentioned this, I would pray you, Sir, seriously to consider, whether that report you had as coming from Mr. Hopkins, of what I told him of my suspicion, was not the sole foundation on which you in length of time gradually framed in your imagination the whole story, which you afterwards reported as being told immediately by me to you, in our journey to Boston.

But you, Sir, have said it, in your first printed letter, and you will stand to it still, that I have in effect owned the very same thing that you have reported, in a variety of terms that are equally full and strong; yea, that you may be sure not to be wanting to yourself, you go further now than before, and say that my terms are fuller and stronger than yours; and are abundant in affirming it, that what I have said of *my opinion* of Mr. Whitefield's aiming at people's forsaking unconverted ministers, and at converted ones being introduced, is most plainly, and manifestly, and fully the same thing as saying, that Mr. Whitefield *told me* that he designed "to turn the generality of ministers in the country out of their places, and bring over ministers from England, Scotland and Ireland, and place them in their room;" so that for me to own the former, and deny the latter, is a most plain, flat, amazing self-contradiction; and represent it as an absurd thing to make any distinction between expressing what I supposed of Mr. Whitefield, as my opinion, and expressing it as a declared design of Mr. Whitefield; and cry out, "What can you mean by this distinction?" If I had only heard this of you from others, I should hardly have believed it: but if I may believe my own eyes, I have seen a gentleman of your understanding, not in jest or only to make sport, but gravely and seriously and in great earnest, go about to show that these two things are exactly the same, and to make it plain, even to a demonstration, by rehearsing over words on both sides, and elaborately finding out, and cutting off evasions, and placing the words one against another in parallel columns, that the world might see the exact identity; and the astonishing contradiction there is in owning one and denying the other.

This cannot be accounted for, any other way, than that you was driven to great straits. You had before reported to the world, in print, that I, in two private letters that I had written to you, had in effect owned the whole matter that you had said concerning me. But now those entire letters were published to the world, wherein the contrary, to the highest degree, appears to be true; that although therein I own it had been my opinion, that Mr. Whitefield would endeavor to promote the forsaking unconverted ministers, and the introducing of converted ones, yet say expressly, that I never mentioned this as a declared design of Mr. Whitefield, but only my opinion; and do in many ways, over and over, and in a great variety of expressions, strenuously and solemnly deny the whole fact that you had reported of me. You therefore doubtless easily saw that there was nothing that you could do to justify yourself, no other way in the world that you could take to maintain the credit of your uprightness and veracity in what you had reported of those private letters, but only stiffly to stand to it (however ridiculously) that for me to say that it was my opinion that Mr. Whitefield intended what I spake of, was to all intents and purposes telling you, that Mr. Whitefield told me that he intended that which you have reported.

But dear Sir, though your circumstances are difficult, and your

temptations great, yet let me entreat you once to look back on what you
have laid down; and after all your positiveness and high charges, to
suffer in yourself a little reflection and exercise of reason.

If I had told you that it was *my opinion* that Mr. Whitefield intended
to do all that which you speak of, would this have been for me to tell
you that Mr. Whitefield *told me* that he intended it, so that you might
truly from thence, in terms, report and affirm that I said the latter, and
so that it is a flat contradicting myself for me to deny such a report? Is it
exactly the same thing for a man to say he has such an opinion of
another's designs, as to say that that other person *told him* they were his
designs? And is it indeed a senseless thing to make a distinction between these two, as you signify? I have been of opinion that the governor of Canada intended to send an army to Annapolis this year, which
I may possibly have told to others; may they therefore go and report in
terms, without hesitation, that I told them, that the governor of Canada told me, that he did intend this? And if I hear of it afterwards, and
deny that I told 'em so, withal declaring what I did say, making the
distinction, am I therefore guilty of the plainest and most astonishing
self-contradiction, even in the very relation I give myself, and of the
greatest absurdity in making the distinction?

Supposing me to be of opinion that Rector [Thomas] Clap has had a
design to do his utmost to ruin my reputation, by artfully misleading
the minds of his unwary, cursory readers, into a belief that I have
evidently perjured myself, by flatly contradicting myself upon oath,
when he himself knew in his heart that there was no real contradiction
at all; I say, supposing this to be my opinion, I can declare it to be my
opinion with truth, but can I therefore truly declare to others that Mr.
Clap told me that this very thing was his design? And if I should
declare so, would not you resent it, as an injurious falsehood and
slander? And if I should excuse myself, and say, "No, I had that opinion of you, and that was the same thing as for me to hear you say so";
would you then think there was no distinction, and that it was a senseless thing to pretend any?

And then besides, I not only don't say in my letters, that Mr. Whitefield told me that he intended to do those things that you reported, but
am far from saying so much as that it was my opinion that he intended
those things. My saying, it was my opinion that Mr. Whitefield did aim
at people's forsaking unconverted ministers, and at the introducing of
converted ones, is surely not the same thing as to say, it was my opinion,
that Mr. Whitefield intended to turn the bigger part of the ministers of
the country out of their places, and bring over ministers from En-

gland, Scotland, and Ireland, and place them in their room. It is my opinion of many persons in the world, that I know of, that they are in the opinion and scheme that popish ministers ought not to preach, and that they would do their endeavor, what in them lies, to have it otherwise, that Protestant ministers should be introduced. But is this the same thing as to say, that 'tis my opinion that they intend to turn out all the popish ministers in the world, and introduce Protestant ministers into their places, mentioning the particular countries whence they intend to bring them? My saying that Mr. Whitefield told me, he intended to bring over a number of young scholars into the Jerseys, to be ordained by the Tennents [William and his sons], don't imply that it was my opinion that he intended to bring ministers from those three countries you mention, or any country or countries, to supply any pulpits in New England, or anywhere else, made vacant by others being turned out; nor ever was it my opinion; nor did ever a thought enter into my heart, of Mr. Whitefield's meaning to bring over one-tenth part enough to supply the greater part of the pulpits in New England; but only a few young men, of the people called Methodists, that were scholars to get ordination.

But you say, it is an immaterial circumstance what countries the ministers were to be brought from, and that it matters not whether I said one word of foreigners supplying the pulpits of other ministers, or no: and therefore insist upon it, that for me to say that it was my opinion, that Mr. Whitefield aimed at people's forsaking unconverted ministers, and introducing converted ministers, was for me to say, that it was my opinion Mr. Whitefield intended all that you have represented; and not only this, but to say that Mr. Whitefield told me so; insomuch that to say otherwise is a flat contradiction; and you represent that to make any distinction is absurd.

Now Sir, if it be really so, I would ask, why, instead of reporting that you heard me say that Mr. Whitefield told me that he intended to turn out the bigger part of the ministers in the country, etc., you did not rather declare plainly and positively, at Boston and Cambridge and elsewhere, that Mr. Whitefield told you this story of his intentions? For you signify over and over in your two printed letters, that it was your opinion that he intended to turn out unconverted ministers and introduce others, before you talked with me. And therefore by your own account it is really true, that Mr. Whitefield told you all that you reported as from me (at least everything that was material, or worthy of any notice in it) and you can't deny it with truth, and without making absurd distinctions, and strange quibbling and equivocation, yea, plain and flat self-contradiction. Surely it would have been more to your purpose to have declared this thing, as one that was an ear-witness; without having recourse to a report you had heard from another. Yea, and not only so, but you might have produced a great many witnesses to vouch the truth of the same, and might have said that you heard a great many persons say that Mr. Whitefield told them so, too. For you speak of the generality of others that were exactly of the same opinion with you and me in this point.

And there is another difficulty that needs to be cleared up with respect to your conduct in this matter. When you first appeared in this controversy in print you represent the matter as though you and I were well-agreed in our private letters, and said the same thing; and signify as much as that it appeared so to you on the receipt of my letters, and that therefore it appeared unaccountable to you that any contradiction should be insisted on between you and me (letter 2nd, at the beginning) and this is almost the only argument you have insisted on in both your printed letters, that your report is true. And yet in the controversy as it was managed between us in private letters, a considerable time before you appeared in public, this was never so much as once mentioned, or pretended. There is no appearance in your private letters to me, as though you supposed that you and I agreed in the least measure, not a lisp of my unaccountably insisting on a contradiction where there was none, no intimation of any difficulty you found in my letters of that nature. Which is something strange, if it was so, that you did really then think that there was such an agreement, and that I in effect owned all, and you was then astonished at a pretense of a contradiction between you and me where there was none, but saw so great and manifest a contradiction between the various parts of my letters, as you speak of. You represent as though you wrote to me in a friendly and pacific manner; but then it was strange you did not mention that which you took so much notice of, that you must think would tend above all things to my conviction. But there is not a hint of any such thing in your private pacific letters (as you call 'em) either for my conviction, or your vindication; but when you come to appear in public, then you are full of it, for my reproach, and insist on scarce anything else.

If you deny this that I have said concerning your private letters, I am willing you should produce them to the world, for your vindication: and if you han't kept copies, I promise to lend you the originals, on your promise that you will publish them.

Now Sir, I desire you to take a view of your conduct in this affair, in the whole series of it from the beginning. You did publicly and abundantly report that I told you, that Mr. Whitefield told me that he intended to make that forementioned general change, and great revolution in the country, and accomplish it in that particular manner: a report, in a peculiar manner tending to render Mr. Whitefield the object of general detestation and abhorrence through the country, and indeed you could have no other end in it; which report had no foundation, because Mr. Whitefield never told me anything of that nature, nor did I ever tell you any such thing. And therefore both of us were greatly injured by it.

If I had really handed this report to you, yet for you to make such an use of it, so to ruin the reputation of a minister of the gospel, and make him the object of general odium, would have been directly in the face of that rule, I Tim. 5: 19, "Against an elder receive not an accusation, but before two or three witnesses." When I understood that you had thus reported, I wrote to you in a friendly manner, expostulating with you about it, declaring to you your mistake, and by all means possible endeavoring to convince you of it, mentioning many things that showed the unreasonableness of supposing it to be true. And when still you did not seem to be convinced, I wrote to you again more largely, mentioning all the ways I could devise that the mistake could possibly arise, hoping some way or other to lead you to a sense of your mistake. But you still immovably persisted in it; and not only so, but instead of retracting, as justice greatly required, and I much insisted in my letters, you on the contrary, against the most earnest remonstrances, go on to declare it more openly than ever, even in the midst of our private correspondence about it, and in a positive and peremptory manner assert it and publish it to the world from the press, and not only so, but tell the world that I had in effect owned the whole matter to you in those very private letters, in which I had been repeatedly and most solemnly denying it, and reasoning and expostulating with you for so greatly injuring Mr. Whitefield and me in the report, and insisting that you should retract it; and which letters were written for that very end, and of which it was the whole drift, as you was very sensible, as appears by your answers written to me, never once pretending to me in those letters, that I owned it, or agreed with you (as you tell the world) or said anything looking that way, but all along going wholly upon the supposition that I denied it only.

When it came to this, I had no other way left for me to take, though it was very contrary to my inclination, but to go into the press too, and from thence declare the matter as it was, and publish those very letters of mine, and endeavor to convince the world that you had greatly abused Mr. Whitefield and me. Upon this you go on still, and resolutely persist in what you said before; and because I say that I once was of opinion that Mr. Whitefield endeavored to promote people's forsaking unconverted ministers, and the introducing of others, but deny that ever he told me what you have reported, or that he ever hinted to me anything like it. You charge me before the world with the most plain, flat, amazing, astonishing, unaccountable self-contradiction, and strange and solemn quibbling and equivocating to amuse and deceive the world; and intimate that I have been guilty of Jesuitical management in a solemn oath. And then when you have done all this, you finish with complaining that I have treated you with very "unhandsome" and "unchristian" reflections; yet say you won't render evil for evil or railing for railing; but that you are so far from it, that you will forgive me without my asking it.

Here I forbear to add any reflections; I trust that your own conscience will be full of those that are proper when you have read this: and if you don't suitably reflect just now, yet I hope the time will come when you will be sedate, and will with solemnity of spirit think of these things, and be enabled to look on your own conduct with real seriousness, as in the sight of God. That you may obtain this mercy is the desire of,

Rev. Sir, your brother and servant,
Jonathan Edwards.

59. TO AN UNKNOWN RECIPIENT

An illustration of Edwards' unending search for current news, as found in the fragmentary close of a letter.

(Beinecke Library, fragment in sermon on Rev. 1:5, June 1745.)

* * *

Northampton, June 4, 1745

[. . .] as you have an opportunity of sending it by some Northampton man, that you see yourselves.

I received the last week's paper; but those of the two preceding weeks I missed: I desire you to send 'em. I am,

Your humble servant,
Jonathan Edwards.

60. TO THE REVEREND BENJAMIN COLMAN

Benjamin Colman, the distinguished pastor of Brattle Street Church, Boston, remained a staunch friend of Edwards' over the years. Here Edwards offers condolences on the death of Colman's daughter.

(Baker Library, Ticknor Coll., ms. 745427, ALS, two quarto leaves, addressed on second verso to the Reverend Benjamin Colman in Boston. For background information, see Ebenezer Turell, *The Life and Character of the Reverend Benjamin Colman* [Boston, 1749]; SIB, *4*, 129; and Clayton H. Chapman, "Benjamin Colman's Daughters," *NEQ* 26 [1953], 169–92).

* * *

Northampton, July 27, 1745[1]

Rev. and Honored Sir,

My lately hearing the news of the death of your daughter [Abigail] Dennie (by which bereavement after so many others God has finished the emptying of your house of all but yourself) is the occasion of my now writing. Such have been your distinguishing afflictions in the decline of life that they are worthy to move the hearts of all that hear of them, and especially the heart of one that has been laid under so many obligations to special regard, and has so many reasons for peculiar esteem and honor as myself. It has pleased the sovereign and infinitely holy God, honored Sir, of late years to be causing his waves and billows one after another to pass over you, first bereaving you of your excellent daughter Turell and her pleasant and hopeful offspring, and then sorely afflicting you in what he permitted and ordered in his providence with respect to your other daughter (your only surviving child), her disposal of herself as to her outward circumstances, and after this laying Madam [Sarah Crisp Clark] Colman (who till then God, by her distinguished virtues and amiable qualities, had made so agreeable a companion, and a great support to you under your afflictions) under a cloud so as to put her out of a capacity thenceforward of being serviceable or comfortable; and then after you had for some years borne this great affliction, bereaving you and your flock of your colleague [William Cooper] and fellow helper in the labors of the gospel, leaving you to bear the burden of the care of so great a congregation and church alone in your old age, and under your great bodily infirmities, and other heavy afflictions: and soon after this taking away her that had

1. The date on the MS (mistakenly) reads July 27, 1744.

been once your desirable consort by death; and quick upon this extinguishing your family by the late death of your daughter.

As God's sovereignty, honored Sir, is to be acknowledged in so great and repeated afflictions, so his power and grace is to be seen and must be owned to be remarkable in so upholding you under them; so that though you are so aged and your bodily infirmities so great, you are kept from sinking, and yet enabled to continue in the service of your congregation, and that the powers of your mind are so remarkably continued and grace, and divine assistance (as seems by your late printed performances) increased. As God has made you a father in our Israel, and a great blessing in your day, so his goodness is to be acknowledged that he continues you to be so, and makes you to be so in some respects more and more; fulfilling his promise in the 92nd Psalm, "They shall still bring forth fruit in old age." There is no reason to doubt, honored Sir, but that he that has so supported you hitherto, will ever proportion his grace and consolations to your trials, and that he that has thus taken away creature-props and supports, one after another on every side, will take such an opportunity to manifest his all-sufficiency.

I desire that while God yet continues you in this world, and is refining you as gold in a furnace, and preparing you for the more eminent station in his eternal glory that he designs you for, you would pray for your sons in the ministry, and for me in particular. That when you are thus deprived of the company of your temporal friends, you may have sweet communion with the Lord Jesus Christ more abundantly, and that as God has gradually been darkening this world to you, putting out one of its lights after another, so he would cause the light of his eternal glory more and more to dawn within you, is the humble prayer of, honored Sir, with humble regard and affectionate sympathy,

Your son and servant,

Jonathan Edwards.

P.S. I have ordered my daughter Jerusha to wait on you with this letter. I desire for her your prayers and blessing.

61. TO FRIENDS IN SCOTLAND

George Whitefield's second visit to Northampton has often been overlooked by Edwards' biographers. Edwards here reports it, placing it in the larger context of the Grand Itinerant's journey through New England in 1744–45. The visit generated a storm of controversy, with attackers and defenders both rushing into print. Edwards notes the reaction in Boston, but makes no mention of the protest from his own Hampshire Association.

But Edwards does praise Whitefield. He found the evangelist's demeanor admirable: irenic, judicious, and actively opposed to revival excesses. Whitefield was still a memorable figure: fervent, eloquent, and magnetic. He attracted throngs, as before, and many lives were changed as a result of his sermons, but no general wave of revival followed. With less opposition, Edwards concludes, Whitefield would have been more successful.

(Published as an "Extract of a Part of the Reverend Mr. Jonathan Edwards' Letter, concerning Mr. Whitefield's Progress, Reception, and Success in New-England," *CMH*, no. 9 [Dec. 1745], 259–63. Although the exact date of the letter has not been ascertained, it was written sometime after September 16, 1745. Edwards refers to Whitefield's visit to Philadelphia, which, as the *New York Post-Boy* reported, began on that date. See Charles H. Maxson, *The Great Awakening in the Middle Colonies* [Chicago, 1920], p. 107.)

*   *   *

[after September 16, 1745]

Mr. [George] Whitefield's late visit to New England has been an occasion of the whole country's being in a great uproar; but, I think, wholly without any fault of his, or at least, any fault committed by him, in this visit. He came ashore at York, in the eastern part of New England, the last year [1744], October 26th; and immediately after his arrival was taken very ill, and had a sore fit of sickness, wherein he was brought near to death; but was wonderfully soon restored, so that he began to preach. Many ministers were more alarmed at his coming, than they would have been by the arrival of a fleet from France, and they began soon to preach and write against him, to warn people to beware of him, as a most dangerous person. Soon after his arrival, the ministers of Boston consulted together how they should treat him; and the greater part of them agreed to invite him to preach in their pulpits. But presently upon it, the president, fellows, and professors of Cambridge College published a testimony against him,[1] warning ministers and people, to beware of him, as an enthusiast, a censorian, and uncharitable person, and deceiver of the people, etc., advertising ministers in their respective associations: through the country, to unite in testifying against him, and warning their people against him. (It is to be noticed, that ministers throughout almost all parts of New England are wont to meet in associations. But the associations on this province and New Hampshire are no part of a legal establishment, as they are in

1. *The Testimony of the President, Professors, Tutors, and Hebrew Instructor of Harvard College in Cambridge; against the Reverend Mr. George Whitefield, and His Conduct* (Boston, 1744).

the Connecticut, but only voluntary societies of ministers for mutual advice and assistance in ecclesiastic and religious affairs.)

There soon followed this a letter from an association of ministers in the eastern parts, to the ministers in Boston, that was published, finding great fault with them for inviting Mr. Whitefield into their pulpits, and earnestly testifying against Mr. Whitefield. After this, testimonies were exceedingly multiplied, and accumulated against him, from associations of ministers all over the country, and many other things written against him by particular persons. In these testimonies and writings, everything was gathered up to object against him, that could by any means be found; everyone strove to find something new, that others had not said before them. Besides, a great deal published in the *Evening-Post,* and in pamphlets, by anonymous authors, wherein Mr. Whitefield was reproached in the most scurrilous and scandalous manner, without observing any measures, or keeping within any bounds. And I question whether history affords any instance paralleled with this, as so much pains taken in writing to blacken a man's character, and render him odious; and all for his old faults, without anything new worth speaking of, that they could find against him; for in his last visit he conducted himself much more modestly, wisely, and inoffensively than before. Many that when he was here before, durst as soon eat fire as speak reproachfully of him, the regard of the people in general was so great to him, now have taken liberty of opposing him, most openly and without restraint. And many that before seemed to have a veneration for him, and spake highly of him in their prayers and sermons, have now appeared zealous against him. He continued in the country much longer than before, being more than three-quarters of an year after his arrival, before his departure. And all the while he stayed, the country was in a kind of constant alarm, as though he was working the country's ruin, and all without any cause; all that he did was only to preach the pure doctrines of the gospel to the people, applying them with proper earnestness, carefully avoiding meddling with their controversies, behaving himself with admirable meekness under all reproaches that were cast upon him, not justifying his former faults, and humbly confessing some of them: but this did not at all abate the violence of his opposers. All the while he continued here, he was treated by many as though he was excepted from the common benefit of rules of truth, justice, and humanity. Though there was a great deal of difference among his opposers, some were much more violent and unjust than others, and doubtless many honest, pious and upright people were drawn in to side with Mr. Whitefield's opposers, being blinded in the midst of the great dust that was raised. And some ministers that favored him at his arrival, were at last overpowered by the multitudes of testimonies, and the great name of the fame of the testifiers; and among all the testimonies that were published, none had so great influence, as a large one published by Dr. [Edward] Wigglesworth,[2] divinity professor at Cambridge in the form of a letter to Mr. Whitefield, he being universally esteemed a very great man, and a Calvinist, and a man of a calm, moderate temper, and his testimony written with more moderation than many others, and with more show of good reason (though I am not far from thinking his testimony just), it has had great influence; but the great opposition made against Mr. Whitefield, had a contrary effect with many, than what was intended. It caused them to cleave the more closely to him, and greatly to pity him, and abhor the spirit and behavior of his opposers; for they looked upon him as persecuted for Christ and the gospel's sake, and many have hereby had their ill thoughts of the generality of the ministry greatly established in them.

Mr. Whitefield wrote several things in his own vindication;[3] and several others published apologies for him; the chief of which were those of Mr. [Thomas] Foxcroft of Boston, and Mr. [William] Hobby of Reading, and Mr. [William] Shurtleff of Portsmouth.[4] But it signified little or nothing to endeavor to oppose and stop the stream that was so violent against him. These apologists were immediately run upon by a multitude, and were ridiculed and lampooned from the press by anonymous authors, in a most scurrilous and vile manner. It was a kind of a miracle, that Mr. Whitefield should appear so little moved by all that he met with, and should in the midst of all possess himself with so much courage and calmness, etc., though he spent the greatest part

2. *A Letter to the Reverend Mr. George Whitefield, by Way of Reply to His Answer to the College Testimony Against Him and His Conduct* (Boston, 1745).

3. *A Letter to the Reverend Dr. Chauncy, on Account of Some Passages relating to the Revd. Mr. Whitefield in His Book Entitled Seasonable Thoughts* (Boston, 1745); *A Letter to the Reverend the President and Professors, Tutors, and Hebrew Instructor of Harvard College* (Boston, 1745); *Some Remarks upon a Late Charge Against Enthusiasm* (Boston, 1745).

4. Thomas Foxcroft, *An Apology in Behalf of the Revd. Mr. Whitefield: Offering a Fair Solution of Certain Difficulties Objected Against Some Parts of His Publick Conduct* (Boston, 1745); William Hobby, *An Inquiry into the Itinerancy, and the Conduct of the Rev. Mr. George Whitefield, an Itinerant Preacher, Vindicating the Former Against the Charge of Unlawfulness and the Latter Against Some Aspersions which Have Been Frequently Cast upon Him* (Boston, 1745); William Shurtleff, *A letter to Those of His Brethren in the Ministry who Refused to Admit the Rev. Mr. Whitefield into Their Pulpits* (Boston, 1745).

of his time while he was in the land in the midst of the hottest battles. He spent much time in Boston and in the parts northeast from Boston; but he visited almost every part of New England, excepting the western part of Connecticut.

He with his lady was here at Northampton, almost a week in July last,[5] and behaved himself so, that he endeared himself much to me; he appeared in a more desirable temper of mind and more solid and judicious in his thoughts, and prudence in his conduct, than when he was here before. He went from hence into Connecticut, but it was so late in the year, that he spent but little time there. What time he did spend there, was mostly in the eastern parts of Connecticut; where he very boldly, plainly and abundantly testified against the opinions and way of the wild and extravagant people there, and has there done a great deal of good; a considerable number have been reclaimed by him. But yet the big part are obstinate, and condemn Mr. Whitefield, as they do other ministers that oppose them. He did not go into the western part of the Connecticut at all; but went out from Lyme (a town at the mouth of Connecticut River), over to Long Island east-end (I think about the beginning of August), and went from thence to the west end of the island, and there went to New York, and from thence through the Province of New Jersey to Philadelphia, intending to travel by land through all the provinces to Georgia. His manner was to preach every day; commonly twice a day; sometimes three times. His preaching was attended in New England with no such remarkable effects, in awakenings and reviving religion as before. There were commonly great and crowded congregations where he preached, and he was heard with great attention, and many affected; but no remarkable alteration has followed; the country in general remains in a great degree of a stupidity, as to any work of conviction on the hearts of sinners. I know of no such work going on anywhere in this land.

It appears to me very probable, that his preaching would have been of great use in many respects, if his adversaries had let him alone, and ministers in general would freely have allowed him their pulpits; and that the consequence would not have been the promoting those errors and disorders that they pretended to fear, and guard against, in making so great an alarm in the country about him; but that on the con-

5. The time is confirmed by Rev. Jonathan Judd, who wrote in his Diary (Forbes Library) for July 15, 1745, "went to town [Northampton], heard Mr Whitefield from Isa. 54:5. Lo[d]ged at Coll Dwights." His entry for July 17 reads, "Mr Whitefield preached here [Southampton] Heb. 4:3."

trary in the temper he was in, it would have very much tended to correct errors and heal breaches. But the manner of his opponents has been to appear full of heat, violence and contention against him, and thereby to fill the churches, towns, and the whole country with contention and confusion, and to lay this strife and uproar to Mr. Whitefield; and cry out, "See what a great flame Mr. Whitefield's coming has put the country into?" And so they would condemn him, as not fit to be borne in human society, for the greatness of the fire which they kindled, and continued to their utmost to blow up. Whereas Mr. Whitefield, in this visit, seemed not inclined to do anybody any harm, some ministers that were more impartial had their hearts filled with fear concerning him, from the abundance they heard; and almost dreaded, lest he should come where they had to do; who, when once they came to see and hear, and converse with him, immediately changed their minds, and had all their fears dissipated at once.

[Jonathan Edwards.]

62. TO A HAMPSHIRE COUNTY MINISTER

(Beinecke Library, in sermons on I Cor. 6:11 [n.d., c. 1746] and I Cor. 11:3 [March 1746].)

* * *

Northampton, October 3, 1745

Rev. Sir,

I heard the last year, that you had very good turnips to sell: if it be so this year, I should be glad to buy six or seven bushels of you. If not, I should be glad if you would inquire who of your people have the best turnips to sell, and send me word in a little time. Herein you will much oblige

Your brother and servant,
Jonathan Edwards.

P.S. You'll have opportunity to bring me word, the next week when you come in to the Association.

63. TO A CORRESPONDENT IN SCOTLAND

In this, his first letter on the Concert for Prayer, Edwards gives the movement his enthusiastic endorsement. It was a cooperative effort begun by ministers in Scotland to enlist all Christians in active intercession before God. Edwards recounts promotional efforts he has already made for the Concert and pledges more. He heralds revivals elsewhere, hoping that the Concert will increase them.[1]

Edwards and all New England were preoccupied at this time with the English military campaign against Louisburg, Cape Breton, Nova Scotia. Reports by church members who were on the scene enable him to supply graphic details. He sees every event as a sign of divine guidance and protection.

(Published in *CMH* 8 [1745], 234–54; *Works*, 5, 444–60. The recipient was probably Rev. John MacLaurin of Glasgow, an initiator of the Concert.)

*   *   *

Northampton, November 1745

Rev. and Most Dear Sir,

I am greatly obliged to you for your large, friendly, profitable and entertaining letter of February last. I esteem my correspondence with you, and my other correspondents in Scotland, a great honor and privilege; and hope that it may be improved for God's glory, and my profit. The church of God, in all parts of the world, is but one; the distant members are closely united in one glorious head; this union is very much her beauty, and the mutual friendly correspondence of the various members, in distant parts of the world, is a thing well becoming this union (at least when employed about things appertaining to the glory of their common head, and their common spiritual interest and happiness), and therefore is a thing decent and beautiful, and very profitable.

When the day is so dark here in New England, it is exceeding refreshing and reviving to hear, by your and other letters, and Mr. [James] Robe's *History*,[2] of religion's being to such a degree upheld in the power and practice of it, in those parts of Scotland that have been favored with the late revival, and of such a number of the persevering subjects of it and of the works now going on in the north of Scotland, under the labors and conduct of such pious, solid, judicious and prudent instruments, that Christ there makes use of; and one thing that has been very joyful to me, that I have been informed of in the letters I have received from you, and my other correspondents, your dear neighbors and brethren, is that Concert that is come into, by many of God's people in Scotland and England, for united prayer to God, for

1. On the Concert for Prayer, see Fawcett, *The Cambuslang Revival*, pp. 210–35.
2. This reference is to *The Christian Monthly History* (Edinburgh, 1743–46), which Robe edited.

the pouring out of his Holy Spirit on his church and the world of mankind. Such an agreement and practice appears to me exceeding beautiful, and becoming Christians; and I doubt not but it is so in Christ's eyes. And it seems to me to be a thing peculiarly becoming us, in the state that things are in at the present day. God has lately done great things before our eyes, whereby he has shown us something of his wonderful power and mercy; but has withal so disposed things, that events have tended remarkably to show us our weakness, infirmity, insufficiency, and great and universal need of God's help; we have been many ways rebuked for our self-confidence and looking to instruments, and trusting in an arm of flesh; and God is now showing us that we are nothing, and letting us see that we can do nothing. In many places where God of late wonderfully appeared, he has now in a great measure withdrawn; and the consequence is, that Zion and the interest of religion are involved in innumerable and inextricable difficulties. And it is apparent that we can't help ourselves, and have nowhere else to go, but to God. II Chron. 20:12, "We know not what to do; our eyes are upon thee." Now how fit is it that God's people, under such circumstances, should go to God by prayer, and give themselves more than ordinarily to that duty, and be uniting with one another in it, agreeing together touching what they shall ask, taking some proper course to act in it with a visible union, tending to promote their offering up their cries with one heart, and, as it were, with one voice. Oh that this duty might be attended with real meekness towards our opposers, lifting up holy hands without wrath; and that we may go to God, self-empty, brokenhearted, looking to God only through Christ, and without making any righteousness of our performances, or any exalting thoughts of ourselves for our secret or social religion, or our differing from others, in being either friends or partakers of the late revival of religion.

I have taken a great deal of pains to promote a falling in with this Concert in New England, at least so far as relates to the quarterly seasons agreed upon. I read those passages of your and your brethren's letters, that relate to this affair, publicly in my own congregation, using many arguments with them to comply with the thing proposed. And many praying societies here have complied. I gave an account of the affair to several of the neighboring ministers, that I thought most likely to fall in with it: two of them seem to like it very well, and to determine to propose it to their people; but one of them [Stephen Williams], who seemed very much to approve of it, the next week was called away to serve as chaplain to the soldiers at Cape Breton, and is not yet returned, and so I suppose nothing is done there. When he was here, I talked with him about this affair, showed him your letters, and urged, wherever he went, to give an account of this Concert to the people of God, and to press their coming into it. He seemed forward to do as I desired; but I have not heard what he has done. I wrote to ——— ——[3] about it, who was then in Connecticut, giving him an account of the proposal, desiring him to mention it to other ministers, that they might promote it among their people. He wrote me word back, that he had mentioned it to several ministers, and desired them to speak to others; but whether anything is done, I have not heard.

I hope, dear Sir, that you will do what in you lies, still to uphold, promote, and propagate this Concert. I should be very sorry to hear of its sinking. I don't think it ought to be let fall, though you should meet with considerable difficulties and discouragements in the affair. Jacob and the woman of Canaan, met with great discouragements, while they were wrestling for a blessing: but they persevered, and obtained their request. I should have more hope from the union, fervency, and unfailing constancy of the prayers of God's people, with respect to the religious affairs of the present day, than anything else; more than from the preaching and writings of the ablest and best friends to the work of God's Spirit. For my part, I am not disheartened with respect to this Concert, though I have met with great discouragements in my endeavors to promote it hitherto: I shall not cease still to do what in me lies to promote and propagate it, according as favorable junctures and opportunities do present. Please to remember me to the correspondent meeting in Glasgow, that you speak of, as one whose heart is with them, particularly in the business of this Concert. Oh! that our hearts, and the hearts of all God's people everywhere, might be united in such an affair, that we might be assisted to be in good earnest in it, and give God no rest, till he shall establish, and make Jerusalem a praise in the earth. I desire you would mention it to this meeting, as my desire, that on the times agreed on for this united prayer, they would pray for America and New England, and (if it be not too much to ask) that they would sometimes think of me in their addresses to heaven. I am sensible it would be too much for me to expect, that they should commonly mention me in particular in their prayers; it would be impracticable for such societies, in all their prayers, to pray particularly for every

3. The original printed version contains a dash; the individual is not further identified.

minister, that is sensible of the worth of the prayers of God's people, and would highly prize them. But I should esteem it a great privilege, to be sometimes thought of by the Christian people there, in their prayers to God. I hope the time is hastening, when God's people in all the different parts of the world, and the whole earth shall become more sensibly, as it were, one family, one holy and happy society, and all brethren, not only all united in one head, but in greater affection, and in more mutual correspondence, and more visible and sensible union and fellowship in religious exercises, and the holy duties of the service of God; and so that in this respect, the church on earth will become more like the blessed society in heaven, and vast assembly of saints and angels there.

I am persuaded that such an agreement of the people of God in different parts, to unite together, to pray for the Holy Spirit, is lovely in the eyes of Jesus Christ the glorious head of the church. And if endeavors are used to uphold, and promote, and enlarge such a Concert, who knows what it may come to at last? Who knows but that by degrees, it may spread all over the British dominions, both in Europe and America, and also into Holland, Zeeland, and other Protestant countries, and all over the visible church of Christ, yea, far beyond the present limits of the visible church? And how glorious a thing will this be, to have the people of God everywhere thus agreeing together, touching such a thing that they would ask! And what blessed fruits and consequences might reasonably be hoped for, from such united prayers! Might it not be hoped, that they would open the doors and windows of heaven, that have so long been shut up, and been as brass over the heads of the inhabitants of the earth, as to spiritual showers; and that God, in answer to such prayers, would speak the word, and say, "Drop down ye heavens from above, and let the skies pour down righteousness"? [Is. 45:8].

As there is a great need of God's people's uniting their cries to God for spiritual blessings at this day, so I can't but think that there is much in the present aspects of divine providence to encourage them in it. For although there are many dark clouds, and God's Spirit is greatly withdrawn from some places where it has lately been remarkably poured out, and Satan seems at present greatly to rage and prevail; yet God is still carrying on his work, if not in one place, yet in another. Though it seems in some measure to cease in the west of Scotland, yet it is carried on in the north, and breaks out in some parts of the United Netherlands. And since the work has ceased very much in New England, it has broke out wonderfully in Virginia, and has prevailed there, for, I suppose, more than a year and half. The work that is lately broke out among them, was begun by the labors of one Mr. [William] Robinson a young minister that went down among them from Pennsylvania, the last year, and spent much time in preaching there, with great success, multitudes being greatly awakened as he preached from place to place, a great thirst appearing in the people after the means of grace, and eagerness to hear the Word preached, and fondness towards the instrument of their awakening. This Mr. Robinson, by all that I can learn of him, from those whose intelligence and judgment I rely upon, is a man of sprightly abilities, fervent piety, and very solid, judicious and prudent.

The governor [William Gooch] encouraged Messrs. [Gilbert] Tennent and [Samuel] Finley to preach in Virginia and invited them to make his house their home, when it was in their way. Accordingly they continued preaching for some time in the country with great success; and, by the last accounts that I heard, the work continued to go on wonderfully there. Mr. [Samuel] Buell, I hear, is gone down into those parts, designing to continue there this winter. He is one that you have probably heard of, has been a zealous and successful preacher in New England.

Besides the work in Virginia, Mr. William Tennent in the Jerseys, has lately had great success among his people; a greater work having been lately carried on among them than at any time these seven years past. And the above-mentioned Mr. Robinson, besides his success in Virginia, has lately had great success in the parts below Philadelphia, in Pennsylvania. The provinces of New Jersey, Pennsylvania, Maryland and Virginia, are become exceeding populous; and there are great numbers in those provinces that show a forwardness to hear the Word preached; but there are few ministers. "The harvest is plenteous, but the laborers few" [Matt. 9:37].

The ministers of the three forementioned presbyteries, that are friends to the late work, who have lately formed themselves into a new synod, who had their first meeting September last, at Elizabeth, in New Jersey; I say these ministers, taking into consideration the very calamitous circumstances of those provinces, by reason of the scarcity of ministers, have formed a design of erecting a college there, for the educating young men for the ministry, hoping, through the influence of some particular gentlemen, to obtain a charter for the establishment of such a society from the king. I think the design to be very glorious, and very worthy to be encouraged, and promoted by all the friends of Zion. In the meantime, these ministers have determined that private academies should be kept in certain ministers' houses, for the instructing and educating young candidates for the ministry, till this design of a more public school can be ripened. Accordingly they have determined that such academy should be kept by Mr. [Jonathan] Dickinson, Mr. [Aaron] Burr, Mr. [Samuel] Blair, and Mr. Finley; all of them excellent men, well capable of, and fitted for such business.

Besides those things that have a favorable aspect on the interest of religion in these parts, among the English, and other inhabitants of European extract, Mr. [David] Brainerd, a missionary employed by the Society in Scotland for Propagating Christian Knowledge to preach to the Indians, has lately had more success than ever. This Mr. Brainerd is a young gentleman of very distinguishing qualifications, remarkable for his piety, and eminent zeal for the good of souls, and his knowledge in divinity, and solidity of his judgment, and prudence of conduct. And I hope he will be improved to be a great blessing. 'Tis [fitting] that he should have all the encouragement from those that employ him, that shall put him under the best advantage in his work.

While I am speaking of the late wonderful works of God in America, I cannot pass over one, which, though it be of a different kind from those already mentioned; yet is that wherein the Most High has made his hand manifest, in a most apparent and marvelous manner, and may be reckoned among the evidences of its being a day of great things, and of the wonderful works of God in this part of the world. What I have reference to, is the success of the late expedition, from New England, against Cape Breton; a place of vast importance, and a place from whence New England, and all the English colonies on the American continent, have been chiefly, and almost only infested by our French enemies since the beginning of the war. I have had much opportunity to be well-informed of the circumstances of this affair, about twenty of my parishioners being present at the siege and surrender of the place: and among others, a major of one of the regiments [Seth Pomeroy], and the general's chaplain [Joseph Hawley], both worthy pious men. There was very discernibly an extraordinary spirit of prayer given the people of God in New England, with respect to this undertaking, more than in any public affair within my remembrance; and many praying pious persons were immediately concerned in it; and among others, several of the chaplains and principal officers. Some of the chief officers that I am well acquainted with, and conversed with a little before they embarked, seemed to have special and extraordinary assistance, to commit themselves to God in the undertaking, to resign their lives to his disposal, and trust in him; and I was informed of the same in many others. Providence made provision for the expedition, by giving us an extraordinary plenty the summer before; and they were remarkable providences that led us into the design. The state of the place was strangely concealed from us, which if it had been known, would have effectually prevented the design. We seem to be under great advantages to be informed; for we had many that very lately had been prisoners there, and others that had traded, and been very conversant there, and some that had dwelt there a considerable time, and our governor [William Shirley] and General Assembly were very diligent in making inquiry, and all seemed to be well satisfied that we had full information; and yet the representations that were relied upon as true, were exceeding wrong. It was unaccountable that so many that had been conversant there, should be kept in such ignorance. If one half of the strength of the place had been known, the expedition had never been thought of; or if they had imagined the number of soldiers and inhabitants there, or if the expensiveness of the undertaking had been conceived of, it never would have been meddled with; for it soon abundantly exceeded the expectations of our General Assembly. After all, when the affair was first proposed to the Assembly, it was not fallen in with; it was thought too great an undertaking. But afterwards, the affair was unexpectedly reconsidered, and then it was carried by a majority of one single vote among fourscore representatives; and such a majority would not have been obtained, had not several of the members of the House, that were against it, been at that time providentially absent; nor yet would it have been, had it not been so ordered, that one of the voters present, that had been against it on a committee, changed his mind and voted for it in the House. After the affair was determined, it was surprising to see how the people were spirited to offer themselves. When the determination of the General Court was first noised abroad, it was not known but that men would be impressed into the service; and many, through fear of being impressed, hid themselves, particularly there were many in a neighboring town, viz. Westfield, that were so afraid of being obliged to go in the expedition, that they ran away, and hid themselves in the woods; and yet afterwards, when orders came for enlisting volunteers, eleven of those same persons that had hid themselves, came and voluntarily offered their service. There were also such instances in other towns.

We were marvelously smiled upon in our preparations for the expedition; so that within two months, from the resolution of the government (which was January 29) the whole military force was under sail. It was wonderful, that during this whole time of preparation, which was in those usually stormy months of February and March, we had a constant series of moderate and fair weather, such as was scarce ever known at that time of year: so that there was hardly any impediment from the weather to our officers, in going about and enlisting, or our soldiers in marching, or our coasters in bringing provisions, or the Committee of War in their various preparations, till all were ready to sail; not so much as the loss of one day, either by snow, rain, or cold. Some who have preserved an account of the weather for more than twenty years, have been surprised to behold the difference between the months of February and March this year, and the foregoing ones; this a continued course of good weather, those as continually intermixed with storms of snow, or rain, or severity of cold. And we seemed in other respects to be strangely succeeded in our preparations. Some have been heard to express themselves with wonder, how things would happen; just as they wanted some kind of materials or provision, an unexpected vessel would come in, and bring them.

It was strange, that while this affair was managing in New England, and the whole country full of the noise of it, it should be concealed from our French enemies, in Cape Breton and Canada. It was very early known in Albany, a place where the Indians that live in Canada are abundantly conversant; so that it was very much concluded by some of the most discerning and judicious of our rulers, that they had notice of our design in Canada, long before our forces embarked; which, if it had been, would in all probability have frustrated the whole design. But it proved afterwards, that it was wonderfully concealed from them, not only till our forces sailed, but a long time after, till it was too late for them to send any succors to their friends. And the design was also kept wholly concealed from the French in Cape Breton; which was in some respects more wonderful; especially considering how many friends they had, French and Indians in Nova Scotia, on the borders of New England; and not only so, but the Indians in the eastern parts of this province, that have always been friends with the French, and have since openly sided with them, and must needs know of our design. 'Tis unaccountable, that none of these should inform our enemies.

Our soldiers were wonderfully preserved from the smallpox, which is a distemper very fatal to the people of New England, and was in

Boston, as our troops were gathering there, both by land and water, and continued all the while they were quartering and anchoring there, very few of the officers or soldiers having had it. And 'tis thought the time was never known, when so many persons, in so many different parts of the town, were ill with this distemper, and it was notwithstanding stopped in its progress. If it had prevailed, and got among the soldiers, it would unavoidably have put an end to the expedition.

When the expedition was first determined by our authority, they were not sure they should have the assistance of one man-of-war; without which our forces would (as it proved by what appeared afterwards) [have] been easily swallowed up by their enemies. Indeed the governor, soon after the expedition was fully determined, dispatched a packet for England, to the Lords of the Admiralty desiring their assistance. And it was so ordered in providence (which was perhaps much in favor to the design), that there had been a change made a little before in the Board of Admiralty, and such commissioners introduced, that were thought to be much spirited for the interest of the nation, and sincerely to seek the success of the war against the French. However, if we had no assistance of men-of-war, till those arrived that the Lords of the Admiralty sent, it would have been too late (as events proved), to have saved our forces from their enemies. Our governor at the same time that he sent a packet to England, sent another to the West Indies to Commodore [Peter] Warren, in hopes of persuading him to send some assistance of men-of-war; but the Commodore sent back the packet-boat with a denial, thinking himself not warranted to come without orders from England. But so wonderfully was it ordered that within a few days after messenger was sent back with his discouraging answer, the Commodore received express orders from the Lords of the Admiralty, forthwith to come to Boston, to act in concert with our governor, for the defense of these northern English settlements; not that they knew anything of the intended expedition against Cape Breton, but only expected, that the French would that spring make an attempt on Annapolis, and would endeavor extraordinarily to annoy our seacoasts. Thus the designs that our enemies were forming against us, were made an occasion of their ruin, and our great advantage. They were taken in the pit that they had digged; for had it not been for their extraordinary designs against us, Commodore Warren would not have had orders at that time to come hither, which if it had not been, our forces must have fallen a prey to the French, and Cape Breton not have been taken. The Commodore having received these orders, with all speed sent the news of it to Governor Shirley; which, when it arrived was like life from the dead to him and others, that were ready to sink in distress and discouragement.

Commodore Warren, after receiving the forementioned orders, soon set sail, with three ships from the West Indies, for Boston. But still if he had not been prevented from coming to Boston, as he intended before he went to Cape Breton, he would have been too late there, to have prevented the *Vigilant* (a strong ship from France of sixty-four guns, with all manner of warlike stores) from getting into the harbor, which if it had done, would (as is judged on all hands) [have] prevented the taking of the place. But so wonderfully was it ordered, that Commodore Warren in his voyage hither, near Cape Sable on April 12th, met with a fisherman, who informed him of our army's being gone to Canso the week before; that on board the fisherman, there was one of the best of pilots, who had got out of the way of our Committee of War, to avoid being pressed for the service. On which information, and being now furnished with a good pilot, so wonderfully thrown in his way, the Commodore dropped his design of coming to Boston, tacked about, and went directly to our forces to Canso, to their great joy; and then without stopping there, went on to his station before Louisburg, to block up that harbor. The Commodore also, by the said fisherman, sent his order for the king's ships that should be found in these ports, forthwith to follow them. The order came to the *Eltham,* a forty-gun ship at Piscataqua, after she was actually got to sea, having set sail for England, as convoy to the mast-fleet. The order reached her by a boat, sent after her from the shore, before she was got quite out of call, on which she bore after the Commodore, and quickly joined him; so that now our army had four men-of-war, under God, to protect them.

It was remarkable, that when so many vessels sailed from this province, New Hampshire and Connecticut, being in all about eighty sail, in a time of year that used to be the most turbulent and tempestuous of any, all arrived safe (through a course of five or six hundred miles on the ocean) at Canso, the place of concourse, a place about sixty miles on this side Cape Breton without the loss of more than one soldier, and three seamen, and fifteen sick. And 'tis to be observed, that the Connecticut forces very narrowly escaped being taken by a French ship of force, that came in sight of them in their voyage; but were kept in play by some vessels of ours, of inferior force, till the fleet of transports got out of reach. And 'tis remarkable, that of all the vessels that have been employed in this affair (who had their voyages at a very difficult time of year), transports and vessels of force from New England, packet-boats to and from England and the West Indies, men-of-war from the West Indies and England to Cape Breton, not one of them failed in any of those voyages, either by being cast away or taken.

It seemed to be ordered wholly in favor to the design, that our forces that went from this government were detained by contrary winds for near three weeks at Canso. If they had sailed before, as appeared, they would have found the harbors and bays full of ice, and could not have landed, so that they would only have discovered themselves to the enemy, and given them timely notice to prepare for their defense, without being able to come near them, which (as after-events confirm) would wholly have defeated the design; and besides, the weather, while they lay in Canso harbor, was exceeding bad, being very cold, with storms and snow; so that if the wind had been fair, and they could have landed at Cape Breton, they could not have lived ashore so ill provided as they were with tents. By this means the enemy would have had a vast advantage against them; but God held them at Canso, till the Connecticut forces and Commodore Warren were come up, and till the bays were clear of ice, and till the time was come that he intended the weather should be good, so that our men could live ashore, and then the wind sprung up fair to carry them to Cape Breton.

While our forces lay at Canso, their cruisers were succeeded to intercept and take many French vessels that were coming to Cape Breton, and in them to take some things that the army greatly needed; and particularly it is judged by some of the officers that were there, that are persons of good judgment, that the army could not have subsisted (so exposed as they were to cold at that time of year in that cold climate) without the rum they took from the enemy.

It was very strange, that when our army lay so long at Canso, within sight of the island Cape Breton, they should be wholly concealed from the French on that island; so that the people of Louisburg had no notice of the expedition against them, till they were surprised with the sight of the fleet coming upon them, and entering the bay where they landed.

Our forces, when they went from Boston, had orders to land in the night, and go upon a certain plan of operations, established on the false representations we had had of the state of the place. Accordingly they set sail from Canso, with a design to land in the night, and pros-ecute their plan; which if they had done, it is judged it would have proved fatal to the design; therefore divine providence prevented it, by causing the wind suddenly to die away, in the midst of their way from Canso to Chappe-rouge Bay, where they intended to land; so that they could not land in the night, but were obliged to land in the daytime, which proved greatly for their advantage.

When they came into the bay, about five miles from Louisburg, in the daytime, in the sight of their enemies, the French were seized with such surprise, that they seemed hardly to know what they did, and were left to act very foolishly. They sent out eighty-eight persons to resist their landing, when, if they had consulted their interest, they should have sent seven or eight hundred, which might have rendered the landing of our men extremely difficult. These eighty-eight men were left to discover themselves, and appear openly; whereas if they had concealed themselves, and lain in ambush, as there were places enough convenient for their so doing, they might have cut off many of our men. Our men were, on this occasion, wonderfully animated with courage, and between twenty and thirty that first landed, boldly encountered those eighty-eight of the French, and killed eight of them, without the loss of a man on their side, and drove the rest back to the town in a great fright, setting all the city and garrison into a terrible consternation; so that in their fright they immediately deserted the Grand Battery, a fort about a mile and half from the city, on the other side the harbor; a fortress of great strength, and the principal fortification that defended the harbor, furnished with thirty-two great cannon, thirty of them forty-two-pounders; a fortress which might have maintained itself alone against all our army. Our men soon perceiving the fortress to be deserted, took possession of it the next morning; and without this, none imagines that ever the city would have been taken. It was principally by the weapons the French left there, that our army annoyed their enemies; and all say they could have done nothing without them. And if the French had kept this fort, they would have had the advantage vastly to have annoyed our army in their siege, and kept them at a distance from the city. 'Tis not imagined, that the French would ever so foolishly have left this fortress, had it not been for their surprise, through the unexpected arrival of our forces, and those that came out to resist our landing, being driven back in so great a fright: so that here appeared the advantage of the above-mentioned concealment of the expedition; and also hereby it appears, how it was in favor to us, that the French came out to oppose our forces at their landing as they did.

The enemy spiked up their cannons before they left the fort, but did not do it effectually. Our men soon got them all clear again. They carried away most of their powder, or threw it into the sea; but left what was much more needed by our men, viz. their balls, suited to the bores of their huge pieces (for our army had none such) and shells, that happened to be suited to the bores of our mortars; and did not knock off the trunnions of their cannon, nor destroy the carriages.

It was a remarkable favor of providence, that our men discovered that the Grand Battery was deserted, and took possession of it, just as they did; for if this discovery had been delayed but an hour or two longer, the enemy would have repossessed themselves of it, and so our whole design probably have been defeated. For just after our soldiers had taken possession of this fort, the enemy, being on consideration aware of their fatal error in leaving of it, were coming out in great numbers in many boats to recover it, but were repulsed by a handful of our men.

Soon after the siege began, the officers of the army, in a council of war, had determined a general assault to be made by scaling the walls; which, though it appeared to be a very adventurous and dangerous attempt, yet was thought necessary to hasten the taking of the city, because, from what they had heard, they were in daily expectation of a strong French fleet, greater than our naval force before the harbor could resist. (The Commodore also was in expectation of orders from England, sending him elsewhere.) But just as they were going to put this in execution, the officers, unexpectedly, changed their minds, and presently after several men-of-war arrived from England, to add to our naval strength (with orders to the Commodore to continue in his present station, at assisting in the siege of Louisburg), and put the army out of fear of the French fleet; and so this desperate attempt was prevented, which if it had gone on, would have proved fatal to our army, as all are sensible since the strength of the city is fully known.

When the army began to fall short of ammunition, and were like to be run out, God sent the *Vigilant*, the strong French ship from France before mentioned, with all manner of warlike stores, and plenty of ammunition, which fell into the hands of our fleet, and so our army was supplied with what they wanted, to enable them to carry on the siege, which otherwise they could not have done. (And the ship itself was added to our fleet, and was the strongest and best ship in the whole fleet.) This ship, and her warlike stores, was intended to be improved against the English settlements. Thus again our enemies fell into the pit which they digged.

Another remarkable incident, by which that which our enemies had done, was an occasion of a great advantage to our army against them, was this: the French, for some reason or other, had sunk a number of cannon in the sea by the Lighthouse Point, over against the Island Battery (a strong battery that defended the mouth of the harbor). These cannon were providentially discovered by our men, which gave them the hint of erecting a battery on the Lighthouse Point. Accordingly they got up these cannon out of the water; and though while they were at work at it, they were right before the mouths of the cannon of the Island Battery, within about half a mile, yet they went through with the business, without the loss of a man. The enemy in the city also seeing what they were about, came out a great number of them in boats to resist them; but after they were landed, our men ran between them and their boats to hinder their return. Upon which the French immediately fled to the woods, and so the town was weakened; and then our men erected a battery on the Lighthouse Point, which being higher ground than the Island Battery, they had a great advantage to annoy them from thence, and did greatly annoy and distress them, which was one of the chief means of their being brought to capitulate.

Our soldiers seemed to be inspired with resolution, eagerness and activity, in a kind of miraculous manner, greatly to the surprise of their enemies, and were marvelously supported, during the long siege of seven weeks, under their extraordinary and Herculean labors and fatigues—in carrying stores, drawing cannon by their own strength over hills and valleys, among rocks, and even drawing great forty-two-pounders for two miles, through morasses, up to the middle in mire, and in digging trenches, and erecting batteries, and watching continually against the enemy, not only in the town, but the French and Indians from the country, in the woods, that were lurking about them seeking advantages against them—our men being unexperienced in war, having never seen a siege before in their lives, and very few of them ever before engaged in any warlike enterprise of any kind, and a great many of them never heard the report of a cannon before.

But the miracle of their preservation, in the midst of so many continued great dangers, was yet greater. Our nearest batteries were erected within thirty rods of the town-wall; and the enemy were constantly, day and night, discharging their cannon and small arms from the town-wall, and their mortars from the many strong fortifications in and about the town; and the air was, as it were, continually full of bombs, and other instruments of death, and our soldiers were abundantly exposed at their batteries, and moving from place to place. But yet the whole number that were killed by the enemy's fire, from the town and forts, during the whole siege (excepting what were killed at an unsuccessful attempt, made in the night, on the Island Battery), did not amount to twenty. Our men at length were so used to their bombs and cannonballs, and found them harmless for so long a time, that they learned at length but little to regard them; so wonderfully did God cover their heads.

Things were wonderfully ordered from time to time, so as tended to keep up the courage of the army, during this long siege, and to revive their spirits, and give new life to them, when their spirits and courage began to fail; when they were very much beat out, and things looked dark, something new that was prosperous or promising would happen to encourage them, either some additional force would arrive, some men-of-war would be added to the fleet, or some new prizes would be taken, or some remarkable advantage gained against the enemy. And as was observed, that such things happened from time to time, at critical seasons, when most needed to encourage the army. Once in digging a trench, our men came upon a rock, which they fatigued themselves in vain, in endeavoring to remove, and labored till they were quite discouraged; and just as they had left it, there came a bomb from the enemy, and fell under that very rock, in the most suitable spot, so as at once to do their work for them, and cast the rock quite out of the way; so that then their work lay fair before them, and they went on with digging their trench.

There once happened something very discouraging to the army, and that was, that they split their large mortar, that they chiefly depended on, and had none but small mean ones left. But it so wonderfully happened, that a mortar of just the same size, was that very day put on board at Boston, to be sent to them, without the people at Boston knowing anything of this special need; which mortar they soon joyfully received; and it was with that mortar, that they afterward chiefly distressed the enemy, from the battery they had erected at the Lighthouse Point, and drove them from the Island Battery, that defended the mouth of the harbor.

God's providence in disposing the circumstances of the surrender of the place, was wonderful. There was an army that had gathered, and laid siege to Annapolis, in Nova Scotia, the last spring, in expectation of a strong naval force from France to assist them, as had been before determined by the French. This army was made up partly of French and Indians from Canada, and partly of the Indians of Nova Scotia, that are at war with us. This army was disappointed of the expected ships from France; some of them were taken by our squadron, under Commodore Warren (the *Vigilant* forementioned was one of them), others were driven away. And the French at Cape Breton sent for this army to come to their relief; so that siege was raised, and Annapolis and Nova Scotia saved, and the army were on their way to Cape Breton, and if they had arrived before the surrender of the city, they had, in all probability, disappointed our enterprise. But our fleet and army before Louisburg, being wearied with the length of the siege, the sea and land officers met in council, and determined, without further delay, to make a general assault upon the city, and attempt to take it by storm. But this desperate attempt was wonderfully and happily prevented; for just as the council of war was broke up, before Commodore Warren was gone off the ground, came out a flag of truce from the city, desiring a cessation of acts of hostility, till they might meet together, to consider what proposals to make to the English, as terms of the surrender of the city; and the consequence was, that they soon agreed to give up the city, and all its fortifications, and king's stores, and the whole country depending, on condition of their being transported, with their movable effects, to France. Thus God gave into our hands the place of greatest importance of any that the French have in North America, the principal fountain of the king of France's wealth, from these parts of the world, and the key to all his northern colonies, and the chief annoyance of the British colonies. When our men entered the city, they were amazed at the strength of it, and to see how they should have been exposed, if providence had not prevented their design that was resolved upon, of scaling the walls. The walls, which were of a most prodigious thickness, they found to be about twenty-five foot high, very much higher than they had imagined, by reason of a trench, of about twelve foot deep, and a vast wraith under the walls, that they were not aware of; so that their ladders would have proved vastly too short; and it would have been a wonder if so much as one of the land army had got into the city. And, besides the strength of the place, it was found, that there were many more soldiers, and others, capable of bearing arms, in the city and country about, than in our whole army.

Another wonderful circumstance of the taking of this place, was this, that during this long siege, our army had almost a constant series of fair good weather, there being scarce any rain, so as to incommode our army during the whole time, which was to the amazement of the French; for it was a time of year, wherein, in all former years, used to be almost perpetual rains and fogs. And the French inhabitants agreed, that there never had been any instance of such weather at that time of the year, since the place was settled. And it was apparent to the French, by this and other things, and much taken notice of by them, that God fought for the English, and some of them said, "that their God was turned an Englishman." Though it was constantly such good weather, during the seven weeks of the siege, yet (as the major general of the army told me)[4] as soon as ever they had entered the city, before the general had reached his quarters, it began to rain, and continued raining almost constantly for eight days together, which, if it had been before the surrender of the city, would have filled our trenches with water, have stopped all business, and extremely incommoded and distressed the army (who were very ill-provided with tents, and very many of them at that time sick), and must have confounded the whole affair. Some of the French took notice of this, and said one to another, "If we had held out a little longer, we should have done well enough"; but others replied, "No; for if the English had continued in the siege, it would still have been fair weather." Thus the clouds and winds, and sun, moon and stars in their courses, from the beginning, fought for us. While we were preparing in New England, for two months, was a constant series of good weather, in February and March, such as was never known at that time of year. And the winds and weather favored us in all our voyages, that were made about this affair; while God detained the army for three weeks at Canso, till the harbors at Cape Breton were cleared of ice; when good weather was not needed, then was a constant series of bad weather, but after they landed at Cape Breton, till the city surrendered, was again constant good weather; but as soon as they entered the city, and did not stand in need of good weather any longer, then they had no more of it.

This place, since it has fallen into our hands, has proved a snare to our enemies abroad; for they not knowing that it was taken, nor imagining that it could be taken, have resorted thither, as they used to do, with their wealth, from the East and West Indies; two East-India ships and one South-Sea man, immensely rich, besides several other vessels, have come there, into our mouths. And now we are freed from the

---

4. The commander-in-chief at Louisburg was Sir William Pepperrell, a friend and correspondent of JE.

noise of the archers, or gunners, on board their ships of war, that infested us, and made havoc on our coasts the last year.

Thus, Sir, I have given you a particular account of this affair, it being perhaps a dispensation of providence, the most remarkable in its kind, that has been in many ages, and a great evidence of God's being one that hears prayer; and that it is not a vain thing to trust in him; and an evidence of the being and providence of God, enough to convince any infidel; and a great argument with me, among other things, that we live in an age, wherein divine wonders are to be expected; and a dispensation wherein God has so apparently manifested himself, that it appears to me it ought not to be concealed, but to be declared in the world amongst his people, to his praise.

We have lately heard of the Pretender's eldest son[5] his entering Scotland, and being joined there by a number of Highlanders. How far God may punish the nations of Great Britain by him, we cannot tell. We have not yet heard of the rebellion's being suppressed, but are ready to hope, by the aspect of affairs, from what we hear, that it is done before this time. It is a day of great commotion and tumult among the nations, and what the issue will be we know not: but it now becomes us, and the church of God everywhere, to cry to him, that he would overrule all for the advancement of the kingdom of Christ, and the bringing on the expected peace and prosperity of Zion.

I desire, honored Sir, that you would favor me with some further accounts of the progress of religion in the north of Scotland, and in the Netherlands, and in general of the state of things on your side the world, relating to late revivals of religion. And please send me a particular account of things relating to the Concert for joint prayer, whether it be like to be upheld, how far it is spread, etc. And remember in your prayers, dear Sir,

> Your respectful, affectionate and obliged brother and servant,
> Jonathan Edwards.

64. TO THE CHURCH AT WEST SUFFIELD

The people of West Suffield, a stronghold of revival spirit, often appealed to Edwards for advice. Here he suspends judgment on John Graham, Jr., a candidate for the pulpit, until he has more facts. West Suffield belonged to

---

5. Prince Charles Edward Stuart (1720–1788), known popularly as "Bonnie Prince Charlie" and "the Young Pretender," led a rebellion, starting in Scotland, to restore his father, James III, "the Old Pretender," to the throne. He was defeated and in 1746 was forced to flee the country.

Massachusetts at this time, hence, the church was in the Hampshire Association. Graham was ordained in 1746 and served as pastor of West Suffield for fifty years.

(Private coll., John F. Gately, Marlboro, Mass., ALS, one leaf.)

* * *

Northampton, January 7, 1745/6

Gentlemen,

As I have heard some things suggested relating to Mr. [John] Graham's prudence and steadiness that I am uncertain of, and doubtful about, but such that, if I should find them true, would make me very much to fear whether he would be likely to serve the interest of religion amongst you, though I never heard anything against his gifts or his morals; and as I would act for you as I would act for myself in a like case of great importance, I can give no advice with regard to further improving of him, till I have had further and more satisfying information concerning him from those that are acquainted with him.

I am your friend and servant for Jesus' sake,
Jonathan Edwards.

65. TO THE REVEREND STEPHEN WILLIAMS

(Haverford College, Magill Library, Charles Roberts Autograph Letters Coll., ALS, two duodecimo leaves.)

* * *

Northampton, February 18, 1745/6

To the Reverend Mr. Stephen Williams, Pastor of the Church of Christ in Long Meadow, to be Communicated

Reverend, Honored and Beloved,

This may certify you that Rachel Parsons (now Bliss) has been admitted a member of this church, in full communion; and so continued, in good standing and without offense during her continuance here. And she having, by the providence of God, been lately removed from hence to dwell at Longmeadow, I would hereby recommend her to be received to the same standing and privileges with you.

Jonathan Edwards, Pastor of the
First Church in Northampton.

66. TO AN UNKNOWN CORRESPONDENT

"Assurance" and "participation in the divine nature" are the main subjects of this theological exposition, in which Edwards clarifies his views while touching as well on election and perseverance. The letter, only a fragment of which remains, is to an unknown inquirer, probably a colonial clergyman. Edwards restates each of the correspondent's queries before giving his answers. The date of writing has been placed between March 13, 1745/6, and September 23, 1747. The publication of *Religious Affections* appears to have prompted the exchange. The opening and close of the letter are missing.

(Trask Library, AL draft, on a full folio sheet, verso of a Mass. proclamation for a fast day, Mar. 13, 1745. Published in *Works*, 8, 631–40. I am greatly indebted to Thomas A. Schafer for an earlier transcription of this letter.)

* * *

[after March 13, 1745/6

[. . .][1] the faith and so also there will be laid up for me a crown of righteousness. And those words (II Tim. 1:12), "I know whom I have believed, and I am persuaded that he is able to keep that which I have committed unto him against that day," are interpreted thus: "Upon supposition that I keep myself through my approaching trial of martyrdom and so approve myself a true believer (which I don't yet know that I shall), then I do know that I have already believed in Christ and have committed my soul to him, and that he is able to keep it against that day." And that in Phil. 1:21, "For me to live is Christ, and to die is gain," is interpreted, "On supposition [that] I live to Christ to the end of my days, then I shall live to Christ (or, for me to live will be Christ) and to die will be gain. Therefore, though I am uncertain whether I shall either live to Christ, or but that I shall go to hell when I die, yet I am in a strait between these two, not knowing which to choose, whether the gain of dying (and so to depart to be with Christ), or to live here, to live to Christ."

I won't charge upon you these absurd interpretations of Scripture; possibly I have misunderstood you when you speak of persons' being unable to say whether they shall persevere through future trials and about the Apostle's speaking in assured strain, on [your] supposition; though I am not able to find out how I should misunderstand you.

1. The opening discussion apparently relates to the *Affections*, Pt. II, sec. 11, on the assurance of one's good estate (*Works*, 2, 167–81).

And if it be as you say, that the apostle Paul expressed himself as uncertain about the state of his soul in the texts you cite, this is a full and clear proof of the thing you seem to deny, viz. that a saint may sometimes have an absolute assurance and yet afterwards be without. For this Apostle, before he uttered those words in Phil. 3:12–13, had abundantly spoken most positively and assuredly, and as one that was certain of his own sincere Christianity and future reward (II Cor. 4:8, 14–18, with 5:1–8, 16–17 and 6:1–11, 1:12, 21–22). And in I Thess. 2:1–10 he most solemnly appeals to God concerning his sincerity and holiness.[2]

Concerning that text in Gal. 2:20, you say, "I know that the Scripture speaks of Christ loving and dying, or giving himself, for those who yet are supposed never finally to obtain the benefits of his death." I shall not undertake in this letter to go through with the controversy about universal redemption and about the interpretation of those scriptures that speak of Christ's dying for all, etc. But I don't remember that the Apostle uses the very same words, of Christ's loving and giving himself, joined in like manner anywhere else, unless it be in Eph. 5:25, where they are used concerning that church of saints that are Christ's spouse, and his body, of his flesh and his bone. And 'tis certain that the Apostle, in this text in Galatians, don't speak of Christ's loving him and giving himself for him only as he might those that have no saving benefits of his death; because in the same sentence he speaks of saving benefits and consequences of Christ's loving him and giving himself for him just as Christ's living in him and his living by the faith of the son of God. And he speaks of those benefits with as much positiveness as of Christ's loving him and giving himself for him.

As to that text, II Pet. 1:10, I shall not pretend in this letter to enter into the controversy between Calvinists and Arminians about the meaning of the word "election" as it is used in the New Testament, whether it signifies a particular election as the Calvinists suppose, or only something general extending to all that live under the gospel, as you suppose the word is used here. Let that be as it will, I think it is plain as it is possible anything should be, by other words in the same sentence, that what the Apostle exhorts to "make sure" in this place is something special and saving.

You say the word *bebaios* is always in Scripture and in all other writings used to signify the certainty and stability of the thing itself, and never used to signify the assurance of knowledge. I am far from pre-

---

2. JE indicated that this paragraph should be inserted in the "last paper, last col.," i.e. the preceding page (now lost) of his letter.

tending to such an universal and perfect acquaintance not only with the Greek Testament but all other Greek writings, as to assert positively, as you do, that this word is used thus or thus always in 'em all, and never any otherwise. I know the word *bebaios* properly signifies "firm" or "sure." Yet I don't suppose there is anything in the Greek word, any more than the English word "firm," that hinders it being used for the firmness of evidence (or judgment, knowledge, or hope), or the firmness of a thing with regard to its evidence to the mind, any more than the firmness [of] the thing in itself. And however it is with all other Greek writings, yet if you had more fully examined the Greek Testament alone, and had not spoken at a venture, you would never have so positively asserted the contrary with regard to the use of the word there.

In II Cor. 1:7 'tis expressly used for the firmness of hope: "Our hope of you is steadfast (*bebaia*)." In Col. 2:7 'tis used for firmness of faith and so of the judgment, as it is also in Mark 16:20 and Heb. 2:3 and in I Cor. 1:6. In Heb. 6:16 the word is used not for ratifying and making things firm in themselves, but firm in their evidence to men's minds. And in Tit. 3:8 διαβεβαιοῦσθαι is put for affirming a thing as evident and certain. And the nature of the thing makes it evident, that the apostle Peter in this very text [II Pet. 1:10] does also use the word in this same sense, when he exhorts those he writes to to make their calling and election sure: not to make the thing firm and established in itself, but firm and sure as to the evidence of it. For neither their calling nor election (in any sense of the words) nor the saving benefits of them, could be made more firm in themselves than they were already, if they were true saints as the Apostle supposes (see v. 1 and 3:1), unless we hold falling from grace.

But if you hold this doctrine and this be the ground of your objection, I think you ought to have explained yourself on this head, that I might have known how to have replied to you in answer to this and other objections. But you not only say that this text is not to my purpose, but that it plainly makes against me; here I confess myself extremely at a loss what you should intend or have respect to, or which way you supposed the words not only did not make for me but against, and that plainly.

As to my saying that the Spirit of God in his saving operation communicates himself to the soul in his own proper nature,[3] implying, as you suppose, God's communicating his essence. After all that is said,

---

3. *Affections, Works*, 2, 201, 233, 236–37.

the objection is only about the use of language and propriety of expressions. It can't be anything else, for I have particularly explained my meaning and expressly declared what I do not mean, that by his proper nature I don't mean his essence; and have also declared particularly what I do mean, viz. that by the Spirit of God's communicating himself in his proper nature, I mean communicating something of his holiness. And this explanation I am careful to give immediately in the place where I first use the expression. And then, further to explain myself, say that "the grace which is in the hearts of the saints, is of the same nature with the divine holiness, as much as it is possible for that to be, which is infinitely less in degree."[4] So that the exceeding great objection is, that I in your opinion signify this that I declare to be my meaning by an improper expression; and if that be still a grand difficulty with you, I hope you will consider the matter more fully.

I confess, my skill in the English tongue does not extend so far as to discern the great impropriety of the word as I have used it. The word "nature" is not used only to signify the essence of a thing, but is used very variously. Chambers in his *Dictionary* observes on this word as follows: "'Nature' (*natura*, φύσις) is a term very variously used. Aristotle has a whole chapter wrote expressly to enumerate the various acceptations of the Greek word φύσις, rendered into English 'nature,' and among Latin writers the different acceptations are so many that a certain author reckons up fourteen or fifteen. Mr. Boyle, in a precise treatise of the vulgarly received notion of nature, gives us eight principal ones."[5] That property which is natural to anyone and is eminently his character, I think, is, without abuse of language or going cross to the common use of it, called his proper nature, though [it] is not just the same with his essence. Thus we say concerning an exceeding good-natured man, that ingenuity is his very nature. I think holiness may, without absurdity, be said to be the proper nature of the Holy Spirit on two accounts: (1) As 'tis his peculiar beauty and glory and so may in a special manner be called his nature, as brightness may in a peculiar manner be said to be the nature of the sun, and [as] that which is in a peculiar manner the nature of honey is its sweetness. (2) 'Tis the proper character of the Spirit above all other things, in that office and work of his wherein we are concerned with him. This is that in his nature which he especially manifests and exercises in his office, acts, and operations towards us; and therefore this in his nature is singled

4. Ibid., p. 202.
5. Chambers, *Cyclopedia*, 2, s.v. "Nature."

out from all other things to denote him by, as he is revealed [to] us; so his name by which he is called in Scripture is the *Holy* Ghost. And this is that in his nature which he communicates something of to the saints, and therefore is called by divines in general a communicable attribute; and the saints are made partakers of his holiness, as the Scripture expressly declares (Heb. 12:10), and that without imparting to them his essence.

Light and heat may in a special manner be said to be the proper nature of the sun: and yet none will say that everything to which the sun communicates a little of its light and heat has therefore communicated to it the essence of the sun, and is sunned with the sun, or becomes the same being with the sun, or becomes equal to that immense fountain of light and heat. A diamond or crystal that is held forth in the sun's beams may properly be said to have some of the sun's brightness communicated to it; for though it han't the same individual brightness with that which is inherent in the sun, and be immensely less in degree, yet it is something of the same nature.

I don't know that I have exceeded the due bounds of a writer in divinity, in expressing that communication that God makes to his saints of his holiness in the very forms that God himself does in his Word, in calling it their being made partakers of the divine nature; and I think the representation I have made of the matter is such as the Scriptures do abundantly warrant in innumerable texts that might be mentioned.

With regard to the objections you make against what I say about a new spiritual sense given to the hearts of the saints, etc., and [my] calling it a new principle, a new habit giving a person ability and disposition to exert the faculties of the soul in exercises of a new kind. This you say is properly to introduce a new faculty. You [. . . .]

[Jonathan Edwards.]

67. TO THE REVEREND JOHN MacLAURIN

Edwards interprets the Jacobite rebellion of 1745–46 in Scotland and England as a divine judgment and warning. The "public calamities" of this letter are events connected with that uprising. He sees a similar message in the epidemic at Louisburg and Indian raids in the American colonies.

His major suggestion, that the Concert for Prayer be extended for seven more years, was heeded. In turn, Edwards vigorously promoted the effort through his *Humble Attempt* and otherwise. Passing mention is made of the journals of David Brainerd, who was still on active missionary duty at the time the letter was written.

(Published as "An Extract of a Letter from the Reverend Mr. Edwards, Minister at Northampton, to a Reverend Minister at Glasgow," *CMH*, no. 10 [Jan. 1746], 296–99. Internal evidence in this letter and the letter which follows points to MacLaurin as the most probable recipient.)

* * *

Northampton, May 12, 1746

The accounts we have had from time to time of the public calamities that Scotland has been subject to by the late rebellion, have been very affecting; God's late dealings with that people have been in wholly and awful severity; manifesting his dreadful displeasure for the backslidings of the land, from the principles, spirit and practices of their forefathers, and for their so despising God's late great mercies, and opposing his Holy Spirit. The distresses you have been the subjects of, must needs be exceeding great; and I believe, such as it is not easy for persons at a distance, that have not felt them, fully to conceive of. I have thought much of you, dear Sir, and your dear brethren, ministers and people in and about Glasgow, since the beginning of these calamities: and long hoped that you would escape that degree of the public calamity, which other places were the subjects of, where the rebels came; but I perceive they have also been in Glasgow.

God has of late distinguished Scotland by his judgments from the neighboring kingdoms subject to the same crown; but his dispensations herein are not so much to be wondered at. God has of late been using the most gracious, gentle and blessed means for winning, drawing, and so reclaiming them; but being despised and rejected in them, he has now changed his hand, and used severity: but yet mercy has been mingled with severity, in that the land together with the rest of the British realm, has not been totally and finally given up into the possession of papists; so wholly removing their candlestick out of its place, we having lately heard that the rebellion is almost wholly suppressed; for which not only you, but we, and all Protestants, have great cause of thankfulness; especially all within the British dominions, which must all have fallen together under the calamity, if the Pretender [Prince Charles Edward Stuart] had gained his purpose.

May God graciously grant that his overflowing scourge that has passed through so great a part of Scotland, may be sanctified to the people, and cause them seriously to consider, and be sensible what is the accursed thing that troubles them, and bring them in good earnest to reflect upon themselves; and that it may be as a refining fire to the true friends of Christ and his interest, purely to purge away their dross, and to take away all their sin; and mightily to quicken and engage them unitedly and earnestly to cry to God for these general and abundant outpourings of his Spirit, which shall subdue all to God, and put an end to all calamities of this nature through the whole world.

And may God's late judgments on Scotland be sanctified to us in New England, and be for our warning, and to excite gratitude in us for God's distinguishing mercies. We have reason to admire God's patience towards us, that we are continued still in such a degree of quietness, and have lately been the subjects of some remarkable smiles, when God is chastening the people in Scotland with such severity; though our circumstances, mercies, privileges, and provocations have been, in so many respects, parallel with theirs, and our sins, in many respects, much more aggravated: not that we have been wholly without public frowns and judgments. We have been awfully frowned on in a sweeping sickness and mortality among our soldiers at Louisburg in Cape Breton, that I suppose has carried off near one half of the garrison, consisting of between two and three thousand. But we have no reason to wonder at it, considering our ingratitude after the receipt of God's goodness in so wonderfully delivering up the place into our hands: which ingratitude has been manifested in the great wickedness prevailing among the soldiers at Louisburg, and our continuing still in our backslidings in the land, without any remarkable alteration. Many families in the land have been made families of mourning, by the death of their friends at Louisburg; and, among others, a family nearly related to me by the death of the Reverend Mr. [Simon] Backus, my brother-in-law, minister of the gospel at Newington in Connecticut, who went to Cape Breton as chaplain to the Connecticut Regiment, and died there last February, having left my sister [Eunice Edwards Backus] a widow, with a family of small children, for whom I desire your prayers.

The French and Indians from Canada, begin early to molest us this spring; the last week they surprised and carried away three men from one of our furthest settlements next to Canada: and the last night we were alarmed with the news of their having beset, and, as is feared, destroyed a new town on the frontiers above the county, called the

Upper Ashuelot: the houses were seen in flames, and the guns heard
from the top of a mountain not far from the town. We in this town were
visited the last summer, fall and winter, with a sore sickness and mortality. There is reason to fear, that if we don't take warning and repent,
and turn from our evil ways, and neither mercies nor judgments will
reform us, that these calamities will prove but the forerunners of those
that are far more terrible, and we shall at last have put into our hand a
far more bitter cup than Scotland has had.

We have heard with grief of the death of the excellent Colonel
[James] Gardiner (of whom you give some account in your last letter),
who fell like a valiant soldier, faithfully doing his duty to God, his king
and country. Happy would it be for the British nation, if their soldiers
in general were like him, not only in valor, but piety!

With respect to the Concert for Prayer, for the pouring out of the
Spirit, the people in this town have of late more generally fallen in with
it. Before the last quarterly season, I preached on a subject tending to
excite to the duty of united prayer for a general outpouring of the
Spirit, endeavoring to persuade all to agree to the proposal from Scotland. What was delivered, seemed to have a great influence on the
congregation: and the first Tuesday of February last was pretty generally observed, in whole or part, as a day of prayer, in private societies,
for the forementioned blessing. I hope the Concert will be upheld in
Scotland and England, and that those who have engaged in it will not
give way to discouragement, but will be like Jacob, in wrestling till the
dawning of the day, though the night should be long and dark. And in
order to the promoting this affair in America, I would humbly propose this, dear Sir, as a proper expedient in order to it, viz. that the
Concert which, with respect to the term first agreed upon, expires the
next November, be renewed and continued for seven years, or, at least,
for a much longer time than what was specified in the former agreement, etc.

As to the state of religion in these ends of the earth, I know nothing
of any remarkable revival in any part of New England. I have lately
seen a journal of Mr. [David] Brainerd's, Scots' missionary to the Indians in Pennsylvania and New Jersey, giving indeed a very remarkable and wonderful account of his success, among these poor, ignorant
people the last summer and fall.[1] But as he is a missionary employed by
the Society in Scotland for Propagating Christian Knowledge, so his

1. Brainerd, *Mirabilia Dei inter Indicos* (Philadelphia, 1746).

journal has doubtless long ere now, been sent thither. I have also received some agreeable account of things getting into a better state on the east end of Long Island; but must refer you for particulars to my letter to Mr. [James] Robe.

I should be glad, dear Sir, if you would, in your next, send me some account of the state of religion in Scotland, and how it has been affected by the late troubles.

I have herewith sent you one of my books on *Religious Affections:* though we dwell at a great distance, one from another here in this world, yet that we may meet together often at the throne of grace here, and have a joyful meeting and eternal co-habitation before the throne of glory hereafter, is the desire and hope of, dear Sir, yours, etc.

[Jonathan Edwards.]

P.S. With respect to the invasion of Ashuelot by the Indians, mentioned in the foregoing letter; it has since proved, that but two Englishmen were killed, and but one taken, but seven houses burnt, and a barn: but the Indians from Canada have of late been continually molesting us, and distressing the new settlements on our borders towards Canada. We have almost daily news of mischief done by them, surprising particular persons, and some families, killing and taking captive, burning houses, and killing cattle. By what we hear it seems probable, that the French are greatly enraged by our taking Cape Breton, and encouraged by what they hear of the rebellion in Great Britain and also by an expectation of an invasion of Boston by a French fleet.

68. TO THE REVEREND WILLIAM McCULLOCH

The people of Scotland had suffered from the uprising led by the Young Pretender. Edwards expresses his sympathy, grateful that Cambuslang was spared. He notes that the Scriptures and history teach that triumph often follows times of tumult, so wonderful events should be expected after these trials. The Concert for Prayer will hasten them.

(Published as "Mr. Edwards's Letter to the Reverend Mr. McCulloch, Minister of the Gospel at Cambuslang," *CMH*, no. 10 [Jan. 1746], 299–302.)

*   *   *

Northampton, May 12, 1746

My dear Friend,

I want much to hear from you; and the more by reason of the great changes that have passed in Scotland, and the great and awful calamities that have come upon that land, since I last heard from you. What we have heard from time to time of the sore calamities and distresses of the poor people there, has been very affecting. But, doubtless those that have felt them, have quite another sense of them than those that only hear of them at a distance. What I have heard has been much more affecting to me, by reason of the correspondence I have been favored with, and the friendship I have by this means been engaged in, with some of the ministers in Scotland; that land has seemed nearer to me, and more as a land that I was interested in on this account; and I look upon my interest to be much the greater in it, because you, dear Sir, are in it. I want to hear how far you and your dear people have shared in the common calamity.

Whether it be more or less, yet there is abundant comfort for you, and all your friends, to be reaped from the consideration of God's late most gracious dealings with Cambuslang, together with the many exceeding great and precious promises that the holy Scriptures are full of, to those that have been the subjects of God's saving grace. From these promises we may learn, that surely it will be well with the righteous; they are in the secret place of the Most High, and dwell under the shadow of the Almighty; there is none like their God, who rideth upon the heaven in their help, and in his excellency on the sky; the eternal God is their refuge, and underneath are everlasting arms; they shall dwell in safety alone: happy are they; who is like unto them? A people saved of the Lord, the shield of their help, and the sword of their excellency. They need not fear, though the earth be removed, and the mountains carried into the midst of the sea.[1] God who foresaw the storm that was coming, has remembered his everlasting love, that is without beginning, to his elect people at Cambuslang, in the care he took of them while he held back the winds, and before he suffered the storm to come, by calling them into their strong refuge and safe hiding place, and sealing them in their foreheads, setting his own stamp and image on their souls; and has empowered you, dear Sir, as the angel that should be the instrument of it, having committed to you the seal of the living God. And, as we have great reason to be comforted concerning God's dear children in Cambuslang, and other parts of Scotland, with relation to the late great calamities God has brought upon that land, so we have no cause of discouragement concerning the church of God in general, in this day of great shaking and tumult. When we see

1. The preceding is a series of paraphrases of Prov. 11:10, Ps. 91:1, Deut. 33:26–29, and Ps. 46:2.

the world, as it were, in travail, and consider that he has the care and disposal of it, is the Covenant-God and heavenly Father, and Redeemer, and spouse of his church, and withal consider how many and abundant the promises are that he has made to his church, of things that he will accomplish for her in this world in the latter days; and also consider what time we are arrived at in the age of the world, we cannot reasonably but have great encouragement and hope with respect to the issue and event of things. Indeed, "it is not for" us "to know the times and seasons which the Father hath put in his own power" [Acts 1:7], but certainly there is much to animate and encourage prayer and hope in them that wait for the consolation of Israel, in the past and present aspect of divine providence; especially if it be considered, that great shakings and commotions have commonly preceded glorious changes in the state of the church of God: as there were great shakings of nations preceded the establishment of God's people in their rest in Canaan, after their cruel bondage in Egypt; so great commotions and revolutions in the kingdoms of the world preceded the return of God's church from the Babylonish captivity. And God did as it were shake the heavens and the earth, the sea and the dry land; he shook all nations, before the introduction of the new and more glorious state of his church, under the Christian dispensation, by Christ and his apostles: so the introduction of the peaceful state of the church, in the days of Constantine the Great, is represented Rev. 6 as being attended with a great earthquake, and stars falling from heaven, etc. And the rising and ascending of the witnesses at the Reformation, is also spoken of as attended with a great earthquake. One thing that especially gives hopes with respect to the issue of the present commotions, is, that God hath lately stirred up so many of his people in Scotland, and some other places, to enter into such a Concert for united prayer for the fulfillment of the glorious promises God has made of an abundant outpouring of his Spirit in the latter days. If at the same time that the creation (that "waiteth for the manifestation of the sons of God" [Rom. 8:19]) appears especially in travail, the church of God appears remarkably as a woman with child, crying, and travailing in birth, and pained to be delivered, wrestling and agonizing with God in prayer, for the promised blessing, there is the more reason to hope that the time is nigh, when she shall bring forth that man-child that is to rule all nations. The prayers of God's people will not be in vain. The prayers of the saints in Scotland began to be offered up, while it was yet a time of silence and peace; and I hope with much incense offered by the angel of the covenant, on the golden altar before the throne. And since that the time of silence and peace has come to an end; the angel has taken the censer, and filled it with the fire of God's wrath, and cast it on the earth, and there have followed voices, and thunders, and lightnings, and an earthquake. But it is greatly to be desired, that God's people should persevere, and continue instant in prayer without discouragement, waiting and hoping for the salvation of the Lord. Certainly at such a day they should increase and abound more and more in faith and fervency in their cries to God, and not to faint, though they have lately been so greatly afflicted, remembering these words of Christ, John 16:20–21, "Ye shall reap and lament, and shall be sorrowful; but your sorrow shall be turned into joy. A woman when she is in travail hath sorrow, because her hour is come: but as soon as she is delivered of the child, she remembereth no more the anguish, for joy that a man is born into the world."

I desire you, dear Sir, to consider of a proposal I have made in my letter to Mr. [John] MacLaurin, respecting the Concert for Prayer, and in order to the promoting it in America, I desire your candid acceptance of my discourse on *Religious Affections,* which I have herewith sent to you.

I should be glad to hear what share you and your people have had in the late troubles. I hope, dear Sir, that you will remember New England in your prayers, praying for the continued exercise of that wonderful patience and long suffering that God has exercised towards us hitherto, and by which he has so distinguished us from Scotland, though no less ill-deserving.

My wife and children join with me in most respectful salutations to you and yours. Remember, dear Sir, that a particular interest in your prayers will be highly prized by,

Your most engaged, loving friend and brother,
Jonathan Edwards.

69. TO THE REVEREND JOSEPH BELLAMY

The Reverend Joseph Bellamy, minister of Bethlehem, Connecticut, was a devoted admirer of Edwards' and one of his closest friends. The bonds between the two were intellectual, theological, and social. Here Edwards seeks Bellamy's practical assistance in raising a flock of sheep. This letter is the first in a sequence on the subject that lasts seven years.

(Beinecke Library, ALS, two quarto leaves, addressed on verso to Mr. Joseph Bellamy at Bethlehem. Published in *NEQ* 1 [1928], 232–33.)

* * *

Northampton, October 3, 1746

Dear Sir,

I have been for some time past in expectation of seeing you here. And though you are not yet come, I hope it will not be long for it. I want to see you very much.

We had some talk with you the last year, concerning buying and letting out some sheep for us; and you was so kind as to put yourself to some trouble for us, and to send us word of an opportunity there was. But having then engaged my brother [Seth] Wetmore, I could not accept the offer that you gave us an account of. But brother Wetmore has failed of procuring for us such a number of sheep as we expected. I should therefore be glad to procure and let out a score of sheep your way; and so would desire you to make some inquiry, and take some pains to know whether any sheep are to be bought, and at what lay, and send me word by the first opportunity. I have the money ready to lay down, and would have enclosed it in this letter, if I were sure of an opportunity of buying your way. But upon an intimation from you, will send the money directly, that you may have it to lay down. I am sensible that in such cases, it is a great advantage for the buyer to have money in his hands; and therefore I am willing, if you buy for us, that you should have this advantage.

I have of late made considerable inquiry, and understand that good sheep are not commonly sold for more than twenty-five pound a score. But I hope to have an opportunity soon to see you in these parts, not only on this, but on some other accounts. And as I understand you have intended a journey here, so I hope you will not fail of it. I am, dear Sir,

Your brother and affectionate friend,
Jonathan Edwards.

70. TO THE REVEREND PHILEMON ROBBINS

Philemon Robbins, minister of the church at Branford, Connecticut, incurred the wrath of the Old Lights by his ardent support of the awakening. Immediately prior to this letter, the local New Haven Consociation had found him "criminally guilty" of questionable conduct and a year later would depose him as pastor. However, because the consociation could not dictate policy to individual churches, the loyal congregation ignored these actions and continued him as minister until his death in 1781.

This letter is of special interest because, three and a half years before Edwards' crisis at Northampton, it predicts strategies he himself would follow: secure as large a council as possible, endeavor to bring in Boston clergy, and publish a full account of the proceedings. Robbins took the counsel to heart.

(CHS, A. R. and P. Robbins Coll., ALS, one folio leaf, letter cover on recto, addressed to the Reverend Philemon Robbins at Branford. See also SIB, *8*, 616–27; Philemon Robbins, *A Plain Narrative of the Proceedings . . . against the Reverend Mr. Robbins of Branford* [Boston, 1747].)

* * *

Northampton, November 3, 1746

Rev. and Dear Sir,

The account you gave me in your letter was very affecting to me; but I received it when it was too late for me to write an answer that should reach you before the appointed meeting of the Consociation, being from home on a journey to Long Island when the letter came to my house, so that I had it not till the day that the Consociation was appointed to meet; and don't know the present circumstances of the affair, only as I lately learned something from Mr. [Joseph] Bellamy, who was here about a fortnight ago.

From all that I can learn of the affair, it appears to me by no means advisable for you to lay down your ministry at Branford, if the major part of the people will stand by you. And if there could be any hope of obtaining a council of churches from towards Boston (including at least three or four of the Boston churches) on representing the affair to them, to come and give you and your church their advice upon it, I should think it would be richly worth the while, and to obtain as large a council as you can. I believe the ministers that way would be very loath to be at the trouble; but if you and your church should apply to 'em, and fairly represent the case, I can't see how they excuse themselves to God and their own consciences in refusing, or how they could reconcile their so doing with many of the rules of God's holy Word, I mean Christian rules of equity, charity, and love to our neighbors as ourselves and pity and relief to the oppressed, etc. There are many of the ministers that way that can't but know the many oppressive measures that have been, and are, from time to time gone into in Connecticut. And shall we never hear the cry of the oppressed, when it is in the power of our hands to do something for their help, but let 'em lie and sink under their oppressions without remedy?

However, if this that I have proposed ben't feasible, I can think of nothing better than something that Mr. Bellamy proposed, viz. that you and your church should apply yourselves to the two associations or consociations of Fairfield County, laying your case before them, and desiring them to give you their judgment, whether you are properly under Saybrook Platform or no, and whether you are bound to submit to the acts and proceedings of the ministers and churches of your county towards you that have been regulated by that platform, since you have publicly renounced it, and also openly denied the jurisdiction of said ministers and churches. And whether you take this or the other course, it appears to me highly needful that a narrative of the whole affair should be published. But others that know more of the present state of your affairs are under greater advantage to give you proper advice.

However, since you have been pleased to ask my thoughts, I desire my good will in what I have written, who am, dear Sir,

>Your affectionate and compassionate brother and servant,
>Jonathan Edwards.

71. TO ESTHER EDWARDS

Edwards' daughters, Sarah and Esther, eighteen and fourteen years old, respectively, were living in East Hampton, Long Island, in 1746. They had probably been there since their father preached the ordination sermon for the Reverend Samuel Buell on September 19, 1746. Extended visits among family and friends were common, and Buell, from the time of his apprenticeship at Northampton, had been regarded as one of the family. At home, wars and alarms marked the year. Soldiers were billeted around town, including at the parsonage. Edwards seeks to reassure his children in their refuge.

(Houghton Library, Autograph File, ALS, one oversize quarto leaf. See also Trumbull, 2, 147–50; and Edwards' Account Book entries for Sept. 30, Oct. 2, and Nov. 3, 1746, Beinecke Library.)

* * *

Mrs. Aaron Burr (Esther Edwards Burr), anonymous, undated, Yale University Art Gallery, bequest of Oliver Burr Jennings

Northampton, November 3, 1746

Dear Child,

We lately received a letter from you dated October 13, and another from Sarah dated October 22, and were much refreshed to hear from you. I not long since wrote a letter to you both, and sent it to Mr. [John] Potwine's for conveyance, and therewith your mother sent an[other][1] for Sarah, as she now with this sends one to you, to be conveyed in like manner.

We are all through mercy in a tolerable state of health. Our house is now forted in, and a watch is kept here every night in the fort, but there has been no mischief done by the enemy in this county, since the taking of Massachusetts Fort.[2] I am ready to think the French and Indians have lately turned their course another way, down towards Annapolis [Nova Scotia], to join the French fleet. But we have lately heard that that fleet have lately been totally confounded by a remark-

1. Conjecture for where MS is damaged.
2. The fort was attacked by the French and Indians on Aug. 19, 1746, and captured. Trumbull, 2, 147–48.

able hand of God against them, in storms and sore sickness; so that they have been quite discouraged and are gone back again, after the two chief men had killed themselves, through melancholy and vexation. 'Tis exceeding wonderful and affecting that God should so appear for so sinful and unworthy a people, to defend us from our enemies and confound them.

We all give our love to you and Sarah. Give mine and your mother's love to Mr. [Joseph] Osborn and his wife [Hannah Hedges Osborn]. I would not have you be discouraged and melancholy, though you are far from home; God is everywhere, and I hope you will walk closely with him, and will have much of his presence. Your circumstances at East Hampton are on some accounts much more comfortable than [those] of your sisters at home, for you lie down and arise and have none to make you afraid. Here we have been in much fear of an army suddenly rushing in upon the town in the night to destroy it. We daily remember you in our prayers to God, who I hope will be with you continually and will in every respect be gracious to you. I am, my dear child,

> Your affectionate father,
> Jonathan Edwards.

72. TO THE REVEREND ROBERT ABERCROMBIE

Abercrombie, a neighboring minister and dependable ally of Edwards', was a founder of the Boston Presbytery of the Presbyterian Church. This is the only known correspondence between Abercrombie and Edwards.

(Beinecke Library, ALS, in "Hebrew Idioms" notebook, one quarto leaf, addressed on verso to the Reverend Robert Abercrombie at Pelham. See also Parmenter, pp. 294–319.)

* * *

> January 8, 1746/7

Rev. and Dear Sir,

I wrote to you a little while ago, desiring you, if you went speedily to Boston, to inquire of Captain McCun[1] for some pamphlets and letters, that I understood were sent me from Scotland, that I had not received, and to bring them with you. I hear you have been to Boston and are

---

1. The captain of a merchant vessel that sailed regularly into Boston. *A Report of the Record Commissioners of the City of Boston, Containing the Boston Marriages from 1700 to 1751* (Boston, 1898), p. 134, lists a George Maccane (McChune), who married Jane Callwell on Jan. 25, 1727.

lately returned. I shall be glad if you would write me word, by the first good opportunity, how you found; and if you brought me any letters or pamphlets, send them; for I want them very much.

Please also to send me word how long it will be 'ere Captain McCun and Captain Scot set sail for Scotland. Herein you'll oblige

Your brother and servant,
Jonathan Edwards.

73. TO THE REVEREND JOSEPH BELLAMY

In a leisurely manner, Edwards moves between business and scholarly affairs, discussing the purchase of sheep and sharing some of his favorite reading with an attentive disciple. He gives early notice of his work on *Freedom of the Will* and sends information about the Concert for Prayer, though mentioning neither by name. Edwards seeks to confer with Bellamy on "many affairs," and invites him either to visit or send further comment.

(Beinecke Library, ALS, one quarto leaf, addressed on verso to the Reverend Dr. Joseph Bellamy at Bethlehem in Connecticut. Published in *NEQ* 1 [1928], 228–32; *PMHS*, ser. 2, XV [1901–02], 12–14.)

* * *

Northampton, January 15, 1746/7

Dear Sir,

I received your letter by Mr. [Job] Strong this day. Mr. [John] Searle was here at my house presently after, and I gave your questions to him, and told him the bearer intended quickly to return.

(As to the affair of sheep, I am much obliged to you for the pains you have taken. I believe you have acted the part of a trusty friend therein. I suppose it is known by this time, whether the man that went to Newtown has succeeded. If he has, and the sheep are bought, we shall rest in what you have done; but if not, and you shall have found no opportunity till this letter reaches you, it is so late in the year, that I desire you would keep the money till shearing time is over and then buy; when I suppose they may be bought much cheaper than now. But I would pray you to send us word by the first opportunity, that if we are not like to have any sheep this year, we may seasonably be looking out, and laying in for wool elsewhere, for the supply of the family. In the spring, if you can give us any encouragement, I should be glad to lay out £60 more for sheep in those parts, as soon as shearing time is over, besides the £30 you have in your hands. But only, if you buy so many sheep for us, it might be perhaps expedient, on some accounts, for the present, not to let it be known who the sheep are for.)

As to the books you speak of: Mastricht is sometimes in one volume, a very thick, large quarto; sometimes in two quarto volumes. I believe it could not be had new under eight or ten pounds. Turretin is in three volumes in quarto, and would probably be about the same price.[1] They are both excellent. Turretin is on polemical divinity; on the Five Points, and all other controversial points; and is much larger in these than Mastricht; and is better for one that desires only to be thoroughly versed in controversies. But take Mastricht for divinity in general, doctrine, practice, and controversy; or as an universal system of divinity; and it is much better than Turretin or any other book in the world, excepting the Bible, in my opinion. I have thoughts of sending, myself, this year, to England for a few books, and have written to Mr. [Edmund] Quincy, a merchant in Boston, about it, to desire his advice and assistance, as to the course to be taken to obtain 'em. If I employ him to send for me, I shall be willing to serve you, as I desire you to serve me about the sheep. I am willing to take your money and put it with my own, and put your books into my catalogue and have the books all come as mine; or shall be willing to serve you, if I can in any respect, by writing to my correspondents in Scotland.

I have been reading Whitby, which has engaged me pretty thoroughly in the study of the Arminian controversy; and I have writ considerably upon it in my private papers. I must entreat you, if possible, to borrow for me Dr. Stebbing, on the Spirit.[2] I had rather pay something for the use of it, than not have some considerable opportunity with it. I have got so deep into this controversy, that I am not willing to dismiss it, till I know the utmost of their matters.

I have very lately received a packet from Scotland, with the several copies of a Memorial, for the continuing and propagating an agreement for joint prayer for the general revival of religion; three of which I here send you, desiring you to dispose of two of 'em where they will

1. The books referred to are Peter van Mastrict, *Theoretica-Practica Theologia*, ed. nova (Utrecht, 1699); and Francis Turretin, *Institutio Theologiæ Elencticæ* (3 vols. Geneva, 1679–85).

2. Daniel Whitby, *A Discourse Concerning I. The True Import of the Words Election and Reprobation. II. The Extent of Christ's Redemption. III. The Grace of God. IV. The Liberty of the Will. V. The Perseverance or Deflectability of the Saints* (London, 1710); and Henry Stebbing, *Treatise Concerning the Operations of the Holy Spirit* (London, 1719).

be most serviceable.[3] For my part, I heartily wish it was fallen in with by all Christians from the rising to the setting sun.

I have returned you Mr. Dickinson's book, but must pray you [to] let me have further opportunity with Dr. Johnson's.[4] If you could inquire of Dr. Johnson, or Mr. [John] Beach, or some other, and find out what is the best book on the Arminian side, for the defense of their notion of free will; and whether there be any better and more full than Whitby, I should be glad; provided you have convenient opportunity. I don't know but I shall publish something after a while on that subject.

Dear Sir, we have so many affairs to confer upon that concern us both, that I would propose that you should come this way again in February or March. You han't a great family to tie you at home as I have. But if you can't come, I must desire you to write fully and largely on all the foregoing particulars of this letter. Herein you will oblige, your cordial and affectionate friend and brother,

Jonathan Edwards.

P.S. It now comes to my mind that I heard that Dr. [Joseph] Pynchon of Longmeadow has Turretin, and that he lately offered to change them away for other books; so that in all probability you may there have those books at a moderate price.

74. TO THE REVEREND WILLIAM McCULLOCH

Edwards sees the divine hand in current English military victories as much as in those of ancient Israel. For him, they fulfill the prophecy in Revelation concerning the pouring out of the sixth vial. He will expand that theme during the year 1747, in the *Humble Attempt*. Edwards agrees with his Scottish friend McCulloch that the Concert for Prayer will hasten the coming of God's glorious day.

(Trask Library, ALS, two quarto leaves; also Dwight ms. transcript. Published in Dwight ed., *1*, 230–32. On the pouring out of the sixth vial, see *Works*, 5, 45–46, 82–85, 298–305, 412–21.)

* * *

3. JE included the Memorial as part of the introduction to *An Humble Attempt*. See *Works*, 5, 324–28.

4. Jonathan Dickinson, *Vindication of God's Sovereign Free Grace* (Boston, 1746); Samuel Johnson, *Letter from Aristocles to Authades Concerning the Sovereignty and the Promises of God* (Boston, 1745).

Northampton, January 21, 1746/7

Rev. and Dear Brother,

The time seems long to me since I have received a letter from you; I have had two letters from each of my other correspondents in Scotland since I have had any from you. Our correspondence has been to me very pleasant; and I am very loath it should fail.

Great changes have been, dear Sir, since I last had a letter from you; and God has done great things both in Scotland and America; though not of the same nature with those that were wrought some years ago, by the outpourings of his Spirit; yet those wherein his providence is on many accounts exceedingly remarkable: in Scotland, in the suppression of the late rebellion; and in America, in our preservation from the great French armada from Brest,[1] and their utter disappointment and confusion, by the immediate and wonderful hand of heaven against them, without any interposition of any arm of flesh: the nearest akin to God's marvelous works of old in defense of his people, in Moses', Joshua's and Hezekiah's time, perhaps of any that have been in these latter ages of the world. I have been writing some account of it to Mr. [John] MacLaurin; but since that, I have seen a Thanksgiving sermon of Mr. [Thomas] Prince's preached on that occasion;[2] in which is a much more distinct, particular, and (I suppose) exact account of the matter (which sermon you will doubtless see). Though there is something that I observed in my letter to Mr. MacLaurin, of the coming of that fleet, its being overruled for our preservation in this part of the land where I dwell, when eminently exposed, and when we have all reason to think our enemies in Canada had formed designs against us, that Mr. Prince does not mention.

In my last letter to you, I wrote you some thoughts and notions I had entertained concerning the pouring out of the sixth vial on the River Euphrates, and the approach of the happy day of the church's prosperity and glory, and the utter destruction of Antichrist, and other enemies of the church, so often spoken of in the holy Scripture. I signified it as what appeared to me probable, that one main thing

1. Duke d'Anville led a French fleet, intent on recapturing Louisburg, conquering Annapolis, Nova Scotia, and wreaking havoc on New England. The original fleet was so decimated by storms and sickness, and disheartened by the death of its commander, that its remnant sailed home without taking any action. Fr. J. Michaud, *Biographie Universelle, Ancienne et Moderne* (Graz, rep. 1966), 2, 97.

2. *The Salvation of God in 1746*, a sermon preached on Nov. 27, 1746, and published that year in Boston.

intended by the drying up the River Euphrates, was the drying up the temporal supplies and incomes of the Antichristian church and kingdom; and suggested it to consideration, whether God's appearing so wonderfully for the taking Cape Breton, and the American fishery thereon depending, out of the hands of the French, and thereby drying up so great a fountain of the wealth of the kingdom of France, and of supply of all popish countries with fish, might not be looked upon as one effect of the sixth vial. I would now also propose it to be considered, whether God's so extraordinarily appearing to baffle the great attempt of the French nation to repossess themselves of this place, ben't some confirmation of it; and whether or no the almost ruining French East India trade, by the dreadful hand of heaven, in burning their stores at Port L'Orient, and the taking so many of their ships by Commodore [Curtis] Barnett, and also the taking so many of their South Sea ships, vastly rich, and several other things of like nature that might be mentioned, mayn't probably be further effects of this vial.

But whatever be thought of these particular events, and the application of prophecies to them, yet it appears to me that God's late dealings, both with Great Britain and the American plantations, if they be duly considered, as they are in themselves and their circumstances, afford just reason to hope that a day is approaching for the peculiar triumphs of divine mercy and sovereign grace, over all the unworthiness and most aggravated provocations of men. If it be considered what God's past dealings have been with England and Scotland, for two centuries past; what obligations he has laid those nations under; and particularly the mercies bestowed more lately; and we then well consider the kind, manner, and degree of the provocations and wickedness of those nations, and yet that God so spares them, and has of late so remarkably delivered them, when so exposed to deserved destruction; and if it be also considered what God's dealings have been with this land, in its first settlement, and from its beginning hitherto, and how long we have been revolting and growing worse; and what great mercy he has lately granted us, in the late remarkable strivings of his Spirit with us, and how his Spirit has been treated, his mercy and grace despised, and bitterly opposed; how greatly we have backslidden; what a degree of stupidity we are sunk into; and how full the land has been of such kinds of wickedness, as have approached so near to the unpardonable sin against the Holy Ghost; and how obstinate we are still in our wickedness, without the least appearances of repentance or reformation; and it be then considered how God has of late made his arm bare, in almost miraculous dispensations of his providence in our behalf, to succeed us against our enemies, and defend us from them: I say, if these things be considered, it appears evident to me, not only that God's mercies are infinitely above the mercies of men; but also that he has in these things gone quite out of the usual course of his providence, and manner of dealing with his professing people. And I confess it gives me great hope that God's appointed time is approaching for the triumphs and displays of his infinite, sovereign grace, beyond all that ever has been before, from the beginning of the world. At least I think there is much in these things, considered together with other remarkable things God has lately done, to encourage and animate God's people unitedly to cry to God that he would appear for the bringing on those glorious effects of his mercy, so often foretold to be in the latter days; and particularly to continue that Concert for Prayer, set on foot in Scotland, and which it is now proposed to continue for seven years longer.

My wife and children join with me in respectful, cordial salutations to you and yours. That we all may be remembered in your prayers, is the request, dear Sir, of

Your most affectionate brother,
Jonathan Edwards.

75. TO THE REVEREND ROBERT BRECK

In eighteenth-century New England, most cases of church discipline were handled quietly by the pastor and a committee. When charges were made, there would be a private hearing; and a confession would be followed by forgiveness as a matter of course. Fornication and drunkenness were the chief offenses; the former was usually settled by marriage and baptism of the baby (the proof of the crime), the latter by promise of sobriety.

Thomas Wait, accused of fornication and found guilty by the Northampton church, appealed the verdict to a council of ministers. Hence, Edwards summons a neighboring clergyman for the meeting. Wait steadfastly maintained his innocence, questioned the basis of taking one person's word over another's, and raised the question of double jeopardy. The plaintiff, Lt. John Miller, spoke on behalf of his daughter Jemima Miller. Wait married Rachel Smith a year later.

(BPL, Chamberlain Mss., ALS, one quarto leaf, addressed on verso to the Reverend Robert Breck of Springfield. See Wait's letter to Edwards of Mar. 9,

1746/7 in Beinecke Library, ALS frag., in sermons on Matt. 12:41 [May 1747] and Titus 3:2 [May 22, 1747].)

*   *   *

Northampton, April 7, 1747

Rev. and Dear Sir,

Thomas Wait of this town, having been judged by this church to be guilty of the sin of fornication, has desired liberty of an appeal to a council of ministers; which the church has allowed him. He desired that the council might consist of ministers without any messengers.

The ministers fixed on are Mr. [Samuel] Hopkins and you, Mr. [Jonathan] Ashley of Deerfield, Mr. [Timothy] Woodbridge of Hatfield, and Mr. [Chester] Williams of Hadley. The time is Thursday the last day of April, to meet at the meetinghouse, at one o'clock in the afternoon. The place where the council is to be provided for and entertained is Asa Wright's. I desire you would come without fail, and be here before noon.

The number of the chosen council is but small, and if some should fail, the design might fail. This, with humble service to Madam, is from your

Brother and servant,
Jonathan Edwards.

76. TO THE REVEREND JOSEPH BELLAMY

In the midst of a year full of study, writing, and domestic distractions, Edwards finds time to locate and forward two volumes to his protégé. In 1747 Edwards' daughter Elizabeth was born on May 6; David Brainerd died on October 9; and the manuscript of the *Humble Attempt* was written and sent to the printer. Edwards' chief concern, however, is for Brainerd and Eleazar Wheelock, both long-time friends of Bellamy's.

(Beinecke Library, ALS, one quarto leaf. Published in *NEQ* 1 [1928], 234–35. Possibly a response to Bellamy's letter to Edwards of Apr. 5, 1747, Beinecke Library, ALS frag., one duodecimo leaf.)

*   *   *

Northampton, June 11, 1747

Dear Sir,

I herewith send you Mastrict, and one volume of Turretin. If you have one of Mr. Beach's and Dr. Johnson's left,[1] I should be glad if you would lend them to me, after you have used 'em sufficiently yourself, and send 'em by some safe hand. I also desire you would send me word what that man has done, that was depended on for buying sheep, etc. I have thought since I saw you whether it would not be proper in the bonds that are taken of the men that hire the sheep, instead of their obliging themselves to deliver so much wool at Mr. [John] Potwine's, to say at Mr. Potwine's, or such other house in Hartford as I shall appoint, that in case Mr. Potwine should die or remove from Hartford, the bond may still oblige them to deliver the wool at Hartford. Give my service to your spouse.

And I hope you will think of what talk we had of your taking a journey in the fall, for the interest of religion. Mr. [David] Brainerd has lately been at my house with Mr. [Eleazar] Wheelock. Mr. Wheelock is very poorly and not able to preach, and so has been for some time; 'tis uncertain whether he [will] ever preach more. Mr. Brainerd is far from being so broken in his understanding, as I have heard. He is capable of conversing very agreeably, and praying in the family most admirably. He is now gone to Boston with my daughter Jerusha. She intends to stay in Boston about a fortnight while Mr. Brainerd goes to the eastward, and then he is to return with her hither again.

Mr. Brainerd is a very desirable man indeed; I am glad I have had such an opportunity of acquaintance with him. Physicians speak of the state of his bodily constitution as very dangerous and difficult, and Dr. [Samuel] Mather of this town gives him over, but Dr. [Joseph] Pynchon is not so positive that he will not recover. For my part I cannot but have some hopes of his recovery. I think it is what all that know him should earnestly pray for. I am, dear Sir,

Your obliged friend and brother,
Jonathan Edwards.

P.S. Please to send me a few lines by the man that comes for Mr. [John] Searle.

1. Probably John Beach, *A Sermon, Shewing, that Eternal Life is God's Free Gift, Bestowed Upon Men According to Their Moral Behaviour* (Newport, 1745); and Samuel Johnson, *Letter from Aristocles to Authades.*

77. TO CALEB CLARK

(Beinecke Library, in "Efficacious Grace" notebook II, n.d. The location of the books that Edwards wanted may have been New Haven; the time, prior to Job Strong's graduation from Yale in 1747.)

* * *

[Northampton, before September 1747]

Mr. Clark,

If you are not like to be overloaden in coming home, I should be glad if you could bring some books belonging to Mr. Darling for me. If you can bring 'em, and speak to Job Strong about 'em, he knows what they be and will procure 'em for you.

Jonathan Edwards.

78. TO THE REVEREND THOMAS GILLESPIE

Edwards, in his theological element, responds to a range of questions arising from *Religious Affections.* At the outset, he explores the complex interconnections of faith and knowledge, love and duty. After a brief consideration of falling from grace, he turns his attention in the last half of the letter to Rom. 8:28, with its many implications for Christian living.

(Trask Library, ALS, six quarto leaves, addressed on verso to the Reverend Thomas Gillespie at Carnock, Scotland. Published in *Edinburgh Quarterly Magazine* 1 [1798], 109–24; Dwight ed., *1*, 232–42; *Works,* 2, 478–89.)

* * *

Northampton, September 4, 1747

Rev. and Dear Sir,

I received your letter of November 24, 1746, though very long after it was written. I thank you for it, and for your offering me a correspondence with you. Such an offer I shall gladly embrace, and esteem it a great privilege, more especially from the character I have received of you from Mr. [Robert] Abercrombie, who I perceive was intimately acquainted with you.

As to the objections you make against some things contained in my late book on *Religious Affections*, I am sorry you did not read the book through, before you made them; if you had, perhaps the difficulties would not have appeared quite so great. As to what is contained in the 175th and 176th pages, I suppose there is not the least difference of opinion between you and me, unless it be concerning the signification and propriety of expressions. I am fully of your mind, and always was, without the least doubt of it,

> That every one, both saint and sinner, is indispensably bound, at all seasons, by the divine authority, to believe instantly on the Lord Jesus, and that the command of the Lord (I John 3:23), that we should believe on the name of his Son Jesus Christ, as 'tis a prescription of the moral law, no less binds the sinner to immediate performance, than the commandment not to kill, to keep the sabbath day, or any other duty, as to the present performance of which, in way of duty, all agree the sinner is bound; and that men are bound to trust the divine faithfulness, be their case, with respect to light or darkness, sight, etc. what it will; and that no situation they can be in, looses them from obligation to glorify the Lord at all seasons, and expecting the fulfillment of his words;

and that the sinner that is without spiritual light or sight is bound to believe, and that it is a duty that [*is*] *at that very time* incumbent upon him to believe. But I conceive that there is a great deal of difference between these two things, viz. its being a man's duty that is without spiritual light or sight to believe, and its being his duty to believe without spiritual light or sight, or to believe while he yet remains without spiritual light or sight: just the same difference that is between these two things, viz. its being his duty that has no faith to believe, and its being his duty to believe without faith, or to believe without believing. I trust there is none will assert the latter, because of the contradiction that it implies. As 'tis not proper to say, 'tis a man's duty to believe without faith, because it implies a contradiction, so I think it equally improper to say 'tis a man's duty to believe without those things that are essentially implied in faith, because that also implies a contradiction. But a spiritual sight of Christ or knowledge of Christ is essentially implied in the very nature and notion of faith; and therefore 'tis absurd to talk of believing in Christ without spiritual light or sight. 'Tis the duty of a man that is without those things that essentially belong to faith, to believe; and 'tis the duty of a man that is without those things that essentially belong to love, to love God; because 'tis an indispensable obligation that lies on all men at all times, and in all circumstances, to love God: but yet 'tis not a duty to love God without loving him, or yet continuing without those things that essentially belong to his love. 'Tis the duty of those that have no sense of the loveliness of God, and have no esteem of him, to love him; and they ben't in the least excused by the want of this sense and esteem, in not loving him one moment; but yet it would be properly nonsense to say 'tis his duty to love him without any sense of his loveliness or any esteem of him. Though it be his duty this moment to come out of his disesteem and stupid wicked insensibility of his loveliness, and love him. I made the distinction, I thought, very plainly, in the midst of those sentences you quote as exceptionable. I say expressly, p. 175, "It is truly the duty of those who are thus in darkness, to come out of darkness into light and believe; but that they should confidently believe and trust, while they yet remain without spiritual light or sight, is an antiscriptural and absurd doctrine." The misunderstanding between us, dear Sir, I suppose to lie in the different application of the particle *without,* in my use of it, and your understanding of it, or what we understand as spoken of and supposed, *without* spiritual light or sight. As I use it, I apply it to the act of believing, and I suppose it to be very absurd to talk of an act of faith *without* spiritual light and sight; wherein I suppose you will allow me to be in the right of it. As you understand it, it is applied to duty or obligation, and you suppose it to be not at all absurd to talk of an obligation to faith without spiritual light or sight, but that the obligation remains full where there is no spiritual light or sight; wherein I allow you are in the right. I think, Sir, if you read what I have said in my book on this head again, it will be exceeding apparent to you, that 'tis thus that I apply the preposition *without,* and not as you before understood it. I thought I had very plainly manifested that what I meant by *being in darkness* was a being in spiritual blindness, and so in a dead, stupid, carnal and unchristian frame and way, and not what is commonly called a being without the light of God's countenance, under the hidings of his face, etc. We have a great number of people in these parts that go on that supposition, in their notions and practice, that there really is such a thing as such a manner of believing, such a kind of faith as this, viz. a confident believing and firm trusting in God in the dark, in the sense mentioned, that is to be sought after, and is the subject matter of divine prescription, and which many actually have. And indeed there are innumerable instances of such as are apparently in a most senseless, careless, negligent, apostate, and every way unchristian and wicked frame, that yet, encouraged by this principle, do retain an exceeding strong confidence of their good state, and count that herein they do their duty, and give much glory to God, under the notion of trusting God in the dark, and hoping against hope, and not trusting in their own righteousness; and they suppose it would show a legal spirit to do otherwise. I thought it would be manifest to every reader that I was arguing against such a sort of people.

You say, "It merits consideration whether the believer should ever doubt of his state, on any account whatever, because doubting, as opposed to believing, is absolutely sinful." Here, Sir, you seem to suppose that a person's doubting of his own good estate, is the proper opposite of faith, and these and some other expressions in your letter seem to suppose that doubting of one's good estate and unbelief is the same thing, and so, that being confident of one's good estate and faith are the same thing; which I acknowledge I don't understand; I don't take faith, and [a] person's believing that they have faith, to be the same thing: nor do I take unbelief, or being without faith and doubting whether they have it, to be the same thing, but entirely different. I should have been glad either you had taken a little more notice of what I say on this head, pp. 177–178, or said something to convince me that I am wrong in this point. *The exercise of faith is doubtless the way to be delivered from darkness, deadness, backsliding, etc.,* or rather is the deliverance; as forsaking sin is the way to deliverance from sin, and is the deliverance itself. The exercise of grace is doubtless the way to deliverance from a graceless frame, that consists in the want of the exercise of grace. But as to what you say, or seem to intimate, of a person's being confident of his own good estate, as being the way to be delivered from darkness, deadness, backsliding and prevailing iniquity, I think, whoever supposes this to be God's method of delivering his saints, when sunk into an evil, careless, carnal and unchristian frame, first to assure 'em of their good estate and his favor, while they yet remain in such a frame, and so to make that the means of their deliverance, does surely mistake God's method of dealing with such persons. Among all the multitudes I have had opportunity to observe, I never knew one dealt with after this manner. I have known many brought back from great declensions, that appeared to me to be true saints, but it was in a way very diverse from this. In the first place, conscience has been awakened, and they have been brought into great fear of the wrath of God, having his favor hid; and they have been the subjects of a kind of new work of humiliation, brought to a great sense of their deservings of

God's wrath, even while they have yet feared it, before God has delivered them from the apprehensions of it, and comforted them with a renewed sense of his favor.

As to what I say of the necessity of universal obedience, or of one way of known sin (i.e. so as properly to be said to be the way and manner of the man), being exception enough against a man's salvation; I should have known better what to have said further about it, if you had briefly shown how the Scriptures that I mention, and the arguments I deduce from them, are insufficient for the proof of this point. I confess they appear to me to prove it as fully as anything concerning the necessary qualifications of a true saint can be proved from the Scripture.

You object against my saying, p. 391, "Nor can a true saint ever fall away, so that it shall come to this, that ordinarily there shall be no remarkable difference in his walk and behavior since his conversion, from what was before." What I say, I think, implies no more than that his walk over the same ground, in like circumstances, and under like trials, will have a remarkable difference. As to the instances you mention of David and Solomon, I don't know that the Scriptures gives us anywhere so much of a history of their walk and behavior before their conversion, as to put us into any proper capacity of comparing their after-walk with their former. These examples are uncertain. But I think those doctrines of the Scripture are not uncertain, which I mention in the place you cite, to confirm the point, which teach that converts are new men, new creatures, that they [are] renewed not only within, but without, that old things are passed away, and all things become new, that they walk in newness of life, that the members of their bodies are new, that whereas they before were the servants of sin, and yielded their members servants of iniquity to iniquity, now they yield them servants of righteousness unto holiness.

As to those doubts and cases of difficulty you mention, I should think it very needless for a divine of your character, to apply yourself to me for a solution of difficulties, for whom it would be more proper to learn of you. However, since you are pleased to insist on my giving my mind upon them, I would observe, as to the first case you mention, of a person incessantly harassed by Satan, etc., you don't say of what nature the temptations are that he is harassed with; but I think it impossible to give proper advice and direction without knowing this. Satan is to be resisted in a very different manner, in different kinds of onsets. When persons are harassed with those strange, horrid injections, that melancholic persons are often subject to, he is to be resisted in a very different manner, from what is proper in case of violent temptations to gratify some worldly lust. In the former case, I should by no means advise a person to resist the devil by entering the lists with him, and vehemently engaging their mind in an earnest dispute and violent struggle with the grand adversary; but rather by diverting the mind from his frightful suggestions, by going on steadfastly and diligently in the ordinary course of duty, without allowing themselves time and leisure to attend to the devil's sophistry, or view his frightful representations, committing themselves to God by prayer in this way, without anxiety about what had been suggested. That is the best way of resisting the devil, that crosses his design most; and he more effectually disappoints him in such cases, that treats him with neglect, than he that attends so much to him, as to engage in a direct conflict, and goes about to try his strength and skill with him, in a violent dispute or combat. The latter course rather gives him advantage, than anything else. 'Tis what he would; if he can get persons thus engaged in a violent struggle, he gains a great point. He knows that melancholic persons are not fit for it. By this he gains that point, of diverting and taking off the person from the ordinary course of duty, which is one great thing he aims at; and by this, having gained the person's attention to what he says, he has opportunity to use all his crafty and subtlety, and by this struggle, he raises melancholic vapors to a greater degree, and further weakens the person's mind, and gets him faster and faster in his snares, deeper and deeper in the mire. He increases the person's anxiety of mind, which is the very thing by which mainly he fulfills all his purposes with such persons.

Concerning the other difficulty you mention relating to the verifying of Rom. 8:28, "All things shall work together for good," etc., in a saint that falls under backslidings and spiritual decays, etc.: it seems to be a matter of some difficulty to understand exactly how this is to be taken, and how far it may from hence be inferred, that the temptations the saints meet with from Satan, and an evil world, and their own declensions and sins, shall surely work for their good. However, since you desire my thoughts, I would express them, such as they are, as follows:

In order rightly to state this matter, there are two things may be laid down, as positions of certain and indubitable truth concerning this doctrine of the Apostle.

I. The meaning cannot be that God's dispensations and disposals towards each saint are the best for him, most tending to his happiness of all that are possible; or that all things that are ordered for him, or done by God with respect to him, are in all respects better for him than anything else that God could have ordered or done, issuing in the highest good and happiness, that it is possible he should be brought to; for that would be as much as to say, that God will bestow on every one of his elect as much happiness as he can, in the utmost exercise of his omnipotence. And this sets aside all these different degrees of grace and holiness here, and glory hereafter, which he bestows according to his sovereign pleasure.

All things may work together for good to the saints, all may be of benefit to them, and may have a concurring tendency to their happiness, and may all finally issue in it, and yet not tend to, or issue in the highest degree of good and happiness possible. There is a certain measure of holiness and happiness, that each one of the elect is eternally appointed to; and all things that relate to him, work together to bring to pass this appointed measure of good. The text and context speak of God's eternal purpose of good to the elect, predestinating them to a conformity to his Son in holiness and happiness; and the implicit reasoning of the Apostle leads us to suppose that all things will surely concur to bring to effect God's eternal purpose. And therefore from his reasoning it may be inferred, that all things will tend to, and work together to bring to pass, that degree of good that God has purposed to bestow upon them, and not any more. And indeed it would be in itself unreasonable to suppose anything else but this. Inasmuch as God is the supreme orderer of all things, doubtless all things shall be so ordered, that with one consent, they shall help to bring to pass his aims, ends and purposes; but surely not to bring to pass what he does not aim at, and never intended. God, in his government of the world, is carrying on his own designs in everything; but he is not carrying on that which is not his design. And therefore there is no need of supposing, that all the circumstances, means and advantages of every saint, are the best in every respect that God could have ordered for him, or that there could have been no circumstances and means that he could have been the subject of, that would, with God's usual blessing on means, have issued in his greater good. Every saint is as it were a living stone, that in this present state of preparation, is fitting for the place appointed for him in the heavenly temple. And in this sense all things undoubtedly work together for good to every one that is called according to God's purpose. He is, all the while he lives in this world, by all the dispensations of providence towards him, fitting for the particular mansion in glory, that is appointed and prepared for him, or hewing for his appointed place in the heavenly building.

II. Another thing which is no less certain and demonstrable than the position that has been already laid down, and indeed follows from it, is this: when it is said, "All things work together for good," etc., thereby cannot be intended that all things, both positive and negative, are best for them, or that it is so universally, that not only every positive thing that the saints are the subjects of, or are concerned in, will work for their good, but also that when anything is absent or withheld from them by God in his providence, that absence or withholding is also for their good in that sense as to be better for them than the presence or bestowment would have been. For this would have the same absurd consequence that was mentioned before, viz. that God makes every saint as happy as possibly he can. And besides, if so, it would follow that God's withholding greater degrees of the sanctifying influences of his Spirit is for the saints' good, and that it is best for them to live and die so low in grace as they do, which would be as much as to say, that 'tis for their good to have no more good, or that it is for their happiness to have no more happiness here and hereafter. If we take good notice of the Apostle's discourse in Rom. 8, it will be apparent that his words imply no such thing. All God's creatures, and all that God does in disposing of them, is for the good of the saint. But it will not thence follow, that all God's forbearing to do is also for his good, or that it is best for him, that God does no more for him.

Therefore, the following things I humbly conceive to be the truth concerning the sins and temptations of the saints being for their good.

1. That all things whatsoever are for the good of the saints, things negative as well as positive, in that sense, that God intends that some benefit to them, shall arise from everything, so that something of the grace and love of God, will hereafter be seen to have been exercised towards them in everything; although at the same time, the sovereignty of God will also be to be seen, with regard to the measure of the good or benefit aimed at, in that some other things, if God had seen cause to order them, would have produced an higher benefit. And with regard to negative disposals, consisting not in God's doing, but forbearing to do, not in giving, but withholding, some benefit, in some respect or other, will ever accrue to the saints, even from these: though sometimes the benefit will not be equal to the benefit withheld, if it had not been bestowed. As for instance, when a saint lives and dies compar-

atively low in grace, there is some good improvement shall be made, even of this, in the eternal state of the saint, whereby he shall receive a real benefit; though the benefit shall not be equal to the benefit of an higher degree of holiness, if God had bestowed it.

2. God carries on a design of love to his people, and to each individual saint, not only in all things that they are the subjects of while they live, but also in all his works and disposals, and all his acts *ad extra,* from eternity to eternity.

3. That the sin, in general, of the saints, is for their good, and for the best, in this respect, that it is a thing that, through the sovereign grace of God, and his infinite wisdom, will issue in a high advancement of their eternal happiness, that they have been sinful, fallen creatures, and not from the beginning perfectly innocent and holy, as the elect angels; and that they shall obtain some additional good on occasion of all the sin they have been the subjects of, or have committed, beyond what they would have had if they never had been fallen creatures.

4. The sin of the saints in this sense cannot be for their good, that it should finally be best for them, that while they lived in this world, their restoration and recovery from the corruption they became subject to by the fall, was no greater, the mortification of sin and spiritual vivification of their souls, carried on to no greater degree, that they remained so sinfully deficient, as to love to God, Christian love to men, humility, heavenly mindedness, etc. and that they were so barren, and did so few good works; and consequently, that in general, they had so much sin and of the exercises of it, and not more holiness and of the exercises and fruits of that (for in proportion as one of these is more, the other will be less, as infallibly, as darkness is more or less, in proportion to the diminution or increase of light). It can't finally be better for the saints, that in general, while they lived, they had so much sin of heart and life, rather than more holiness of heart and life. Because the reward of all at last will be according to their works, and he that has sowed sparingly shall reap sparingly, and he that has sowed bountifully shall reap also bountifully; and he that builds wood, hay and stubble, shall finally suffer loss, and have a less reward, than if he had built gold, silver and precious stones, though he himself shall be saved. But notwithstanding this,

5. The sins and falls of the saints may be for their good, and for the better, in this respect, that the issue may be better than if the temptation had not happened, and so the occasion not given, either for the sin of yielding to the temptation, or the virtue of overcoming it; and

yet not in that respect (with regard to their sins or falls in general) that it should be better for them in the issue, that they have yielded to the temptations offered, than if they had overcome. For the fewer victories they obtain over temptation, the fewer their good works, and particularly of that kind of good works to which a distinguished reward is promised in Rev. 2 and 3 and in many other parts of Scripture. The Word of God represents the work of a Christian in this world by a warfare; and 'tis evident by the Scripture that he that acquits himself as the best soldier shall win the greatest prize. Therefore, when the saints are brought into backslidings and decays, by being overcome by temptations, the issue of their backslidings may be some good to them, they may receive some benefit by occasion of it, beyond what they would have received if the temptation had never happened; and yet their backslidings in general may be a great loss to them in that respect, that they shall have much less reward than if the temptations had been overcome, and they notwithstanding had persevered in spiritual vigor and diligence. But yet this don't hinder but that,

6. It may be so ordered by a sovereign and all-wise God, that the saints' falls and backslidings, through their being overcome by temptation, in some particular instances, may prove best for them; not only that the issue may be greater good to them than they would have received if the temptation had not happened, but even greater, in that instance, than if the temptation had been overcome. It may be so ordered that their being overcome by that temptation, shall be an occasion of their having greater strength, and in the whole, obtaining more and greater victories, than if they had not fallen in that instance. But this is nowhere promised, nor can it be so, that, in the general, it should prove better for them that they are foiled so much, and do overcome so little, in the course of their lives, and that finally their decay is so great, or their progress so small. From these things it appears,

7. That the saying of the Apostle, "All things work together for good to them that love God," though it be fulfilled in some respect to all saints, and at all times, and in all circumstances, yet is fulfilled more especially and eminently to the saints' *continuing in the exercise of love to God,* not falling from the exercises, or failing of the fruits of divine love in times of trial: then temptations, enemies and sufferings such as be, will be best for them, working that which is most for their good every way; and they shall be more than conquerors over tribulation, distress, persecution, famine, nakedness, peril and sword (Rom. 8:35–37).

8. As God is carrying on a design of love to each individual saint, in all his works and disposals whatsoever, as was observed before, so the particular design of love to them that he is carrying on, is to fit them for, and bring 'em to their appointed place in the heavenly temple, or that individual, precise happiness and glory in heaven, that his eternal love designed for them, and no other (for God's design of love or of happiness to them, is only just what it is, and is not different from itself). And to fulfill this particular design of love, everything that God does, or in any respect disposes, whether it be positive, privative or negative, contributes, because doubtless everything that God does, or in any respect orders, tends to fulfill his aims and designs. Therefore, undoubtedly,

9. All the while the saint lives in the world, he is fitting for his appointed mansion in glory, and hewing for his place in the heavenly building: and all his temptations, though they may occasion, for the present, great spiritual wounds, yet at last, they shall be an occasion of his being more fitted for his place in glory. And, therefore, we may determine, that however the true saint may die, in some respects, under decays, under the decay of comfort, and of the exercise of some religious affections, yet every saint dies at that time when his habitual fitness for his place in the heavenly temple is most complete, because otherwise, all things that happen to him while he lives, would not work together to fit him for that place.

10. God brings his saints at the end of their lives to this greatest fitness for their place in heaven, not by diminishing grace in their hearts, but by increasing it, and carrying on the work of grace in their souls. Otherwise, that cannot be true, that where God has begun a good work, he will perform it, or carry it on to the day of Christ, for if they die with a less degree of grace than they had before, then it ceases to be carried on before the day of Christ comes. If grace is finally diminished, then Satan so far finally obtains the victory, he finally prevails to diminish the fire in the smoking flax. And then how is that promise verified, that God will not quench the smoking flax, till he bring forth judgment unto victory? So that it must needs be, that although saints may die under decays in some respects, yet they never die under a real habitual decay of the work of grace in general. If they fall, they shall rise again before they die, and rise higher than before; if not in joys, and some other affections, yet in greater degree of spiritual knowledge, self-emptiness, trust in God, and solidity and ripeness of grace.

If these things that have been observed are true, then we may infer from them these corollaries:

First. That notwithstanding the truth of that saying of the Apostle, Rom. 8:28, the saints have cause to lament their leanness and barrenness, and that they are guilty of so much sin; not only as it is to the dishonor of God, but also as that which is like to their own eternal loss and damage.

Secondly. That nothing can be inferred from the forementioned promise, tending to set aside, or make void the influence of motives to earnest endeavors to avoid all sin, to increase in holiness, and abound in good works, from an aim at an high and eminent degree of glory and happiness in the eternal world.

Thirdly. That though it is to the eternal damage of the saints, ordinarily, when they yield to, and are overcome by temptations, yet Satan and other enemies of the saints, by whom their temptations come, are always wholly disappointed in their temptations, and baffled in their design to hurt the saints, inasmuch as the temptation, and the sin that comes by it, is for the saints' good, and they receive a greater benefit, in the issue, than if the temptation had not been, and yet less than if the temptation had been overcome.

As to Mr. Boston's view of the covenant of grace, I have had some opportunity with it, and I confess I did not understand his scheme delivered in that book. I have read his Fourfold State of Man, and liked it exceeding well.[1] I think he therein shows himself to be a truly great divine.

Sir, hoping that you will accept my letters with candor, to remember me in your prayers, I subscribe myself, your affectionate and obliged

Brother and servant,
Jonathan Edwards.

79. TO THE REVEREND JOSEPH BELLAMY

Following up his letter of June 11, Edwards updates Bellamy on Brainerd's condition and requests a visit from Bellamy before Brainerd's death.

(CHS, ALS, one quarto leaf, addressed on verso to the Reverend Mr. Joseph Bellamy at Bethlehem.)

*   *   *

---

1. Thomas Boston, Sr., *A View of the Covenant of Grace, from the Sacred Records: wherein the parties in the Covenant . . . and the administrations thereof, are distinctly considered* (Edinburgh, 1742), and *Human Nature in its Fourfold State . . . in several practical discourses* (Edinburgh, 1720).

Northampton, September 14, 1747

Dear Brother,

Having a direct opportunity, I could not let it pass without writing a line. We are through mercy pretty well. My wife kindly salutes you and your spouse.

Mr. [David] Brainerd is now at my house, and has been here a long time, in a very low state, growing weaker and weaker; he is like to be here till he dies. His feet and legs a few days ago began to swell, and that symptom is increasing. He gives his hearty love to you; and desires you to write back by the bearer of this, who says he shall return the week after next. When he went from Kaunaumeek, he left some of his things, books and other things, at Mr. [John] Sergeant's, to be sent to your house and committed to your care. He desires you to write and inform whether they are there, and what things they are. What if you should come and see him before he dies? I should be glad to see you here.

Mr. John Brainerd came from the Jerseys hither the week before last, and is now here, and presents his hearty and humble regards to you. He has thoughts of returning this week to the Jerseys and returning hither again the next. If you don't come hither this fall (as I would not have you put by going to the eastward for it), please to write a little more fully about the business I committed you. My kind love to your spouse. I am,

Your affectionate friend and brother,
Jonathan Edwards.

80. TO THE REVEREND WILLIAM McCULLOCH

Edwards had completed the *Humble Attempt* by this time. In fact, the book was advertised in Boston only a day after the letter was written, as "now in the press." Consequently, he mentions a number of topics in that work: military victories, spiritual declension, and the prophecies of Scripture, beginning and ending with the Concert for Prayer. Edwards closes on his usual optimistic note: signs strongly suggest that the great age of the Spirit is at hand.

(Trask Library, ALS, two quarto leaves, no address, but notation at bottom of p. 4 in Edwards' hand, to the Reverend Mr. William McCulloch. See Edwards to McCulloch, Jan. 21, 1747 [No. 74], above; *BNL*, Sept. 24, 1747, 2. The two letters mentioned by Edwards are not extant.)

*   *   *

Northampton, September 23, 1747

Rev. and Dear Sir,

I thank you for your letter of March 12, 1747, which I suppose lay a long while at Mr. [Thomas] Prince's in Boston before I received it, through Mr. Prince's forgetfulness. It seems he had forgotten that he had any such letter; and when I sent a messenger to his house on purpose to inquire whether I had any letters lodged there for me from Scotland, he told him "no"; when I suppose this letter had been long in his house; and I should probably never have had it at last, had not one of my daughters occasion to go to Boston, who made a visit at the house, and made more full inquiry.

I am sorry to hear of your affliction through your indisposition that you speak of, and desire to be thankful to the God of all mercy, for his goodness in restoring you again to health.

I have, in my letter to Mr. [John] MacLaurin, given a particular account of what I know concerning the propagation of the Concert for United Prayer in America; which you will doubtless have opportunity to see. The propagation of it is but slow, but yet so many do fall in with it; and there is that prospect of its being further spread, that it is a great encouragement to me. I earnestly wish and hope that they that have begun extraordinary prayer for the outpouring of the Spirit of God, and the coming of Christ's kingdom, will not fail, or grow dull and listless in such an affair, but rather that they will increase more and more in their fervency. I have taken a great deal of pains to promote this Concert here in America, and shall not cease to do so, if God spares my life, as I have opportunity in all ways that I can devise. I have written largely on the subject, insisting on persuasives and answering objections; and what I have written is gone to the press. The undertaker for the publication encourages me that it shall speedily be printed. I have sent to Mr. MacLaurin a particular account of it.

You desire to hear how it was with the people of New England, when we were threatened with an invasion by the French fleet the last summer. As to the particular circumstances of that wonderful deliverance, the fullest and best account I have ever seen of it, is in Mr. Prince's Thanksgiving sermon on that occasion;[1] which in all probability you have seen long before this time. Nor need you be informed by me of the repeated mercy of God to us, in confounding our enemies in their renewed attempt this year, by delivering up their fleet, in its way

1. See above, Letter No. 74, JE to McCulloch, Jan. 21, 1746/7, n. 2.

hither, into the hands of the English. In all probability, that fleet was intended for the execution of a very extensive design against the English colonies, in conjunction with the French forces in Canada. For there was an army lay waiting at Nova Scotia, which on the news of the taking of their fleet, immediately left the country and returned to Canada. And another army of about 3,000 came from Canada, over the Lake Champlain, towards New England and New York. And they, or a part of them, attacked the fort at Saratoga, in New York government, and killed or took about fifty men that were drawn out of the fort; but desisted from any further attempts, about the time we may suppose they received the news of the defeat of their fleet. And very soon after they received this news in Canada, the French there released most of our captives; and sent one ship loaden with them, to the number of 170, to Boston, and another ship with about sixty, if I remember right, to Louisburg. The reasons that induced them so to do are not known, and can only be guessed at by us. But by their doing it very soon after they received the news of the loss of their fleet, it looks as though that had great influence in the affair. New England has had many other surprising deliverances from the French and Indians, some of which I have given a particular account of in my letter to Mr. MacLaurin; which it would be needless for me to repeat, seeing you have such frequent opportunities with him.

These deliverances are very wonderful and affecting; our enemies own that the heavens are on our side, and fight for us; but there are no such effects of these mercies upon us that are the subjects of 'em, as God requires and most justly expects. The mercies are acknowledged in words, but we are not led to repentance by them. There appears no such thing as any reformation or revival of religion in the land. God's so wonderfully protecting and delivering a people, whose provocations have been so great, and who do so continue in apostasy and provocation, is very marvelous. And I can think of no account that can be given of it so probable as this, that God has a design of mercy to the rising generation, and that there are a great many of the elect among our children, born and unborn; and that for these elect's sake, God will not suffer us to be destroyed, having a design to bring forth a seed of the posterity of this people, to inherit and dwell in this land, that shall be a holy seed, and a generation of his servants. And so that those words are applicable to us, Is. 65:8–9, "Thus saith the Lord, as the new wine is found in the cluster, and one saith destroy it not, for a blessing is in it; so will I do for my servants' sakes, that I may not destroy them all. And I will bring forth a seed out of Jacob, and out of Judah an inheritor of my mountains: and mine elect shall inherit it, and my servants shall dwell there." I am full of apprehensions that God has no design of mercy to those that were left unconverted of the generation that were on the stage, in the time of the late, extraordinary religious commotion and striving of God's Spirit, unless it be perhaps a small gleaning from among them. But it may be when their little ones, the generation that was then in their childhood, are brought fully on the stage of action, God will abundantly pour out his Spirit, and revive and carry on his work here and elsewhere in the Christian world.

I thank you for taking the pains of writing to me your thoughts of the forty-two months of the treading down of the holy city [Rev. 11:2], which are new and entertaining. The chief objection against what you propose, that I can think of, is that the forty-two months of the treading down the holy city, seems to be the same period with the 1,260 days of the witnesses' prophesying in sackcloth, mentioned in the very next verse in immediate connection with this; and *that* the same with the 1,260 days of the woman's being in the wilderness, ch. 12:6; and that the same with the time, times, and an half, of the woman's being in the wilderness, v. 14; and *that* the same with the time, times, and an half, of the reign of the little horn, Dan. 7:25; and with the forty-two months of the reign of the beast, Rev. 13:5; and that this evidently signifies the duration of the reign of Antichrist, which is a thing entirely diverse from the sum of the times of the city of Jerusalem's being under the dominion of pagans, Saracens, Persians, and Turks as you represent.

However, 'tis possible that what you mention may be one way wherein that prophecy, Rev. 11:2, may be fulfilled. For God's Word is oftentimes fulfilled various ways: as one way wherein the prophetical representation of the beast with seven heads is fulfilled, is in the seven successive forms of government that idolatrous Rome is under; and another way that it was fulfilled was by Rome's being built on seven hills. One way wherein the prophecy of the seventy years captivity of the Jews was fulfilled, was in its being seventy years from Jehoiakim's captivity to Cyrus' decree; and another way that it was fulfilled was in its being seventy years from Zedekiah's captivity to Darius' decree, Ezra 6; and another way that it was fulfilled was in its being seventy years from the last carrying away of all, Jer. 52:30, to the finishing and dedication of the temple.

But I expect no certainty as to these things, or any of the various conjectures concerning the time of the calling of the Jews, and fall of the kingdom of the Beast, till time and fulfillment shall decide the matter. However, I cannot think otherwise, than that we have a great deal of reason to suppose that the beginning of that glorious work of God's Spirit, which before it is finished, shall accomplish those things, is not very far off. And there is very much in the Word of God, and in the present aspects of divine providence, to encourage us greatly in our begun Concert for extraordinary united prayer for the coming of Christ's kingdom.

Let us, therefore, go on with what we have begun in that respect, and continue instant in prayer with all perseverance, and increase more and more in faith and fervency, and not keep silence, nor give God any rest, till he establish and make Jerusalem a praise in the earth. And remember in your prayers, dear Sir,

Yours in great esteem and affection,
Jonathan Edwards.

81. TO THE REVEREND STEPHEN WILLIAMS

David Brainerd arrived at Edwards' home on May 28, 1747, ravaged by tuberculosis. Part of the treatment advised by physicians was horseback riding. Combining this prescription with a desire to report to his missionary sponsors, he left for Boston on June 9, returning to Northampton on July 25. Throughout the nineteen weeks between his first coming and his death on October 9, his constant companion and nurse was Jerusha, Edwards' second daughter, who was then seventeen years old.

No doubt a number of funeral invitations similar to this letter were sent out, for "eight of the neighboring ministers, and seventeen other gentlemen of liberal education, and a great concourse of people" attended the last rites. Edwards delivered the sermon, *True Saints, When Absent from the Body, Are Present with the Lord,* which was published in Boston in December 1747.

(Drew University, Rose Library, ALS, one quarto leaf, addressed on verso to the Reverend Stephen Williams at Longmeadow. See *Works,* 7, 68, 445–76, 543*n.*)

* * *

Northampton, October 9, 1747

To the Reverend Stephen Williams:

It has pleased God to remove by death that eminent servant of his, the Reverend Mr. David Brainerd, about six o'clock this morning. You may remember that you desired me, if I had opportunity, to give you notice of the time of his funeral. It is, God willing, to be the next Monday, the lecture before the funeral to begin at one o'clock.

When Mr. Brainerd in his lifetime was speaking of the circumstances of his own funeral, and desiring that the neighboring ministers of his acquaintance might be sent for, I mentioned what you had said, manifesting a disposition to attend his funeral, if it might be conveniently. He seemed in a considerable degree to take a thankful notice of it; and desired me to take some pains to find an opportunity to give you notice. I mention these things to you, reverend Sir, leaving it with you to conduct yourself according to your own discretion. But if you can be present, I should be very glad, who am,

Your humble servant,
Jonathan Edwards.

82. TO THE REVEREND JOHN BRAINERD

Edwards was so impressed with David Brainerd that he resolved to write his biography. Brainerd's exemplary life embodied ideals he admired: doctrinal fidelity, missionary zeal, vital religious experience, indomitable courage in overcoming obstacles, and radiant spirit. Here, Edwards seeks the fullest factual background possible from John Brainerd on his brother's life. He shows meticulous attention to detail for the book already taking shape in his mind.

The Life of David Brainerd, an outstanding success, has been reprinted more often than any work of Edwards', confirming his instincts about its interest and value. Gov. Jonathan Belcher of New Jersey declined to accept the dedication, but his name prominently heads the list of subscribers.

(Trask Library, ALS, two quarto leaves, addressed on verso to Mr. John Brainerd at Cranbury, New Jersey. Published in *Works*, 7, 587–90. The volume edited by Edwards was first published as *An Account of the Life of the late Reverend Mr. David Brainerd* [Boston, 1749].)

* * *

Northampton, December 14, 1747

Dear Sir,

I have read through your deceased brother's papers, containing his life, and have determined to publish an abstract of them. I have with this sent to you a letter to Gov. [Jonathan] Belcher, desiring his leave to dedicate the book to him; which I desire you to wait on His Excellency with. If he should consent to have the book dedicated to him, it might not only tend to make it the more taken notice of, and so the more useful, but also may do honor to your brother's memory, whom many, in his lifetime, strove to lay under disgrace. I have sent my letter to the Governor open, that you may see it; but desire you handsomely to seal and deliver it.

In writing your brother's Life, it will be unavoidable but that mention must be made of your brother's expulsion from the College: and therefore I think it is necessary that a just and particular account be given of that matter. So that I should be glad that when you come hither in the spring, you would come furnished to give me a just, exact and certain account of that affair, that the Rector may have no cause, nor find any room to complain of the least misrepresentation in any respect. I should be glad also to know particularly what offers your brother made to the Rector from time to time of satisfaction, in order to his being restored to College. There is mention made in his private journals of his making attempts to be reconciled several times, one in June and another in July 1743. And particularly, I think I have heard him speak of a confession he offered (or something of that nature) to the Trustees at Hartford, the May after his expulsion, at the time of the election, but there is no account what it was. There is indeed in his diary, a copy of the confession he offered at last, at the time of that commencement that his class took their degrees, but no other. Perhaps Mr. [Isaac] Burr may be able to give a particular information of some of these matters, and Mr. [Jedidiah] Mills. I should be glad that when you are on your journey hither you would inquire of him, or any other that you think would be likely to inform. I think your brother told me that the Rector acknowledged that the confession he offered at last was Christian satisfaction. However, I should be glad to be more fully informed of that matter.

I want also to be more particularly informed of some things in your brother's life: something more particular concerning his parentage, his mother in particular, who she was, and whence descended. And if there was anything remarkable in his childhood, any remarkable dangers, deliverances, or restorations, or any other thing worthy to be noted in writing his Life: a particular account of his mission to the Indians; how the Society in Scotland came first to appoint a number of commissioners in New York and the Jerseys; how the Commissioners came to hear of, and improve Mr. Brainerd; how they came first to send him to Kaunaumeek; how he came afterwards to be called thence and sent to the Forks of Delaware. And perhaps Mr. [Gilbert] Tennent and some others that were well acquainted with him, may be able to inform of some remarkable things of him, of his character, behavior, or speeches that may be worthy to be inserted in his Life. And I want to be more particularly informed of your brother's illness last winter at Mr. [Jonathan] Dickinson's, for there his journal is very short. I want also to [be] informed whether your brother's public *Journal* be continued till he left the Indians, or whether anything further was published by him, or prepared for the press, beyond what was printed at Philadelphia.[1] If there was, I should be glad to see it, that I mayn't publish the same thing over again out of his diary. I should be glad that you would bring me an account of these things when you come in the spring. And also bring any other of your brother's papers that may contain what may be worthy to be inserted. Some of his letters to his friends that I have seen are remarkable, and well worth publishing, and I doubt not but there were many others that were, that I have not yet seen. I desire that you would bring some of them, such as you think are most worthy to be taken notice of, to yourself or others; and particularly I desire you would, as you come along, in my name request of Esther Sherman[2] that she would send me some of his letters to her. Your brother in his diary often mentions his writing on divine subjects, and I perceive he spent abundance of time in writing; I don't know how to think that all that he meant was writing sermons: I should be glad to see some of these his composures on divine subjects.

On further considering your brother's diary, since I wrote the preceding part of this letter, I find that I want to be informed of some further particulars, in order to writing his Life, which probably Mr. [Ebenezer] Pemberton or Mr. [Aaron] Burr can give information in:

There is mention made of a meeting of ministers that examined him at New York, in November 1742. I want to know what meeting of ministers that was; whether a meeting of the Presbytery, or of the Commissioners.

Why the Commissioners gave him so long a space, after he was examined at New York concerning his qualifications for the mission, before they actually sent him on the business, as from November to the next April; whether it was because they looked on the winter season unfit to engage in such business.

1. Brainerd, *Mirabilia Dei inter Indicos.*
2. Esther Sherman was mentioned in Brainerd's diary as a correspondent with whom he felt close. She later married Job Prudden, his college friend (DEX, *1,* 742–43).

It seems by your brother's diary, that when he was examined at the time forementioned, the design was that he should be sent to the Indians in Pennsylvania and he [appeared][3] to have that expectation all winter, of going to those Indians. I would be informed, how the Correspondents came to change their minds, and when the spring came, send him to Kaunaumeek.

What your brother's special business to New York and the Jerseys was when, the next spring, he went thither from East Hampton, before he went to Kaunaumeek. And what meeting of ministers that was that he, at that time, met at Woodbridge; whether a meeting of the Presbytery, or of the Correspondents; and what instructions he there received.

He took three journeys from Kaunaumeek to New York and the Jerseys: one in May 1743; another in September following, when he went no further than New York; another at the latter end of March, the next year. I want to know: what was the special occasion of these journeys; who his interpreter was at Kaunaumeek, an Englishman or Indian; what encouragement the Commissioners saw in the state of the Delaware Indians, that should incline them to send a missionary to them rather than any other Indians.

I suppose my funeral sermon on your brother is by this time printed. Mr. [Edward] Bromfield writes me word, in a letter dated December 1, that it was then in the press, and would be finished in about ten days from that time; and that Maj. [Daniel] Henchman had agreed to print it without any subscription, and to send me my part of them; and also that he with some other gentlemen had determined to send fifty of them as a present to you. I am, Sir,

> Your affectionate friend,
> Jonathan Edwards.

P.S. If I had received one of my sermons on your brother's funeral, I would now send one to Gov. [Jonathan] Belcher. If he consents that I should dedicate his Life to him, it may not be amiss perhaps for you to make a present of one of yours to him, when you receive them.

83. TO THE REVEREND EBENEZER PARKMAN

Edwards must report another death in his household, this time of his daughter Jerusha, who may have contracted tuberculosis from Brainerd while she was caring for him.

---

3. MS damage.

(National Library of Scotland, Edinburgh, ALS, one quarto leaf, shorn on left side, addressed on verso to the [Reverend] Mr. Ebenezer [Parkman] of Westb[orough] per the Reverend [John] Brainerd.)

* * *

[Northampton,] March 4, 1747/8

[Dear] Brother,

[It has] pleased a holy God of late sorely to [try our] family, by taking away by death [our] daughter, Jerusha. The Reverend Mr. John [Brainerd], the bearer of this (who lately was [appointed] missionary to succeed his deceased brother) [can tell] you of the circumstances. This is [to ask your] prayers for us under our great [affliction], that it may be sanctified to us and [that God] would fill up the melancholy vacancy [made] by death in this family, with his [gracious] and comfortable presence. My surviving children join with me in salutations to you, Madam, and your family: [begg]ing your sympathy and prayers and [that] you would remember our youngest [who] is under threatening circumstances. [I am,] dear Sir,

Your afflicted brother,
Jonathan Edwards.

84. TO THE REVEREND JOSEPH BELLAMY

Throughout 1748 Edwards was writing two books, *The Life of David Brainerd* and *Humble Inquiry*, which were published the following year. No record exists of communication from Bellamy after mid-1747. Edwards seeks a response from him regarding materials for the Brainerd book, subscriptions to it, and word of his participation in the Concert for Prayer.

(Beinecke Library, one quarto leaf, addressed on verso to the Reverend Mr. Joseph Bellamy at Bethlehem. Published in *NEQ* 1 [1928], 235–36.)

* * *

Northampton, April 4, 1748

Rev. and Dear Brother,

I here send a couple of bags to put our wool into, to be sent to Hartford to Mr. [John] Potwine's, desiring you to take care of that matter as you have very kindly manifested yourself willing to do. I trust entirely in your friendship and faithfulness in that matter.

You have probably before now heard of our sore affliction in the death of our daughter, Jerusha, who died after five days' illness, February 14. I have great satisfaction concerning her state, from what I know of her in life, and what appeared in her at death. Mr. David Brainerd, who had much intimate acquaintance with her, she having constantly been with him as his nurse, nineteen weeks before his death, expressed great satisfaction concerning the state of her soul, and that he looked on her not only as a saint, but as a very eminent saint. I desire your prayers for us that God would make up our great loss in spiritual blessings.

Please to accept of one of my books on prayer for the revival of religion,[1] which I here send you. And send me word whether the proposal for united prayer be complied with in your parts.

I wrote you some time since informing that I was about to publish Mr. Brainerd's *Life* from his private writings, desiring you to send me any letters of his worthy to be inserted;[2] but have had no answer. I would now renew that request, and also that you would send me word whether you will allow me to mention your name in the printed proposals for subscription, as one that will take in subscriptions in your parts. This with respectful salutations to Mrs. [Frances Sherman] Bellamy, is from, dear Sir,

> Your affectionate friend and brother,
> Jonathan Edwards.

85. TO SARAH PIERPONT EDWARDS

On a visit to Boston, Edwards' wife, Sarah, was the guest of Edward Bromfield, a merchant and a frequent host of the family. Edwards sends news from home concerning sick children. His uncle and good friend Col. John Stoddard had died in Boston on June 19. Uncertain of arrangements, Edwards leaves the timing of his wife's return up to her judgment.

(Beinecke Library, ALS, two irregular fragments. The left side of each is sheared, so words on that margin usually lack a letter or two, which are supplied by the editor. Published in Faust and Johnson, p. 384. On Stoddard, see SIB, 5, 118.)

* * *

1. I.e. *An Humble Attempt* (*Works*, 5, 309–436).
2. Bellamy would have had access to Brainerd's letters to Esther Sherman, who was the sister of Bellamy's wife. DEX, *1*, 525, 743.

Northampton, June 22, 1748

My Dear Companion,

I wrote you a few lines the last sabbath day by Ensign [Timothy] Dwight, [Jr.,] which I hope you will receive. By this I would inform you that Betty [Elizabeth Edwards] seems really to be on the mending hand. I can't but think she [is] truly better, both as to her health and her sores, since she has been at Mrs. [Miriam] Phelps'. The first two or three days, before she was well acquainted, she was very unquiet; but now more quiet than she used to be at home. This is lecture-day morning, and your two eldest daughters went to bed last night, both sick, and rose beat out and having the headache. We got Hannah Root to help them yesterday in the afternoon, and expect her again today. How Sarah [and] Esther do today I can't tell, for they are not up. We have been without you almost as long as we know how to be, but yet are willing you should obey the calls of providence with regard to Col. [John] Stoddard.

If you have money to spare, and it ben't too late, I should be glad if you would buy us some cheese in Boston and [send it] with other things if it can be safely.

Give my humble service to Mr. [Edward] Bromfield and Madam [Abigail Coney Bromfield] and proper salutations to other friends.

I am your most affectionate companion,
Jonathan Edwards.

86. TO THE REVEREND JOHN ERSKINE

John Erskine was one of a circle of leading Scottish ministers who established bonds of friendship with Edwards. The two had much in common. Both were skilled, prolific writers and eloquent speakers. They shared a doctrinal solidarity, love of people and ideas, and evangelical fervor. Erskine's loyalty lasted for years beyond Edwards' lifetime: he sponsored Edwards' writings and disseminated his views. Although we have no extant letters from Erskine to Edwards, a number of letters from Edwards to Erskine are available. This is the earliest extant.

(Trask Library, ALS, one folio leaf. Published in Dwight ed., *1*, 251–52; Faust and Johnson, pp. 385–87).

* * *

John Erskine, by Henry
Raeburn, undated,
National Portrait Gallery
of Scotland

Northampton, August 31, 1748

Rev. and Dear Sir,

I this summer received your kind letter of February 9, 1748, with
your most acceptable present of [John] Taylor on *Original Sin,* and his
Key to the Apostolic Writings, with his *Paraphrase on the Epistle to the Romans,* together with your *Sermons* and *Answer to Dr. Campbell.* I had your
Sermons before, sent either by you or Mr. [John] MacLaurin.[1]

I am exceeding glad of those two books of Taylor's. I had before
borrowed and read Taylor on *Original Sin;* but am very glad to have
one of my own. If you had not sent it, I intended to have sought
opportunity to buy it. The other book, his *Paraphrase,* etc., I had not
heard of; if I had, I should not have been easy till I had seen it, and
been possessed of it. These books, if I should live, may probably be of
great use to me. Such kindness from you was unexpected. I hoped to

1. John Taylor, *The Scripture-Doctrine of Original Sin Proposed to Free and Candid Examination*
(London, 1740; 3d ed., Belfast, 1746), and *A Paraphrase with Notes on the Epistle to the Romans.
To Which Is Prefix'd A Key to the Apostolic Writings* (London, 1745; Dublin, 1746); John Erskine,
The People of God Considered as All Righteous: in three Sermons preach'd at Glasgow, April 1745
(Edinburgh, 1745), and *The Law of Nature, sufficiently promulgated to the Heathen World . . . ; in
some miscellaneous reflections, occasioned by Dr. Campbell, Professor of Divinity at St. Andrew's,
Treatise on the Necessity of Revelation* (Edinburgh, 1741).

receive a letter from you, which alone I should have received as a special favor.

I have for the present been diverted from the design I hinted to you, of publishing something against some of the Arminian tenets, by something else that divine providence unexpectedly laid in my way, and seemed to render unavoidable, viz. publishing Mr. [David] Brainerd's *Life,* of which the enclosed paper of proposals gives some account.

It might be of particular advantage to me here in this remote part of the world, to be better informed what books there are that are published on the other side the Atlantic, and especially if there be anything that comes out that is very remarkable. I have seen many notable things that have been written in this century against the truth, but nothing very notable on our side of the controversies of the present day, at least of the Arminian controversy. You would much oblige me, if you would inform me what are the best books that have lately been written in defense of Calvinism.

I have herewith sent the two books of Mr. [Solomon] Stoddard's you desired.[2] The lesser of the two was my own; and though I have no other, yet you have laid me under such obligations, that I am glad I have it to send to you. The other I procured of one of my neighbors.

I have lately heard some things that have excited hope in me that God was about to cause there to be a turn in England, with regard to the state of religion there, for the better; particularly what we have heard that one Mr. [Gilbert] West, a clerk of the Privy Council, has written in defense of Christianity, though once a notorious deist; and also what Mr. [George] Lyttelton, a member of the House of Commons has written.[3] I should be glad if you would inform me more particularly in your next concerning this affair and what the present state of infidelity in Great Britain is.

It has pleased God, since I wrote my last to you, sorely to afflict this family by taking away by death, the last February, my second daughter [Jerusha] in the eighteenth year of her age, a very pleasant and useful member of this family, and that was generally esteemed the flower of the family. Herein we have a great loss; but the remembrance of the

2. The books are identified in JE's duplicate letter to Erskine, Oct. 14, 1748 (No. 90), below, as Solomon Stoddard, *Benefit of the Gospel to the Wounded in Spirit* (Boston, 1713), and *A Treatise concerning the Nature of Saving Conversion* (Boston, 1719).

3. Gilbert West, *Observations on the History and Evidence of the Resurrection of Jesus Christ* (London, 1747), and *A Defence of the Christian Revelation* (London, 1748); and George Lyttelton, *Observations on the Conversion and Apostleship of St. Paul* (London, 1747).

remarkable appearances of piety in her, from her childhood, in life, and also at her death, are very comfortable to us, and give us great reason to mingle thanksgiving with our mourning. I desire your prayers, dear Sir, that God would make up our great loss to us in himself.

Please to accept of one of my sermons on Mr. Brainerd's death, and also my sermon on Mr. [Samuel] Buell's installment.[4] I desire that for the future your letters to me may be directed to be left with Mr. Edward Bromfield, merchant in Boston, and not with Mr. [Thomas] Prince, who is so forgetful, that his care is not to be depended on.

My wife joins with me in respectful and affectionate salutations to you and Mrs. [Christian Mackay] Erskine. Desiring that we may meet often at the throne of grace in supplications for each other. I am, dear brother, your obliged friend,

Fellow laborer, and humble servant,
Jonathan Edwards.

P.S. I desired Mr. Prince to send to you one of my books on the subject of the Concert for Prayer, for a general revival of religion, the last year;[5] and he engaged to do it; but I perceive he forgot it, and it was long neglected. But I have since taken some further care to have the book conveyed; so that I hope that ere this time you have received it.

In the conclusion of your letter of February 9, you mention a design of writing to me again by a ship that was to sail the next month for Boston. That letter I have not received.

87. TO THE REVEREND ELEAZAR WHEELOCK

In addition to writing books, Edwards also promoted their sale. In the case of *The Life of David Brainerd*, he was phenomenally successful, securing a total of 1,953 subscribers, including the Reverend David McGregore, who ordered one for himself and thirty for his parishioners. One hundred thirty-nine clergy are listed among the subscribers at the front of the book. Edwards probably did not write to each of them but relied instead on key ministers to rally colleagues. Even so, a prodigious amount of correspondence must have been required to produce these results. This letter is the sole example known to survive of the effort. Wheelock did subscribe, but the printer gave him the wrong first name (Ebenezer).

4. *True Saints, When Absent from the Body, are Present with the Lord* (Boston, 1747), and *The Church's Marriage to her Sons, and to Her God* (Boston, 1746).
5. *An Humble Attempt.*

(Beinecke Library, ALS, addressed on verso to the Reverend Mr. Eleazar Wheelock, Pastor of the Church of Christ at the Crank in Lebanon.)

* * *

New Haven, September 14, 1748

Rev. and Dear Sir,

Having understood that you was willing to take in subscriptions for the printing Mr. Brainerd's *Life*, I have inserted your name in the printed proposals; some of which I have here enclosed to you, desiring you to take some pains to promote subscriptions in your parts. I can't but think that an account of the life of this extraordinary person, as taken from his own private writings, will not only have a very great tendency to promote the interest of true religion in general; but in a peculiar manner, and vastly more than anything that has ever yet been published, to open the eyes of the common people with regard [to] that wild sort of religion that has so much prevailed in your parts of the country.

I think the book at the price proposed will be very cheap, considering how books are now sold, which I have lately had special occasion to know. I believe there will be so many subscribers that there will be no books left for non-subscribers.

I desire that the proper titles of subscribers, together with their place of abode, may be added to their names, and that you would collect the subscriptions and forward them to Boston as soon as may be. Herein I am persuaded you will much serve the interest of religion as well as oblige your

Friend and brother,
Jonathan Edwards.

88. TO DEACON MOSES LYMAN

The ongoing struggle between revivalist members of the Goshen, Connecticut, church and their traditionalist pastor Stephen Heaton had reached the crisis stage. Heaton had been exonerated of charges by a council. Dissension still prevailed, however, as parishioners continued to seek his dismissal. Unable to find relief through Congregational channels, they proposed affiliation with the Church of England.

Edwards, true to his Puritan heritage, pronounces the option anathema. He musters an array of arguments against that course of action and warns of the ultimate peril, being burdened with an Arminian minister.

(Private collection of John H. Edwards, Woodbridge, Conn., ALS, two quarto leaves. It is reasonable to assume, first, that this advice to Goshen was sent again through Moses Lyman, who was from Northampton originally and who served as a liaison with Edwards, and, second, that it was sent with a cover, now missing, which explains the lack of a salutation. See Edwards' letters to Lyman, Aug. 31, 1741 [No. 34], and May 10, 1742 [No. 38], above. See also DEX, *1*, 480–82.)

* * *

Northampton, September 30, 1748

Question. Supposing a society or congregation of people, who have been educated in the doctrines and way of worship, generally professed by the people of New England, are subject to the following calamitous circumstances, viz. that they are under a minister who is wholly unqualified, and notoriously unfit for that sacred office, with regard both to natural and moral qualifications; which has been made very evident by many uncontestable facts, that have been properly and abundantly proved, in a public proceeding: but still they are held under this minister, are not allowed to settle another, or statedly to enjoy any other public means for the good of the souls of them and their children; and are obliged, though small, and not of great ability, to maintain this minister; and so to expend their money, wholly to no purpose, but only, in effect, to maintain a public nuisance and their own calamity; and this people have long been thus grievously distressed while they have been waiting and hoping for redress in the use of all possible means, and all in vain; and there is no prospect of their ever obtaining any help, unless by turning to the Church of England: whether or no it be lawful or advisable for such a people publicly, to renounce a stated union with the churches of the country, and join themselves to the Church of England?

I answer in the negative, for the following reasons.

There are many ceremonies practiced and established in the Church of England which are not lawful, and cannot be complied with, as established by the laws and canons of that church, with a well-informed and good conscience; they being properly human additions to the ordinances of God; and those that worship of God in the use of them, their fear, or worship toward God is taught by the precept of men, which is unlawful, and provoking to God, as is evident by Is.

29:13. A people ought not to do any evil or unlawful thing that good may come, or to deliver themselves from evil.

If such a people subject themselves to the Church of England, they cannot have the choice of their own minister; but must be subject to such an one as shall be sent them. And as the state of the Church of England now is, they can't reasonably have the least expectation of any other minister, than one that is an Arminian, or worse than an Arminian; one who in his teaching shall wholly neglect many of those doctrines that are most essential to be known in order to salvation; and that shall teach and inculcate those doctrines that shall tend to corrupt and infect the minds of their hearers with such principles as are directly contrary to the scheme of the gospel, and tend especially to hinder their souls' salvation, which will be an infinitely terrible calamity to themselves and their children. And if they, under these circumstances, by their own act, put themselves under the Church of England, they will be guilty of bringing this calamity on themselves and their posterity, so far as in them lies, to all generations. They will not be merely passive in it, but it will be their own doings: which they can never justify; they will be guilty of the blood of their own souls, and the souls of their children, and perhaps of their posterity to the latest generation, who, if they should eternally perish by this means, they must expect to have all rising up in judgment against them, accusing them as the murderers of their souls.

If such a people shall say their calamity is as great already as they are, and it is like to continue; they are not taught the necessary doctrines of the gospel now; and it can't be any worse in the Church of England, I answer: If it be so indeed, their misery now is not theirs by their own act; they are purely passive in it; and are, or ought to be, praying and waiting for deliverance from it. And though now there appears no prospect of their deliverance, yet there are many ways that they may be delivered in divine providence; which often brings very great and unexpected changes in a short time. But by taking the forementioned course, they take the matter out of the hands of providence, and take it into their own hands, and take a course forever to preclude all deliverance, and to prevent their receiving any benefit that might be received by providential events and to fasten their calamity forever on themselves and their posterity. But if they had no hope that God in his providence would ever appear for their help, and had reason to think he would not, yet that would not justify their making so great misery to themselves and posterity, as was before mentioned, [by] their own doings: they are guilty of no sin in being purely passive in their calamity, when they cannot help it; but it is a great sin, for men, by their own act, to make themselves miserable. As, for instance, if a man were in a miserable captivity under severe taskmasters, and esteemed his bondage worse than death, and had no prospect of deliverance, it would not be lawful in such a case for a man to kill himself, to free himself from slavery.

As to any temporal loss such a people may sustain, which by paying their money for nothing, which they can't avoid any other way than by turning to the Church of England: the gaining or saving of money ought not to come into consideration in such an affair as this. The worship of God, the doctrines of the gospel and affairs of our eternal salvation, surely ought not to be put into the scales with so many shillings or pounds in bills of the old tenor, or in silver and gold: it is a shameful thing even to mention it; it is madness indeed when men will sell their religion for a little money: to do so is to sell God and heaven, and their own souls, and symbolize with Judas, who sold Christ for thirty pieces of silver.

Whereas some may possibly say, the Church of England had a divine blessing in and after the times of the Reformation, I answer: While Calvinistical doctrines were generally taught and professed among them, and the way of salvation thoroughly preached amongst them— which was once the case—these things were attended with the divine blessing. But the case is now altered; these doctrines have long been almost universally exploded in the Church of England, and the divine blessing has departed with them.

For these reasons, and many others, I think a people in the forementioned circumstances, cannot be in God's way, nor in the way of God's blessing, in seeking redress of their grievances by joining with the Church of England; but ought still to wait on God in the way of importunate prayer, though they have already waited long, and see nothing but midnight darkness. And 'tis to be hoped no such people will act suddenly and rashly in an affair of such vast consequence, but will first thoroughly acquaint themselves with the present state of the Church of England, that they mayn't act blindfold. And to that end I would recommend them *The Dissenting Gentleman's Answer to Mr. White's Three Letters.*[1]

Jonathan Edwards.

1. [Micaiah Towgood], *The Dissenting Gentleman's Answer to Mr. White's Three Letters* (London, 1746), a response to John White, fellow of St. John's College, Cambridge, whose three Letters (one originally published in 1743, the other two in 1745) were bound together as *Three Letters to a Gentleman Dissenting from the Church of England* (London, 1748).

89. TO THE REVEREND WILLIAM McCULLOCH

Edwards welcomes news that various individuals are beginning a new spiritual life, but his eye is on the millennium, which will bring benefit to everyone. He hopes that the Concert for Prayer and revival will usher in the golden age. Speculation on prophecy is of keen interest to him, but he defers judgment on controversial interpretations.

(Trask Library, ALS, two quarto leaves. Published in Dwight ed., *1*, 261–64. This letter relates to "Events of an Hopeful Aspect" in "Notes on the Apocalypse" and the *Humble Attempt*. See *Works*, 5, 285–97, 308–436.)

* * *

Northampton, October 7, 1748

Rev. and Dear Sir,

I thank you for your letter of February 10, 1748, which I received the week before last. I had also long before that received the letter you speak of, which you wrote the spring before, dated March 12, 1747, which I wrote an answer to, and sent it to Mr. [Thomas] Prince of Boston, and committed it to his care; and am very sorry that you never received it.[1]

I am far from being weary of our correspondence. I ever looked on myself as greatly honored and obliged by you in your beginning this correspondence; and have found it pleasant and profitable: and particularly your last letter that I have but now received has been very agreeable and entertaining, especially on account of the good news it contains.

I cannot but think that many things mentioned in your letter, and the letters of my other correspondents in Scotland which came with yours, are great things, worthy to be greatly taken notice of, and to be an occasion of much rejoicing and praise to all that love Zion, viz.: the remarkable change in one of the clerks of the Privy Council [Gilbert West]; God's stirring up him and Mr. [George] Lyttelton to write in defense of Christianity;[2] the good effect of this among men of figure and character; the good dispositions of the King, the Prince and Princess of Wales; the late awakening of two of the princesses, Amelia

---

1. See Letter No. 80, JE to McCulloch, Sept. 23, 1747, above.

2. West, *Observations on the History and Evidence of the Resurrection of Jesus Christ;* idem, *A Defence of the Christian Revelation;* and Lyttelton, *Observations on the Conversion and Apostleship of St. Paul.*

and Caroline, and the hopeful conversion of one or both of them; the hopeful, real piety of the Archbishop of Canterbury [Thomas Herring], and his good disposition towards Calvinism, experimental religion and the dissenters; several of the clergy of the Church of England, their lately appearing to preach the doctrines of grace; several of the magistrates in various towns in England, their exerting themselves with uncommon zeal to put the laws in execution against vice; and the eminent piety of the Prince of Orange, now Stadtholder of the seven United Provinces. These things (at least some of them) are great in themselves, and are of that nature that they have a most promising aspect on the interest of Zion, and to be happy presages and forerunners of yet better and greater things that are coming. They look as if the tide were turning, and glorious things approaching, by the revolution of the wheel of God's providence.

I think we and all others that have lately united by explicit agreement in extraordinary prayer for a general revival of religion and the coming of Christ's kingdom, may without presumption be greatly encouraged and animated in the duty we have engaged in, by the appearance of such a dawning of light from such great darkness; and should be ungrateful, if we did not acknowledge God's great goodness in these things, and faithfulness in fulfilling the promises of his Word; such as these in particular, "If any two of you shall agree on earth as touching anything you shall ask, it shall be done of my Father which is in heaven" [Matt. 18:19]; and "Before they call, I will answer; and while they are yet speaking, I will hear" [Is. 65:24]. I have already communicated these things to some belonging to this town and other places. Some have appeared much affected with them, and one that belongs to another town has taken extracts of these passages. I design, God willing, to communicate these things to my congregation, before the next quarterly day for prayer; and also to the neighboring ministers, who, according to our stated agreement will be met together on that day, to spend the former part of the day in prayer among ourselves, and the latter part in public services in one of our congregations; and shall also probably communicate these things to some of my correspondents in New Jersey and elsewhere. And I can't but think they will tend to do a great deal of good in various respects, and particularly will tend to promote the Concert for Prayer in these parts of the world. I desired Mr. [Thomas] Prince of Boston to send you one of my books on the

Concert,[3] soon after it was published; who engaged to do it; but long forgot it, as I perceived afterwards to my surprise. But since that more thorough care has been taken about that matter; and I hope you and each of my other correspondents in Scotland, have before now received one of those books.

I thank you, dear Sir, for sending me your thoughts on some things in the prophecies of the Revelation of St. John, and for being at so much trouble as to send it twice (supposing the first letter had miscarried). This I take as a particular mark of respect, for which I am obliged to you. I received, as I said before, your former letter (which contained the same observations) and sent an answer to it, wherein I gave you my thoughts, such as they were, on those subjects. But if you have received my book on united prayer, etc., therein you have seen more fully my thoughts on some things in the Revelation, but have a near relation to the same matters that you write about; the substance of which I before had written to you in a large letter, desiring your opinion of what I wrote. The letter I think you received, by some intimations contained in yours of March 12, 1747, but you was not pleased to favor me with anything at all of your thoughts of what I had so largely communicated to you, to that end, that I might have your opinion. But I am not the less willing again to communicate my thoughts of your remarks.

As to what you observe concerning the number 666, and that number being found in the name of the present King of France: it is indeed something remarkable that that number should be found both in his Latin and French names, as you observe; and I don't know but that the omniscient Spirit of God (who doubtless in his predictions has sometimes his eye on several things, in which he knows they will be fulfilled) might have some respect to his name in the prophecy. But yet I can hardly think that this individual King of France, or any other particular prince in Europe, is what is chiefly intended by the Beast, so largely described in the 13th chapter of Revelation, whose number is said to be 666. Of all the conjectures concerning the number of the Beast, that I have lit on in my small reading, that of Mr. [Francis] Potter's seems to me the most ingenious, who supposes the true meaning is to be found by extracting the root of the number.[4] But after all, I have ever suspected that the thing chiefly aimed at by the Holy Spirit was never yet

3. *An Humble Attempt.*
4. Francis Potter, *An Interpretation of the Number 666* (Oxford, 1642); see *Works*, 5, 113, n. 4.

found out, and that the discovery is reserved for later times. The chief cause why Mr. Potter's conjecture don't fully satisfy me is the difficulty about adjusting the fractions in the root when extracted.

With respect to your very ingenious conjectures concerning the period, forty-two months or 1,260 days, of the outer court and holy city's being trodden under foot of the Gentiles; you know, Sir, that that forty-two months or 1,260 days spoken of, Rev. 11:2, has been universally understood, as being the very same period with the 1,260 days of the witnesses prophesying in sackcloth, spoken of in the next verse, and the 1,260 days of the woman's being fed in the wilderness (ch. 12:6) and of the time, times, and half a time, of her being nourished in the wilderness from the face of the serpent (v. 14) and the forty-two months of the continuance of the beast (ch. 13:5). But it does appear to me probable that this forty and two months of the continuance of the beast, means the sum of the diverse periods in which the plot of ground whereon the ancient literal Jerusalem stood, was under the dominion of the Romans, Saracens, Persians, and Turks; but the space of time during which the reign of Antichrist, or the popish hierarchy, continues. And as to the particular time of the downfall of Antichrist, you see reasons in the forementioned pamphlet, why I think it certain that it will not be known till it be accomplished. I cannot but think that the Scripture is plain in that matter, and that it does in effect require us to rest satisfied in ignorance till the time of the end comes.

However, I should be very foolish if I were dogmatical in my thoughts concerning the interpretation of the prophecies; especially in opposition to those who have had so much more opportunity to be well acquainted with things of this nature. But since you have insisted on my thoughts, I conclude you will not be displeased that I have mentioned them, though not altogether agreeable to yours. I am nevertheless greatly obliged to you for your condescension in communicating your thoughts to me. If we don't exactly agree in our thoughts about these things, yet in our prayers for the accomplishment of these glorious events in God's time, and for God's gracious presence with us and his assistance in endeavors to promote his kingdom and interest in the meantime, we may be entirely agreed and united. That we may be so, is the earnest desire of, dear Sir, your obliged and affectionate

> Brother and servant in our common Lord,
> Jonathan Edwards.

90. TO THE REVEREND JOHN ERSKINE

Letters in the eighteenth century were sometimes lost in transit, those sent overseas being most vulnerable. Consequently, to insure delivery, Edwards on occasion wrote a duplicate, either to the same person or to another. This letter resembles his letter of August 31, 1748 (No. 86) also to Erskine, with the addition of two extracts of letters from New Jersey governor Jonathan Belcher and descriptions of missionary efforts.

(Trask Library, ALS, four quarto leaves. Published in Dwight ed., *1*, 265–70.)

* * *

Northampton, October 14, 1748

Rev. and Dear Sir,

A little while ago I wrote a letter to you, wherein I acknowledged the receipt of your letter, and the books that came with it, viz. [John] Taylor on *Original Sin,* and on the *Romans;* with your *Sermons* and *Answer to Mr. Campbell,*[1] for which most acceptable present I would now renewedly thank you. I sent my letter to Boston, together with one of Mr. [Solomon] Stoddard's *Benefit of the Gospel to the Wounded in Spirit,* and his *Nature of Saving Conversion,* with a sermon on Mr. [David] Brainerd's death, and some account of a history of his life now in the press, to be sent to Scotland by the first opportunity.[2] Whether there has been any opportunity or no, I cannot tell.

I have very lately received another letter from you, dated April 6, 1748, which was indeed exceeding acceptable, by reason of the remarkable and joyful accounts it contains of things that have a blessed aspect on the interests of Christ's kingdom in the world: such as the good effects of the writings of Mr. [Gilbert] West and Mr. [George] Lyttelton on some at Court; the religious concern in Mr. [Thomas] Randall's and Mr. Gray's parishes; the hopeful true piety of the Archbishop of Canterbury [Thomas Herring]; his and the King's disposition, not only to tolerate, but comprehend the dissenters, and their

1. Taylor, *The Scripture-Doctrine of Original Sin;* idem, *A Paraphrase with Notes on the Epistle to the Romans;* Erskine, *The People of God Considered as All Righteous,* and *The Law of Nature, sufficiently promulgated to the Heathen World; or an Inquiry into the Ability of the Heathens to discover the being of God, and the immortality of human souls; in some miscellaneous reflections, occasioned by Dr. Campbell, Professor of Divinity at St. Andrew's, Treatise on the Necessity of Revelation* (Edinburgh, 1741).

2. Stoddard, *Benefit of the Gospel to the Wounded in Spirit,* and *A Treatise concerning the Nature of Saving Conversion;* JE, *True Saints.* The proposal described what was to be published as *The Life of David Brainerd.*

indifference with respect to the liturgy, ceremonies and episcopal ordination; the piety of the Prince, who is now advanced to the
stadtholdership, and has it established in his family forever; the awakening of the Princess Caroline; and the good dispositions of the
Princess of Wales. I think it is very fit that those who have lately entered
into an union for extraordinary prayer for the coming of Christ's
kingdom and the prosperity of Zion, should inform one another of
things which they know of that pertain to the prosperity of Zion, and
whereby their prayers are in some degree answered: that they may be
united in joy and thanksgiving, as well as in supplication; and that they
may be encouraged and animated in their prayers for the future, and
engaged to continue instant therein with all perseverance.

I think those things forementioned, which you have sent me an
account of, are worthy greatly to be observed by those that are united
in the Concert for Prayer, for their comfort, praise and encouragement. I intend to communicate these things to my own people before
the next quarterly season for prayer, and to the neighboring ministers,
who are united in this affair; and also to my correspondents in this
province, and other provinces in America. I doubt not but they will
have an happy tendency and influence in many respects. I hope, dear
Sir, you will continue still to give me particular informations of things
that appear relating to the state of Zion and the interest of religion, in
Great Britain or other parts of Europe. In so doing you will not only
inform me, but I shall industriously communicate any important informations of that kind, and spread them amongst God's people in this
part of the world; and shall endeavor to my utmost to make such an use
of them as shall tend most to promote the interest of religion. And
among other things, I should be glad to be informed of any books that
come out, remarkably tending either to the illustration, or defense of
the truth, or the promoting the power of godliness, or in any respect
peculiarly tending to advance true religion.

I have given an account of some things which have a favorable aspect
on the interest of religion in these American parts of the world, in my
letters to Mr. [James] Robe and Mr. [John] MacLaurin sent with this;
which you will have opportunity to see.

In your last letter you desire to be particularly informed of the
present state of New Jersey College, and of things remarkable of a
religious nature respecting the Indians. As to the former, viz. the state
of New Jersey College, by the last accounts I had, it was in something of
an unsettled state. Gov. [Jonathan] Belcher had a mind to give them a

new charter, that he thought would be more for the benefit of the society. Accordingly, a draft of a new charter was drawn, wherein it was proposed to make considerable alteration in the Corporation of Trustees; to leave out some of the former trustees; and that the Governor for the time being should be a trustee, and three or four of the Council of that province. Those two things made considerable uneasiness, viz. leaving out some of the former trustees, and making it a part of the constitution that the Governor and so many of the Council should be members of the Corporation. Some feared that this would not be for the health of the society; because the men in chief authority in that province ben't, for the most part, men of no religion, and many of them open and professed contemners of it. How this matter has been settled, or whether these difficulties are got over, I have not been informed. As to Governor Belcher himself, he appears thoroughly engaged to promote virtue and vital religion in those parts, which already has had some good effects: vice and open profaneness, by the means, is become less fashionable among the great men, and virtue and religion more credible. The disposition of Governor Belcher may in some measure be seen by the following extract of a letter from him, in answer to one I wrote to him on a special occasion:

Burlington, New Jersey, February 5, 1748

You will, Sir, be sure of me as a friend and father to the missionaries this way, and of all my weight and encouragement for spreading the everlasting gospel of God our Savior, in all parts and places where God shall honor me with any power or influence. As to myself, Sir, it is impossible to express the warm sentiments of my grateful heart for the mercies without number with which I have been loaded, by the God which has led me all my life long to this day. And my reflection upon his goodness covers me with shame and blushing, for I know my utter unworthiness, and that I am less than the least of all his mercies. I would therefore abhor myself, and repent in dust and ashes. You are sensible, my good friend, that governors stand in a glaring light, and their conduct is narrowly watched by friends and enemies: the one often undeservedly applaud them, while the other perhaps too justly censure them. Yet in this I am not anxious; but to approve myself to the searcher of hearts, from whose mouth I must hear pronounced, at the great and general audit, those joyful words, "Enter Thou," etc., or that terrible sentence, "Depart from me," etc. Join with me then in thankfulness to God for all the blessings and talents he has entrusted me with, and in prayer that I may employ them to his honor and glory, to the good of the people over whom he hath placed me, and so to the comfort of my own soul; that I may always remember that he that ruleth over men must be just, ruling in the fear of God.

In another letter which I since received, dated Burlington, N.J., May 31, 1748, he says as follows:

I will prostrate myself before my God and Savior, and on the bended knees of my soul (abhorring myself in every view) I will beg for a measure of divine grace and wisdom; that so I may be honored in being an instrument of advancing the kingdom of the blessed Jesus in this world, and in that way be bringing forth fruit in old age.[3]

I bless God my heavenly Father, that I am not ashamed of the cross of Christ; and I humbly ask the assistance of sovereign grace, that in times of temptation, I may never be a shame to it: I mean that my conversation may always be as becometh the gospel of Christ. And I tell you again that all such as minister at the altar, and in the course of their ministry approve themselves faithful to the great head of the church, will not only find my countenance and protection, but my love and esteem.

As to our embryo college, it is a noble design; and if God pleases, may prove an extensive blessing. I have adopted it for a daughter, and hope it may in time become an "Alma Mater," to this and the neighboring provinces. I am getting the best advice and assistance I can in the draft of a charter, which I intend to give our infant college. And I thank you, Sir, for all the kind hints you have given me for the service of this excellent undertaking. And, as St. Luke says of Mary, "She kept all these things and pondered them in her heart" [Luke 2:19], so you may depend, what you have said about the College will not be lost with me; but, as far as God shall enable me, I shall exert and lay out myself in every way to bring it to maturity, and then to advance its future welfare and prosperity: for this I believe will be acceptable in the sight of God our Savior; a relish for true religion and piety being great strangers to this part of America. The accounts I receive from time to time give me too much reason to fear Arminianism, Arianism and even Socinianism, in destruction to the doctrines of free grace, are daily propa-

---

3. He was sixty-six years old the 8th day of January last—JE's note.

gated in New England colleges. How horribly and how wickedly are these poisonous notions rooting out those noble pious principles on which our excellent ancestors founded those seminaries! And how base a return is it of the present generation, to that God who is constantly surrounding them with goodness and mercy! And how offensive is it in the eyes of that God, who is jealous of his glory, and will take vengeance on his adversaries, and reserveth wrath for his enemies! And from these things I am led to thank you for your book wrote in consequence of the memorial from Scotland for promoting a Concert in Prayer. I am much pleased with this proposal and invitation to all good Christians, and with your arguments to encourage and corroborate the design. The two missionaries you mention, Messrs. [Elihu] Spencer and [Job] Strong, I am told are at present at Boston. I have once and again desired Mr. [John] Brainerd to assure 'em of my kindness and respect: but their affairs have not yet led them this way. I rejoice in their being appointed to carry the gospel in its purity to the Six Nations. And when Mr. Brainerd, and they, proceed to Susquehanna, they shall have all my assistance and encouragement; by letters to the King's governors where they may pass, and my letters to the Sachem or Chief of those Indians.

With regard to the two missionaries Governor Belcher mentions: the Commissioners in Boston of the Corporation in London for the Propagation of the Gospel among the Indians in New England and Parts Adjacent, a little before Mr. David Brainerd went to Boston, the summer before his death, had received a sum of money from the estate left by the famous Dr. [Daniel] Williams, for the maintenance of two missionaries among the Six Nations. And having entertained a very great esteem of Mr. Brainerd, from the opportunity they had of acquaintance with him while in Boston, they committed to him the affair of finding and recommending the persons proper to be employed in this business. Accordingly he, after much deliberation, recommended one Mr. [Elihu] Spencer belonging to Haddam, his native town; and Mr. [Job] Strong belonging to this town, Northampton; who are undoubtedly well-qualified persons, of good abilities and learning, and of pious dispositions.

The Commissioners on his recommendation accepted these persons; and after Mr. Brainerd's death, sent to 'em; and they went down to Boston, and accepted the mission. But the Commissioners did not think proper immediately to send 'em forth among the Six Nations; but ordered them to go and live, during the winter, in New Jersey, with Mr. John Brainerd among the Christian Indians; there to follow their studies, and get acquaintance with the manners and customs of Indians; and in the spring to go with Mr. Brainerd, to Susquehanna, to instruct the Indians on that river, before they went to the Six Nations. Accordingly, they went and lived in New Jersey, but were discouraged as to their intended journey to Susquehanna, for they understand that the Susquehanna Indians greatly objected against entertaining missionaries without the consent of the Six Nations (to whom they are subject and of whom it seems they stand in great fear) and insisted that the missionaries should go to the Six Nations first.

Therefore in the spring, Messrs. Spencer and Strong returned to Boston for new orders from the Commissioners: who saw cause to order them to come and live at my house, till the time of an appointed interview of the governors of Boston and New York with the chiefs of the Six Nations at Albany, in the latter part of summer: when it was proposed that some that should go to Albany with Gov. [William] Shirley, should, on the behalf of the Commissioners, treat with the Six Nations concerning their receiving missionaries.

Messrs. Spencer and Strong did accordingly. They lived with me in the summer, and went to Albany at the time of the treaty: and the nation of the Oneidas in particular were dealt with concerning receiving these missionaries, who appeared free and forward in the matter. Mr. Spencer and Strong at that time got some acquaintance with the chiefs of the tribe, who appeared fond of them, and very desirous of their going with them. But the grand difficulty then in the way was the want of [an] interpreter; which occasioned their not going with the Indians at that time, but returning again to New England. Mr. Strong also was taken much out of health, which discouraged him from entertaining any thoughts of throwing himself into the fatigues and hardships of this undertaking till the next spring. But the difficulty of the want of an interpreter is now got over; a very good one has been found; and Mr. Spencer was ordained on the 14th of the last month, and is gone with the interpreter, to go to the country of the Oneidas, about 170 miles beyond Albany, and about 130 miles distant from all settlements of the white people.

It is a thing that has a favorable aspect on the design of propagating the gospel among the Indians, that many of late have been remarkably spirited to promote it, and liberally to open their hands in order to it. Mr. Brainerd's going to Boston before his death, and people there having some acquaintance with him and with his labors and success among the Indians, gave occasion to a considerable number in Boston, men of good substance and of the best character, and some of them principal men in the town, to form themselves into a charitable society, that by their joint endeavors and contributions they might promote the instruction and spiritual good of the Indians: who have done some very liberal things for the Indians in New Jersey and also the Six Nations. The people of Northampton have also had their hearts remarkably opened to contribute to the maintenance of Mr. Spencer's interpreter. And a particular man at Springfield, has been moved to devote a considerable part of his estate to promote the propagation of the gospel among the Six Nations.

As to my writing against Arminianism: I have hitherto been remarkably hindered; so that probably it will be a considerable time before I shall have anything ready for the press; but do intend, God allowing and assisting, to prosecute that design; and I desire your prayers for the divine assistance in it. The books you sent me will be a great help to me; I would on no account have been without 'em.

I condole with you and your dear spouse, [on] the loss of your noble and excellent father:[4] which is doubtless a great loss to the church of God. But the glorious King of Zion, who was dead, is alive and lives forevermore, and can raise up others in exalted stations to favor Zion; and seems to be so doing at this day, by things you give an account of in your letter.

I have been the subject of an afflictive dispensation of late, tending to teach me how to sympathize with the afflicted; which I think I mentioned in my last letter to you, viz. the death of my second daughter [Jerusha] the last February.

Please to present my most affectionate and respectful salutations to your dear consort [Christian Mackay Erskine]. That I and mine may be remembered in your and her prayers, is the request of your affectionate and

> Obliged friend and brother,
> Jonathan Edwards.

4. JE refers to John Erskine's father-in-law, George Mackay, third Baron Reay, who died in 1748.

91. TO THE REVEREND JOSEPH BELLAMY

Edwards replies to an inquiry from Bellamy and adds further news regarding John Searle, a native of Northampton and one of a number of pupils who had studied theology with Edwards. Searle is busily searching for a pastorate. As it turned out, he did not become permanent minister at any of the places mentioned here, settling instead in Sharon, Connecticut. Edwards was invited to preach at his installation but was unable to attend.

Edwards has recently completed his *Life of David Brainerd* and is about to plunge into *Freedom of the Will*. That plan would be interrupted by a year of controversy on the communion question and the writing of the *Humble Inquiry*.

(HSF, Joseph Bellamy Papers, ALS, one quarto leaf.)

* * *

Northampton, January 9, 1748/9

Rev. and Dear Sir,

I received your letter dated January 1, by Mr. [Job] Strong: but as to your other letter you mention, that you sent by the way of Hartford about a fortnight before, I have not received it.

Mr. [John] Searle is not in these parts: I suppose he is at Norwich, a place as far distant from hence as Bethlehem is. He was here about a month or six weeks ago: and I perceive that the ministers in the neighborhood of the place where he has been at Norwich, are desirous of his staying longer there, which is a large congregation, where has been great and long continued difficulty and division; and the people in general, of different parties, greatly united in him; excepting the separatists, and they are friendly to him and have passed him for a good man. He is earnestly desired by the people of Quabin, and has been applied to lately by the people of Ellington and of Old Windsor. And, for my part, I am wholly at a loss at present where he can best serve the interest of religion; and if he should ask my advice, should not know what advice to give him, without further information from him or others.

If I live till the spring, I shall probably have occasion for Mastrict and Turretin, being engaged in studies on the Arminian controversies and preparing to write something upon them. I hope you will come and bring the books yourself for I should rejoice to see you here.[1]

1. The books referred to here are Mastrict's *Theoretico-Practica Theologia*, and Turretin's

I have here sent a sermon directed by Madam [Prudence Chester] Stoddard to her brother [Anthony Stoddard] at Woodbury; I desire you take care of the conveyance of it: you will have opportunity to read it by the way if you see cause.

I am exceeding sorry you did not go to Long Island as you proposed: but I wish you contrive to make out a journey there still, and travel as you proposed from one end of the island to the other.

My wife and one of my younger children have lately been in very dangerous circumstances, but through mercy are now all moving about.

Give my love to Mrs. [Frances Sherman] Bellamy.

> I am, Sir, your brother and most affectionate friend,
> Jonathan Edwards.

92. TO THE REVEREND THOMAS FOXCROFT

Foxcroft is shepherding the *Humble Inquiry* through the press. With this note, Edwards forwards subscription proposals and promises an abstract of Foxcroft's long letter, marshaling arguments against the Halfway Covenant. It was published as an appendix to the book.

(Beinecke Library, ALS, one quarto leaf, addressed on verso to [the Reverend Thomas] Foxcroft, [Minister of th]e Gospel [at Bos]ton. Abstract of Foxcroft's letter, dated June 26, 1749, published in *Humble Inquiry*. See *Works*, *12*, 326–48.)

* * *

Northampton, May 12, 1749

Rev. and Honored Sir,

I received your letter of May 3rd the day before yesterday, since I wrote to Mr. [Edward] Bromfield by Mr. [Benjamin] Alvord. I humbly thank you for your letter. My warning now is exceeding short, and I have but just time to send a draft of proposals for subscription, intending very shortly to write largely to you and send an abstract of your former letter to be added to my book as an appendix, if you please, and an answer to three more objections, taking up about a sheet and an half in manuscript. But now I must break off by subscribing myself

> Your obliged brother and humble servant,
> Jonathan Edwards.

Institutio Theologiæ Elencticæ. JE probably owned a revised edition of the latter work. See *Works*, *13*, 384, n. 5.

Thomas Foxcroft,
anonymous, undated,
Harvard University
Portrait Collection,
bequest of Henry H.
Edes to the University,
1935

93. TO THE REVEREND JOHN ERSKINE

After reporting on Indian missions, the College of New Jersey, and the Concert for Prayer, Edwards introduces the communion controversy. He realistically assesses the dispute and anticipates, a year ahead of the event, that it may cost him his position. His book on the question, *Humble Inquiry,* is in press. Until it is published, the Northampton church has declined to take further action.

(Trask Library, ALS, two quarto leaves. Published in Dwight ed., *1,* 273–76.)

* * *

Northampton, May 20, 1749

Rev. and Dear Sir,

The day before yesterday I received your letter of February 14, with the packet containing the pamphlets you mention in your letter, for which I am greatly obliged to you. I have not yet had opportunity to read these books, but promise myself much entertainment by them, from the occasions on which they were written, and the subjects they are upon. The last letter I received from you before this was dated

April 6, 1748, so that I suppose the two letters you say you wrote to me since those which I acknowledge the receipt of, have miscarried. Which I much regret, as I much value what comes from your hand.

In one of your last letters which came to hand, you desire to be particularly informed concerning the state of religion in these parts of the world, and particularly concerning the mission to the Indians, and the infant college in New Jersey. As to the affair of preaching the gospel to the Indians, Mr. [Elihu] Spencer went the last fall, far into the western wilderness; to the Oneidas, one of the tribes of Indians called the Six Nations, living on Susquehanna River, towards the head of the river, to a place called by the Indians, Onohquauga, about 180 miles southwest from Albany on Hudson's River, where he continued almost through the winter; and went through many difficulties and hardships, with little or no success, through the failing of his interpreter [Rebecca Kellogg Ashley]; who was a woman that had formerly been a captive among the Caghnawauga Indians in Canada, who speak the same language with those Oneidas, excepting some small variation of dialect. She went with her husband [Benjamin Ashley], an Englishman, and is one of the people we here call Separatists: who showed the spirit he was of there, in that wilderness, beyond what was known before. He differed with and opposed Mr. Spencer in his measures, and had an ill influence on his wife; who I fear was very unfaithful, refusing to interpret for Mr. Spencer more than one discourse in a week, a sermon upon the sabbath; and utterly declined assisting him in discoursing and conversing with the Indians in the week-time. And her interpretations on the sabbath were performed very unfaithfully, as at last appeared, so that Mr. Spencer came away in discouragement in the spring, and returned to Boston, and gave the Corporation there, who employed him, an account of his unexpected difficulties and disappointment; and became obliged to them to wait three months, to see if they could procure a fellow missionary, and another interpreter, to go with him to the Indians; which I believe is not much expected. If these are not obtained within the limited time, Mr. Spencer is free from any further engagements to them. Mr. Spencer is now preaching at Elizabethtown in New Jersey, in the pulpit of the late Mr. [Jonathan] Dickinson; and I believe is like to settle there. He is a person of very promising qualifications, and will hopefully in some measure make up the great loss that people have sustained by the death of their former pastor.

As to the mission in New Jersey, we have from time to time had comfortable accounts of it. And Mr. John Brainerd, who has the care of the congregation of Christian Indians there, was, about three weeks ago, at my house; and informed of the increase of his congregation, and of their being added to from time to time by the coming of Indians from distant places, and settling in the Indian town at Cranbury, for the sake of hearing the gospel; and of something of a work of awakening being all along carried on, among the Indians to this day; and of some of the newcomers being awakened, and of there being instances from time to time of hopeful conversion among them; and of the general good and pious behavior of the professing Indians. But he gave an account also of some trouble the Indians meet with from some of the white people; and particularly from Mr. [Robert Hunter] Morris, the Chief Justice of the Province, a professed deist, who is suing them for their lands, under pretext of a will made by their former king, which was undoubtedly forged. However, he is a man of such craft and influence, that it is not known how the matter will issue.

I have heard nothing new that is very remarkable concerning the college in New Jersey. It is in its infancy. There has been considerable difficulty about settling their charter. Gov. [Jonathan] Belcher, who gave the charter, is willing to encourage and promote the college to his utmost; but differs in his opinion concerning the constitution which will tend most to its prosperity, from some of the principal ministers that have been concerned in founding the society. He insists upon it that the governor, for the time being, and four of His Majesty's Council for the Province, should always be of the Corporation of Trustees; and that the governor should always be the president of the Corporation. The ministers are all very willing that the present governor, who is a religious man, should be in this standing. But their difficulty is with respect to future governors, who they suppose are as likely to be men of no religion and deists, as otherwise. However so the matter is settled, ['tis] to the great uneasiness of Mr. Gilbert Tennent in particular, who it is feared will have no further concern with the college on this account. Mr. [Aaron] Burr, the President of the College, is a man of religion and singular learning, and I hope the college will flourish under his care.

I have taken a great deal of pains in communicating to others, in various parts, the pleasing accounts you, and my other correspondents in Scotland, gave me last year of things of promising aspect on the interest of religion on your side of the ocean; which have been very affecting to pious ministers and people in New England, and also in the provinces of New York and New Jersey; and hope some considerable good has been done by such tidings; particularly in animating many in the duty of extraordinary united prayer for a general revival of religion, and promoting the Concert for Prayer proposed from Scotland; which prevails more and more in these parts of the world; which together with other things in some places, are cause of thankfulness, and bode well to the interests of Zion (of which I have given a more particular account in my letters to Mr. [John] MacLaurin and Mr. [James] Robe and Mr. [William] McCulloch, sent with this), though it be in general a very dead time as to religion, and a time of the prevailing of all manner of iniquity.

I shall send orders to Boston, that one of my books on Mr. [David] Brainerd's life may be sent to you with this letter, if any of them are ready, as I hope they are or will be very speedily.

I have nothing very comfortable to inform of concerning the present state of religion in this place. A very great difficulty has arisen between me and my people, relating to qualifications for communion at the Lord's table. My honored grandfather [Solomon] Stoddard, my predecessor in the ministry over this church, strenuously maintained the Lord's Supper to be a converting ordinance; and urged all to come who were not of scandalous life, though they knew themselves to be unconverted. I formerly conformed to his practice, but I have had difficulties with respect to it, which have been long increasing; till I dared no longer to proceed in the former way: which has occasioned great uneasiness among my people, and has filled all the country with noise; which has obliged me to write something on the subject, which is now in the press.

I know not but this affair will issue in a separation between me and my people. I desire your prayers that God would guide me in every step in this affair. My wife joins with me in respectful salutations to you and your consort.

I am, Sir, your obliged and affectionate brother and servant,

Jonathan Edwards.

94. TO THE REVEREND WILLIAM McCULLOCH

This letter, to one of the prime supporters of the Concert for Prayer in Scotland, is unusual in showing specific results of the promotional efforts made to get it going. Edwards quotes reports from three ministers, who write about the warm reception given by their congregations and fellow clergy for revival through the Concert.

(Trask Library, ALS, two quarto leaves. Published in Dwight ed., *1*, 276–78.)

* * *

Northampton, May 23, 1749

Rev. and Dear Brother,

The last letter I received from you was dated February 10, 1748, to which I wrote an answer the latter end of last summer; which I suppose you received, because I perceive by letters sent me this spring by some others of my correspondents, your neighbors, they had received letters I sent to them at the same time, and in the same packet. Your letters to me have been very acceptable; I should be glad to receive 'em oftener.

The letter I last received from you, and others that came with it, were peculiarly agreeable on the account of the good news they contained concerning Mr. [Gilbert] West and [George] Lyttelton, the Archbishop of Canterbury [Thomas Herring], some in the royal family, the Stadtholder, etc. These things I have taken a great deal of pains to communicate to others; and they have been very entertaining, and I hope profitable to many. I was at the pains to extract, from all the letters I received at that time, those things which appeared with a favorable aspect on the interest of religion in the world, and to draw various copies to send to different parts, to such as I supposed would be most likely to be entertained and improved by them, and to do good with them. And I believe they have been of great benefit, particularly to excite and encourage God's people in the great duty of praying for the coming of Christ's kingdom; and to promote extraordinary united prayer in the method proposed in the memorial from Scotland. I read these articles of good news to my own congregation, and also to the association of ministers to which I belong, when met on one of the quarterly seasons for prayer; and read them occasionally to many others; and sent a copy of one of the forementioned abstracts to Connecticut, which was carried into various parts of that government, and shown to several ministers there. I sent one to Mr. [David] Hall of Sutton, a pious minister about the middle of this province, who, according to my desire, communicated it to other ministers, and I suppose to his people. I sent a copy to Mr. [John] Rogers of Kittery, I suppose about seventy miles to the eastward of Boston, who in reply wrote to me and in his letter says as follows:

> Yours of the 22d of December came not to my hand till the 19th of this; with which I was well-pleased, and had some sweet sense of the sovereign free grace of God in the instances you mentioned, with some going forth of heart after further displays of it in the mighty and noble of our nation, and the great ones of our own country; and indeed that the kingdom of our exalted Redeemer might prevail in all the world. And, dear Sir, I am full in the belief that so many of the Lord's people agreeing upon a time to unite in prayer for the pouring out of the Holy Spirit, and the coming of the Redeemer's kingdom, is from the Lord; and can't but hope the day draws near, when he will pour out of his waters upon the thirsty, and his floods upon the dry ground; as also that all his ministers and people who are engaged in so delightful a work for so noble an end, will give him no rest till he shall make his Jerusalem a quiet habitation, etc., name, and praise in the earth.

I sent another copy into New Jersey to Mr. John Brainerd, missionary to the Indians there, with a desire that he would communicate it to others as he thought would be most serviceable. He writes in answer, March 4, 1748, as follows:

> I received yours of January 12 on sabbath morning, February 5, and desire to acknowledge your kindness with much thankfulness and gratitude. It was a great refreshment, as well as encouragement to me; and I trust has been so to many others in these parts, who are concerned for the prosperity of Zion. The next Tuesday after (as perhaps, Sir, you may remember) was the quarterly day appointed for extraordinary prayer; upon which I called my people together and gave them information of the most notable things contained in your letter. And since, I have endeavored to communicate the same to several of my neighboring ministers, and sundry private Christians, as I had opportunity. I have also thought it my duty to send an extract, or rather a copy of it, to Gov. [Jonathan] Belcher. I have likewise (for want of time to transcribe) sent the original to Philadelphia by a careful hand, that the Reverend Mr. Gilbert Tennent might have the perusal of it; where a copy was taken, and the original safely returned to me again. I can't but hope that this letter (as it contains many things wherein the power and goodness of God do appear in a most conspicuous manner) will be

greatly serviceable in stirring up the people of God in these parts, and encouraging their hearts to seek his face and favor, and to cry mightily to him for the further outpouring of his gracious Spirit upon his church in the world. For my part, I think the remarkable things which your letter contains might be sufficient to put new life into anyone who is not past feeling; and as a means to excite a spirit of prayer and praise, in all those who are not buried in ignorance, or under the power of a lethargic stupor. And 'tis looked upon by those whom I have had opportunity to converse with, whether ministers or private Christians, that what God has done is matter of great thankfulness and praise, and might well encourage his people to lift up the hand of prayer, and be instant therein.

Mr. [James] Davenport, minister of a part of Elizabethtown in New Jersey, writes thus upon it, in a letter dated April 1, 1749:

> I thank you for sending your letter to Mr. Brainerd open, that I might see it, which I took a copy of; and have found it again and again refreshing and animating. I read it to the ministers who met at my house for prayer, on the first Tuesday of February, and sent it afterwards to Long Island. Mr. [Samuel] Buell took a copy of it and read it in his congregation on the Island.

I hope, dear Sir, these things will encourage you to continue your correspondence, and to go on to give me information of whatever appears in your parts of the world, favorable to the interests of the kingdom of Christ. It will not only be entertaining to me, but I shall endeavor, whenever I receive such tidings, to communicate it for the entertainment and profit of God's people as I have opportunity.

I must refer you, dear Sir, to my letters to other correspondents in your neighborhood, for other particulars relating to the state of religion in these parts of the world, and hope when you are before the throne of grace you will not forget your very affectionate

Friend and brother and servant,
Jonathan Edwards.

P.S. I hope some of my books on Mr. [David] Brainerd's life will be ready, so that one of them may be sent from Boston to you with this letter: I shall send orders to my friends in Boston accordingly.

95. TO THE REVEREND JAMES ROBE

This letter opens with a wistful longing for the exhilaration of revival: a vivid awareness of one's needs and of divine resources, a deeper understanding, and a transformed life. Edwards, heartened by reports of these effects occurring in distant places, trusts that an awakening will once more sweep over his somnolent town.

The association covenant, held up by Edwards as a model, was transmitted to him by the Reverend Joseph Emerson of Groton, later Pepperrell, Massachusetts. It calls for repentance and rededication by both clergy and laity to curb moral declension and the apparent weakening of ministerial authority. Personal interest in others' behavior and welfare is urged, in the spirit of John Winthrop's *A Model of Christian Charity.*

(Trask Library, ALS, three quarto leaves. Published in Dwight ed., *1*, 279– 83. See also Edwards to Parkman, Sept. 11, 1749 [No. 101], below.)

*   *   *

Northampton, May 23, 1749

Rev. and Dear Sir,

Mr. [John] MacLaurin, in a letter I received from him the last week, dated March 10, 1749, informs me of a letter you had written to me, sent to him; which he had taken care of. This letter, by some means or other has failed, and has never reached me. I intend to make inquiry after it, to see if it ben't left at Boston, and forgotten to be sent. I have reason to hope (though I have not received your letter) that you and your family are well, because Mr. MacLaurin and Mr. [John] Erskine (the only correspondents from whom I have received letters this time) inform of nothing to the contrary.

As to the present state of religion in these parts of the world, it is in the general very dark and melancholy. But yet there are some things which appear comfortable and hopeful. Particularly, the Concert for extraordinary prayer for the coming of Christ's kingdom, is spreading and prevailing. And we hear of awakenings and revivals of religion in some places. We have had accounts from time to time of religion being in flourishing state in the Indian congregation in New Jersey, under the care of Mr. John Brainerd, of the congregation's increasing, by the access of Indians from distant parts, of a work of awakening carried on among the unconverted, and additions made to the number of the hopefully converted, and the Christian behavior of professors there. Mr. Brainerd was at my house a little while ago, and represented this to be the present state of things in that congregation.

I had a letter from Mr. [James] Davenport (who is settled now as a minister over a congregation belonging to Elizabeth in New Jersey) dated April 1, 1749, wherein he says as follows:

> Mr. [Thomas] Lewis told me that there has been a remarkable work of conviction prevailing in his place, ever since last December. I think he spoke of about forty under soul-concern, a considerable number of 'em under strong convictions and some hopefully converted. I heard lately a credible account of a remarkable work of conviction and conversion among whites and negroes, at Hanover in Virginia, under the ministry of Mr. [Samuel] Davies, who is lately settled there, and has the character of a very ingenious and pious young man; whose support in his preparation for service, Mr. [William] Robinson[1] contributed much, if not mostly to; and on his deathbed gave him his books, etc.

Mr. [Samuel] Buell of East Hampton on Long Island, was here last week, and gave account of a very considerable work of awakening at this time in his congregation, especially among the young people; and also of a yet greater work at Bridgehampton, under the ministry of one Mr. [James] Brown, a very pious and prudent young man lately settled there. These congregations are both pretty large. He also gave an account of religion's continuing in a very prosperous state at a part of Huntington, another town on Long Island, where was a great and general awakening last year.

An association of ministers between this and Boston, seem of late to have applied themselves something earnestly to invent means for the promoting religion. The following is a copy of something they have agreed upon for this end, as it was put to me by a minister that lives that way.

> The sum and substance of the answers given by the Association to this question, *What things shall be done by us for preventing the awful threatening degeneracy and backsliding in religion, in the present day?*
>
> These we apprehend may be reduced to the following heads, viz. those that respect ourselves personally, and those which concern the Association as such, and those which relate to our people in our respective churches and congregations.

---

1. This Mr. Robinson was a young minister of eminent gifts and grace; I think, belonging to Pennsylvania, but had sometimes preached with great success in Virginia in various parts; but died three or four years ago, in his youth—JE's note.

Samuel Davies, by James Massalon, 1874, the Art Museum, Princeton University

I. As to what respects ourselves personally:

1. We ought surely to get a deep and affecting sense of this, whether there is not in ourselves defection and great danger of further degeneracy; for otherwise we shall with little heartiness undertake, or earnestness endeavor, reformation.

2. We are not to think it amiss that we ourselves be excited to look, with a proper attention and concern, into our own state, into our own experiences in the divine life, and into what little proficiency we make, or declension we fall into, ourselves.

3. We must by all means see to it that we be sound and clear in the great doctrines of the gospel, which are the life of our holy religion (we here intend those doctrines which are exhibited in our excellent Westminster Catechism and Confession of Faith); and that we all boldly and impartially appear in the defense thereof. At the same time, we must take heed and beware of the dangerous errors which many have run into; particularly the Armi-

nian and neonomian on the one hand, and the antinomian and enthusiastical on the other.

4. We must be very faithful in every part of our ministerial works, and make conscience to magnify our office. In a particular manner, we must take good heed to our preaching; that it be not only sound, but instructive, savory, spiritual, very awakening and searching, well adapted to the times and seasons which pass over us; laboring earnestly herein. We must therefore dwell much upon the doctrine of repentance and conversion; the nature, necessity and evidence thereof; and much urge the duty of self-examination, and open the deceits of the heart: bringing the unconverted under the work of the law, that they may be prepared to embrace the offer of the gospel. Moral duties must be treated of in an evangelical strain; and we must give unto everyone his portion, and not shrink from it, under the notion of prudence; in special, in the important duty of reproving sinners of all sorts, be they who they will. Again, we must not be flighty in our private conference with souls, and examining candidates for the communion, or other special privileges; and we must carefully and wisely suit our endeavors to the several ages and conditions of persons, the elder and younger. And in a very particular manner, we must set ourselves to promote religion among our young people. And in a word, we must see whether we are animated to all these things by the grace of God in us.

5. We are impartially to see what evils are to be found among ourselves, and remove 'em. Let us be seriously thoughtful whether (among our defects) we have not been, in some respect or other, the blamable means of discouragement to those who have been under religious concern; or whether we have not given strength and boldness to the ungodly, when we have been testifying against extravagancies and disorders of the late times.

6. We must conscientiously be exemplary in our whole behavior and conversation. 'Tis necessary that we be serious and grave, as what highly becomes gospel-bishops. And especially, we must be very watchful over our frame and conduct on the Lord's day. We must therefore look well to our sabbatizing, both at home and abroad, both

before our own and other people. Our example is of vast consequence in magnifying our office, before recommended.

7. We ought to stir up the gifts which are in us, and to grow more and more, according to the sacred injunction, II Tim. 1:6.

8. We should follow all our endeavors with fervent prayer to God; especially our labors in preaching and teaching: the seed of the Word is to be steeped in tears.

II. As to what concerns the Association as such:

1. We must lay aside disgust one with another, and study brotherly love, that it may revive and continue. We must endeavor to be as near as we can of one mind, and go on harmoniously; and then we shall be the more strongly united in all, but especially in our *present* proceedings. There must be respectful treatment one of another, the persons and characters of one another; and we must be careful of ministerial characters, which is of greater consequence than at first sight may appear. And when we have occasion to dispute, let it be under a very strict guard, avoiding all censuring reflections.

2. That we manifest our approbation of the Westminster Assembly's Catechism, as containing an excellent system of divinity: and we purpose to preach agreeable to the doctrines of the Bible exhibited therein.

3. As we must be very careful of our conversation in general as abovesaid, so especially must we respecting our conduct while together in association.

4. It is proposed that a course of our associations be turned into fasts, upon this great account.

5. We agree to be more especially fervent in continual prayer for the advancement of the kingdom of Christ.

6. Some special new and prudent care must be taken to guard our pulpits.

7. 'Tis proposed that we agree to endeavor to introduce the public reading of the holy Scriptures, the manner and time to be left to discretion.

III. With regard to what may be done among the people we stand related to:

1. We conceive that whatever public exercises are to be

agreed on, or whatever concerns the public, the people are to be informed of, and acquainted with our design.

2. That it be earnestly recommended to the people to consider the worth of their privileges, and the danger of being deprived of 'em; which there is partly by the spreading of evil doctrines among 'em, and partly by the conduct of too many people towards their ministers.

3. Let pragmatical, factious spirits, fomenting division, be duly frowned upon.

4. We must guard them against the temptations of their several employments, and the special seasons wherein they are most exposed.

5. We must consider what evils there are to be found among them, which do especially need reforming; as the profanation of the Lord's day, which is enough to destroy all religion; tavern-haunting, company-keeping, chambering, uncleanness, profaneness, etc. And we ought loudly to testify against 'em. And that what we do may be effectual, let us endeavor to convince their consciences of the evil of sin, and of these sins. We are not to fail to warn people solemnly against the dreadful guilt of unthankfulness under God's signal mercies, and of incorrigibleness under heavy and sore judgments. Could we in wisdom do it, we should also warn 'em against their oppressing the Lord's ministers in their maintenance.

6. Let us endeavor to revive good customs and practices among 'em; particularly, the ancient good practice of catechizing, family order, worship and government, religious societies under good regulation, godly conference and conversation among Christians; and in brief, whatever is laudable and of good tendency.

7. Church discipline should be revived; brotherly watchfulness and admonition. Nor are we to forget to take special care of the children and youth of the flock.

8. We may do well to engage, as far as we are able, all persons of distinction and influence to unite with us in this work of reformation, e.g. justices, schoolmasters, candidates for the ministry; and especially to assist us by their example.

9. Solemn renewal of covenant hath been advised to as very

useful upon this occasion (vid. Synod 1679 for reformation),[2] but we leave this to each one's discretion.

Finally, in these things we should think ourselves bound to exert ourselves, and use uncommon fervency, to preserve what remains of religion, and prevent further decay.
October 1748

Thus far this Association.
The members of this Association, as their names were sent to me, are as follows.

The Reverend Messrs. Loring of Sudbury.
Cushing of Shrewsbury.
Parkman of Westborough.
Gardiner of Stow.
Martyn of Westborough.
Stone of Southborough.
Seecomb of Harvard.
Morse of Shrewsbury.
Smith of Marlborough.
Goss of Bolton.
Buckminster of Rutland.
Davis of Holden.

I must refer you, dear Sir, for other particulars relating to the state of religion in these parts of the world, to my letters to my other correspondents in your neighborhood.

My wife and family join with me in very affectionate and respectful salutations to you and yours. Desiring a continued interest in your prayers for us all, and for this part of the Zion of God, I remain, dear Sir,

Your loving brother and obliged friend and servant,
Jonathan Edwards.

P.S. I intend to send order to Boston with this letter, that one of my books on Mr. [David] Brainerd's life may be sent to you with it; hoping that some of 'em are ready, or will be speedily. I crave your acceptance of it.

2. See *The Necessity of Reformation . . . Agreed upon by the Elders and Members of the Churches . . . Sept. 10, 1679* (Boston, 1679).

96. TO THE REVEREND THOMAS FOXCROFT

Of the three letters to Foxcroft in May and June 1749, this is the most conversational. Edwards cites colleagues who concur with him on the communion controversy, weighs possible consequences of it, and reaffirms his determination to pursue his course. He seeks Foxcroft's intervention to stop Elisha Williams from writing against him. Williams never did so. Instead, he went to England on business, turning his notes over to his half-brother, Solomon, who wrote *The True State of the Question* in opposition to Edwards.

(Beinecke Library, ALS, two folio leaves, addressed on verso to the Reverend Mr. Thomas Foxcroft in Boston. On Elisha Williams, see SIB, 5, 593.)

* * *

Northampton, May 24, 1749

Rev. and Honored Sir,

I have herewith sent an answer to three other objections against the doctrine maintained in my discourse now in the press; which objections I find, by further consideration and conversation, there is a necessity should be answered. I have also sent a short preface, and an abstract of your letter to me on this subject. I have taken such things from the letter as I desire may be published. If they are published as something that I add to my own book, as an abstract of a letter which I received from you (in the form wherein I have here sent it), it may be best to be as an appendix. But if it be published as something that you would add in your own name, I should think it would be better to be in a preface. I should choose the latter, viz. that you should add these things in a preface in your own name; but I must leave it with your judgment. I should be glad that something may be observed concerning the opinion of the late and present divines in England and Scotland. Some things I have observed, that lead me to suppose that their opinion is generally agreeable to Mr. [Richard] Baxter's.

In my narrative of the work of God wrought here fourteen years ago,[1] which was sent to Dr. [Isaac] Watts and Dr. [John] Guyse, I observed something of the manner of our church to admit members without a profession of conversion. They, in some of their letters written to Dr. [Benjamin] Colman, appeared much offended at it. I have a sermon of Dr. Guyse, preached at the ordination of Mr. [Thomas]

---

1. *Faithful Narrative* (*Works*, 4, 157).

Gibbons in London,[2] wherein he plainly manifests his mind with regard to the qualifications of the members of a Christian church. And I have seen a practical discourse of Mr. [John] Willison's of Dundee,[3] wherein he is much in warning graceless persons not to presume to approach the Lord's table. But you have vastly greater opportunities of full information, concerning the present principles and practice in England and Scotland, than I. And an account of this would be more likely to have influence on some, than an account of what was in the last and preceding centuries.

You speak in your last letter, as though Mr. [Solomon] Stoddard's opinion was far from being the prevailing opinion in your parts. If it be so, I should be glad if this also might be inserted; for people in general here are not sensible but that their opinion is become the established opinion almost all over New England. You say, you believe the generality of the churches and elderly ministers your way hold to the first principles of New England in this matter. If you mean not only with respect to qualifications for the Lord's Supper, but also baptism, 'tis what I was by no means aware of and quite otherwise than I supposed. I did suppose it to be the universal, and long established custom of the country, to admit to baptism on lower terms than to the Lord's Supper; excepting those churches where Mr. Stoddard's principles were established. And particularly that it was the custom to admit parents who desired baptism for their children into the church in a state of education, on their owning the covenant, as it is called; which they do, not as professing or pretending to saving faith and repentance or regenerating grace. I should be glad to be more particularly informed as to that matter. And if it be otherwise than I have conceived, I think it had best by all means be published in the book; for 'tis undoubtedly very diverse from what is universally received to be fact in these parts.

The greatest difficulty of all relating to my principles is here, respecting baptism. I am not sure but that my people, in length of time and with great difficulty, might be brought to yield the point as to the qualifications for the Lord's Supper, though that is very uncertain. But with respect to the other sacrament, there is scarce any hope of it. And this will be very likely to overthrow me, not only with regard to my

---

2. John Guyse, *A Sermon Preached at the Ordination of the Rev. Mr. Thomas Gibbons* (London, 1743)

3. Among several of Willison's works on the Lord's Supper, the one most likely to have been referred to here is *A Sacramental Directory* (Edinburgh, 1716), which went through several editions.

usefulness in the work of the ministry here, but everywhere; if the case *be,* as I supposed it *was* in the country. The ministers in New Jersey and Pennsylvania are many of them strict with regard to qualifications for the Lord's Supper. But I understand they are not so with regard to baptism; but do admit all, on owning the covenant, not under the notion of a profession of true godliness.

If I should be wholly cast out of the ministry, I should be in many respects in a poor case. I shall not be likely to be serviceable to my generation, or get a subsistence in a business of a different nature. I am by nature very unfit for secular business; and especially am now unfit, after I have been so long in the work of the ministry. I am now comfortably settled, have as large a salary settled upon me as most have out of Boston, and have the largest and most chargeable family of any minister, perhaps within an hundred miles of me.

I have many enemies abroad in the country, who hate me for my stingy principles, enthusiasm, rigid proceedings and that now are expecting full triumph over me. I need the prayers of my fathers and brethren who are friendly to me, that I may have wisdom given me by my great master, and that I may be enabled to conduct with a steady faithfulness to him, under all trials and whatever may be the issue of this affair. I seem as it were to be casting myself off from a precipice; and have no other way, but to go on, as it were blindfold, i.e. shutting my eyes to everything else but the evidences of the mind and will of God, and the path of duty; which I would observe with the utmost care.

This western part of New England is exceeding full of noise about this affair, and few are indifferent. Some of the ministers in Connecticut, that have been chief favorers and promoters of the late work of God, have a spirit of opposing zeal excited on this occasion (from whom I should have least expected it), and appear strangely ready to entertain groundless surprises, and receive false reports and misrepresentations concerning me, which the country is very full of.

As to the three objections to which I have now sent answers, I think the *first* of them may properly be placed the first of all the objections. As to the placing of the other two, I must leave it to your discretion, who have the book before you, and see the order of the objections, and can better judge where they will most properly come in, than I, who don't fully remember their order.

If you see Rector [Elisha] Williams at Boston, I hope you will endeavor to dissuade him from writing against me, as he has given out. Not that I am afraid of the strength of any fair arguing against the doctrine I maintain; but such are my peculiarly disadvantageous circumstances, that he doubtless has it in the power of his hands to do me a great deal of hurt, let his arguments be never so weak. Yea, if they should be far worse than nothing in the esteem of observing and discerning readers, yet its only being said that Rector Williams has written an answer to me, will do me great hurt with my people. It would be a very likely way to discourage Mr. Williams from writing, if he could be made to believe that it would not be for his honor; and particularly if he could be artfully led to think that my books would go to Great Britain, to England and Scotland; and that his opposing me in this matter would be offensive to learned men there, and not for his honor in that part of the world.

I should be glad if his writing might be prevented, not only for the reason already mentioned, but also on this account, that it would save me a long and perhaps almost endless labor of replying. For though I have been with great reluctance brought to begin to write, yet since divine providence has compelled me, and I have put my hand to the plow, I shall look upon it [as] my duty to pursue the matter to the end; and to write as long as I see there is any need of writing, in order to defend this important doctrine, and God gives me ability and opportunity.

If you observe any expressions in my manuscript not respectful enough to my grandfather, I would pray you to inform me of it. I would in no degree be guilty of the sin of Canaan, in his disrespect to his grandfather.

I desire you to inform Messrs. [Samuel] Kneeland and [Timothy] Green, [Jr.], that Capt. [Benjamin] Church and Mr. [John] Potwine of Hartford, when I lately saw 'em together there, desired me, if there should be occasion for it, to inform my undertaker, that they would jointly take off an hundred of the books and send him the money, and Mr. John Brainerd of New Jersey has engaged to take fifty; and Mr. [Joseph] Bellamy of Bethlehem in Connecticut has engaged to take fifty more, provided the undertaker will wait for the money till the fall of the year.

I thank you for the pains you have taken to forward the printing of this book, and your readiness to take pains to get subscriptions, and to take care of and correct the impression. Under these obligations, and in hope of your future friendliness to me, and prayers for me under my present difficulties, I subscribe myself, honored Sir, your respectful and most obliged

> Brother and servant,
> Jonathan Edwards.

97. TO THE REVEREND THOMAS FOXCROFT

The *Humble Inquiry* is about to be sent to the printer. As pledged in his note of May 12, 1749, Edwards dispatches the last few corrections to Foxcroft. Sometimes Foxcroft included quotations verbatim in the treatise. At other times, he rephrased while preserving the thought. Edwards trusted his urbane, erudite colleague to carry out his authorial intent.

(Beinecke Library, ALS, two quarto leaves, addressed on verso to the Reverend Mr. Thomas Foxcroft, a pastor of the First Church in Boston.)

* * *

Northampton, June 5, 1749

Rev. and Honored Sir,

I observe that Dr. [Cotton] Mather, in his *Ratio Disciplinæ*,[1] speaks of the churches of Christ in all ages and the greatest lights in the churches both ancient and modern, as concurring in this principle, that baptism is of larger extent than the Lord's Supper, and that many within the visible church may have the former for their children, when they themselves yet want some actual fitness for the latter (p. 81). And if I remember right, the synod in New England that first introduced the custom of half-members, say to the same purpose, as the same Dr. Mather gives an account of their proceedings, in his *Magnalia*,[2] so that I believe what Mr. [Richard] Baxter says to the contrary will be disputed. And though I don't know but that, notwithstanding this, it may be well to mention what Mr. Baxter[3] says with relation to this in a prefix or appendix, yet I don't think 'tis best for me (who am so little read in church history) in the body of my discourse, to assert, or say anything that implies an assertion, that it has been the current opinion

1. Cotton Mather, *Ratio Disciplinæ Fratrum Nov-Anglorum* (Boston, 1726).

2. Cotton Mather, in the *Magnalia*, Pt. V, devotes 100 pages to a discussion of church discipline, including the Synod of 1662 that instituted the halfway covenant. He notes that, according to the Cambridge Platform, persons baptized should make a profession before being admitted to the Lord's Supper (ch. 12, #7, pp. 70–71, Prop. IV). At the same time, the severity of excommunication is to be avoided (p. 32).

3. See Foxcroft's treatment of Baxter in *Humble Inquiry, Works, 12,* 344–46.

of the Reformed churches, that what justifies for one sacrament, does for the other also, as I think I have done in a clause of my answer to one of the last objections which I sent by my wife, which clause therefore perhaps had best be left out.

In my answer to the objection from the perplexity of communicants, through their doubting of their state, I desire that these words may be added, somewhere in a proper place in my answer to that objection, viz.:

> Mr. [Solomon] Stoddard often taught his people that assurance was attainable, and that they who are true saints might know it if they would, i.e. if they would use proper means and endeavors in order to it. And if so, certainly it is not just to charge those perplexities on God's institutions, which arise through men's negligence; and would not be just, on the supposition of God's institutions being such as I suppose them to be.[4]

I don't know but that in my answer to the objection from the Passover, I said to this purpose: *that while the Israelites were in Egypt, sacrifices had not as yet been instituted.* If I did say so, I desire (if it ben't too late) it may be altered, thus: *The people offered no sacrifices to the true God in Egypt; as is evident by Ex. 8:25–26*, or words to that purpose, if they can be added with good connection.[5]

Excuse, for being so many ways troublesome,

Your most obliged servant,
Jonathan Edwards.

98. TO THE REVEREND JOSEPH BELLAMY

This series of brief news flashes, probably written in haste, deals with matters of immediate concern to Edwards and Bellamy.

(PCUSADH, ms. copy by Richard Webster. Printed in Bellamy, *1*, 55.)

* * *

Northampton, July 18, 1749

Dear Sir,

I will take care of your proposals for subscription for your book[1] and send 'em by the first opportunity, with a letter or letters recom-

4. The Stoddard quotation appears with minor differences in ibid., p. 299.

5. These statements are adapted by Foxcroft in his comparison of Passover with the Lord's Supper. Ibid., pp. 274–83.

1. Bellamy, *True Religion Delineated* (Boston, 1750).

mending the affair. Mr. [John] Searle will give you an account of the reasons why I cannot come to his ordination. I am very sorry it happens so, for I have found a great inclination to go; and much the greater because I believe Mr. Searle and the people are oppressed.

I hope you will go and talk with Mr. [John] Sergeant and wish you would cultivate an acquaintance with him. I should be glad to talk with you about your going to Boston and about several other affairs. If my wool is not yet sent to Hartford, I desire you would take some care about it.

Give my love to Mrs. [Frances Sherman] Bellamy and remember me in your prayers; you know my difficult circumstances. The printer in Boston told me my book on the sacrament would be done in about three weeks, i.e. now next week, but I understand their language and don't expect it till the beginning of September.[2]

I am, Sir, your brother and entire friend,
Jonathan Edwards.

99. TO MARY EDWARDS

No matter how pressing the demands or cares of the moment, Edwards always put his paternal and pastoral responsibilities first. Here he writes to his fifteen-year-old daughter Mary, who is in Portsmouth, New Hampshire, and offers her assurance and exhortation. When he delivered the sermon there for the ordination of Job Strong on June 28, 1749, Mary had preceded him to visit friends and remained after he left. The first paragraph of the letter shows the direct, Puritan approach to death, characteristic of a number of Edwards' letters. He urges her to stop a while in Boston en route home. Lengthy visits to relatives and friends were common for young people in the eighteenth century.

(Trask Library, ALS, two quarto leaves. Published in Dwight ed., *1*, 285–86; extracts in *PMHS*, ser. 2, XV [1901–02], 19–20.)

*   *   *

Northampton, July 26, 1749

Dear Child,

You may well think that it is natural for a parent to be concerned for a child at so great a distance, so far out of view, and so far out of the reach of communication; where, if you should be taken with any dan-

2. According to JE's letter to Parkman, Sept. 11, 1749 (No. 101), below, the *Humble Inquiry* books were actually available in Northampton the week of Aug. 21.

gerous sickness that should issue in death, you might probably be in your grave before we could hear of your danger.

But yet my greatest concern is for your soul's good. Though you are at so great a distance from us, yet God is everywhere. You are much out of the reach of our care, but you are every moment in his hands. We have not the comfort of seeing you, but he sees you. His eye is always upon you. And if you may but be sensibly nigh to him, and have his gracious presence, 'tis no matter though you are far distant from us. I had rather you should remain hundreds of miles distant from us and have God nigh to you by his Spirit, than to have you always with us, and live at a distance from God. And if the next news we should hear of you should be of your death (though that would be very melancholy), yet if withal we should hear of that which should give great grounds to hope that you had died in the Lord, how much more comfortable would this be (though we should have no opportunity to see you, or take our leave of you in your sickness), than if we should be with you in all your sickness, and have much opportunity to tend you, and converse and pray with you, and take an affectionate leave of you, and after all have reason to apprehend that you died without God's grace and favor! 'Tis comfortable to have the presence of earthly friends, especially in sickness and on a deathbed; but the great thing is to have God our friend, and to be united to Christ, who can never die anymore, and whom even death can't separate us from.

My desire and daily prayer is that you may, if it may consist with the holy will of God, meet with God where you be, and have much of his divine influences on your heart wherever you may be, and that in God's due time you may be returned to us again in all respects under the smiles of heaven, and especially in prosperous circumstances in your soul; and that you may find all us alive. But that is uncertain; for you know what a dying time it has been with us in this town, about this time of year, in years past. There is not much sickness prevailing among us as yet, but we fear whether mortal sickness is not beginning among us. Yesterday Eliphaz Clap's remaining only son died of the fever and bloody flux, and is to be buried today. May God fit us all for his will.

I hope you will maintain a strict and constant watch over yourself and against all temptations: that you don't forget and forsake God; and particularly that you don't grow slack in secret religion. Retire often from this vain world, and all its bubbles, empty shadows, and vain amusements, and converse with God alone; and seek that divine grace and comfort, the least drop of which is more worth than all the riches, gaiety, pleasures and entertainments of the whole world.

If Madam [Prudence Chester] Stoddard of Boston, or any of that family, should send to you to invite you to come and remain there on your return from Portsmouth, till there is opportunity for you to come home, I would have you accept the invitation. I think it probable that they will invite you. But if otherwise, I would have you go to Mr. [Edward] Bromfield's. He and Madam [Abigail Coney Bromfield] both told me you should be welcome. After you are come to Boston, I would have you send us word of it. Try the first opportunity, that we may send for you without delay.

We are all through divine goodness in a tolerable state of health. The ferment in town runs very high concerning my opinion about the sacrament: but I am no better able to foretell the issue than when I last saw you. But the whole family has indeed much to put us in mind and make us sensible of our dependence on God's care and kindness, and of the vanity of all human dependences. And we are very loudly called to seek his face, trust in him, and walk closely with him. Commending you to the care and special favor of an heavenly Father, I am

> Your very affectionate father,
> Jonathan Edwards.

Your mother and all the family give their love to you.

100. TO EDWARD BROMFIELD

This fragment seems to indicate that Edwards' daughter Mary had not yet returned home. It also reflects Bromfield's role in sending books abroad on behalf of his Northampton friend, as well as rendering other kinds of assistance.

(Beinecke Library, ALS, two duodecimo leaves, sermon on Prov. 6:22 [1] for Jan. 1749/50, shorn on left side, addressed on verso to [Edwa]rd Bromfield [i]n Boston.)

* * *

Northampton, August 29, 1749

[. . . a]re that you would convey [. . .] act as soon as may be [. . . m]onth. But if my daugh[ter . . .] should be returned to [. . .] have it be sent, I desire you [. . . op]en the packet and take out [. . .] directed to her; and deliver to [. . . e]nclose the rest in a cover to [. . .]burne, and send them along. [. . . wi]th kind respects to you and [. . . your fa]mily, from me and mine, is [. . .]

> [Y]our obliged friend and servant,
> Jonathan Edwards.

[. . .] thanks for the care you have [. . .]ut the books I desired might [. . .] for to England and am glad [. . .] that they are like to come in [. . .]g.

101. TO THE REVEREND EBENEZER PARKMAN

This letter gives a vivid description of a difficult journey that Edwards took to Portsmouth, New Hampshire, and back. He relates the story to explain why he was unable to visit Parkman. The purpose of the trip was to preach the ordination sermon for Job Strong. "Mr. Lyman" is not further identified, but he may have been Isaac, who was called to the church at York, Maine, that December. Isaac Lyman did not return with Edwards and, if he was the person mentioned here, he could have gone on to meet with the people of York or speak in the church.

Edwards comments that copies of the *Humble Inquiry* have been circulating throughout his parish for about three weeks, temporarily silencing the communion controversy. On the bright side, he observes signs of awakening among the young people of his congregation.

(AAS, Curwen Family Papers, box 3, f. 2, ALS, four pages on two quarto leaves.)

* * *

Northampton, September 11, 1749

Rev. and Dear Brother,

I doubt not but you very much wonder that I did not call to pay my respects to you in my late journey to Portsmouth. And indeed you have reason to wonder at it. For truly it was very strange that circumstances should so happen as to afford a sufficient excuse for such a neglect. However, when you have heard the circumstances, I doubt not but your wonder will be lessened.

When I set out from home, it was what I had in view to spend a night at your house in my journey down. When I set out from home, I intended to go to Brookfield the first day, and the next to Westborough and lodge at your house. But I met with a great deal of difficulty with my companion, Mr. Lyman. After we came to Cold Spring, he was so terrified with accounts we there met concerning the drought in the parts below, that he was very loath to go forward; I had hard work to persuade him; yea, he was so discouraged that we actually rode back three miles, and I could get him no further than Cold Spring that night. By the next morning, he was persuaded to go forward, and we went as far as Worcester that day. And understanding that the way to Portsmouth was through Concord, and supposing your house to be much out of the way thither, and being loath to put Mr. Lyman out of his way, with whom I had met with so much difficulty to get him along, I determined to leave my visit at your house till my return; and accordingly laid out my affairs, and hoped to set out from Boston on Wednesday, so as to be sure of having time enough afore me. But when in Boston, I found I could not finish my business so as to begin my journey before Thursday. However, [I] intended to come and lodge at your house on Thursday night. But when Thursday came, it proved a very rainy day. It began to rain in the night, and continued raining pretty freely and plentifully most of the day, which, though a very merciful and happy event after so extreme a drought, yet gave me some exercise of mind concerning my journey. I had publicly told my people that I hoped to return to 'em after two sabbaths, and I concluded they would be destitute if I was absent. And I was especially loath to leave 'em destitute at this critical and difficult time with me and them. I therefore resolved to strive to perform the journey in the two remaining days of the week; and accordingly, laid out myself very much in order to it. I disturbed Mr. [Edward] Bromfield's family between three and four in the morning, and called up his son to send him for my horse to Roxbury. My horse I found was become poor and dull by being so long kept in pastures burnt up with drought. But by the way I happily fell in with company, which seemed to encourage and help forward my horse, and with their help just made it out to reach Worcester that night, without being much exposed to the malignant influence of the evening air. My company were strangers, and had their way through Marlborough; and if I had forsaken them for the sake of coming through Westborough, I could have had no time at all with you, and should at last have found myself unable to reach Worcester, and so wholly have defeated my design of getting home that week.

However, it proved unhappy that I strove so much for it, for I almost ruined my horse (he has not got over it yet) and worried myself exceedingly, and the next day was again hindered by the rain, so that after all I could not get home.

I not long since received a letter from you (dated May 18), a long time after it was written. However, I thank you for it. I had heard before of the endeavors of your association for a reformation. Mr. [Joseph] Emerson of Groton sent me a copy of the articles you agreed upon; and I sent a copy of them to Scotland, to some of my correspondents there.[1]

It has been a time of great ferment among my people for a long time on account of my principles relating to the qualifications for Christian sacraments. My books on that subject[2] have been among them about three weeks; by which the fermentation seems to be much quelled for the present. They seem not to know what to say to my book; but are waiting to see what somebody else will say to it in some answer they suppose will be written to it. It is uncertain what the issue of the affair will be.

However, there has of late appeared some degrees of awakening on the minds of some of our young people, more than has been in five years before, which I look upon very remarkable, at so unlikely a time of great uneasiness of the people with their minister. I desire, dear Sir, your prayers both for me and my people in our present difficult circumstances. And I desire we may, from time to time, remember one another according to your kind proposal, formerly made. My wife joins with me in respectful and cordial salutations to you and Mrs. [Hannah Breck] Parkman. I am, dear Sir,

> Your obliged and very respectful friend and brother,
> Jonathan Edwards.

102. TO THE FIRST PRECINCT, NORTHAMPTON

On October 16, 1749, a petition presented to the Northampton Precinct requested that a meeting be held "as quick as may be" to consider matters relating to the pastor. In placing the matter before the Precinct, Edwards' opponents accomplished a tactical coup. The Precinct meetings continued until Edwards was dismissed the following June.

As the minister, Edwards was not allowed to attend these meetings and received the report referred to here only the evening before it was to be considered at the meeting. Having no opportunity to confer with members of the committee, he forwarded this letter (which did him little good).

1. See Letter No. 95, JE to James Robe of May 23, 1749, above.
2. *An Humble Inquiry.*

(Trask Library, Dwight ms. transcript of Edwards' "Narrative of Communion Controversy," pp. 18–20. Published in Dwight ed., *1*, 322–23; *Works, 12*,
518–20. See also Trumbull, *2*, 205–09.)

* * *

Northampton, November 9, 1749

Dear Friends and Brethren,

I never heard that any such thing was proposed, or thought of by the
Committee of the Precinct, as is proposed in their report, until yesterday; their determination was shown me last night, by a messenger
from them, one of their number; and I have had no opportunity to
confer with the Committee about it or to offer any objection to them
against their proposal. I therefore think it requisite that I should at this
time signify to you the reasons why the thing proposed by them appears to me not to be regular or reasonable.

1. As the proposal of the Committee is expressed, they desire that a
church meeting should be warned, to see if the church will not call a
council or meeting of ministers to advise to measures to be taken by the
church in order to issue the dispute between the minister of the Precinct and the Precinct, which I think is not proper. If the church call a
council, it will doubtless be in order to be assisted with regard to some
controversies or difficulties of its own, and not to remedy the disputes
of the Precinct. The business of a precinct meeting is to manage the
affairs of a precinct; and the business of a church meeting is about the
affairs of a church and not about the affairs of civil societies. It is not
yet certain that there is any dispute or difference between the pastor
and the church, for this has never been properly tried.

2. If I do not misunderstand the report of the Committee, it is
therein proposed that the church meeting should in the warning be
limited to a particular method of managing the business they meet
upon, viz. to consider whether to call a council of neighboring ministers to advise to measures, etc. I am not against warning a church
meeting, if you desire to consider of proper measures to be taken to
secure and promote the interests of religion, and the church's own
welfare under its present circumstances. But I do not know, why the
church should be limited to any certain method of proceeding which
the Precinct has thought of. The Precinct has no more business to limit
or direct the church to a certain method in managing its affairs, than
the church has to direct and limit the Precinct in the management of

its affairs. It is not yet known, that the church will not themselves agree on some measures, to bring their own difficulties to an end, and they will not think proper to choose a committee of their own, to that end, who may be successful [in contriving] a method, to which the church may agree, which may supersede the need of a council.

My end in sending this writing to you is not to perplex you, nor clog any reasonable proceedings, but to do my [duty] to you as your guide in religious matters and that I may do what is proper to prevent any just blame that you or I myself might hereafter fall under; and there-fore I hope that what I have said will be taken in good part, from your affectionate pastor, who desires that you may go in the way of your duty, and in the way of God's blessing, and may be a people happy in God's favor.

Jonathan Edwards.

103. TO THE NORTHAMPTON CHURCH COMMITTEE

The church meeting of November 13, 1749, resulting from the Precinct meeting, was stormy. Edwards' proposal that a council of mutually chosen churches be created was recommended by the committee but defeated at an adjourned meeting of the church. The church also voted to suspend obser-vance of the Lord's Supper.

(Williams College Library, Williamsiana Coll., ALS, one-half quarto leaf, signed, on verso, committee recommendation. Published in Dwight ed., *1*, 324–26; *Works, 12*, 520–23. For background, see Trumbull, 2, 209–11.)

*   *   *

Northampton, November 13, 1749

[To the Committee:]

That a council be called, mutually chosen, to consider of the present circumstances of this church, relating to the controversy subsisting between pastor and people, concerning the qualifications of commu-nicants; and to give their advice what course we shall take to bring this dispute or controversy to an issue: and in general, what is to be done in our present circumstances in order to the church's peace and pros-perity.

Proposed by
Jonathan Edwards.

104. TO THE REVEREND THOMAS FOXCROFT

After offering consolation to Foxcroft on the death of his wife, Edwards gives a review of developments in the communion controversy since the summer. He writes candidly and confidentially, listing events as well as personal reactions. Edwards sees dismissal as inevitable, but he wants first to follow "all proper procedures" to ensure that his position is understood and, if possible, judged by an impartial council.

An interesting sidelight is his hope that the Commissioners will send a man of "sound principles and pious character" to replace the late John Sergeant at Stockbridge. Edwards' "hints" about the requirements for a new missionary suggest that he was jockeying for the post.

(Beinecke Library, ALS, three double quarto leaves. The events described here are recounted in *Works*, *12*, 511–23.)

* * *

Northampton, November 21, 1749

Rev. and Honored Sir,

I condole you on the awful breach God has made in your family, since I last saw you, in the death of Mrs. Foxcroft. By what I have heard of the amiable qualities and endowments she was possessed of, your loss, and the loss of your whole family must needs be exceeding great. The breach made in a family by the death of such an one, in such a place and relation, must be great, and as it were wide as the sea. Yet those excellent qualifications that render your loss very great, must in a peculiar manner afford you comfort in your affliction; as they give you confidence that death has been an happy change to her, and that now she is in blissful circumstances, though she be taken from you, and her body molders in the dark and silent grave. So that although your sorrow be great, yet you mourn not for her but for yourself; and in mourning for yourself, as left by her alone in this evil world, your sorrow has this alleviation, or rather blessed consolation attending it, that your separation from her is not final and perpetual; for those that sleep in Jesus will God bring with him; and then you shall again meet her in joyful circumstances, and be caught up together with her to meet the Lord in the air, and shall both together be ever with the Lord. In the meantime, dear Sir, may you have much of the presence of her and your God and Savior, who is all in all; and who is the unfailing fountain of all that is amiable and comfortable and profitable in the most desirable of creatures.

My afflictions and troubles are also very great, though of another kind. The difficulties in this church relating to my opinion about the qualifications of communicants are come to great height indeed. Our circumstances are not easily conceived of by those that are at a distance. On the sabbath on October 15, I proposed that a day should be set apart by the church for solemn fasting and prayer, to seek to God for his direction and help under our present difficulties, and that the services of the day should be carried on by the neighboring ministers; which I proposed, as supposing that their services would be more acceptable than mine: and it seemed to be unanimously agreed to. And there being several persons in the town that desired to come into the church, who are hopefully converted, and stood ready to make a profession of godliness, who had hitherto been kept out because a committee of the church had refused to consent that they should make any public profession of godliness, and chose rather that they should not come in at all, than come in in that way, I proposed that the neighboring ministers that assisted at the fast should be applied to for advice in that matter, to see if they could not direct us into some method wherein these persons might be admitted consistent with a good conscience in both pastor and people. This was objected against. Then it was proposed by one of the brethren that these ministers should be applied to for advice with respect to a method of the churches being informed of the reasons of my opinion; because it was said the people had not generally read my book, nor were like to; and that great part of the church were never like to be informed of my reasons unless they were directed into some way by ministers. There was then considerable discourse of the people's hearing my reasons delivered from the pulpit, seeing it was confessed that a very great [part] of the church had not read, and were not like to read my book. But this also was objected against, and nothing was determined. Therefore the meeting was adjourned till the next sabbath for further consideration of these matters; and the fast was appointed to be on the Thursday following that sabbath. The people went away, as appeared, many of them in a great ferment of mind. On Monday, the next day, a considerable number of them met together, and subscribed a writing, directed to the committee of the parish or Precinct, demanding a Precinct meeting, the next Thursday, to take into consideration my opinion respecting qualifications of members of the church; and to apply to me, and desire me to recede from my principles; and if I refused, to see if the Precinct would not use endeavors for a separation between the pastor and people. Accordingly the Precinct meeting was warned and convened on the next Thursday. At the meeting it was moved and insisted upon by (I suppose) two or three persons, that it should be put to vote whether I should be desired to deliver the reasons of my opinion from the pulpit, and it passed in the negative. Then some of the more considerate objected against the Precinct's proceeding to the business for which the meeting was warned before the fast which we had appointed to seek direction and help from God. Accordingly, the meeting was adjourned for a fortnight.

The next sabbath the church was stayed according as had been determined the sabbath before; and we entered on some further discourse on things that had been discoursed on the sabbath before; and it was in the first place put to vote whether the church would consent that such amongst us as were able and willing to make a public profession of godliness should be admitted into the church with such a profession (rather than not be admitted at all) for the present, till our unhappy controversy could be brought to an issue: and there was but a very few votes for it. Then it was put to vote whether the neighboring ministers that were expected at the fast should not be sought to for their advice in this matter, to see if they could not find out a way that these persons whom all agreed to be qualified, should be admitted in some way that might be safe and satisfying to both sides. For this also there was but very few votes. Then it was put to vote whether the church would not consent to hear the reasons of my opinion from the pulpit on lectures appointed for that end (for they would look upon it profaneness to hear 'em on the sabbath), seeing it seemed to be a thing beyond dispute, that a great part of the church had not been informed, nor were like to be informed of my reasons any other way. But this also passed in the negative. Then I proposed that it should be referred to the neighboring ministers whether it was not reasonable that I should be thus heard, all things considered. Very much was said against it, with much warmth, and some injurious reflections; and then it was put to vote and passed in the negative.

The next Thursday we had our fast. And the Thursday following, November 2, the Precinct met according to adjournment, and chose a committee of nine men to consider what course to take, and confer with me, and make report to the next meeting; and then adjourned themselves for a week. The committee chosen were many of them some of those that were most violently engaged in this controversy. The next day this committee came to me, and told me that they had all agreed to make me this proposal or offer; which if I would consent to, they would endeavor to bring the Precinct to yield to; viz. that the people should hear me preach in defense of my opinion, provided I would first draw out each sermon at length, in a legible character, and give it to them, and give them opportunity to carry it to some minister, that he might see it, and prepare an answer to it, before I delivered it; and that then I might deliver it, provided I would consent that he should deliver his answer immediately after it. I told them that at present I could not think it to be my duty to comply with this proposal, unless it were also provided that I should also see the discourses of my antagonist; as he was to see mine. I then told them what I thought of the irregularity of the Precinct's taking this ecclesiastical affair into their hands. But they strenuously justified it. And then the committee went away without concluding anything, after long continued uncomfortable disputing, and some harsh reflections and injurious charges. And several of them afterwards did very industriously endeavor to make me appear in the highest degree ridiculous by much misrepresenting my talk at that time. This committee met afterwards at another house, by themselves; and drew up a report, wherein they declare it to be their opinion that the Precinct should endeavor that there should be meeting of the church to see if the church would not apply to some of the neighboring ministers, for their advice what was to be done to issue the dispute between me and the Precinct respecting the admission of members into the church.

On November 9, the Precinct met to receive their report and I having understood what the report was, sent a letter to the Precinct, informing them that I was not against warning a church meeting if they desired it, to consider of proper measures to be taken to secure and promote the interest of religion and the church's welfare under its present circumstances; but did not think it was proper for me to call the church together to take measures to issue disputes of the Precinct, as was proposed; and that I did not think the church should be limited or directed by the Precinct in the management of its affairs. But my letter was taken in very ill part, and wholly disregarded. They therefore accepted the report of the committee and appointed two of the deacons to come to me to desire a church meeting: 1. To determine, by a vote whether the church were of my mind with respect to qualifications, etc. 2. To see if the church will apply to some neighboring ministers for advice what course to take. And then proceeded to add ten more to the Precinct committee, but without giving them any instructions, or appointing them any business; which I suppose was an oversight. But I conclude their design was that this large committee of nineteen should in general take care of their affairs, and see that they were managed effectually. Then they adjourned their meeting for four weeks.

The next day, the two deacons came to me with a copy of the vote of the Precinct, desiring me to warn a church meeting, etc. as aforesaid.

The sabbath following I warned a church meeting to be the next day, to consider what course ought to be taken by this church under its present difficulties, with respect to the admission of members into the church. The church accordingly met. The meeting was opened by prayer. Then one of the principal brethren[1] showed himself greatly displeased that I had used such general terms in my warning of the meeting, and had not warned it in such terms as the Precinct had directed me; and uttered several very injurious reflections and charges; and declared that if I would not warn a church meeting for the purposes the Precinct directed, they would warn one themselves. After I had given some reasons of my conduct, I told the church that I thought the state of the church did greatly demand the assistance of a council; and that we needed the advice of a large council, that should look into our circumstances and give us advice in general, what we should do for our peace and welfare; and insisted that I should be allowed to nominate half the council. After much debate upon it the meeting was adjourned for a week; and a committee of five persons chosen to consider of the matter, and confer upon it with the pastor, and report their opinion at the next meeting. The committee all excepting one agreed to my proposal of a council mutually chosen.

Yesterday the church met according to adjournment, and after prayer, the report of the committee was read; and then the dissenting committeeman got up, and gave the reasons why he did not agree to it, with some very reproachful charges on me. And suggested that there was some snare laid to entrap the people in my proposal of a council mutually chosen, which seemed to alarm the people, and they greatly insisted that the council should all be of neighboring ministers. And a very uncomfortable meeting we had. After long debating they determined to add ten to the church committee and chose the warmest-spirited men they could find, and would accept of no others: when men of calm tempers were nominated, they would not vote them. This

1. Maj. Seth Pomeroy.

committee are further to consider what to do, and the meeting was adjourned for a fortnight; after they had voted that the sacrament of the Lord's Supper should be discontinued, and no more administered during the continuance of the present controversy.

Thus things have gone on. The alienation of the people is exceeding great. They have had, not a little to increase the flame from some gentlemen abroad; and particularly from Col. [Elisha] Williams of Wethersfield and Mr. [Jonathan] Ashley of Deerfield. A great part of my people seem to be industriously engaged to reproach me at home and abroad; and represent all that I say and do in the darkest colors. And seek my separation from 'em very much as a man would strive to gain his point, in a great lawsuit. And indeed, I have not the least expectation of continuing their minister; though I believe my people think I am struggling to my utmost for it. I think the people seem to be in awful circumstances, and in the highway to ruin, for the present and future generations; and I durst not leave them without first using all proper endeavors that they may be saved from ruin, in the use of suitable means, as by the advice of an able and proper council, etc. And then besides, since I am in so many respects reflected upon and re-proached for my conduct, and so many misrepresentations are contin-ually carried abroad in the country, I think it greatly concerns me, before I leave this people, that our affairs should be looked into and judged of by an impartial council. And indeed, I greatly need the advice of such a council to know how to conduct myself in so difficult a situation. I earnestly desire your prayers, and desire you would lay my case before other ministers, that you think are friendlily disposed, and desire their prayers for me, that I may have God's presence and be guided by his counsel in these great trials and temptations, and wish you would write me your thoughts.

And I desire you would lend me Mr. Baxter, and Langley,[2] and any other good book you have on this controversy, and commit them to the care of Col. [Timothy] Dwight; who will convey them safely.

There is another affair I would say something of, and that is con-cerning the Indians and Stockbridge. I wish that the Commissioners would now take care that there may be a man sent them of sound principles, and a pious character. There has been so much contributed

---

2. Richard Baxter, *Certain Disputations of Right to Sacraments and the True Nature of Visible Christianity* (2d ed., London, 1658); Samuel Langley, *Suspension Reviewed, Stated, Cleered and Setled upon Plain Scripture-Proof* (London, 1658). These books, among others, are discussed by Foxcroft in his appendix to the *Humble Inquiry* (*Works*, *12*, 326–48).

towards an Indian school there, that if the affair may be under the care of a missionary of good character, there seems to be the best door for gradually propagating the gospel among the Indians that is opened at present. If the school flourishes, 'tis very likely some of the Six Nations would send their children there to be instructed, and that the good effects would be very extensive: I hope, Sir, you will accept these hints with candor and ever remember with Christian charity and compassion before God,

> Your respectful son and obliged servant,
> Jonathan Edwards.

105. TO THE NORTHAMPTON CHURCH COMMITTEE

The church committee met privately on November 27, 1749, and passed eight votes, plus two addenda. All were designed to shackle Edwards in his defense and deliver him to his opponents. They forbade him from preaching on his views of church membership, limited a council to churches within the county, and restricted the council's agenda to the question of the pastor's dismissal.

With the parry and thrust of a skilled fencer, Edwards uses logic against these motions in his address to the committee. He points out their inconsistencies and contradictions. They prejudge him, render a verdict before he has received a fair hearing, and deny basic tenets of Christianity, including the Golden Rule. He invokes the spirit of the Enlightenment, placing heavy reliance on "plain reason," "universally established maxims of equity," and "the most acknowledged rights of mankind." The church committee, however, is in no mood for discussion or reconciliation, doubtless sensing that it is no match for him and intent on his departure.

(Trask Library, Dwight ms. transcript of "Narrative," pp. 27–35. Published in Dwight ed., *1*, 327–33; *Works*, *12*, 525–30. For the church committee's votes, see *Works*, *12*, 523–24. See also Trumbull, *2*, 211–12.)

*   *   *

Northampton, December 5, 1749

Dear Brethren,

I would now lay before you some reasons why I think that your votes at your late meeting, on November 27, are not to be approved of; which I would do in the spirit of meekness, and desire that they may in the same spirit be weighed and considered.

I. It is manifest that in these votes, you are in various instances inconsistent with yourselves.

First. Your votes imply that it is your mind that a council should be called, previous to any endeavors after a separation between pastor and people, and also previous to what you call a "definitive council"— that is, previous to a council which shall determine whether pastor and people shall be separated or not. And yet, in your seventh vote, you have voted that it shall be proposed to the first council whether the church shall not use means immediately for a separation: which implies that this first council should pass their judgment whether minister and people ought not to be speedily separated, which is the very business of the last council who, as you yourselves suppose, are to determine that matter. If the first council are to have no power to determine it, then why should they take it upon them publicly to inquire and judge and give their voice, how it ought to be determined?

If there be a certain consistory to whom it does not belong to decide a matter, and it is also determined beforehand that they shall not decide it, but that it shall be decided by other judges, I think they would but do the part of busybodies to meddle with it so far as publicly to take cognizance of it and pass their judgment on it. According to Congregational principles, on which the church seem to insist, the utmost which any council under heaven has to do, is only to give their judgment without laying any proper obligation on those whom they advise.

Second. In your concluding vote in your second paper, you have given your voice that, if I do not agree to what you shall finally insist upon, or to that purpose, it shall be proposed to the church immediately to call a council to dismiss me. And surely such a council, if they have anything to do as counselors, will have to judge whether I ought to be dismissed or not, and whether it be consistent with the interests of religion and the peace of the town and church, that I should continue here. And yet, in the same vote, you have voted to propose it to the church to take this work of the council into their own hands, and to determine themselves, in the first place, whether my continuance here is consistent with the interests of religion and the peace of the town and church, and whether a separation ought not to be sought: which is first judging the very thing which they are to call a council to judge of and direct them in. Herein you are inconsistent with yourselves; and, if you persist in such a vote, will be inconsistent with[1] the rules of decency and order, and all usual methods of proceeding. In so great an affair as the separation of a pastor and a people, it is by no means proper for a people, whatever their private thoughts may be, to proceed to de-

1. The phrase, "yourselves and . . . inconsistent with," is taken from the Dwight ed., *1*, 329. There is a lacuna in the Trask copy.

clare their judgment in public votes until they have had the voice of a council to lead and conduct them.

Third. You yourselves, the gentlemen of the committee, have taken it upon you to do that which is properly the business of what you call the "definitive council," in your third vote; wherein you vote that, if I continue in my principles, I ought not to continue the pastor of this church. This vote you have passed as a committee of this church, and if you persist in it, it must be a part of your report to the church, intended for their direction; nor can such a vote of yours be of any other use. And so herein you give your judgment and direction to the church directly, in that very matter which the last council is to judge of and direct the church in.

Fourth. You vote that a council should be called previous to any *endeavors* after a separation; and yet, in this third vote, you yourselves do at the same time, before any council is called, immediately proceed to that which is properly and directly of the nature of an endeavor, that I should be separated, provided I do not retract my opinion. For it must be supposed that you had some end in it, and passed this vote as a means to some public effect; and the effect directly looked at, is no other than a separation in such a case.

Fifth. The only proviso made in the said third vote, wherein it is voted that I ought not to continue the pastor of this church, is, "If I continue of the principles which I have advanced," without adding, "or the church be *brought to be of my mind,*" or anything of that nature: whereby it is plainly supposed that it is a thing already determined and out of the question, that the church never will be of my mind. And yet you afterwards vote that a council shall be called for that very end: to judge whether the church shall take any longer time to study and peruse my book; which, if they do advise to, it must be as requisite in order to a proper trial whether the church, on proper information, will not be brought to be of my mind. So that, putting both these votes together, it comes to this: that you would call a council to judge whether there has already been a fair trial whether the church, on proper information, will be brought to be of my mind; and yet would tell them at the same time that you have decided this matter already, and have determined that it is no longer worthwhile to make a question of it, and that it is clear enough already to be taken as a ground of public votes and acts. And this is, in effect, to tell the council, at the same time you call them, that you do not need them, having thoroughly determined the matter already yourselves, in which you have called them to advise.

II. You are not only inconsistent with yourselves, but I think several of your votes are inconsistent with reason and justice.

First. Your votes imply that I should be allowed to choose none who live out of the county of Hampshire to be members of any council which shall have anything to do in judging of our affairs, either in giving advice for our conduct, or to determine and finish our controversy; which, as the case stands, is contrary to plain reason and universally established maxims of equity, and inconsistent with the most acknowledged rights of mankind. For it is apparent that all matters of difficulty, concerning which the judgment or advice of any council is needed or proposed, are wholly things appertaining to a controversy between me and the church concerning qualifications of candidates for Christian or ecclesiastical communion; and it is well known that the ministers of the county are almost universally on one side, and against me, in this controversy. And I desire you impartially to consider whether, if you should persist in these conclusions, it would be doing as you would be done by? Supposing that it had happened on my side, as it has on yours, that the ministers of the county had been as generally and as fully on my side, in the original controversy, as now they are on yours: would you think it reasonable if I should in that case insist upon it, that you should not be suffered to go out of the county to bring ministers for any council which was to have any hand in judging, advising or determining in our affairs?

Second. If I understand your votes, you have determined that the council which shall be called to advise us to what course to take under our present difficulties, shall be so limited, that they shall have no liberty to judge of our circumstances in general and to advise to proper expedients for our welfare as they shall think requisite; and that particular care shall be taken that they shall not give any judgment or advice with regard to some things which have been matters of difficulty and controversy between me and the church. And I think you, in effect, have voted that they shall be limited to that one single thing, viz. whether the church shall take longer time to study or peruse my book. For, as was observed before, the other things which you mention cannot belong to the business of the previous council, but are the proper business of the last council. Now against this, I object the following things:

1. To call a council and limit them in this manner, does not at all answer the present circumstances and exigencies of this church. The present sorrowful state of the church greatly requires a council which shall have liberty to look into the whole state of our case, without

keeping some parts of our difficulties out of their sight, that they may give us advice what course we shall take for our welfare. If ever it was requisite that the whole case of a patient, under a most terrible and threatening disease, should be laid before physicians, it is requisite that our whole case should be laid before a council for their advice with regard to our difficulties in general. What we need a council for, if we need any at all, before a council comes to determine whether we shall be separated or not, is, if possible, to find a remedy for our broken, confused and perplexed circumstances, so that pastor and people may either walk together in peace, or at least, that things may be so regulated that there may be some peace while we are continued together; and if finally there should appear a necessity for a separation, that things may be prepared for an equitable and peaceable parting. But to tie up a council to such a single particular as is mentioned in your votes, is utterly to disable them from answering these ends.

2. It would be very absurd in itself for the church to come into such a determination. It would be for the church to set itself up in a sort of supremacy and self-sufficiency, as above all control and advice. It would be in effect to say, "In these and those parts of the controversy between us and our pastor, we need no advice, nor will we allow a council to give us any." And it would be unhandsome treatment of any council, under any circumstances, thus to tie them up. The language of it would be: "We in these things are not willing to trust your judgment, esteeming ourselves wiser than you." If you say that these parts of our controversy, which the council was tied up from meddling with, are very clear and plain, then so much the less reason have you to fear leaving them to the determination of a council—unless you are confident that you are wiser than they.

3. For you to insist on these limiting votes, will be very unequal and unfair dealing with me. As the council is to be called to advise in matters controverted between you and me, one party has no more right to limit the other party, as to controverted points which shall be referred, than the other party has to limit the one. If I should claim a power to decide in this matter, and should single out a particular point, such as I thought would best serve my purpose, and say, "I will have this matter, and this only, judged of by a council; and as to other matters which you desire that they should advise in, I will not suffer it," would you hearken at all to it, or bear such treatment?

One thing more I think it my duty to observe to you before I conclude. After your other votes, you conclude all this with an enforcement of the whole, that, provided the proposals of the committee respecting a council, etc. should not be agreed to by me, and there should be nothing else agreed to respecting said council and the ends for which they are to be called, you will propose it to the church to vote my principles so and so pernicious, and to manifest a desire of separation and to call a council to dismiss me. I think that this vote, with these circumstances, is properly of the nature of a threatening that, if I do not comply with what you, the committee, shall finally insist upon, you will propose to the church to deal thus with me. As you are a committee chosen to confer with me concerning a method of proceeding, I might reasonably expect, as you are Christians, and Christians to whom I stand in the relation of a pastor, you would first have seen whether, by friendly conference, we could not have amicably agreed on measures to be taken. If you had thought it proper to pass any other vote at all, and to let me see it, one would have thought that at least it should have been forborne, until you had found, by conference, that I would agree to nothing reasonable, and that this should have been the last thing you did. But at the very first interview, to come with such menaces to terrify me into a compliance with you, before a word of conference between us, is indeed carrying things with a high hand, of which I entreat you seriously and calmly to consider.

On the whole, I desire you would not persist in the votes you have passed, and that you would consider again whether the proposals, which were agreed to by me and the former committee of the church, are not just and reasonable, and the measures therein proposed such as our circumstances require. But if not, if you can think of any other measures which are equitable and have any tendency to answer the exigencies of our present circumstances, I think you will not find me difficult or backward to a compliance.

Jonathan Edwards.

106. TO THE REVEREND JOSEPH BELLAMY

In the midst of the uproar at Northampton, Edwards dashes off this summary of latest incidents and his own emotions. Between innumerable meetings, he manages to eke out time to annotate Bellamy's manuscript of *True Religion Delineated* (Boston, 1750). His view of events is clear, and, despite insult and humiliation, he is not intimidated. The concluding note is one of faith and equanimity.

(Beinecke Library, ALS, two quarto leaves. Published in *NEQ* 1 [1928], 237–40.)

*   *   *

Northampton, December 6, 1749

My Dear Friend,

The expected opportunity of sending your manuscripts to New Haven has failed, and having now an opportunity by Simeon Lyman of Salisbury of sending them directly to his brother at Goshen, I now embrace it and here send with your manuscripts the notes I have made.

As for the present state of things here with regard to our controversy, 'tis not very easy for me to give you an idea of it, without writing a sheet or two of paper. But in brief, things are in great confusion: the tumult is vastly greater than when you was here, and is rising higher and higher continually. The people have got their resentments up to a great height towards you since you have been gone; and you are spoken of by 'em with great indignation and contempt. And I have been informed that Col. [Elisha] Williams of Wethersfield has written a letter to one of the principal men of this church, wherein he speaks contemptibly and with resentment of your and Mr. [John] Searle's last visit here.

There have been abundance of meetings about our affairs since you was here: society meetings, and church meetings, and meetings of committees; of committees of the parish and committees of the church; conferences, debates, reports, and proposals drawn up, and replies and remonstrances. The people have a resolution to get me out of town speedily, that disdains all control or check. To make the matter strong, there is a Precinct meeting kept alive by adjournment. They have already had three or four conventions, and have a standing committee of nineteen men (chiefly of such as are strongly engaged) to oversee and manage the affair effectually. And we have another committee of the church of fifteen men (in the choice of which they picked out those that are most violent) and these appointed for the same end. But notwithstanding such great doings, nothing is yet done or concluded. The two grand difficulties that the people stick at about calling a council, are: first, that they would have a council all on their own side in the controversy, and are contriving and struggling to their utmost to cut me off from liberty of choosing my part of the council of such as are of my opinion; and secondly, they are utterly against a council having liberty to look into the whole state of our case, and giving advice in general; but would tie them up to some particulars, in judging of which they think they can have no power to look into and condemn anything in their conduct, or to thwart their designs. I have been openly reproached in church meetings, as apparently regarding my own temporal interest more than the honor of Christ and the good of the church.

As to the affair of a public dispute, it was quickly at an end after you went from hence. The people at their next parish meeting rejected it, as what would tend to make parties among us. They seem to be determined that the arguments for my opinion shall never be publicly heard, if it be possible to prevent it. And the church committee have voted expressly that no council shall have power to give advice in that matter, i.e. whether I shall preach on the subject or no: and have drawn up a writing, containing nine or ten votes or conclusions of theirs, manifesting what they would have as to the measures that shall be taken relating to a council to be called; and in the same writing have added at the end a threatening, that if they and I don't agree, they will report it to the church as their opinion that the church should vote that my opinion is so and so pernicious, and declare their desire of a speedy separation, and immediately call a council themselves to dismiss me.

I might have observed before that I have been informed that Rector Williams wrote 'em up advice, not to have a public dispute; because it would tend to parties.

You may easily be sensible, dear Sir, that 'tis a time of great trial with me, and that I stand in continual need of the divine presence and merciful conduct in such a state of things as this. I need God's counsel in every step I take and every word I speak; for all that I do and say is watched by the multitude around me with the utmost strictness and with eyes of the greatest uncharitableness and severity, and let me do or say what I will, my words and actions are represented in dark colors. And the state of things is come to that, that they seem to think it greatly concerns 'em to blacken me, and represent me in odious colors to the world, to justify their own conduct. They seem to be sensible that now their character can't stand unless it be on the ruin of mine. They have publicly voted that they will have no more sacraments; and they have no way to justify themselves in that, but to represent me as very bad. I therefore desire, dear Sir, your fervent prayers to God. If he be for me, who can be against me? If he be with me, I need not fear ten thousands of the people. But I know myself unworthy of his presence and help, yet would humbly trust in his infinite grace and all-sufficience.

My love to your spouse. I am your brother and near friend,

Jonathan Edwards.

107. TO THE NORTHAMPTON CHURCH COMMITTEE

Edwards responds to the church committee's recommendations of December 5, 1749 (*Works, 12,* 531). He cannot accept them, and instead contends for a small council of local ministers who would advise the Northampton church whether he could choose members of a second council from outside the county.

(Trask Library, Dwight ms. transcript of "Narrative," pp. 37–38. Published in Dwight ed., *1,* 334–35; *Works, 12,* 532.)

* * *

Northampton, December 7, 1749

Dear Brethren,

The reasons which I have given, showing it to be just that all councils called to judge or advise in our present affairs should be mutually chosen, and that I should have liberty to nominate some of the members out of the county, I think of most undeniable evidence, and that indeed the matter is so plain that it does not properly admit of any dispute. Yet since I find you are so resolved not to comply with what I so reasonably urge, I now, for sake of peace and to avoid great tumult and confusion, make you the following offer, viz. that the ministers of this Association should be consulted—that is, the *seven* ministers who live nearest, or the five nearest, if you think seven too many—and that it shall be left to their judgment whether it be not reasonable and best in this case that I should be allowed to go out of the county for ministers and churches, to be some of the members of the council who are to judge whether I shall be dismissed from my pastoral office here or not; and that, if it should be determined that it is best that this should be allowed, then their judgment be asked whether the state of things be ripe for such a council being called; and, if they judge that we are not ripe for it, that we should ask their advice how we shall conduct ourselves for the present.

These ministers are, in the most proper sense, the ministers of the vicinity and are all, save one,[1] professedly on your side in our main controversy. If we go from these, in the way of mutual choice, I insist on the liberty of going out of the county. If you accept this offer, I now promise that, whatever the judgment or advice of these ministers shall be in the forementioned particulars, I will [make] no objections against your choosing any of them to be of the future council.

As to your last conclusion of December 5, my present determination is not to consent to it, nor to put any such thing to vote, nor in any respect to have any hand in the matter unless first advised to it by these ministers.

[Jonathan Edwards.]

108. TO THE NORTHAMPTON CHURCH COMMITTEE

Edwards concedes that a council should be called to determine whether pastor and people ought to be separated. In doing so, he bows to his church's wish that the first council be chosen from among Hampshire County ministers. He urges the church to accept his conciliation, despite his recognition of the many irregularities there have been in the negotiations thus far.

(Trask Library, Dwight ms. transcript of "Narrative," pp. 40–44; Beinecke Library, fragment, one leaf. Published in Dwight ed., *1*, 335–38; *Works*, *12*, 534–37.)

* * *

[Northampton, December 11, 1749]

Dear Brethren,

You very well know that what has been insisted upon heretofore by my people, was that the neighboring ministers should be consulted as a previous council, to give us advice what course we should take before the calling of a council to determine whether pastor and people should be separated; and that I objected against it, these ministers being almost universally, *by their open profession,* on your side in the grand controversy between you and me; and that I insisted on it, as just and equal, that I should have a choice with you in the council of advisers; and that if those whom you choose were known to be on your side in the main controversy, I should have liberty to nominate as many who should be on my side; and that this was [as] just in a council which should be called to give previous advice, as in a council which should

1. I.e. Edward Billing, the pastor of Cold Spring.

judge concerning the affair of our separation, because such a foundation might be laid by the previous advice of the first council as might in
effect finish the whole affair. But, however, I have not been hearkened
to in this matter; and one thing urged in opposition to what I have
insisted on, was that, according to the Platform of Church Discipline,
such affairs should be judged of by those who were of the vicinity or
neighborhood.[1] And finding, after long urging what I looked upon as
my due and might claim as one of the common rights of mankind, that
all my reasonings were in vain, I have now at length yielded that point
and, for the sake of peace, which in the whole course of this affair I
have earnestly pursued, have complied with that you first insisted
upon, viz. that the neighboring ministers should be desired to give us
advice what course to take, previous to the council called to judge
whether pastor and people shall be separated; and that I would leave it
to them to judge, on a full view of our case, how we shall conduct
ourselves. Now I think you ought not to reject what I offer, and attempt to constrain me to a compliance with the new measures in which
the committee have agreed, for the following reasons:

1. It would be a very unjust proceeding. The neighboring ministers,
on whom you first insisted, have indeed much to prejudice them
against me in these affairs, being declaredly against me in the main
controversy. But it is well known that many of the ministers of the
county, who are out of the neighborhood, have had much more to
prejudice them. These neighboring ministers are all Calvinists in their
persuasion and friends to the late revival of religion, and those who
have lived in good neighborhood and peace with me, which has not
been interrupted by any remarkable breach between me and them, or
any known affront or disgust which they have taken. But with regard
to the other ministers of the county, it is well known that four or five of
them have heretofore had the reputation of Arminians.[2] Some others
of them are known to be strenuous opposers of the late revival of
religion,[3] for which I have been so public an advocate. And you know

1. The reference is to ch. 8, § 8 of the Cambridge Platform. Williston Walker, *The Creeds
and Platforms of Congregationalism* (New York, 1893), p. 215.

2. County ministers reputed to be Arminians included Jonathan Ashley of Deerfield,
Joseph Ashley of Sunderland, Robert Breck of Springfield, and Noah Merrick of Wil-
braham.

3. Ministers opposed to the awakenings included Jonathan Ashley, Robert Breck, William
Rand of Kingston, and even JE's brother-in-law Samuel Hopkins of West Springfield (*Works,
4*, 22–23).

that the dispute about the late work in the land, is a controversy which has greatly engaged the feelings of men. There are no less than six of them,[4] who have either had a particular difference or controversy with me, or have in time past openly manifested some affront or disgust which they have taken. Another of them, one of the senior ministers of the county,[5] has shown a strong prejudice in this particular affair in something which he has said to two of the brethren of the committee of this church, as I have been well-informed. Another of them has an own father in the town who is one of the committee;[6] and several of his brethren are greatly engaged in this controversy.

2. If the church, at the same time that they agreed to the report of the committee, should withal say that, if I had any reasonable objection against any particular minister, he should not be chosen; still, proceeding on this plan would be in many ways of unhappy consequence. It would necessitate me publicly to point out particular ministers of the county and openly to object those things against them, which would naturally tend to excite unpleasant feelings between these ministers and me, to beget new prejudices and revive and establish old ones. And then it is wholly uncertain what the church would esteem *reasonable objections;* and they would open a door for new difficulties and endless controversy about the particular members to be chosen, concerning the principles and past conduct of ministers, and probably with regard to some ministers, whether they be in the county or not: it being a matter of controversy not yet decided, concerning *three,* who used[7] to be reckoned to be of the county, whether they indeed be of the province.[8]

3. If the church should now depart from what they formerly insisted on and I have now offered in compliance with them, and should insist on the measures proposed by the committee, they would act very absurdly and inconsistently. For the Platform has heretofore been insisted on as directing [to] ministers of the neighborhood, and seems still to be insisted on in the report of the committee under the name of the *Constitution of these Churches;* and yet this same committee, in this

4. See above, nn. 2 and 3.

5. Jonathan Ashley, according to JE in his letter to Foxcroft, Nov. 21, 1749 (No. 104).

6. Possibly Rev. John Woodbridge of South Hadley (*Works, 12,* 535, n. 6).

7. Dwight's MS transcript reads "need," but printed version (Dwight ed., *1,* 337) reads "used."

8. In May 1749, the Massachusetts towns of Enfield, Somers, and Suffield were annexed to Connecticut.

very report, insist on liberty to go out of the neighborhood without being limited by any other bounds than those of the county. Whereas it is those ministers whom I have proposed, and they only, who are properly the ministers of the neighborhood. The Platform speaks of *neighborhoods*, but says nothing of counties. Many of the churches of the county are no more in the way of communication with us than some churches out of the county. The churches in Sheffield, and some others in this county, are no more in the way of mutual concern and intercourse with us in our religious affairs than the churches in Boston, nor indeed not near so much. So that the committee insist upon the Platform and our being confined to the neighborhood, and yet at the same time insist on liberty to deviate from the Platform and to depart from the neighborhood. Yea, they are yet more absurd: for one grand point that is in controversy between us is whether we shall have liberty to go from the neighborhood for any council. And yet they insist upon liberty to go from the neighborhood, in the first place, for a council to determine whether we shall have liberty to go from the neighborhood, which is the most gross and palpable inconsistency.

As to the determination of your forefathers, thirty-six years ago, that they would be subject to a council of the churches of the county: you, of this generation, never looked on it as any constitution for you,[9] nor have you ever, in one instance, conformed to it; for you never have yet, in any one controversy since I have been your pastor, referred anything to a council of churches, but to consistories of another nature. And besides, the plain design of that vote was that all the churches of the county taken together should be consociated as a standing council, agreeable to Mr. [Solomon] Stoddard's Presbyterian principles, who was the first mover in that affair. And moreover, what I now offer, viz. that our affairs should be referred to the ministers of that Association that we belong to, is much more agreeable to the plain design of that vote, since the state of the county is so exceedingly altered from what it was then, is become so much bigger, and the churches more at a great distance one from another and divided into different associations.

On the whole, I renewedly insist upon it, that the offer I make you is highly reasonable and fair, yea, that I do therein evidently depart from my just right in compliance with you that, if possible, our affair may be

9. An original fragment of the "Narrative" (Beinecke Library) begins here.

proceeded in with peace and without tumult. That which I now propose is what you yourselves have till now insisted on; and I apprehend there can be no imaginable reason why it should now be departed from, unless it be to lay me under still greater disadvantages, and to have opportunity to bring in such into the council, as are more prejudiced against me.

One thing further I would observe as an objection against the report of the committee, is this: it is known that the two main things for which the previous council is to judge in are these, viz. first, whether things are now ripe for a council that shall judge whether pastor and people should be separated; second, whether 'tis not best that I should be allowed to nominate some that live out of the county to be members of that council. But the committee in their report have taken care that if this council don't determine the first point according to their mind, they shall have nothing to do with the second, which would be a very unfair and partial determination. This don't seem to be because they suppose that if the first council don't judge things ripe for a decisive council, that it will then be unreasonable for this council to proceed to direct as to the method of choosing that second council; because they, the committee, in some votes they themselves have passed, did proceed to determine the method of choosing the second council, and voted that it ought to be chosen wholly out of the county—though at the same time, in another vote, they determined to leave it with a previous council whether things are now ripe for the calling of the last council in order to an immediate separation. And if it is not too soon for the committee to judge of this point and advise the church in it, then it is not too soon for a council to judge of it and advise the church in it.

[Jonathan Edwards.]

109. TO THE COUNCIL OF CHURCHES

On the second day of the preliminary council meeting at Northampton, Edwards submitted this offer to resign on certain conditions. In its report, the council concurred with him that the Lord's Supper should be "speedily" restored. It found his request for admission of new members to be too sensitive and advocated waiting. The council also chided the church for not being willing to hear Edwards preach on the subject and for not making its views clear. The time was not ripe for a definitive council to be called. The council instead recommended that public harmony be restored, one of Edwards' suggestions.

(Trask Library, Dwight ms. transcript of "Narrative," pp. 88–89. Published in Dwight ed., *1*, 367–68; *Works*, *12*, 570–71. The ms. report of the council is at the Beinecke Library, two folio leaves; published in *Works*, *12*, 571–74.)

*   *   *

Northampton, December 27, 1749

[Dear Brethren,]

I, the subscriber, do make the following declaration and offer: that if my people, being so advised by the council of churches now sitting, will hear me deliver the reasons of my opinion from the pulpit and consider further of the matter of controversy between me and them until the spring, when it shall be comfortable traveling, laying aside all public agitation until then, and then desire a council of churches in order to bring our controversy to a final issue; and will consent, being also so advised by this council, that I shall have an equal hand in the choice of the council with them, and that I should go out of the county into the other parts of New England for my choice; and this council on a full hearing and thorough consideration of our case, can find out no way for a composition or accommodation, either by satisfying my conscience in yielding some points to the people or by making them easy in some things in a compliance with me, or any other way which the council in their wisdom may devise; but the people shall, after all, declare their unwillingness that I should be their pastor: I will declare it before the council as my desire that the people should be left entirely at their liberty as to my continuing their pastor, and will move it to them to gratify the people's desire in dissolving my pastoral relation to this church—provided the Precinct will first engage to free me from rates—and will, the council so advising, resign my pastoral office. This is that to which I humbly propose and desire this reverend council to advise this people to consent, withal strongly advising that in the meantime quietness and peace be maintained, and jangling agitations and public proceedings, tending to enkindle or uphold strife, be laid aside; and that the Lord's Supper be restored, if the people can find it in their hearts freely to consent to it on the advice of the council; and that this council also endeavor to find out a way that those who are able and willing to make a profession of godliness may be admitted into the church in a way consistent with a good conscience in both pastor and people; and that all parts of the public service of God be quietly, steadily and regularly upheld and attended.

Jonathan Edwards.

110. TO DEACON NOAH COOK

Edwards stands ready to meet with individuals in order to discuss differences, but he believes that conferring with a committee or its representatives would be contrary to the recent council's advice to suspend public debate.

(Trask Library, Dwight ms. transcript of "Narrative," pp. 91–92. Published in Dwight ed., *1*, 369–70; *Works, 12*, 575.)

* * *

Northampton, January 2, 1749/50

[Dear Brother,]

On mature consideration, I am confirmed in the same mind which I expressed the last night concerning the committee chosen to confer with me. It appears to me altogether of the nature of a public proceeding, with respect to the present controversy. The appointment and choice of the committee are a public proceeding. The committee are the representatives of a public society, and if you come and confer with me as a committee of the Precinct, you therein will act in a public capacity, in the name and behalf of the Precinct; and all from beginning to end will be a public proceeding, and so plainly contrary to the advice of the council. The appointed interview of the committee with me cannot be understood otherwise than as a meeting appointed for a sort of public dispute. For though the whole parish won't be actually present, yet they will be present by their representatives. And 'tis to be a debate or discourse managed in behalf of the whole. The committee are to hear my arguments in some sort as the ear of the society, that the whole may be influenced by it; otherwise I don't see how they can, in hearing, act in behalf of the Precinct. And if they don't act in behalf of the Precinct, how do they act as a committee for the Precinct? This I think is not a reasonable way of proceeding for the information of the whole parish, not tending to light and peace but the contrary, and contrary to the express words of the council's advice, and disagreeable to the plain design of it, and tending to supersede and set aside the thing they aimed at. Therefore I must decline conferring with such a body of men together, chosen to come as a committee of the Precinct; but stand ready at any time to confer with freedom and friendliness

318 Letters

with each of these brethren, or any others, coming in a private capacity and in their own name only. I am

> Your friend and servant, for Jesus' sake,
> Jonathan Edwards.

111. TO THE REVEREND JOSEPH BELLAMY

Edwards' discussion of praise and blame in this letter is elaborated in *Freedom of the Will*, Part IV, sections 3 and 4. He summarizes the work and findings of the preliminary council and concludes that he does not expect to continue at Northampton after April.

(Library of Congress, Manuscript Div., ALS, two quarto leaves.)

* * *

Northampton, January 15, 1749/50

My Dear Friend,

I thank you for your two letters by Mr. [Simeon] Lyman. As to your questions in your last letter, I would say, that the difficulty that is in them seems to arise from the ambiguity, or want of a fixed meaning to some phrases.

Your second question is, *Are we to blame for that wherein we are not voluntary?* I say yes, as the word *voluntary* is often used, viz. to signify that which arises *from* a bad or good will, or things that are *the fruits* of the will. For we are to blame for something else besides the fruits of a bad will, or a bad disposition or temper, and we are to blame for the bad will itself. Blame or faultiness consists primarily in the *being* of a bad will or disposition, and not only in the effects of it. And therefore we may be to blame for that which don't arise from a bad temper: viz. the bad temper itself. For if the bad temper itself was not blameworthy, I think the effects of it, or those things that arise from it, could not be blameworthy. But as the word *voluntary* may be understood, we are to blame for nothing but what is voluntary, as if by voluntary we understand both that which consists in the will, and also that which arises from it. We are to blame for that which consists in the will or which the will consists in, and so we are to blame for a bad temper or bad disposition; not because a bad temper is the fruit of a bad will, but because a bad will consists in it. A bad temper of mind is nothing else but the habit of a bad will.

You inquire whether it is not inconsistent to say that a sense of the divine beauty arises from a good temper, and a good temper arises from a sense of the divine beauty. I answer yes, as the expressions may be understood. If by a sense of the divine beauty, you mean an habitual sensibility of moral beauty, I say, in this sense, a sense of the divine beauty don't arise from a good temper, for an habitual sensibility of moral beauty (or an habitual good taste of mind) and a good temper of mind are the very same thing: 'tis what goodness of temper does primarily consist in. And therefore a good temper in that primary notion of it don't arise from a sense of the divine beauty, for a good taste or habitual taste of moral good don't arise from a taste of moral good. But in another sense, a good temper does arise from a sense of the divine beauty, viz. everything else that belongs to what we call a good temper, excepting the good taste and relish of the mind, as good desires, inclinations to good resolutions, a disposition to a good choice and to good actions and behavior, a disposition to proper meditations, and proper and suitable affections to a right fear, sorrow, joy, hope, dependence, etc. All these things arise from a sense of the divine beauty.

I thank you for your care in dispersing my books.[1] As to the present state of things in this town, we have had a great deal of struggle and difficulty about calling a council, whether I should be allowed in my choice of half the council to go out of the county, in order to having my half on my side in the main controversy. Finally, we agreed to call a council of five out of the seven next neighboring churches, which five churches should be mutually chosen, and to leave it to them whether in the choice of the decisive council that is to determine whether I shall be dismissed from my pastoral office, I may go out of the county, and whether the state of things be now ripe for such a council. The council met the 26th of last month, and sat two days. As to the latter question, they determined that the state of things was not ripe for a decisive council, for two reasons: 1. that the people were not in a proper temper for such a proceeding; and 2. thorough means had not yet been used to convince me of my supposed error. With regard to this latter, they signified that they expected an answer to my book speedily from the press, which they hope might be a means of reconciling minister and people. The person they expect this answer from, as I understand, is Mr. [Peter] Clark of Salem-Village [Danvers]. But whether he is truly writing an answer or no, I cannot certainly learn.

As to the first question, viz. I might go out of the county in choosing

---

1. Copies of *The Life of David Brainerd*, published in 1749.

my part of the council, this council did not determine but referred it
for further consideration; and to that end adjourned themselves to
the first Wednesday in February, when they are to meet again to determine this point. The churches of which this council consists are the
church of Hatfield, the First Church in Hadley, the church in Sunderland, the church of Cold Spring, and the church in Newhampton.
What this council will determine, in this remaining point, I know not.
But let their determination be what it will, I don't suppose it will make
any alteration as to my continuing here. I expect to[2] leave my pastoral
office here when this year is out, which ends at the last of April, as the
people have reckoned from the beginning for the payment of my
salary.

I desire your fervent and constant prayers. Give my love to Mrs.
Bellamy. I am your very affectionate

> And obliged friend and brother,
> Jonathan Edwards.

P.S. I hope to see [you] here in the spring.

112. TO THE REVEREND THOMAS FOXCROFT

Edwards brings his Boston mentor up to date on developments of the past
three months. He is already planning for the creation of the definitive council
and solicits Foxcroft's attendance. This letter marks the emergence of Col.
Israel Williams as a protagonist in the unfolding drama.

(Beinecke Library, ALS, two quarto leaves.)

*   *   *

Northampton, February 19, 1749/50

Rev. and Honored Sir,

I thank you for your kind letter of January 22. I before had received
the books by Col. [Timothy] Dwight; which I am very glad of, and
think they will be very useful to me.

The council that first sat on our affairs, December 26, consisted of
five churches, viz. the First Church in Hadley, and the Second Church
in Northampton, and the churches of Hatfield, Sunderland and Cold
Spring. This council was agreed upon with a vast deal of difficulty, by
reason of the people's extreme caution and jealousy, and care to have

---

2. JE started to write "be dism[issed]," then crossed it out.

such a council as they could depend on, to determine as they would have 'em. Three things were referred to 'em:

1. Whether, in the calling a council to determine whether I should be separated from my people, it was not reasonable that I should be allowed to choose some ministers or churches that are out of the bounds of this county?

2. Whether the state of things be now ripe for the calling such a council?

3. If not, how we shall conduct ourselves for the present.

The council after hearing the debates, and about forty-eight hours' consultation, drew up their result, wherein they declare themselves unresolved as to the first thing, about the calling a decisive council. As to the second, they judged that the state of things was not ripe for such a council, for three reasons, viz. *first*, that means should be first used for my conviction, of my supposed error; which they supposed had been fully done. *Secondly,* they supposed it probable that an answer to my book would in a short time be published; which they hoped might be a means of reconciliation between pastor and people. *Thirdly,* they thought we were not in a proper temper to go about so great and important an affair, as a separation between pastor and people: there being evidently a great want of meekness and calmness of spirit, etc. And as to the third thing, how we should conduct ourselves for the present, they advise to a better temper and more Christian behavior, and to converse freely and friendlily together about the point in controversy, and to restore the sacrament of the Lord's Supper. And then the council adjourned themselves to the first Wednesday in February, further to consider of the first thing referred to them, about the choice of a decisive council, about which they were now unresolved. And accordingly they met again according to adjournment; and heard further debates and pleadings of the parties on the subject. And after consulting, and debating the matter among themselves about twelve hours, when the question was put, they found themselves equally divided upon it, and so left us as we were. But some of the members, as Christian friends, advised to yield something one to another, and advised that the people should consent that I should go out of the county for some of the members of the future council, and content themselves with having the major part of the council brought from within the county.

One thing that I urged before the council at their first sitting, as a reason why the state of things was not ripe for a decisive council, was that a very great part of my church had never read my book, and that the church had from time to time refused to consent to hear my reasons from the pulpit, and I thought they could not properly proceed so far, till they had some way or other been informed of my reasons for my opinion. I expected the council would have said something about it in their result; but they saw cause to be wholly silent. Therefore at their last sitting I openly declared before the council and the committee of the church that I could not be easy in my conscience to leave this people without making trial whether my people would hear my reasons from the pulpit, for that which I was persuaded was the counsel and will of God, unless they, the council, would give their voice against it and declare it as their judgment, that I had no right to preach my opinion to my people. I told them that if they would consider the matter and give this as their judgment, I should be easy; but otherwise I was determined to do it. And because I thought it would be most offensive to my people for me to preach upon the sabbath, I would first try whether they would hear me on lectures appointed for that end, as I earnestly sought peace; but if not I would reserve liberty to myself to do it on the sabbath. One of the council said that they had not expressly declared whether the people ought to hear me, but that it was supposed that they had sufficiently intimated their minds, that they ought, in a clause in their result, wherein they mentioned it as one occasion of alienation, etc., that the people had opposed my preaching. And several of them spake of it as a thing out of doubt that I had a right to preach what I thought was the counsel of God, and a right that I ought not to give up, and should not leave to the judgment of any council. I accordingly appointed a lecture the next Thursday (which is now the last Thursday) and preached it. There was a very thin congregation of our own people, but a very great number of strangers, and the more because the court was then sitting here. I appointed another lecture to be the next Thursday. Many of the people are extremely uneasy at my preaching, and are diligently contriving some way or other to put a stop to it. I purpose by the will of God to preach three or four more lectures. And then, if my people insist upon it, I shall not refuse to join with them in calling a council to determine about a separation, if they will allow me to choose three churches abroad in other parts of New England. And I don't know but I shall make 'em this offer, that they on their part may choose who they please without my objecting against any, if they will allow me the same liberty. And if it should be thus, I shall probably much desire, dear Sir, that you should be one of the council, if by sending to your church I might be sure that you will come, and not Dr. [Charles] Chauncy, and also a delegate that will be friendly. And I desire, Sir, that you would write me word whether you would consent to come some time about the latter end of April, if sent to; and whether if the church should be sent to, I might be secure as to the minister and messenger. I hope you will not be unwilling to deny yourself for our help in our great distress.

My youngest child [Elizabeth], about three years old, is in a very languishing, dangerous state, and my wife is pretty near her time. I desire your prayers for them; and for me under all my trials. I am, honored Sir,

> Your obliged and most respectful son and servant,
> Jonathan Edwards.

Please to send your answer to Mr. [Edward] Bromfield, that he may send it by the bearer, that he may not know that it comes from you.

February 20.

Since I wrote the preceding, I have been informed that Col. [Israel] Williams of Hatfield, when here at court the last week, did in open court with very great heat and vehemence, express himself concerning my appointing lectures to deliver the reasons of my opinion; spoke of it as unsufferable lording it over my people, called me a tyrant, etc. And was very angry that the Court of Common Pleas had adjourned themselves in order to attend the lecture. The same was proposed in the Court of General Sessions of the Peace, of which Colonel Williams is one, and the major part were against it, and did not adjourn themselves. Colonel Williams had several turns of talking angrily about it. He is, I believe, disposed to exert himself to his utmost against me. He has great influence on many of the neighboring ministers: and his thus appearing will doubtless greatly embolden my people, and will have influence on many of the principal men in neighboring towns; for he is chief colonel of the regiment; and all other military offices are dependent on him; and he has now commissions to give out according to his pleasure.

I also perceive that both my people and neighboring ministers seem to be contriving to put a stop to my lectures, or at least to put a stop to people's attending them. They have several times gone over to Mr. [Chester] Williams of Hadley (who is especially engaged against me, and very much under Colonel Williams' influence) to consult him. He, as I am told, advised them to come to me to stay the church on the sabbath, to see if they would not call the Association together to advise 'em what to do under present circumstances; and if I refused, then to get as many as they could to subscribe a request to the Association to come together. Accordingly two of the deacons came to me last Saturday near night, to desire me to stay the church, etc. I told them I intended not to have any hand in calling any more councils on our affairs, unless I might choose some of them, who favored my opinion. And I understand that yesterday they went about with a paper for subscriptions, to call together the Association. Such are our confusions. I much desire that Mr. [John] Webb and you would confer together, and give me your advice, whether, if the people will not attend my lectures, I had best to take opportunity to deliver the reasons of my opinion on the sabbath, and give me advice what I shall do in other respects.

Jonathan Edwards.

113. TO DEACON NOAH COOK

Edwards and the Northampton church had reached an impasse in meetings held on March 26 and 27, 1750. He wanted to select three (later two) churches for the "final" council, thereby including churches from outside the county, so that his case might be heard by a fairer tribunal. The church committee opposed both proposals. Here Edwards assures Deacon Cook of his readiness to negotiate whenever the church is willing.

(Beinecke Library, ALS and ms. draft, one folio leaf, two quarto leaves. Published in *Works, 12,* 604–06.)

* * *

Northampton, March 30, 1750

Dear Brother,

I now make the following declaration, which I am willing you should show to any of the members of this church, whom you please, as you have opportunity.

I declare I have no disposition to continue in the pastoral relation to this church, they retaining their present settled aversion to it, after such a council as I have insisted on have had fair opportunity, on a view of our calamitous state, to judge whether it don't admit of some other remedy, and to give their own judgment and advice, and use their own means (if they shall think fit to use any) in order to a reconciliation, and in order to your consenting to continue longer under my ministry: I say, if after this you appear still fixed in an aversion to my being any longer your minister, my private inclination and judgment is that you should be gratified by an immediate separation. Though, at the same time, I don't think it proper to bind myself by any promises, or come to any absolute determination, before I have had the advice of a council in so great and important an affair; because for either of us to do thus, and then send for a council to advise us, would be preposterous and inconsistent.

I declare that as the above-mentioned is at present my private inclination and judgment, so I fully expect that it will be the judgment and advice of the council when they come, provided such a council be called as I insist on.

I declare I have no scheme or secret design in view, in any step I take, to bring the church into any snare; so that they should at last be obliged to continue under my ministry, contrary to what shall finally appear to be their fixed inclination, after any means the council may think proper to be used. And if the council advise to any such thing, it will not be in the least owing to any design or contrivance of mine, and will be altogether unexpected to me: that is, it will be unexpected to me, if they advise to my finally continuing contrary to the church's fixed inclination, etc.

I declare that I do not decline setting aside the vote passed the last Monday, because it was my own draft, or because I desire to get my will, or obtain any victory over others, or because I am fond of those very words or phrases; but because I insist on the things therein contained, they being only essential things. I studied, when I drew the vote, barely to express such things as the nature of the case absolutely requires the judgment and advice of a council in. And I think to set aside the vote, when passed, after its being so fully and particularly debated and considered, unless it be with a view to some material alteration, would be to open a door for the lengthening out our controversy with frivolous jangling and strife.

I declare that I have no desire that the time should be lengthened out before a council is called, in order to bringing our matters to some issue; but on the contrary, I desire that the calling such a council may be hastened.

And whereas many of the church have expressed a fear or suspicion that if the council should have so large a liberty of judging and advising as is expressed in the forementioned vote, they would persuade me to comply so far with the church, as to go on to admit members into the church in our former manner, though not fully brought off from my opinion; and some (one at least) intimated a suspicion that I expected it myself and had long acted with this view; I now declare that I have never taken one step with this view or expectation; and that I have not, and never had any such expectation; and that it is not because I would make a reserve for such an event that I insist on such liberty of judgment and advice in the council as is expressed in the forementioned vote, and oppose their being limited as is proposed in Maj. [Seth] Pomeroy's draft; but because I am not willing to have any hand in what I judge to be in its own nature unfit and preposterous; for which I am satisfied I should be much blamed abroad, as laying myself under disadvantages, and should not be able to vindicate myself; and also because I doubt whether members of a council will be willing to come from a distance, if tied up in such a manner from giving advice and acting their own judgment.

As I declared things to the same purpose with these above before in the church meeting, so I now renew the declaration, and know of nothing further I can do at present to convince my brethren that these things are true, than by declaring that I speak uprightly and in the simplicity of my heart.

If there remains a fixed resolution, either that the council called shall not have liberty of giving advice for a remedy of our calamities according to their own judgment (not that I desire the church to bind themselves to stand to their advice) and judging for themselves whether an immediate separation be best, or to confine me wholly to this county in my choice, I don't think it will be to any purpose to call another church meeting, unless it be to prolong fruitless wrangling and strife. But if it be thought there is a disposition further to consider of these matters, I stand ready to call the church together to that end at any time I shall be desired.

Jonathan Edwards.

114. TO THE REVEREND THOMAS GILLESPIE

A vigorous discussion with his overseas correspondent provides Edwards with a welcome respite from the round of protracted meetings. The theme of this letter is whether to believe or doubt one's good estate. He draws illustrations from, among others, Jonah, Hosea, and Job. The postscript was written after his dismissal.

(Trask Library, ALS, six quarto leaves. Published in *Edinburgh Quarterly Magazine* 1 [1798], 337–54; Dwight ed., *1*, 287–97; *Works*, 2, 501–13.)

* * *

Northampton, April 2, 1750

Rev. and Dear Sir,

I received your favor of September 19, 1748,[1] the last summer, and would now heartily thank you for it. I suppose it might [have] come in the same ship with the letters I had from my other correspondents in Scotland, which I answered the last summer; but it did not come to hand till a long time after most of the others, and after I had finished and sent away my answers to them, and that opportunity for answering was past. I have had no leisure or opportunity to write any letters to Scotland from that time till now, by reason of my peculiar and very extraordinary circumstances, on account of the controversy that has arisen between me and my people concerning the profession that ought to be made by persons that come to Christian sacraments, which is likely speedily to issue in a separation between me and my congregation. This controversy, in the progress of it, has proved not only a controversy between me and my people, but between me and a great part of New England; there being many far and near warmly engaged in it. This affair has unavoidably engaged my mind, and filled up my time, and taken me off from other things. I need the prayers of my friends, that God would be with me, and direct and assist me in such a time of trial, and mercifully order the issue.

As to the epistolary controversy, dear Sir, between you and me, about faith and doubting, I am sorry it should seem to be greater than it is, through misunderstanding of one another's meaning, and that the real difference between us is so great as it is in some part of the controversy.

As to the dispute about believing without spiritual light or sight, I thought I expressed my meaning in my last letter very plainly: but I

1. Printed in *Edinburgh Quarterly Magazine*, 1 (1798), 181–95.

kept no copy, and it might perhaps be owing to my dullness that I think so. However, I perceive I was not understood. I cannot find out by anything you say to me on this head, that we really differ in sentiments, but only in words. I acknowledge with you that "all are bound to believe the divine testimony, and trust in Christ—and the want of spiritual light or sight does not loose from the obligation one is laid under by the divine command, to believe instantly on Christ and at all seasons, nor excuse him in any degree for not believing. Even when one wants the influence and grace of the Spirit, still he is bound to believe: ability is not the rule of duty." I believe the obligation to believe, lies on a person who is remaining without spiritual light or sight, or being in darkness. No darkness, no blindness, no carnality or stupidity, excuses him a moment from having a strong and lively faith and love as ever was exercised by the apostle Paul, or rather renders it not sinful in him that he is at that same moment without such a faith and love. And yet I believe it is absurd, and of very hurtful consequence, to urge persons to believe in the dark, in the manner and in the sense in which many hundreds have done in America, who plainly intend, a believing strongly with such a sort of strong faith or great confidence as is consistent with continuing still, even in the time of these strong acts of faith, without spiritual light, carnal, stupid, careless, and senseless. Their doctrine evidently comes to this, both in sense and effect, that it is a man's duty strongly to believe with a lightless, sightless faith; or to have a confident, although a blind, dark, and stupid faith. And such a faith has indeed been promoted exceedingly by their doctrine; and has prevailed with its dreadful effects, answerable to the nature of the cause. We have had, and have to this day, multitudes of such strong believers, whose bold, proud and stupid confidence, attended with a very wicked behavior, has given the greatest wound to the cause of truth and vital religion that ever it suffered in America.

As to what follows in your letter, concerning a person's believing himself to be in a good estate, its being properly of the nature of faith: in this there seems to be some real difference between us. But perhaps there would be none, if distinctness were well observed in the use of words. If by a man's believing that he is in a good estate, be meant no more than his believing that he does believe in Christ, does love God, etc., I think there is nothing of the nature of faith in it. Because knowing it or believing it depends on our own immediate sensation or consciousness, and not on divine testimony. True believers, in the hope they entertain of salvation, make use of the following syllogism: *Whosoever believes, shall be saved; I believe, therefore,* etc. Assenting to the major proposition is properly of the nature of faith; because the ground of my assent to that is divine testimony. But my assent to the minor proposition, I humbly conceive, is not of the nature of faith, because that is not grounded on divine testimony, but my own consciousness. The testimony that is the proper ground of faith is in the Word of God. Rom. 10:17, "Faith cometh by hearing, and hearing by the Word of God." There is such a testimony given us in the Word of God, that *he that believes shall be saved;* but there is no such testimony in the Word of God, as that such an individual person, in such a town in Scotland or New England, believes. There is such a proposition in Scripture, as that *Christ loves those that love him;* and therefore this everyone is bound to believe; and a firm believing it on divine testimony is properly of the nature of faith; and for anyone to doubt of it, is properly the heinous sin of unbelief: but there is no such proposition in Scripture, or that is any part of the gospel of Christ, that such an individual person in Northampton loves Christ. If I know I have complacence in Christ, I know it the same way that I know I have complacence in my wife and children, viz. by the testimony of my own heart, or inward consciousness. Evangelical faith has the gospel of Christ for its foundation; but that *I love Christ* is a proposition not contained in the gospel of Christ.

And therefore, that we mayn't dispute in the dark, 'tis necessary that we will explain what we mean by a person's believing he is in a good estate. If thereby we mean only believing the minor of the foregoing syllogism (or such like syllogisms), *I believe* or *I love God,* 'tis not of the nature of faith; but if by a man's believing himself to be in a good estate, be understood his believing not only the minor, but the consequence, *therefore I shall be saved,* or *therefore God will never leave nor forsake me,* then a man's believing his good estate partakes of the nature of faith; for these consequences depend on divine testimony in the Word of God and gospel of Jesus Christ.

Yea, I would observe further, that a man's judging of the faith or love he finds in himself, whether they are that sort of faith and love which he finds, [to] be saving, may depend on his reliance on Scripture rules and marks, which are divine testimonies, which he may be tempted not to rely upon from the consideration of his great unworthiness. But his judging that he has those individual inward acts of understanding and exercises of heart that he has, depends on inward sensation, and not on any testimony of the Word of God. The knowing present acts depends on immediate consciousness, and the knowing past acts depends on memory. And therefore the fullness of my satisfaction that I now have such an inward act or exercise of mind, depends on the strength of the sensation, and my satisfaction, that I have had 'em heretofore, depends on the clearness of my memory, and not on the strength of my reliance on any divine testimony. And so my doubting whether I have, or have had, such individual inward acts, is not of the nature of unbelief: though it may arise from unbelief indirectly; because if I had had more faith, the actings of it would have been more sensible, and the memory of them more clear, and so I should have been better satisfied that I had them.

God seems to have given Abraham's servant a revelation that the damsel in whom he found such marks, viz. coming to draw water with a pitcher to that well, her readiness to give him and his camels drink, etc. should be Isaac's wife, and therefore his assenting to this was of the nature of faith, having divine testimony for its foundation. But his believing that Rebekah was the damsel that had those individual marks, his knowing that she came to draw water, and that she let down her pitcher, etc. was not of the nature of faith. His knowing this was not from divine testimony, but from the testimony of his own senses. You speak of a saint's doubting of his good estate, as "part of unbelief, and the opposite of faith, considered in its full compass and latitude, as one branch of unbelief, one ingredient in unbelief," and of assurance of a man's good estate, as "one thing that belongs to the exercise of faith." I don't know whether I take your meaning in these expressions. If you mean, that a person's believing himself to be in a good estate is one thing that appertains to the essence of saving faith, or that saving faith, in all that belongs to its essence, yea, and perfection, cannot be without implying it, I must humbly ask leave to differ from you. That a believing that I am in a good estate is no part or *ingredient* in the essence of saving faith, is evident by this, that the essence of saving faith must be complete in me before it can be true that I am in a good estate. If I han't as yet acted faith, yea, if there be anything wanting in me to make up the essence of saving faith, then I am not as yet in a state of salvation, and therefore can have no ground to believe that I am so. Anything that belongs to the essence of saving faith is prior in the order of nature to a man's being in a state of salvation, because 'tis saving faith that brings him into such a state: and therefore believing that he is in such a state, can't be one thing that is essential or necessary in order to his being in such a state; for that would imply a contradiction. It would be to suppose a man's believing that he is in a good estate to be prior in the order of nature to his being in a good estate. But a thing cannot be both prior and posterior, antecedent and consequent, with respect to the very same thing. The real truth of a proposition is in the order of nature first, before its being believed to be true. But till a man has already all that belongs to the essence of saving faith, that proposition, *that he is in a good estate*, is not as yet true. All the propositions contained in the gospel, all divine testimonies that we have in God's Word, are true already, are already laid for a foundation for faith, and were laid long ago; but that proposition, *I am in a good estate*, not being one of them, is not true till I have first believed: and therefore this proposition can't be believed to be true, till saving faith be first complete. Therefore the completeness of the act of saving faith won't make it take in a belief of this proposition, nor will the strength or perfection of the act cause it to imply this. If a man in his first act of faith has ever so great a conviction of God's sufficiency and faithfulness, and let his reliance on the divine testimony in the gospel be never so strong and perfect, all will have no tendency to make him believe this proposition, *I am in a good estate*, to be true, till it be true; which it is not till the first act of faith is complete, and has made it true. A belief of divine testimony in the first act of faith, may be to any assignable degree of strength and perfection, without believing that proposition; for there is no such divine testimony then extant, nor is there any such truth extant, but in consequence of the first act of faith. Therefore (as I said), saving faith may be with all that belongs to its essence, and that in the highest perfection, without implying a belief of my own good estate. I don't say it can be without having this immediate *effect;* but it is rather the *effect* of faith, than a *part, branch,* or *ingredient* of faith. And so I don't dispute whether a man's doubting of his good estate may be a consequence of unbelief (I doubt not but it is so in those who are in a good estate); because if men had the exercise of faith in such a degree as they ought to have, it could not but be very sensible and plain that they had it. But yet I think this doubting of a good estate is entirely a different thing from the sin of unbelief itself, and has nothing of the nature of unbelief in it; i.e. if we take doubting one's good estate in the sense in which I have before explained it, viz. for doubting whether I have such individual principles and acts in my soul. Take it in a complex sense, and it may have the sin of unbelief in it; as thus: If, although I doubt not I have such and such qualifications, I yet doubt of those consequences for which I have divine testimony or promise; as when a person that doubts not that he *loves Christ,* yet doubts whether *he shall receive a crown of life.* The doubting of this consequence is properly the sin of unbelief.

You say, dear Sir, "The Holy Ghost requires us to believe the reality of his work in us in all its parts just as it is"; and a little before, "The believer his doubting whether or not he has faith, is sinful because it is belying the Holy Ghost, denying his work in him; so there is no sin to which that doubting can so properly be reduced as unbelief."

Here I would ask leave thus to express my thoughts in a diversity from yours. I think, if it be allowed to be sinful for a believer to doubt whether he has faith, that doubting is not the sin of unbelief on any such account as you mention, viz. as belying or denying any testimony of the Holy Ghost. There is difference between doubting of the being of some word of the Holy Ghost, and denying the *testimony* of the Holy Ghost, as there is a difference between doubting concerning some other words of God and denying the testimony of God. 'Tis the work of God to give a man great natural abilities; and if we suppose God *requires* such a man *to believe the reality of his work, in all its parts, just as it is;* and so that 'tis sinful for him at all to doubt of his natural abilities being just as good as they are; yet this is no belying any testimony of God (though it be doubting of a work of God) and so is diverse from the sin of unbelief. So, if we suppose a very eminent saint is to blame in doubting whether he has so much grace as he really has, he indeed don't believe the reality of God's work in him, in all its parts, just as it is; yet he is not therein guilty of the sin of unbelief, against any testimony of God, any more than the other.

I acknowledge, that for a true saint in a carnal and careless frame, to doubt of his good estate, is sinful, as it were mediately and indirectly, as the cause of it is sinful, viz. the lowness and insensibility of the actings of grace in him, and the prevalence of carnality and stupidity. 'Tis sinful to be without assurance, as (as we say), *'tis his own fault,* he sinfully deprives himself of it, or foregoes it. As a servant's being without his tools is his sin, when he has carelessly lost 'em, or as 'tis his sin to be without strength of body, or without the sight of his eyes, when he has deprived himself of these by intemperance; not that weakness or blindness of body in their own nature are sin, for they are qualities of the body and not of the mind, the subject in which sin is inherent.

'Tis indirectly the duty of a true saint always to rejoice in the light of

God's countenance, because sin is the cause of his being without this joy at any time. And therefore it was indirectly David's sin that he was not rejoicing in the light of God's countenance, at that time when he was in the bed of adultery with Bathsheba. But yet 'tis not directly a believer's duty to rejoice in the light of God's countenance when God hides his face, but it rather then becomes him to be troubled and to mourn: so there are perhaps many other privileges of saints that are their duty indirectly, and the want of 'em is sinful, not simply but completely considered. Of this kind I take the want of assurance of one's good estate to be.

I think no words of mine either in my book or letter implied that a person's deliverance from a bad frame, don't begin with renewed acts of faith or trusting in God: if they did, they implied what I never intended. Doubtless if a saint comes out of an ill frame, wherein grace is asleep and inactive, it must be by renewed actings of grace. 'Tis very plainly impossible, that grace should begin to cease to be inactive in any other way than by its beginning to be active. It must begin with the renewed actings of some grace or other: and I know nothing that I have said to the contrary, but that the grace that shall first begin sensibly to revive shall be faith, and that this shall lead the way to the renewed acting of all other grace, and to the further acting of faith itself. But a person's coming out of a carnal, careless, dead frame, by or in the reviving of grace in his soul, is quite another thing from a saint's having a strong exercise of faith, or strong hope, or strong exercise of any other grace, while yet remaining in a carnal, careless, dead frame; or in other words, in a frame wherein grace is so far from being in strong exercise, that 'tis asleep and in a great measure without exercise.

There is a *holy hope,* a truly *Christian hope,* that the Scripture speaks of, that is reckoned among the graces of the Spirit: and I think I should never desire or seek any other hope but such an one; for I believe no other hope has any holy or good tendency. Therefore this hope, this grace of hope only, can properly be called a duty. But 'tis just as absurd to talk of the exercise of this holy hope, the strong exercise of this grace of the Spirit, in a carnal, stupid, careless frame, such a frame yet remaining, as it would be to talk of the strong exercises of love to God, or heavenly-mindedness, or any other grace, remaining in such a frame. 'Tis doubtless proper, earnestly to exhort those who are in such a frame to come out of it, in and by the strong exercises of all grace; but

I should not think it proper to press a man earnestly to maintain strong hope, NOTWITHSTANDING the prevailing and continuance of great carnality and stupidity (which is plainly the sense of the people I opposed). For this is plainly to press people to an unholy hope, a strong hope that is no Christian grace; and that is strong wicked presumption. And the promoting of this has most evidently been the effect of such a method of dealing with souls, in innumerable multitudes of awful instances.

You mean, Sir, to suppose (pp. 6 and 7 of your letter) that 'tis God's manner of dealing with his saints, while in a SECURE, CARELESS frame, first to give 'em assurance of their good estate, while they remain in such a frame, and to make use of that assurance as a means to bring 'em out of such a frame. Here again I must crave leave to differ from you, and to think that none of the instances or texts you adduce from Scripture, do at all prove the point. I think it is God's manner first to awaken their consciences, and to bring 'em to reflect upon themselves, and to bring 'em to feel their own calamity which they have brought upon themselves by so departing from God (by which an end is put to their carelessness and security), and again earnestly and carefully to seek God's face before they find him, and before God restores the comfortable and joyful sense of his favor. And I think this is abundantly evident both by Scripture and experience. You much insist on Jonah as a clear instance of the thing you lay down. You observe that he says, ch. 2:4 and v. 7, "I said, I am cast out of thy sight; yet will I look again towards thy holy temple"; "When my soul fainted within me I remembered the Lord: and my prayer came in unto thee, even into thine holy temple." You speak of these words as "demonstrating an assurance of his good estate and of God's favor" (I will not now dispute whether they do or no). And you speak of this exercise of assurance, etc., as *his practice in an evil frame, and in a careless frame; for he slept securely in the sides of the ship,* manifesting *dismal security, awful carelessness, in a carnal frame.* That Jonah was in a careless, secure frame when he was asleep in the sides of the ship, I don't deny. But, dear Sir, does that prove that he remained still in a careless, secure frame, when in his heart he said these things in the fish's belly (ch. 2:4, 7)? Does it prove that he remained careless after he was awaked, and saw the furious storm, and owned it was the fruit of God's anger towards him for his sins? And does it prove, that he still remained careless after the whale had swallowed him, when he seemed to himself to be "*in the belly of* hell"? when *the water compassed him about, even to the soul;* and, as he says, all God's waves and billows passed over him, and he was ready to despair; when he went down to the bottoms of the mountains, was ready to think God had cast him out of his sight, and imprisoned in a prison that he could never escape ("The earth with her bars was about me forever") and his soul fainted within him. He was brought into this condition after his sleeping securely in the sides of the ship, before he said, "I will look again towards thine holy temple," etc. [Jonah 2:2–6]. He was evidently first awakened out of carelessness and security, and brought into distress, before he was comforted.

The other place you also much insist on, concerning the people of Israel, is very much like this: before God comforted them with the testimonies of his favor, after their backslidings, he first, by severe chastisements, together with the awakening influences of his Spirit, brought 'em out of their *carelessness* and carnal *security*. It appears by many scriptures, that this was God's way of dealing with that people. So Hosea, ch. 2, God first *hedged up her way with thorns, and made a wall that she could not find her paths.* And took away her corn and wine and wool and flax, destroyed her vines and fig trees, and caused her mirth to cease, and by this means brought her to herself, brought out of her security, carelessness and deep sleep, very much as the prodigal son was brought to himself. God *brought her first into the wilderness,* before *he spake comfortably to her,* and opened to her *a door of hope* [Hos. 2:4]; by her distress first brought her to say, I will go and return to my first husband; and then, when God spake comfortably to her, she called him, "Ishi, my husband"; and God did as it were renewedly betroth her unto him [v. 7]. That 2nd of Hosea is very parallel with Jer. 3. One place serves well to illustrate and explain the other. And that it was God's way of dealing with his people Israel, after their apostasy and carnal security, first to awaken them, and under a sense of their sin and misery to bring them solicitously to seek his face, before he gave them sensible evidence of his favor, and not to awaken out of security by first making manifest his favor to 'em, is evident by many Scriptures; as Lev. 26:40–42; Deut. 32:36–39; I Kgs. 8:47–51; Jer. 29:12–14, 30:12–22, ch. 50:4–8; Ezek. 20:35–37; Hos. 5:15 with ch. 6:1–3, 13:9–10, ch. 14 throughout.

And besides, I would observe that in Jer. 3 the prophecy is not concerning the recovery of backsliding saints, or the mystical church, which though she had corrupted herself, still continued to be God's

wife; but concerning the apostate Israel, that had forsaken and renounced her husband, and gone after other lovers, and whom God
had renounced, put away and given her a bill of divorce (v. 8). So that
her recovery could not be by giving her assurance of her good estate, as
still remaining his wife, and that God was already married unto her;
for that was not true, and is not consistent with the context. And
whereas it is said, v. 14, "Return, O backsliding children, saith the
Lord; for I am married unto you, and I will take you one of a city," etc.
Indeed, "I am married," in the Hebrew, is in the preter perfect tense;
but you know, Sir, that in the language of prophecy, the preter tense is
very commonly put for the future. And whereas it is said, v. 19, "How
shall I put thee among the children? . . . and I said, Thou shalt call me
my father," I acknowledge this expression here, "my Father," and that,
Rom. 8:15, is the language of faith; 'tis so two ways: 1. 'tis such language of the soul as is the immediate *effect* of a lively faith: I acknowledge that the lively exercises of faith do naturally produce satisfaction
of a good estate, as their immediate effect. 2. 'Tis language which in
another sense does properly and naturally *express* the very act of faith
itself; yea, the first act of faith in a sinner, before which he never was in
a good estate; as thus, supposing a man in distress, pursued by his
enemies that sought his life, should have the gates of several fortresses
set open before him, and should be called to from each of them to fly
thither for refuge, and viewing them all, and one appearing to him
strong and safe, but the rest insufficient, he should accept the invitation to that one, and fly thither with this language, *This is my fortress, this
is my refuge. In vain is salvation looked for from the other. Behold I come to this;
this is my sure defense.*[2] Not that he means that he is already within the
fortress, and so in a good and safe estate; but "this is my chosen
fortress, in the strength of which I trust, and to which I betake myself
for safety." So if a woman were at once solicited by many lovers, to give
herself to them in a married state, and beholding the superior beauties
and excellencies of one far above all the rest, should betake herself to
him, and fly into his arms with this language, "This is my husband:
behold I come unto thee. Thou art my spouse." Not that she means
that she is already married to him, but that he is her chosen husband,
etc. Thus God offers himself to sinners as their Savior, God and Father; and the language of the heart of him that accepts the offer by a

2. See II Sam. 22:2; Ps. 18:2, 46:1, 91:2, 9; Jer. 3:23.

true faith, is, *Thou art my Savior;* in vain is salvation hoped for from others that offer themselves, *Thou art my God and Father.* Not that he is already his child, but he chooses him, and comes to him, that he may be one of his children. As in Jer. 3:19, Israel calls God her Father, as the way to be *put among the children,* and be one of them, and not as being one already. And in vv. 21–23 she is not brought out of a careless and secure state by knowing that the Lord is her God; but she is first brought to consideration and sense of her sin and misery, weeping and supplications for mercy, and conviction of the vanity of other saviors and refuges, not only before she has assurance of her good estate, but before she is brought to fly to God for refuge that she may be in a good estate.

As to the instance of Job, I would only say that I think he, while in his state of sore affliction, though he had some great exercises of infirmity and impatience under his extreme trials, yet was very far from being in such a frame as I intended, when I spoke of a *secure, careless, carnal* frame, etc. I doubt not, nor did I ever question it, that the saints' hope and knowledge of their good estate, is in many cases of excellent benefit to help them against temptation and exercises of corruption.

With regard to the case of extraordinary temptation and buffeting of Satan, which you mention, I don't very well know what to say further. I have often found my own insufficiency as a counselor in such like cases, wherein melancholy and bodily distemper have so great a hand, and give Satan so great advantage, as appears to me in the case you mention: if the Lord do not help, whence should we help? If some Christian friends of such afflicted and (as it were) possessed persons would from time to time pray and fast for them, it might be a proper exercise of Christian charity, and the likeliest way I know for relief. I kept no copy of my former letter to you, and so don't remember fully what I have already said concerning this case.[3] But this I have found with such melancholy people, that the greatest difficulty don't lie in giving them good advice, but in persuading them to take it. One thing I think of great importance, which is that such persons should go on in a steady course of performance of all duties, born of the general and particular calling, without suffering themselves to be diverted from it by any violence of Satan, or specious pretense of his whatsoever, properly ordering, proportioning and timing all sorts of duties, duties to

3. See Letter No. 78, JE to Thomas Gillespie, Sept. 4, 1747, above.

God, public, private and secret, and duties to man, relative duties, of business and conversation, family duties, duties of friendship and good neighborhood, duly proportioning labor and rest, intention and relaxation, without suffering one duty to crowd out or entrench upon another. If such persons could be persuaded to this, I think in this way they would be best guarded against the devil, and he would soonest be discouraged, and a good state of body would be most likely to be gained, and persons would act most as if they trusted and rested in God, and would be most in the way of his help and blessing.

With regard to what you write concerning immediate revelations, I have thought of it, and I find I can't say anything to purpose, without drawing out this letter to a very extraordinary length: and I am already got to such length, that I had need to ask your excuse. I have written enough to tire your patience.

It has indeed been with great difficulty that I have found time to write so much: if you knew my extraordinary circumstances, I doubt not you would excuse my not writing more. I acknowledge the subject you mention is very important: probably, if God spares my life, and gives me opportunity, I may write largely upon it. I know not how providence will dispose of me: I am going to be cast on the wide world with my large family of ten children. I humbly request your prayers for me under my difficulties and trials.

As to the state of religion in this place and this land, it is at present very sorrowful and dark. But I must for a more particular account of things refer you to my letter to Mr. [John] MacLaurin of Glasgow, and Mr. [James] Robe. So, asking a remembrance in your prayers, I must conclude, by subscribing myself, with much esteem and respect,

Your obliged brother and servant,
Jonathan Edwards.

P.S. July 3, 1750. Having had no leisure to finish the preparation of my letters to Scotland before this time, by reason of the extraordinary troubles, hurries and confusions of my unusual circumstances; I can now inform you, that the controversy between me and my people, that I mentioned in the beginning of my letter, has issued in a separation between me and my people. An ecclesiastical council was called on the affair; who sat here the week before last; who, by a majority of one voice, determined an immediate separation to be necessary; and accordingly my pastoral relation to my people was dissolved on June 22. If I can procure the printed accounts from Boston of the proceedings of the council, I will give order to my friend there to enclose them with this letter, and direct them to you. I desire your prayers that I may take a suitable notice of the frowns of heaven on me and this people (between whom was once so great an union), in the bringing to pass such a separation between us; and that these troubles may be sanctified to me; that God would overrule this event for his own glory (which doubtless many adversaries will rejoice and triumph in), that God would open a door for my future usefulness, and provide for me and my numerous family, and take a fatherly care of us in our present unsettled, uncertain circumstances, being cast on the wide world.

J.E.

115. TO THE REVEREND SAMUEL HOPKINS (OF SPRINGFIELD)

The Northampton Precinct has asked advice about the controversy between Edwards and the church from ministers in the vicinity of Springfield. Edwards attempts to put the situation in perspective for his brother-in-law, doubtless to discourage his becoming involved: only a few members of the Northampton church are active, speaking for the many; one council of churches has already approved Edwards' going out of the county to find other council members; and the nearby ministers declined to intervene.

(Beinecke Library, ALS draft, one quarto leaf.)

* * *

Northampton, April 3, 1750

Dear Brother,

I understand that our people had on yesterday a Precinct meeting for the managing our ecclesiastical affairs (as they have had a great many such the fall and winter past). And that at this meeting a committee was chosen to write to the Association in the lower part of the county to desire their judgment and advice in some things concerning the controversy subsisting between me and this church, and have appointed a messenger to carry the letter. The whole meeting, as I was informed, consisted of forty-four persons; and the majority that voted this was twenty-six, as I was informed by one that counted 'em. They gave me no notice of the meeting or their design in it, so that I had no opportunity either to concur or remonstrate. They have given me no notice of what they have done or what particulars they intend to ask the judgment of the Association in. It was proposed by one in the meeting, as I was informed, that I should be notified of what they had determined, that I might have opportunity to send also if I thought fit. But the motion was rejected with much dislike. Why they chose to send to your Association rather than our own, I don't know. Only as I am informed that Maj. [Ebenezer] Pomeroy, Jr., said he had conversed with several of the ministers and by their conversation he was persuaded that Association would take cognizance of their affairs.[1] I conjecture that one main thing that they would have your judgment in is a controversy between me and the church, whether I ought not to be allowed to choose without the bounds of this county, two of the members in ten of the council that shall have power to issue our affairs. I am persuaded that if you knew all circumstances, you would be fully satisfied we needed no previous council to decide this controversy, or any further advice than we have had, or, if we did, that it was proper I should have some hand in this previous council in calling them and representing things before [them]. And that 'tis especially needless for them, if they will have this controversy judged by a council in which they only have a hand, to have this Association to go to yours. But if you judged these things were proper, yet I am persuaded you would not think this offer properly brought to you when referred only by about twenty-six of the Precinct at a Precinct meeting, instead of being referred by the church, which consists of about 300 male members. But if you would allow 'em all those forementioned things, yet doubtless you would not think it proper to undertake to judge this matter, or anything else that has been matter of controversy between me and the church concerning our mutual rights, only as being the representations of one side. It would be impossible you should have a just view of our affairs, so as to put you into a proper capacity to judge or advise in matters relating to our controversy, without a very long rehearsal; to be sure, can't expect a just view of 'em only on the representation of one side.

The church and pastor have already by mutual choice called a council of churches chiefly to decide this very point in controversy between us, viz. whether I had a right to go out of the county for a part of the council that shall have power to issue our affairs, who were so far from thinking that there was no need of hearing both parties in order to decide it, that they at their first sitting spent about two days in hearing and considering what each had to say. And then, being at a loss what to determine, adjourned themselves for about six weeks to take time to

1. Here JE drew a symbol, but the intended insertion has not been found.

consider of it. And at their second meeting, spent another day in further hearing each party and in deliberation and finally were at a loss, being equally divided as to question whether I had a proper right to go out of the county, which was all they had power to judge of as a council; but as to its being prudential, that I should be allowed to go out for a minor part, they did (to all appearance with a concurring) judge[2] and did advise that it should be allowed.[3]

About fifty of my people did lately subscribe a request to the ministers of our Association to come together to give 'em advice, what they should do under present circumstances, and in their draft made such a representation as moved the ministers that they met at Hadley and actually passed a vote that they would give advice. But some of them thought it necessary to hear my representation of things before they proceeded to act, and accordingly came over hither; and having heard my representations, altered their minds and determined that it was best to act nothing, and accordingly they broke up and did nothing.

But I believe, Sir, I need say no more (and probably needed not to have said anything) to make you sensible how far you are from having a proper call at present to judge of any matters in controversy between me and this church.

I am

Your loving brother,
Jonathan Edwards.

116. TO THE REVEREND PETER CLARK

Edwards seeks to dissuade Clark from writing a reply to his *Humble Inquiry,* as had been requested by the Precinct. The effort proved successful. On May 21, 1750, Clark, in answer to the present letter, not only said that Edwards' views had been misrepresented but in essence agreed with them, writing that "it is a visible profession of faith . . . which is the only door . . . of admission to the communion of the visible church."

(MHS, Bostonian Society Deposit, Colburn Autograph Coll., ALS, two folio leaves. Beinecke Library, autograph extract, half of one quarto leaf. Published in full in *NEQ* 29 [1956], 228–33. Extracts published in Edwards' *Farewell Sermon* [1751; Dwight ed., *1,* 627–28] and *Misrepresentations Corrected* [1752; *Works, 12,* 360].)

* * *

2. Idem.
3. Idem.

Northampton, May 7, 1750

Rev. and Honored Sir,

There having been application made to you from time to time by my people, in an affair that most nearly concerns me, occasioned (I suppose) by intimations they have received from some of the neighboring ministers of what they knew of your abilities, and something they had heard you had said particularly relating to this affair; and there having been an intercourse by letters between you and my people, and also the neighboring ministers about this matter: I thought it not amiss for me also to write to you, and say something for myself. I don't know what has been said to you by those who have applied to you, nor what representations they have made of my principles and conduct, but I know some of them have been greatly engaged in opposition to me in this affair, and have been apt to view things which I say and do in a most disadvantageous light; and therefore I have reason to expect they make an answerable representation of them to others. I know by your letters, which I have seen, you have had some great misrepresentations made to you, and know not how far your mind may be prepossessed with such prejudices as mankind in general are very liable to in cases of controversy, by receiving accounts from time to time, from such as are on one side only; but nevertheless am encouraged to write on my own behalf, from the esteem I have long entertained of your judgment, from some of your writings, particularly your defense of infant baptism against my classmate [John] Walton,[1] and also by the appearances I saw of candor in your late letters to Major [Ebenezer] Pomeroy, [Jr.,] and Mr. [Edward] Billing. And my writing appeared to me the more requisite from what you signify in your letter to Major Pomeroy of your thoughts of writing and sending to my people your opinion of my book, lately published, after you should have had opportunity to read it.

I have taken a great deal of pains to explain myself both in what I have written and spoken; but yet I am so unhappy as to be misunderstood by many. Notwithstanding all I can say for myself, there appears (as seems to me) a strange disposition to take me wrong, and to entertain uncharitable and injurious thoughts of my meaning, and also concerning the principles and dispositions I act from, and the ends they suppose I secretly aim at. By which means many at a distance have conceived very disadvantageous and injurious notions of me.

1. Peter Clark, *The Scripture-Grounds of the Baptism of Christian Infants* (Boston, 1735).

I am far from pretending to a discriminating judgment of men's spiritual state, so as infallibly to determine who are true converts and who are not, or imagining that I, or anybody else is sufficient for the execution of any such design as the setting up a pure church consisting only of true converts. Nor do I claim any power above my neighbors in that respect. I have seen enough of my own fallibleness, and of the uncertainty of my judgment in things of this nature, I think, forever to guard me from such folly, as to assume to myself the divine prerogative in this respect. I have constantly borne a full testimony in preaching, writing, and conversation against the assuming and arrogance of such as set up themselves to be discerners of men's hearts, and have promoted separations under a notion of setting up pure churches. I have ever been an enemy to all pretenses of knowing men's spiritual state, and other secret things, not revealed in the Word of God, or manifested by the events of providence, by any supposed immediate revelation, impulse, or suggestion. I have always [been] nauseated [by] the presumption and folly of such as appeared forward to be quick and peremptory in their decisions concerning the state of men's souls, from a pretended extraordinary skill in the secret methods of the Spirit's operation. And the older I have grown, the more and more has experience and observation of the event of things taught me the contemptibleness and folly of such pretenses. I have much disliked the tyranny of those who set up their own experiences as a rule to judge others by, and of such as insist on a particular account of the time of conversion, and of the order and method of their experiences, in order to a cordial embracing [of] persons, who profess the main principles or virtues wherein godliness consists, and are of answerable conversation, in the arms of charity, as true Christians and brethren in Christ. I have long borne testimony against these things. I have ever been an enemy to a separating, divisive, factious, uncharitable spirit; and have exerted myself in many ways against such things, as they have abundantly appeared in the country of late years. I have not set myself to oppose ministers, or to encourage a disaffection between ministers and people, under a pretense of their not being converted, not being lively preachers, etc. I have heretofore lived in an happy union with the ministers of this neighborhood; which I have industriously cultivated, and looked upon as one of the special blessings of my life; but I fear this controversy has in some measure interrupted it, or at least the happy fruits of it. A state of controversy is peculiarly disagreeable to me, and I look upon it as my great calamity, and desire to take it as a frown of providence that should deeply humble me, that I am obliged to enter into such a controversy with my own people. I dreaded it greatly before it began, and nothing could make it tolerable to me, but that I have the testimony of my conscience that I could not avoid it, and so that 'tis an affliction that God lays upon me and calls me to bear.

I am often (and I don't know but pretty generally in the country) represented as of a new and odd opinion with respect to terms of Christian communion, and as being for introducing a peculiar way of my own; whereas I don't perceive that I differ at all from the scheme of Dr. Watts in his book entitled *The Rational Foundation of a Christian Church, and the Terms of Christian Communion,* which he says is the common sentiment and practice of all Reformed churches.[2] I had not seen this book of Dr. Watts' when I published what I have written on the subject; but yet I think my sentiments, as I have there expressed them, are as exactly agreeable to what he lays down, as if I had been his pupil. Nor do I at all go beyond what Dr. Doddridge plainly shows to be his sentiments in his *Rise and Progress of Religion,* and his Sermons on Regeneration, and in his Paraphrase and Notes on the New Testament.[3] Nor indeed, Sir, when I consider the sentiments you have expressed in your letters to Major Pomeroy and Mr. Billing, can I perceive but that they come exactly to the same thing that I maintain. You suppose, "The sacraments are not converting ordinances; but that as seals of the covenant they presuppose conversion, especially in the adult; and that 'tis visible saintship, or in other words a credible profession of faith and repentance, a solemn consent to the gospel covenant, joined with a good conversation, and competent measure of Christian knowledge, is what gives a gospel right to all sacred ordinances; but that it is necessary to those that come to these ordinances, and in those that profess a consent to the gospel covenant, that they are sincere in their profession," or at least should think themselves so.

The great thing which I have scrupled in the established method of this church's proceeding, and which I dare no longer go on in, is their publicly assenting to the form of words rehearsed on occasion of admission to the communion, without pretending thereby to mean any such thing as an hearty consent to the terms of the gospel covenant, or

2. Isaac Watts, *The Rational Foundation of a Christian Church, and the Terms of Christian Communion* (London, 1747).

3. Philip Doddridge, *The Rise and Progress of Religion in the Soul* (London, 1745; Boston, 1749); *Practical Discourses on Regeneration . . . in ten sermons, preach'd at Northampton* (London, 1742); and *The Family Expositor: or, A Paraphrase and Version of the New Testament* (London, 1739–56).

to mean any such faith or repentance as belong to the covenant of grace, and are the grand conditions of that covenant; it being, at the same time that the words are used, their known and established principle, which they openly profess and proceed upon, that men may and ought to use these words and mean no such thing, but something else of a nature far inferior, of which I think they have no distinct determinate notions, but something consistent with their knowing that they don't choose God as their chief good, but love the world more than him, and that they do not give themselves up entirely to God, but make reserves; and in short, knowing that they don't heartily consent to the gospel covenant, but live still under the reigning power of the love of the world, and enmity to God and Christ. So that the words of their public profession, according to their openly established use, cease to be of the nature of any profession of gospel faith and repentance, or any proper compliance with the covenant; for 'tis their profession that the words as used, mean no such thing. The words used under these circumstances do at least fail of being a "credible profession of these things." I can conceive of no such virtue in a certain set of words, that 'tis proper, merely on the making these sounds, to admit persons to Christian sacraments, without any regard to any pretended meaning of those sounds: nor can I think that any institution of Christ has established any such terms of admission into the Christian church. It don't belong to the controversy between me and my people, how particular or large the profession should be that is required. I should not choose to be confined to exact limits as to that matter; but rather than contend, I should content myself with a few words, briefly expressing the cardinal virtues or acts implied in a hearty compliance with the covenant, made (as should appear by inquiry into the person's doctrinal knowledge) understandingly, if there were an external conversation agreeable thereto. Yea, I should think that such a person solemnly making such a profession, had a right to be received as the object of a public charity, however he himself might scruple his own conversion, on account of his not remembering the time, not knowing the method of his conversion, or finding so much remaining sin, etc. And if his own scruples did not hinder his coming to the Lord's table, I should think the minister or church had no right to debar such a professor, though he should say he did not think himself converted: for I call that a profession of godliness, which is a profession of the great things wherein godliness consists; and not a professing his own opinion of his good estate.

When I say in my book that a "positive charity" is requisite, my meaning has been misunderstood by some, as though by "positive," I had meant "peremptory," whereas I meant no more than "positive" in opposition to a mere "negation" of a contrary determination. I think there should not only be no evidence against a man, but some positive exhibition or visibility implying probability, or some worthiness of a real act of the charitable judgment of the church in a person's favor as a true Christian, agreeable to his profession. I think you express the very same thing, when you speak of a "credible" profession as what entitles a man to admission. "Credible" is that which is worthy of "credit" or "belief."

Sir, if you write to my people your opinion of my book as you proposed in your letter, I desire you would do it before the council that is to meet here on June 19, to judge whether or no I ought immediately to be dismissed from my pastoral office. And I ask the favor of you, of sending me a copy of your letter to them, otherwise 'tis probable I may never know what you write and that the people will never see it, at least not before the council, unless it be plainly in their favor. It was not without some difficulty that your last letter to Major Pomeroy was communicated even to the Precinct, though you directed that it should be communicated. However, they yet stand to it that you are on their side. The state of this people is very unhappy. I would not speak to their disparagement; I know it is a day of great temptation with them; and allowances must be made for them on many accounts.

In your letter to Mr. Billing, you say, reverend Sir, that "He speaks as one that knows the heart of a minister," but there [are] but few that know the heart of a minister under my circumstances.

It would be tedious, and would tire your patience for me to give a particular account of the state of things. But if you had fully known them, and how ready a people in such a state are to catch at every word, from a man they have received such a character of, and to make much of little things, you would probably have forborne, on so uncertain a report of my principles, to say to them, "They might easily be reduced to an absurdity," though it was only on supposition you had been rightly informed. Some things which you have said have been improved to my disadvantage, both by ministers and people, though I confess without your having given them much occasion.

I conclude with asking your fervent prayers to the God of all light and grace for me under my great troubles. I am, honored Sir, with much esteem and respect,

Your son and servant,
Jonathan Edwards.

117. TO THE REVEREND JOHN ERSKINE

In the wake of his dismissal, Edwards reviews the circumstances surrounding it for his friend. Erskine seems willing to recommend Edwards for a position in Scotland, but Edwards has reservations.

(Trask Library, ALS, six quarto leaves; Dwight ms. transcript, six quarto leaves. Published in Dwight ed., *1*, 405–13.)

* * *

Northampton, July 5, 1750

Rev. and Dear Brother,

I now acknowledge the receipt of three letters from you since I last wrote to you; one of September 12, another of September 20, another of December 22, all of the year 1749. The two first I received in the winter, with Mr. Glas' *Notes on Scripture Texts,* Ridgley on original sin, Wheatly's *Schools of the Prophets,* Davidson's Sermon occasioned by the death of Mr. Harrison, and Mr. McKaile's Sermon.[1] Your letter written in December I received a little while ago.

I have greatly regretted the want of opportunity to answer you till now, but such have been my extraordinary circumstances, the multitude of distracting troubles and hurries that I have been involved in (which I can't easily represent to you), that I have had no leisure. I have been very uneasy in neglecting to write to my correspondents in Scotland; and about two months ago I set myself to the business; but was soon broken off; and have not been able to return to it again till now.

1. John Glas, *Notes on Scripture-Texts* (Edinburgh, 1747–60); on JE's use of this work, see *Works, 13,* 137, n. 9. Thomas Ridgley, *The Doctrine of Original Sin Considered, Being the Substance of Two Sermons Preached at Pinners Hall* (London, 1725); Charles Wheatly, *The Schools of the Prophets: A Sermon* (Oxford, 1721); Thomas Davidson, *The Triumphant Exit of a Faithful Servant of Jesus Christ, Set Forth in a Sermon Preach'd on Occasion of the Death of the Revd. John Harrison* (London, 1749); Hugh McKaile, *The Last Publick Sermon, Preached by Hugh MacKaile upon the Sabbath Immediately Preceeding that 8th of September 1662, the Day Affixed for the Removal of the Ministers of Edinburgh from Their Kirks, and Themselves and Their Families from the City in the Days Thereafter with the Last Speech and Testimony Delivered by Him on the Scaffold* (Edinburgh, 1749).

And now Sir, I thank you for your letters and presents. The books you sent me were entertaining to me, and some of them will be of advantage to me, if God should give me opportunity to prosecute the studies I had begun on the Arminian controversy. There were various things pleasing to me in Glas' *Notes,* tending to give some new light into the sense of Scripture. He seems to be a man of ability, though I can't fall in with all his singularities.

The account you say Mr. [Thomas] Davidson gave of the absurdities of the Moravians are not very surprising to me. I have seen here in America so much of the tendency and issue of such kind of notions and such sort of religion as are in vogue amongst them, and among many others in many respects like 'em, that I expect no other than that sin, folly, absurdity, and things to the highest degree reproachful to Christianity, will forever be the consequence of such things. It seems to me that enough, and enough of this kind, has lately appeared, greatly to awaken the attention of Christian divines, and make 'em suspect that the devil's devices in the various counterfeits of vital experimental religion, have not been sufficiently attended to, and the exact distinctions between the saving operations of the Spirit of God, and all its false appearances, not sufficiently observed.

There is something now in the press in Boston, largely handling the subject. I have had opportunity to read the manuscript and, in my humble opinion, it has a tendency to give as much light in this matter as anything that ever I saw. It was written by Mr. [Joseph] Bellamy, minister of Bethlehem in Connecticut,[2] the minister which Mr. [David] Brainerd sometimes speaks of as his peculiarly dear and intimate friend (as possibly you may have observed in reading his *Life*). He was of about Mr. Brainerd's age; and it might have been well, if he had more years over his head. But as he is one of the most intimate friends that I have in the world, and one that I have much acquaintance with, I can say this of him: that he is one of very great experience in religion, as to what has passed between God and his own soul; one of very good natural abilities, of closeness of thought, and extraordinary diligence in his studies, and earnest care exactly to know the truth in these matters. He has long applied his mind to the subject he has wrote upon, and used all possible helps of conversation and reading. And though his style is not such as is like to please the

2. Bellamy, *True Religion Delineated.* JE wrote the preface, reprinted in *Works, 4,* 569–72.

polite world; yet if his youth, and the obscurity of his original, and the place that he lives in, etc., don't prevent his being much taken notice of, I am persuaded his book might serve to give the church of God considerable light as to the nature of true religion, and many important doctrines of Christianity. From the knowledge I have of him, I am fully satisfied his aim in this publication is not his own fame and reputation in the world; but the glory of God, and the advancement of the kingdom of his Redeemer.

I suspect the follies of some of the Seceders, which you mention in both your letters of September 20 and December 22, arise in considerable measure from the same cause with the follies of the Moravians, and the followers of the Wesleys, and many extravagant people in America, viz. false religion, counterfeit conversions, and the want of a genuine renovation of the spirit of their minds. I say as to many of them, not to condemn all in the gross. The spirit seems to be exactly the same with what appears in many, who apparently, by their own account, have had a false conversion.

I am a great enemy to censoriousness, and have opposed it very much in my preaching and writings. But yet I think we should avoid that bastard, mischievous charity, by which Satan keeps men asleep, and hides their eyes from those snares and crafty works of his, which it is of the utmost consequence to the church of God to discover and be aware of; and by which, for want of their being discovered, the devil has often had his greatest advantages against the interest of religion. The Scripture often leads us to judge of true religion, and the gracious sincerity of professors, by the genius, the temper, and spirit of their religion. Jas. 3:17; Eph. 5:9; Gal. 5:19–25; I Cor. 13:4, etc.; Rom. 8:9; I John 4:16; John 13:35; I John 2:10; I John 3:14 and 18–19, and 23–24; ch. 4:7, 12–13; and very many other places. I have been greatly grieved at a spirit of censoriousness; but yet I heartily wish that some sorts of charity were utterly abolished.

The account you give of Archbishop [Thomas] Herring, the moderate, generous, truly catholic, and Christian principles appearing in him and some others of the dignified clergy, and other persons of distinction in the Church of England, are very agreeable. 'Tis to be hoped that these things are forerunners of something good and great to be brought to pass for the church of God.

I have seen some accounts in our public prints published here in America, of those conversions and baptisms in the Russian Empire, which you mention in your last letter; and should be glad of further information about that matter.

We have had published here an extract of a letter, written by Dr. [Philip] Doddridge to Mr. [Richard] Pearsall, of Taunton in Somersetshire, and transmitted by him to Boston, in a letter to Mr. [Thomas] Prince;[3] giving a surprising account of a very wonderful person, a German by nation, a preacher of the gospel to the Jews, lately in London; whom he (Dr. Doddridge) saw and conversed with and heard preach (or rather repeat) a sermon there; who had had great success in preaching to those miserable people in Germany, Poland, Holland, Lithuania, Hungary, and other parts; God having so blessed his labors that in the various parts through which he had traveled, he had been the instrument of the conversion of about 600 Jews; many of whom are expressing their great concern to bring others of their brethren to the knowledge of the great and blessed Redeemer, and beseeching him to instruct their children, that they may preach Christ also. I should be glad, if you hear anything further of the affair, to be informed of it by you. I think such things may well be improved to animate and encourage those who have engaged in the Concert for Prayer for the reviving of religion. I rejoice to hear what you write of some appearances of awakening in Mr. [John] Gillies' church in Glasgow, and if it continues should be glad to be informed.

I am very glad to hear what Mr. [John] MacLaurin informs of the encouragements likely to be given from Scotland to New Jersey College, a very hopeful society; and I believe what is done for that seminary is doing good in an eminent manner.

Mr. MacLaurin tells me of some prospect of your being removed to a congregation in Edinburgh; which I am pleased with, because I hope there you will act in a larger sphere, and will have more opportunity to exert the disposition that appears in you, to promote good, public designs for Zion's prosperity.

I thank you for the concern you manifest for me under my difficulties and troubles, by reason of the controversy between me and my people, about the terms of Christian communion. This controversy has now had that issue which I expected; it has ended in a separation between me and my people. Many things have appeared that have

3. On the revival in Russia, see *Boston Gazette*, Jan. 16, 1750. *Boston Weekly News-Letter*, Mar. 22, 1750, "Extract out of a Letter [by Philip Doddridge] from the Rev. Mr. Pearsall of Taunton in Somersetshire in England, October 31st, 1749, to the Rev. Mr. Prince in Boston."

been exceeding unhappy and uncomfortable in the course of the controversy. The great power of prejudices from education, established custom, and the traditions of ancestors and certain admired teachers, and the exceeding unhappy influence of bigotry has remarkably appeared in the management of this affair. The spirit that has actuated and engaged my people in this matter is evidently the same that has appeared in your own people in their opposition to winter communions, but only risen to a much higher degree; and some of the arguments that have been greatly insisted on here have been very much of the same sort with some of those urged by your people in your affair. There have been many things said and done during our controversy that I am willing should be buried in oblivion; and therefore shall not now declare 'em. But would only say in the general, that there has been that prejudice, and spirit of jealousy, and increasing engagedness of spirit, and fixedness of resolution to gain the point in view, viz. my dismission from my pastoral office over them, upheld and cherished by a persuasion that herein they only stood for the truth and did their duty; that it has been an exceeding difficult thing for me to say or do anything at all, in order to their being enlightened, or brought to a more calm and sedate consideration of things, without its being misinterpreted, and turned to an occasion of increasing jealousy and prejudice; even those things wherein I have yielded most, and done most to gratify the people and assuage their spirits, and win their charity. I have often declared to the people and gave it to 'em under my hand, that if after all proper means used and regular steps taken, they continued averse to continuing under my ministry, I had no inclination to do anything as attempting to oblige them to it. But I looked on myself bound in conscience before I left them (as I was afraid they were in the way to ruin), to do my endeavor that proper means should be used to bring 'em to a suitable temper, and so to a capacity of proceeding considerately and with their eyes open, properly and calmly and prayerfully examining the point in controversy, and also weighing the consequences of things.

To this end I have insisted much on an impartial council, in which should be some of the elderly ministers of the land, to look fully into our state, and view it with all its circumstances, with full liberty to give both me and them such advice as they thought requisite and proper. And therefore I insisted that the council should not wholly consist of ministers and churches that were professedly against me in the point in controversy; and that it should not consist wholly of ministers and churches of this neighborhood, who were almost altogether in opposition to me; but that some should be brought from abroad. This I also insisted on, as I thought it most likely an impartial council would do me justice in the public representation they would make of our affairs in their result. The people insisted that the council should be wholly of the neighborhood, undoubtedly because they supposed themselves most sure that their judgment and advice would be favorable and agreeable to them. I stood the more against it, because in this country we have no such thing as appeals from one council to another, from a lesser to a larger; and also because the neighboring ministers were all youngerly men. These things were long the subject matter of uncomfortable troubles and contests. Many were the proposals I made. At last, they complied with this proposal (after great and long-continued opposition to it), viz. that I should nominate two churches to be of the council, who were not within the bounds of this county. And so it was agreed that a council of ten churches should be called, mutually chosen, and that two of my half should be called from abroad. I might have observed before that there was a great and long dispute about the business of the council, or what should be left to them: and particularly, whether it should be left to them, or [whether] they should have liberty to give us what advice they pleased for a remedy from our calamities. This I insisted on, not that I desired that we should bind ourselves beforehand to stand to their advice, let it be what it would; but I thought it absurd to tie up and limit the council, that they should not exercise their own judgment, and give us their advice according to their own mind. The people were willing the council should make proposals for an accommodation; but that if they did not like them, the council should be obliged immediately to separate us, and would not have 'em have any liberty to advise to wait longer, or use any further means for light, or take any further or other course for a remedy from our calamities.

At last a vote was passed in the church in these words: "That a council should be called to give us their best advice for a remedy from the calamities arising from the present unsettled, broken state of this church, by reason of the controversy here subsisting, concerning the qualifications for full communion in the church: and, if upon the whole of what they see and find in our circumstances, they judge it best that pastor and people be immediately separated, that they proceed to dissolve the relation between 'em." Accordingly, a council was agreed upon to meet here on this business on June 19. I nominated two out of this county, of which Mr. [Thomas] Foxcroft's church in Boston was one. But others were nominated provisionally, in case these should fail. Those that came were Mr. [David] Hall's church of Sutton, and Mr. [William] Hobby's church in Reading. One of the churches that I nominated within the county refused to send a delegate, viz. Mr. [Edward] Billing's church of Cold Spring. However, Mr. Billings himself (though with some difficulty) was admitted into the council.

The people, in managing this affair on their side, have made chief use of a young gentleman of liberal education and notable abilities and a fluent speaker, of about seven or eight and twenty years of age, my grandfather Stoddard's grandson, being my mother's sister's son [Joseph Hawley, Jr.], a man of lax principles in religion, falling in in some essential things with Arminians, and is very open and bold in it. He was improved as one of the agents for the church, and was their chief spokesman before the council. He very strenuously urged before the council the necessity of an immediate separation. And I, knowing the church the most of them to be inflexibly bent on this event, I told the council that I should not enter into the dispute, but should refer the matter wholly to the council's judgment. I signified that I had no desire to leave my people on any other consideration than their aversion to my being their minister any longer. But they continuing so averse, had no inclination or desire that they should be compelled, but yet should refer myself to their advice.

When the church was convened in order to the council's knowing their minds with respect to my continuance, about twenty-three appeared for it; others stayed away, choosing not to act either way. But the generality of the church, which consists of about 230 male members, voted for my dismission. My dismission was carried in the council by a majority of one vote.

The ministers were equally divided; but of the delegates one more were for it than against it. And it so happened that every member of the council that were of the churches of the people's choosing voted for my dismission, but every one that were of the churches that I chose were against it. And there happening to be one of these fewer than the other, by the church of Cold Spring's not sending a delegate (which was through that people's prejudice against my opinion), the vote was carried that way, by the vote of one delegate. However, on the 22nd of the last month, the relation between me and this people was dissolved. I suppose the result of the council, together with the protestations of some of the members, are printed in Boston by this time.[4] I shall endeavor to procure one of the printed accounts to be sent with this letter to you, together with one of my books on the point that has been in controversy between me and my people. Two of the members of the council who dissented from the result, yet did not sign the protestation, viz. Mr. [Peter] Reynolds and his delegate, which I suppose was owing to Mr. Reynolds' extraordinary cautious and timorous temper.

The last sabbath I preached my farewell sermon. Many in the congregation seemed to be much affected and some are exceedingly grieved. Some few I believe have some relentings of heart, that voted me away. But there is no great probability that the leading part of the church will ever change. Besides their own fixedness of resolution, there are many in neighboring towns to support their resolution, both in the ministry and civil magistracy, without whose influence I believe the people never would have been so violent as they have been.

I desire that such a time of awful changes, dark clouds, and great frowns of heaven on me and my people may be a time of serious consideration, thorough self-reflection and examination, and deep humiliation with me. I desire your fervent prayers for me and those who have heretofore been my people. I know not what will become of them. There seems to be the utmost danger that the younger generations will be carried away with Arminianism, as with a flood. The young gentleman I before spoke of is high in their esteem, and is become the most leading man in the town; and is very bold in declaring and disputing for his opinions; and we have none able to confront and withstand him in dispute: and some of the young people already show a disposition to fall in with his notions. And 'tis not likely that the people will obtain any young gentleman of the Calvinistical persuasion to settle with them in the ministry that will have courage and ability to make head against him.

And as to the older people, there never appeared so great an indifference among them about things of this nature. They will at present be much more likely to be thorough in their care to settle a minister of principles contrary to mine, as to terms of communion, than to settle one that is sound in the doctrines of grace. The great concern of the

4. A brief notice of JE's dismissal appeared in *The Boston Gazette*, July 31, 1750, followed by the full reports by the majority and minority in the issue of Aug. 7. A pamphlet by JE, entitled *The Result of a Council of Nine Churches met at Northampton, June 22, 1750. With a Protest against the Same. By a Member of the Said Council*, was published in Boston later in 1750.

leading part of the town at present will probably be, to come off with flying colors in the issue of the controversy they have had with me, and of what they have done in it; for which they know many condemn them.

An end is put for the present by these troubles to the studies I was before engaged in, and my design of writing against Arminianism. I had made considerable preparation, and was deeply engaged in the prosecution of this design, before I was rent off from it by these difficulties. And if ever God should give me opportunity, I would again resume that affair. But I am now as it were thrown upon the wide ocean of the world, and know not what will become of me and my numerous and chargeable family; nor have I any particular door in view, that I depend upon to be opened for my future serviceableness. Most places in New England that want a minister would not be forward to invite one with so chargeable a family, nor one so far advanced in years, being forty-six the fifth day of last October. I am fitted for no other business but study: I should make a poor hand of getting a living by any secular employment. We are in the hands of God, and I bless him. I am not anxious concerning his disposal of us. I hope I shall not distrust him, nor be unwilling to submit to his will. And I have cause of thankfulness, that there seems also to be such a disposition in my family.

You are pleased, dear Sir, very kindly to ask me whether I could sign the Westminster Confession of Faith, and submit to the Presbyterian form of church government; and to offer to use your influence to procure a call for me to some congregation in Scotland. I should be very ungrateful if I were not thankful for such kindness and friendship.

As to my subscribing to the substance of the Westminster Confession, there would be no difficulty: and as to the Presbyterian government, I have long been perfectly out of conceit with our unsettled, independent, confused way of church government in this land. And the Presbyterian way has ever appeared to me most agreeable to the Word of God, and the reason and nature of things, though I cannot say that I think that the Presbyterian government of the Church of Scotland is so perfect that it can't in some respects be mended. But as to my removing with my numerous family over the Atlantic, it is, I acknowledge, attended with many difficulties that I shrink at. Among other things, this is very considerable, that it would be on uncertainties whether my gifts and administrations would suit any congregation that should send for me without trial. And so great a thing as such a removal had need to be on some certainty as to that matter. If the expectations of a congregation were so great, and they were so confident of my qualifications as to call me at a venture, having never seen or heard me, their disappointment might possibly be so much the greater and the more uneasy after acquaintance and trial. My own country is not so dear to me, but that if there were an evident prospect of being more serviceable to Zion's interests elsewhere, I could forsake it. And I think my wife is fully of this disposition.

I forgot to mention that in this evil time in Northampton, there are some of the young people under awakenings; and I hope two or three have lately been converted: two very lately, besides two or three hopefully brought home the last year.

My wife and family join with me in most respectful and cordial salutations to you and your consort. And we desire the prayers of you both for us under our present circumstances. My youngest child but one [Jonathan, Jr.] has long been in a very infirm, afflicted, and decaying state with the rickets and some other disorders. I desire your prayers for it. I am, dear Sir,

> Your most affectionate and obliged friend and brother,
> Jonathan Edwards.

P.S. For accounts of the state of religion in America and some reasons of my conduct in this controversy with my people, I must refer you to my letters to Mr. [James] Robe and Mr. MacLaurin.

118. TO THE REVEREND WILLIAM McCULLOCH

McCulloch is one of the circle of Scottish ministers with whom Edwards feels a close kinship. Here, Edwards resumes correspondence with McCulloch for the first time in a year. Following the trauma of the communion controversy, he finds the religious outlook in New England discouraging. Yet there are signs of revival elsewhere, and his confidence is ultimately unshaken.

(Trask Library, ALS, two quarto leaves, addressed on verso to the Reverend William McCulloch, minister of the gospel in Cambuslang, Scotland, care of Reverend Mr. MacLaurin of Glasgow. Published in Dwight ed., *1*, 413–14.)

*   *   *

Northampton, July 6, 1750

Rev. and Dear Sir,

'Tis now long since I have received a letter from you; the last was dated March 10, 1749. However, you having heretofore manifested that our correspondence was not unacceptable to you, I would not omit to do my part towards the continuance of it. Perhaps one reason of your neglecting to write, may be the failing of such agreeable matter for correspondence as we had some years ago, when religion was flourishing in Scotland and America, and we had joyful informations to give each other of things pertaining to the city of our God. 'Tis indeed now a sorrowful time on this side the ocean: iniquity abounds, and the love of many waxes cold; multitudes of fair and high professors, in one place and another, have sadly backslidden; sinners are desperately hardened; experimental religion is more than ever out of credit with the far greater part; the doctrines of grace, those principles in religion that do chiefly concern the powers of godliness, are far more than ever discarded; Arminianism and Pelagianism have made a strange progress within a few years; the Church of England in New England is, I suppose, treble of what it was seven years ago; many professors are gone off to great lengths in enthusiasm and extravagance in their notions and practices; great contentions, separations, and confusions in our religious state prevail in many parts of the land. Some of our main pillars are broken, one of which was Mr. [John] Webb of Boston, who died in the latter part of last April. Much of the glory of the town of Boston is gone with him. And if the bereavements of that town should be added to by the death of two or three more of their remaining older ministers, that place would be in a very sorrowful state indeed, like a city whose walls are broken down, and like a large flock without a shepherd, encompassed with wolves, and many in the midst of it.

These are the dark things that appear; but on the other hand, there are some things that have a different aspect. There have in some places appeared revivings of religion. Some little revivings have been in some places towards Boston. There has been some reformation not long since in one of our colleges. And by what I hear, there has been much more of this nature in some other parts of the British America than in New England: something considerable in several towns on Long Island; and also in some other parts of the province of New York near Hudson's River; something in several parts of New Jersey, particularly through the labors of Mr. [Nehemiah] Greenman, a young gentleman educated by the charitable expenses of the pious and eminent Mr. David Brainerd, mentioned in his *Life;* which I think I sent to you the last summer. And since I last wrote to Scotland, I have had accounts of the prevailing of a religious concern in some parts of Virginia.

And I must not forget to inform you, that although I think it has of late been the darkest time in Northampton that ever was since the town stood, yet there have been some awakenings in the minds of some of the young people here, and two or three instances of hopeful conversion the last summer, and as many very lately.

When I speak of its being a dark time here, I have a special reference to the great controversy that has subsisted here, for about a year and half between me and my people, about the terms of communion in the visible church; which has now at length issued in a separation between me and my people—for a more particular account of which, I must refer you to my letters to Mr. [James] Robe and Mr. John Erskine. Besides, I shall endeavor to preserve the printed copies of the result of the council, that sat here the week before last, with the protestation of some of the members, that these may be sent to you with this letter, together with one of my books published on the point in debate between me and my people; of which I crave your acceptance.[1]

I am now separated from the people, between whom and me there was once the greatest union. Remarkable is the providence of God in this matter. In this event, we have a great instance of the instability and uncertainty of all things here below. The dispensation is indeed awful in many respects, calling for serious reflection, and deep humiliation, in me and my people. The enemy far and near will now triumph; but God can overrule all for his own glory. I have now nothing visible to depend upon for my future usefulness, or the subsistence of my numerous family. But I hope we have an all-sufficient, faithful, covenant God to depend upon. I desire that I may ever submit to him, walk humbly before him, and put my trust wholly in him.

I desire, dear Sir, your prayers for us under our present circumstances. I am, Sir,

> Your respectful and affectionate friend and brother,
> Jonathan Edwards.

---

1. *The Result of a Council . . . With a Protest Against the Same;* and *An Humble Inquiry.*

P.S. My wife and family join with me in cordial salutations to you and yours.

119. TO THE REVEREND THOMAS FOXCROFT

Edwards requests Foxcroft, overseer of his Boston publications, to secure newspaper coverage of his dismissal and of the minority report opposing it. The day he wrote this, *The Boston Gazette* carried an extract of the two reports and a week later printed both reports in full, in three columns spread across the front page.[1] In a bizarre twist, Edwards reports that the church has called on him to preach three times to date since his "farewell sermon."

(Beinecke Library, ALS, one quarto leaf.)

*   *   *

Northampton, July 31, 1750

Rev. and Honored Sir,

I am sorry that the result of the council that sat on my affair, with the protest against it, was not published in the newspapers; as I think it would be to my advantage that they should be known and made public in all parts of the country; and if they had been published in the public prints that would undoubtedly have made them much more public, and generally known; so that in that case, probably twenty would have seen them where one will see them as they are now printed by themselves. I can't but still desire that they may be so published, and therefore desire you to persuade some or other of the publishers of newspapers to put them into their papers; as they are not so long, but that they may conveniently do it; and I suppose they will be no disadvantage to their papers.

There is no manner of prospect at present of this people's altering their minds. The committee for supplying the pulpit have got me to preach three sabbaths since I preached my farewell sermon; but it is with great reluctance. They from week to week do their utmost to get the pulpit otherwise supplied. They have taken much pains to get the neighboring ministers to take their turns to preach here, but meet with difficulty. They have talked of hiring somebody for the present, that they have no thoughts of settling, till they can hear of some likely candidate to hire on probation; but they don't know who to get. And

1. *Boston Gazette,* July 31 and Aug. 7, 1750, and *The Result of a Council . . . With a Protest Against the Same.*

therefore they have had of late, both a Precinct and church meeting, and have determined with all possible speed to get a candidate for settlement; and have sent Deacon [Ebenezer] Pomeroy to Cambridge, to consult the President [Edward Holyoke] concerning a candidate; and I suppose hope the Deacon will bring one with him, who may supply the pulpit next sabbath, that they mayn't be obliged to ask me to preach anymore.

I should be glad of a line from you by Mr. [Nathan] Graves, who brings this. And desire you will still remember in your prayers, your most obliged

Friend and servant,
Jonathan Edwards.

120. ENCLOSURE

The following is a note, probably for Thomas Foxcroft, Thomas Prince, or one of Edwards' Boston contacts, that was sent with letters intended for England. It demonstrates Edwards' continuing contact with eminent leaders within the English dissenting community.

(Beinecke Library, one leaf.)

*   *   *

[Northampton, after June 1750]

I would intreat you, Sir, before you seal up the packets to Dr. [John] Guyse and Dr. [Philip] Doddridge, to procure of Mr. [Samuel] Kneeland, two of the printed copies of the *Result* of our council, with the *Protest;* and put one into each packet.[1] I have an account with Mr. Kneeland, and I desire him to set them down to my account.

Yours,
Jonathan Edwards.

121. TO THE REVEREND WILLIAM RUSSELL

Edwards calls on his brother-in-law to clarify the stand he has taken on qualifications for church membership. Edwards believes that Russell agrees with his own view, but he remembers hearing that Russell has said that in the event of conscientious disagreement no profession of faith is necessary. A restatement of Russell's position will help remove the ambiguity.

---

1. *The Result of a Council . . . With a Protest Against the Same.*

(Beinecke Library, two quarto leaves, addressed on verso to the Reverend William Russell, Pastor of the First Church in Middletown.)

* * *

Middletown, September 14, 1750

Rev. and Dear Sir,

You may remember that when I was at your house the last week, I was talking with you concerning my opinion, with regard to the visible qualifications for Christian sacraments; and that you signified that you agreed with me in supposing that, by the institution of Christ, it was a saving faith or a cordial reception of Christ and self-dedication to him, which should be professed.

I then mentioned what Mr. [Stephen] Williams of Longmeadow had told me that you said to him, viz. that you thought that although this, you supposed, was the truth; yet if my people, and candidates for communion at Northampton, continued to be of another mind, after I had declared to them my opinion with the reasons of it, and they declared to me their conscientious desire to be admitted to full communion without any such profession, I might with a good conscience take 'em in according to their own judgment. But you said Mr. Williams was mistaken and had misrepresented you, etc. And that the next morning, I brought on the discourse again, and desired you plainly to tell me your real sentiments as to that matter, viz. whether I, being of the forementioned opinion with respect to the institution of Christ, appointing a profession of saving faith, etc. (which you also supposed he had appointed), I could with a good conscience, acting as a minister of Christ and one appointed and sent by him, in the service of his house to execute his institutions, be active in receiving persons to sacraments, and administering sacraments to them, who in the profession they made did not pretend to signify anything of such a nature as a saving faith, or a cordial reception of Christ, and entire self-dedication to him, but declared that they meant something of a vastly different nature, and acted on those principles, that persons might and ought to make such a profession as they made, who included no such thing, but were conscious to themselves that they were real enemies to Christ; and loved the world better than him.

I desired to know your mind, and have your advice as to that matter, as it was an affair that it highly concerned me to be well informed in, and because I looked on you as a person of judgment, and I thought it very natural under my difficult circumstances and having such an opportunity to consult so near a friend and relation. And I thought you then complied with my desire, and told me your mind, very plainly expressing your sentiment. You may remember what you said to what I proposed concerning a steward's attending his master's orders, in giving the portion of meat appointed to each member of the household, and the comparison you yourself brought concerning the king's officers admitting persons to the privileges of subjects, their attending the king's instructions as to the qualifications that should appear and the profession they should make. In the time of it I thought you spoke plainly. But since that, something has passed, which has made me suspect, that after all, I never understood you, and that indeed you concealed from me your real sentiments. This suspicion arose in my mind in my journey from New Haven hither.

My request therefore, dear Sir, is that you would write to me, and inform me whether I rightly understood you or not, and express your mind with plainness in this matter. The reasons why I desire it are these two, viz. 1. I truly desire to know your mind for my own benefit, for which reason I asked it at first. 2. Misunderstandings often tend to weaken and interrupt friendship; which plain dealing prevents. And 'tis doubtless desirable that friendship and good understanding should be maintained and cherished between brethren. I am, Sir,

Your affectionate brother,
Jonathan Edwards.

P.S. I desire your prayers for me and my family under our great difficulties and trials.

122. TO THE REVEREND JOSEPH BELLAMY

One of Edwards' more mundane letters, this note reflects his activity in the business of sheep raising. It also attests to the depth of his friendship with Joseph Bellamy.

(Beinecke Library, ALS, one quarto leaf, addressed on verso to the Reverend Joseph Bellamy at Bethlehem.)

* * *

Canaan, November 5, 1750

Rev. and Dear Sir,

My wife seems to be very unwilling that our sheep should be sold. She chooses rather that they should be let out at a lower rate, if none will still hire them at the rate of a pound of wool a sheep. I should be glad (if they can't be let out so), they may not be sold, any of them, as yet. If I should settle anywhere in this western part of the country, possibly I may find some way to dispose of 'em myself. I am Sir, your

Affectionate and grateful friend and brother,

Jonathan Edwards.

123. TO THE REVEREND JOHN ERSKINE

Deprived of his position and with uncertain prospects, Edwards is grateful for a gift of books from John Erskine as well as for the moral support they represent. He repeats the optimistic sentiments he has expressed to other Scottish friends. The idea of frequent communion holds particular appeal, as the sacrament has not been observed at Northampton for over a year.

(Trask Library, ALS, two folio leaves; Dwight ms. transcript, four quarto leaves. Published in Dwight ed., *1*, 415–18. The vote to suspend communion was taken Nov. 20, 1749; *Works, 12*, 523.)

*   *   *

Northampton, November 15, 1750

Rev. and Dear Sir,

Some time in July last I wrote to you, and ordered one of my books on the qualifications for communion in the church, to be sent to you from Boston with the letter.[1] In my letter I informed of what had come to pass in the issue of the late controversy between me and my people, in the dissolution of my pastoral relation to them; and ordered the printed *Result* of the ecclesiastical council that sat on our affairs, and the *Protest* against the said *Result*,[2] to be put up with the letter; and also, at the same time, sent letters to my other correspondents in Scotland, with the books, etc.

I have as yet had no call to any stated business elsewhere in the ministry, although of late there has been some prospect of my having invitations to one or two places. This people of Northampton are hitherto destitute of a minister. They have exerted themselves very much to obtain some candidate to come and preach to them on probation, and have sent to many distant places; but have hitherto been disappointed, and seem to be very much nonplused. But the major part of 'em seem to continue without any relentings or misgivings of

1. *An Humble Inquiry.*
2. *The Result of a Council . . . With a Protest Against the Same.*

heart concerning what has been done; at least the major part of the leading men in the congregation. But there is a number whose hearts are broke at what has come to pass; and I believe are more deeply affected than ever they were at any temporal bereavement. It is thus with one of the principal men in the parish, viz. Col. [Timothy] Dwight. And another of our principal men, viz. Dr. [Samuel] Mather, adheres very much to me; and there are more women of this sort than men. And I doubt not but there is a number, who in their hearts are with me, who durst not appear, by reason of the great resolution, and high hand with which things are carried in the opposition, by the prevailing part. Such is the state of things amongst us, that a person cannot appear on my side, without greatly exposing himself to the resentments of his friends and neighbors, and being the object of much odium.

The committee, that have the care of supplying the pulpit, have asked me to preach the greater part of the time since my dismission, when I have been at home; but it has seemed to be with much reluctance that they have come to me, and only because they could not get the pulpit supplied otherwise. And they have asked me only from sabbath to sabbath; in the meantime, they have taken much pains to get somebody else to preach to 'em.

Since I wrote to you in July last, I received your letter, dated 30th of April last, with your generous and acceptable presents of Fraser's *Treatise of Justifying Faith,* Mr. Crawford's *Manual against Infidelity,* Mr. Randall's *Letter on Frequent Communicating,* Mr. Blair's Sermon before the Society for Propagating Christian Knowledge with an Account of the Society, and the Bishop of London's Letter to the Cities of London and Westminster.[3] The view the last-mentioned gives of the wickedness of those cities, is very affecting; and the patience of God towards such cities, so full of wickedness, so heinous and horrid in its kinds, and attended with such aggravations, is very astonishing. That these cities, and the nation, and indeed Christendom in general, are come to such

3. James Fraser, *A Treatise on Justifying Faith, Wherein is opened the grounds of believing or the sinner's sufficient warrant to take hold of what is offered in the everlasting gospel* (Edinburgh, 1749); William Crawford, *A Short Manual against the Infidelity of this Age* (Edinburgh, 1734); Thomas Randall, *A Letter to a Minister concerning Frequent communicating, occasioned by the late Overture to the Synod of Glasgow and Air upon that subject* (Edinburgh, 1749); Hugh Blair, *The Importance of Religious Knowledge to the Happiness of Mankind. A Sermon Preached before the Society for Propagating Christian Knowledge . . . To Which is Subjoin'd a Short Account of the Present State of the Society* (Edinburgh, 1750); and Thomas Sherlock, *A Letter from the Lord Bishop of London to the clergy and people of London and Westminster; on the occasion of the late Earthquakes* (London, 1750).

a pass as they are, seems to me to argue that some very remarkable dispensation of divine providence is nigh, either of mercy or judgment; or perhaps both: of great mercy to an elect number, and great wrath and vengeance towards others; and that those very things you take notice of in Is. 59 are approaching, appears to me very probable. However, I cannot but think, that at such a day, all such as truly love Zion and lament the wickedness that prevails in the earth, are very loudly called upon to united and earnest prayers to God, to arise and plead his own cause, that he would make bare his own arm, that that may bring salvation. That now, when the enemy comes in as a flood, the Spirit of the Lord may lift up a standard against him. When the church of Christ is like the ship wherein Christ and his disciples were when it was tossed with a dreadful tempest, and even covered with waves, and Christ was asleep, certainly it becomes Christians (though not with doubting and unbelief) to call on their Redeemer, that he would awake out of sleep, and rebuke the winds and waves. There are some things that afford a degree of comfort and hope in this dark day, respecting the state of Zion. I can't but rejoice at some things which I have seen, that have lately been published in England, and the reception they have met with in so corrupt a time and nation—some things of Dr. [Philip] Doddridge's (who seems to have his heart truly engaged for the interest of religion), particularly his *Rise and Progress of Religion,* and *Colonel Gardiner's Life,* and also Mr. Hervey's *Meditations.*[4] And I confess, 'tis a thing that gives me much hope, that there [are] so many on this side the ocean united in the Concert for Prayer proposed from Scotland; of which I may give a more particular account in a letter to Mr. MacLaurin, which I intend shall be sent with this. I had lately a letter from Gov. [Jonathan] Belcher, and in the postscript he sends me the following extract of a letter he had lately received from Dr. Doddridge:

> Nor did I ever know a finer class of young preachers, for its number, than that which God has given me this year to send out into the churches. Yet are not all the supplies here, or elsewhere, adequate to their necessities; for many congregations in various parts of England remain vacant. But I hope God will prosper the schemes we are forming for their assistance. . . . I bless God, that in these

4. Philip Doddridge, *Rise and Progress of Religion in the Soul,* and *Some remarkable passages in the life of the Honourable Col. James Gardiner, Who Was Slain at the Battle of Preston* (London, 1747); and James Hervey, *Meditations among the Tombs* (London, 1746).

middle parts of our island, peace and truth prevail in sweet harmony: and I think God is reviving our cause, or rather his own,
sensibly, though in a gentle and almost unobserved manner.

This which the Doctor speaks of I hope is a revival of real religion;
though many things, in many places, have been boasted of as glorious
revivals, which have been but counterfeits of religion. So it has been
with many things that were intermingled with, and followed our late
happy revival. There have been in New England, within this eight
years past, many hundreds, if not thousands of instances very much
like that of the boy at Tiptry-Heath, mentioned by Mr. [Thomas]
Davidson, as you give account in your letter.

We ought not only to praise God for everything that appears favorable to the interest of religion, and to pray earnestly for a general
revival, but also to use means that are proper in order to it. And one
proper means must be allowed to be a due administration of Christ's
ordinances: one instance of which is that which you and Mr. [Thomas]
Randall have lately been striving for, viz. a restoring the primitive
practice of frequent communicating. I should much wonder (had it
not been for what I have lately found myself of the force of bigotry,
and prejudice arising from education and custom), how such arguments and persuasives as Mr. Randall uses, can be withstood. But
however they may be resisted for the present, yet I hope those who
have begun will continue to plead the cause of Christ's institutions.
And whatever opposition is made, I should think it would be best for
them to plead for nothing at all short of Christ's institutions, viz. the
administration of the Lord's supper every Lord's day. It must come to
that at last; and why should Christ's ministers and people, by resting in
a partial reformation, lay a foundation for a new struggle, and an
uncomfortable labor and conflict, in some future generation, in order
to a full restoration of the primitive practice?

I should be greatly gratified, dear Sir, by the continuance of your
correspondence, and by being informed by you of the state of things
relating to the interest of religion in Europe, and specially in Great
Britain; and particularly whether the affair of a comprehension [in
Latin] is to go on, or whether the Test Act is like to be taken off, or if
there be anything else done or published in England or Scotland, that
remarkably affects the interest of religion.

I have with this letter sent Mr. [Joseph] Bellamy's *True Religion Delin-*

eated, with a sermon of mine at Mr. [Job] Strong's ordination;[5] of which I ask your acceptance as a small testimony of gratitude for your numerous favors to me.

I ask a constant remembrance in your prayers, that I may have the presence of God under my unusual trials, and that I may make a good improvement of all God's dealings with me. My wife joins with me in most cordial salutations to you and Madam. I am, dear Sir,

> Your affectionate and obliged friend and brother,
> Jonathan Edwards.

124. TO THE REVEREND JOSEPH BELLAMY

After Edwards' dismissal from Northampton, a small group of his former parishioners, numbering about twenty families, adhered to him. Edwards frequently preached to them in their homes. Despite grave doubts, Edwards, at the group's incessant urging, agreed to gather a council to advise him on whether he should accept a call as their pastor in a newly constituted church. In this letter, Edwards invites Bellamy to be part of such a council. News of this proposed council caused bitter feelings toward Edwards to erupt again in Northampton.

(Ms. last at Marietta College, Ohio, sold at auction in 1992, and currently unlocatable, ALS, one quarto leaf.)

* * *

Northampton, [April 1751]

Rev. and Dear Sir,

I much desire to see you here this spring, and should be glad you would come so to be here on the third Thursday in May, when it is agreed to desire a council to meet here, to look into the state of things, and give me advice with regard to my duty in my circumstances; and also to give advice to the people here that have adhered to me, what course they shall take under their very difficult circumstances. I hope, Sir, you will not fail. I shall think it of great importance that some ministers should be here that give a fair representation of things relating to Canaan and Stockbridge. I suppose that the ministers that will be called will be Dr. [Joseph] Sewall, Mr. [Thomas] Prince, Mr. [Peter]

---

5. Bellamy, *True Religion Delineated,* and JE, *Christ the Great Example of Gospel Ministers. A Sermon Preach'd at Portsmouth, at the Ordination of the Reverend Mr. Job Strong* (Boston, 1750).

Clark, Mr. [William] Hobby, Mr. [Edward] Wigglesworth, Mr. [John] Walley of Ipswich, Mr. [David] Hall of Sutton, Mr. [Edward] Billing, Mr. [Robert] Abercrombie. I am, Sir,

Your friend and brother,
Jonathan Edwards.

125. TO THE REVERENDS JOSEPH SEWALL AND THOMAS PRINCE

Edwards solicits the participation of clergy and lay representatives from the Third Church, Boston, in the forthcoming council, to advise him on whether he should become pastor to the Northampton families that sided with him in the communion controversy. Edwards clearly lacks enthusiasm for such a move, and seems more interested in asking the council to give him advice about "divers doors opening" for him elsewhere—primarily in Stockbridge. Edwards had visited and preached there, to the approbation of both colonists and Indians, in October 1750 and again from early January to late March 1751.

(AAS, Curwen Family Papers, box 3, f. 2, ALS, one folio leaf; facsimile in Winslow, opposite p. 264. The letter was "to be communicated," that is, read to the church. Note on verso in Prince's hand: "April 26, complied with [by a] general vote." It accompanied another letter, written by Edwards but signed by the Northampton minority; Beinecke Library, AL draft, one octavo leaf. It begins: "We, the subscribers of the First Church of Northampton, being under many difficult and distressed circumstances." A similar document, beginning "We, the subscribers" and addressed to Hobby and his church, is in the Trask Library [1751 file], in Edwards' hand, one folio leaf and one octavo leaf.)

*   *   *

Northampton, April 10, 1751

Reverend, Honored and Beloved,

My brethren in this place, who now apply to you for your advice under their distressing circumstances, being those whom I think myself obliged to be tenderly concerned for, they having long been under my pastoral care, and having adhered to me when most of their neighbors have been alienated from me and have renounced my ministry, and have manifested themselves especially friendly under very great trials; I do concur with them in desiring that they, under their present difficulties, may have the advice of a wise and judicious council, which I am sensible their case greatly requires. And *though my settlement in the pastoral office, over so small a number, under their circumstances, appears to me to be a thing attended with great difficulty and darkness,* yet I am willing to *resign myself in that affair,* to the direction of a council of such ministers and churches as they now apply themselves to. And if I should finally leave them, my obligations to them and affection for them make me unwilling to leave them in such extremely difficult circumstances, without some advice from such as may be confided in as persons of the best ability and integrity, to direct them what to do and which way to turn themselves. *I also desire an opportunity to lay my own case before such a council, to ask their judgment of it, and to be advised by them how to conduct myself with regard to my settlement in the work of the ministry;* there seeming at this time, through a merciful providence in the time of my great troubles, to be divers doors opening for my improvement and serviceableness in that great work.

Hoping for an opportunity to lay before you my circumstances, and to receive your advice in these important concerns, at the time and place specified in my brethren's letter, in conjunction with the reverend elders and messengers of such other churches as they apply to; and asking an interest in your prayers for me and them, and for the whole church and congregation in this place in their present dark state, I am, with much honor and respect,

Your brother and servant,
Jonathan Edwards.

126. TO THE REVEREND THOMAS FOXCROFT

Edwards makes an apparently unusual request of Foxcroft: that he counteract the influence of Chauncy, his fellow pastor at First Church, Boston, and promote attendance at the coming Northampton council by, among others, Joseph Sewall, the associate of Thomas Prince. Edwards had already asked Prince himself to encourage the participation of Sewall and his parishioners in his letter to them of April 10, 1751, but he depended on Foxcroft for loyal, energetic reinforcement.

(Beinecke Library, ALS, one quarto leaf, addressed on verso to the Reverend Thomas Prince [sic], minister of the gospel in Boston.)

* * *

Newbury, April 23, 1751

Reverend and Honored Sir,

It has been suggested to me by several ministers, since I came from Boston, that there is great danger of Dr. [Charles] Chauncy's influencing Dr. [Joseph] Sewall and Mr. [John] Hubbard to oppose their church's sending to the council at Northampton. And if their church fails, I think Mr. [Peter] Clark and Mr. [Edward] Wigglesworth will not go, and so all will fail.

This therefore is humbly to request of you that you would take an opportunity this week to confer with Dr. Sewall, Mr. Hubbard, the Secretary [Josiah Willard], and Maj. [Daniel] Henchman and Mr. [Edward] Bromfield about it; the matter being to be determined the next sabbath. I think the matter is of great importance and therefore I hope you will excuse

Your obliged brother and servant,
Jonathan Edwards.

127. TO THE REVEREND WILLIAM HOBBY

The tempestuous days of the May 1751 council were over. Edwards was back in the peaceful atmosphere of Stockbridge, his direction settled, his appointment official. He has one more record to set straight concerning the communion controversy, and he does so in this letter.

(Trask Library, AL draft, two quarto leaves, envelope covers addressed to Edwards at Stockbridge; Dwight ms. transcript, four quarto leaves, with supplied closing. Published in Dwight ed., *1*, 453–56. There is no evidence to support Dwight's claim of contemporary publication of the letter.)

* * *

[Stockbridge, June 1751]

Sir,

I think myself obliged, in the most public manner I am able, to correct a great and very injurious representation made a public fact concerning me, in a late pamphlet entitled, *A Letter to the Reverend Mr. Hobby, In Answer to his Vindication of the Protest against the Result of an Ecclesiastical Council met at Northampton*, etc. signed by Robert Breck, Joseph Ashley, Timothy Woodbridge, and Chester Williams.[1]

1. William Hobby, *A Vindication of the Protest Against the Result of the Northampton-Council*

These gentlemen who were members of the council that dissolved the relation between me and First Church in Northampton, in giving an account in p. 16 of their pamphlet what declarations both the church and I made before that council of our principles, say that Mr. Edwards declared that he could not in conscience be active in admitting any into the church unless they first made a profession "that they were indeed sanctified." Whereas I declared the reverse of this, openly and publicly and very particularly before that council in the meetinghouse, a great multitude being present. For this reason, because I had heard that such reports had been made abroad of my opinion, but carefully corrected 'em, and expressly denied and contradicted 'em. But told the council that there was no truth in such reports, that the thing I insisted on was not that a person should SAY THEY WERE CONVERTED OR WERE GODLY, that this was not what I ever intended by a person making a profession of godliness, and that I should not think it became persons to come and make such a profession as this. But what I insisted on as a proper profession of godliness was his professing the great things wherein godliness consists; or that he found such things in his heart which, though he might think them not to be godliness, yet were truly such things as the Scripture represents as the essentials of true piety. And that if they had these in appearance seriously and understandingly, I should think they ought to be accepted, though they at the same time should very much doubt of their being converted. Yea, if they should through melancholy or any temptation determine against themselves and say they did not think they were converted, if their own scruples did not hinder them, I should think they ought to be accepted and should be ready to admit them.

I here subjoin two or three testimonies of this:

> Mr. Edwards declared before the council that dismissed him that the thing he insisted on was not that a person should say he was converted or was godly, and that this was what he called profession of godliness, and that he should not think it proper or becoming in persons to make such profession. But what he called a profession of godliness was professing the great things wherein godliness consists, and if they did this to appearance seriously and understandingly, he should think they ought to be accepted, though they

(Boston, 1751); Robert Breck et al., *A Letter to the Reverend Mr. Hobby, in Answer to His Vindication of the Protest, Against the Result of an Ecclesiastical Council, Met at Northampton, etc.* (Boston, 1751).

should very much doubt of their being converted; yea, if they should through melancholy or any temptation determine against themselves and say they did not believe they were converted, if their own scruples did not hinder them, I should think they ought to be accepted and should be ready to admit 'em.

I declare that these things I heard Mr. Edwards declare before the said council.

Josiah Clark

I desire it may be noted that this person is not one of those that ever appeared to be on my side or of my opinion.

I declare that, according to the best of my remembrance, what Mr. Edwards declared before the council that dismissed him from the people of Northampton, in the sitting of [the] previous council in the meetinghouse in Northampton, and that what he insisted on to be professed was the great and essential things wherein godliness consists, not that a person should profess that he was converted or believed he was godly. To the same purpose I have heard him often, before the council sat at their sitting, and afterwards, express himself.

Supply Kingsley

I remember clearly that Mr. Edwards declared before the council that dismissed in the meetinghouse, that a man's professing of himself that he was sanctified or in a state of grace was unbecoming or unreasonable, but that a man should profess those great things wherein true godliness consists, and that such a profession ought to be accepted, let a man think of himself as he will, as to his being converted or not.

Timothy Dwight, Jr.

But because I would take the utmost possible care that what I said might be well observed and understood by the council, and this false report sufficiently corrected, I sent the same thoughts into the council in writing. I sent an extract of a letter I had before written to Mr. [Peter] Clark of Salem Village in the following words:[2]

It don't belong to the controversy between me and my people, how particular or large the profession should be that is required. I

2. MS of extract in Beinecke Library, one quarto leaf. Published in preface to *A Farewell Sermon* (Boston, 1751) and *Misrepresentations Corrected* (*Works*, *12*, 360). See Letter No. 116.

should not choose to be confined to exact limits as to that matter. But rather than contend, I should content myself with a few words, briefly expressing the cardinal virtues, or acts implied in a hearty compliance with the covenant of grace: the profession being made (as should appear by inquiry into the person's doctrinal knowledge) understandingly, if there were an external conversation agreeable thereto. Yea, I should think that such a person, solemnly making such a profession, had a right to be received as the object of a public charity, however he himself might scruple his own conversion, on account of his not remembering the time, not knowing the method of his conversion, or finding so much remaining sin, etc. And (if his own scruples did not hinder) I should think a minister or church had no right to debar such a professor, though he should say, he did not think himself converted. For I call that a profession of godliness, which is a profession of the great things wherein godliness consists, and not a profession of his own opinion of his good estate.

This writing, I was informed, was handed round and was read by the members of the council. This abundant care did I take that the council might fully understand that I by no means insisted that a man should profess that he was sanctified or converted, that I was so far from such a profession, that I disliked such a kind of profession, as the condition of communion. Yet now some of the gentlemen that are the members of that council declare to the world from the press that I declared that very thing to that council, that I could not in conscience admit persons unless they first made a profession THAT THEY WERE INDEED SANCTIFIED. It may be some may say that although I produce testimonies to the contrary, yet there are four that write in this declaration which is sufficient to balance all my testimonies. To this I say that the extract of my letter to Mr. Clark of Salem Village, which was laid before the council, wherein the contrary is expressly declared, was in writing and they can't and dare not deny that this extract in these very words was laid before them. And if they do, there is the original letter written long before in Clark's hands, which will speak for itself, if they deny that I have truly represented it.

That they make such a declaration as they have done is the more remarkable because the extract of that letter was printed long before in the preface to my *Farewell Sermon* as a designed refutation of such kind of reports of my opinion and was referred to, to the same purpose, in the printed *Result* of the council that sat at Northampton,[3] which these gentlemen confess they had seen (p. 18). And these things from the press were very much known and taken notice of in that part of the country where these ministers live, long before. So that if it were possible for me to defend myself from such injurious representations and reports and assertions as these gentlemen have made, one would think it was most effectually done. But notwithstanding all this, but yet it must be, they nevertheless boldly assert to the world that I declared that which I, instead of declaring, did at this time so expressly, carefully, publicly denied; declaring the reverse of it by word of mouth in their hearing and by writing of [in] their seeing, and afterwards from the press before the world.

If I had perfectly held my peace and made no declaration of anything, and they had then told the world that I declared this, it would not have been injurious as now, since I have with so much [pains] declared the contrary and taken so much care that they should [have] full notice of my denying and abhorring the thing they say I asserted and insisted on.

> [I am your friend and brother,
> Jonathan Edwards.]

128. TO THE REVEREND JOSEPH BELLAMY

Edwards writes with the terms of his new salary; he also announces donations from overseas both for him personally and for the maintenance and education of the Indians.

(HSF, Joseph Bellamy Papers, ALS, one quarto leaf, addressed on verso to the Reverend Joseph Bellamy at Bethlehem.)

*   *   *

> Stockbridge, June 28, 1751

Dear Brother,

I have been to Boston and have agreed with the Commissioners. They engage £70 sterling per annum, besides the small matter that Stockbridge people engage. The installment is appointed on the second Thursday in August, when I hope to see you here. I came hither the last week. I am, Sir,

> Your most affectionate friend and brother,
> Jonathan Edwards.

3. *The Result of a Council . . . With a Protest Against the Same.*

P.S. I met in Boston many very kind letters from Scotland, with a present of £60 sterling in goods, which will come to perhaps a third more, as it may be disposed. It came free of all charge, freight and insurance being paid. Ten pounds sterling more is coming.

Thus, it proves that we need not fear to trust God in the way of duty. Admiral [Peter] Warren has appropriated £700 sterling for the use of the Mohawks here, and Mr. [Isaac] Hollis has engaged £180 sterling for the same use.

129. TO THE REVEREND JOHN ERSKINE

In the first letter to Erskine from his new location, Edwards acknowledges receipt of an additional packet of books and sermons. He shares news of the work of Dutch ministers in America and of signs of awakening, a favorite theme. One must ever be on guard, he warns, against the peril of false religion amid revival enthusiasm. Although Edwards expects to be installed at Stockbridge in August, his family is still living in Northampton.

(Trask Library, ALS, two quarto leaves; Dwight ms. transcript, five quarto leaves. Published in Dwight ed., *1*, 458–62.)

* * *

Stockbridge, June 28, 1751

Reverend and Dear Brother,

I have lately received a *Treatise of the Restoration of the Jews*, and a pamphlet entitled *A Serious Address to the Church of Scotland;* and a sermon on *The Qualifications of the Teachers of Christianity*, preached by you before the Synod, with Glas' *Notes on Scripture Texts, No. 5*.[1] These pamphlets were enclosed in a wrapper superscribed by your hand. There was also in the packet a brief advertisement concerning one of the pamphlets, written in your hand, though without any date or name or any letter in the packet. But yet I conclude these pamphlets were sent by you. And accordingly I now thank you for them. Your discourse on *The Qualifications of Teachers of Christianity* is a very acceptable present. Glas' *Notes on Scripture Texts* contains some things that are very curious, and discover close study, and a critical genius.

The Treatise of the Restoration of the Jews, if written by a Christian

1. Samuel Collett, *A Treatise of the Future Restoration of the Jews and Israelites to Their Own Land* (London, 1747); *A Serious Address to the Church of Scotland, with Relation to the Growth of Deism and Immorality* (London, 1739); John Erskine, *The Qualifications necessary for teachers of Christianity* (Glasgow, 1750); John Glas, *Notes on Scripture-Texts* (see *Works, 13*, 137, n. 9).

divine, is a strange and unaccountable thing: by reason of there being nothing at all said or hinted about the Jews' conversion to the Christian faith, or so much as one mention of Jesus Christ; and his supposing that the prophecies of Ezekiel are to be literally fulfilled in the building such a temple and city as is there described; and the issuing of such a river from the threshold of the temple, and running into the East sea; and the Jews' offering sacrifices, and observing other rites spoken of in Ezekiel; and that the Messiah is yet to come and to reign in Jerusalem as a temporal prince, etc. And I am wholly at a loss as to the author's real design, whether it was to promote Judaism or Deism; or only to amuse his readers.

Since I received these pamphlets, I have received letters from all my other correspondents in Scotland; but none from you. Mr. [John] MacLaurin speaks of your writing, or designing to write; but suggests that possibly your letter would not arrive so soon as the rest. So that I hope I shall yet, ere long, receive a letter from you.

The letters I have received from my other correspondents make mention of a great revival of religion in Gelderland; and Mr. Mac-Laurin has sent me printed accounts of it, published, as I understand, by Mr. [John] Gillies, his son-in-law, being extracts of letters from Holland.[2] I had some notice of it before in a letter from Mr. [James] Davenport, who for the most part resides in New Jersey. The account he wrote was brought over from Holland, by a young Dutch minister whose name is John Frelinghuysen, born in New Jersey, second son to an eminent and successful Dutch minister there [Theodore Frelinghuysen]. His elder brother [Theodore, Jr.] is settled at Albany and by all accounts is an able and faithful minister there. This second son had been in Holland two years, I suppose to perfect his education in one of their universities, where his brother at Albany had his education. He came over into America the last summer, having first been married and ordained in Holland, in order to take the pastoral charge of some of the places that had been under his father's care. The accounts Mr. Davenport gives from him are not so particular as those that are published by Mr. Gillies. But there is one material and important circumstance which he mentions, not taken notice of in the accounts from Scotland, viz. that the Stadtholder was much pleased with the work.

2. John Gillies, *Good News from the Netherlands. Extracts of Letters from Two Ministers of Holland Confirming and Giving Accounts of the Revival of Religion in Guelderland.* Reprinted in Boston in 1751.

At the same time that we rejoice in this glorious work and praise God for it, it concerns us earnestly to pray that God's ministers and people there may be directed in such a state of things, wherein wisdom and great discretion is so exceedingly needed, and great care and skill to distinguish between true and false religion; or those inward experiences which are from the saving influence of the Spirit of God and those that are from Satan transforming himself into an angel of light. Without this, it may be expected that the great deceiver will gradually insinuate himself; acting under disguise, he will pretend to be a zealous assistant in building the temple, yea, the chief architect, when his real design will be to bring all to the ground, and to build Babel instead of the temple of God, finally to the great reproach, and grief of all true friends of religion, and the haughty triumph of its adversaries. If I may be allowed my conjecture in this affair, there lies the greatest danger of the people in Gelderland who are concerned in this work. I wish they had all the benefit of the late experience of this part of the church of God here in America.

Mr. MacLaurin informs, dear Sir, that you have a correspondence in the Netherlands, and as you know something of the calamities we have suffered from this quarter, I wish you would give 'em some kind admonitions. They will need all the warnings that can be given them: for the temptation to religious people in such a state of things to countenance the glaring, shining counterfeits of religion, without distinguishing them from what is true and genuine, is so strong, that they are very hardly indeed restrained from it. They will at last find the consequences not to be good of an abundant declaring and proclaiming their experiences on all occasions and before all companies, if they get into that way, as they will be likely to do without special caution in their guides. I am not so much concerned about any danger the interest of the revival of religion in Gelderland may be in from violent, open opposition, as from the secret, subtle, undiscerned guile of the old serpent.

I perceive pious ministers in the Netherlands are concerned to obtain attestations to the good, abiding effects of the late awakenings in Scotland and America. I think it is fit they should know the very truth of the case, and that things should be represented neither better nor worse than they are. If they should be represented worse, that would give encouragement to unreasonable opposers. If better, that might prevent a most necessary caution of the true friends of the awakening. There are undoubtedly very many instances in New England, in the whole, of the perseverance of such as were thought to have received the saving benefits of the late revival of religion; and of their continuing to walk in newness of life, and as becomes saints; instances which are uncontestable; and which men must be most obstinately blind not to see. But I believe the proportion here is not so great as in Scotland. I cannot say that the greater part of supposed converts, give reason by their conversation to suppose that they are true converts. The proportion may perhaps be more truly represented by the proportion of the blossoms on a tree which abide and come to mature fruit, to the whole number of blossoms in the spring.

In the forementioned letter which I lately had from Mr. Davenport, he mentions some degrees of awakening in some places of New Jersey. The following are extracts from his letter:

> I returned last month from Cape May, where I had been laboring some time, with little or no success, as to the unregenerate; except somewhat encouraging the last day of my preaching among them. Yet, blessed be God, I hear of the success of several ministers in the Jerseys, and the revival of religion in some places, though it is a very dull time in most. Mr. [Israel] Read of Bound Brook has, I hear, some encouragement by reason of some souls in his place being under conviction. Mr. [Samuel] Kennedy, who is likely to settle at Basking Ridge, I hear has more encouragement in this way. And Mr. John Frelinghuysen, more yet among the Dutch. He is the second son of that Frelinghuysen you speak of in your narrative, who died a few years ago. This second son came over from Holland, where he had been two years, and was ordained a little before he came over last summer. . . .
>
> Pious ministers among the Dutch our way, I think, increased faster of late than among other people. I was at the house of such an one, Mr. [Samuel] Verbryk, as I came along in this journey; who was ordained last fall, about five miles beyond Dobbs' Ferry, in New York government. . . . Mr. William Tennent told me that Mr. John Leydt, a pious young Dutch minister in New Jersey, was translating accounts from Holland into English. . . . Mr. [John] Brainerd has had some special success lately through mercy; so that nine or ten Indians appear to be under convictions, as he tells me; and about twelve of the white people near them, that used to be stupid like the very heathen; and many others more thoughtful and serious. Mr.

[Samuel] Sackett has lately been favored with particular success in reducing a number drawn away and infected by the Separatists. And some endeavors I used since that, and with him, have I trust not been altogether in vain. The good Lord grant that false religion may cease, and true religion prevail through the earth.

This letter of Mr. Davenport's was dated April 26, 1751.

The Dutch people in the provinces of New York and New Jersey have been famed for being generally exceeding ignorant, stupid, and profane, little better than the savages of our American deserts. But 'tis remarkable that things should now begin to appear more hopeful among them, about the same time that religion is reviving among the Dutch in their mother country. And certainly the revivals of religion which have very lately appeared, especially that among the Dutch in Europe, do verify God's holy Word, which gives such great encouragement to his people to pray for such mercies. And I must think these things not only afford great encouragement to those who have engaged in the Concert for United Prayer begun in Scotland, to go on with that affair, but binds it strongly upon them so to do; and that it will be an aggravated fault, if, after God does such glorious things, so soon after we have begun in an extraordinary manner to ask them, we should grow cold and slack and begin to fail. And I think what God has now done may well cause those who seemed at first with some zeal to engage in this affair, but have grown careless about it and have left off, to reflect on themselves with blushing and confusion. What if you, dear Sir, and other ministers in Scotland who have been engaged in this affair, should now take occasion to inform ministers in the Netherlands of it, and move them to come into it; and join with us in our united and extraordinary prayers for an universal revival of religion?

As to my present circumstances, I came the last week to this place, having undertaken the business of a missionary to the Indians here, having been chosen the pastor by this church, and chosen missionary by the Commissioners for Indian Affairs in Boston. My installment is appointed to be on the second Thursday in the next month.[3] I don't expect to get ready to remove my family till winter. But I must refer you, dear Sir, to my letters to Mr. MacLaurin and Mr. [James] Robe, for a more full account of my circumstances, and of the things which have passed relating to 'em. I have with this sent you the *Gazette* containing

3. JE was installed at Stockbridge on Aug. 8, 1751.

the Result of a late council at Northampton and intend to order one of my *Farewell Sermons* to be put up for you.[4]

My family were in their usual state of health when I left 'em, excepting my youngest child [Pierpont Edwards] who had something like an intermitting fever.

Please to present my cordial respects and Christian love to your dear consort. And remember me in your prayers, with regard to the trials and changes I am called to pass through, and the new and important business I have undertaken. I am, dear Sir,

> Your most united and obliged friend and brother,
> Jonathan Edwards.

130. TO THE REVEREND THOMAS GILLESPIE

Edwards presents a cool analysis—historical, social, psychological, and religious—of the causes leading to his dismissal. He assumes a major share of blame, which he attributes to youth, inexperience, and timidity. Although he venerates Solomon Stoddard, he is convinced that his grandfather's profound but detrimental influence over the town kept him from success.

(Trask Library, ALS, four quarto leaves; Dwight ms. transcript, six quarto leaves. Published in Dwight ed., *1*, 462–68; *Works, 4*, 561–66.)

* * *

Stockbridge, July 1, 1751

Rev. and Very Dear Sir,

I am very greatly obliged to you for your most kind, affectionate, comfortable and profitable letter of February 2, 1751. I thank you, Sir, for your sympathy with me under my troubles, so amply testified, and the many suitable and proper considerations you suggest to me for my comfort and improvement. May God enable me to make a right improvement of them.

'Tis not to be wondered at, dear Sir, that you are shocked and surprised at what has happened between me and the people of Northampton. 'Tis very surprising to all impartial and considerate persons that live near, and have the greatest advantage to know the circumstances of the affair, and the things that preceded this event and made way for it. But no wonder if it be much more so to strangers at a distance. I doubt not but that God intends his own glory, and the safety

---

4. The Result of the council of May 16, 1751, published in the *Boston Gazette*, June 11, 1751; and *A Farewell Sermon*.

and prosperity of Zion, and the advancement of the interest of religion, in the final issue of this event; and, I trust also, my good. But it is best that the true state of the case should be known, and that it should be viewed as it is, in order to receiving that instruction, which divine providence holds forth in it, and in order to proper reflections and a right improvement.

As there is a difference among particular persons as to their natural temper, so there is some difference of this kind to be observed in different countries, and also in different cities and towns. The people of Northampton are not the most happy in their natural temper. They have, ever since I can remember, been famed for a high-spirited people, and close, and of a difficult, turbulent temper. However, though in some respects they have been a stiff-necked people, yet God has been pleased in times past to bestow many special and distinguishing favors upon them. The town has stood now near an hundred years. Their first minister, Mr. Eleazer Mather (brother to Dr. Increase Mather of Boston, and Mr. Samuel Mather of Dublin in Ireland), was a very eminent man of God. After him came Mr. [Solomon] Stoddard, my grandfather; a very great man, of strong powers of mind, of great grace, and great authority, of a masterly countenance, speech, and behavior. He had great success in his ministry, there being many seasons in his day of general awakening among his people. He continued in the ministry at Northampton about sixty years. But God was pleased in some respects especially to manifest his power in the weakness of his successor, there having been a more remarkable awakening since his death that ever had been till then in that town. Although since that also, a greater declension, and more awful departures from God in some respects than ever before: and so the last minister has had more to humble him than either of his predecessors. May the effect be answerable to God's just expectations!

The people, having from the beginning been well-instructed, have had a name for a long time, for a very knowing people; and many have appeared among them persons of good abilities; and many that have been born in the town have been promoted to places of public improvement. They have been a people distinguished on this account. These things have manifestly been abused to nourish the pride of their natural temper, which has made 'em more difficult and unmanageable. There were some mighty contests and controversies among them in Mr. Stoddard's day, which were managed with great heat and violence; some great quarrels in the church, wherein Mr. Stoddard, great as his authority was, knew not what to do with them. In one ecclesiastical controversy in Mr. Stoddard's days, wherein the church was divided into two parties, the heat of spirit was raised to such a height, that it came to hand-blows: a number of one party met the head of the opposite party, and assaulted him and beat him unmercifully.

In later times, the people have had more to feed their pride. They have grown a much greater and more wealthy people than formerly, and are become more extensively famous in the world, as a people that have excelled in gifts and grace, and had God extraordinarily among them; which has insensibly engendered and nourished spiritual pride, that grand inlet of the devil into the hearts of men, and avenue of all manner of mischief among a professing people. Spiritual pride is a most monstrous thing. If it ben't discerned and vigorously opposed in its beginning, it very often soon raises persons above their teachers, and supposed spiritual fathers, and sets 'em out of the reach of all rule and instruction, as I have seen in innumerable instances. And there is this inconvenience attends the publishing of narratives of a work of God among a people: such is the corruption that is in the hearts of men, and even of good men, that there is great danger of their making it an occasion of spiritual pride. There is great reason to think that Northampton people have provoked God greatly against them by trusting in their privileges and attainments; and the consequences may well be a warning to all God's people, far and near, that hear of them.

Another thing which probably has contributed in some measure to the unhappiness of the people's manners, was that Mr. Stoddard, though an eminently holy man, was naturally of a dogmatical temper; and the people being brought up under him, and with a high veneration for him, naturally were led to imitate him. Especially their officers and leading men seemed to think it an excellency to be like him in this respect.

It has been a very great wound to the church of Northampton, that there has for forty or fifty years been a sort of settled division of the people into two parties, something like the Court and Country Party in England (if I may compare small things with great). There have been some of the chief men in the town, of chief authority and wealth, that have been great proprietors of their lands, who have had one party with them. And the other party, which commonly has been the greatest, have been of those who have been jealous of them, apt to envy 'em, and afraid of their having too much power and influence in town and church. This has been a foundation of innumerable contentions among the people from time to time; which have been exceeding grievous to me; and by which doubtless God has been dreadfully provoked, and his Spirit grieved and quenched, and much confusion, and many evil works have been introduced.

Another thing that evidently has contributed to our calamities is, that the people had got so established in certain wrong notions and ways in religion, which I found them in and never could beat them out of. Particularly, it was too much their method to lay almost all the stress of their hopes on the particular steps and method of their first work, i.e. the first work of the Spirit of God in their hearts in their convictions and conversion, and to look but little at the abiding sense and temper of their hearts, and the course of their exercises and fruits of grace, for evidences of their good estate. Nor had they learned, and many of them never could be made to learn, to distinguish between impressions on the imagination, and truly spiritual experiences. And when I came among them, I found it to be too much a custom among them without discretion, or distinction of occasions, places, or companies, to declare and publish their own experiences; and oftentimes to do it in a light manner, without any air of solemnity. This custom has not a little contributed to spiritual pride, and many other evils. When I first settled among the people, being young and of but little experience, I was not thoroughly aware of the ill consequences of such a custom; and so allowed it, or at least did not testify against it as I ought to have done.

And here I desire it may be observed that I would be far from so laying all the blame of the sorrowful things that have come to pass to the people, as to suppose that I have no cause of self-reflection and humiliation before God on this occasion. I am sensible that it becomes me to look on what has lately happened, as an awful frown of heaven on me, as well as on the people. God knows the wickedness of my heart and the great and sinful deficiencies and offenses which I have been guilty of in the course of my ministry at Northampton. I desire that God would discover them to me more and more, and that now he would effectually humble me and mortify my pride and self-confidence, and empty me entirely of myself, and make me to know how that I deserve to be cast away as an abominable branch, and as a vessel wherein is no pleasure; and, if it may consist with his holy will, sanctify me, and make me a vessel more meet for my Master's use, and yet improve me as an instrument of his glory and the good of the souls of mankind.

One thing that has contributed to bring things to such a pass at Northampton, was my youth and want of more judgment and experience, in the time of that extraordinary awakening above sixteen years ago. Instead of a child, there was want of a giant in judgment and discretion among a people in such an extraordinary state of things. In some respects doubtless my confidence in myself was a great wrong to me; but in other respects, my diffidence of myself injured me. It was such that I durst not act my own judgment, and had no strength to oppose received notions and established customs, and to testify boldly against some glaring false appearances and counterfeits of religion, till it was too late. And by this means as well as others, many things got footing which have been a dreadful source of spiritual pride, and other things that are exceeding contrary to true Christianity. If I had had more experience and ripeness of judgment and courage, I should have guided my people in a better manner, and should have guarded them better from Satan's devices, and prevented the great spiritual calamity of many souls, and perhaps the eternal ruin of some of them, and should have done what would have tended to lengthen out the tranquillity of the town.

However, doubtless at that time there was a very glorious work of God wrought in Northampton, and there were numerous instances of saving conversion; though undoubtedly many were deceived, and deceived others; and the number of true converts was not so great as was then imagined. Many may be ready from things that are lately come to pass to determine that all Northampton religion is come to nothing, and that all the famed awakenings and revivals of religion in that place prove to be nothing, but strange tides of a melancholy and whimsical humor. But they would draw no such conclusion if they exactly knew the true state of the case, and would judge of it with full calmness and impartiality of mind.

There are many things to be considered in the case of Northampton:

1. That many of those who have been most violently engaged, and have chiefly led and excited others in it, though they have been leading men in the town, and have been esteemed considerable for their knowledge, estate and age, and have been professors of religion, yet have not been the most famed for piety.

2. The leading men, who have been most engaged in this matter, who have taken vast pains to stir up others that are inferior, have had this great advantage in their hands: that the controversy was a reli-

gious controversy. That which I opposed was that they always had supposed to be a part of divine truth, a precious and important doctrine of the Word of God, and that the cause of my opposers was the cause of God. This has led the more ignorant and less considerate people to look on their zeal against me a virtue, and to christen even their passions and bitterness in such a cause with sanctified names, and to let 'em loose and prosecute the views of their bitterness and violence without check of conscience.

3. They have also had the great advantage of the vast veneration the people had for Mr. Stoddard's memory, which was such that many of them looked on him almost as a sort of deity. They were all (i.e. except the young people) born and brought up under his ministry, and had been used from their infancy to esteem his sayings all as oracles. And he, they knew, maintained that doctrine which I oppose, with great positiveness and zeal, and opposed the contrary which I maintain, as an exceeding pernicious doctrine. Under these circumstances, I naturally appear as a dangerous opposer of the cause of God, and my teaching and insisting on the doctrine which Mr. Stoddard opposed appears to 'em a sort of horrid profaneness.

4. Crafty designing men have abundantly filled the ears of the more ignorant with suggestions that my opinion tends to overthrow all religion, and to ruin the present and future generations, and make all heathen, shutting them out of the church of Christ.

5. Not only many of the leading men in Northampton have used their utmost endeavors to engage the minds of the common people in this controversy, but they have also been put forward by the neighboring ministers all round. My opposers have also been assisted and edged on by some at a greater distance, persons of note; and some great men in civil authority have had a great hand.

6. It is to be considered, that the contrary opinion to mine had not only long been established in Northampton, without so much as one opposer to it, but it had also been fully and quietly established for a long time in all the neighboring churches and congregations, and in all the country round, even to a great distance. So that my opinion, when first broached, appeared to the people exceeding singular. Their views being very narrow, it appeared to them that all the world almost was against me. And my most crafty opposers have improved this advantage, and have abundantly represented me, as all alone in my opinion.

7. Many of the people, who at length came to have their spirits much

raised, and were brought to join in violent measures, yet came slowly into it, after having [been] long practiced with, and indefatigable endeavors used to engage and inflame 'em.

8. There are about twenty heads of families, besides others that were women and young people, who ever appeared openly against the proceedings of the town; and many others have appeared friendly to me. And there is not a little reason to think that there are many more, especially women and youth, that would appear so, if they dare. For a person, by appearing my friend at Northampton, so much as openly to discountenance my being turned out of the pulpit, exposes himself to immediate persecution of his neighbors, and perhaps of his nearest friends. I mean he falls under their great resentment, loses all their friendship, and is everywhere the object of reproach.

9. 'Tis to be considered that these things have happened when God is greatly withdrawn, and religion was very low, not only at Northampton, but all over New England.

10. I believe the devil is greatly alarmed by the opposition made to Mr. Stoddard's doctrine, and the agreeable practice, which had been so long established at Northampton, and so extensively in the country: in which he found his account, and hoped for greater consequences, and more agreeable to him. And God for wise ends, has suffered him to exert himself in an extraordinary manner in opposition, as God ordinarily does when truth is in the birth.

But I am drawn out to an unexpected length in my observations on these things, and have not left myself room nor time for some other things, that I would willingly write, and must therefore refer you to my letters to my other correspondents in Scotland, particularly Mr. [John] MacLaurin, Mr. [James] Robe, Mr. [William] McCulloch, and Mr. John Erskine.[1] To some of them I have been [sending] a particular account of my present circumstances, and things which have lately passed relating to 'em. I would only say in general, that I have had a call to settle at Stockbridge, a place in the western borders of New England, next to the province of New York, about thirty-six miles from Albany, and about forty miles west from Northampton, the place where Mr. [John] Sergeant was minister and missionary to the Indians. I am both called by the church here, constituted partly of English and partly of Indians, and am appointed missionary to the Indians by the Commissioners for Indian Affairs in Boston: agreeable to what you suggest in

---

1. Only the letter to Erskine of June 28, 1751 (No. 129), survives.

your letter, as though you had been able to foresee future events, when you say, "Perhaps you are to be employed where the gospel has been little understood, or attended to." I suppose this place will for the future be the place of my ordinary abode, though it will be some months before I can remove my family.

I have no leisure at present to write on that subject you speak of, viz. impressions and supposed immediate revelations, though I own the vast importance of the subject. I had begun to write something against the Arminians, before the late controversy broke out with my people; which broke me off from it, and obliged me to write on that controversy. And now lately, Mr. [Solomon] Williams of Lebanon has wrote a book in answer to mine on that subject,[2] which I think myself obliged to answer, if God gives opportunity.

I have much to teach me to behave as a pilgrim and stranger on the earth. But in the midst of troubles and difficulties, I receive many mercies. Particularly I have great reason, with abundant thankfulness, to take notice of the great kindness of friends in Scotland. Blessed be God who never forsakes those that trust in him, and never wants instruments for the conveyance of his goodness and liberality to those who suffer in his cause.

I shall take care that there be conveyed with this letter to you, one of my *Farewell Sermons,* and the Result of the council, that sat at Northampton the last May.[3]

Remember me, dear Sir, at the throne of grace, with regard to all my trials, and with regard to my new circumstances, and the important service I have undertaken in this place. And please in your next to inform me what family you have and of their state. I am, Sir,

> Your most affectionate friend and brother,
> Jonathan Edwards.

131. TO THE REVEREND ISAAC HOLLIS

Edwards introduces himself in this first letter to the chief sponsor of the Stockbridge school. After giving thanks for Hollis' patronage, he reviews recent events and discloses his plan to emphasize English in educating the Indians.

2. Solomon Williams, *The True State of the Question* (Boston, 1751); JE responded with *Misrepresentations Corrected.*
3. See *A Farewell Sermon;* and the *Boston Gazette,* June 11, 1751.

(Trask Library, ALS draft, one folio leaf, letter on verso from Timothy Dwight to Edwards, July 10, 1751; Dwight ms. transcript, two quarto leaves. Published in Dwight ed., *1*, 469–71.)

*   *   *

Stockbridge, Summer 1751

Rev. and Honored Sir,

Having seen your late letter to Mr. [Thomas] Prince of Boston and another to Capt. [Martin] Kellogg, received this summer, and having lately been appointed missionary to the Indians in this place, I thought myself obliged to take the first opportunity to write to you, who have exerted yourself in so extraordinary a manner to promote an interest here, to serve which I am now devoted: partly to offer my thanks for what you have done and have lately offered to do with so fervent and enlarged a heart and bountiful a hand, for the advancement and enlargement of Christ's kingdom of grace among these poor people and the eternal welfare of their souls; which may well excite the joy and admiration of all good Christians and deserve the thanks of all that make the interest of Zion their own, and especially of him who has the souls of Indians in this place committed to his more immediate care.

And partly to inform you of what I have had opportunity to observe of the state of things here relating to the affair of the instruction of the Indians, which you have a right to know, it being an affair which you have been pleased so greatly to interest yourself in, and which depends so much on the effects of your most generous and Christian benefi- cence. I have had considerable opportunity to see the state of things; for though 'tis but about a month since I came here after I had under- taken the work of the ministry here as the stated missionary, yet I had been here before two months in the winter and then spent much time with the Indians, particularly the Mohawks under Captain Kellogg's care.

There are two schools for the instruction of the Indian children, one under the care of Mr. Timothy Woodbridge, which began soon after Mr. [John] Sergeant began to preach to these Indians. His school consists wholly of the children of the Proper Housatonic Indians. The other [is] under the care of Captain Kellogg, which he began with Stockbridge Indians on the plan which Mr. Sergeant projected. But the changeable, unsettled state that things have been in since Mr.

Sergeant's death, has altered [it] from that form; and the Housatonic boys have left it, and it now consists wholly of Mohawk children, that have been brought down hither by their parents from their own proper country, about eighty miles distant, to that end, that they might be taught to read and write and be instructed in the Christian religion.

There are some things give a hopeful prospect with regard to these Mohawk Indians, particularly the forward inclination of the children and their aptness to learn. But that which has evidently been the greatest defect from the beginning in the method of instruction here, is that no more proper and effectual measures have been taken to bring the children that are here taught, to the knowledge of the English tongue; which has not been the fault of the teachers, who I suppose have done what they could in the business to which they have been appointed and in the improvement of the means and advantages which have been put into their hands. However, for want of this, all the labor and cost that has been expended in schools here for about fourteen years has been consequently to but little effect or benefit. When the children are taught to read—but many of them, for want of the English language, know nothing what they read (the books being all in the English tongue)—they only learn to make such sounds on the sight of such marks, but know not the meaning of the sounds, and so have neither profit nor pleasure in reading; and will, therefore, be apt soon to lose even what they have learned, having no benefit or entertainment in the use of it.

'Tis on many other accounts of great importance that they should be brought to the English language, as this would greatly tend to forward their instruction, their own barbarous languages being exceeding barren and very unfit to express moral and divine things. And their being brought to the English language would open their minds, and bring 'em to acquaintance and conversation with the English, and would tend above all things to bring that civility which is to be found among the English.

Some pain has been taken to teach the children the English tongue, but nothing very considerable has been accomplished, and I can think of but two ways in which it can be effected: either the introducing a number of English children into their schools to learn with them and be their mates; or the disposing the Indian children into the English families to live there a year or two, where they must be obliged to speak the English and nothing else, and then return into the Indian school to perfect them in reading, writing, and knowledge of the principles of religion, and other useful knowledge. The latter (if their parents can be persuaded to it, as probably they may) will be much the most effectual.

I would therefore, Sir, humbly propose that some such method should be taken with regard to the children that have the benefit of your liberality, and that part of your benefaction should be expended in this way under the care of some prudent and faithful trustees: for in order to the business being managed thoroughly and effectively, a great deal of care and authority will be necessary, vastly more than the schoolmaster can have leisure for. There are many things pertaining to the regulation of the affair of the instruction of the Indian children that seem greatly to require the care of a number of persons, who shall be entrusted to dispose things according to the best of their discretion, sending from time to time a particular and exact account of the manner in which they have laid out your money. I thought myself obliged to give you these intimations, you being at a great distance and not capable of knowing the exact state of things any otherwise than by the information of those that are on the spot; and it being fit you should know those circumstances that are of such importance in the affair, that without a proper regard to 'em, the great expense you are at is liable to [be] in a great measure in vain.

I humbly request your prayers to [the] fountain of all light and grace for his direction and assistance in that important service I have lately undertaken in this place. I am, honored Sir, your most humble servant and

> Affectionate brother in the gospel ministry,
> Jonathan Edwards.

132. TO WILLIAM HOGG

Edwards expresses deep appreciation to a man who helped him in his hour of greatest need. He also sketches for this generous Scottish benefactor his current situation and the outlook at Stockbridge.

(Sterling Library, Anson Phelps Stokes Autograph Coll., ALS, two quarto leaves, notation on verso, "Answered 8th May 1752 to Mr. Prince's Care," presumably in the recipient's hand.)

* * *

William Hogg, by Alan Ramsay, undated, private collection of Mr. J. G. B. Gibson, Duns, Berwickshire, Scotland

Stockbridge, July 13, 1751

Dear Sir,

The accounts which I have lately received from correspondents in Scotland, of the respect to me and my family, which you have, in various ways, testified, both by word and deed, may well deeply affect us with gratitude, and excite our admiration. And in the first place, we have reason to admire and be most gratefully affected by, the providence of God, which in the time of our peculiar and uncommon troubles, has appeared for us in so wonderful and unexpected a manner; in that, when, according to a human view of things, nothing was to be expected but difficulties and straits; and friends that were near at hand, which we formerly should have expected most from, stood at the greatest distance, and seemed to rejoice at our trouble, and to be ready, on every occasion, to increase them; others who are perfect strangers, that we never so much as heard of, and at so great a distance, are raised up, have most friendly affections excited, and hearts enlarged towards us, to extend their kindness to our relief and bountiful supply, even beyond the ocean. How true, in this instance, does it appear to be, that God is, as he declares himself in his Word to be, an all-sufficient and faithful God, and that his promise never fails; that we need not fear to trust him in the way of obedience to him; though, according to an human appearance, we seem to run the greatest ventures by cleaving to him.

In the next place, our gratitude is due to his people, to whom he has given so much of his Spirit of love and kindness, and made the instruments of his bounty. I would by this, dear Sir, in particular render thanks to you; to whom they are due, in some respects, in [a] peculiar manner.

I, with my family, have for this two years past gone through many troubles: but I hope the Lord has not forsaken us, nor suffered us to sink under our trials. He has in many respects exercised a fatherly care of us in our distresses. A door seems to be opened for my further improvement in the work of the ministry, in this place; which is situated in the northwestern frontiers of New England about 150 miles west from Boston, and about thirty-six miles southeast from Albany, on Hudson's River, in the province of New York. It is a place where an Indian mission has been for some time established, and a church settled, made up partly of English and partly of Indians, formerly under the pastoral care of the Reverend Mr. John Sergeant, who died the summer before last. I have been invited to take the pastoral charge here, and desired by the Commissioners for Indian Affairs, to undertake the business of a missionary. And this henceforward is like to be the place of my settled abode. There are some things remarkable in divine providence, that afford a prospect of good things to be accomplished here for the Indians, and give reason to hope that God has mercy in store for them; particularly that [of] God so enlarging the hearts of some gentlemen in England to contribute of their substance for this end. Sir Peter Warren has lately given £700 sterling, that the annual interest of it may be improved to this end, and particularly to promote the instruction of the Mohawks here (one of the chief tribes of Indians in North America, about fifty of which, old and young, came down hither the last fall to live here for the sake of instruction, at eighty miles' distance from their proper country). And the Reverend

Mr. Isaac Hollis of High-Wycombe in Buckinghamshire, in letters lately sent, which I have received, has offered 180 pounds sterling per annum, for the support and instruction of Indian children (boys) in a boarding school here. And [he] also desires that if any boys can be found of forward genius, that they may be put to learning, and have a liberal education, to fit them for the work of the ministry; and promises to be at the charge of it, over and above the forementioned £180 sterling per annum. And besides, Mr. [Thomas] Coram of London (who had been a correspondent of Mr. Sergeant's in his lifetime) had laid a plan of a boarding school for the education of Indian girls here; and gave great encouragement as to a sufficient subscription to be obtained in London for the building and supporting it. But he, dying the last spring, committed the care of the affair to the Reverend Mr. Chandler of London, who has undertaken it. And also the Society in London for the Propagating the Gospel among the Indians in New England and Parts Adjacent, have lately manifested a disposition to expend liberally, to promote the gospel here, as there shall be occasion. And the governments of Massachusetts and Connecticut have done considerable for the encouragement and support of the Mohawks here. And among other things done by this province of the Massachusetts, they have appointed a committee to provide them a sufficiency of land to settle on.

I shall have reason, dear Sir, much to value the prayers of one who has so much of a Christian spirit, as you have manifested towards me, and who has given so much evidence of a disposition to unmerited, disinterested benevolence. I particularly desire your prayers with regard to this important business, which I have now undertaken.

I conclude with fervent prayers to the God of all grace and love, and fountain of all good, that he would abundantly reward you with the blessings of his goodness, spiritual and temporal. And am, Sir,

Your most obliged friend and humble servant,
Jonathan Edwards.

P.S. I have here enclosed a copy of a Result of a late council at Northampton, and shall order one of my *Farewell Sermons* preached at Northampton to be put up at Boston,[1] and conveyed to you—a very small testimony of gratitude.

---

1. *Boston Gazette*, June 11, 1751; and *A Farewell Sermon*.

133. TO SPEAKER THOMAS HUBBARD

At Stockbridge, Edwards played a key role in Indian affairs, under the partial supervision of the government. In this wide-ranging survey to the Speaker of the Massachusetts House of Representatives, Edwards reports on conditions at Stockbridge. He gives his insights on a recent conference in Albany between the English and Indians and he also discusses military, political, educational, and practical matters. In the years to come, Hubbard proved to be a stalwart friend, who exercised his considerable influence on Edwards' behalf.

(Trask Library, AL draft: part of one folio leaf [f. ND1, #12.1], envelope cover addressed on verso to Edwards, to be left at Rev. Samuel Hopkins' or Aaron Sheldon's at Sheffield for conveyance; fragment [f. ND1 #12.2] on envelope cover addressed to Edwards at Stockbridge; one small leaf [f. ND1, #12.3], 13 cm.; one folio leaf [f. 1751, #13], letter of Joseph Pynchon, Aug. 7, 1751, addressed on verso to Col. Ephraim Williams and Edwards at Stockbridge. Also at Trask Library, Dwight ms. transcript, eight quarto leaves. Published in *CMHS* 10 [1809], 142–53; extract published in *BWNL*, Oct. 3, 1751.)

* * *

Stockbridge, August 31, 1751

Honored Sir,

I would now give you particular information of what has lately passed relating to the Indian affair in this town, and of the present situation, circumstances and exigencies of this affair; it being absolutely necessary that some persons of influence in the General Assembly be informed of these things.[1]

When the Commissioners of the General Assembly were going to Albany, to the treaty with the Six Nations, they came by way of Stockbridge, being directed so to do to that end, that they might treat with the Mohawks here, concerning their settlement in this place. But when they came hither, found that Hendrick, and almost all the heads of families, were gone to their own country, so that they had no opportunity for any such treaty at that time. And therefore, when they met them at Albany, they proposed to 'em to return with them, that they might have opportunity to treat with them here on those matters. I

---

1. This paragraph is not in the MS, but is taken from the MHS published version, which is close, with some variations, to Dwight's transcript.

Thomas Hubbard, by John Singleton Copley, c. 1767, Harvard University Portrait Collection, gift of Mrs. Sarah Appleton to Harvard College

being at Albany, with the Commissioners, having been invited thither by them, I by their allowance talked with Hendrick and Nicholas alone about the affair, using arguments with them to persuade them to endeavor to get as many of their chiefs as they could to come to Stockbridge, and treat of this affair with the Commissioners of the Massachusetts. And this matter was further urged afterwards by the Commissioners themselves. Hendrick made answer, that it was necessary, according to their manner, before they determine to meet with the English, to treat about so public a concern, first to have some time of consideration, and then to hold a council among themselves; therefore they would return to their own country; and after consultation, would send word to Stockbridge, and give notice of their determination, in twenty days. Accordingly, in about twenty days, Nicholas and several others came down, and brought word that the chiefs of their nation would be here in about a week to treat with the English about the affair proposed. And by Nicholas' account, they seemed to expect, or at least to desire, here to meet not only with the General Court's Committee formerly chosen to provide 'em with lands, but also with

Etaw Oh Koam (Nicholas),
by John Verelst, 1710,
Archives Nationales du
Canada, Ottawa

the same Commissioners they saw at Albany; and mentioned Col.
[Joseph] Dwight of Brookfield in particular. Upon this, I desired the
principal English inhabitants of this town to meet together to consider
what was to be done on this occasion. And considering that this was a
very critical juncture, and perceiving that the tribes of the Mohawks
now expected to come to a decisive conclusion, whether to go on with
the design of seeking instruction and care at Stockbridge or no, we all
were of one mind, that it was necessary forthwith to give notice to the
Committee of the Assembly formerly appointed, and also to [the]
Commissioners that were at Albany, and represent to 'em this, and
signify what appeared to us of the importance of their coming to meet
the Indians, with Capt. [Martin] Kellogg of Suffield as an interpreter,
on this occasion. And accordingly sent one messenger to Albany for
Col. [Jacob] Wendell, not knowing he was gone from thence; and
another to Springfield and Brookfield, for Brig. [Joseph] Dwight, Col.
[Joseph] Pynchon, Col. [William] Brattle, Capt. [Timothy] Dwight,
[Jr.,] and Captain Kellogg; and another to Sheffield to Capt. [Ben-
jamin] Ashley.

Hendrick (Tee Yee Neen Ho Ga Row), anonymous engraving, 1755, John Carter Brown Library, Brown University

On Saturday, August 10, arrived here Brigadier Dwight, Colonel Pynchon, Captain Dwight, and Captain Kellogg; and Captain Ashley came at the beginning of the next week. When on Tuesday arrived almost all the chiefs of the tribe of the Mohawks from their two towns, Canajoharie and Tiononderoge, they came with a great train; so that, together with what were here before, there were ninety-two in all. After the Committee had made their first speech to them, and generally proposed the affair they would treat with them about, and they had taken time to consider of the matter, [the chiefs] signified that the Committee had heretofore proposed to 'em the affair of settling in New England and sending their children to school here, but then they were but few here, and therefore could do nothing in behalf of their tribe: but now the council of the nation were present, and they had full power to act. But in the first place, they put 'em in mind, how the English had failed of those things, that they had been encouraged with the hopes of heretofore; and desired that now nothing might be said but what should stand, and be made good: and that therefore, they should thoroughly consider what was determined, and let everything be fully settled. And after these and some other things said by way of preface, they thanked them for their offer; they signified their falling in with the proposal that had been made them, of sending their children here to be instructed, and coming a number of them to live here, and gave a belt of wampum in consideration of it, and that what they did in this matter, not only was done on their own behalf, [but] for all nations of Indians; that by this they opened the door for all nations, that they might come and bring their children hither to be instructed, and as a confirmation that they would do what they could to persuade other nations to send their children hither.

After this the gentlemen of the Commission had much free discourse with the Indians from day to day, till they went away. They and the Stockbridge Indians had also many friendly meetings. They went away on Thursday, August 22.[2] They appeared in good humor and came away well satisfied, so far as appeared. The day before they went away, a present was made to them in the name of the province. I was sorry it could be no greater. Perhaps never was there an occasion more requiring a present to the Indians, and whereon a very liberal present might have been made to better purpose. About fifty, old and young, stayed behind, and others that went away declared a design, some of coming themselves, others of sending their children in the fall and winter.

Some considerable uneasiness has arisen since the chief of the Mohawks went away, concerning the distribution of the present; which was left entirely to the Indians themselves. Their chiefs distributed the present chiefly among those that went away and told those who stayed behind that the English would provide for them. But since they understand that there are no promises of clothing, only for those which belonged to the school, several of them are gone away in disgust: and I don't know what the consequences may be. But in general the aspect of divine providence appears exceeding favorable on the design; some of the chiefs of the Mohawks seemed to be much engaged in the design; especially Abraham Conaughstansey, Hendrick's elder brother, who I can't but look upon as a remarkable man; and in many things he has done seems to manifest great solidity, prudence, and acts very much as a person endowed with [the] humility, simplicity, self-denial and zeal of a true Christian. The Church of England seem to be very jealous of the Mohawks; and greatly against their coming hither and (so far as I can

2. JE mistakenly wrote the date as "Aug. 21."

learn) effectually engage Abraham against it, and induce him to do what in him lies to keep 'em in their own country. They have advanced him to an office, and made him a reader in the Church of England, to carry on divine service in the absence of the minister, and give him a salary. But instead of the effect upon Abraham the Church of England intends, Abraham to his utmost improves it to a contrary purpose, and while he officiates among his people, he from sabbath [to sabbath] exhorts them to come down hither for instruction, tells them that there they live in darkness, but here in light; [that] he knows but very little, and can teach them but little, but here are those that can give 'em vastly greater degrees of knowledge.

Besides the tribe of the Cauneengcheys, or proper Mohawks, there are some appearances among some of the tribe of the Oneidas. A number of these that live at Onohquaga, about 200 miles from Albany, where Mr. [Job] Spencer went, manifested a religious disposition to our commissioners at Albany. One of their chief men have been to visit this place; he appeared a very sober, conscientious man; and returned with messages from us to his brethren at home, and I am sorry we had not wherewith to make him an handsome present. Abraham told me of others, considerable men, of the nation of the Oneidas, in other places, and also some of the Tuscororas, that are religiously disposed.

God in his providence seems now to be opening the door for the introducing the light of the gospel among these nations, more than ever [he] has done before. And if we, the English, don't fail in our [part], there is a prospect of great things being done. And probably this present season is our *now* or *never*. 'Tis evident the French are now using extraordinary efforts to draw all those nations over and engage 'em in their interest. The king of France has lately made extraordinary provision for them, that the presents made them in Canada may be very bountiful. And they are indefatigable by the endeavors of their emissaries. They are building forts in all the western parts of North America, in the carrying places between the lakes and rivers, and in all the most advantageous places to bring them into dependence and to draw their trade. Col. [William] Johnson and Maj. [John Henry] Lydius, who are above all others acquainted with the state of these Indians, in the time of the treaty at Albany spake of it [as] a gone case, a thing beyond all doubt or dispute, that these nations were lost to the British interest, unless something extraordinary was done that was never like to be done. By all accounts, about one half of the Onondagas have actually left their old habitations, and are gone to live in Canada, the French having provided land for them; and many others of the far nations are resorting to settle there. Abraham told me that the Cayugas, the Onondagas, and the Chamnloowanees or Senecas are generally in the French interest. He says, they come to Albany[3] and flatter the English and speak smooth words, pleasant words, but their hearts are with the French. He said concerning the last of those nations, viz. the Chamnloowanees, who are vastly the greatest of the Six [Nations], that the governor of Canada (meaning by his emissaries) was always there with them. Four Indians have lately been in this town from among the Caughnawaugas in Canada, two of them related to Captain Kellogg, and two of them the kinsmen of Capt. [Ebenezer] Carter of Norwalk. Two of these especially appeared to be uncommonly intelligent men. These told me that the Indians that used formerly to appear on the side of the English are continually in great multitudes flocking to Canada, and informed [me] in what manner the French, particularly the priests, dealt with [them]. They said all the far nations that used to be our friends, had lately left us, and had entered into alliance with the French.

And we have had credible information from the Mohawks, that the French are now gone with an army of 600 men into the southwestern parts of North America, 400 French, and 200 Indians, intending to augment their army to a thousand as they go along, in order to strengthen their interest there, and particularly to kill a certain Virginia trader, who has lately gained the affections of the Indians and drawn their trade that way, and to draw off the nation of the Miamis that are very friendly to the English; and that Colonel Johnson, having had undoubted intelligence of this fully by a Frenchman who deserted the army, and some of others, had sent a belt of wampum to all the Five Nations, to alarm them. Thus great are that politic nation, in their endeavors to establish their interest among all the Indian nations in North America, and to alienate them from the British interest. I was credibly informed while at Albany, that the Indians there in the time of the treaty gave that as one reason why they deserted the English, and came to the French, that the English gave 'em so much rum, that they could not live with them or near them, as they had found by long experience it was an occasion of their being greatly wasted.

Now 'tis remarkable that in this situation of things, the only remain-

---

3. The extract printed in 1751 reads: "He says, They indeed come to *Albany* and treat with the *English* as Friends; but then go directly to the Governour of *Canada*, and tell Him all that has pass'd."

Sir William Johnson, by
John Wollaston, c. 1750,
Albany Institute of
History & Art, gift of
Laura Munsell
Tremaine

ing means that divine providence hath left us to repair and secure
these Indians in the British interest, is this very thing: viz. to our
utmost, to prosecute the design of instructing them thoroughly in the
Protestant religion, and educating their children. Colonel Johnson,
though I suppose a man of not much religion, owns this and says he
knows it will be for the British interest for them to bring their children
to Stockbridge, and therefore he will promote it to his utmost. And
now God seems to be opening this door in an unusual manner.

This opportunity may easily be lost by our negligence. There is a
party among the Mohawks at home that violently oppose the Indians
that are praising the design of their going [for] instruction here, and
Abraham too suffers a sort of persecution from them. They ridicule
him and others that are religiously disposed, and tell 'em the English
will fail, all their pretenses of kindness to 'em will come to nothing, and
stand ready to insult 'em on our disappointing them.

There are many things, which, in the present situation of this affair,
greatly need to be done without delay. The boarding school needs
much to be done to it. The house, furniture, and school itself should be
in better order. The Indians themselves took notice of the deficiencies

and irregularities. The house is in [a] miserable state; and much needs to be done to it to finish it. And not only so, but there is a necessity of the house being enlarged. 'Tis far from being sufficient for the boarding and lodging of an English family and necessary teachers, and the scholars which, according to Mr. [John] Sergeant's plan, are to be boarded and lodged there. And the house should be furnished with seats, writing tables, and beds and bed clothes, for the children. Mean lodging will do; yet they should be such as that they may be kept clean and warm. The boys also should have tools for their work: and the place where the school should be kept should be at some distance from the place where they lodge and are boarded. This is necessary that the school, in school hours, may not be hindered by the family, and by the Indian families who have their wigwams round about the boarding house; and also that the master's family may have more liberty in school hours. There is also a necessity of another master to be employed to teach the Indian boys to work at certain hours.

Care had need to be taken, and some orders given about these things directly. There seems to be a necessity that these things should be done before winter. If there be such an increase of the school as is expected, the state of things will be attended with difficulty and confusion, which if they remain till next summer, 'tis to be feared it will tend much to discourage the Indians.

I would also humbly propose that a young gentleman, a scholar, a man of good genius and of fervent piety, be sought for and sent hither as soon as possible, to be learning the Mohawk language, to fit him to be a missionary (if need be, to go amongst the Six Nations in their own country); in the meantime, to be assisting in instructing the Indians and their children here, in all necessary knowledge, and teaching two or three of the forwardest and most promising of the Indian boys, in order to their being brought up to learning and fitted for the ministry, the charge of which Mr. [Isaac] Hollis has offered to be at in a late letter to Captain Kellogg; and that a salary be offered him sufficient to encourage him: and also, that a couple of likely English boys be sent hither, to be under the care and instruction of this young gentleman, to be learning the Mohawk language, and also trained up in other useful learning, to fit them to be interpreters for the country, and also to be employed as schoolmasters or missionaries. This would be of excellent service, as it would tend to introduce the English tongue. This I suppose may be done without any additional charge, excepting the charge of their board. Brig. [Joseph] Dwight of Brookfield has a son, he has declared he should be willing [to] send hither to be so instructed. Colonel Pynchon speaks of him as an extraordinary likely boy.

And there is another thing that is most apparently of absolute necessity in order to the prosperity of the Indian affair in this town, yea, indeed to the keeping it alive: viz. that there should [be] some persons of wisdom and integrity here on the spot, or very near, who should be appointed by the Commissioners and the General Assembly, a sort of curators, to have the immediate inspecting and directing of affairs relating both to the Mohawks and Stockbridge Indians, who shall in a considerable degree be entrusted with moneys, and should be themselves paid for extraordinary labors, going journeys, and the like. The Indian affair here does as much need the immediate continual care of a number of persons who are empowered to inspect it, as a college or great hospital; and in some respects much more. Things have heretofore gone into vast confusion for want of it, and now the necessity of it is greatly increased, as the objects of care are multiplied. No person that has any tolerable view of the affair, can imagine it to be sufficient to answer its necessities, that there is a corporation that has the care of it 150 miles off. What renders it more necessary that things here should be under the immediate care of trustees here, is the misunderstanding and jealousies that here subsist between some of the chief of the present English inhabitants of the town; which is one of our greatest calamities. Things, on this account, do much more need constant inspection; and therefore the gentlemen entrusted ought to be such as are perfectly impartial, no way interested in, related to, these contending parties.

'Tis very probable that gentlemen might be found very properly qualified that would be willing, only on some intimation from the honorable Commissioners and the General Assembly, to come and live here: as Dr. [Israel] Ashley of Westfield, a gentleman of great discerning and activity in business and of an upright and pious character; and Col. [Timothy] Dwight of Northampton, who, though he have a rough way of talking, yet not of acting, is [a] very religious, conscientious man, of a public spirit of great activity and resolution in public affairs, and very discerning. And there is some hope that Brig. [Joseph] Dwight and Colonel Pynchon of Brookfield would be willing to come and live here, who are excellently qualified for the business which needs to be done here. The Mohawks greatly insist that these two gentlemen should be improved to treat with them for the future.[4] The Assembly and Commissioners for the greater safety might, if they saw fit, entrust these curators for a limited time, and with their power limited according to discretion, requiring an exact and particular account of their acts and expenses to be laid before their constituents from time to time.

One of the greatest and most hurtful defects in the method of instruction in the schools here is that no more effectual measures are taken to teach the children to the English tongue. The instructions that have been given at school here this fifteen years past, have been in a great measure in vain for want of this. The children learn to read, to make such sounds on the sight of such marks; but know nothing what they say, and having neither profit nor entertainment by what they read, they neglect it when they leave school, and quickly lose [it]. There are but two ways to remedy this mischief: either the bringing in a number of English children into the school with the Indians; or the putting the Indian children, while young, into good English families, where they should hear nothing but English, and after they have been there a year or two, then return 'em into the school here. This would be far the most effectual way. And there is no doubt but most of the Indians might be persuaded to it. Some of the Mohawks have moved it of their own accord. But this method can't be gone into without the care of a number of trustees to manage it, to take [pains] to find proper places, to ride from time to time to visit the children and see how they are looked after, and the like. I have strongly recommended it to Mr. Hollis, that the boarding school, so far as he is concerned in it, should be committed to the care of a number of trustees. For want of these, it happens from time to time, that the Mohawks and their instructors are run out of provisions, and have nothing to eat. Now this week they have had nothing to eat but squash and Indian corn and bread. Something must also be done at providing clothing for others of the members of the school. And when the Indians have their lands laid out, there will be a necessity of a great deal of care to be taken of 'em at their first settlement, by helping them, at first, in bringing to their land, etc. And innumerable new things constantly occur, requiring the care of some body that has some power.

In the time of the treaty here, Hendrick manifested a desire to go to Boston; which was fallen in with. And it was proposed that his brother

4. JE added, in brackets: "Mr. Hopkins of Sheffield."

Abraham should go with him, and be there in the time of the sitting of the General Assembly. It was thought it would be a satisfaction to the Assembly and Commissioners to have opportunity to see 'em, and converse with them about those religious affairs; and might tend greatly to promote the grand design. They insisted that Nicholas should go with them, because he was the first to come and live here, and would be very much offended if he was neglected. So that, I suppose, they will come at the beginning of October.[5]

I desire, Sir, that you would excuse my troubling you with so long a letter. I thought it of great importance that you should have a particular knowledge of the state of things here. Please to give my duty to the Commissioners.

I am, honored Sir, Your Honor's most

> Humble and obedient servant,
> Jonathan Edwards.

134. TO SPEAKER THOMAS HUBBARD

Although this published extract contains no address or salutation, it appeared in the *Boston Weekly News-Letter* just three weeks after the publication of a similar extract from a letter to Thomas Hubbard. Apparently, Hubbard found Edwards' intelligence regarding French and Indian affairs worth relating to the public.

(Published in *Boston Weekly News-Letter*, Oct. 24, 1751.)

* * *

Stockbridge, September 26, 1751

Some of the Mohawks are come this day to Stockbridge from their own country, and bring an account of their brethren at home, that they continue in a disposition and design to bring their children hither to be instructed. . . . A number of the far nations are just now coming to treat with the Five Nations, with a very great belt of wampum, which is a sign of great and important business: and they say the army that lately went to extirpate the nation of the Miamis, are returned without success; their design being discovered by that nation before they came: and that the army in their return stopped at a place a little above Oswego, and had sent to the chiefs of all the Five Nations to come to

---

5. Dwight's MS transcript continues here with a page and a half of deleted text that does not appear in JE's MS draft and that repeats, in only slightly different language, JE's recommendations for trustees.

'em; and particularly, that the governor or general of the army, had sent very earnestly for Hendrick to come, but that he utterly refused, and declared that none of his tribe should stir. And, if the account which these men give is true, the other nations decline this proposed interview with the French general, and say, if he has any business with them, he must come to them. These men also give an account, that the small-pox, and fever and flux rage exceedingly at this day among the Five Nations, through the greater part of their countries, and prove very mortal; and that great multitudes are swept off: that the small-pox was brought among them from the country of the Flat-Heads, by some that went thither to war: that the tribe of the Cauneebyenkees, or Proper Mohawks, had hitherto escaped.

[Jonathan Edwards.]

135. TO SIR WILLIAM PEPPERRELL

Edwards presents his philosophy of educating children, based on the Socratic method, as opposed to rote learning, and designed to win the support of his renowned recipient. Edwards was aware that the hero of Louisburg could offer a wise evaluation of the proposals. Pepperrell's prestige and influence made his approval of the highest value.

(Trask Library, AL fragment, one quarto leaf with notes in Edwards' hand on verso: "Things to be brought from Northampton in the winter / Lucy's shoes / Dripping pan / Bags"; Dwight ms. transcript, eight quarto leaves. The text follows the draft where available, as indicated; otherwise, Dwight's transcript. Notes for this letter are in the Beinecke Library, two quarto leaves. Published in Dwight ed., *1*, 474–81.)

* * *

Stockbridge, November 28, 1751

Honored Sir,

When I had the opportunity the last spring of waiting on Your Excellency at your seat at Kittery,[1] and was there gratified and hon-

---

1. Pepperrell expressed deep interest in the Stockbridge school at the time of JE's visit, and promptly wrote to prestigious persons in London, among them his old friend, Admiral Peter Warren. Pepperrell wrote: "I have this day been favored with a visit from Rev. Jonathan Edwards, a worthy minister of the gospel, who has, the last winter, been preaching to some of the Six Nations, the Housatonics of Stockbridge. He tells me he has great encouragement, that many of them incline to embrace the Protestant religion. This seems to be a token for good, and will not only tend to make them our fast friends, and keep them from going over

ored by the kind and hospitable entertainment of your house, I was favored with some conversation with you, concerning the affairs of the Indians at Stockbridge, and the business of the mission here, to which I had then been invited. And you were then pleased generously to assure me of your good offices, in affording me any assistance in this employment, which you could render me, through your acquaintance and correspondence in London.

I have lately been favored with a letter from the Hon. Andrew Oliver, of Boston, wherein he was pleased to send me an extract of a letter he had seen, which was sent to you from Joseph Paice, Esq., of London, concerning a proper plan of a school for Indian girls in this place, and to propose to me to write to you on the subject of the said extract. This encourages me to hope that a letter from me, on this subject, to Your Excellency will be kindly received.

With this hope, I would take leave to say, that I think that, as the boarding schools here are now in their commencement, and are yet to receive their form and character, and that among a people hitherto unaccustomed to any method of instruction whatsoever, it is a great pity but that the method actually adopted should be free from the gross defects of the ordinary method of teaching among the English.

One of these grand defects, as I humbly conceive, is this, that children are habituated to learning without understanding. In the common method of teaching, so far as my observation extends, children, when they are taught to read, are so much accustomed to reading, without any kind of knowledge of the meaning of what they read, that they continue reading without understanding, even a long time after they are capable of understanding, were it not for an habit of making such and such sounds, on the sight of such and such letters, with a perfect inattentiveness to any meaning. In like manner they are taught their catechism, saying over the words by rote, which they began to say, before they were capable of easily and readily comprehending them, being long habituated to make sounds without connecting any ideas with them. They so continue, even until they come to be capable of well understanding the words, and would perhaps have the ideas, properly signified by the words, naturally excited in their minds on hearing the words, were it not for an habitual hearing and speaking them without any ideas; so that, if the question were put in phraseol-

to the French, but may be a means of building up the kingdom of our glorious Redeemer, which is far more important." Pepperrell's letter persuaded Warren to contribute £700 to the Stockbridge mission. Parsons, pp. 245–46.

ogy somewhat new, to which they have not been accustomed, they would not know what to answer. Thus it happens to children, even with regard to the plainest printed catechisms, even those which have been contrived with great care and art, so that they might be adapted to the lowest capacities.

I should therefore think that, in these boarding schools, the children should never read a lesson, without the master or mistress taking care, that the child be made to attend to, and understand, the meaning of the words and sentences which it reads; at least after the child begins to read without spelling, and perhaps in some degree before. And the child should be taught to understand *things*, as well as *words*. After it begins to read in a Psalter, Testament or Bible, not only the words and phrases should be explained, but the things which the lesson treats of should be, in a familiar manner, opened to the child's understanding; and the master or mistress should enter into conversation with the child about them. Familiar questions should be put to the child, about the subjects of the lesson; and the child should be encouraged, and drawn on, to speak freely, and in his turn also to ask questions, for the resolution of his own doubts.

Many advantages would arise from this method. By this means, the child's learning will be rendered pleasant, entertaining and profitable, as his mind will gradually open and expand with knowledge, and his capacity for reasoning improved. His lesson will cease to be a dull, wearisome task, without any suitable pleasure or benefit. This will be a rational way of teaching. Assisting the child's reason enables him to see the use, and end, and benefit of reading, at the same time that he takes pains from day to day to read. It is the way also to accustom the child, from its infancy, to think and reflect, and to beget in it an early taste for knowledge, and a regularly increasing appetite for it.

So also, with regard to the method of catechizing children; besides obliging them to give the answers in the printed catechism, or in any stated form of words, questions should be asked them from time to time, in the same familiar manner, as they are asked questions commonly about their ordinary affairs, with familiar instructions, explanations, and rehearsals of things intermixed; and, if it be possible, the child should be led, by wise and skillful management, into the habit of conversation on divine things, and should gradually be divested of that shyness and backwardness, usually discovered in children, to converse on such topics with their superiors. And when the printed catechisms are used, as I am far from thinking they ought to be entirely neglected, care should be taken, that the child should attend to the meaning of the words, and be able to understand them; to this end, not only explaining the words and sentences, but also from time to time varying the phraseology, putting the question in different words of the same sense, and also intermixing with the questions and answers, whether printed or not, some improvement or application, in counsels and warnings given to them, founded on the answers that have been given.

Beside the things already mentioned, there are other things, which, as it appears to me, ought to be done, with regard to the education of children in general, wherein the common methods of instruction in New England are grossly defective. The teacher, in familiar discourses, might, in a little time, give the children a short general scheme of the scriptural history, beginning with the creation of the world, and descending through the various periods of that history, informing them of the larger divisions, and more important events of the story, and giving them some idea of their connection one with another; first, of the history of the Old Testament, and then of the New. And when the children had in their heads this general scheme, then the teacher might, at certain times, entertain them, in like familiar discourse, with the particular stories of the Scriptures, sometimes with one story, and then with another, before they can obtain the knowledge of them themselves, by reading; for example, at one time the story of the creation, at another time the story of the flood, then the dispersion of the nations, the calling of Abraham, the story of Joseph, the bringing of the children of Israel out of Egypt; and in the New Testament, the birth of Christ, some of the chief acts of his life, his death, his resurrection, his ascension, the effusion of the Holy Spirit at the day of Pentecost and some of the chief of the Acts of the Apostles; withal, pointing out to them the place which each event has in the general scheme, and the connection it has with other main parts of it, the teacher in[2] a familiar manner applying the events of the story discoursed [upon], for informing of the child's understanding, influencing his heart, and directing its practice. And children, that are able to read their Bibles, might be set to read a particular scriptural story, sometimes one, and sometimes another, diligently observing it. And when it had done, it

2. Here begins the fragment of JE's MS draft.

might be called to the master or mistress, and inquired of, concerning the particulars of the story, to see that the child has taken good notice, and is able to give an account of it.

And I can't see why children in general, besides the Scripture history, should not, in a like familiar way of conversation, be taught something of the great successive changes and events in the Jewish nation and world of mankind that connect the history of the Old and New Testaments. Thus they might be informed, in short, of the manner in which the four great monarchies succeeded each other, the persecutions the Jews suffered from Antiochus Epiphanes, and the principal changes that happened in their church and state, till Christ came, and might be shown how such events were a fulfillment of such and such prophecies. And when they learn the history of the New Testament, they might, with much profit and entertainment, have pointed forth to 'em, many plain prophecies of the Old Testament, which have their fulfillment in him. And I can see no good reason, why children can't, or mayn't, be taught something in general of ecclesiastical history, and be informed how things, with regard to the state of religion and the church of God, have gone on, as to some of the main events, from the time when the Scripture history ended to the present time, and how certain prophecies of Scripture have been fulfilled in some of those events; and they may also be told what may yet be expected to come to pass, according to Scripture prophecies, from this time to the end of the world.[3]

It appears to me obvious, also, that, in connection with all this, they should be taught somewhat relating to the chronology of events, which would make the story so much the more distinct and entertaining. Thus, they may be taught how long it was from the creation of the world to the coming of Christ; how long from the creation to the flood; how long from the flood to the calling of Abraham, etc.; how long David lived before Christ; how long before the captivity in Babylon; how long the captivity, before Christ, etc.; how long since the birth of Christ, how old he was when he began to preach, and when he was crucified; how long after his resurrection, before he ascended; how[4] long it was after the destruction of Jerusalem by Nebuchadnezzar, till Babylon was destroyed by Cyrus; how long after the beginning of the Persian Empire, before that empire was overthrown by Alexander; when was the great oppression of the Jews by Antiochus Epiphanes;

3. MS draft ends.
4. MS draft resumes.

when Judea was conquered by the Romans; how long after Christ's resurrection, before the destruction of Jerusalem; and how long before the empire became Christian; how long after Christ,[5] before the popes claimed such and such powers; when the worship of images was introduced; how long before the Reformation, etc., etc. All children are capable of being informed, and having an idea of these things, and can much more easily learn them, if endeavors were used to that end, than many things which they do learn.

And with like ease, and with equal benefit, they might be taught some of the main things in geography: which way the land of Canaan lies from this; how far it is; which way Egypt lay from Canaan; which way Babylon lay from Jerusalem, and how far; which way Padan-Aram was from Canaan; where Rome lay from Jerusalem; where Antioch, etc., etc.

And I cannot but think it might be a pretty easy thing, if proper measures were taken, to teach children to spell well, and *girls* as well as *boys*. I should think it may be worth the while, on various accounts, to teach them to write, and also to teach them a little of arithmetic, some of the first and plainest rules. Or, if it be judged that it is needless to teach all the children all these things, some difference might be made in children of different genius, and children of the best genius might be taught more things than others. And all would serve, the more speedily and effectually, to change the taste of Indians, and to bring them off from their barbarism and brutality, to a relish for those things, which belong to civilization and refinement.

Another thing, which properly belongs to a Christian education, and which would be unusually popular with them, and which would in several respects have a powerful influence, in promoting the great end in view, of leading them to renounce the coarseness, and filth and degradation, of savage life, for cleanliness, refinement and good morals, is teaching them to sing. Music, especially sacred music, has a powerful efficacy to soften the heart into tenderness, to harmonize the affections, and to give the mind a relish for objects of a superior character.

In order to promote the salvation of the children, which is the main design of the whole Indian establishment at this place, I think that, beside their attending public worship on the sabbath, and the daily worship of the family, and catechizing in the school, and frequent

5. MS draft ends.

counsels and warnings given them, when all together, by their teachers; each child should, from time to time, be dealt with singly, particularly and closely, about the state and concerns of his soul; and particular care should be taken to teach and direct each child, concerning the duty of *secret prayer*, and the duty pressed and enforced on every one; and care should be taken, that all may have proper opportunity and convenience for it.

I would say nothing concerning buildings, lodgings, household stuff, cattle, servants, husbandry instruments and utensils for the children's work, as it is agreed on all hands that these are necessary; and the providing of them will doubtless be left to the care and direction of trustees that shall be appointed.

But I would beg leave to say further, with regard to methods to forward the proficiency of the children in their learning, that I cannot but think measures might be devised, greatly to encourage and animate them in it, and excite a laudable ambition to excel. One thing I have thought of, which, as appears to me, might have a happy tendency this way, in each of the boarding schools: at certain periods, there should be a sort of public examination in the school, on a day appointed for the purpose, which shall be attended by all the trustees, and all in the town who are in any respect connected with Indian affairs, and some of the neighboring ministers, and gentlemen and ladies; and also that the chiefs of the Indians be invited to attend; at which there should be a public trial of the proficiency, which each one has made, in the various branches which have been taught, as in reading, writing, spelling, arithmetic, knowledge in the principles of religion, knowledge of church history, etc.; and that a premium shall be given to such as are found to excel, which may be done in something, that will very much please Indian children, with but little expense. And likewise, that the works of the children be then produced, to be judged of, that it may be determined who has made the greatest proficiency in learning to sew, to spin, to knit, etc.; and that a reward be given to such as have excelled. And perhaps, also, that a reward be then given to such as, by the testimony of their teachers and governors, have excelled in virtue or diligence, in care to speak the truth, in strictly observing the sabbath, in good manners, in respect to their superiors, etc. And that, on the day of public trial, there be something of an entertainment made for the members of the school, and those who are invited to attend. This might tend, not only greatly to stimulate the children in their learning, but would be very pleasing and animating to the tribes of Indians, and would have great influence in rendering them very favorably disposed to the affairs of the schools.

But Your Excellency will easily see that, in order to the practicableness of these things, in any tolerable degree and manner, it is necessary that the children should be taught the English tongue; and indeed this is the most absolute necessity, on almost every account. Indian languages are extremely barbarous and barren, and very ill-fitted for communicating things moral and divine, or even things speculative and abstract. In short, they are wholly unfit for a people possessed of civilization, knowledge and refinement.

Besides, without their learning English, their learning to read will be in vain; for the Indians have not the Bible, nor any other book, in their own language. Without this, their teachers cannot converse with them, and so can have no advantage to instruct them. Hence, all possible means must be used, in the first place, to introduce the English tongue among the children. To this end, much pains should be taken to teach them the English name for every thing, and English words that signify such and such actions; and an interpreter might be used for a while, to interpret their lessons to them, and to teach them to construe them, or turn them into Indian. And a number of English children might be put into the school with the Indian children. But the most effectual method of all would be, to put out some of the Indian children, first, into some good English families, one at a place, to live there a year or two, before they are brought into the school; which would not only be above all others the most successful method, but would be absolutely necessary, at least at first; but truly a great deal of care must be taken to find good places for them, and to look well to them, and to see that they are well taken care of, in the families to which they are sent. It is probable, that the parents of the children might, with proper endeavors, be persuaded to such a measure.

But it will doubtless be very easily and quickly determined by Your Excellency that if such methods as those which have been mentioned, or any like them, or indeed any other effectual measures, are taken, it will be absolutely necessary that the school should be under the constant care and inspection of trustees, who live upon the spot, or very near at hand. It will be in vain for any to expect that any woman can look after such a school, and provide for and govern so large a family, and take care continually to order and regulate so many and great affairs pertaining to it, within doors and without, without much assistance of some always at hand, who are able and faithful, and are interested and duly empowered. If she has under her a second, or a kind of usher, and has servants of both sexes, yet still she will be under the necessity of having some superior assistance. And as to the precise method of teaching, and regulating the discipline of the school and family, it must be left very much to their discretion; for experience alone can certainly determine the fittest methods of ordering such an establishment, so new and untried, though many probable conjectures may be made. And experience will doubtless direct to some new measures, which cannot now be thought of. Hoping that Your Excellency will excuse the particularity and minuteness into which I have unintentionally been led, on a subject, about which I cannot but feel the deepest interest, I remain, with very high respect,

Your most humble servant,
Jonathan Edwards.

136. TO LADY MARY PEPPERRELL

Edwards was always careful to curry favor with the aristocracy, but in writing to Lady Pepperrell, Sir William Pepperrell's wife, he eschews "flattery and ceremony" and instead composes an apostrophe to Christ to console her on the loss of her son. Assuming the familiarity of a personal chaplain, Edwards counsels her to contemplate Jesus, placing characteristic emphasis on his excellencies, beauty, and love. The letter breathes calm and comfort, gentleness and healing. Edwards assures the grieving mother that rest, refreshment, and confidence are her rightful heritage as a Christian.

(Trask Library, ALS, two quarto leaves, one a letter cover addressed to Edwards at Stockbridge; Dwight ms. transcript, four quarto leaves, with text often at variance from Edwards' ms. Published in Dwight ed., *1*, 481–85; abridgement in Parsons, pp. 247–50.)

*   *   *

[Stockbridge, November 28, 1751]

Madam,

When I the last spring was at your house in Kittery, among other instances of your kind and condescending treatment of me was this, that when I had some discourse with Sir William concerning the Indian affair and Stockbridge, and he generously offered me any assistance in the business of my mission here that his acquaintance and correspondence in London gave him advantage for, and to propose my writing to him on our affairs, you were pleased on this occasion to invite me to write to you at the same time. If I should neglect to do as you then proposed, I should not [only] neglect doing a Christian duty to you, but fail of doing myself a great honor. But as I know from the small acquaintance I had with you that a letter of compliments would not be agreeable to a lady of your disposition, especially under your present melancholy circumstances; so the writing of such a letter is very far from my intention or inclination.

When I saw the evidences of your deep sorrow under the awful frowns of heaven in the (then late) death of your only son, it made an impression on my mind that turned my disposition to quite other things than flattery and ceremony. When you mentioned my writing to you, I soon determined what should be the subject of my letter. It was that which appeared to me to be the most proper subject of contemplation for one in your circumstances, and the subject which above all others appeared to me to be a proper and sufficient source of consolation to one under your heavy affliction: and this was the Lord Jesus Christ—with regard especially to two things, viz. his amiableness and love, or his infinite worthiness, and that we should love him and take him for our only portion, rest, hope and joy; the other, his great and unparalleled love to us. And I have been of the same mind ever since, being determined, if God favored me with opportunity to write to Your Ladyship, these things should be the subject of my letter.

I will now, therefore, begin with the former of these. Let us think, dear Madam, a little of the loveliness of our blessed Redeemer and his worthiness, that our whole soul should be swallowed up with love to him and delight in him, and that we should salve our hearts in him, rest in him, have sweet complacence and satisfaction of soul in his excellency and beauty whatever else we are deprived of. The Scripture assures us abundantly of his proper divinity, so that we consider him that came into the world in our nature and died for us, as truly possessed of all the fullness of that infinite glory of the Godhead, his infinite greatness and majesty, his infinite wisdom, his infinitely perfect holiness and purity, righteousness and goodness. He is called "the brightness of God's glory and the express image of his person." He is the image and exhibition of the infinite beauty of the [Deity], in the viewing of which God the Father had all his infinite happiness from eternity. The eternal and immutable happiness of the Deity himself is represented in Scripture as a kind of social happiness, in the society of the persons of the Trinity. Prov. 8:30, "Then was I by him as one brought up with him: and I was daily his delight, rejoicing always before him." This glorious person, in the perpetual and eternal view of whose beauty God the Father is infinitely happy, has God sent into the world to be the light of the world, that by him the beauty of the Deity might shine forth in the brightest and fullest manner to the children of men. And infinite wisdom has contrived that we should behold the glory of the Deity in the face of Jesus Christ to the greatest advantage and in such a manner as should be most adapted to the capacity of poor feeble worms, and so as should tend most to engage and invite our attention, to encourage and allure our hearts and give us the most full and perfect acquiescence and delight. For Christ by his incarnation having come down as it were from his infinite height above us, having become one of us, our kinsman and brother, and his glory shining to us through his human nature, the manifestation is marvelously qualified to suit the nature of the human sight; the effulgence of his glory is attempered to our sight. He is indeed a person of infinite majesty to fill our souls with the greatest reverence and adoration. But there is nothing in it that needs to terrify us. For his infinite majesty is joined with as it were infinite meekness, sweet condescension and humility. So that in the whole there is nothing terrifying or forbidding. There may be the utmost possible reverence and abasement and at the same time our hearts be drawn most sweetly and powerfully to the most free access, the most intimate embrace. When we view his greatness and majesty and other attributes, we are kept free from fear and flight by the view of his gentleness and humility. And when we view his marvelous love and abasement and are encouraged and comforted with that, we are kept from an indecent familiarity by the view of his infinite majesty. And by all together we are filled with most reverential love, humble boldness and familiarity, delightful adoration, and sweet surprise. The glory of Christ is properly, and in the highest sense, divine. He shines in all the brightness of glory that is the Deity, who is light, a luminary infinitely bright. Such is the exceeding brightness of this Sun of Righteousness, that the brightness of the natural sun is as darkness in comparison of it, yea, black as sackcloth of hair. And, therefore, when he shall appear in his glory, the brightness of the sun shall disappear as the brightness of the little stars do when the sun rises (Is. 24:23, Matt. 24:29, Rev. 6:12). But although his light is so bright and his beams go forth with infinite strength, yet as they proceed from Christ in the character of the Lamb of God and shine through his meek and lowly humanity, they are infinitely gentle and mild, not dazzling and painful to our feeble eyes, but vivifying and healing, like smooth ointment or a gentle eye salve. Then the Sun of Righteousness arises on them that fear God's name with healing in his wings, i.e. in his beams (Mal. 4:2). It is like the light of the morning, as a morning without clouds; as the dew on the grass, under whose influence the souls of the people are as the tender grass, springing out of the earth by clear shining after rain. Thus are the beams of his beauty and brightness fitted for the support of the healing and reviving of the afflicted. He heals the broken in spirit and bindeth up their wounds. He comes down on the spirits of his people that are as it were cut down by the scythe of adversity—like the rain on the mown grass, and as the showers that water the earth (Ps. 72:6).

But especially are the beams of Christ's glory infinitely softened and sweetened by that other thing which I proposed to consider, viz. his love, his unparalleled, dying love. And here many things are to be considered: one is that the glory of Christ's person very much consists in that infinite goodness and grace, which has so marvelous a manifestation in his love to us. The apostle John tells us that God is light (I John 1:5) and that he is love (I John 4:8, 16), and his light is an infinitely sweet light because it is the light of love and especially appears so in the person of our Redeemer, who was infinitely the most wonderful instance of love that ever was seen. All the perfections of the Deity have their brightest manifestation in the work of redemption, vastly more than in the work of creation. In other works we see God's back parts, but here shines the glory of his face (II Cor. 3:18). Yea, in this work are opened the infinite treasures of God's heart (Eph. 3:8–10). This work is a work of love to us and a work that Christ is the author of. His loveliness and his love have both their greatest and most affecting manifestation in those sufferings he endured for us at his death. Therein above all appeared his holiness, his hatred of sin, and his love to God in that when he desired to save sinners, rather than that a suitable testimony should not be borne against it, he would submit that strict justice should take place in its condemnation and punishment in his own soul's being poured out unto death (Rom. 8:3). And such was his regard to God's honor that, rather than the desired happiness of himself should injure it, he would give up himself a sacrifice for sin. Thus, in the same act he appears in the greatest conceivable manifestation of his infinite hatred of sin and also infinite grace and love to sinners. His holiness appeared like a fire burning with infinite vehemence against sin, at the same time that his love to sinners appeared like a sweet flame burning with an infinite fervency of benevolence.

'Tis the glory and beauty of his love to us filthy sinners, that 'tis an infinitely pure love and it tends to the peculiar sweetness and endearment of his infinite holiness; that it has its greatest manifestation in such an act of love to us. All the virtues of Christ, both divine and human, have their greatest manifestation in that marvelous act of his love, his offering up himself a sacrifice for us under those extreme sufferings. Herein especially appears his infinite wisdom. Herein he has abounded towards us in the riches of his grace in all wisdom and prudence (Eph. 1:8). Herein appears most his strict justice. Herein, above all other things, appeared the humility of his human nature in being willing to descend so low for us. In his behavior under those last sufferings, above all other things, appeared his obedience to God, his submission to his disposing will, his patience. Herein appeared his meekness when he was [taken] as a lamb to the slaughter and opened not his mouth, but only in prayer that God would forgive his crucifiers. And what an affecting and endearing [thing] is the manifestation of his excellency and amiableness when it chiefly shines forth in such an act of love to us.

The love of Christ another way tends to sweeten and endear all his virtues and excellencies, viz. as his love has brought him into such a relation to us as our friend, our elder brother, our Lord, our head and spiritual husband, our Redeemer, and hath brought us into so strict an union with him that our souls are his beloved bride. Yea, we are the members of his body, his flesh and his bone (Eph. 5:30).

Now, Madam, let us consider what suitable provision God has made for our consolation under all our afflictions in giving us a Redeemer of such glory and such love, especially when it is considered what were the ends of that great manifestation of his beauty and love in his death. He suffered that we might be delivered. His soul was exceeding sorrowful even unto death, to take away the sting of sorrow and that we might have everlasting consolation. He was oppressed and afflicted that we might be supported. He was overwhelmed in the darkness of death and of hell, that we might have the light of life. He was cast into the furnace of God's wrath, that we might swim in the rivers of pleasure. His heart was overwhelmed in a flood of sorrow and anguish, that our hearts might be filled and overwhelmed with a flood of eternal joy.

And now let it be considered what circumstances our Redeemer now is in. He was dead but is alive, and he lives forevermore. Death may deprive of dear friends, but it can't deprive us of this, our best friend.

And we have this friend, this mighty Redeemer, to go to under all affliction, who is not one that can't be touched with the feeling of our afflictions, he having suffered far greater sorrows than we ever have done. And if we are vitally united to him, the union can never be broken; it will remain when we die and when heaven and earth are dissolved. Therefore, in this we may be confident, we need not fear though the earth be removed. In him we may triumph with everlasting joy; even when storms and tempests arise we may have resort to him who is an hiding place from the wind and a covert from the tempest. When we are thirsty, we may come to him who is as rivers of waters in a dry place. When we are weary, we may go to him who is as the shadow of a great rock in a weary land. Having found him who is as the apple tree among the trees of the wood, we may sit under his shadow with great delight and his fruit may be sweet to our taste. Christ told his disciples that in the world [they] should have trouble, but says he, "In me ye shall have peace." If we are united to him, our souls will be like a tree planted by a river that never dieth. He will be their light in darkness and their morning star that is a bright harbinger of day. And in a little [while], he will arise on our souls as the sun in full glory. And our sun shall no more go down, and there shall be no interposing cloud, no veil on his face or on our hearts, but the Lord shall be our everlasting light and our Redeemer, our glory.

That this glorious Redeemer would manifest his glory and love to you, and apply the little that has been said of these things to your consolation in all your affliction, and abundantly reward your generous favors, as when I was at Kittery, is the fervent [prayer] of, Madam, Your Ladyship's most obliged and affectionate friend,

> And most humble servant,
> Jonathan Edwards.

137. TO THE REVEREND TIMOTHY EDWARDS

Edwards' principal concern in this letter is for his sister, Eunice Backus, an impoverished widow who has just suffered the loss of two children. He urges his father to seek greater financial assistance for her. Eunice raised the rest of her seven children, including a son, Simon, who graduated from Yale first in his class in 1759. The letter provides an intimate glimpse into the family's experience of life in Stockbridge.

(Trask Library, Dwight ms. transcript, one quarto leaf. Published in Dwight ed., *1*, 485–87. See also Henry R. Stiles, *The History, Genealogies and Biographies of Ancient Windsor, Connecticut* [2 vols. New York, 1891–92], 2, 38; DEX, 2, 567, 571–72.)

*   *   *

Stockbridge, January 27, 1751/2

Honored Sir,

We have lately heard the sorrowful tidings of the death of two of sister [Eunice] Backus' children, as we are informed both at your house; which is the occasion of cousin Eunice[1] returning from Stockbridge at this time; she having a desire to see her mother and surviving sisters at Windsor, on this melancholy occasion. We are much affected with sister's great and heavy afflictions, and lament the death of two such likely promising children in their early youth. It is my earnest desire that it may be sanctified to us of this family. I desire your prayers, that it may be so; particularly to those that are young in the family; that they may be awakened by it to diligent preparation for death; and that we all may take notice of our distinguishing mercies, with a becoming thankfulness to God. I look upon it as a great favor of heaven, that you, my parents, are still preserved in the land of the living to so great an age. I hope by the leave of divine providence, to make you and sister Backus a visit in the spring.

We are, through mercy, in our ordinary state of health, except that little Betty don't seem of late to be so well, as she was in the summer. If she lives till spring, I believe we must be obliged to come again to the use of the cold bath with her. My wife and children are well pleased with our present situation. They like the place far better than they expected. Here, at present, we live in peace; which has of long time been an unusual thing with us. The Indians seem much pleased with my family, especially my wife. They are generally more sober and serious than they used to be. Beside the Stockbridge Indians, here are above sixty of the Six Nations, who live here for the sake of instruction. Twenty are lately come to dwell here, who came from about two hundred miles beyond Albany. We expect our son and daughter [Elihu

1. JE is here using the terminology of his children to speak of his niece, the daughter of Eunice Edwards Backus, born in 1733.

and Sarah] Parsons will remove hither in a short time. Many of their goods are already brought up. [. . .][2]

I hope some of her friends will be kind to her in this respect. There are perhaps none of her uncles but are much better able to help her than I am at this time; who, by reason of lately marrying two children, and the charge of buying, building and removing, am, I suppose, about 2,000 pounds in debt, in this province's money.[3]

I should be glad if sister Mary would suggest it to brother [John] Ellsworth to do something for her. If she don't care to do it in her own name, let her do it in mine, as doing the errand from me. Please to give my duty to my mother, and my love to sister Mary. My wife is at this moment from home. My children give their duty to their grand-parents, and aunts, and love and affectionate condolence to their mournful surviving cousins. I am, honored Sir,

Your dutiful son,
Jonathan Edwards.

138. TO BRIG. JOSEPH DWIGHT

The brevity and formality of this note to an erstwhile friend attest to the cooling of the relationship in the short time since Dwight's arrival.

(RIHS, mss. V, p. 160, ALS, one quarto leaf, addressed on verso to the Honorable Joseph Dwight, Esq., in Stockbridge.)

*   *   *

Stockbridge, February 10, 1751/2

Honored Sir,

I have some apprehensions, from some things I have lately heard and observed, that there is a design of dismissing Mr. [Benjamin]

2. Sereno Dwight here interpolated, "After alluding to the indigent circumstances of his sister Mrs. Backus and her family, and mentioning that himself and Mrs. Edwards had done every thing for his niece, which was in their power, he proceeds." Dwight ed., *1*, 486. In the Dwight MS transcript, a line and a half are blotted out and unreadable.

Dwight explained the situation of Mrs. Backus: "Her husband, the Rev. Simon Backus of Newington (Wethersfield), was designated by the Connecticut Legislature, as chaplain to the troops sent to Louisburg in 1746, to prevent its recapture by the French. He died there soon after his arrival. The vessel, containing his effects, and a considerable sum contributed by the gentlemen of the army for his family, was cast away on its return; and the family were left in very indigent circumstances." Dwight ed., *1*, 485–86n.

3. Dwight commented: "I suppose that this means £2000 *old tenor,* as it was then called; the value of which continually varied, but has been commonly estimated at 6*s*. 8*d*. sterling to the pound." Ibid., 486n.

Ashley and his wife [Rebecca Kellogg Ashley] from their business at the boarding school, very speedily and suddenly. If it be so, I entreat Your Honor to give me opportunity to speak with you concerning that affair, before it be put in execution. Appoint me a time and place, and I will wait upon you.

If my apprehensions are groundless, I ask pardon. I am, Sir,

> Your very humble servant
> Jonathan Edwards.

139. TO SEC. ANDREW OLIVER

This letter begins a series of lengthy reports that are concentrated over the next two years to the Commissioners in Boston. The present letter was sent with the one following. It was directed to the Secretary of the Commissioners personally, to be used at his discretion, while the following letter was intended for the Commissioners as a whole. In both, Edwards offers an assessment of the Stockbridge schools. The first letter is more pointed in remarks about Brigadier Dwight and Mrs. Sergeant. Funds have been misused, mismanagement has prevailed, and progress has been hindered. The Indians are already dissatisfied with Mrs. Sergeant. Edwards fears they will be further alienated if she is appointed head of the female school and that the entire purpose of the enterprise will thereby be defeated.

(Trask Library, AL draft, one folio sheet, a letter cover addressed on verso to Edwards in Stockbridge, and a 1750 Yale broadside announcing master's candidates and theses; Dwight ms. transcript, eight quarto leaves. Excerpted and paraphrased in Dwight ed., *1*, 489–92.)

* * *

[Stockbridge] February 18, 1751/2

Sir,

I think it is absolutely necessary that I should let you into some of the secrets of our affairs.

In my letter that I wrote to Your Honor after the interview with the Mohawk chiefs the last August, and also in my letter to Mr. Speaker [Thomas] Hubbard, I earnestly insisted on the necessity of some persons being on the spot or very near, appointed by the Commissioners and General Assembly, a sort of curators to have the immediate inspection and care of our affairs. And concerning this affair I used these words, "What renders it more necessary that things here should be under the immediate care of trustees, is the misunderstanding and jealousies that here subsist between some of the chief of the present English inhabitants of the town, which is one of our greatest calamities. Things on that account do much more need constant inspection, and therefore the gentlemen entrusted ought to be such as are perfectly impartial, no way interested in or related to those contending parties."

I recommended Col. [Joseph] Dwight of Brookfield, but then knew not of what now appears, that he would be the furthest of any gentleman whatsoever from having that most necessary qualification I mentioned, by his being like to be the son-in-law of one of these contending parties by his marrying Mrs. [Abigail] Sergeant, which match there is reason to apprehend will be of extremely hurtful consequences to the important affairs of Stockbridge. There are already very hurtful consequences of this new alliance and many things that showedly forbode those that will be much more hurtful.

There was the last year a very formal pacification between Col. [Ephraim] Williams and Deac. [Timothy] Woodbridge, with solemn promises made by Colonel Williams that he would henceforward live quietly and friendlily with Deac. Woodbridge and no more speak ill of him or attempt anything against him or in any wise molest him: but this alliance, and his daughter's being the mistress of the female school, and Col. [Elisha] Williams of Wethersfield's being yet alive, and he himself being joined with the Commissioners in the care of that school, have so elevated him that he has now very much thrown off all appearances of peace with Deac. Woodbridge and revived the misunderstanding with him, by strangely affronting him in a very open manner. And there appears of late a very sudden and strange alteration in the temper and conduct of Colonel Dwight, who has had, ever since the appointment of the Committee by the General Assembly, the sole management of all our affairs, so that nothing has been done but he is the doer of it. As for Col. [Joseph] Pynchon, he stays at home. And this is much the case with Capt. [John] Ashley; and when he is home, he leaves things wholly with Brigadier Dwight. I know not what the late great alteration in him can be owing to, unless it [be] female counsels. He now appears to approve that which Colonel Williams and Mrs. Sergeant approve, which a little while ago he greatly condemned; and to condemn what they condemn (in some instances), which before he approved. And things are carried on in some respects [in] a very strange manner.

The Indians here have a very ill opinion of Colonel Williams and the deepest prejudice against him, he having often molested 'em with respect to their lands and other affairs, and, as they think, done very unjustly to 'em; and Madam Sergeant partakes of no small degree of the same prejudice. This has appeared by things they have said of her at my house, of their own accord, without anybody saying anything to lead 'em to it. They say that Mr. [John] Sergeant did very well till he married her; but that afterwards there was a great alteration in him and he became quite another man. They speak of her as proud and covetous and not to be trusted; and Mr. Sergeant had much lost his interest in the esteem and affections of the Indians in the latter part of his life. There is this among other evidence of their prejudice against Mrs. Sergeant, that though great pains have been taken to get children for her female school, she has not been able to get above four: three Stockbridge Indians and one Mohawk. And there have already been loud complaints among the Indians of her treatment of the children, which justly or not I will not determine. But if not, it shows the effect of their prejudice and what it may be expected will be effects of it[1] here-after. In order that the school may flourish, it is of great importance that the person, who is to be the mistress, be one against whom the Indians have no prejudice and ill opinion. Their prejudices are hardly eradicated. It is easy to gain their friendship; but when once they receive an impression that any individual is dishonest, they will hardly ever trust him again.

Mrs. Sergeant is undoubtedly a woman of very considerable abilities, and her natural temper disposes her much more to dominion than subjection. She loves to have a hand in the management of public affairs and she had a vast ascendance over Mr. Sergeant, and she had very much the disposal of Mr. [Isaac] Hollis' monies—at least she made bold to dispose of 'em according to her own discretion in some instances. As to her manner of disposing them, I will not assert that she is not at all wronged in representations that are made by some that know. But this is past doubt, that she made more bold with his money, and with the public benefactions of some others to the poor Indians, than I should have dared to have done.

And I could wish that the manner of spending Mr. Hollis' money since Mr. Sergeant's death, by another person into whose hands they have fallen, were thoroughly known. The longer I continue here and the more insight I get into the management of these affairs in Stock-bridge, the more am I filled with astonishment. When one considers

1. The text for the remainder of the paragraph, missing from JE's draft, is based on Dwight's MS transcript.

the noble spirit of charity Mr. Hollis has shown, and the large remittances [which] have been made by him to this place, and to how little good purpose, especially of late, and how ignorant he is of the true state of his affairs here, and how far his conceptions of them probably are from the truth—it is enough to make one sick.

I would say everything in Capt. [Martin] Kellogg's favor that is his just due. I believe he has done good service by his endeavors, the summer before last, to persuade the Mohawks to come hither; and that Mr. Sergeant's letters in his lifetime, seconded by Captain Kellogg's after his death, was the first means of persuading some of the Mohawks to come and visit this place. And the last winter, though he kept no school, yet I believe he, being animated with the Mohawks' coming, took a great deal of pains in his way to teach 'em to read. But he could never be persuaded to set up a school or turn out of his own disorderly way. No government was maintained; very little manners taught; but all was suffered to go on in wildness, nastiness and confusion, to the great offense of such as have visited the place. And though he has been much urged, he never could be persuaded to keep any particular accounts of his expenses for the satisfaction of the world. I never have seen any of the accounts which he sent to Mr. Hollis; but was informed by one of the late Committee, from another of the same Committee that had seen one of them, that he was extremely dissatisfied with it.

And as to the particular design that Mr. Hollis had in view in his most generous benefaction and which he supposes is pursued to good and happy effect—I mean the educating the boys that Captain Kellogg has pretended to teach and maintain at his cost—this money has been entirely lost. At least it has been so, if his way of management before was as it has been since I have been here. I don't mean that his scholars have learned nothing at all by him. But I mean they have had no better education nor near so good as they might and probably would have had without any of that cost. So that, in effect, I believe Mr. Hollis' money has rather prevented and clogged his great design, than promoted it. Captain Kellogg has, with promises of a free maintenance, enticed away a number of Stockbridge boys from Deacon Woodbridge's school, where they were regularly instructed and governed and taught good manners, for the sake of making up the number of Mr. Hollis' boys, by which he might draw his pay for the boarding school, where they were much more neglected and have grown more wild, disorderly and vicious, which is a mere cheat to Mr. Hollis, a

perfect wasting of his money and doing mischief with it. He taught the
boys nothing more than Deacon Woodbridge too would have taught.
The boys were not taught to wash as Mr. Hollis [directed], nor anything at all done towards it; and other commendable things which
Deacon Woodbridge taught were neglected. And then he has been
absent near half his time since the beginning of last August, leaving the
care of his boys to one body or other.

The irregularity and disorderly manner of Captain Kellogg's management of the boys has been what the Mohawks have found great
fault with, and has been a chief discouragement to 'em.

And now another schoolmaster is come and has set up a regular
school, and has suddenly made a great and happy alteration in the
state of things, which the Mohawks are greatly taken with. And now it
is known that the Indians will send all the children to Mr. [Gideon]
Hawley and none to Captain Kellogg. Yet Captain Kellogg is there still,
and calling the boys he formerly had his boys still; and looks upon
them as under his care; and looking on himself a superintendent with
respect to them, to the manifest entwining and entangling the affair
and not helping it, as is already found by experience. And whether he
intends to draw Mr. Hollis' pay, others can judge as well as I. He has
nothing to do there as a master or teacher, though he may still take
some care of their clothing and in some measure do the part of a
steward. In the way we are in, we are like to have superintendents
multiplied here, drawing great salaries and expecting great honors
and having but little business. Captain Kellogg looks on himself a sort
of a superintendent of the whole school and Madam Sergeant expects
to be superintendent of the female school.

Brigadier Dwight had his eyes as open to see Captain Kellogg's
defects as anybody, and used to be abundant in speaking of his uselessness, his exceeding unfitness for the business he was in, the disorder
and nastiness in which things were kept under his care, and how that it
was high time he was gone, etc., etc. But now, suddenly his tone is
turned. Colonel Williams and Mrs. Sergeant were always in the same
box with Captain Kellogg and have ever appeared his great friends.
But still Colonel Pynchon's eyes are open, who, though he has been but
little here, can inform Your Honor something of these things, if he
should be inquired of.

The management has been something strange with respect to Mr.
Hawley. Before he came, very dark representations were carried to
him from hence, misrepresentations of things tending greatly to discourage his meddling at all with the business. For what reason I know

not, unless because he was one of my nominating and so it was supposed he would naturally fall under my influence and not be governed
by them. When Colonel Dwight came, which was soon after Mr.
Hawley had begun his school, the conduct at first was as if he was at a
loss whether to smile or frown upon him, whether to discourage or
encourage him; and it was given out by some that are conversant with
Colonel Williams and his daughter that it was doubtful whether Mr.
Hawley would not soon be removed. And if it had not been for Mr.
Hawley's courage, prudence, and steadiness of temper in so difficult a
situation, he would undoubtedly have been laid under some lasting,
unspeakable disadvantages. And I feel still it will be the endeavor of
some to make his work difficult, to the end that they may discourage
him, unless they can draw him over to such an attachment to 'em as to
be their tool. Just before Colonel Dwight went away he discourses with
Mr. Hawley in Captain Kellogg's presence, as Mr. Hawley himself informs me, and warns him not to have his dependence too much on me;
and offers his own friendship and assistance, tells him that he might
see cause hereafter to alter his opinion of some persons; and assures
him that he is much more able to support him and assist him than I,
two to one; that he had authority to direct him and order how he
should conduct in the school; and that I had no authority to intermeddle in his concerns; and that, when I introduced him into the school, I
did it without authority; that the Commissioners had no authority in
the affair; but that the authority was all vested in the Committee of the
General Assembly and he had their authority, for they expected he
should act for the rest; and adds repeated charges that he should by no
means tell me of these things that he had said to him, but without
getting any promise from Mr. Hawley. Here appears a sudden, wonderful change in Colonel Dwight with respect to me. He has constantly
for many years professed the highest respect to me, far beyond what I
could with any modesty expect. He expressed an esteem of me beyond
any other minister in New England, and has very lately expressed his
great desires of living under my ministry. And I never have had one
word of difference with him, nor with Madam Sergeant, Colonel Williams, or Captain Kellogg, though they greatly opposed my coming to
Stockbridge before I came. But since have all declared themselves to
me well-pleased with it, though they have said contrary things behind
my back. Mrs. Sergeant has pretended to a great extravagance in her
professions of esteem and regard to me to my face, though from time
to time I have found by what she has said to others her heart was not at
all in it.

I suppose Colonel Williams of Wethersfield has greatly established the character of his uncle [Col. Ephraim Williams] and cousin [Abigail] Sergeant in London and that he has raised and confirmed Mr. Hollis' good opinion of Captain Kellogg, who has always been his great friend. And it may be expected that when Colonel Williams comes, he will be exceeding busy and active in our affairs, taking much upon him, agreeable to his natural temper. But I can't think his influence on our affairs will be very happy. The Society in London, if they had any true view of the case, would never have appointed Madam Sergeant to be the mistress of the girls' school; and her own father and near kinsman, the Committee to look after her and her accounts. But things are like to [be] situated more preposterously still. According to the course things are in, viz. that Madam Sergeant should be the mistress, and her own husband, in effect, the whole Committee of the General Assembly to receive her accounts, make representations to his constituents, and to [be the] sole sovereign manager of that and all other affairs here; or rather, this power will be in Madam Sergeant's hands with the family of the Williamses for her counsel, and her husband her instrument to execute her designs, as he intends to settle here for the sake of his wife's being the mistress of the female school. And I confess I have no hopes of seeing the affair prosper if things are carried thus; I expect nothing but perpetual dissensions, undermining, and counterworking of one another among the inhabitants of the town, which probably will soon bring all to the ground; and probably they will think themselves so strong that they will attempt nothing short of purging the town of all that stand in their way. For my part, I have no reason to expect that they except me from such an attempt, as they well know, and know already, that I am not for their turn, and they doubtless only think me a great nuisance here.[2] They now strive to the utmost to confine my usefulness to as narrow a sphere as possible. They find fault behind my back with my preaching to the Mohawks, and instructing their children, as an intermeddling where I have no business. Things are now so situated, that they think the day is their own, and therefore are less and less cautious in their conduct, and seem resolved to have all in their own hands. This is but too agreeable to a temper and conduct, which I have long been acquainted with in many of the family.

The affair at Stockbridge being great and being much taken notice of in the world makes some people very fond of having a hand therein, and eager to engross the management of all to themselves, and so

2. The text for the remainder of the paragraph, missing from JE's draft, is based on Dwight's MS transcript.

impatient of every person and thing that stands in their way. The Brigadier is exceedingly engaged about his wife's being the mistress and therefore pushes that affair with great vigor. He's already bought a great number of boards and brought 'em on her land to build a schoolhouse there. But how imprudent will it be to set up a public building on a particular person's property.

I write these things, honored Sir, because I am satisfied you have not heretofore been enlightened in the true state of things as you ought to have been. It was my knowledge of some of these matters—though but little in comparison—that occasioned me when last in Boston, so earnestly to press the Commissioners' frequently visiting the place. I have been slow to speak. My disposition has been entirely to have suppressed what I know that would be to the disadvantage of any of the people here. But I dare not hold my tongue any longer. You doubtless will own, Sir, that 'tis but doing you justice for somebody or other to let you know the true state of things in a matter of such vast importance that is under your care, which you, being at so great a distance, never can know but by the information of some that live here. And I know of none you can more reasonably expect it from, than from the missionary you have put here to have the special care of the interest of religion among the Indians. I did not intend to have intermeddled with the affair of Mrs. Sergeant's being the mistress, or to say anything that should tend to hinder it, and therefore avoided everything of such a tendency in my letter to Sir William Pepperrell. But being now applied to again by the honorable Commissioners, and the tendency of her influence more and more evidently appearing, I thought this was the time that God called me to speak; and that, if I should hold my tongue now, I should perhaps lay a foundation for great uneasiness to my conscience all my life after; when I might groan under the view of the continued consequences of my silence and when it might be too late to speak.

I [leave it] with you, to judge whether things which I have mentioned, together with Colonel Williams' laying out his £500 to produce an effect so very small, may be a sufficient warning to you to take care who you entrust with the money of the Society. Selfish designs and intrigues for private interest are the ruin of our affairs. 'Tis of the utmost consequence that persons improved here should be of the most proved and approved character for faithfulness and simplicity.

'Tis necessary that it should be known whether the Committee of the General Assembly here act as your committee as well as the committee of the province, as things are often carried in the Assembly by particular parties and interests. It will not be likely to be for the health of the affair for the Assembly to take the matter entirely out of the hands of the Commissioners. It must needs be a great defect if you have no instruments here under your direction that have any power to dispose of your money to your minds and put your orders in execution, but that all should fall into the hands of others that don't look on themselves at all accountable to you.

And now, Sir, I leave it to your discretion how to use this letter. You are sensible of the difficult situation I am in and how much trouble it might be an occasion of to me if this letter should be made public, especially if Brigadier Dwight should settle, as he is resolved to do if Madam Sergeant be the mistress of the girls' school, and which there is no probability of if she be not. However, I am not afraid that some of the Commissioners that I am acquainted with and know to be my friends should see this letter, as Secretary [Josiah] Willard, Mr. [Edward] Bromfield, and Mr. [Thomas] Foxcroft. And as to others, you know them better than I.

And if you judge it to be absolutely necessary for the public good that it should be read, some of it or all of [it], [to] all the Commissioners, I will not forbid it, though I should suffer greatly by it. If you are satisfied that Mrs. Sergeant is not like to be established as the mistress, there may be no need of it. But I will lay Your Honor under no absolute restriction, but trust myself in your hands and leave the affair to your wisdom, depending that in the first place you will do the part of a friend to the interest of religion and Christ's kingdom and after that the part of a faithful friend to me.

[Jonathan Edwards.]

140. TO THE COMMISSIONERS

This letter accompanied the previous one but unlike it was meant to be read publicly, at the Commissioners' general meeting in Boston. Edwards is more businesslike and less personal here. He opens with praise of Gideon Hawley. He appreciates the invitation to submit a plan for the female school and will do so as soon as he can confer with the Committee. Abigail Sergeant seems uninterested in the instructional activity. He considers her unfitted by temperament, preparation, and responsibilities to head the female school.

(Trask Library, AL draft, one folio sheet, on back of the Feb. 18, 1752, draft to Oliver, address side of the letter cover; Dwight ms. transcript, four quarto leaves.)

*   *   *

Stockbridge, February 19, 1751/2

Honored and Rev. Sirs,

Immediately after the receipt of Mr. [Andrew] Oliver's letter of December 31, I wrote to Mr. [Gideon] Hawley and sent him an extract of the letter, that part of it that related to him. It was some time before the letter reached him. But the week before last Mr. Hawley came. Several of the sachems of the Mohawks were then present, and Abraham [Conaughstansey] who is chief among them in religious affairs. I went with Mr. Hawley to the boarding school and called the Mohawks and Onohquagas together and told 'em what was designed as to Mr. Hawley's services among them. They appeared very highly pleased. They declared that they had been very uneasy at the confusion things had been in, that there had been no good order, no regularity, and their children not taken care of, and this was what they [had] long been waiting and wishing for, to have a regular school set up. I never saw such marks of satisfaction and well pleasedness among them on any occasion whatsoever. And they have since appeared highly pleased with Mr. Hawley and very forward to assist him and strengthen him in ordering and governing his school. He appears to [be] a young man of uncommon prudence and steadiness of mind, spirit of government, and faculty of teaching; and has his heart much in the affair and seems disposed greatly to exert himself in it. I had heard him much recommended but his qualifications appear beyond my expectation. He has a large school, about thirty-six in all, yet desires me to employ him on the best terms I can and to inform you what allowance he would expect if confirmed in the service. He has left good business that he was in as a candidate for the ministry, where he had 20*s* a week York money, besides his board and housekeeping, while preaching on probation, and a prospect of a very comfortable settlement if he had continued. And his services here are extraordinary as, besides teaching his scholars to read and write, he labors to teach them the English tongue, and to instruct 'em in religion, also instructing two English boys that by the order of the government are put into the school. And he himself [is] taking pains to learn the Mohawk language, and sometimes preaching to 'em as they have desired him, being willing to hear preaching oftener than I can attend it, though I constantly preach to 'em once every sabbath and go once a week to instruct their children. I should think he ought, while he is here upon probation, to have as much as candidates for the ministry ordinarily have while preaching on probation. For his service is much greater than theirs

and he has left such business for this. And if he settles in the business, I
should think he ought to have what is commonly accounted a comfortable and honorable maintenance for a minister, in the settlement and
salary.

In Mr. Oliver's last letter nothing is said, whether Your Honors have
agreed to what I proposed in one of my letters concerning things to be
allowed for premiums to encourage and engage the children in their
learning, which was proposed for Deac. [Timothy] Woodbridge's
school. I would now humbly request the same for Mr. Hawley's school,
where they will be no less useful and necessary.

But[1] then 'tis necessary that Mr. Hawley should know what authority the Commissioners have with respect to him, and who he is to look
to for orders with respect to his business in the school, [in] disposing of
premiums, in other [affairs] wherein he will need orders on emergen-
cies from time to time. For this is a matter of dispute, for Mr. Hawley
has been informed by a gentleman of no inferior character[2] that the
Commissioners have no authority at all in such matters and that when I
introduced him into the school, by your order, I acted wholly without
authority; but that all authority is vested entirely in the Committee of
the Assembly.

I gratefully acknowledge the unmerited honor the Commissioners
have done me in desiring me to draw up a plan for a female school,
after conferring with Col. [Joseph] Dwight, Col. [Joseph] Pynchon,
and Col. [Ephraim] Williams, to be transmitted hence. I have yet had
no opportunity for the proposed conference. Colonel Dwight has
lately been here but [I] neglected a particular conversation with him
and Colonel Williams about the affair because I was [in] daily expectation of Colonel Pynchon, when I hoped to have opportunity to confer
with 'em all together. But the last week, Colonel Dwight suddenly went
away without giving me any information of it but the night before. 'Tis
now wholly uncertain when I shall have opportunity to [see him].

But I am still in expectation of Colonel Pynchon and Captain
Dwight. If opportunity should [be present] and we should have a
conference, 'tis expected in about a fortnight when I hope to have
opportunity for the desired conference. But I apprehend a probability
of difference of sentiment about the affair. Madam [Abigail] Sergeant,
who is Colonel Williams' daughter and with whom Colonel Dwight is
entering into strictest engagements and nearest relations, has notions

1. JE drew a vertical line through this paragraph.
2. Colonel Dwight is meant, but JE is trying to avoid a direct charge at this point.

of the affair very wide from mine. Her notions of the state and business and attendants of the chief mistress appear to me to be such as it would be hardly prudent to put in execution at present. When I wrote my letter to Sir William Pepperrell concerning a female school, I purposely avoided mentioning my thoughts concerning those things because I was not willing to give offense. But since I was again applied to by vote of the Commissioners, I looked upon it that I was called in providence to take matters into my most deliberate consideration and speak my mind freely.

Officers, servants, and tenements should not be multiplied needlessly because the charge will be hereby needlessly enhanced, but the care of the affair will be the greater and attended with greater difficulty and encumbrances. Things will be more apt to run into the confusion and it will be more difficult to keep 'em in order. It would not be prudent to be at great pains and cost to make a machine that is very complex, when one that is much more simple will reach the end as well. I humbly conceive that the beginnings should be moderate. 'Tis easier to add what an experience is found to be wanting than to undo or remove what is once done if found too much. Things with respect to the Mohawks are at present in a great manner unsettled and uncertain, and therefore moderation at the beginning is more requisite as there will be the less venture. Mrs. Sergeant seems to expect not to be much concerned in the immediate instruction of the children [in] teaching them to read, etc., and only to do the part of a kind of superintendent over the affair. But it appears to me absolutely necessary that the mistress of the female school, as well as the male, should devote herself to the business of teaching. The business, if it be well done, will require all the care and strength and skill and constant attendance of a woman of superior abilities and education. The art of teaching, and more especially little children at the first opening of their understanding, requires superior talents. And the cultivating and new forming the minds of those that come out of such great wildness will require great prudence, faithfulness, and constant application. A large salary given to maintain a female superintendent will be wholly thrown away, and perhaps laid out rather to clog than help the affair. The Committee will be sufficient for superintendence and therefore the mistress should be one whose circumstances will allow her to devote herself to the business, not having any very great care upon her hands besides. And then it will be a hard thing to find a gentlewoman in New England of sufficient talents for the business of teaching in this school that will be willing to serve under Mrs. Sergeant and be subject to her.

But I am sensible [that] these sentiments will be very disagreeable, and I fear provoking, to some that you have directed me to confer with, as it will not consist with Madam Sergeant's intention nor circumstances, as she is about marrying to Colonel Dwight and so will immediately have the care of two families of her own and probably after a while must have the care of a third; and she is a very weakly person and not used to a laborious way of living. And it will be wholly impossible for her to do the part of a school mistress in this school by herself, to give any constant attendance to the business, and I know by what she has said to me she does not expect it. However, I intend to confer with those gentlemen you mentioned as soon as I can get opportunity.[3]

I have no interest of my own or of my friends to serve in this affair. I have nothing but my conscience that should dispose me to say or do anything [which] will probably be displeasing to any of the General Court's Committee and such as are of 'em like to be my parishioners, and to expose myself to new troubles and difficulties in the place wherein I am now settled, after I have so lately emerged from those that were so great and larger in the place where I formerly was.

But[4] I desire some new instructions from you, respecting this affair. If it be desired that I should put my thoughts respecting a plan [on paper], I am ready to do [it]. And if, notwithstanding there being the highest probability of a wide disagreement, it will be desired that I should confer with the forementioned gentlemen, I will do it.

[Jonathan Edwards].

141. TO JOSEPH PAICE

Joseph Paice, a merchant and Presbyterian layman of London, had expressed interest in missions to Indian girls. The Boston Commissioners forwarded to Edwards three of his letters on the subject that were written to Sir William Pepperrell. The Commissioners suggested that Edwards write to Paice about Stockbridge.

Surprisingly, Edwards opens this letter with a wide-ranging comparison of the English and French colonists in North America. He reviews the strategic situation of the two great powers but concentrates on an indictment of the English. Identifying himself as English, he complains that they are compla-

3. JE drew a vertical line through this sentence.
4. JE drew a vertical line through this paragraph.

cent, lack initiative, and exploit the Indians. Despite their superior numbers and many other advantages over the French, the French excel in military alertness and attention to the natives. It is high time that the English were aroused to pursue decisive, positive action.

Then Edwards shifts from the overall picture to focus on Stockbridge. The opportunity to win and hold the friendship of Indians is immediate. At the crest of his optimism, he envisions mission schools there as centers of learning, radiating Christianity and civilization and bringing benefits of lasting value.

Edwards probably little dreamed that his letter would be brought to the attention of the Archbishop of Canterbury himself. Paice sent on a copy of the letter, sensing that the larger implications of Edwards' warning to the English, and his plea on behalf of Indian missions, were more important than the unfavorable estimate of Church of England missionaries.[1] Anti-Anglican rhetoric, long commonplace among colonials, would not be thought unusual by London dissenters.

(London, Lambeth Palace Library, Secker Coll., ms. 1123, Part I, No. 60, ms. copy by Joseph Paice, four folio leaves; Trask Library, AL draft, on three commencement broadsides for: (1) Yale, 1750 (2) Princeton, 1750 and (3) Yale, 1748; and Trask Library, Dwight ms. transcript, twelve quarto leaves.)

* * *

[Stockbridge,] February 24, 1751/2

Sir,

I have been so favored and honored by some of the Commissioners in Boston of the honorable Society for Propagating Christian Knowledge in New England and the Parts Adjacent, that they have sent me copies of three of your letters to Sir William Pepperrell, one dated 9th

1. Paice sent the copy of JE's communication with his own cover letter, dated July 18, 1752, to the Archbishop of Canterbury, Thomas Herring, which included this comment: "I have taken the freedom to enclose a copy of [Mr. Jonathan Edwards' letter] for your perusal, and must ask pardon for troubling you with so long a piece, which I should not have done did it not appear to contain some particulars of importance. I would have sent the original, but it is wrote in a hand hardly legible. As I have the original, I beg you will not take the trouble to return the enclosed. Permit me, Sir, farther to mention that I do not patronize his observation on the Episcopal missionaries in New England, but, as that is part of his letter, I could not avoid transcribing it with the rest." (London, Lambeth Palace Library, MS Coll. 1123, no. 61, ALS.) Moreover, as reflected in his letter to John Erskine of July 5, 1750 (No. 117), JE already knew something of the Archbishop, and seems to have been favorably disposed. Erskine had reported that Herring was a man of "moderate, generous, truly catholic, and Christian principles."

of April, another 8th of June, the last 13th of August, all of the year
1751, together with three other papers drawn up on the subject of the
school for the instruction of Indian girls, with letters sent to me by the
Commissioners on the same subject, proposing to me to write to you
on our Indian affairs, and encouraging me, that probably a letter from
me would not be taken amiss, which together with the spirit which
appears in your letters, and a hope that, by my writing to one of such
capacity and disposition, might serve to promote the great and important design of the settlement of this place, is what encourages and
induces me to write, and is what I have to offer in excuse for my
troubling you with this.

And to begin with what should be uppermost in my heart, I thank
God that has excited such an uncommon concern for the enlargement
of the kingdom of Christ in America among the poor Indians in some
at so great a distance, so able to help us, who are immediately concerned in their instruction; and I thank you, Sir, for taking the interest
of religion among the American Indians and the British interest in
America, so near your heart and exerting yourself so much in it, for
which you merit the thanks of all British subjects and Christians in
these parts and especially of missionaries to the Indians. I think the
concern that is manifested by some in Great Britain about these things,
and the zeal and activity that appears in them to spread the gospel in
the dark parts of this continent, may well shame us that are the inhabitants of the British America. If we regard only our temporal interest
and safety, without any respect to the enlargement of Christ's kingdom, it certainly greatly concerns us to do our utmost to propagate the
Protestant religion among the Indians. I rejoice to find in your letters
and papers, sent to Sir William, such just sentiments on this head.

The English have not only greatly failed of their duty in so neglecting the instruction of the Indians, but we have been extremely impoli-
tic, and by our negligence in this matter have brought the whole British America into very difficult and dangerous circumstances, which I
am much more sensible of since I have been in this place, where I have
been now for about a twelvemonth, during which space I have had
much acquaintance with many of the Iroquois or Six Nations (as we
call them); and have had frequent conversation with some of their
chiefs, who have a great acquaintance with the state of those nations,
and the nations beyond them. While we have been asleep, our most
dangerous and inveterate enemies, the French, have been awake; they
have discerned and taken the advantages which we have overlooked

and neglected, to our unspeakable, and as 'tis to be feared, irreparable damage. The English have heretofore had vastly greater advantages in their hands to gain the Six Nations, and most of the other nations of North America, and establish them in their interest, than the French, as the British settlements are abundantly more numerous and populous, and better situated, as we possess the sea coasts, and the more powerful Indian nations are much nearer to us, and could have a better market for their commodities, and be very easily supplied with such goods as they need, and at a much cheaper rate. And the Six Nations or Iroquois (which are the powerful body of Indians in these northern parts of the continent) have ever since the settlement of America, till of late, been much more inclined to the English than the French; and though the French have been indefatigably laboring to draw 'em over to their interest for perhaps a whole century past, and we all the while very negligent, yet they have made but slow progress till of late. Instead of our improving the advantages, divine providence has put, and so long left in our hands, to consult our own safety, by using means to secure these nations in our interest, we have on the contrary been constantly taking courses to alienate them. 'Tis true we have traded a great deal, but our trade has been carried on with them in a way that has naturally tended to beget in them a distrust of us, and aversion to us. Most of our Indian traders, being persons of little conscience, the Indians have been abundantly defrauded, and commonly that has given 'em, in exchange for their skins and furs, that [which] has done 'em no good, but been their greatest plague, viz. rum in vast quantities, which, though pleasing to their appetites, they are sensible is their undoing, and serves nothing to gain their affections, but the contrary. They themselves give it as a reason why they are under a necessity of deserting us, that we destroy them. Nothing has been more common than for our traders first to make them drunk, and then to trade with them and defraud 'em of their goods, when they have lost the use of their reason and [are] unable to defend themselves. Though the king annually gives £500 sterling as a present to the Six Nations, yet (I suppose it to be very apparent), there is all reason to think, the money is embezzled, and used for the advance [of] the private gain of those into whose hands it falls; and of that part that is given [to the Indians], 'tis bestowed in that which issues [in] no good end, viz. in rum to make 'em drunk.

And as to instructions in religion, very little has been done among those people by the missionaries of the Society for Propagating the

Gospel in Foreign Parts. And that Society have been vastly imposed upon (as appears by printed accounts of the Society which come over [hither]) by the representations of the Society. The Iroquois themselves have often in my hearing complained greatly of their negligence. The monies of that given Society, instead of being used to propagate the gospel among the heathen, are chiefly spent to promote the church party in opposition [to] those of the Presbyterian and Congregational persuasion in New England. Those of the Church of England here, especially their clergy, being almost wholly high church men, and great bigots, use all manner of methods to promote their particular party, to encroach upon and root out dissenters, and engross everything to themselves; wherein they are no less active, than the Papists are to build up themselves here on the ruins of the Protestant and British interest, which is a thing worthy to be considered in any projection for a coalition of the Church of England and dissenters in the affair of the instruction of the Indians, and in the establishment of school for the education of their children and youth.

The French here in America have been more faithful to those by whom they have been entrusted than the English. The French government in Canada have been more faithful to their king, and the French missionaries more true to the interest of their religion. They have had their missionaries for many years constantly amongst the most powerful of these nations, who have been great in their labors among them, using all the arts and subtle devices of the clergy of the Church of Rome, prejudicing them against the Protestants and English by innumerable Jesuitical falsehoods. And the French fail not, as the Mohawks tell me, to make great use of our negligence, as an advantage to prejudice the Indians against us, telling them that 'tis apparent that the English care not for their good in that they take no pains to instruct 'em in religion; at the same time offering their own assistance and labors for the salvation of their souls, if they will be their friends.

The vast difference of the temper of the French and English nations, as it has appeared in the different conduct towards these people, has been very strange. While they have been so exceeding vigilant, we have been like men in a lethargy, even so as to make us the objects of the mirth of the French and, of late, the contempt of the Indians. For they often, in my hearing, have made mention of this remarkable difference, and have told me how the French laugh at us. We have seen the advantages the French were taking, in one instance and another and have stood by, and let 'em go on quietly when we might easily have prevented 'em, till it has been too late, and then we lament it. Thus, when they were about building their fort at Crown Point on our own land (which has been our greatest annoyance in the late war), it was known before, of our anticipating and preventing them talked of, but all ended in talk, and nothing was done; and in a little time we most severely suffered for our sloth. Besides our great trouble and loss of blood, and diminution of our bounds, that fort has cost us to defend ourselves against it, perhaps ten times so much as the charge of building and maintaining a fort there ourselves.

The great advantage the French have by their interest in the Indian nations never so sensibly appeared as in the late war, for by means of them they were much too hard for these British colonies, though the French in Canada are but a handful in comparison of them. The things we suffered in the war have raised the Indians' opinion of the strength of the French, and given a notion of our impotence; many things that happened in the war served to render us contemptible in their eyes, and to disincline 'em more and more to a strict alliance with [us]; and especially our [making] such a pretense of our invasion of Canada, and making such great preparations for it, and treating with them so much about it, and at last failing without putting anything in execution, and so, greatly disappointing those of the Indians that we had engaged, and were ready to assist us. And then after that, making another pretense of besieging the fort at Crown Point, and also making great preparations for that, and doing much to engage their [the Indians'] assistance, and finally dropping that also, without ever going against the place. Besides some notable instances of unfaithfulness to the Mohawks, who proved themselves our faithful allies in the late war, of which they have loudly and often complained. When these things are considered, 'tis no wonder they have been followed with such sad effects, in so great an alienation of most of the northern tribes from the British interest; especially when it is also considered, that the French stand ready to aggravate these things to the Indians, to put their own constructions upon them, and to heighten the contempt, and blow up the resentment which they saw naturally rising in their minds on these occasions.

The French have been mightily encouraged by these things; and this encouragement, together with the late experience they have of the advantage of the alliance of the Indians to them and the disadvantages, have exceedingly engaged them to lay out themselves to finish the business of alienating from the English all the nations of Indians in

North America from us, and fixing them strongly in a friendship with them.

I believe the people of England are in no measure sensible how much the Court of France have exerted themselves, and what cost they have been at to this end since the last war. The presents that are made them at the French king's cost are very large, and such as we can have little hope to vie with them in; and the Mohawks tell us of great things they have been doing in the two past years to the west of us; in building forts at the carrying places between the lakes and rivers, and in the most important places. In treaties they have had with the nations, the presents they have made them, they have so extended their settlements and fortified places, that they have now in effect joined their settlements in Canada and those on Mississippi River, and hemmed us all in; and have had great success in gaining over the greater part of the Iroquois, and almost all the nations about the Great Lakes, by which they are become very formidable to the few Indians that are yet our friends, who blame the British Governors for their negligence, and commend the Governor of Canada for his superior wisdom. The French have left no stone unturned, no method neglected, to gain their purpose. They have not only sent forth their missionaries and other emissaries, but they have of late, gone with armies to do their business the more thoroughly. Their way is, when they have gained the friendship of a nation, to persuade some of 'em to come and settle in Canada and inveigle 'em to permit their building forts in their territories, whereby they in effect become some of the French dominions, so they are constantly enlarging the French empire in America, and curtailing the British dominions more and more. In time of war, they are far more active and thorough than we; and they are no less active to establish and enlarge their interest in time of peace, when we are soundly asleep. In war, they drive us in. 'Tis found by experience we can't maintain our frontiers against them, but where they once get footing, they hold their own and never give back.

What will be the consequences of these things in future times, God only knows. But if another war should break out, unless the Most High should remarkably interpose in our defense, there is a great probability of our being brought into before-unexperienced distress. Indeed, as things are now situated, there is a great prospect of the French king's having the greatest part of North America in his possession; though the king of Great Britain has much the greatest number of subjects here, and has had heretofore vastly the greatest advantage to enlarge his dominions here. Yea, it would have been an easy thing in the time of the late war with the naval forces of Great Britain to have taken the possession of the whole. Certainly the French in the like case would not have neglected the opportunity. But we must look to God, and not to earthly princes for defense. That things are brought to this pass is both the natural consequence, and also a just punishment, of our so much neglecting the eternal welfare of those people [the Indians].

Divine providence seems now to have left us but one way to help ourselves, and to do anything considerable towards regaining these nations to the British interest, and that is in applying ourselves now at length (though it be late in the day) in good earnest to our duty, in instructing them in the principles of the true religion, cultivating the minds of their children, and storing them with useful knowledge. There seems still to be an opportunity for us to do much in this way towards attaching them to our interest, as well as promoting their own true happiness, if we have but a heart to improve it, and prudence sufficient for the conduct of the affair.

The Indians, wild as they are, have some sense of the shamefulness of vice, and of the value of virtue, order and civility. And they have some sense of the worth of knowledge. If anyone among them is able to read and write, it is looked upon as a great attainment, and they esteem it a thing much to be valued to be able to read and understand the Bible. And therefore, many of them are fond of their children's learning the English tongue to that end, that they may understand what they read. Therefore, herein we can outdo the French. For they, however great expense they are at, in bestowing presents upon them, yet agreeable to the genius of their religion and maxims of their church, keep the Indians in ignorance. They forbid 'em the use of the Bible; nor do they teach 'em to read and write. If we should go on, and many among them by our means should have these attainments, and it was seen by the nations that there was such a difference between such as have been under our care and those under theirs, it would [be seen] that the greatest benefit was obtained by those that are on our side; and seeing the difference, and taking notice that the French keep their Indians in ignorance, and refuse to enable [them] to read the Bible, would naturally excite their jealousy of the French, as not truly seeking their good, but as having some ill design in their pretenses of kindness to 'em; and that the rather, because they have so much discerning that they are sensible that the French are a designing, crafty, treacherous people; and though our presents of clothing, arms and ammunition should not equal those of the French, yet if we vigorously prosecuted this design of instructing them, they would soon see the benefits they receive from us are more substantial, and of greater value than those they receive from the French, for they are a *discerning people*. And we have also this advantage, that our religion would recommend itself more to their reason and to the light of nature in 'em than the religion of the French, though not so much to their corruptions. As this way of dealing with these nations would be in itself the most Christian and benevolent, so therein we might expect God's blessing, and might hope that his anger would be turned away which has been provoked by our past negligence, from whence we have reason to fear God will make them a sore scourge to us as a just punishment of our cruelty to their souls and bodies, by our withholding the gospel from 'em, defrauding them of their goods, in addition to that of learning, with prejudicing them against Christianity by our wickedness; and killing multitudes of 'em, and easily diminishing their numbers with strong drink.

And this method would not only be the most becoming Christians, and so most pleasing to the great Governor of the world, but if we look only to the natural tendency of it in the present situation of things, I am persuaded there is no course in the world that can be devised by any policy or art, that would be so likely to gain and attach these nations to us. I think this is the voice of providence, and the intimation which God gives us in the present state of things, that if ever North America is regained from a subjection to Antichristian powers, it must be more by the spreading of the light of the gospel than by any policy, wealth or arms of the British Empire. If the king's annual bounty of £500 sterling (the greater part of which, it is to be feared, is embezzled, and great part of the remainder spent to make the Indians drunk) were laid out for their instruction, it would be ten times so effectual to gain the desired end.

And divine providence seems now in a remarkable manner to be opening a door in this place for the successful prosecution of this method of gaining the Indians by instructing them; and to give us a better opportunity at least in some respects than ever was given before. Here they see the congregation of the Housatonic Indians, now consisting of above 200[2] souls, who have sat under the care of the English

2. The Paice copy reads "250."

above sixteen years, and have been constantly well treated by us, and see in them many happy effects of our care of 'em, and kindness to 'em in things that concern their temporal interest, and none of those ill consequences which Indians are ready to fear. They have before their eyes, in the Housatonic Indians, a confutation of that which commonly [are] the greatest objections of the Indians against putting their children under the care of the English, viz. that the English will make slaves of 'em, and the eyes of many of them [the Iroquois] seem to be turned this way; and there seems to be some special influence on the minds of many of them at this time, inclining them to seek greater degrees of light than they have hitherto lived in. Besides those that are of the tribe of the Conneenchees or proper Mohawks, there lately is come to us above twenty old and young of the Oneidas (another of the Six Nations), from Onohquaga, a place about 200 miles southwest from Albany, on Susquehanna River near the head of it, on an invitation that was sent to 'em from hence the last summer. There is something wonderful in these Onohquaga Indians. Of late years, through some remarkable influence on their minds, they have had a strange turn of mind; several of them that have been notorious drunkards have reformed, and they have generally left their former inclination to war and bloodshed, and turned their minds to religion, and have been seeking after instruction. And those of them that are come hither show the best disposition of any of our Indians. They, above all others, [are] sober and serious and show a thirst after knowledge and delight much in instruction. They are well pleased with what they find here, and the chief of 'em, who is a very serious man, intends to go home in the spring, and invite others of his people hither, and thinks it probable that he shall bring many with him.

And we begin now to get into more happy circumstances as to the method and means of their instruction than heretofore. Things have been in no small degree of confusion, for want of a proper person to be their schoolmaster. We have been some time in quest of a proper person for this business. At length one is obtained, who I hope is well qualified for it. He's one Mr. Gideon Hawley, a young gentleman of liberal education, of about twenty-four years of age, who is now here, and has set up a regular school here for the instruction of the Iroquois, greatly to the satisfaction of the Indians. He appears to be a person of good abilities, remarkable piety, prudence and steadiness of temper, of good reputation, of a happy talent in teaching, and of a good spirit of government, is one that has long had an inclination to the business of instructing Indians, and has an proclivity for it. He has a school of about thirty-six. He applies himself with great zeal and diligence to teach the children to read and write, to instruct 'em in the English language and in the principles of religion, to regulate their manners, and himself to learn the Iroquois tongue, and to teach a couple of English boys, who are put into the school by the Government to fit 'em for serviceableness to the Indians in due time.

There is already a happy alteration apparent amongst these Indians since he came, though he has been here but about three weeks.[3] And he has got a considerable interest in the Indians' affection. And their chiefs have diligently applied themselves to assist him, and strengthen his hands in governing their children, and bringing them to good order. Some of the chiefs of the Mohawks have been here of late, who manifested great satisfaction and will doubtless carry home a good report of what they have seen.

Another thing that appears very favorable to our design, and that is the happy union that appears between these Iroquois and the Stockbridge Indians, the latter making the other welcome, and doing all that they can to encourage them. They had a meeting the week before last. So that now, if the English don't fail of their duty, and if private views and designs, and some unhappy misunderstandings which subsist between some of the chief English inhabitants of Stockbridge (which is the greatest calamity that attends the affair), I say if these things don't prevent, there is a most hopeful prospect of much good being done to these interests, and also much being done for the British interest in America. If things go on under a wise conduct, 'tis to be hoped, that instead of one male school and one female, there may after some [time] be several schools for each sex, and means found for giving some of the children of best genius (for there are some very forward geniuses among 'em) a superior education, to fit them to be instructors, schoolmasters, or missionaries to their own people. And here might be erected in time a kind of academy for this end. And if this should take effect, and I see not at present [why] it may not, it will probably be found necessary with these people to go out [of] the usual methods of a scholastic and academical education, and particularly not to begin with teaching the boys the learned languages, unless it be some that have a peculiar genius for learning of languages, but to begin with more entertaining and rational studies, which will better

---

3. The draft has a dash, often made by JE to indicate text to be supplied later. The "three weeks" in the Paice copy is amply corroborated by other sources (SIB, *12*, 393).

suit the genius of these people, instructing them something in geography and history, and then perhaps to proceed to something of the easier parts of the mathematics, the first rudiments of astronomy, and after that, something of grammar and logic, etc., natural philosophy, then in the study of divinity. But no particular method can now be fixed. This must be left to be found, by the united help of discretion and experience, in such as have the care of the business. Doubtless more happy methods might be found for the instructing both the girls and boys than are commonly gone into among the English. And I should think it is no matter how soon that a couple of good terrestrial globes, and good maps of places mentioned in Scriptures, were procured for their use. If such things as these should go forward (as I know nothing why they mayn't, if we don't hinder by our own negligence or folly and private designs), this probably would have a powerful influence to draw the nations of Indians to us and engage them in our interest. This would by degrees open the eyes of the nations and convince them that greater benefits were to be received from us than [from] the French. Possibly it may be thought I am in too much haste, too forward in my projections, and that it is time enough to talk of an academy, etc., a many years hence. But certainly, if we consider how active the French are, and what amazing progress they have made of late, and are daily making, it may be sufficient to convince us that we had need not to be dilatory; not that I suppose the state of things is already ripe for the putting all these things in execution. Things are not sufficiently settled and certain with respect to the Iroquois. But, if things remain with their present good appearance one twelvemonth longer, I should think it high time to begin to lay new foundations for a more enlarged design.[4] Some of the boys and young men among the Iroquois have made pretty swift progress in learning the English tongue, and 'tis to be hoped Mr. Hawley will be able in time to get a good acquaintance with their language. He is disposed, as soon as he has any considerable knowledge of it, to go up into their country, taking some of the best of the Indians with him, to assist him to persuade the people there to bring their children hither for instruction, Abraham Conaughstansey has notified himself willing to go with

---

4. The passage beginning with "too forward in my projections" and ending here is not in the draft, but is supplied by the Paice copy. It may have been prepared by JE on a separate piece of paper but, in any case, as with other Paice "additions," was most likely in the fair copy. The draft has symbols at different points, unrelated to copy on the three broadsides, which could indicate other notes.

him,[5] which it is to be hoped will be of happy effect. I don't suppose that instructing the Indians is all that we should do to secure 'em in our interest. With them, undoubtedly, many other things might be done, which joined with this might serve greatly to forward the design. Besides the kindness bestowed on their children, in boarding and clothing them at school, kindness may be shown to those parents that bring their children, and presents may sometimes be made to those of their chiefs that assist in the affair. And still forts might be built by the government, in some important places not yet possessed by the French, but which, if we neglect 'em much longer, we may expect they will not be neglected by them. If our old obstinate negligence be continued much longer, we may expect the French will come closer and closer upon us with their fortifications; our supineness will not only embolden them but, as it were, tempt and draw them on.[6] Trading houses might be erected, whence they might be supplied with goods at a cheap rate, much cheaper than the French can afford them; and care might be taken that they should be dealt with, with an inviolable, honest fairness, which would have a mighty influence upon 'em. And no rum should be sold to 'em.[7]

Dear Sir, before the full copies of your three letters to Sir William were sent to me by some of the Commissioners in Boston, the Honorable Andrew Oliver, Esq., their secretary and treasurer, was pleased to send me an extract of the first of those letters, and to propose that I should send my thoughts concerning a female school to Sir William. Accordingly I did so, which may receive improvement and perhaps be corrected by your thoughts in one of the papers sent with your letters. I think that one school of girls should not consist of more than fifteen or twenty. Only I humbly conceive it is necessary, as to the children of the Iroquois at least, whose parents have no lands or tenements in this place, that they should be boarded and lodged in an house built for that purpose[8] at the expense of the charitable funds; which give the mistress much greater advantage to have influence upon them, to form their minds, change their manners, and bring them to a civil, orderly and Christian way of living.

5. This phrase, beginning with "Abraham Conaughstansey" and ending here, is in the Paice copy, not the draft.

6. The part of this sentence beginning with "our supineness" and ending here is in the Paice copy, not the draft.

7. This sentence is in the Paice copy, not the draft.

8. The phrase "in an house built for that purpose" is in the Paice copy, not the draft.

I agree with you, Sir, that one mistress, with a female assistant, who shall be subject to her, will be sufficient for one school. But then there will be need that the mistress be generally present in the school, and devote herself to the business of teaching, which, in order to be done with good effect with respect to those that are taken out of such wildness and barbarity, will require the constant application of a woman of superior talents. And therefore I humbly differ from you in supposing that missionaries' wives should be preferred for this business, it being ordinarily impossible that women, that are married and have the care of families of their own, should be sufficiently devoted to this business.

But I fear I have quite tired your patience. I ask pardon for troubling you with so tedious a letter. I have been drawn on to so great a length by the great importance of the subject, and the many important things pertaining to it which present themselves to the view of one in my situation, together with the view of your pious and charitable concern about it, though [you are] at so great a distance, and have so [much] less to excite and oblige your concern than[9] he, who is, Sir, with respect and gratitude,

Your most humble servant,
Jonathan Edwards.

142. TO COL. TIMOTHY DWIGHT

The sale of Edwards' house in Northampton relieved him of the fiscal strain of the previous two years. In the wake of the controversial council of May 1751, Edwards exhorts Dwight to remain steadfast in his principles; they will, he is confident, prevail with the townspeople. Edwards is preparing *Misrepresentations Corrected* and anticipates publication in the summer.

(Trask Library, ALS, one quarto leaf.)

*   *   *

9. The Paice copy ceases to follow the draft from this point. In the Paice copy, the words immediately following are, "we that are on the spot." Then JE's draft contains an alternate ending (written below his signature), which reads: "Hoping that some good improvement may be made of the particular informations I have given, being one so able and willing, which I leave to your wisdom. Hoping for your candid acceptance of what I have written, with an honest intention, I am, Sir." The passage beginning "being one so able" and ending with "Hoping" is excluded, as are the last seven words. In place of the latter, he simply substituted, "I remain, Sir." The traditional closing, "Your most humble servant," is the same in both versions.

Stockbridge, February 27, 1751/2

Dear Sir,

I thank you for your letter, for your care of us respecting the sale of my homestead, and in sending me those ten dollars. I send you such a note for it as you desire. Please to return my hearty thanks to Deac. John Smith, for the dollar he sent me, when you have opportunity. I shall need a great deal more joinery work done this spring or summer; but am as yet uncertain when I shall have stuff prepared. If John Pomeroy or some other good and pretty quick workman could be engaged, I should be glad.

Mr. [William] Hobby's copy of the Remonstrance was through mistake sent to me, and I have sent it to you by Capt. [Jonathan] Sheldon. You desire me to give a few hints from the minutes I took of the objections justly arising from the tenor of the Remonstrance,[1] but seem to have forgotten that I drew up those minutes and gave 'em to you when at Northampton last. I beseech you not to patch up a mock reconciliation with the church, accepting of something from them that is nothing but a mere sham. Nothing ought to be accepted but proper Christian satisfaction made to you and me, and made as public as the offense committed. And I desire you never would consent to the settlement of a minister that is of principles contrary to yours; you thereby will bring yourselves into a great shame. I can't believe that Mr. [Solomon] Stoddard's principles will ever have a quiet establishment again at Northampton, or that people will ever prosper again in that way; but 'tis probable that the small company that adhered to me, if they hold their own, will prosper and prevail. I believe there will be two societies there. Yours may be the smallest at first, but if you are steadfast, and act prudently, I believe at last they will be the biggest and will get the meetinghouse. I have been extremely hindered of late; otherwise should have near finished the first draft of my answer to Mr. [Solomon] Williams. However, I hope to get it into the press this summer. I am, Sir,

Your affectionate and obliged brother and servant,
Jonathan Edwards.

1. See JE's "Notes on the Remonstrance of a Committee of the Northampton Church against the Proceedings of the Council, May 1751" (Firestone Library), which was apparently used to draft "Vindication from the Church's Accusations" (Beinecke Library).

143. TO JASPER MAUDUIT

Edwards adamantly opposed the appointment of Abigail Sergeant as head of a school for Indian girls. The Williams family was equally determined to install her. Sergeant's cousin Col. Elisha Williams was able, while in London, to secure her appointment to the post and to have himself and her father designated commissioners for the mission.

This letter is the only one of record from Edwards to Mauduit, Treasurer of the New England Company in London. Edwards furnishes a review of the history of the Indian mission. He conspicuously does not name Ephraim Williams, Joseph Dwight, or Abigail Sergeant or reveal his disapproval of her. The report reinforced the good opinion of the Boston Commissioners for Edwards, and they continued to stand by him. The Londoners never changed their position, however, but were unable to enforce it. In a noncommittal response, Mauduit hoped that Edwards would receive "wisdom for a right behavior in the difficult situation."

(Trask Library, AL draft, on four envelope covers: three folio leaves, each addressed on verso to Edwards at Stockbridge, and one quarto leaf, addressed on verso to Mrs. Sarah Edwards at the house of Mr. Edmund Quincy in Boston; Dwight ms. transcript, eight quarto leaves. See also Alderman Library, New England Company Letterbook, Mauduit letters for July 10, 1751, Apr. 19, 1753, Mar. 7, 1754, and Mar. 30, 1754, pp. 267–68, 274, 282, 284.)

* * *

Stockbridge, March 10, 1751/2[1]

Sir,

It has been proposed to me by some of the honorable Commissioners of Indian Affairs in Boston to write to you, giving you a particular account of the state of things relating to the instruction of the Indians in this place, and the prospects that attend that affair, as what may have a tendency to promote the design. I readily fall in with a proposal, by which I esteem myself much honored by those that made it; and because I think [it is] what is fit and reasonable, and what would tend to your satisfaction, to have a just and full account of the state of things relating to affairs of this place (which is the principal affair your

1. Though the date written at the close of the draft is Mar. 4, 1752, JE sent the letter on Mar. 10, as is indicated by his insertion of the later date at the head of the letter, just below the salutation.

Jasper Mauduit, by
Samuel Webster, 1758,
Dr. Williams' Library,
London

honorable Commissioners have made their care), by some person that
lives on the spot and so may be supposed to be under the best advantage to see the state of affairs, with all its attending circumstances. And
this is the more requisite at this time, as there is a probability of the
need of a considerable increase of supplies for the support of this
affair. And since our dependence for supplies is so much on the charitable fund under your care, the nature of the case, and justice to you,
who are so greatly concerned, require that you have as just and full
idea of the affair as can be given you by such as have opportunity for
the most full acquaintance with it, both with regard to those circumstances that are prosperous and appear with an hopeful and promising [aspect] and also the difficulties and dark clouds that attend. I am
persuaded from long observation that 'tis a common fault of accounts
that are sent home to England by missionaries, to be laid before those
who employ 'em or support 'em, that in their accounts they take little
notice of anything else but things that pertain to the prosperity and
success of the affair they are employed in, omitting those things that
are of a contrary nature, so that those that are informed by 'em never

have any just notion of the true state of their affairs in America. This has been notoriously the case with regard to the accounts sent home from time to time by the missionaries of the Society for the Propagating the Gospel in Foreign Parts.[2]

There are many things that appear with a hopeful and promising aspect on our affairs. With regard to the Housatonic or Stockbridge Indians, who are a part of the tribe of the River Indians (as they are called because they heretofore have chiefly lived near Hudson's River on each side of the river): when Mr. [John] Sergeant first came hither there were but about fifty of them young and old, but they have been gradually increasing by others of the tribe coming in to settle here for the sake of instruction; so that now there are about 250, so that this town may now be looked upon as the headquarters of the nation of the River Indians, there being many more here than are together in any other place. And 'tis not unlikely that in time the most of that nation may be got together here and brought to submit to instruction. And these Indians have now entirely got over all their jealousies and suspicions of some ill design of the English upon them, in persuading them to submit to instruction, and particularly that the English intended to make slaves of them and their children. They are much more civilized than formerly and of late there seems to be an increasing seriousness among them. There has [been] from the beginning a school maintained for the instruction of their children under the care of Mr. Timothy Woodbridge, a man of very good abilities, and a gentleman of a manly, honest, and generous disposition; and by an agreeable conduct has established himself very much in the affections and confidence of the Indians. But his school, till of late, has not been in so happy circumstances as might be desired; which has been very much owing to great difficulties he has been under, being much straitened in his circumstances and under many discouragements by reason of some peculiar, unhappy circumstances in the state of things amongst some of the English inhabitants of Stockbridge. But of late his school is brought into much better circumstances. He has now the encouragement of a better support and seems to be much animated and engaged in his business. He has a large school, and an Indian for his usher, whose name is John Wauwaumpequunnaunt, who is also my interpreter, an extraordinary man on some accounts; understands English

2. These were missionaries of the Church of England under the supervision of the Bishop of London. Deprecation of their efforts, and of the Anglican church in general, was almost a ritual among colonial Dissenters.

well, [is] a good reader and writer and is an excellent interpreter. And perhaps there was never an Indian educated in America that exceeded him in knowledge, in divinity, [and] understanding of the Scriptures. He heretofore had not been so strictly temperate as he ought to have been, but there seems now to be an alteration in him in this passion and he is much more careful. The things of religion seem to lie with much weight on his mind, and he seems to be very diligent and faithful in his business.

As to the Iroquois or Indians of the Six Nations (as we call them), the greater part of which (whom we have had concern of late), though many of them have lately been much alienated from the English and have been drawn over to the French interest—particularly most of the Senecas and Cayugas, some of the Oneidas and all the Onondagas— yet there has of late years appeared in many of the rest, as among the Conneenchees or Proper Mohawks, in some of the Tuscaroras, a growing inclination to religion and desire of knowledge and instruction. The nearest of these nations, namely, the Conneenchees, when at home in their own country, are about eighty miles from us, Stockbridge being about forty miles southeast from Albany, and their nearest town about forty miles on the other side of Albany.

Mr. Sergeant, after he had been settled here some years, projected another school for the effectual cultivation of the minds and change of the manners of the Indians. His design was that a house should be built in which the children [should] be boarded and maintained at the expense of the English and be constantly day and night under the instruction of their master and governors; and that they should not only be instructed in reading, writing, the principles of religion, and the English [language], but be brought up to work; and that their time should be divided between study and work, under different masters. But he met with many difficulties which clogged his design, and particularly was very much hindered by the late war, so that he lived [not] to see his design put in execution. Indeed, something was done at the expense of the Reverend Mr. Isaac Hollis. He first took a number of boys under his own immediate care and boarded and clothed and instructed 'em himself at Mr. Hollis' cost. And some of those afterwards were sent abroad and put to English families, there to be instructed and maintained at Mr. Hollis' expense. After that, Mr. Sergeant procured Capt. Martin Kellogg for the present exigency till a house could be built, the foundation of a boarding school could be properly laid, and a proper person (a man of learning) could be obtained to be the schoolmaster. Captain Kellogg, though a man of pretty good understanding for one that was being an illiterate man, and a man in years; but the more easily obtained, being lame and not so well able on this account to follow other business that required more action; Captain Kellogg was a little while here before the beginning of the war, and when the war broke out, he took a number of the Stockbridge boys with him to Newington, about seventy miles from hence, who still were maintained at Mr. Hollis' cost.

When the war ended, Mr. Sergeant applied himself anew to the prosecution of his design of a boarding school, and went about building a house which he left but in its beginnings. He also wrote letters to the Mohawks, inviting them to bring their children hither to be instructed in his intended school. But he did not live to see anything brought to effect. His boys were left in Captain Kellogg's hands; and after Mr. Sergeant's death, Captain Kellogg wrote to the Mohawks, showing Mr. Sergeant's letters that he wrote in his lifetime; and the year before last a number of the Mohawks came down, about twenty old and young, which was a little before I came to this place. It had then [been] long since anything had been heard from Mr. Hollis and many supposed he was probably dead. And therefore Captain Kellogg dismissed his boys that he had before taken care of at Mr. Hollis' cost and applied himself wholly to the care of the Mohawks, who were soon taken notice of by the government and taken under their care; and Captain Kellogg went on to instruct 'em at the government's expense, but not in so happy a manner as was to be desired. He never set up any school, but very much left the children to their liberty to come to him to read their books when they pleased. He never could be persuaded to go out of this way in a more regular method of teaching. The children were very much neglected as to instruction in civility and good manners, and thus things continued in great confusion. Captain Kellogg's inactivity was not so much to be wondered at, considering his lameness and age, he being about sixty-five years old and the business new to him.

However, there was a very extraordinary disposition appeared in the Mohawk children to learn. They, many of them, appeared greatly to delight in it and their late coming so far for instruction and appearing so desirous of [it,] seemed much to engage the Captain, so that he the [year] before last took much pains with them in his way. But the Mohawks much disliked his irregular way. They were desirous of a regular school. Nevertheless, the number of the Mohawks which came down hither continued to increase the winter, so that through the greater part of the winter there were about ninety, old and young.

The last summer, Mr. Hollis having been informed of the Mohawks coming hither, a letter was received from him by Captain Kellogg, directing him to increase the number of boys that were to be instructed and maintained to twenty-four, Mr. Hollis it seems not knowing but that there was then a boarding school under Captain Kellogg maintained at his cost.

In June last, an interview was appointed between Commissioners from the several English governments and the Six Nations at Albany. When the General Assembly of the Massachusetts chose their Commissioners for this conference, they gave them instructions to visit Stockbridge, to confer with the Mohawks here concerning their settlement in New England and putting their children under the instruction of the English. Accordingly, some of their chiefs were discoursed with at Albany by the Commissioners of the Massachusetts; and it was moved to 'em that they should, after the treaty there, come down hither and give them their return opportunity to see 'em and treat with them here at Stockbridge about this affair. They objected that it would be inconvenient for some reasons to come immediately on this business and desired it might be deferred for forty days. And at the forty days end, there came down almost all the chiefs of their nations and met the Committee of the government here, and manifested an uncommonly good disposition with respect to the affair proposed for 'em, and promised to promote it to their utmost; but objected the confused state that they observed things were in, that no regular school was set up and no more thorough means taken for the well educating their children. But [they] were encouraged by the Committee, that they would endeavor to obtain an alteration in that respect. None of the Committee thought that Captain Kellogg would be sufficient for the regular education which the Mohawks insisted on and therefore determined that another master, a man of learning, must be sought for. However, Captain Kellogg, having received the forementioned letter from Mr. Hollis, proceeded to take up a number of boys, to be taught and maintained at his charge; but still went on with them in his former manner.

The General Assembly of the province and your Commissioners in Boston were informed of what had passed at this treaty with the Mohawk chiefs at Stockbridge. You have doubtless heard how the Assembly have exerted themselves and what a forward disposition they have manifested to do what they can to promote the design of their instruction. The Commissioners also on this occasion endeavored to find a proper person for a schoolmaster and treated with a young gentleman [Eli Forbush] of good reputation for his learning and piety to this end. And his coming was much expected and long waited for, but things so happened that he finally failed. And things continuing long in their former neglected and confused state, the Indians, many of them, were much discouraged. Some of them took their children away, giving this reason for it. And the affair of the Mohawks seemed to be under a dark cloud and in a declining state, and so continued through [a] great part of the last winter.

But yet in the midst of this darkness, some new things appeared of a very hopeful aspect, with respect to the design of promoting knowledge and religion among the Iroquois or Six Nations. There had been here the last summer a man whose name was Jonah [Tonaughquunnaugus] from Onohquaga, a town of the Oneidas situated on Susquehanna River near the head of the river about 200 miles southwest from Albany. He was one of the principal inhabitants of the town, who, having heard of the things which were doing here for the instruction of the Indians, came to visit this place and make report to his people. I sent a letter by him to the inhabitants of Onohquaga, inviting them to come and bring their children hither for instruction; in consequence of which, there came twenty-one of them—men, women, and children—through so long and tedious a journey, in the very depths of a most severe winter, to live here for the sake of instruction. Something very remarkable has of late years appeared among those Onohquagas, as appears from information we have from others of the Iroquois, particularly Abraham Conaughstansey, the Mohawk who in his honesty and simplicity prefers them to his own tribe. Many among them that used to be notorious drunkards and blood-thirsty warriors have of late strangely had their dispositions and manners altered through some wonderful influences in their minds. They seem to be averse to war and do the utmost to dissuade others of the Iroquois that go to war with the Southern Nations, and have entirely forsaken their drunkenness and have a religion and thirst after instruction. These Onohquagas came hither in the latter part of December.

Soon after this, something happened of a dark aspect. Hendrick, the chief speaker of the Mohawks, was coming down with some others of the chiefs of the Mohawks with him, and three of the sachems of the Oneidas and a number of children both of the Mohawks and Oneidas to be instructed here, and came as far as Kinderhook, a place about twenty miles from here; and being there met by some of the Mohawks that were here, particularly by one of the chief men here who is not so well disposed, who gave 'em such an account of the state of things here that Hendrick and all the Oneidas that were coming with him and most of the children returned back again in great disgust. However, Abraham Conaughstansey, who has more solidity and prudence than most of them, came forward with one or two more of the chiefs of the Mohawks and about ten in all.

Soon after they arrived, the great defect which had been so discouraging to the Mohawks was supplied: a schoolmaster was obtained, one Mr. Gideon Hawley, a young gentleman of liberal education, twenty-four years of age, who appears to be well-qualified for the business. He came hither and set up a regular school, greatly to the joy of the Iroquois. I never saw so great marks of satisfaction in them on any occasion. Mr. Hawley has a school of about thirty-six children and youth, which indeed is too great for him, considering the manifold business he has to do. For besides his teaching his children to read and write, and teaching the English tongue, the principles of religion and good manners, and teaching a couple of English boys, who are put into the school by the government to learn the Iroquois tongue and other things necessary to fit 'em to be serviceable to Indians, as missionaries or schoolmasters in due time; he himself is laboring to learn the Indian tongue. There is already a happy alteration among the Indians since he came. He has gained a considerable interest in their affections; and their chiefs have diligently applied themselves to assist him and strengthen his hands in governing the children and bringing them to good order.

Another thing appears very favorable to our design, viz. the happy union that there subsists between these Iroquois and the Stockbridge Indians, the latter having lately of their own accord had a meeting to see what they could do on their part to encourage the Iroquois in coming hither for instruction. I have given a particular account in a letter to Mr. Joseph Paice of London, which you will probably have opportunity to see. The Onohquaga Indians are especially well-pleased in what they find here and are well-satisfied in their coming, and intend to invite the rest of their brethren that they left at Onohquaga to follow them. Jonah, who is a very serious man, is soon going to Onohquaga on that business and thinks he shall bring many with him.

Mr. Hawley intends, sometime in the approaching summer, to go up into the country of the Iroquois and take with him some of the best of the Indians to endeavor to persuade 'em to bring their children hither to be instructed. Abraham Conaughstansey encourages him in the design and offers his assistance. This Abraham is indeed an extraordinary man for his uprightness, prudence, and Christian zeal and self-denial. Things now in many respects seem to be in prosperous circumstances. The children in each school, both of the Stockbridge Indians and Iroquois, are making sensible advances in their learning; and increase in their knowledge of the principles of religion and the English tongue; and are more and more inured to order and good manners. These things, together with the forward disposition that appears in the government to promote their design, and God's so wonderfully opening the hearts of some in England to contribute so liberally to it, and bringing so many there of such ability to exert themselves for our help, give us reason to hope that God has a design of doing some great thing for these unhappy people.

The difficulties and clouds of darkness that attend this affair are of two sorts: those that are from without or those [that] arise from within. The former are either from the French, such as the late, mighty, and successful endeavors of that nation to alienate the Indians from the British interest and to attach them to themselves, of which I have written largely to Mr. Paice; or from the Dutch in the neighboring province of New York that lies next to the Iroquois and are the people that, of all the British subjects, have ever had chiefly to do with those people and are fond of keeping them to themselves: for the Dutch in Albany subsist almost wholly by the profits of their trade with those Indians. They are, therefore, very jealous of the English in New England and utterly averse to their having anything to do with them. Yea, many seem to be very averse to their changing their manners from their present wildness and intemperance to a sober and civil way of living, probably fearing that this would make the Indians more careful of their interest in trading; and also because it would be an occasion of their gradually leaving off their hunting and living by husbandry, which would deprive them of the benefit of their trade in skins and furs. On these accounts the Dutch exceedingly oppose their coming here, so that those that come, as they are obliged to come through the Dutch settlements, are obliged to rise through great opposition they must meet from 'em.

As to difficulties that arise from within, they are also of two sorts.

There are some that arise from among the Indians with whom we have to do. These are of different minds. Some of the tribe of the Mohawks are great enemies to the design here on foot and oppose and laugh at those that come hither. And of those that come, all are not alike disposed. 'Tis manifest that some come only for the sake of a free maintenance and the presents the English bestow upon them. This seems to be the case with some of the chief men, which causes a good deal of difficulty.

But worse than these are difficulties that arise from among the English, particularly a very great and open misunderstanding and discord that has for several years past subsisted between some of the chief of the English inhabitants of Stockbridge. The opposition of one side to the other has proceeded a very great length indeed and has been made very public all over New England, and this contention has very great and extensive influence. The two contending parties are very considerable men, men of influence. One of them is a man of good understanding, of a very considerable estate and of great activity, and has many in New England that are related to him. They are men of figure and influence, and some of 'em have great influence in our affairs. The other is a man of superior abilities and has great interest in the Stockbridge Indians, and he has perhaps greater influence upon them than all other Englishmen put together. They [the Indians] have been mightily engaged on his side in this controversy and have the deepest prejudice against the other men, so that of late they have several times talked of breaking up and leaving the town because of him. And it seems to be a growing [thing]. The latter also has on his side most of the English inhabitants in the town.

The breach between those contending parties is such that there appears no hope of its being healed. Great attempts have been made to heal it and there has been a very formal pacification, but it soon appeared to be but a palliative cure. It is again broken out to a great degree.

This misunderstanding does greatly in many respects affect the affair of the instruction of the Indians in this place, and [is] the darkest cloud, the most pernicious thing that attends it, the chief hindrance of success, and what endangers the affair more than anything, and sometimes seems to threaten the subversion of it. And, therefore, I thought it was not just to conceal it from you, who have a right to know the true state of our affairs, though by informing you we may expose our own shame. This contention first began about the management of the great affair of the instruction of the Indians, which was the design of the settlement of the town. And as such misunderstandings frequently arise from private views, so such are the infirmities of mankind that, by long and continued contention about public affairs, we are apt to lose sight of the public interest and to be wholly engaged in the pursuit of our private designs.

This contention does particularly affect the affair of a female school and brings [it] under a great deal of difficulty. And the unhappy influence of it in the affairs of the male boarding school appears more and more dark, which causes, in the continuance and progress and series of things that belong to it, that [contention] more naturally and directly affects this affair. I am more afraid of the unhappy influence of this affair than of all the French and Dutch can do.

'Tis not unlikely that, by reason of the influence of this contention, you may have sent to you different and inconsistent accounts of the state of things here. But I would humbly say, that I conceive the way of your greatest security from being imposed upon, will be to rely much on your Commissioners in Boston who are not much in the way of being biased [or] corrupted by the influence of our shameful contentions.

I'll make bold to trouble [you] with a brief extract of a letter I sent the last summer to [the] Treasurer of the Commissioners in Boston and another to the Speaker of the House of Representatives, in both [of] which I had these words:

> What renders it more necessary that things here should be under the immediate care of trustees here is the misunderstanding and jealousy here subsisting between some of the chief of the present English inhabitants of the town, which is one of our greatest calamities. Things on this account do much more need constant inspection and, therefore, the gentlemen entrusted ought to be such as are perfectly impartial, no way interested in or related to those contending parties.

It must be left to the honorable Society in London to make what further inquiry, into the true state of things with regard to this contention, they think proper. Perhaps when they have inquired so as to satisfy themselves, they may think it most safe, to leave the nomination of all parties in New England to be improved and concerned in our affairs in any respect, to the Commissioners in Boston themselves, who have more knowledge of the state of this difference and its influence in our affairs than is to be expected in those that are on the other side of the ocean.

'Tis the view I have in my situation of the importance of the grand affair I am here engaged in, and a deep concern for its interest, that have obliged me to give this information, trusting to your candor to put a favorable construction on my so doing and to forgive me wherein you may think I have done amiss. I trust you are not unwilling to know the true state of this principal affair that is under your care, and hope you will consider that 'tis impossible you should know it, but by information either directly or indirectly from hence.

If our misunderstandings and private designs don't prevent, 'tis probable we still should soon need to have a great number of persons employed in the instruction of the Indians, and there will be a necessity of a great increase of our expenses and so of an answerable increase of our supplies. And it appears very evident that if discretion be used in laying out what is bestowed in this affair, it will be money bestowed to the greatest and most excellent purpose. Leaving you, Sir, to make what use of the information I have given in this letter which shall be most agreeable to your wisdom, I am, Sir,

Your most humble servant,
Jonathan Edwards.

144. TO SPEAKER THOMAS HUBBARD

Throughout 1752 and 1753, Edwards desperately tried to hold his position at Stockbridge. Having been through one dismissal procedure, he was not anxious to experience another. To protect himself, he here writes at length to leaders in government (Hubbard, Willard) and the mission board (Mauduit, Oliver), as well as to the foremost underwriter (Hollis). Portions of these defenses are often repeated in letters to other recipients. In one of the manuscript pages for this communication, Edwards wrote Hubbard's name at the top and Hollis' name at the bottom of the same page.

(AL draft, the two parts of which are found in different locations: (1) Trask Library, one irregular folio leaf, and one quarto leaf on a letter of Samuel Hopkins to Edwards, Mar. 11, 1752; and (2) Beinecke Library, one irregular folio leaf and one irregular quarto leaf. Partial Dwight ms. transcript also at Trask Library, four quarto leaves, with variations from the original wording.)

* * *

[Stockbridge,] March 30, 1752

Sir,

I would pray you not to let any know anything of this letter till you have read it through.[1]

The present circumstances of the great affair of the instruction of the Indians here seem to require my giving you a particular account of our state. In order to you having a just understanding of things, 'tis necessary that I should give you some history of things which perhaps you may not have been perfectly acquainted with.

Mr. [John] Sergeant in his lifetime exerted himself to promote the putting in execution his prized plan of a boarding school. He used many endeavors to find a proper master, a man of learning, for he always supposed such an one would be necessary. But meeting with disappointments and the war coming on, the affair lay dormant for several years. But before the end of the war Mr. Isaac Hollis urged that the matter should be no longer deferred, having made considerable remittances to Dr. [Benjamin] Colman, urged that his money should not be unimproved. Whereupon Mr. Sergeant, in the year 1748, agreed with Capt. Martin Kellogg of Newington, near Wethersfield in Connecticut, a good friend of Col. Elisha Williams, for the present exigency.

Captain Kellogg, being a man in years above sixty-two and being lame and not well able to follow other business, was the more easily obtained; and so twelve boys were carried down from here to Newington to be taken care of by Captain Kellogg at Mr. Hollis' charge, where they continued a year. In the spring of the year 1749, the business being concluded, Captain Kellogg brought his boys hither.

When Mr. Sergeant came to reckon with Captain Kellogg as agent for Mr. Hollis, he was extremely uneasy at some things in his conduct and accounts, and expressed a resolution to set things on some other foot, that more effectual care might be taken that Mr. Hollis should have justice done him in the expense of his money. But that summer, on July 27, Mr. Sergeant died before he had executed his design, and left the boys in Captain Kellogg's hands in the house intended for the boarding school, but in its first beginning and just sufficient to shelter them from the weather, where a kind of boarding school was kept, but in a very broken, confused manner, and nothing was taught the boys

1. JE drew a vertical line through this sentence, which often indicates a deletion. In this case, he may have concluded that the statement was not necessary, or that it was superseded by the final paragraph of the letter.

more than they might have been taught in a much better manner in the regular school that is maintained by the Commissioners under the care of Mr. [Timothy] Woodbridge, and no benefits received by them but what they would have had without any of that extraordinary [effort]. So that 'tis beyond dispute that Mr. Hollis' money was entirely thrown away.

The winter following began that great misunderstanding between Col. [Ephraim] Williams[2] and Captain Kellogg on one side and Mr. Woodbridge on the other, which first began concerning Captain Kellogg and his manner of spending Mr. Hollis' money. The parents of Captain Kellogg's boys and the Indians of the town in general were extremely uneasy at Captain Kellogg's conduct and have often loudly complained in my hearing of Captain Kellogg's ill treatment of their children, his neglecting them as to their board, clothing, and instruction, and why he little cares that their children should be kept clean and orderly. And by this means, the Indians of the town in general have been imbibed a deep prejudice against Captain Kellogg.

In that confused state things continued till the fall of the year 1750. And it then having been a considerable time since Captain Kellogg heard anything from Mr. Hollis, Captain Kellogg, supposing that he was dead, and that no further supplies were to be expected from him, dismissed all his boys. And some of the Mohawks being lately come, he applied himself wholly to the care of them, expecting his pay from the government.

In this state things were when I first came hither, which was in the beginning of January 1750/1. When the people here were seeking after me, Colonel Williams and Captain Kellogg and Madam [Abigail] Sergeant showed themselves extremely averse, expressed themselves with much engagedness and exerted themselves to their utmost to hinder it. After I had been here a month or two, there appeared a very universal earnest desire among the Indians that I should be their minister, and among almost all of the English people; and Colonel Williams and Madam Sergeant seemed to fall in also. But afterwards, Colonel Williams said things to some persons that manifested great uneasiness at the prospect of my settling after my call. Whether it was through some sudden change of mind, I will not determine. Madam Sergeant also from time to time has uttered things to one and another that manifested that she was far from being well-pleased, and Captain

2. This and all subsequent references in this letter to Colonel Williams are to Col. Ephraim Williams of Stockbridge.

Kellogg has also manifested the utmost aversion to my settled ministry in this place.

Captain Kellogg at first seemed much animated by the Mohawks' coming and took a great deal of pains with them to teach 'em to read, but his method was unhappy. He set up no school but left the children to themselves, to come and read and go when they pleased. He never could be persuaded to go out of this way into a more regular method of teaching, though much pains has been taken with him to persuade him, and seemed by degrees to grow more and more negligent as the influence of the newness of the Mohawk affair diminished. The children under his care have all along been most woefully neglected as to instruction in writing, in good manners, or any manner of care of their cleanliness and decency in their manner of living, which according to the character Captain Kellogg generally has, as an ill husband in his own business.[3] The Mohawks have been very uneasy at this neglected and confused state of things relating to the instruction of their children and have grown more and more so, being desirous of a regular school and some proper method to bring their children to an amendment of manners.

The last summer, Captain Kellogg received a letter from Mr. Hollis directing him to increase the number of boys maintained and instructed by him from twelve to twenty-four, seeming to suppose that Captain Kellogg had then twelve under his care at his cost.

In August last was that notable interview of the chiefs of the Mohawks and the Committee of the Assembly, which I gave you a particular account of in a former letter. The Indians then manifested themselves exceedingly well disposed to what we proposed relating to the instruction of their children, and promised to promote it to their utmost, not only among their own people but among other nations, yet objecting [to] the confused state they observed things to be in: their children much neglected, no regular school maintained, nor those measures taken for the instructing their children which they had observed the English looked upon necessary in teaching their own children; but were encouraged by the Committee of the province that they would endeavor that there should be an alteration in that respect; the Committee being all of one mind that Captain Kellogg was very unfit for the business he was in, and Brig. [Joseph] Dwight who, though not

3. Here JE inserted a cue mark and the words "see papers at the end." The papers referred to may well have been intended for inclusion at this point. Unfortunately, they have not been located.

one of the Committee at the time, yet was present in all negotiations, he then was much in speaking in my hearing of Captain Kellogg's unfitness, how it was necessary he should be removed, and high time he was gone, etc.

The Brigadier was at that time exceeding friendly to me, as indeed he had been my great friend for perhaps more than twenty years past, expressing an high opinion of me, far beyond what I could with any modesty expect, as though he esteemed me above all other ministers in New England, etc., and under my late difficulties at Northampton has often expressed great friendship.

The Commissioners in Boston, understanding the great need of a schoolmaster for the Mohawks, endeavored to find a proper person and treated with Mr. [Eli] Forbush of Westborough, for whom we long waited, but he finally failed.

Things continuing long in their former neglected, confused state, the Mohawks, many of them, were much discouraged. Some of them took their children away, giving this negligence as a reason of it, and the affair of the Mohawks seemed to be under a dark cloud through [a] great part of the last winter.

But yet in the midst of this darkness some new things appeared which seemed to be remarkable smiles of heaven on our design.

There have been here the last summer an Indian from Onohquaga on the Susquehanna River, near the head of it, about 200 miles south-west from Albany, whose name was Jonah Tonaughquunnaugus, who, hearing of things that were doing here, came to visit the place that he might make a report to his people. Letters were sent from here by him to the inhabitants of Onohquaga to invite [them] to come and bring their children hither for instruction; in consequence of which, twenty-one of them, young and old, came hither through so long and tedious a journey in the depths of a most severe winter, and arrived in the latter part of December.

Something very remarkable of late has appeared among these Onohquagas, who are some of the nation of the Oneidas: a strange turn or change of disposition and reformation, from the drunkenness and blood-thirstiness to virtue and religion and a thirst after instruction, of which Abraham [Conaughstansey], the Mohawk, gave me a particular account agreeing with the accounts we have from others. These Onohquagas are by far, the best disposed Indians we have.

In the beginning of February last, the great defect which had been so discouraging to the Mohawks was supplied. A schoolmaster was obtained, one Mr. Gideon Hawley, a gentlemen of liberal education, of about twenty-four years of age, who appears excellently qualified for the business, both as to abilities, and moral and religious endowments. He has set up a regular school greatly to the joy of Mohawks and Onohquagas. I never saw such appearances of satisfaction in 'em on any occasion. Their chiefs have much exerted themselves to assist him and strengthen his hands in governing their children and bringing them to order.

Another[4] thing that seems to show a remarkable hand of heaven in favor of our design is this. The last February, the Stockbridge Indians, entirely of their own accord, met together to consider whether they had done their duty in order to promote the Iroquois coming hither for instruction in Christianity, and what remained for 'em still to do; and in the issue of their consultation desired a conference with the Iroquois, and when [they] met with them they told 'em that they observed that the English had done a great deal that they might be instructed in religion, which made [them] to reflect on themselves as not having done their part; that as to themselves, they now for some time had had experience of the great benefit of the instructions of the English; that once they were in a state of great darkness, but now were brought into light, and knew that it was good, and therefore earnestly desired 'em to give heed to the instructions of the English, and not to listen to objections, particularly to give way to no suspicions of the English as though they intended to make slaves of them or their children; told 'em that they themselves at first were full of such suspicions, but now had been so long under the care of the English and found that they were wholly without grounds, and to encourage 'em offered 'em the use of some of their lands near the boarding school.

There now also began to appear a very great alteration in Brig. Dwight, a strange turn of mind and change of sentiments as to many things and a new and particularly an unaccountable alteration as to his friendship toward me, without ever anything being passed between us whereby he signified any dislike or uneasiness to me at anything in any conduct. He used great endeavors to alienate Mr. Hawley from me and to beget in him uneasiness and jealousy towards me. Discoursing with Mr. Hawley in Captain Kellogg's presence, he warns him not to have his dependence too much upon me; tells him that he might see cause hereafter to alter his opinion of some persons; and offers him his own

4. JE drew a vertical line through this paragraph.

friendship and assures him that he is much more able to support him and assist him than I, two to one; that he had authority to direct him and order how he should conduct himself in the school; and that I had no authority to intermeddle in his concerns. And since then, in discoursing with him a long time alone about me, he endeavored to persuade him that I intermeddled with that which I had no business with, in coming from time to time to instruct the Mohawks (though I was desired so to do by the express vote of the Commissioners, till some other person had learned the language and was fitted to preach to 'em in their own tongue), that I herein did him an injury and [insulted his person] and that he would have the less salary and that it might [impress them as][5] an affront to him. On Mr. Hawley's replying that he rejoiced in it and that he was glad of the advantage he had by hearing me preach that he might learn by it, the Brig. replied with an air of contempt. His words I don't remember, but it seemed to signify as though it was beneath him to learn of me in preaching. All this was before ever he had expressed to me the least dissatisfaction at any part of my conduct.

Another dark cloud that has lately risen is a late great increase of uneasiness in the Indians here with Colonel Williams. They have long had a rooted, universal prejudice against him, but it has lately risen to a great height by some things that have happened, so that they have talked of breaking up and leaving this town and seeking habitation elsewhere because of him.

Another thing that threatens even the total subversion of the affair of the Mohawks and the boarding school is this: neither Captain Kellogg nor Colonel Dwight were here when Mr. Hawley first set up his school among the Mohawk (I introduced him, by order from the Commissioners). But they both came soon after. When he came, it appeared that Captain Kellogg was resolved not to grant his station; and though it was very apparent that the Indians would insist on Mr. Hawley's being the schoolmaster that should have the care of all their children, so that his upbuilding a distinct school was apparently impractical, yet he claimed the boys he formerly had, which I suppose was the greater part of Mr. Hawley's school; calls them his boys; challenges a superior authority over 'em; and a kind of superintendence under the Brigadier's countenance and encouragement, to the very

5. The two groups of words here in brackets are conjectural readings.

great embarrassing and confounding of the affair. I will leave you, Sir, to judge whether he intends to draw Mr. Hollis' pay. He is away from his family and business at Newington; is at the boarding school with a son and daughter; [and] spends his time here, which heretofore he has set a high price upon. But certainly that business he is [in] now, if it can be called a business, is not that for which Mr. Hollis has hired him, and his spending his time here now is of no service to the design Mr. Hollis and the government have in view, but very much the contrary. He pretends in some measure to do the business of a steward, but is very unfit for it, being naturally very slack and negligent, and his inactivity greatly increased by his lameness and age, being about sixty-six. The stewardship under his care is managed in a very miserable manner, greatly to the wasting of the country's money (for he has the care of the provision not only for Mr. Hollis' boys but for the Mohawk and Iroquois families that are nursed by the government), and waste of things made there, to the great observation of such as have opportunity to see how things are managed. Such poor provision is made that the schoolmaster cannot live there, when it is very necessary he should, as the master of a boarding school, in order to sustain his children in an orderly, civil way of living, agreeable to the design of that school. And Captain Kellogg has been exceeding slack as to his accounts and has appeared very obstinate in this slackness, though there has been much reasoning and expostulating with him about the matters. And he is now a great impediment to Mr. Hawley in his business. His lordly disposition, together with the notion he has of his authority here, keeps everything uneasy and unsettled.

'Tis[6] apparent that Captain Kellogg is not pleased in Mr. Hawley's being there and evidently counteracts him and embarrasses him in his [efforts] in many respects. When he pleases, he has drawn [all] of the boys out of the school to serve his occasion. And sometimes calls 'em off pointedly to take the care of them and instruct 'em himself; and that he might have the [appearance] of the constant care of them himself, sends [some] away from him into another room to study, where they sometimes sit on the beds; others get up and dance about the room. Such a way of management keeps things in a broken, confused state. 'Tis impossible for Mr. Hawley in such a state of things to accomplish any steady order and government. 'Tis in vain for him to

6. All of the bracketed words in this paragraph are conjectural due to the illegibility of the MS.

pretend to keep some of the boys in order while others can attend in disorder. Mr. Hawley has a disposition to invent methods for a happy reputation of the school and seems to have a genius for it, but 'tis wholly in vain for him to pretend to any such things. The boys are so [confused] that many of them know not who to submit to as their master. And nothing goes on successfully. Mr. Hawley is so discouraged that he would by no means continue, were it not for the hope of an alteration. And while things remain [so], Mr. Hollis' money and the country's too is spent in great measure in vain; and if there be no remedy, all will undoubtedly prove to be worse than in vain. 'Tis never to be hoped that any gentleman fit for the business will be moved to keep the school under such circumstances. The unhappiness of the state of things at the boarding school by reason of Captain Kellogg's being there is too manifold to be fully declared in this letter. Our circumstances are more lamentable than can easily be conceived of in many respects. And all seems in great measure to spring from one source, viz. that great quarrel between Colonel Williams and Captain Kellogg, and Deacon Woodbridge, and the same cause which that quarrel arose from, which is a breach wide as the sea that cannot be healed. I have not the least expectation that ever Colonel Williams will be reconciled to Deacon Woodbridge. It need not be wondered at that the Brigadier shows himself entirely on their side in this contention, considering his circumstances. I can conceive of no other cause of the strange alteration of his abundant care of me, I having always been looked upon with a suspicious eye because Deacon Woodbridge had a main hand in getting me to be a missionary here and Colonel Williams and Captain Kellogg were known to oppose it much.

'Tis certainly very unfit that all our affairs should be at the arbitrary disposal of one only and he only so greatly engaged with a party in that contention which has its influence in everything that is done here and having that party for his counsel in all affairs. If things are continued in this situation, the country had as good throw their money into the sea.

There is indeed now a glorious opportunity given in divine providence for doing good amongst the Six Nations. But 'tis in vain to expect any good if things go on in this course. 'Tis not difficult to foresee what will soon be the consequence. Mr. [Benjamin] Ashley and his wife [Rebecca Kellogg Ashley] in this case are fully determined to go away and to go and live among the Mohawks in their own country, whom all the Iroquois love, and especially the Onohquagas are exceeding fond of and have manifested it in their public speeches from time to time. I am very apprehensive that their going away and going to live in the Iroquois country would entirely break up the Mohawk affair, that it would at once drive most of those that are here away and keep others back and give 'em a very great disgust to the English. They have long shown themselves very jealous for Mr. Ashley and his wife, that they are not well treated by those that have the management of things, and have very publicly complained of it. And then Mr. Hawley also is in the forementioned case fully determined to go away; which would be another fatal stroke under our circumstances.

If a few Mohawks should after all continue (which I much doubt of), yet the affair would have a mortal stroke and would doubtless languish to death. The design of making a settlement of 'em in the Hoplands, which the country has bought for 'em, would entirely fail, for none now appear willing to settle there but the Onohquagas. And if they lead the way, probably a few Mohawks would follow 'em. But they are above [all] attached to Ashley and his wife, and 'tis beyond all doubt they will not settle here, if those persons are not with 'em, and that the fairest prospects will be dashed. The glorious opportunities divine providence is giving us will be lost, and so all that we have done will prove worse than in vain: for the consequence will be the establishing a prejudice in the minds of the Six Nations against any attempts of the future, and putting all designs of this nature more effectually out of our reach, it may be, for two or three generations and, according to the genius of that people, they will never trust us again.

Yea, I apprehend more than this. The Stockbridge Indians are in such a rustle and so uneasy by reason of some things belonging to the present situation of affairs, that I think there is real danger that if there be no alteration, they, the great part of them, will break up and leave the town.

'Tis probable, Sir, you may have very different representations made of things, very different from these. These things may be called [a] very wild, extravagant account of things. The representations I have made, they are such as can be warranted as to most material things by sufficient testimony if inquiries should be made and such as you, Sir, will doubtless see (if things go on as they are) confirmed by the future events and consequences of things. As there are many in New England of a certain family that are extremely uneasy at my being here, so I expect to be represented by many of them and those that are related to 'em as very unfit for the place I am in, a mischief maker, etc., and should not wonder if they should strive to remove me.[7]

However, I will endeavor always to discharge a good conscience, at the same time endeavoring so far as may be consistent with this to live peaceably with all men. We are here in a remote and hidden corner, where a vast deal of public moneys, and moneys given for charitable and pious purposes, have been expended, and I am satisfied that the world is in no measure sensible after what manner much of it has been spent. 'Tis absolutely necessary that those that are first in the ordering and governing of our affairs should know the state of things, which they never can know but by information from some that live here; which never would be given, if fear of incurring the displeasure of particular persons must always be sufficient to prevent.

Colonel Dwight, notwithstanding all that has been forementioned, professes still to be my hearty friend and declares that what he has said and done has not been from disaffection but judgment: to which I have nothing to say, but only if he is not mistaken through ignorance of his own heart (as many times persons are), it strangely happens that friendship in him acts like enmity in other folks.

I shall prescribe to Your Honor no limitations in the use you shall make of this letter but what are set by your own discretion, entirely trusting your wisdom to use it so as to do good and not hurt with it. I am, Sir,

Your most humble and obliged servant,
Jonathan Edwards.

145. TO SEC. ANDREW OLIVER

The Stockbridge squabbles reached a crescendo in 1752. The Williamses supported Capt. Martin Kellogg as the head of the male boarding school while seeking to demoralize and discredit Gideon Hawley. The Indians disliked the former and approved of the latter, and the Mohawks left in disgust by the end of the year. In this letter, Edwards accurately predicts the results and the direction matters will take at the assembly.

---

7. JE drew a vertical line through the following: "It has of late been abundantly given out that I am seeking the female school for some of my family, which is perfectly a groundless premise." The next two sentences, which begin the last MS page, end in an incomplete thought and were no doubt meant to be deleted also. They read: "I have not the least inclination to any such thing. When they knew [me] to be no fit matter to be made a tool to serve their designs."

This was also the year of maximum stress for Edwards, whose position was threatened. His emotional state is reflected in the chirography of this draft, which contains many ampersands, run-on sentences, and uncertain crossouts.

(Trask Library, AL draft: one folio leaf, fragments missing; letter cover, addressed on verso to Edwards at Stockbridge; and one large quarto leaf, irregular, on a note from Samuel Hopkins of Sheffield to Edwards, May 3, 1752. Dwight ms. transcript, six quarto leaves. Published in part in Dwight ed., *1*, 493–94.)

*   *   *

[Stockbridge,] May 1752

Sir,

Affairs amongst us have gone on in great confusion since I last wrote to Your Honor. We have one difficulty and disturbance after another.

The[1] Mohawks, who were quite weary of a long continued state of confusion, seemed greatly pleased with Mr. [Gideon] Hawley's coming and everything for a little while seemed to appear with the most pleasing, promising aspect. But this appearance soon vanished, confusions returning, and to a greater degree than ever has had a tendency to discourage them much more than [instruction].

One half of the Mohawks went away. And there is little probability, as to most of them, that they will return any more. Some went away in a great disgust with Capt. [Martin] Kellogg, especially for some of his conduct. Other things happened, one after another, greatly to disturb the minds of such as were left.

Mr. [Jonathan] Hubbard of Sheffield, a great friend with Captain Kellogg and his party, being at the boarding school, struck [a child of the] chief sachem [of the] Onohquagas on his head with his cane, without any manner of provocation (his mother is a remarkably serious woman), which put the Indians into a terrible ruffle, so that they seemed resolved, all of them, immediately to pack up and be gone. Mr. Hawley and Mr. [Benjamin] Ashley came to me to inform me of it, to ask my advice what to do to calm their minds and to prevent its proving the utter ruin of the affair. I told them that Col. [Joseph] Dwight had blamed me much for intermeddling with the affairs of the Mohawks and told me that herein I meddled with what was none of my business. I, therefore, advised 'em to go to him and declare the whole affair to

---

1. JE drew a vertical line through this paragraph.

him, that he might use proper means to prevent the fatal consequences. On my advice they went to him, but their coming was taken as the fruit of a disposition to find fault with persons on that side, and what had happened was supposed by the Brigadier to be a mere trifle, and that indeed there was no great remaining uneasiness among the Mohawks, in which he was greatly mistaken to my knowledge. The chief of those that were here came that day to my house to complain of the treatment, and Mr. Hubbard happened at the same time to be present and showed very great uneasiness. Mr. Hubbard was persuaded to give some money to pacify 'em.

However, the Brigadier was provoked and his passions roused.[2] He went down to the boarding school in the afternoon and came into the school in school [time] and fell upon Mr. Hawley in the presence of the whole in a very fervid manner, and continued him under his chastisement for three hours together by the watch, so as wholly to break up the school and alarm all the Mohawks. He told Mr. Hawley he was of no judgment, of no prudence; that he was unfit for the business he was in; that if he had any regard to [the] prosperity of it, he would quit it immediately; that he was a mischief-maker. When Mr. Hawley desired that his conduct might be then examined and looked into, he told him he should not take so much notice of him. His talk was full of menaces. He told him he would inform of his ill conduct and that my recommendation would not do his turn.

The Mohawks in general heard it; the Brigadier's talk was very loud and he did not endeavor to conceal it from 'em. They were very much concerned about it and said they did not know but that great man would kill their schoolmaster, and were very much afraid Mr. Hawley would go away. They had several meetings about the affair. The chief of 'em went to Captain Kellogg and expressed their great uneasiness to him, and desired to have opportunity to speak to the Brigadier about the affair, and told 'im they were afraid that Mr. Hawley would go away. Captain Kellogg told 'em he hoped they would get another as good. They told 'im they did not; they were acquainted with Mr. Hawley and did not like new things. Mr. Hawley that very day was going a journey into Connecticut, but the Indians insisted on opportunity to speak with him about this affair before he went. And when they met him they, entreating him not to be discouraged nor to leave them, said that if he went away, they would go also.

2. JE deleted "and his passions roused."

The[3] Brigadier's end seemed to be to discourage Mr. Hawley and drive him [off], and indeed, he was greatly, his spirit very much overcome, for a while after this strange treatment. The Mohawks seem to have imbibed a great disgust toward the Brigadier from this thing. The Brigadier has made himself disagreeable to the Mohawks and to all the Indians in the town by this and some other conduct of his.

The Stockbridge Indians have had some things that have put [them] into a great ruffle this winter past and this spring. They were considerably ruffled by what they perceived of a great opposition made to something that was done about a seat in the meetinghouse, which they had a hand in, and much insisted on, insomuch that they had a meeting about it among themselves of their own accord. Everything is kept in a tumult and uneasiness through a high-handed, passionate way of managing affairs.

Col.[4] [Joseph] Pynchon seems long ago entirely to have forsaken the business, [which] I surmise is through his dislike of the spirit and conduct of one that is joined with him as of the same Committee. Captain Ashley expresses a great dislike of the management, and I can't perceive that he has any hand in the management of affairs. He is discouraged and declares he will do his utmost that the Mohawks affair shall be thrown up by the government.[5] Captain Kellogg has informed [me] that the Brigadier intends that Captain Ashley should be dismissed from the business and probably Col. [Oliver] Partridge is to be introduced as one of the Committee in his stead. Thus, all things are left to the arbitrary disposal of one man.

He has done everything of importance, without taking the voice of the rest of the Committee, if we may credit Captain Ashley as to the following particulars. Everything that gives this any clog or brings the least clog to designs seem to provoke [him] to a high degree.[6] Captain Kellogg has lately given out that he has had it from a certain great man that [I] was not like to be here four years hence. It has also been said by gentlemen of the party of Hatfield, that I was wholly unfit for the business I was in and was not like to be continued in it long.[7] Colonel Elisha Williams is now come home, which probably gives new spirit to those menaces. However, sometimes what they see among the Indians

3. JE drew a vertical line through this paragraph.
4. Idem.
5. The phrase "and declares he will . . . by the government" was crossed out by JE.
6. JE drew a vertical line from the beginning of the paragraph to this point.
7. JE drew a vertical line from this point to the end of the paragraph.

seems to convince 'em that the affair is languishing and like to come to
an end, and then they lay the blame to us as the causes of its ruin.
Doubtless all that are around that ben't tools will have many things laid
to their charge. But still I think there is no necessity of the affair's
breaking up unless Colonel Dwight and Captain Kellogg are resolved
to have it so, and are determined when they leave it, to leave it in ruins,
to make the world believe the life of the affair depended on them. And
they are determined to have their wills in that, that if they have not the
government of the affair, nobody else shall. But undoubtedly, if they
don't leave the business soon, they will leave the affair in ruins, and the
affair by going to ruin will leave them.

The[8] dependence of the affair as to continuance and prosperity is
chiefly on the Onohquagas, who are much best disposed, and most
likely to come in considerable number, and have not been here so long
to see so much to discourage 'em, and who alone are willing to settle at
the Hoplands. The affair is not at all desperate as to them and some of
the Mohawks, if there be a speedy alteration. But if the Brigadier and
Captain Kellogg continue here, there is no hope of Mr. Hawley's and
Mr. Ashley's and his wife's [Rebecca Kellogg Ashley's] continuance,
who will not continue under one whom they esteem so despotic and
terrible an inspector; there will be no way to keep any of the Indians
here, unless it be some that are entirely mercenary and who may be
persuaded to stay for the sake of presents that are made 'em, to [be
maintained][9] and have their fill there in mere [idleness],[1] which it is
now very apparent is all that moves many of the Conneenchees in
coming and continuing here.

There have been many and great consultations among the party
here with Colonel Partridge of Hatfield. And there is reason to think
that great things are to be pushed in the approaching Assembly.
Doubtless the utmost endeavors will be used to make interest in the
court.[2] It has been said in some discourse that has been overheard
among them, that some particular members will not act without their
[wills] being opened with money, etc.

The Brigadier has plainly discovered many designs tending to bring
money into his own pocket, viz.[3] a design of being the steward of both

8. JE drew a vertical line through this paragraph.
9. MS damage; words supplied from Dwight transcript.
1. MS damage; word supplied from Dwight transcript.
2. JE drew a vertical line through the remainder of the paragraph.
3. JE deleted: "a design of taking care of Mr. Hollis' boys."

boarding schools, by which he will have opportunity to supply the Indians out of his own shop, and getting his pay from public funds, in these hard times for shopkeepers by reason of a scarcity of a medium for [exchange]. He has had a design of introducing his son as the master of the boarding school under the notion of a present supply, another proper person not appearing.[4]

Captain[5] Kellogg has given hints of an agreement between him and the Brigadier to resign the care of Mr. Hollis' scholars to him when things are ripe for it (whether this be that he may draw Mr. Hollis' large benefactions), he providing for their maintenance and taking care of their instruction by his son. These things, besides his wife's being mistress of the female school, and two of their sons maintained and educated at the public charge, and a couple of their girls in like manner maintained in the female school; probably one of the family to be his wife's usher, and his servants paid for as under the notion of servants employed in the affairs of the female school; the house to be set on Madam [Abigail] Sergeant's land; and the farm to be bought by the country for a school, from advantage to sell it at an high rate, yet the family in great measure to be maintained on the produce of it; and besides the advantage of carrying on a trade with both Stockbridge Indians and Mohawks—there is clear evidence of most of these things. A man had need to have a great stock of uprightness to manage a public affair well, under so manifold temptations of private interest.

However, the Brigadier the last summer was abundant in expressing his sense of the extreme unfitness of Captain Kellogg for the business he was in and the necessity of his being speedily dismissed, yet 'tis most manifest he has no design of his going away so long as Mr. Hawley is here. He told Mr. Hawley he looked upon him as of more importance here than all of us and that he intended to write to Mr. Hollis, to inform him of his good qualities.

The Indians appear more and more averse to Mrs. Sergeant's having any of their girls. They have been very uneasy with respect to those three, which she took up in the fall and put out at Brookfield. Two of their parents have in their great uneasiness gone down to Brookfield

4. JE drew a vertical line through this paragraph. At the end of the paragraph, he included the following sentence in brackets, evidently intending to move it to another, undisclosed location: "He has manifested an expectation of diverting the channel of the King's bounty to the Six Nations from New York." Dwight interpolated, in MS transcript, that the King's bounty to the Six Nations from New York was £500 sterling.

5. JE drew a vertical line through this paragraph.

to bring 'em home. The parents of one of them, who was brought home [at that] time, are greatly disgusted at the treatment.[6]

The people of the town have unanimously, both English and Indian, desired Mr. [Timothy] Woodbridge to go to the General Assembly at the approaching session as their representative, supposing that, although his presence be needed in the school, yet the present extreme state of things will justify their desiring him to be absent for a season, to be at court while the great and important things relating to this town are considered, which it is supposed will be determined this session. Therefore, I hope the Commissioners will not resent his coming till they have candidly heard the reasons of his coming. Then, perhaps, they may think the great ends of his school and the mission here, and everything done here for Indians, did more require his going to court [at] that juncture than his continuance in the school. He goes presuming upon it that the court will be ready to release him as soon as the consideration of our affairs is over.

I have advised Mr. Hawley to go to Concord to join some of the Commissioners, that they may have opportunity to see him and confer with him concerning the business they have here improved him to, and to agree with him, provided the Commissioners see fit further to improve him. There should be a probability of the state of things being so altered that he can see any encouragement to continue longer in the business. And also, to vindicate his own character, the Brigadier having threatened to accuse him, I have here sent some testimonials of his character from some gentlemen in Connecticut that have had acquaintance with him.

John Wauwaumpequunnaunt, the interpreter and usher of the school, has long complained of the insufficiency of his salary to support his family. He is [so] constantly employed in his business that he says he can't hunt nor yet follow husbandry, and that what he has is not sufficient to support his family without those, which probably is true. He seems excellently qualified for his business on every other account, unless that he has heretofore been apt sometimes to drink too hard; but has now for a considerable time appeared serious and very careful as to that matter. I hope he will reform. I would, therefore, humbly propose it to the consideration of the honorable Commissioners,

6. Here follows in JE's draft a list of topics to be discussed: "Mr. Woodbridge & Mr. Hawleys Journey/ My salary/ Testimonials of Mr. Hawleys character/John's salary/Capt. Joseph Kellogg is brought here." The draft discusses only the first item and "John's salary," but the other items may have been included in the sent letter.

whether it might be best to allow him something more, to be continued so long as he shall carry himself well.

[Jonathan Edwards.]

146. TO THE REVEREND AARON BURR

Burr's rapid courtship of and marriage to Edwards' daughter Esther took place the month after this letter was written. Here, Edwards gives no hint that he expected such events. Burr's proposed trip abroad to raise funds for the College of New Jersey never materialized. Edwards' eldest son, Timothy, did enter the college and graduated in 1757. The letter is also noteworthy for its advocacy of smallpox inoculation, which was later responsible for Edwards' death.

(Firestone Library, Jonathan Edwards Collection, ALS, two-thirds of a folio leaf, ms. damage to left edge.)

* * *

Sheffield, May 6, 1752

Rev. and Dear Sir,

I thank you for your favor by [Elijah] Williams your pupil, and also for your other letters received before. My not answering them before now was not in the least owing to want of respect, or any disposition to uphold any misunderstanding; but partly from the multitude of affairs which have continually pressed my mind, which yet would not have prevented my writing if I had known of any good opportunity. I heard nothing of Mr. Josiah Williams' going in the winter, till after he was gone. If I had, I should doubtless have wrote by him.

As to the affair of the report of what you said concerning my book on the terms of communion, etc., from the credit I give you, in [you]r representation, I fully believe you have been misrepresented: and therefore don't think it worth [the while][1] to make an uproar in tracing the mat[ter to the] original. I would pray you to give your[self no fur]ther uneasiness about that matter, as though anything remained with me to occasion disaffection. I assure [you] there is nothing of that nature.

You are pleased to ask my thoughts concerning your proposed voyage to Great Britain for the sake of New Jersey College. You have those nearer to you that know ten times as much of the circumstances and

1. The bracketed items in this paragraph are conjectures due to MS damage.

Aaron Burr, Sr., by
Edward Ludlow
Mooney, undated, the
Art Museum, Princeton
University

necessities of the College, that are vastly more able and in fitter circumstances to advise you; Gov. [Jonathan] Belcher and the trustees in particular. There doubtless might great advantages be obtained by your going to England and Scotland, and spending about a year in Great Britain, more than by all letters that can be written. The only doubt is whether the College won't extremely suffer by your being so long absent. But of that I am not a fit person to judge. One thing I will venture to give you my thoughts in, viz. that since you have not had the smallpox, if you can find a skillful, prudent physician, under whose care you can put yourself, you would take the smallpox by inoculation before you go, after properly preparing your body for it, by physic and diet.

If you go, it will be necessary you should take some companion with you. I know not who you have there, but I have been favored with some acquaintance with Mr. [John] Wright, whom I should think would be a very suitable person to go as your companion on such a design. If I were going, he would be very agreeable to me; I should not expect to find one more agreeable or fitter for the purpose.

I heartily thank you for your kind offer with respect to the education of my son. 'Tis prob[able that][2] I shall send him before long: I have de[sired Mr.] Wright to take care to provide a good place. [He is] obliging and ready to be helpful. And from [the kind] and generous disposition you have manifested, I shall have dependence on your fatherly care of him.

If you go to Great Britain, I shall be ready to do my utmost to forward the design of your going in my next letters to Scotland.

Mr. Wright can inform you something of the state of things in Stockbridge. You may perhaps do much to promote our affairs in London. But I hope to write to you again about these matters before you go. In the meantime, asking your prayers, I am, dear Sir,

Your friend and brother,
Jonathan Edwards.

147. TO THE FIRST CHURCH OF CHRIST, NORTHAMPTON

In an epistle to his former Northampton congregation, printed as an appendix to his *Misrepresentations Corrected,* the rejected shepherd counsels his late flock to follow sound doctrine. While refusing to attack Solomon Williams personally, Edwards warns that his views are pernicious. The congregation should remember the teaching of Solomon Stoddard. Over and over, he repeats the refrain "You have been taught," that is, by his grandfather. Then he contrasts the patriarch's instruction with Williams'.

Edwards does not conceive of Christianity as a spectator activity, family formality, or social custom. Rather, it is a dynamic experience, in which the Almighty imparts life to the soul, transforming the affections and making all things new. On these essentials and most others, excepting qualifications for church membership, Edwards agrees with Stoddard. He concludes by urging the church to reject Williams' teaching, which are full of errors, and return to Stoddard.

(Beinecke Library, AL draft, appendix to ms. "Answer to Williams"; Trask Library, Dwight ms. transcript, five quarto leaves. Published in *Misrepresentations Corrected and Truth Vindicated* [Boston, 1752], pp. 167–73; Dwight ed., *4,* 597–609; *Works, 12,* 498–503.)

*   *   *

---

2. Idem.

[June 1752]

Dear Brethren,

Though I am not now your pastor, yet having so long stood in that relation to you, I look on myself obliged, notwithstanding all that has of late passed between us, still to maintain a special concern for your spiritual welfare. And as your present circumstances appear to me very evidently attended with some peculiar dangers, threatening the great wounding of the interest of vital religion among you; which probably most of you are not well aware of: I look on myself called to point forth your danger to you, and give you warning. What I now especially have respect to, is the danger I apprehend you are in, from the contents of that book of Mr. [Solomon] Williams of Lebanon, to which the foregoing performance is a reply;[1] which I perceive has been written and published very much by your procurement and at your expense; and so (it may naturally be supposed and expected) is dispersed in your families, and will be valued, and much made use of by you as a book of great importance. What I have respect to, is not so much the danger you are in of being established by that book in your former principles, concerning the admission of members (though I think these principles are indeed very opposite to the interest of true piety in churches); but what I now mean is the danger there is, that while you are making much of that book as a means to maintain Mr. [Solomon] Stoddard's doctrine concerning the terms of communion, you, and especially your children, will by the contents of it be led quite off from *other* religious principles and doctrines, which Mr. Stoddard brought you up in, and always esteemed as of vastly greater importance, than his particular tenet about the Lord's Supper; and be naturally led into notions and principles, which he ever esteemed as of fatal tendency to the souls of men.

By the way, I would have it observed, that when I take notice of these things in his book, my aim is not to beget in you an ill opinion of Mr. Williams as though he were as corrupt in his settled persuasion, as one would be ready to think, if we were to judge only by things delivered in some parts of this book; and especially if it should be supposed, that he embraced all the consequences of what he here maintains. Men often don't see or allow the plain consequences of their own doctrines. And therefore, though I charge very pernicious consequences on some things he says, yet I don't charge *him* with embracing these conse-

---

1. Solomon Williams' book was *The True State of the Question;* "the foregoing performance" was JE's *Misrepresentations Corrected,* a rebuttal of Williams. For information on these works, and for useful background information on this controversy, see *Works, 12,* esp. pp. 68–77.

quences: nor will I undertake to explain how it could come to pass, that he should maintain things now in this book in opposition to me, which are so contrary to the good and sound doctrines he has formerly delivered in other books. Let that be as it will, and however orthodox the principles may be, which he more ordinarily maintains; yet the ill and unsound things he delivers here, may do never the less hurt to you and your children, who may read this book without having in view the more wholesome doctrines of his other writings.

For instance, you have ever been taught, that unconverted men don't really believe the gospel, are never truly convinced of its truth; and that 'tis of great importance that sinners should be sensible of the unbelief and atheism of their hearts. But contrary to this, Mr. Williams' book abundantly teaches you and your children this notion, that unsanctified men may really be convinced of the divine truth of the gospel, and believe it with all their hearts.

You have been ever taught, that Christless sinners, especially when under some more slight awakenings, are very ready to flatter themselves that they are willing to accept of Christ as their Savior; but that they must be brought off from their vain imagination, and be brought to see that the fault is in their own wills, and that their not being interested in Christ is owing to their obstinacy and perverseness, and willful wicked refusal of God's terms; on which account they are wholly inexcusable, and may justly be cast off by God. But contrary to these things, this book of Mr. Williams abundantly teaches you, that men, in an unconverted state, may indeed cordially consent to the terms of the covenant of grace, may comply with the call of the gospel, may submit to its proposals, may have satisfaction in the offer God makes of himself as our God in Christ, may fall in with the terms of salvation propounded in the gospel, and renounce all other ways, and may sincerely and earnestly desire salvation in this way; and that some unconverted men are not willful obstinate sinners (p. 21b). Which doctrines, if embraced and retained by your children as true, will tend forever to hinder that conviction of the opposition and obstinacy of the heart, which Mr. Stoddard ever taught you to be of such importance in order to the soul's humiliation, and thorough conviction of the justice of God in its damnation.

You have ever been taught, that the hearts of natural men are wholly corrupt, entirely destitute of anything spiritually good, not having the least spark of love to God, and as much without all things of this nature, as a dead corpse is without life: nevertheless, that 'tis hard for sinners to be convinced of this; that they are exceeding prone to imagine, there is some goodness in 'em, some respect to God in what they do: yet that they must be brought off from such a vain conceit of themselves, and come to see themselves utterly depraved and quite dead in sin. But now this book of Mr. Williams leads you to quite other notions; it leads you to suppose, that some natural men are above lukewarmness in religion, that they may truly profess to be the real friends of Christ, and to love God, more than his enemies, and above the world.

It was a doctrine greatly inculcated on you by Mr. Stoddard as supposing it of great importance for all to be convinced of it, that natural men are not subject to the law of God, nor indeed can be; that they never do truly serve God, but are wholly under the dominion of sin and Satan. But if sinners believe Mr. Williams' book, they won't be convinced of these things; nay, will believe quite contrary things, viz. that sinners, while in a state of nature, may have a cordial subjection to Jesus Christ, and may be subject to him with all their hearts, and may be so devoted to the service of Christ as to be above those that serve two masters, may give up themselves to be taught, ruled, and led by him in a gospel way of salvation, and may give up all their hearts and lives to him. And is it likely, while sinners believe these doctrines of Mr. Williams, that they will ever be brought to a thorough humiliation, in a conviction of their being wholly under the power of enmity against God? Which Mr. Stoddard taught you to be of such great importance.

You know, it was always a doctrine greatly insisted on by Mr. Stoddard as a thing of the utmost consequence, that sinners who are seeking converting grace, should be thoroughly sensible of God's being under no manner of obligation, from any desires, labors, or endeavors of theirs, to bestow his grace upon them; either in justice, or truth, or any other way; but that when they have done all, God is perfectly at liberty, whether to show them mercy, or not; that they are wholly in the hands of God's sovereignty. (See *Guide to Christ,* p. 75 c, d and *Benefit of the Gospel,* pp. 64 and 75–76.) Whereas, if a sinner seeking salvation believes Mr. Williams' book, it will naturally lead him to think quite otherwise. He (in p. 28) speaking of such sincerity and earnestness of endeavors as may be in natural men, to qualify 'em to come to the sacrament, and of the great encouragement God has given, that he will bestow his saving grace on such as use such endeavors, adds these words (near the bottom of the page), "God never will be worse than his encouragement, nor do less than he has encouraged; and he has said, 'To him that hath shall be given.'" Naturally leading the awakened sinner, who is supposed to have moral sincerity enough to come to the sacrament, to suppose, that God is not wholly at liberty; but that he has given so much encouragement, that it may be depended upon he will give his grace; and that it would not be reasonable or becoming of God to do otherwise; because if God should do so, he would be worse than his encouragement, and would not fulfill that word of his, "To him that hath shall be given." And how will this tend effectually to prevent the sinner's looking on God as absolutely at liberty, and prevent his resigning himself wholly into the hands of God, and to his sovereign pleasure?

It is a doctrine which has ever been taught you, and made use of for the warning, awakening and humbling of gospel sinners, that they have greater guilt, and are exposed to a more terrible punishment, than the heathen. But this is spoken of by Mr. Williams as an unsufferable treatment of visible saints: naturally tending to alleviate and smooth the matter in the consciences of those that are not scandalous persons, though they live in unbelief and the rejection of Christ under gospel light and mercy.

If you will believe what Mr. Williams says (p. 56), those blessed epithets and characters in the epistles of the apostles, which you always, from the first foundation of the town, have been taught to be peculiar and glorious expressions and descriptions of the blessed qualifications and state of true saints, and heirs of eternal happiness; such as "being elected," "chosen before the foundation of the world," "predestinated to the adoption of children through Jesus Christ"; "quickened, and made alive to God, though once dead in trespasses and sins"; "washed, sanctified, justified"; "made to sit together in heavenly places in Christ"; "begotten again, to an inheritance incorruptible, undefiled";[2] with innumerable others the like: I say, if you believe Mr. Williams you have been quite mistaken all your days, and misled by all your ministers; these things are no more than were said of the whole nation of the Jews, even in their worst times! Which is (as I have observed) exactly agreeable to the strange opinion of Mr. [John] Taylor of Norwich in England, that author who has so corrupted multitudes in New England. Thus you are at once deprived of all the chief texts in the Bible, that hitherto have been made use of among you, as teaching the discriminating qualifications and privileges of the truly pious, and the nature and benefits of a real conversion; too much paving the way for the rest of Taylor's scheme of religion, which utterly explodes the doctrines you have been formerly taught concerning

---

2. See Eph. 1:4–5, 2:1, 5–6; I Cor. 6:11; and I Pet. 1:4.

eternal election, conversion, justification; and so, of a natural state of death in sin; and the whole doctrine of original sin, and of the mighty change made in the soul by the redemption of Christ applied to it.

And this, taken with those other things which I have observed, in conjunction with some other things which have lately appeared in Northampton, tend to lead the young people among you apace into a liking to the new, fashionable, lax schemes of divinity, which have so greatly prevailed in New England of late; as wide as the east is from the west, from those great principles of religion, which have always been taught, and have been embraced, and esteemed most precious, and have justly been accounted very much your glory by others.

If this book of Mr. Williams with all these things, is made much of by you, and recommended to your children, as of great importance to defend the principles of the town, how far has your zeal for that one tenet, respecting natural men's right to the Lord's Supper, transported you, and made you forget your value and concern for the most precious and important doctrines of Jesus Christ, taught you by Mr. Stoddard, which do most nearly concern the very vitals of religion!

I beseech you, brethren, seasonably to consider how dark the cloud is that hangs over you, and how melancholy the prospect (especially with regard to the rising generation) in many respects. I have long been intimately acquainted with your religious circumstances, your notions and principles, your advantages and dangers; having had perhaps greater opportunity for it than any other person on earth. Before I left you, it was very evident, that Arminianism, and other loose notions in religion, and Mr. Taylor's in particular, began to get some footing among you; and there were some things special in your circumstances, that threatened a great prevailing of such like notions: which if they should by degrees generally prevail, will doubtless by degrees put an end to what used to be called saving religion.

Therefore let me entreat you to take the friendly warning I now give you, and stand on your guard against the encroaching evil. If you are not inclined to hearken to me, from any remaining affection to one whose voice and counsels you once heard with joy, and yielded to with great alacrity; yet let me desire you not to refuse, as you would act the part of friends to yourselves and your dear children.

I am, dear brethren, he who was once (as I hope through grace) your faithful pastor,

> And devoted servant for Jesus' sake,
> Jonathan Edwards.

148. TO COL. TIMOTHY DWIGHT

The money that Edwards expected from the sale of his home in Stockbridge was temporarily blocked,[1] another frustrating monetary setback for him. Accordingly, Edwards takes steps to liquidate a landholding in Winchester, Connecticut, a transaction that was not completed until April 1754. He could take some satisfaction in the fact that *Misrepresentations Corrected* was on its way to the press, although he feared that his opponents would try to destroy the manuscript.

(Trask Library, ALS, one quarto leaf, addressed on verso to Col. Timothy Dwight in Northampton, and one octavo leaf.)

* * *

Stockbridge, June 30, 1752

Dear Sir,

I request of you the favor of endeavoring to sell my land at Winchester. My deed of the land, together with a plan of it, is in the hands of your son. I shall be in great need of money, and therefore must endeavor to procure it that way, or some other. The town of Stockbridge sent in a petition by Deacon [Timothy] Woodbridge, to the General Assembly, that they would buy my house and house lot for a parsonage. But it was not granted; 'tis supposed the granting it was prevented, very much by Capt. Ephraim [Williams] who was at Concord the whole time of the sitting of the Assembly, constantly busy with the representatives, with his lime-juice punch and wine. Objections were made against the petition, which could come from none but he. By this means I shall be in greater need of money than I expected.

I have wrote a letter to Capt. Benjamin Sheldon, another to Charles Phelps, another to Capt. [Joshua] Leavitt of Suffield, desiring them to endeavor to obtain some more subscriptions for the printing of my book and to send what they got to you, to be forwarded to Mr. [Thomas] Foxcroft; which I now desire you to do, if any subscriptions are sent to you. Herein you will oblige

Your affectionate brother,
Jonathan Edwards.
Give my love to sister [Experience King] Dwight.

1. Payment was approved by the House of Representatives on Dec. 4, 1752 (Petition, MAR, vol. 32, pp. 258–61; *JMHR*, 29 [1752–53], for 1752: p. 14, June 2; p. 25, June 4; p. 57, Dec. 4).

Sir,

I have sent the copy of my answer to Mr. [Solomon] Williams,[2] by my son [Elihu] Parsons, to be conveyed by you to Mr. Foxcroft. I need not tell you that extraordinary care had need be taken in the conveyance. There are many enemies who would be glad to destroy it. I know not how in the world it can be well got to Mr. Foxcroft's hand, especially by reason of the smallpox, but I desire you would do the best you can.

J.E.

149. TO THE REVEREND THOMAS FOXCROFT

Edwards forwards the manuscript of *Misrepresentations Corrected* to Foxcroft, who he knows will once again exercise reliable supervision of the printing. He is concerned that he has treated Solomon Williams fairly in the treatise, and requests Foxcroft to alert him if he has done otherwise. Significantly, he is unable to afford extra copies of his own work.

(Beinecke Library, ALS, one folio leaf, addressed on verso to the Reverend Mr. Thomas Foxcroft.)

* * *

Stockbridge, June 30, 1752

Rev. and Honored Sir,

I have now at length sent you my answer to Mr. [Solomon] Williams and must request the favor of you, added to all your other condescending and most obliging favors, to correct the press. A little while ago, I wrote you a letter from Northampton, and sent a draft of proposals for subscription to be printed, and sent a few subscriptions. Since that, Mr. [Nathaniel] Hazard of New York has desired me to set him down for four dozen. I expect many more subscriptions. There are but few of the written proposals I have sent abroad yet come in. Three or four have appeared willing to subscribe in this town. I should be glad that the printed proposals when done might be forwarded to Col. [Timothy] Dwight of Northampton, with all convenient speed.

I should be glad that you would endeavor that this book may be printed in a pretty good paper and character, and may be printed correctly, and that particular care may be taken that the printer don't skip over a whole line as they sometimes do. And if the bookseller can be agreed with to let me have a number for the copy, it would be pleasing. If not, I must go without. With respect to any alterations that

2. *Misrepresentations Corrected.*

you may think needful to be made; it becomes me much to prefer your judgment to my own. But it is very difficult, and almost impossible, for another to enter into all the views of a writer, or to know everything he has in view in all that he says; and therefore a little variation of sentiment, may much thwart and disappoint his design, insensibly to another. But this I should take as a very friendly part and much desire, that if you observe, that in any instances I have mistaken Mr. Williams' meaning, and misrepresented him, or in any respect injured him, or delivered myself unhappily in any other respect, you would inform me of it via Colonel Dwight of Northampton; who has often opportunities to send to me. I have another copy by me, much like that I now send to you, and can make needed alterations and send 'em to you.

I desire you would use some endeavors to promote subscriptions in other places, where you think it feasible, and that, to that end, you would speak or write to the Rogerses [John Rogers, Sr. and Jr.], to Mr. [William] Hobby, Mr. [David] Hall, Mr. [Joshua] Eaton, [Mr. David] Goddard, etc.

If [I] have not erred in my calculation, this book will be considerably less than my former, which may be some encouragement to subscribers. I thank you for your late letter of June 4 and the care you took of the packet from Mr. [John] Erskine. He mentions another packet sent before, which never came to hand. If you hear of it, I desire you would send it. Asking your continued prayers, and presenting humble respects to your family, and Mr. [Edward] Bromfield and his family, I am, Sir,

> Your obliged brother and servant,
> Jonathan Edwards.

I will hereafter send the Table mentioned in the Preface.[1]

150. TO THE REVEREND THOMAS PRINCE

The learned pastor of the Third Church, Boston, had been a close friend of Edwards' and a strong supporter for many years. Here Edwards sends condolences on the loss of his fourth child.

(MHS, John Davis Papers, ALS, two quarto leaves, one cut and irregular, addressed on verso to the Reverend Thomas Prince, pastor of a church in Boston, in care of Colonel Dwight of Northampton.)

*   *   *

1. See *Works, 12,* 353.

Stockbridge, July 2, 1752

Rev. and Honored Sir,

We have lately heard of the death of your daughter, Mrs. Mercy; and the report seems to be credible, though we have heard very little of the circumstances. We live now at so great a distance from Boston, that we are not [at an][1] advantage to seek certain and speedy information from thence, as we used to be.

Dear Sir, the dispensations of heaven have indeed, in some respects, been distinguishingly afflictive toward you and your family. So is God often wont to deal with his people: before they leave the world, the enjoyments of the world gradually leave them; and the world, while they continue in it, is made more and more of an empty place to 'em. But your comfort, Sir, may be that in God is a fullness that don't diminish, and is subject to no variableness, through the dark and gloomy clouds that pass over us. I trust that God's design in thus dealing with you is to fit you to be more and more filled with that fullness, and so to bring forth more fruit to God's glory in this world, and perfectly[2] [. . .] world where [. . .] where all tears [. . .] eyes of God's people [. . .] shall flee away; [. . .] with pious [. . .] endearment, and in[3] perfect and glorious prosperity, and a more perfect enjoyment of 'em than in this world; and yet, such an enjoyment as will be no temptation to any withdrawment of the heart from God; but so as to draw the heart to God, and give an enjoyment of God in them. May God grant this may be the issue of your sore afflictions, which are such as call for the condolence of your friends, especially such as have been laid under such special obligations as I have been.

Please to present my most affectionate salutations to Mrs. [Deborah] Prince, and your only surviving child, as from a cordially condoling friend. I hope they will not sink under their affliction, or give way to melancholy. My desire is that the God of all comfort would be your and their support and light in your darkness. May God make me thankful for all distinguishing mercies which I have received in the midst of many troubles and difficulties which have in some respects been distinguishing.

My wife and daughter Esther and oldest son [Timothy] are gone to New Jersey, have been gone a fortnight. My son and daughter are gone to abide there. She was married to President [Aaron] Burr on the 29th

1. MS damage at fold.
2. MS damage; the lower left corner of the first page is missing.
3. End of missing portion; the full text resumes.

of last month. Desiring a remembrance in your prayers, I remain, dear Sir,

> Your obliged friend and humble servant,
> Jonathan Edwards.

151. TO THE REVEREND JOHN ERSKINE

This letter is unusual in not conveying any information about Stockbridge or the unsettled situation there. After acknowledging books and letters from overseas, Edwards describes religious activities in the colonies, adding details about an offer made to him by a church in Virginia. He is eager to resume writing and is working on *Freedom of the Will*.

(Trask Library, ALS, two folio leaves; Dwight ms. transcript, four quarto leaves. Published in Dwight ed., *1*, 496–99; and partially in Wellwood, pp. 515–16.)

* * *

Stockbridge, July 7, 1752

Rev. and Dear Brother,

The last spring I received a letter from you, dated at the beginning July 17, and at the end, September 5, 1751. And the week before last, I received another letter dated February 11, 1752, with a packet containing Arnauld, *De la Fréquente Communion*, Goodwin's sermon at the ordination of Mr. Pickering, Mr. Some's *Sermon on Methods for Reviving Religion, Reasons of Dissent from the Sentence of the General Assembly*, Edwards on *Christ God-man*, Mr. Hartley's sermon, Parrish on the Assembly's Catechism, and Dr. Gill's *Sermon on Is.* [*21*]:*11–12*.[1] I heartily thank you for these letters and pamphlets. Arnauld On Frequent Communion will not be very profitable to me, by reason of my not understanding the French. But several of the rest have been very agreeable to me. That letter which you mention in your last, dated

---

1. Antoine Arnauld, *De la Fréquente Communion. Où les Sentimens des Pères, des Papes, et des Conciles, touchant l'usage des sacremens de Pénitence et d'Euchariste, sont fidèlement exposez* (Paris, 1643; 11th ed., Lyon, 1731); JE disbound this volume and used it for note-taking. No information could be found on "Goodwin's sermon at the ordination of Mr. Pickering." David Some, *The Methods to be taken by Ministers for the Revival of Religion* (London, 1730); *Reasons of Dissent from the Sentence of the Reverend Commission of the General Assembly on March 11th, 1752* (Edinburgh, 1752); Joseph Edwards, *Christ God-Man. A Sermon . . . With a preface, occasioned by a book . . . entitled, Memoirs of the Life and writings of Mr. W. Whiston* (London, 1749); Thomas Hartley, *A Sermon preach'd in Northampton before the President and Governors of the County Infirmary* (Northampton, 1750). No information could be found on "Parrish on the Assembly's Catechism." John Gill, *The Watchman's Answer to the Question, What of the Night?* (London, 1750).

February 11, as sent about a twelvemonth before, containing some remarks on the decay of the power of the papal clergy, and an abstract of Venema's _Reasonings,_ to prove that Judas was not present at the Lord's Supper, I never received and regret it much that I missed of it. And request that you would still send me those Remarks on the Decay of the Papal Clergy.[2]

I am obliged to you for the particular informations you have given me concerning Mr. Adams of Falkirk's affair.[3] Though it is pity so deserving a person should suffer at all from his brethren, only for not acting contrary to his conscience; yet 'tis matter of thankfulness that the Assembly of the year 1751 showed a so much better temper than that of the preceding year. I shall be glad to hear concerning the temper and conduct of the Assembly of this present year, 1752.

I am sorry to hear that there is so much reason to fear that the revival of religion in the Netherlands will be hindered and brought under a cloud through the prevailing of imprudences. It is what I was afraid I should hear. I should be glad to see the pastoral letter you mention against fanaticism, though written by one disaffected to the revival. I wish I could see a history of enthusiasm, through all ages, written by some good hand, a hearty friend of vital religion, a person of accurate judgment and large acquaintance with ecclesiastical history. Such a history, well-written, might doubtless be exceeding useful and instructive, and of great benefit to the church of God; especially if there [be] united with it a proper account and history of true religion. I should, therefore, choose that the work should be a history of true, vital, and experimental religion and enthusiasm; bringing down the history from age to age; judiciously and clearly making the distinction between one and the other; observing the difference of source, progress, and issue; properly pointing out the limits; and doing justice to each, in every age, and at each remarkable period. I don't know that there is any such thing extant, or anything that would in any good measure answer to the same purposes. If there be, I should be glad to hear of it.

2. The author is probably Hermann Venema (1697–1787), whose main work was _Dissertationum Sacrarum, Libri tres in quibus de Rebus Varii et Selecti Argumenti Libere Disputatur_ (Harlingen, 1731). While no publication of his answers the description, the topic was one JE addressed in _Misrepresentations Corrected._ No information could be found on "Remarks on the Decay of the Papal Clergy."

3. John Adams, minister of Falkirk, Scotland, since 1744, joined the majority of the Torphichen congregation in 1748 in opposing the General Assembly's forced settlement of James Watson over them. In 1750 Adams was called before the bar of the General Assembly and made to apologize. The following year, Watson was settled at Torphichen under military guard. _Fasti Ecclesiae Scoticanae_ (5 vols., Edinburgh, 1915), _1,_ 207, 231.

I thank you for the account you give me of Mr. [John] Taylor's writings and the things which he is doing to propagate his opinions. It now appears to be a remarkable time in the Christian world; perhaps such an one as never has been before. Things are going downhill so fast; truth and religion, both of heart and practice, are departing by such swift steps that I think it must needs be, that a crisis is not very far off. And what will then appear, I will not pretend to determine.

The last week, I sent away my answer to Mr. [Solomon] Williams.⁴ If I live till it is published, I will endeavor to send one to you, and some other friends in Scotland.

I hope now, in a short time to be at leisure to resume my design of writing something on the Arminian controversy. I have no thoughts of going through with all parts of the controversy at once. But the subject which I intended, God willing, first to write something upon, was free will and moral agency; endeavoring, with as much exactness as I am able, to consider the nature of that freedom of moral agents, which makes them the proper subjects of moral government, moral precepts, counsels, calls, motives, persuasions, promises and threatenings, praise and blame, rewards and punishments: strictly examining the modern notions of those things, endeavoring to demonstrate their most palpable inconsistency and absurdity; endeavoring also to bring the late, great objections and outcries against the Calvinistic divinity, from these topics, to the test of the strictest reasoning. And particularly that grand objection, in which the modern writers have so much gloried, and so long triumphed, with so great a degree of insult towards the most excellent divines and, in effect, against the gospel of Jesus Christ, viz. that the Calvinistic notions of God's moral government are contrary to the common sense of mankind. In this essay, I propose to take particular notice of the writings of Dr. [Daniel] Whitby and Mr. [Thomas] Chubb. And the writings of some others, who though not properly Pelagians, nor Arminians; yet, in their notions of the freedom of the will, have, in the main, gone into the same scheme. But if I live to prosecute my design, I shall send you a more particular account of my plan after it is perfected.

I suppose there has been a trial before now whether a national collection can be obtained in Scotland for New Jersey College; unless it has been thought prudent, by such as are friends of the affair, to put it off a year longer; as some things I have heard seem to argue. There was a design of Mr. [Ebenezer] Pemberton's going to England and

---

4. *Misrepresentations Corrected.*

Scotland. He was desired by the trustees, and it was his settled purpose to have gone the last year: but his people and his colleague, Mr. [Alexander] Cumming, hindered it. His intention of going occasioned great uneasiness among his people, and created some disaffection towards him in the minds of some of 'em. Since that, President [Aaron] Burr has been desired to go, by the unanimous voice of the trustees. Nevertheless, I believe there is little probability of his consenting to it; partly on the account of his having lately entered into a married state. On the 29th of last month, he was married to my third daughter [Esther Edwards].

What you write of the appointment of a gentleman to be Lieutenant Governor of Virginia [Robert Dinwiddie], who is a friend of religion, is an event that the friends of religion in America have great reason to rejoice in; by reason of the late revival of religion in that province, and the opposition that has been made against it, and great endeavors to crush it, by many of [the] chief men of the province. Mr. [Samuel] Davies, in a letter I lately received from him, dated March 2, 1752, mentions the same thing. His words are, "We have a new governor, who is a candid, condescending gentleman. And as he has been educated in the Church of Scotland, has a respect for the Presbyterians, which I hope is a happy omen."

I was, in the latter part of the last summer, applied to with much earnestness and importunity, by some of the people of Virginia, to come and settle among them in the work of the ministry; who subscribed very handsomely for my encouragement and support, and sent a messenger to me with their request and subscriptions. But I was installed at Stockbridge, before the messenger came. I have written some account of the state of things at Stockbridge to Mr. [John] Mac-Laurin, which you doubtless will have opportunity to see.

July 24

Northampton are still destitute of a minister, and in broken, sorrowful circumstances. They had the last winter one Mr. [Daniel] Farrand, a young gentleman from New Jersey College, but contended much about him, so that he has left them. They are now in a state of contention; my warmest opposers are quarreling among themselves. I hear they have lately sent for a young preacher, one Mr. [Joseph] Green, [Jr.,] of Barnstable, who is soon expected; but I know nothing what his character is.

Another minister has lately been dismissed from his people, on the same account that I was dismissed from Northampton, viz. Mr. [Edward] Billing of Cold Spring. Many of Cold Spring people were originally of Northampton, were educated in the same principles, and have followed the example of the people there.

I heartily thank you for the account you have from time to time sent me of new books, that are published in Great Britain. I desire you would continue such a favor. I am fond of knowing how things are going on in the learned world.

Mr. John Wright, a member of New Jersey College, who is to take the degree of Bachelor of Arts the next September, is now at my house. He was born in Scotland; has lived in Virginia; is a friend and acquaintance of Mr. Davies; has a great interest in the esteem of the religious people of Virginia; and is peculiarly esteemed by President Burr; has been admitted to special intimacy with him; and is a person of very good character for his understanding, prudence, and piety. He has a desire to have a correspondence with some divine of his native country, and has chosen you for his correspondent, if he may be admitted to such a favor. He intends to send you a letter with this, of which I would ask a favorable reception, as he has laid me under some special obligations.

My wife joins with me in affectionate salutations to you and Mrs. Erskine. Hoping that we shall continue to remember each other at the throne of grace, I am, dear Sir,

> Your affectionate and obliged brother and servant,
> Jonathan Edwards.

152. TO THE REVEREND ISAAC HOLLIS

Edwards repeats to his English patron what he has told others about the history of the Stockbridge mission, dwelling on the deficiencies of Capt. Martin Kellogg as he perceives them. He cites specific ways the Williams family opposed Gideon Hawley and Timothy Woodbridge and stresses the need for impartial trustees. Edwards is striving to retain Hollis' interest so that he will not withdraw his patronage because of the contention. For confirmation of his views, he refers Hollis to Thomas Prince and the Boston Commissioners.

(Trask Library, AL draft, five folio leaves, one shorn, one an envelope cover addressed to Edwards at Northampton; Dwight ms. transcript, fourteen quarto leaves. See Edwards' letter to Hubbard, Mar. 30, 1752 [No. 144], and other letters, for many similar, sometimes identical, expressions.)

* * *

Stockbridge, July 17, 1752

Rev. and Honored Sir,

I wrote a letter to you the last summer, giving you some account of the state of things in this place relating to the great affair of the instruction of the Indians, when I had been but a little while here. But the state of our affairs being in many respects much altered since I wrote that letter and having now had opportunity for a much more full acquaintance with the state of things, both with regard to their present situation and as relating to things that have been in times past; and our present circumstances being such that justice to you as well as the interest of the important affairs of this place does in a special manner require you having particular information: this is what induces and obliges me again to write to you at this time.

Some things have happened, since I last wrote, that may well be looked on as remarkable smiles of heaven upon our design; but on the other hand some things have opened to me, both with regard to what has happened now, and things past that I have now gained a particular acquaintance with, that are matters of no small grief and surprise, and which cannot be concealed from you who have had so great an interest in our affairs without a high degree of injuriousness.

Some things which I then knew of I did not mention to you, hoping there would be no necessity to betray our shame to such as [were] abroad; but I see that you can't [be] dealt justly with, without having a full account of our state, though it be much to our reproach.

I shall now therefore endeavor, as much as in me lies, to give you an exact account of our affairs, both of those things that are prosperous and may be looked upon as smiles of heaven, and those things that are of a contrary aspect, that you may have a just view of the state of things here; only in giving the account I shall endeavor (as much as is consistent with justice to you and the cause you are embarked in), to avoid injuring the character of particular persons.

Some things I have observed have led me to think that you supposed that here has been for some years a regular boarding school maintained on the plan of Mr. [John] Sergeant's printed proposals, in which the money you have remitted hither for two or three years past has been expended; which (if it be so) must be for want of proper information. Indeed, Mr. Sergeant in his lifetime did something towards it. He several years before his death used many endeavors to find and procure a proper master, a man of liberal education (for he always sup-

posed such an one would be necessary). But meeting with disappointments, and you, Sir, having already made considerable remittances
and urging that something should be done speedily; Mr. Sergeant, in
the year 1748, agreed with Capt. Martin Kellogg of Newington, near
Wethersfield in Connecticut, a great friend of Col. Elisha Williams, for
the present exigency till a house could be built and the foundation of
his designed boarding school properly laid, and a proper person could
be obtained to be a schoolmaster. Captain Kellogg (though a man of
good understanding for one of his education), being an illiterate man
and a man in years, being then about sixty-two years of age, he being
lame and not well able on that account to follow other business that
required more action, was the more easily obtained for this business.
The peace with France not being then concluded[1] and this being an
exposed place, twelve Indian boys were carried down from hence to
him at Newington, to be maintained and instructed by Captain Kellogg at his own house where they continued a year. In the spring of the
year 1749, the peace being settled, Captain Kellogg brought his boys
hither, the foundation of an house being now laid. When Mr. Sergeant
came to reckon with Captain Kellogg as agent for you, he was extremely uneasy at some things in his conduct and accounts. But it must
be noted in justice to Captain Kellogg that by reason of Mr. Sergeant's
great dissatisfaction at his accounts, Captain Kellogg abated fifty
pounds in our currency, professing that he did it in complaisance to
Mr. Sergeant. But Mr. Sergeant expressed a resolution to set things on
some other foot, that more effectual care might be taken that you
should have justice done you in the expense of your money. But that
summer, on July 27, he died before ever he had executed his design,
and left the boys in Captain Kellogg's hands, in the house intended for
the boarding school, but in its first beginnings and just sufficient to
defend them from the weather, where a kind of boarding school was
kept, but in a very broken and confused manner, and where nothing
was taught the boys more than they might have been taught, in a much
better manner, in the regular school that is maintained in this town at
the expense of the Society in London for Propagating the Gospel in
New England and Parts Adjacent; and where no additional benefits at
all were received by 'em (excepting a free maintenance), but what they
would have had without the expense you were at about them, and
without any additional cost to the Society. So that 'tis very manifest that

1. The Treaty of Aix-la-Chapelle was signed Oct. 8, 1748.

money was spent without anything done to further the great design [in] your mind, but would have been done to better purpose without it.

That winter following, began an exceeding unhappy misunderstanding and great contention between some of the chief English inhabitants of the town concerning Captain Kellogg and his manner of spending your money, in which Captain Kellogg was naturally very deeply engaged on one side. The parents of the children were extremely uneasy, and the Indians of the town in general, and have often loudly complained in my hearing of Captain Kellogg's ill-treatment of their children, in so greatly neglecting them as to their board and clothing and instruction, and taking so little care that their children should be kept clean and orderly. And by this means, the Indians of the town have in general imbibed a great prejudice against Captain Kellogg. In this state, things continued till the fall of the year following, A.D. 1750.

Mr. Sergeant before his death had wrote letters to the Mohawks, inviting them to bring their children hither to be instructed in his intended boarding school. Those letters after Mr. Sergeant's death were seconded by a letter from Captain Kellogg and one Mr. [Benjamin] Ashley and his wife [Rebecca Kellogg Ashley]. (She is Captain Kellogg's sister, had long been in captivity among the Mohawks, was well acquainted with their language, and has a great interest in their affections.) These had lately been occasionally amongst the Mohawks in their own country and endeavored to persuade [them] to come into New England. In consequence of these things, in the latter part of the year about twenty old and young of the Mohawks came down, which was but a little time before I came hither on the business of a missionary.

In the fall of that year, it being a considerable time since anything had been heard from you; and Captain Kellogg, suspecting that you were not in the land of the living and that no further supplies were to be expected from you, dismissed all the [Housatonic] boys that he had kept at your charge and applied himself to the care of the Mohawks, who were soon taken notice of by the government and taken into their care. And Captain Kellogg went on to instruct them, expecting his pay from the government, though no agreement had been made with him. Mr. Ashley and his wife also dwelt with him, to assist in the affair of their instruction, she being our interpreter for the Mohawks.

In this state things were when I first came hither, which was in the beginning of January 1751. Captain Kellogg, during that winter, seemed much animated and engaged by the late coming of the Mohawks and took much pains, in his way, in teaching them to read. But his method was unhappy. He set up no school, but left the children to themselves, to come and read and go when they pleased. He never could be persuaded to go out of this way into a more regular method of teaching, though much pains has been taken with him, and seemed by degrees to grow more and more negligent. The children have been very much neglected, as to instruction in civility and good manners.

Thus things continued in great confusion so long as he was the only master, which was till very lately. Captain Kellogg may partly be excused for his inactivity and awkwardness in the business by reason of his lameness and age, he being now about sixty-six years old and the business new to him. But the Mohawks much disliked his way, being desirous of a regular school and some proper method to bring their children to order and an amendment of manners. Nevertheless, the number of Mohawks which came down hither in the fall and winter increased, so that through the greater part of the winter we had near fifty, old and young.

The last summer, Captain Kellogg received a letter from you, directing him to increase the number of boys maintained and instructed by you from twelve to twenty-four, you seeming, Sir, to suppose that he had then the care of twelve at your charge.

In August last, was a notable interview between the Committee of this Province of the Massachusetts and almost all the chiefs of the nation of the Mohawks, who came hither from their own country with a great train; being invited hither to treat concerning their settlement in New England and putting their children under the instruction of the English. The Indians manifested an uncommonly good disposition with respect to the affair proposed to 'em and promised to promote it to the utmost, not only among their own people, but among all nations of Indians; yet objecting the confused state that they observed things to be in: their children much neglected, no regular school maintained, nor those measures taken for the instructing their children which they had observed the English thought necessary in teaching their own children. But [they] were encouraged by the Committee of the Province that they would endeavor that there should be an alteration in that respect: the Committee being all of one mind that Captain Kellogg was very unfit for that regular education of their children which the Mohawks insisted on, and therefore all determined that another master, a man of learning, must speedily be sought for. However, Captain Kellogg, having received the forementioned letter from Mr. Hollis, proceeded to [take] up a number of boys to be taught and maintained at your expense, but still went on in his former, irregular manner. With the promise of a free maintenance, he enticed away some of the scholars of Deacon Woodbridge's school, where they were regularly and well-instructed, greatly to their disadvantage, their children being much more neglected, and soon, to the common observation of the Indians, became far more disorderly than before.

The General Assembly of the Province and the Commissioners in Boston were informed of what had passed at the treaty with the Mohawks in August last. You may probably, Sir, have heard how the Assembly exerted themselves thereupon to promote the design of the instruction of the Mohawks. The Commissioners also endeavored to find a proper person to be their schoolmaster and treated with a young gentleman [Eli Forbush] of good reputation for his learning and piety to that end. But things so happened that he finally failed. Things continuing long in their former neglected and confused [state], the Mohawks (many of them) were much discouraged. Some of 'em took their children away, giving this negligence and confusion as the reason of it. And the affair of the Mohawks seemed to be under a dark cloud through [a] great part of the last fall and winter.

But yet in the midst of this darkness some new things appeared, which seemed to be remarkable smiles of heaven on the design of instructing the Iroquois or Six Nations in this place. There had been here the last summer an Indian whose name was Jonah Tonaughquunnaugus from Onohquaga, a town of the nation of the Oneidas (one of the Six Nations) situated on the Susquehanna River, near the head of the river about 200 miles southwest from Albany. He was one of the chief inhabitants of the town who, having heard of things that were doing here for the Indians, came to visit the place that he might satisfy himself and make report to his people, and also to see Mr. Ashley and his wife, with whom he had had some acquaintance. I sent a letter by him to the inhabitants of Onohquaga, inviting them to come and bring their children hither for instruction. Mr. Ashley also wrote to the same purpose. In consequence of which there came twenty-one of them, men, women, and children, through so long and tedious a journey in the very depths of a most severe winter and arrived in the latter part of December. One of the women being big with child fell in travail by the way and brought her child alive with her hither.

Something very remarkable has of late years appeared among these

Onohquagas. Many of them, that used to be notorious drunkards and blood-thirsty warriors, have of late strangely had their dispositions and manners changed through some wonderful influence on their minds. They are now averse to war, and do their utmost to dissuade others of the Iroquois that go to war with the southern nations, and have entirely forsaken their drunkenness, and have a disposition to religion and a thirst after instruction.

In the beginning of February last, the great defect which had been so discouraging to the Mohawks was supplied. A schoolmaster was obtained, one Mr. Gideon Hawley, a gentleman of liberal education of about twenty-four years of age, who appears to be well-qualified for the business; of good abilities, and learning, and serious piety, and of uncommon prudence for one of his years, disposed to exert himself greatly to do good and promote the interest of religion in the world; and has long had a peculiar inclination to be employed in instructing Indians. He has set up a regular school, greatly to the joy of the Iroquois. I never saw such appearances of satisfaction in 'em on any occasion. Mr. Hawley has a school of about thirty children and youth. He labors in teaching the children to read and write and in teaching them the English tongue, the principles of religion and good manners, while teaching a couple of English boys, who are put into the school by the government to learn the Iroquois tongue, and other things necessary to fit 'em to be serviceable to the Indians as missionaries or schoolmasters in due time. He himself also is learning the Iroquois language. He has already gained interest in the affections of the Indians, the chief of which have diligently applied themselves to assist him and strengthen his hands in governing their children and bringing them to good order.

Another thing appears very favorable to our designs, viz. the happy union which subsists here between the Iroquois and the Stockbridge Indians. The latter lately of their own accord met together to consider whether they had done all that it was proper for them to do to encourage the Mohawks coming hither for instruction; and after consultation they determined and did as follows: they gave notice to the Iroquois that are here that they desired a conference with them; and after all were convened they told 'em that they observed that the English had done much that they might be instructed in the Christian religion, which made 'em to reflect on themselves and to think that they had failed of doing their part; that as to themselves, they now for some time had had experience of the great benefit of the instruction of the

English; that once they were in a state of great ignorance and dark-ness, but now were brought into the light and know that it was good, and therefore earnestly desired 'em to give heed to instruction and not to listen to any objections, and particularly not to give way to suspi-cions of any ill designs in the English, fearing that they intended to make slaves of them or their children; that they themselves at first were full of such suspicions, but found that they were wholly without grounds; and to encourage 'em, offered 'em the use of some of their lands near the boarding school as long as they pleased; and concluded with saying to this purpose, "We have but a little time to continue here. Let us give diligent heed to the instructions that we have and do our utmost to practice accordingly, and it may be, if we do so, we may hereafter meet together in heaven."

The Onohquaga Indians are especially well-pleased in what they find here, at least since Mr. Hawley came, and intend to invite the rest of their brethren which they left at Onohquaga to follow them. Jonah Tonaughquunnaugus, who is a remarkably pious and devout man, is soon going thither on that errand, and thinks he shall bring many with him in his return.

Mr. Hawley intends, if providence allows, some time in the ap-proaching summer or fall to go up into the country of the Iroquois, taking with him several of the best of the Indians, to endeavor to persuade the Indians there to bring their children hither to be in-structed.

The things forementioned, together with the forward disposition of the government, and that so many in England have been lately moved to exert themselves for our help, and have had their hearts and hands so oped[2] in and to it, seem to be tokens for good and give reasons to hope that God has a design of doing some great things for those poor Americans.

But yet there are some great difficulties [which] attend our affairs, particularly the great and successful endeavors of the French of late to alienate the Iroquois from the English and attach 'em to themselves; the great opposition of the Dutch, in the government of New York that lies between us and the Iroquois, to the Indians coming here, being afraid they shall lose the benefit of their trade; and the evil disposition which appears in some of the Iroquois themselves.

But worse than all these are the difficulties that arise from among

2. Archaic for "opened."

the English, particularly a great misunderstanding that has for more than two years subsisted between the chief English inhabitants of Stockbridge, of which I before gave some hint. The opposition of one side to the other has proceeded a great length indeed, in the attempts which one has made against the other, and has been made very public all over New England. And this contention has great and extensive influence, the contending parties being both considerable men: one of them a gentleman [Col. Ephraim Williams] of good understanding and very considerable estate, and of great activity, and has many in New England who are related to him that are men of distinction, and some of them have great influence in our affairs. This gentleman is in strict union with Captain Kellogg. The other is a man of superior abilities [Deacon Timothy Woodbridge], has a great interest in the esteem of the Stockbridge Indians, and has perhaps greater influence upon them than all other Englishmen put together. They have been mightily engaged on his side in this controversy and have for many years had the deepest prejudice against his antagonist, which seems to be increasing and has risen to that height of late that the Indians talk of breaking up and leaving the town because of him. And most of the English inhabitants are engaged on the same side with the Indians.

The breach between these two contending parties is as wide as the seas. There seems to be no new hope of its being healed. Great endeavors have been used to heal it, and there has been a very formal pacification, but it soon appeared to be but a palliative cure. It has again broke out to a great degree.

This misunderstanding does very much affect the affair of the instruction of the Indians in this place and is the darkest cloud and the most pernicious thing that attends it, the chief hindrance of success. It keeps the affair unsettled and in a great deal of confusion and not a little threatens the entire subvention of it. It especially affects the affair of the boarding school, as it began first about that affair.

'Tis not unlikely, Sir, that through the influence of this contention you may have sent to you different and inconsistent accounts of the state of your affairs here. But I humbly conceive, the way of your greatest security is to rely much on the Reverend Mr. [Thomas] Prince of Boston, whom you have chosen especially to be your correspondent in these affairs, or to inquire of the Commissioners for Indian Affairs in Boston who are not so much in the way of being corrupted and biased by the influence of our shameful quarrels as may others, being at a distance from us and not being related or engaged with either party. 'Tis indeed of great necessity that those who are interested in our affairs to any considerable degree should be impartial with respect to this pernicious quarrel.

I wrote largely the last summer to the Honorable Andrew Oliver, Esq., Treasurer to the Commissioners, and to the Speaker of the House of Representatives [Thomas Hubbard]. In both my letters I had these words:

> What renders it more necessary that things here should be under the immediate care of trustees, is the misunderstanding and jealousy here subsisting between some of the chief of the present English inhabitants of the town, which is one of our greatest calamities. Things on this account do much more need constant inspection. And therefore the gentlemen entrusted ought to be such as are perfectly impartial, no way interested in or related to these contending parties.

The boarding school ever since Mr. Hawley came is subject to a peculiar unhappiness that keeps it in a disadvantageous, uncomfortable, unsettled state; which there is reason to think is much owing to the influence of this contention. The great difficulty it labors under is this, that although when Mr. Hawley came and had set up a regular school, it was apparent that the Indians would insist on Mr. Hawley's having the care and instruction of all their children, which Captain Kellogg therefore could not hinder; yet he never resigned the boys. But although Mr. Hawley has their instruction, yet Captain Kellogg lives there still, calls the boys his own, and claims a superior power and command over them, and acts as though he looked on himself as a superintendent over all affairs of the house, and plainly shows himself not pleased in Mr. Hawley's being there; don't at all assist him in the affairs of the school, but in many respects counteracts him and greatly clogs and hinders him. When he pleases, he will call the boys down out of the school to serve him in his occasions; and sometimes calls 'em off, pretending to take the care of them himself. Which keeps things in a very broken, unsettled state, makes it very difficult for Mr. Hawley to maintain order and government, it not well appearing to the boys who is their master or whom they ought to obey. Captain Kellogg claims the greatest part of the boys as his own, and by often breaking in by his pretended superior authority, makes it extremely difficult for Mr. Hawley to get into any established, happy methods of teaching and regulating the school; which otherwise, for aught appears, it might be easy for him to do. Mr. Hawley [is] so discouraged with such a situation of things that he by no means will continue, but for the hope of an alteration. Nor is it a thing ever to be hoped for, that any gentleman fit for the business will be obtained to keep the school under these circumstances. And if this disease has no remedy, it threatens ruin to the whole affair.

This difficulty is probably much owing to the influence of the forementioned contention. There are some that are by no means willing he [Captain Kellogg] should go away. And it may well be supposed his continuance is desired to maintain and strengthen a party. There is a great understanding between Captain Kellogg and his brother Ashley and his wife, the interpreter, so much owing to the forementioned great contention. I would by no means wrong Captain Kellogg in any respect or do him the least injustice, but just that you who have so great a concern with him should know something of his infirmities as well as good qualities. He is a person of high resentments and has some other peculiar unhappiness in his temper that renders it very difficult to manage with him.

I who see this state of things and see how sad the consequence is like to be, if there be no alteration, have had many doubts and conflicts in my own mind with respect to my thus giving you a full account of our state.[3] I have been very backward to speak to the wrong of any person's character, and besides, I did not know but I might lay myself under suspicion, and might discourage you from expending anything further in the Stockbridge affairs. But my concern for the Indian affair of Stockbridge, which is of greater importance than mine or Captain Kellogg's reputation, and my remembrance of that great rule of our Savior, of doing to others as we would that they should do to us, have conquered.

The forementioned unhappiness, which attends the affair of the boarding school and which threatens its overthrow, is what none here can remedy without your help; you being Captain Kellogg's sole constituent, to whom only he looks on himself as accountable, and he claiming the highest authority over the greater part of Mr. Hawley's school. And you, Sir, can on the plainest grounds challenge a right to know the true state of your affairs here. And it would be the greater injury and abuse to conceal it from you, as your liberality is so great. And 'tis impossible that you ever should know, but either directly or

3. JE interlineated, "See p. 1. e," but the corresponding passage meant for insertion has not been located.

indirectly by information from hence. We may determine, Sir, that you would not willingly dispose of your money in such a manner as would be equivalent to throwing it away. Much less so, that it should only be an occasion of hindering good, and greatly clogging and embarrassing the affair of the instruction of the Indians.

I would humbly propose, Sir, that your bounty should be committed to the care and into the hands of some persons that are near at hand, that are not related to the contending parties here or at all engaged in their quarrel, and that your appointment of the persons should be under the direction of Mr. Prince or the Commissioners in Boston. I mention this, because I so well know the state of things, that it is abundantly evident to me 'tis necessary in order to your safety. And if it were in the hands of two or three faithful trustees, there now seems to be an opportunity for bringing it to most excellent and indeed glorious progress, far beyond what ever had been before, and therefore I hope, Sir, that the account I have given will not be discouraging to you. Michael and his angels and the dragon seem to be remarkably at war about our affairs. And I believe it is a token for good, and that something very good and great is like to be the issue. I think it [not] suitable for such as have entered on Michael's side to sit in discouragement. [. . .]

[Jonathan Edwards.]

P.S. to my letter to Mr. Hollis written in the summer, 1752.
Sir,

Since I wrote the preceding letter of July 17, some things have appeared which have convinced me that it is necessary that I should more particularly explain some things hinted at or generally mentioned in the preceding letter.

As to the controversy between me and my former people (the influence of which reaches Stockbridge affairs in no small degree), the enclosed Result of a council will give you some light.[4] It is, as you will see, the result of a council called by a number of brethren at Northampton that adhered to me, to give their advice about a twelvemonth after my separation from that people under the conduct of another council, in the calling of which no small degree of violence was used.

The family of note I mentioned in the preceding letter, as deeply engaged in that controversy on the side of my opposers, is the family of the Williamses. The controversy had begun some time before Elisha

4. *Boston Gazette*, June 11, 1751.

Williams went to England, and he was much resorted to for advice by my opposers and was their chief adviser till he set out for England, and had begun to write against me. But when he had determined to go to England, he committed his papers to his brother, Mr. [Solomon] Williams of Lebanon, who finished what the Colonel had begun, and published a book against me written with no small degree of bitterness and contempt. Another of his brothers, viz. Col. Israel Williams of Hatfield, exerted himself very much with great zeal against me after his brother Elisha was gone, and was much resorted to by my opposers at Northampton. They also made much use of their brother [Jonathan] Ashley of Deerfield and Col. [Oliver] Partridge, another of the same family, and their kinsman, Mr. Chester Williams of Hadley, who were very busy and active in that affair. With these joined Mr. [Jonathan] Hubbard, the minister of the Lower Sheffield, who was moderator of the council at Northampton that led the people there to dismiss me from the ministry in that church. He has shown himself very opposite to my coming to Stockbridge.

When my being the minister at Stockbridge was first proposed, Col. Ephraim Williams of this town (uncle to Colonel Elisha, Colonel Israel, and Mr. Williams of Lebanon, and great uncle to Colonel Partridge), together with his daughter, Mrs. [Abigail] Sergeant, very greatly opposed it. But when they saw the stream was too strong for them and this was like to come to pass, they appeared as if they were friendly to it; and by many things, it was evident they were still in their hearts very opposite and that my being the minister here was very cross to 'em. Probably their opposition was the greater because Mr. [Timothy] Woodbridge, that Colonel Williams had been in great contention with, was very much for it. These were the two gentlemen between whom arose that great contention in Stockbridge I mentioned, which began about the manner of Captain Kellogg's spending, viz. Col. Ephraim Williams with Captain Kellogg on one side, and Mr. Woodbridge on the other. Captain Kellogg had long been a great favorite of the family of the Williamses. At that time, Colonel Williams had a joint interest in the management of some affairs here relating to the Indians, wherein Mr. Woodbridge thought public injury was done. His finding fault greatly provoked them. Whereupon Colonel Williams entered a complaint against Mr. Woodbridge to the Commissioners in Boston, laid many charges against him, [and] endeavored to have him turned out of the school, on which Mr. Woodbridge was cited to Boston. Many of the chief Indians went with him to defend him, and not Colonel Wil-

liams, before the Commissioners. The whole county was filled with the
noise of this affair. In the issue, Deacon Woodbridge was justified and
established in this place, and the conduct of Colonel Williams in this
affair was greatly disliked by the Commissioners. Mr. Woodbridge
from his childhood has had the character among all that have been
acquainted with him as a person of uprightness, of a generous disposition, one that greatly abhors any mean, clandestine, injurious management from private views, and of a very easy, placable, natural temper. And by his long-proved justice and integrity, he has gained a vast
esteem with the Indians, who are a people peculiar in that respect, if
once they find a man is mean, [and] deceitful, never will trust him
again; but their friendship is mightily gained by upright dealing.

After the interview with the Indians here in August was twelvemonth,[5] the General Assembly appointed Col. [Joseph] Dwight, Col.
[Joseph] Pynchon, and Capt. [John] Ashley their Committee to take
care of the Mohawk affair here on their behalf, and lay out the money
they had granted for their support, boarding school stuff, etc. These
were all united in their sentiments of Captain Kellogg's uselessness
here and none more full in it, and more zealous to have him speedily
removed and another master procured, than Colonel Dwight. The
same gentleman had been for many years one of the greatest friends I
had in New England, and appeared my zealous friend in the controversy with my people at Northampton, and expressed an higher opinion of me than of any other minister in Massachusetts; till he had
entered deeply into engagements with Mrs. Sergeant, that he has since
married. And then there was a sudden, strange alteration, both with
regard to his friendship towards me and his disposition with regard to
Captain Kellogg's continuance. He is a gentleman of a very susceptible
constitution, warm passions, and beyond measure captivated by Mrs.
Sergeant. The rest of the General Court's Committee are generally
against Captain Kellogg's continuance here. The Indians have a great
and rooted prejudice against Colonel Williams and Mrs. Sergeant,
alias Mrs. Dwight, and are most firmly attached to Mr. Woodbridge.

Colonel Dwight and the family of the Williamses now seem mightily
engaged to have Captain Kellogg continued here. What their particular ends are I will not determine. However, 'tis apparent that they
think it necessary, in order to promote certain designs of theirs relating to the Indians, particularly Mrs. Dwight's being the mistress, which

5. I.e. a year past.

the Indians in general—both the Stockbridge Indians and Mohawks—are very opposite to. The Indians have their particular prejudices against her, besides their dislike to the family she belongs to,
which is greater than to any family in the world.

Many have been the devices of Captain Kellogg and those that abet
him, to put some good color on his continuance here at your charge,
without being in the employ you appointed him to.

'Tis pretended and greatly insisted that he has peculiar talents for
the management of the Mohawks, and such great interest in them that
his going away would be the ruin of the Mohawk affair. But in this they
are entirely mistaken. I have been long enough acquainted with the
Mohawks to know that 'tis far otherwise. There is no person that is
around with them, that they are [so] frequently contending with, and
whose conduct they have been so frequently disgusted by.

The Captain and his abettors have much insisted that he was the
chief instrument of the Mohawks first coming hither, when this does
not appear. Mr. Ashley and his wife seem to have a much fairer claim
to that honor, though I deny not that the Captain had some hand in it.

One while it was given out, that Mr. Kellogg had a scheme for uniting the Six Nations one to another, and attaching them to the British
interest; and that it was necessary he should be continued here, that he
might have opportunity to prosecute that scheme. Then it was said, he
must be here as a steward, though that be a business he is wholly unfit
for by reason of his age, lameness, and great inactivity, and a business
he does little at. Another pretense is, that 'tis needful he should be
here to superintend your affairs and see that they be well looked after
by the master that teaches them. Sometimes, that he might have some
show of being in employ, he has sent out some Indian boys to work in
the fields, but without any overseer and so to no purpose. Sometimes
for several days together, he has called some of the boys out of Mr.
Hawley's school and pretended to teach 'em himself, to the vast breaking and putting into confusion the affair of their instruction. Of late,
Mr. Kellogg insists that 'tis of importance that he should be here to
promote the affair of the female school, which as yet has no being, nor
is like to have in the way things now are going.

I have from time to time expostulated with Captain Kellogg about
those things, and dealt very plainly with him (though with moderation
and calmness), and have told him plainly if he persisted in his resolution of continuing here under these circumstances, I should think
myself bound to send you a very full and particular [account] of the

state of things here. My discourse with him has sometimes seemed almost to bring him to a resolution to go away. But then he goes to Colonel Dwight and the Williamses and they strongly advise him to continue, as he himself tells me. It has been given out that if I write to you, as good gentlemen as I will write against me, who can have greater influence on Mr. Hollis than I.

The people of the town have been very uneasy, who, some of them, have with this sent some testimony concerning the present state of your affairs. These are all English inhabitants of Stockbridge that are heads of families, except their children and some late comers, and Colonel Williams' family. It might have been easy to have obtained the voice of all the rest, if this had been necessary. The letter from Mr. Ashley is the Ashley whose wife is our interpreter for the Iroquois. With this also comes: a letter from Mr. [Samuel] Hopkins, the minister of the Upper Sheffield, the nearest minister to Stockbridge, a gentleman of a very prudent and pious character, a great friend of vital religion, long intimately acquainted with Mr. Sergeant and with Stockbridge affairs; the letter from Mr. Woodbridge, etc.

So much would not be done in making representations to you concerning Captain Kellogg were it not that the whole of this important affair of the Iroquois, as its well-being and being, is greatly concerned in the matter that is represented. You doubtless will receive other representations, perhaps in abundance, and probably will be greatly surprised at the receipt of so many letters from contesting parties, containing such jarring representations, and not a little damped in your spirit at the sudden appearance of so great contest about your affairs here [in] which, Sir, you have so exerted yourself and from which you have entertained such hopes. And indeed it is very lamentable, and I have been exceeding loath to be the occasion of that surprise and gloom, which will probably be brought in your mind on the receipt of these letters. I have hung back very much about the matter, hoping that our difficulties might some way be terminated, but at present there appears no prospect of it. I hope, Sir, you will not at once take up a resolution to do no more in our affairs. I would pray you to consider that the unsuccessfulness of your endeavors here has not arisen from the nature of the affair itself, which has indeed afforded the most glorious opportunity, but wholly from the hands that have managed it for you, it being left so much to one and not being under the care of any trustees.

But whatever may be the effects of these letters, as to your determining and tendering your future conduct with respect to future disbursements, I insist that you have given such extraordinary demonstrations [of] so great sincerity and zeal in your desires of the prosperity of Stockbridge affairs, [that] you would earnestly pray for us to him who is the Great Shepherd and Bishop of souls [I Pet. 2:25], who is able to bring order out of confusion, and cause every valley to be exalted, every mountain and hill to be made low, that crooked things should be made straight and rough places plain, and to reveal his own glory [Is. 40:4–5] and cause the light of it to shine through the darkest clouds.

Perhaps it will be represented in some letters you may receive, that I have fallen under an unhappy bias by evil-minded persons. But the general knowledge you have of New England will naturally lead you [to] suppose that the Commissioners in Boston, who are the chief men in New England, and Mr. Prince, are not much in the way of being biased by parties here, and probably you will not be afraid to rely much on words you receive from them.

Having done what I find necessary to disburden my own conscience, I must leave the event with the infinitely wise and gracious head of the church, remaining, reverend Sir, with much esteem,

> Your brother and fellow servant in the labor of the gospel,
> Jonathan Edwards.

153. TO SEC. JOSIAH WILLARD

The outspoken nature of this letter indicates Edwards' level of trust in his friend, the Secretary of the Province. Spurning circumlocution, he frankly lays out his concerns about the machinations of Brig. Joseph Dwight against him.

(Trask Library, one folio leaf, a letter cover addressed on recto to Edwards at Northampton in New England; Dwight ms. transcript, with liberties, two quarto leaves.)

* * *

Stockbridge, July 17, 1752

Honored Sir,

I have some reason to suppose that some discourse of Brig. [Joseph] Dwight, representing me as of a very stiff, inflexible temper, has made some impression on your mind. I know that others, in some respects, are better able to judge of my qualifications and character than I myself; and it becomes me to be jealous of myself and suspicious of my own judgment of myself, wherein it is any instance in my favor. But yet whether this be my just character or no, I humbly conceive I have given him no occasion to observe it in any of my conduct towards him. He never conversed with me but once concerning any of these affairs, which have been the occasion of misunderstanding. Then, it is true, he endeavored to satisfy [me] with respect to his past conduct, his secret endeavors to divide Mr. [Gideon] Hawley from me, and so much opposing my preaching to the Mohawks. And all the reason he had to say I was stiff was, that when he insisted upon it, that I should say whether the reasons he had given [me] were satisfying, that I did not appear satisfied, which I had certainly no reason to be; for he then, at [that] very time, before he put the question to me whether I was satisfied, with much spirit told me I had no business to preach to 'em, I did no good there, and did in a threatening air signify a design of taking some effectual course to hinder me; and did with much of an upbraiding air, blame me for my conduct in some instances.

I know that I am stiff and inflexible is what was abundantly said of me at Northampton during my late, long controversy with my people at Northampton, and by those that espoused their cause, particularly by the family of the Williams. But the only reason they had to say so was, that I durst not violate a good conscience in complying with what they insisted on, as to the terms of communion; and that I did not yield to them and the ministers that were against me in that controversy, rendering by that means, that town and that part of the county filled with this cry of my stiffness and inflexibleness. And in several other cases of religious controversies that have been before with several ministers and some with other persons, wherein I was reproached for a good conscience, this has been said of me. And I don't remember that ever on any other occasion.

You are doubtless, Sir, sensible that in all ages this has been the cry, in cases of persecution of persons for conscience's sake, that they are froward, perverse, stiff, willful, and inflexible.

The Brigadier has seen cause on this occasion, and since he has entered into so strict [an alliance] with that family of the Williams, to give into the report, and adopt the reproach that my enemies have cast upon me, to represent as though there was no dealing with me. The Williams now on this occasion, especially some of them, are abundant in their insisting on this endeavor, to make the utmost of it, as some of them talk of my being removed from this place. And I have observed that some that join with them take this course to wound my reputation. Where they think harshness will not be relished, they make way for the wounds they intend to give by saying some good of me, and then introduce the ill that they have to say of me as an exception, as it were with much tenderness, as what is grievous, etc. But with other persons, who don't insist on any caution, they take another course; they don't lay themselves under such restraints.

As [to] a reconciliation with the Brigadier, if by a reconciliation is meant foregoing all personal resentment, I hope there would be no difficulties on my side. But if thereby be meant, my being of the opinion that he is a fit person to be here, or that this cause will ever flourish under his hands, that opinion it may be hard for me to be of, though perhaps some will account it an instance of my stiffness and inflexibleness, that I cannot.

But to be of that opinion is at present [not] in my power, because I think I see abundant evidence of the contrary. I think [him] not fit upon these accounts: he is naturally a person of too sovereign and arbitrary a disposition, naturally exceedingly inclined to engross all power and manage all things by himself. This appears by the many impetuous things he has done of his own head here, since [he] has been one of the committee. Of his own head, instead of building a school-house for the male school, he has erected a large house, as large as the building that was before, that cost at least a thousand pounds, and [is] not yet finished. For what end he has built it so large, I know not. Of his own head, [he] has gone about another large house, instead of a schoolhouse, for the female school; has determined the place of it, viz. on Madam [Abigail] Sergeant's land, that being but near his own land. [He] has ordered the timber to [be] carried thither, and thereto framed. Of his own head, he had Mr. [Japheth] Bush to live here to set the boys to work, who, though a very honest man, is a man of no authority and is not regarded, but despised, by the Indians. But [he] is a pretty zealous friend on Colonel Williams' side in the Stockbridge contentions. Of his own head, he sent for some of the sachems, to have a treaty with them; and brought up Capt. Joseph Kellogg from Suffield to interpret; and had the treaty alone with them, a very unhappy one, the chief thing being to know what [he] should do to attach the Six Nations to the British interest. He distributed the country's presents alone, of his own mind, and I think in such a manner [as did] much hurt. [. . .]

[Jonathan Edwards.]

154. TO COL. ELISHA WILLIAMS

Elisha Williams, returned from London and ready to resume his political career, comes to aid his Uncle Ephraim and exercise his new authority as a commissioner to Stockbridge from the London Society. Edwards is not intimidated. In the first of a series of exchanges, he courteously but firmly refuses to submit to his old tutor's jurisdiction and insists that an impartial judge is needed to remedy affairs at Stockbridge.

(Beinecke Library, ALS, two quarto leaves, addressed at top to Col. Elisha Williams, now in Stockbridge.)

* * *

Stockbridge, August 15, 1752

Honored Sir,

The more I think of it, the more I am confirmed in it, that it will answer no good purpose, either for the forming a right judgment of our affairs, or the bringing them to an happy issue, to take accounts of 'em from particular persons, of contrary judgments, privately and separately. I think it is high time that the affairs of Stockbridge, which have been [a] matter of misunderstanding and controversy, should be thoroughly examined, even from their first foundation, and searched to the very bottom; and that it should be done here on the spot, all parties being face to face, and the inhabitants of the town in general present: and that this is the only method that will tend to any good. But then I humbly conceive that the persons that should make this inquiry, either as judges or mediators, should be such as may justly be looked upon as wholly impartial, and in such circumstances as have not a visible tendency to bias them on one side or the other. This certainly is requisite in the nature of things, and in order to the just confidence of persons concerned, and the satisfaction of the world.

Now, Sir, I trust you will not take it as any reflection upon you, or any evidence of want of due respect, that I say you cannot justly be esteemed such a person; being nearly related to the family chiefly concerned in these controversies and being known to have been long united to Capt. [Martin] Kellogg, in a peculiar and very intimate friendship. As to my judgment on these affairs, it is the reverse of that which I have reason to think you are fixed in. I own that I am full in it, that for Mrs. [Abigail] Dwight to undertake the care of the female boarding school will in no wise answer the design or expectation of the society in London, with regard to such a school. And though I would maintain the utmost care not to injure her in any respect, yet I think a public, important interest ought not to be sacrificed for her sake.

And I think that Captain Kellogg's staying here, at Mr. [Isaac] Hollis' charge, while he is not in the business that Mr. Hollis appointed him to (and for the support of which business alone he makes his remittances hither) and without any stated, visible employment whatsoever, which has been the case ever since the beginning of last February, is a just and great offense to all Christians that observe it; and must, if it continues, become more a scandal in the eyes of the whole country, and all far and near that know of it.

Now, Sir, if I should submit the reasons of my opinion and conduct, in these and other things relating to our affairs, to your judgment, and we should give you the desired opportunity to inquire into, and judge of our affairs, I have the greatest reason to think that the judgment you would pass on them, on such a hearing, would be the foundation of a representation you would make of them home to England. And you will not be offended if I think that it concerns me, as I regard my reputation in the world, that the judgment which is made on our affairs for such a purpose, should be a true and impartial one. I have reason to stand on my guard in this matter: for I know many of your friends here have their spirits greatly engaged in these affairs, and that I am looked on by them as a person not a little obnoxious; that some of them have not spared my character; that one of them, who has lately spent much time with you at Wethersfield, is in effect no other than my open and avowed enemy. And I have good evidence that another of them has drawn up a letter to Mr. Hollis, in which I am not a little reflected upon, and various things are said to my disadvantage (I don't say this by mere conjecture), and I have reason to think that others are privy to the contents of this letter.

Therefore, I hope Sir, that you will excuse me that I wholly decline having any hand in such an opening of our affairs before you as you have proposed, which I profess I don't refuse from any disrespect to you, whom I ever desire to treat with honor, with your excellent consort [Elizabeth Scott Williams] now with you: on the mention of whom, I cannot but renewedly congratulate myself and my country, on her becoming one of its inhabitants; as I hope she brings no small degree of the blessing of heaven into New England with her.

But that the good end which you propose by inquiring into our affairs may not fail of being obtained, with the best advantage, I would now humbly make you this offer; viz. to join with you in an earnest application to the body of the Commissioners, that they would appoint a committee, to come on the spot, and make thorough inquiry into our present difficulties, and the management of Stockbridge affairs, from the very beginning, by all the living inhabitants or residents in the town that have had any hand in them in any respect. In which case, I am ready to promise freely to open myself, and declare openly the reasons of my judgment concerning the affairs of the two boarding schools, and give all the light in the state of our affairs, in every respect, that lies in my power. And it shall be no objection, if you are present, and hear all that is said. I am willing that all affairs should be determined and settled by the judgment of such a committee, and that the Commissioners should make such a representation to England as they think proper on their report. This, with the most cordial respects to Madam is, honored Sir, from

> Your respectful and most humble servant,
> Jonathan Edwards.

155. TO COL. ELISHA WILLIAMS

Elisha Williams' response to Edwards' previous letter has not survived, but its contents may be inferred from this reply. Williams called for a meeting at which Edwards would explain his opposition to Abigail Dwight as headmistress of the female school.

The issue, Edwards rejoins here, goes deeper than a conflict over why he is not obliged to tell Williams his reasons why Dwight should not be the headmistress. The missionary's proper supervisors are the Boston Commissioners, who have not notified him of the colonel's commission or granted permission for a proceeding such as the one requested. If a hearing is to be held, it should be sponsored by the Commissioners, the duly constituted authority, before a neutral tribunal.

Williams replied the next day that Edwards had misunderstood him. He simply desired an amicable "interview." The London Society has appointed Abigail Dwight; he is delegated to secure information about her. Any questions about her competence should be discussed privately, before being aired to the Commissioners. He closed with his version of a conversation with Sarah Pierpont Edwards.

(Beinecke Library, ALS, two folio leaves; RIHS, ms. 1129, copy in unknown hand, two folio leaves. See also RIHS, ms. 1130, copy of reply, Aug. 19, 1752, two folio leaves.)

* * *

Stockbridge, August 18, 1752

Honored Sir,

An Indian lately picked up a letter in the street, directed to me, not knowing what, nor from whom it was. However, it is come to my hands. I have had some doubt in my mind whether I had any right to it, coming to me in such a manner: for it seems it went out of the hands of the possessor of it accidentally, and not designedly. However, seeing it inscribed to me, I opened it, and found it a letter from you; and presuming you intended I should have it, I would now make some reply to it.

In the beginning of your letter, you speak of an interview with Col. [Joseph] Dwight, your uncle [Col. Ephraim Williams, Sr.], and Capt. [Martin] Kellogg, in your presence, as what I myself had mentioned. In which you seem to have taken the matter very wrong. When you mentioned the misunderstandings here subsisting, and desired some account from me of them, I signified as much, as that if I did at any time give an account, I should choose that all parties concerned in these misunderstandings should be face [to] face, but mentioned the name of no one person: much less did I single out these names; which would have been to exclude others concerned in our controversies. And I spake of the thing in general, and not as being at this time, or in any particular person's presence. But it was you, Sir, that did this in your reply, as near as I can remember, in these words, *Well, why can't that be now?*

After taking the matter into consideration, I have given you my reasons why I think it is not best to be done now before you, as a judge or mediator. You seem to think yourself injured; and particularly in my not giving you the reasons why I think it will not answer the design and expectation of the society for Mrs. [Abigail] Dwight to undertake the care of the female school; and are pleased in your letter to tell me once and again, that you have a right to know my reasons, and therefore that you insist on my giving you the reason why I judge, etc. To which I would say, if you are truly vested with this high authority, I was not aware of it; and therefore, if I have erred in not submitting to you in this manner, I have transgressed ignorantly. However, I am willing to be informed, if I have had mistaken notions concerning the common rights of mankind, as well as been ignorant of the extent of your commission. I should think it might be a matter of doubt whether the Society themselves have so great authority. If they should desire to know my sentiments concerning such an affair, and I in compliance with their desire should tell them my judgment, then to insist on my reasons as what they have a right to demand, not allowing me to judge for myself whether it be best to suppress them, but to determine for me that I can have no sufficient reason for my silence: without doubt the Society would have a right to pay as little regard as they please to my judgment, and as much less as they please for my not giving the reasons of it, and to establish a mistress and maintain any person they think best in the school, without regard to my judgment. But this will by no means amount to a power to demand the secrets of my heart in this matter; which for ought they know I have good reason to conceal.

But whatever power of this kind the Society has, I suppose they have committed it to no single person in America. It is known that there is a body of Commissioners, to whom they have committed their authority in many respects; who are able to exercise it, acting jointly, but not singly. If they have committed their authority to any single person, acting alone, in any particular affair, in that affair, they have made him their sole commissioner. And if there be any such commissioner in the affair of establishing a mistress of the female school, who therefore has power to demand and judge of all reasons pro and con in this affair, I may be excused for not supposing it in my conduct hitherto, the commission not having been published, or at least not made known to me. I have acted according to the best light and information I have had. I know not who to look to for directions, with regard to my duty in my present station here, but (under Christ) to the body of Commissioners that have introduced me into it; who have signified to me that I am to receive my directions from them, and am accountable only to them, and not to [be] dictated to by any here. I trust that they that sent me hither are able to inform me to whom I am accountable better than others that are comparatively strangers to our affairs. And therefore, till I have further instructions, I shall act accordingly. To them I refer myself; to them I am ready to give my reasons, etc. at any time when they shall ask for them. To their judgment I refer all our difficulties and misunderstandings so far as I have any concern in them; and so far as I have no concern in them, I am willing to let them alone. If our affairs are represented before any in order to our receiving the benefit of their wisdom, friendly interposition, and mediation, in the manner you proposed to have our affairs represented before you, I think they are the properest persons, much more suitable than a single gentleman, nearly related to the family that from the beginning have been chiefly interested in the lamentable controversies which have been the bane of the Indian affairs. With respect to those that they employ, they may act authoritatively; and as to others, let 'em hear our affairs as you proposed to hear 'em. I can see no more difficulty in their represent-ing affairs before them for their advice and friendly mediation, than in all parties representing affairs before you for such a purpose, which you proposed, and seemed to think there was no difficulty in the way of. To insist on this objection of some persons concerned not being under the authority of the Commissioners, will be in effect to insist that none shall ever come hither, either to judge or advise, or in any respect to take knowledge of our affairs, to use their wisdom to put an end to our confusions, because all the controverting parties are not subject to the same constituents.

As an objection against my giving my reasons, why I think it would not answer the end for Mrs. Dwight to be the mistress of the school, before a committee appointed by the Commissioners, you suppose that this would be to endeavor in an open manner to hurt her reputa-tion, to which I would say: it will be time enough to mention and consider the objection, when it is known that my reasons are taken from things that would be to her reproach. And if that be supposed to be the tendency of an open hearing before some of the Commis-sioners, then I would humbly inquire, why you thought well of such an open hearing now, all misunderstanding parties being present, while you are in town? Certainly you could not reasonably think all the misunderstanding parties, better friends to Mrs. Dwight than the Commissioners.

I mentioned some things as reasons why I should stand on my guard. You are pleased to speak of these things as groundless surmises and jealousies, though I told you expressly I did not speak by conjec-ture. It will be no affront to you, Sir, that I say that I understand the affairs of Stockbridge better than you can do. And besides those things that I mentioned concerning your friends, I might have added that even as to yourself, I have, at least, some reason to suspect that your mind had been so prepossessed and prejudiced by means of them, or by some other means, that you did not come to town with a mind altogether calm and friendly towards me and my family, from your treatment of my wife, at your first coming to my house in my absence, after your having been so long absent from New England; when, as one of the first compliments, you did in effect peremptorily give her the lie, in telling her before all the company with an assured air, that "she knew better," on her saying something which she doubtless supposed to be fact, and wherein she asserted nothing injurious to you, and though she treated you, after her known manner, with all possible respect. Certainly [this was]¹ charging her with asserting contrary to her own knowledge.

I don't mention this because I desire to lay it up against you, but as one thing that will justify my caution. And for this reason did I mention what has appeared in the temper of some of your friends towards me. I have no disposition to anything else but peace and friendship with them. This I have sought hitherto and this I am resolved to pursue hereafter, so long as there can be any hopes of it—though I don't think our meeting to represent the grounds of our misunderstanding before you as a mediator, would be a proper expedient in order to it. Indeed, I need no mediator as to my own part. I am already fully disposed to peace. I require no humble confessions or lowly submissions, and insist on no terms with them, but only that henceforth they don't act the inimical part.

As to your kinsman [Col. Ephraim Williams, Sr.], though it be a matter of plain and known fact, that he freely and openly, and without restraint or reserve, declares by words and actions his disesteem and great dislike of me, and his resolution to injure my character, and this without my ever having injured him in the least degree; yet I have not the least disposition to be his enemy, or to lay up any of these things against him, but am ready freely to forgive him, and desire to live in peace with him, and bury everything in oblivion from this day forward: and there has been no day wherein this has not been my disposition. I utterly disclaim proceeding on the foot of personal resentment in these affairs, or saying or doing anything from a spirit of opposition, desire of victory, or any delight in forbearing to comply with others' desires. I wish with all my heart that all such principles of acting, and all selfish principles whatsoever, were utterly and forever banished from Stockbridge; which must necessarily be very provoking to God, and pernicious to the great design of enlarging the kingdom of Christ here. If I know my own heart, I have for more than thirty years, set my heart on the advancement and enlargement of Christ's kingdom on earth, as a kingdom of light, love, and peace, and have preferred these things to my chief joy. If I am influenced in anything I do, from principles contrary to these, my earnest prayer to God, the

1. MS damage; reading supplied from copy.

searcher of hearts, is, that God would cleanse me from such secret faults. I remain, Sir, with all respect,

Your most humble servant,
Jonathan Edwards.

156. TO SEC. ANDREW OLIVER

Edwards and the Boston Commissioners shared a relationship of appreciation and trust. In this letter he recapitulates events at Stockbridge of the past year. Whole sections are lifted from different letters, including those to Speaker Hubbard (Mar. 30 and Aug. 29, 1752) and Rev. Isaac Hollis (July 17, 1752). Edwards includes a minute account of his dealings with Col. Elisha Williams and stands ready to supply any further information needed, including all correspondence. He alerts the Commissioners to the fact that Williams may bypass them and attempt to exert pressure through the London Society. No doubt the Commissioners were amused by Edwards' description of his encounter with Capt. Martin Kellogg, who ingenuously disclosed that he had been coached to give various reasons to the Commissioners for his presence, including the preposterous claim that he had a scheme to unite the Six Nations and persuade them to support British interests.

(Trask Library, AL draft, one folio leaf, a letter cover, addressed on recto to Edward Bromfield, merchant in Boston, and one quarto leaf, a letter cover, addressed on verso to Mrs. Esther Edwards at Northampton; Dwight ms. transcript, eight quarto leaves.)

*   *   *

Stockbridge, August 27, 1752

Sir,

I received your letter of the 29th of June, with a copy for Mr. [Gideon] Hawley. I humbly thank the Honorable Commissioners for their esteem, manifested in the confidence they put in me. I take it as a great obligation upon [me] to faithfulness and care, not to fail their expectations.

I will now endeavor to give Your Honor as just an idea as I can of the state of things here and the manner in which they have gone since the last April, leaving it to you to make what use, of the account I shall give, you think proper.

Capt. [Martin] Kellogg went away to his family at Newington about the same time that Col. [Joseph] Dwight set out from hence in order to go to Concord. But before they went away, they sent for Capt. Joseph Kellogg of Suffield, to be here during their absence. Capt. Martin Kellogg was gone about two months, during which time his brother was here, but in no business or employ of any kind whatsoever. And we can but guess at the ends for which he was sent for hither, and can conceive of nothing, but that Captain Martin might have some color to draw Mr. [Isaac] Hollis' pay, during the time of his absence, unless it be to persuade the Mohawks to entertain a good opinion of Colonel Dwight, for which [he] used his endeavors; and of which there was great need, if it was needful, that the Colonel should continue, for he had much lost the esteem of the Indians by his conduct.

When the Brigadier went away, he left orders with Mr. Bush, a carpenter, to go on in his work, in order to the building an house for the female boarding school on Mrs. [Abigail] Sergeant's land; not merely a schoolhouse, but, as I understand, a large house with diverse apartments. Accordingly, Mr. Bush went on to hew and draw the timber to the place. Before Colonel Dwight returned, he wrote a letter to Mr. [Timothy] Woodbridge, to move him to endeavor a reconciliation between him and me, which Mr. Woodbridge showed me; on which I said to him to this purpose: If, by a reconciliation, was meant dismissing all personal resentment and treating him with all respect and benevolence, there was nothing in my disposition in the way of it. But if by a reconciliation, he meant my concurring in his measures, I insisted on the liberty of having my own judgment. If he insisted that I should declare, that I thought him my cordial friend as he has done, I should think I am not to blame in not being convinced of this, if his actions showed the contrary.

I made such an answer the rather, because I perceived by Mr. Hawley he had been secretly working against me, even in that journey to Concord. However, when he returned, that I might show a placable spirit, presently after he came to town, I went to wait upon him and pay my respects to him at his lodging, but he introduced no discourse concerning any of the misunderstanding, and he has never once been at my house to this day. For a little while after he came to town, he appeared resolute to go on with the building on the hill, and many men were employed continually about it; but, in about a fortnight or three weeks, came suddenly to a stand and dismissed all his workmen, and never has done anything more at the building. What was the cause of thus suddenly desisting, I never knew.

Though he comes not near me, yet, by what I hear from others, he appears very much out of humor. He has talked with Deacon Wood-bridge and Mr. Hawley, and has signified that he expects that things will take a new turn, and still insists that it must be that the ordering of the affairs of the school must be wholly in the hands of the General Court's Committee, and has plainly manifested his persisting in a de-sign of turning out Mr. Hawley.

The people of the town, both Indian and English, are all happily united in opinion and affection, excepting only Col. [Ephraim] Wil-liams' family, though there have been great attempts from that fam-ily—in which Brigadier Dwight has an apparent hand—to break this union, and particularly to beget a disaffection in the people towards their minister. Their representations seemed to make some little im-pression, on the minds of two or three persons a short time; but this effect of their talk was soon over, and the persons that were a little moved were soon convinced of the injuriousness of what was said against [me], and the ill spirit it proceeded from.

Captain Kellogg and the people on the hill seem to have great de-pendence on Col. [Elisha] Williams of Wethersfield. Captain Kellogg declared, before Colonel Williams' arrival, that he should be deter-mined very much, as to his continuance here, by his advice. Since his arrival they have all resorted to him. First Col. Ephraim Williams went to him to Wethersfield, then Captain Kellogg, and then Mrs. Sergeant, and then Captain Ephraim, the Colonel's eldest son. Colonel Elisha, talking with Mr. [Thomas] Strong, minister of one of our neighboring towns, as Mr. Strong informed me, concerning our affairs, expressed a determination to come to Stockbridge and inquire into affairs and know the bottom of them, expressing his confidence of his influence in England [being] superior to that of anyone else. However, Brigadier Dwight, Mrs. Sergeant, and Captain Kellogg, a little while ago, ap-peared to be very much disheartened. Colonel Dwight and Mrs. Ser-geant talked much of going away to live at Brookfield. Captain Kel-logg, the beginning of this month, seemed to be resolved immediately to go away, and to that end went about the town to make up accounts with people. But on Saturday, the 8th of August, Col. Elisha Williams and his lady came into the town and continued here near a fortnight. [The] Captain spent the greater part of his time with him, from day to day, while he was here. On Wednesday, the 12th of August, the Briga-dier was married to Mrs. Sergeant, as we are informed.

On Friday the same week, Col. Elisha Williams came to my house to discourse with me concerning the difficulties subsisting in the place;

told me it was supposed I was against Mrs. Dwight being the mistress of the female school, and desired to know the reasons. And discoursing on the misunderstandings here, he expressed a desire of knowing the state of things and of being the instrument of composing and settling these differences. I desired some time to consider before I gave an answer. The next day I sent him an answer in writing. I chose that the intercourse should be carried in writing to avoid misrepresentations. In my letter to him (endeavoring to treat him with due honor and respect), I declined making a representation of our affairs before him, and particularly giving my reasons why I thought it would not be best for Mrs. Dwight to undertake the care of the female school. And humbly offered to join with him in an earnest representation to the body of Commissioners, that they would appoint a committee to come on the spot, to make thorough inquiry into our present difficulties, as being more proper to have them either as judges or mediators, than one that was nearly related to the family chiefly interested in these contentions. And proposed that the Commissioners, by their committee, should be desired to look into the management of Stockbridge affairs, from the beginning, by all the living inhabitants and residents in the town, that had had any hand in them in any respect, declaring myself ready to open myself with freedom, before such a committee.

In his reply, he told me he could not join with me in what I proposed of applying to the Commissioners, etc.; that it could not be reconciled with that text, "Study to be quiet"; that the General Assembly's Committee would not subject themselves to a committee of the Commissioners, to whom they were no-ways accountable. And told me, once and again, that, being desired by the Society in London to inquire into the state of things here, he had a right to know my reasons, why I thought it not proper that Mrs. Dwight should undertake the care of the girls' school, and that he was sorry that I had not informed him; that he still insisted upon it, that I should inform him; and that, though he wished to be returning home, yet he would wait to give me opportunity; and that he should be very sorry to be obliged to inform the Society in London of the unhappy state of things here.

In reply, I still insisted on my former proposal, of referring these things to the Commissioners, as the properest persons to inquire into our affair, and give us their advice and using their wisdom to compose things here by their friendly advice, without disputing about authority; which there surely could be no more difficulty in all parties yielding to, than in their yielding to laying matters before him to this end, that he might attempt a composition by his friendly advice, which he had appeared desirous of, and seemed to think there was no difficulty; that to determine we never would yield to have our affairs heard by any person, in order to the help of their advice under our great contentions, unless they were persons that all parties were accountable to, would be in effect to say, that we would accept of the assistance and advice of none at all, because all parties were not subject to the same constituents.

I signified that it was not evident to me, that he had authority to demand the reasons of my judgment respecting Mrs. Dwight, and gave him several reasons why I doubted it; which, because my discourse was pretty long, I shall not stand to repeat, but told him in the conclusion that whatever authority the Society had, or their Commissioners in New England had from them, acting jointly, I supposed one acting singly could not be looked upon as having this high authority; told him that, to the Commissioners that were my constituents, I referred myself; who had lately told me, that they looked upon persons employed by them as accountable to them only.

'Tis not unlikely that he and his friends here are much displeased at my declining what he demanded and so much insisted on; and possibly he may make representation of the affair, to my disadvantage to the Society in London, and Colonel Dwight to the Commissioners in Boston. If there should be occasion, I am willing to lay copies of the letters at large, that passed between Mr. Williams and me, both before the Commissioners, and their constituents in London. As Colonel Williams seems to have a distrust of the Commissioners in Boston, and utterly refuses on any terms to have a hand in referring Stockbridge difficulties to their judgment or advice; so possibly [he] will not at all apply himself to the Commissioners in Boston in the affair of Mrs. Dwight; but, in a total neglect of them, will apply himself directly to the Corporation in London, and, relying on his great influence on them, will endeavor to persuade them, to oblige their Commissioners here to establish a mistress or to do it themselves, without concerning themselves with the Commissioners.

Though as I observed before Colonel Williams came, Brigadier Dwight, Mrs. Sergeant, and Captain Kellogg seemed to be very much disheartened as to a continuance here, yet now they all seem to be reestablished on a purpose of continuance. Captain Kellogg, though he seemed just going before, has now altered his purpose and declares he is advised to continue here. I have sometimes talked freely with the

Captain about his conduct, and expostulated with him about his continuing here at Mr. Hollis' charge, when not in the employ Mr. Hollis appointed him to. And have reasoned with him about the ill consequences and confusions that his being here is the occasion of. And told him I should think myself obliged to write to Mr. Hollis, and give him full information of the state of his affairs here, if he still continued here. He says he should not continue were it not for others' advice. Many have been the devices of these his advisors, to put some good color on his continuing here at Mr. Hollis' expense. One pretense was that he had a scheme to unite the Six Nations and attach 'em to the British interest, and that it was of importance that he should continue here to have opportunity to prosecute that scheme. And then it is pretended that he must be here as a steward, though [he] is very poorly capable of that business and does very little at it. Another pretense is that he must be here to superintend Mr. Hollis' affairs. Sometimes, that he might have some show of being in employment, he has sent out some boys to work, but without any overseer. Sometimes for some days together, he calls some of the boys out of Mr. Hawley's school and proceeds to instruct 'em himself, tending only to the putting things in a state of confusion. Sometimes [he] sends his son into the school. It has often been urged that 'tis absolutely necessary he should be here by reason of his great interest in the Mohawks, and that this is so great, that if he should go away all would break up, when the case is manifestly much otherwise. He has very little interest in the Mohawks' esteem and affections. No person here that has concern with [them] appears to be less agreeable to them, as there is none that they are so often displeased with and finding fault with. Lately, the Captain insists that 'tis of importance he should be here to promote the design of the female school, and that Mrs. Dwight desires him not to go away as she shall want his assistance. But finally, he is advised, as soon as he can get boys, to set up a distinct, independent school; which yet he himself owned to me, tended to confusion.

Thus things go on in a state of confusion, which those at a distance can scarcely have any idea of. In the meantime, the affair of the Six [Nations] is languishing to death. The affair as to the Mohawks is in a manner dead and, I fear, past recovery. They seem to be discouraged, are most of 'em gone, and I don't expect they will come up again, unless it be to get presents, and fill their bellies in the present time of great scarcity in their own country. They have apparently done very much with the notion of coming here for instruction. The Onohquagas han't been here so long, to be discouraged by our management. But if things go on in this manner much longer, it may be expected that they will be discouraged also. The management of things has a great while been in wrong hands. They ought to be conducted by the Commissioners, who have had the care of Stockbridge affairs; but here are others that seem to aim to engross all to themselves. They seem to be very agreed in a forward, assuming, grasping disposition, indefatigably active in prosecuting their particular designs, and impatient of every thing that stands in their way. Dr. [Joseph] Pynchon has never been here since the last October, and Capt. [John] Ashley has several times to me shown an unwillingness to coming here, to concern himself about these affairs, without Dr. Pynchon.

Very much depends on the affair of the establishment of a mistress of the girls' school. If that affair be settled to their minds, their influence here will [be] established and things always will be very much in their hands. They are sensible that affairs depend very much on that single point, and therefore that is the point they drive with all their might. The wisdom of the Commissioners will easily discern, that this is the juncture wherein the foundation [is] to be laid of the future state of things in Stockbridge, either their prosperity or calamity, and perhaps without any opportunity of future redress. I look on myself called to speak something freely at such a juncture; and therefore I hope my so doing will be candidly interpreted by the Commissioners. I don't think our affairs will ever prosper, if they must be under the hands of Brigadier Dwight and the family of the Williamses. As to the former, he is apparently not of a temper fitted for this business: too sovereign and arbitrary, too sanguine and precipitant, too passionate; has not simplicity enough, too unsteady, of a very suspicious, jealous temper; which was very remarkably the temper of the family at Northampton, which he came of on the mother's side; and has not a temper and manner that suits Indians; and he is too uxorious. And then he has too many private schemes in view, to be so free of a temptation as those ought to be, that are employed in our affairs. His private interest, and the interest of his family, would be greatly advanced indeed, if he could have brought all his schemes to bear: his wife, a large salary as a mistress, without immediately doing the business of a schoolmistress (and whether Mrs. Sergeant's assistant was to be one of the family, I never was told), £10 sterling towards finishing her house, two children maintained and educated at the country's charge; and he has had in view being himself not only a committeeman but steward of both the schools, as he has proposed this to me, which would be a great profit to a shopkeeper; and [he] had a design of introducing his son to be master of the male school and sent him to that end with a letter to me, to desire me to introduce him, though it was only under the notion of a present supply: but if he had once been introduced, I leave to others to judge, whether 'tis likely he would have been for continuing him. But it happened that before his son came, I had letters from the Commissioners, to send for Mr. Hawley; so that his son was forced to go back again. He has also had a scheme for getting Mr. Hollis' monies into his own pocket. Captain Kellogg told Mr. Hawley that it was a thing concerted between him and Colonel Dwight [for] him to resign Mr. Hollis' affair into his hands. I suppose the design was that he was to have the care of 'em as steward, and his son as teacher. Besides, Mrs. [Dwight] has a design that the farm her house stands upon should be bought by the country for a school lot; and if so, they would [have] had advantage to have sold it probably for great profit, and yet to have lived upon it and upon the incomes of it, as officers concerned in the business of the school. And as their family and the school would be blended, the provisions of the school would have been their provisions, and the servants of the school their servants. And besides, the Brigadier has had it in mind (for he has signified it to me) to divert the channel of the King's bounty to the Six Nations, of £500 sterling, from going by the way of New York. He did not tell me [that] he intended it should come through Stockbridge and through his hands, and be dealt to the Indians out of his shop. If all these things could have been brought to pass, the profit, to him and his family, would indeed have been very great. And one that has so many schemes of private interest must be under more temptations than is desirable, in a public affair of such vast importance.

And as to Mrs. Dwight herself, if I am or ever can be called to give my opinion of her qualifications for the business, I think I may lawfully now express my mind. However, I had rather that the Commissioners without resting on my judgment make thorough inquiry here on the spot, she being present, of those that have been longest acquainted with [her] and with her management, disposal of money, etc. heretofore, viz. the English inhabitants of this town in general. I leave it with the Commissioners to judge whether what I proposed to Col. [Elisha] Williams ben't most safe, viz. that some of the Commissioners should come on the spot, and inquire into the management of Stockbridge affairs from the beginning, by all the living inhabitants.

If Mrs. Dwight is not like to be settled in the school here, it would be well if she would soon dismiss the expectation of it; for the continuance of the expectation is the continuance of all our contentions. If she had done with this expectation, she and the Brigadier would doubtless soon leave the town; and then Captain Kellogg would also leave it; and there would be an end to these lamentable consequences of their presence here; which, if they are continued much longer, would bring the affairs of the Six Nations quite to nothing. Indeed it is a wonder, that she is not perfectly discouraged: the fixed prejudice of the Indians against her is so apparent, and has been made so manifest, since she has tried to get their children into her school. They reproach Deacon Woodbridge and Mr. [Benjamin] Ashley, as if they dissuaded the Indians from sending their children; but I must needs have perceived it not, if it were. The Indians have undoubtedly drunk in their prejudice of themselves, from their own observation, and the Mohawks have taken it from the Stockbridge Indians.

It appears [to] me very necessary, that Deacon Woodbridge should go again to Court, at the next sitting. 'Tis apparent, that the Brigadier forbore to bring in his accounts or [mention] anything in Court, about Stockbridge affairs, the last sitting, because Deacon Woodbridge was there; but he has evidently still a design of making a violent push in Court, to carry his points there.

And there is another thing, Sir, I would humbly suggest, that it should be proposed to Gov. [Spencer] Phips, to make Deacon Woodbridge a justice of the peace,[1] as 'tis very necessary for the keeping good order among the Indians. They were brought to submit to the English government some years ago; and Col. [Ephraim] Williams was put in justice; supposing that this might tend to the suppression of vice, and maintaining good order amongst them. But it has never done any good that way; for the Indians have such prejudice that they will not bear his government. And there is no man in the world, that they would so readily submit to, as to Deacon Woodbridge. His being a justice, is indeed most necessary, in order [to] any good effect at all of the English laws among them. [. . .]

[Jonathan Edwards.]

---

1. Woodbridge was approved as Justice of the Peace for the Housatonic Indians at Sheffield, Berkshire County, and commissioned Jan. 3, 1753. Later he was Judge both of Probate and Common Pleas. MAR, vol. 3, p. 333; Electa F. Jones, *Stockbridge, Past and Present* (Springfield, 1854), p. 135.

157. TO SPEAKER THOMAS HUBBARD

In this letter Edwards nominates Timothy Woodbridge for a resident trustee, in the hopes that Woodbridge will help stabilize the Stockbridge situation. Edwards accuses Joseph Dwight of forging ahead without consultation and executing projects and disbursing funds for personal benefit rather than the purposes intended. Edwards exhorts prompt action to save the Mohawk school.

(Trask Library, AL rough draft, one folio leaf; ALS second draft, two folio leaves; Dwight ms. transcript, six quarto leaves.)

* * *

Stockbridge, August 29, 1752

Sir,

The special end of my writing to Your Honor at this time is humbly to propose to you that you would use your influence that Deacon [Timothy] Woodbridge may be added to the General Court's Committee for the taking care of the Mohawk affair in this place. Probably you will not wonder that I should propose it, when you have understood the present state of things here, by which the necessity of it appears. I informed you something of the calamities which attend the Mohawk affair in my letter of last spring; which, as I then signified, were owing very much to the affairs falling almost entirely into the hands of one man [Col. Joseph Dwight], who was entering into a strict alliance with Col. [Ephraim] Williams' family, by his engagements with his daughter, Mrs. [Abigail] Sergeant, and who was almost constantly here, while the rest of the Committee kept at a distance. Our confusions continue, and grow worse and worse, and from the same cause. Colonel Dwight takes up his constant abode here; and as we are informed was lately married to Mrs. Sergeant, and so is now become Colonel Williams' son-in-law, and appears in all respects to be strongly attached to, and engaged with that family. He claims and has used a sort of sovereign arbitrary power here with regard to the Mohawks, and both the boarding schools. He denies all authority of the Commissioners in these affairs, and says all is in the hands of the General Court's Committee; and that he only of the Committee being resident here, it must be looked upon that they leave affairs with him. Accordingly, he has done most things of consequence of his own head, without the voice of either of the other gentlemen of the Committee since the Committee were first appointed, so far as I can learn from the information of the rest of the Committee. And almost everything has been done in an unhappy manner. Instead of building two schoolhouses, agreeable to the vote of the Assembly, [he] has framed two large houses with the various apartments; each of which will doubtless cost as much as three schoolhouses: for what purpose, I know not. The state of things is apparently such, as makes it very doubtful whether we shall have any occasion for so much as one schoolhouse for the Mohawks anywhere in New England; and if anywhere, probably not here, but at the Hoplands.[1]

I think the case required the mature consideration of the whole Committee before the foundation of any house, schoolhouse or other house, had been laid; and it should have been inquired of the Indians, whether, if they settled in the Hoplands, they would be willing their children should be at school here. For I think there is little probability of this. The Colonel has determined the place, as well as the form of these houses by himself alone, if I am rightly informed. He has of his own head, I think in a very precipitant manner, framed a large house for a female boarding school, on his wife's home lot, near her house; when it remains yet undetermined whether she shall be the settled mistress, and when indeed there is not the least prospect of her ever having a school. One would think they have made trial enough to convince them that the Indians, both Stockbridge Indians and Mohawks, have such a prejudice against her, that they will not let her have their children. The house is framed big enough, not only for a schoolhouse, but to entertain and lodge all the scholars.[2]

He in the winter, of his own head, sent for some of the chiefs of the Mohawks to come hither from their own country, and sent for Capt. Joseph Kellogg of Suffield in order to a treaty with them: which treaty he managed by himself alone. And the chief business of it was to know what we should do to secure the Six Nations in the British interest: than which no business could have been devised more unhappy for the interest of our great and important affairs with them in this place. For they are exceeding apt to suspect, that in all we do for them, we act not from any kindness to them, but from a regard only to our own interest,

1. A section of Great Barrington, later Lee, Massachusetts.

2. JE deleted: "Though the Society in London granted £10 sterling to prepare her house for their entertainment and lodging, that house has been lately finished in a pretty sumptuous manner; but not with lodgings for Indian girls. But the Colonel nevertheless expects the £10 sterling to help defray the charge of it."

and because we need their help, which they have often expressed since they have been here. I have labored much to convince 'em that in this affair we evidently acted the part of friends to them and sought their real and best interest: and they seemed in some measure convinced; but such a treaty as this, in the boarding school here, by one they supposed acted and spoke in the name of the country, tended fully to establish them in their former suspicion, and so to defeat our own designs. The Colonel, singly and according to his own discretion, distributed the £200 old tenor the General Court granted in the winter to the Onohquagas, who were newly arrived; not giving all to them, but some to them, and some to the chiefs of the Mohawks, in such a manner as did more to create uneasiness among them, so far as I could learn, than to gain their affections. And so far as it was used to the last-mentioned purpose, it was to gain their affections to himself, and to establish his own interest with them, and not to excite their gratitude to the government, if the Onohquagas understood him right, and speak true. For they all (i.e. all their heads of families) with one voice declared to me, that he delivered the present to them in his own name and as his own kindness to 'em; that he said to 'em that he had gathered up a little in one place, and a little in another, till he had got so much for them, which he now gave them. The Colonel of his own head did also again send for Capt. Joseph Kellogg, and kept him here about ten weeks in the spring and summer, without any visible business or employ whatsoever: and as to his secret business we can but guess at that. And many other things have been done of great consequence, and which have had a most unhappy influence, without the voice of the rest of the Committee, if Capt. [John] Ashley may be credited. 'Tis apparent that this affair cannot prosper under his hands, if it should continue under his management as it has been. And indeed it is already brought to the very brink of ruin, and will soon be past recovery, and all the cost [of] the country and Commissioners will be lost, if there ben't some alteration. The Colonel is too sanguine, self-sufficient, and confident, too hasty and precipitant in his measures, too unsteady, of too passionate and fiery a temper, which tends to keep everything in a ruffle and tumult; too sovereign and arbitrary. He is not of a disposition and manner that at all suits Indians, who don't seem at all pleased with him, but have shown much of the contrary. They don't love a man of his sovereign and forbidding airs, nor have they at all liked his conduct. Though he has taken pains to gain an ascendant in their esteem, he is of a very suspicious, jealous temper; which was remarkably the temper of the family at Northampton, which he came from on the mother's side. And he is too uxorious; and has had too many things in view for the promoting his private interest in the management of our affair, to consist with his being so free of temptation, as those ought to be who have the management of Stockbridge affairs. His wife expects the salary of £30 sterling as mistress of the girls' school, without immediately doing the business of a schoolmistress, as she has manifested to me; and whether the mistress under her was to be one of the family, I cannot tell. Two of their children they expect should be both boarded and educated at the country's charge. And he has had it in view, not only to be a committeeman (and so chief manager of all affairs) but also steward of both boarding schools, as he has signified to me; which would have been a great profit to him, as a shopkeeper and otherwise, besides what he would expect from the country, as the reward of his services. He had a design that his son should be master of the male boarding school, and actually sent him up from Brookfield to Stockbridge for that end, with a letter to me, desiring me to introduce him into the school, though it was only under the pretense of a necessary, present supply. I leave it to others to judge whether he would not have been for continuing him if he had been introduced. But it happened, that before his son came, I had a letter from the Commissioners, to send for Mr. [Gideon] Hawley; so that his son was forced to go back again. He has also had a scheme for the getting Mr. [Isaac] Hollis' monies into his own pocket. Capt. [Martin] Kellogg told Mr. Hawley in the spring, that it was proposed that he should resign Mr. Hollis' affair into the Colonel's hands, when things were ripe for it, or to that purpose. I suppose the design was, that he was to have the care of Mr. Hollis' boys, and would see that they should be instructed by his son, and would himself take care of 'em as steward, and so draw the pay for the whole. Besides, his wife had a design that the farm her house stands upon should be bought by the country, for a school lot for the female school (for she signified this to me), and so they would have had the advantage of selling it for good pay, and a good price, and yet still to have lived upon it, and upon the income of it, as officers concerned in the business of the school; and the family and the school being blended, the provision of the school would have been their provision, and the servants of the school to take care of the school farm, would have been their servants. Besides all these things, the Brigadier has had it in his mind (as he intimated to me) to turn the channel of the King's bounty of £500 sterling to the Six Nations, from going by the way of New York. He did not say that he intended it should come through Stockbridge, and through his hands as the resident agent for the government, and be dealt forth to the Indians, out of his shop. If all these things could have been brought to bear, the profit to him and his family would have been great indeed.

In the course things are now in, everything is going into such a channel, and forming into such a shape, as tends to establish a dominion of the family of the Williamses over Stockbridge affairs, and bring all things in a great measure into their hands, as 'tis apparent that this is what they are eagerly grasping at. By their natural disposition they are sufficiently apt to assume and engross all power, profit, and honor to themselves. Col. [Elisha] Williams of Wethersfield, since his arrival, has been very busy about our affairs. He [has] been abundantly resorted to by his friends in Stockbridge. He has lately spent near a fortnight here; and assumed more to himself than I thought he had a right to do, in demanding accounts concerning our affairs.

These things show the necessity of some other committeeman, that shall be resident here, and have a hand in the management of affairs, besides Colonel Dwight, with the family of the Williamses for his counsel. 'Tis apparent the other gentlemen of the Committee don't incline to have anything to do with Colonel Dwight, without greater strength on their side. Col. [Joseph] Pynchon has not been here since last December; and I have reason to think the cause is, he don't like such a companion in the committee. And Captain Ashley has said to me several times, that he don't care to have anything to do, without Colonel Pynchon. I know Colonel Pynchon would rejoice to be joined in commission with Mr. Woodbridge. The latter is a person well capable of the business, and in some respects better than any man in New England; for he has, more than almost any man in these western parts of New England, been acquainted with Indians, and has demonstrated that he has great skill in managing them, by the vast ascendant he has gained and constantly maintains over them. And he has certainly the character of strict integrity, among all that have been longest acquainted with him. That he has no disposition to lay schemes for his private interest to the prejudice of the Indians, he has demonstrated by the best proof, viz. long trial. He has had the fairest opportunities to have made an estate by the Indians, of any man in these parts, but he has not taken his opportunities; but on the contrary, has often given up his own interest for their sakes. Much has been said against him, but if reports should be followed, all would probably [be] found to come from one family to whom he has been obnoxious, as standing in the way of their particular designs. He is known to be a gentleman of good discerning, and there is no great danger of his being wheedled, and made a dupe or tool, by such as craftily build up themselves on the ruin of public designs. Colonel Pynchon is acquainted with him, and knows his character. I would propose to Your Honor to discourse with him about the matter. Perhaps adding Deacon Woodbridge to the Committee is the only expedient that is feasible for the delivering Stockbridge affairs from present dreadful embarrassments. It may be none will care to move that Colonel Dwight should be turned out; but if Mr. Woodbridge is added, it may be as effectual a relief as if the other were dismissed. Then Colonel Pynchon and Captain Ashley will be encouraged to come to Stockbridge, and be active in the business of the committee; and in all probability the Brigadier will soon dismiss himself, and have no more concern in the business. But if we have no redress at all, 'tis past all doubt, the Mohawk affair will soon be past recovery.

I leave it to Your Honor to make use of this letter as your wisdom shall direct. I ask your candid interpretation of the freedom I have used in this case of extremity. My wife joins with me, in most respectful and affectionate salutations to you, Madam, and your family. I am, honored Sir,

Your obliged and most humble servant,
Jonathan Edwards.[3]

158. TO SEC. ANDREW OLIVER

Edwards brings the Commissioners up to date on the activities of a number of Stockbridge personalities. To bolster his own position, he frequently invokes the name of Isaac Hollis, the chief English benefactor of the community. He finds fresh evidence of Martin Kellogg's shortcomings as teacher, his misuse of funds, and his efforts to undermine Gideon Hawley.

(Trask Library, ALS draft, two envelope covers inscribed to Edwards at Stockbridge: one folio leaf addressed on the recto, and one large quarto leaf addressed on the verso; Dwight ms. transcript, four quarto leaves.)

* * *

3. JE deleted the following postscript, dated Oct. 14: "Though Capt. Ashley in talk with me, in a variety of expressions, signified that the building the female schoolhouse on the hill was against his mind, and that he should never consent to it; yet I hear since he has owned he did consent. Possibly it may prove so concerning some other things. This I observe that I may in nothing injure the Brigadier."

October 1752

Sir,

Since my other letter of August 27 has long been waiting for an opportunity for conveyance, various things have appeared in our affairs, which it may not be improper to inform you of. It looks as though there were resolutions in the people on the hill to drive their schemes to effect, though the earth should be removed for it.

Col. Ephraim Williams has lately made a very extraordinary, vigorous, and vehement attempt suddenly to change the English inhabitants of the town by buying out at once the old inhabitants in general. He arose; he went out before day and called some out of their beds, offering to buy their interest here; and so went from one to another, and went to most of the inhabitants that forenoon, offering very high prices, vehemently pressing with cash, that the bargain should be immediately closed, writings drawn, and the affair completed without delay, urging secrecy on each one. One completed and finished the affair with him. Some others came into a verbal agreement on conditions. One was offered double wages to go immediately to carry [a] letter first to Hatfield, then to Mr. Elisha Jones of Weston, then to Col. [Elisha] Williams of Wethersfield. But notwithstanding the secrecy and extraordinary vigor with which this matter was carried on, yet the design was discovered before it could be completed, and so disappointed. And then his friends and he himself were glad to lay this conduct to distraction.

His son, Ephraim, has expressed a great resolution that I should be removed out of town, declared he would gladly spend £500 of his money to accomplish it, offered Mr. [Thomas] Ingersoll of Sheffield £500 if he would find out a way for it. Col. Israel Williams said to one of my neighbors of Stockbridge that a way was devised for the sending me out of town in a little time, that would doubtless be effectual.

A scheme is plainly laid entirely to thrust Mr. [Gideon] Hawley out of business, let his friends and constituents do what they will to prevent. Col. [Joseph] Dwight has told Mr. Hawley that 'tis Capt. [Martin] Kellogg's design to set up a distinct, independent school under another schoolmaster; that he shall provide to keep the school on Mr. [Isaac] Hollis' behalf; and that he intends to take up all the boys that come, to clothe 'em well, etc., better than heretofore. Probably he presumed that the clothing and presents that will be offered will tempt all to subject themselves to Captain Kellogg rather than Mr. Hawley.

Captain Kellogg is now gone to Newington, but the Brigadier's talk plainly supposes that he intends to come again, though Colonel Dwight in some of his talk plainly manifests that he has still thoughts of taking (after a while) Mr. Hollis' affairs into his own hands and providing Mr. Hollis a schoolmaster.

I have lately been a journey to Newark in New Jersey, where I saw Mr. [Nathaniel] Hazard, a merchant in New York, who told me that he the last June received and answered two bills Captain Kellogg has drawn on Mr. Hollis of £80 sterling apiece. By which it appears that Captain Kellogg has drawn full pay from Mr. Hollis for the two years past, as much as he had in the preceding years, without clothing [the boys] in the least, imposing on Mr. Hollis in an almost unexampled manner, considering the greatness of the injury, the plainness of the case, and the obstinacy with which he has proceeded to such a step, after this part of the country has been for so long a time so full of objections [to] his being here at Mr. Hollis' [expense,] without being in the business to which Mr. Hollis has appointed and agreed to send him his money for. In the beginning of the year before last, he professedly threw up Mr. Hollis' school and dismissed all his boys, supposing that Mr. Hollis was dead, it having been long before he had heard anything from him. And what he did afterwards in teaching the Mohawks, he did not pretend to proceed on Mr. Hollis' plan or with any expectation of any pay from him; and never pretended to take up any boys afterwards, on Mr. Hollis' account, till about a year after this, viz. the last fall, after he had received a letter from Mr. Hollis; and 'tis but little he has done since. The charge he has been at in clothing the boys has been but a trifle. He has never kept any school at all, though sometimes he has pretended to teach some children to read, in a most confused manner. But through [a] great part of the year, he has not done even this, nor had so much as the shadow of a school.

He has been absent at least one third of the year; and [a] great part of the time that he has been here, he has not had so much as the shadow of a school nor been in any business whatsoever.[1]

I leave it to Your Honor to judge whether it tends to promote the noble designs the Society and Commissioners have in view here, to support any officers here, male or female, that do from private view with all their might encourage such iniquity in our affairs.

1. JE deleted: "I have some time ago wrote a letter to Mr. Hollis, giving him some account of the state of his affairs here, attended with letters from some others here. I have desired Mr. [Thomas] Prince to show the letters to some of the commissioners."

Colonel Dwight is very open in his finding fault with the Commissioners' management, particularly in writing such a letter to me as that which was wrote last June, and the instructions they there gave to Mr. Hawley.[2]

Col. [Joseph] Pynchon has lately been here two or three days, but while he was here there was little else but altercation and warm contest between his brother Dwight and him concerning the method of managing affairs, and particularly concerning the female school. And he is gone away entirely discouraged, with a resolution to have no more to do in Stockbridge affairs, which he says are blown up already.

If it be not altogether so, yet I think it is high time the Honorable Commissioners had full information of the state of things here. We have long waited for an opportunity to send, but none has presented. Mr. Hawley meets with many very discouraging things. [His] circumstances here are very difficult and precarious, and he greatly needs the Commissioners' advice, and has a great intention to see the Commissioners, and to confer fully and freely with them about affairs he is concerned in. And it appeared to me necessary that he should, both for the public interest and on his own account. He is kept out of business, and probably very good business, wherein he might settle elsewhere, and I don't wonder he is uneasy and thinks it necessary to talk with the Commissioners. We have had thoughts of his staying till Deacon Woodbridge went to Court, the necessity of whose going appears more and more. But the Court's being prorogued, and not knowing for how long a time, the important matter of intelligence to the Commissioners and to Mr. Hollis having been so long delayed for want of opportunity, which so much require their speedy notice; our calamities continuing and growing worse and worse, and it being now a time wherein most of the Mohawks are gone, and so a time wherein Mr. Hawley can be absent with far less inconvenience than some times hence, when many of the Mohawks are expected down by reason of the want of provisions in their own country; and considering that probably the Commissioners might have a freer opportunity to hear and consider Mr. Hawley's representations now than in the time of the sitting of the Court, and also that it might be some convenience for the Commissioners to have notice of the state of our affairs, so as to ripen their thoughts on them before the sitting of the Court: I say, consider-

2. JE deleted: "'Tis apparent by what he says that he has done of taking Mr. Hollis' affairs into his own hands in case Capt. Kellogg leaves it, and providing a schoolmaster for Mr. Hollis himself."

ing these things, it was thought advisable for Mr. Hawley not to delay his journey.

Praying that the Most High by his unerring wisdom would give wisdom and counsel and success to the Commissioners in their consultations on our affairs, and direct and assist us here that are employed by them in so important a service, is the humble and earnest prayer of, honored Sir,

Your most obliged, humble servant,
Jonathan Edwards.

159. TO THE REVEREND JOHN ERSKINE

During an apparent lull in local hostilities, Edwards takes the opportunity to resume correspondence with his Scottish friends, writing four letters to them in three days. In three of these letters, Edwards comments on revivalism abroad and at home, and touches on various items of church and personal news.

(Trask Library, ALS, two folio leaves; Dwight ms. transcript, four quarto leaves. Published in Dwight ed., *1*, 507–12.)

* * *

Stockbridge, November 23 N.S., 1752

Rev. and Dear Brother,

In August last I wrote to you,[1] and sent away the letter (with letters to some of my other correspondents) to Boston, to be conveyed to Scotland. Therein I acknowledged the receipt of two letters from you, one of July 17, 1751, another of February 11, 1752; with the pamphlets sent with the last letter. And now acknowledge the receipt of another letter from you of May 13, 1752, and the pamphlets you sent with the last. The letter I received the latter end of September; the pamphlets I did not receive till very lately; they were forgotten by Mr. [Thomas] Prince. Stinstra *Against Fanaticism*[2] I shall have no benefit by, because I am not acquainted with the French language. What the Jewish convert has published of his conversion,[3] etc. is very agreeable. And I now heartily thank you for this letter and packet.

I am very glad to see what you write concerning the state of religion

1. JE's letter was dated July 7, 1752, at the beginning, July 24 at the close, and may not have been carried to Boston before August. See above, No. 151.
2. Johannes Stinstra, *Lettre Pastorale, contre le Fanatisme* (Leiden, 1752).
3. No information on this publication has been found.

in the Netherlands. But I believe there is more of a mixture of what is bad with the good that appears in that land than Mr. [Hugh] Kennedy, and many other ministers there, are aware of; and that they will find that the consequence of their not carefully and critically distinguishing between the good and the bad, and guarding with the utmost caution and diligence against the latter, will prove worse than they now conceive of. By your account, 'tis now exactly with Mr. Kennedy, as it was with many pious ministers in America in the time of the great religious moving here. They looked upon critical inquiries into the difference between true grace and its counterfeits, or at least a being very busy in such inquiries and spending time in them, to be impertinent and unseasonable, tending rather to damp the work of the Spirit of God than promote it, diverting their own minds and the minds of others, as they supposed, from that which God at such an extraordinary time did loudly call 'em more especially to attend. The cry was, "O, there is no danger, if we are but lively in religion and full of God's Spirit and live by faith, of being misled! If we do but follow God, there is no danger of being led wrong! 'Tis the cold, carnal, and lifeless that are most likely to be blind and walk in darkness. Let us press forward and not stay and hinder the good work, by standing and spending time in these criticisms and carnal reasonings!" etc., etc.

This was the language of many, till they ran on deep into the wilderness and were taught by the briars and thorns of the wilderness. However, 'tis no wonder that divines in Europe will not lay very much weight on the admonitions they receive from so obscure a part of the world. Other parts of the church of God must be taught as we have been; and when they see and feel them, they will believe. Not that I apprehend there is in any measure so much enthusiasm and disorder mixed with the work in Holland, as was in many parts of America, in the time of the late revival of religion here. But yet I believe the work must be more pure, and the people more thoroughly guarded from his wiles, who beguiled Eve through his subtlety and corrupts the minds of zealous people from the simplicity that is in Christ, before the work goes on to a general conquest and is maintained in its power and glory for a great length of time. But God will have his own way; who being his counselor hath taught him? [Is. 40:13]. We must expect confusion and uproar before we have that abundance of peace and truth which the Scripture speaks of. Many must run to and fro, and knowledge will be increased [Dan. 12:4].

The Dutch ministers in America, which you speak of, which I have acquaintance with, are some of the younger ministers and such as were born in America (though several of them have had part of their education in Holland). I have not acquaintance enough with them to know their sentiments particularly about those corrupt mixtures abovementioned, and the care which is to be used in guarding against them. However, 'tis not very likely, if some of them should write to their brethren in Holland, that their letters would have more influence upon them than letters from you, and some others of the ministers of Scotland. Nevertheless, there is a prospect that there will in time be very happy effects of the growing acquaintance and union there is between a very considerable number of very hopeful and pious Dutch ministers in the provinces of New York and New Jersey, and many English and Scotch ministers in America. The number of well-disposed Dutch ministers in those provinces has of late remarkably increased; so that I think when they meet together in their coetus, they make the major part. Some of the elder ministers seem to be of quite contrary sentiments and dispositions, not appearing friendly as the other to what they esteem the power of religion, nor approving of awakening, searching, strict and experimental preaching; which has occasioned various contests among them. However, the stricter sort, being the prevailing part, are like to carry the day.

The Dutch churches in these provinces have hitherto been so dependent on the classis in Holland, that whenever any among them have been educated for the ministry, and any churches have been desirous of their administrations, they could not receive their orders on this side of the water, but have been obliged to go to Holland for ordination; which has been a great encumbrance that has attended the settlement of ministers among them, and has undoubtedly been one occasion of such multitudes of the Dutch living wholly without ministers. Application was made not long since, through the influence of the forementioned serious younger ministers (as I take it) by the coetus here to the classis in Holland, for their consent that they might unite themselves to the Presbyterian Synod of New York, which now consists of English and Scotch. But the success of their application was prevented by a letter written by one of their elder ministers, remonstrating against it, very falsely representing the New York Synod as no proper Presbyterian synod, but rather a company of independents. On which, the classis of Holland advised them by no means to unite themselves with that synod.

The last September I went a journey into New Jersey and had opportunity in my journey of seeing some of these younger Dutch ministers, and conversing with them on this subject. They seem resolved, by some means or other, to disengage themselves and their churches from the forementioned great encumbrance of being obliged to cross the ocean for the ordination of every minister. I was much gratified, during the little opportunity I had, to observe the agreeable disposition of these ministers.

There were also many other things I had opportunity to observe in those parts which were very agreeable. I was there at the time of the public commencement in the College [of New Jersey], and the time of the meeting of the Trustees of the College, the time of the meeting of the Correspondents of the Society for Propagating Christian Knowledge, and the time of the meeting of the New York Synod, so that I had opportunity to converse with ministers from Long Island, New York, New Jersey, Pennsylvania, and Virginia. The College is in flourishing circumstances, increases apace, and is happily regulated. The Trustees seemed engaged to their utmost to promote learning, virtue, and true religion in it; and none more than Gov. [Jonathan] Belcher, who is the President of the Trustees, and was at the commencement and Trustees' meeting. But they very much want further supplies for the convenient support of the College. I had considerable opportunity with Governor Belcher; was several times at his house at Elizabeth. He labors under many of the infirmities of age, but savors much of a spirit of religion and seems very desirous of doing all the good he can while he lives.

The New York Synod is in flourishing circumstances, much more so than the Philadelphia Synod. They have the greatest body of ministers now and increase much faster than the other. They are in higher credit with the people in almost all parts, and are chiefly sought to for supplies by destitute congregations. With respect to the proceedings of the Correspondents, they have dismissed Mr. [Azariah] Horton from his mission on Long Island, and he is about to settle in a congregation in New Jersey. He was dismissed by reason of his very much failing of employ, many of the clans of Indians he used to preach to having dwindled away by death or dispersion, and there [being] but little prospect of success among others that remain; and some being so situated that they may conveniently be taken care of by other ministers. The Correspondents have it in their view to improve the money by which he used to be supported, to support a mission among the Six Nations, after they have found a suitable person to undertake the business of such a mission, and he is fitted for it by learning the language. They used endeavors to obtain a suitable person for the purpose in New Jersey. But meeting with no success, they voted to empower Mr. [Joseph] Bellamy, Mr. [Samuel] Hopkins of Sheffield, and myself, to procure a suitable person (if we can find such an one) in New England, for the present to come and live at Stockbridge, to be here learning the Mohawk language with Mr. [Gideon] Hawley, our schoolmaster for the Mohawks, to fit him for this mission. Persons proper to be employed, and such as may be obtained, are very scarce; and 'tis doubtful whether we shall be able to obtain one.

There is a very dark cloud that at present attends the affair, relating to the Indians at Stockbridge, occasioned very much by some of the General Court's Committee (at least the chief of them, who is a gentleman that has lately married Mrs. [Abigail] Sergeant, and has removed and lives at Stockbridge) pursuing measures very contrary to the measures of the Commissioners of the Society in London. The opposition is maintained not with a small degree of stiffness and resolution, and the contest is become so great that it has brought things into very great confusion. The foresaid gentleman is a man of some note; and his wife's relations earnestly engage with him; and many of these are persons of considerable figure in the country. The Commissioners all very much dislike this gentleman's conduct. This contest occasions no misunderstandings among the people in Stockbridge in general; all, excepting those nearly related to that family, both English and Indians, are happily united to me and my family. It would be very tedious for me to write, and for you to read all the particulars of this uncomfortable affair; and the more undesirable as it would tend to hurt the reputation of some persons. The Commissioners are exerting themselves to relieve us of this calamity; and it is probable they will be successful.

I thank you for the account you give of some valuable books published; I desire you would continue to favor me in this manner.

I began the last August to write a little on the Arminian controversy, but was soon broke off; and such have been my extraordinary avocations and hindrances, that I have not had time to set pen to paper about this matter since. But I hope God in his providence will favor me with opportunity to prosecute this design; and I desire your prayers that God would assist me in it, and in all the work I am called to, and enable me to conduct myself to his glory and acceptance under all difficulties and trials.

My wife joins with me in most hearty and affectionate salutations to you and Mrs. Erskine. I am, dear Sir,

> Your most affectionate and obliged brother and servant,
> Jonathan Edwards.

P.S. I propose with this to send you Mr. Hobart's *Second Address to the Members of the Episcopal Separation in New England,* and my answer to Mr. [Solomon] Williams,[4] which I would desire you to give your neighbors, my correspondents, opportunity to read if they desire it.

160. TO THE REVEREND WILLIAM McCULLOCH

(Trask Library, ALS, two quarto leaves; Dwight ms. transcript, three quarto leaves. Published in Dwight ed., *1,* 516–18.)

* * *

Stockbridge, November 24 N.S., 1752

Rev. and Dear Sir,

I thank you for your letter of March 3, 1752, which I received this fall. I thank you for your friendly and instructive observations on God's dealings with me and my family. Though God's dispensations towards us have been attended with some distinguishing trials, yet the end of the Lord has been very gracious. He has ever manifested himself very pitiful and of tender mercy, in the midst of difficulties we have met with, in merciful circumstances which they have been attended with, and also in the event of them.

Our circumstances here at Stockbridge are in many respects comfortable. We here live in peace and friendship with the generality of the people, but we are not without our difficulties and troubles here. The Indian affair, which the last year was attended with so pleasing and glorious a prospect, has since been unspeakably embarrassed, through the particular schemes of some great men that have had concern, who are divided and opposite in their counsels and measures from the Commissioners of the Society in London, and are to their utmost striving to accomplish their designs in opposition to them, and in this great contest I am looked on as a person not a little obnoxious. There are some of a certain family of note, who vigorously abetted and set forward my opposers at Northampton, and were a chief occasion of

4. Noah Hobart, *A second address to the members of the Episcopal Separation in New-England* (Boston, 1751), and JE, *Misrepresentations Corrected.*

my removal from that town, to whom my settlement at Stockbridge was very grievous, who now take occasion to exert themselves to their utmost to weaken my interest and influence; and I have all reason to think, would, if it were possible, undermine me, and procure my removal far hence. Many endeavors have been used to disaffect my people towards me; but all in vain; they are all firmly united to me, excepting a few who are of the forementioned family, or nearly related to 'em. Endeavors have been used also to disaffect some of the Commissioners, but wholly in vain. They seem to have their eyes very wide open, as to their particular designs and schemes, and the true springs of their opposition. We hope for an end to this lamentable contest before long, but its effects hitherto have been very sorrowful, especially with regard to the affair of the Mohawks.

Some other things have happened which have much prejudiced the cause of religion among the Indians, and, among other things, the late discovery of the famous Tartarian root, described in Chambers' *Dictionary*, called "ginseng,"[1] which was found in our woods the last summer, and is since found in the woods in many of these western parts of New England and in the country of the Six Nations. The traders in Albany have been eager to purchase all that they could of this root to send to England, where they make a great profit by it. This has occasioned our Indians of all sorts, young and old, to spend abundance of time in wandering about the woods, and sometimes to a great distance, in the neglect of the public worship and of their husbandry; and also of their going much to Albany (which proves worse to them than their going into the woods) to sell their roots: where they are always much in the way of temptation to drunkenness, especially when they have money in their pockets. The consequence has been, that many of them have laid out their money, which they have got for their roots of ginseng, for rum, wherewith they have intoxicated themselves.

God has been very gracious to my family of late, when some of them have been visited with sore sickness. My wife has lately been very dangerously sick, seemed to be brought to the very brink of the grave, had very little expectation of life; but seemed to be assisted to

1. Chambers has a long article extolling the presumed virtues of ginseng and describing the physical characteristics of the plant itself. "The *Gin-seng* is one of the principal Curiosities of the *Chinese*, and *Tartars:* . . . It is known among them by divers other Names, as the *only spiritous;* the *pure Spirit of the Earth;* the *Plant that gives Immortality,* &c." Chambers, *Cyclopedia, 1,* 147–48.

an unmoved resignation to the will of God, and unshaken peace and joy in God, in the expectation of a speedy departure. But God was pleased to preserve her, and mercifully to restore her to a pretty good state of health. My youngest daughter [Elizabeth] also (who has ever been a very infirm child) was brought nigh unto death by a sore fit of sickness, but is now also restored to her former state. My daughter [Sarah] Parsons, my eldest daughter who with her husband [Elihu] has removed from Northampton and dwells in Stockbridge, has also very lately been very sick, but is in considerable measure restored. My daughter Esther's marriage with Pres. [Aaron] Burr, of Newark, seems to be very much to the satisfaction of ministers and people in those parts, and also our friends in Boston, and other parts of New England.

As to the state of religion in America, I have but little to write that is comfortable. But there seem to be better appearances in some other colonies, than in New England. When I was lately in New Jersey in the time of the Synod there, I was informed of some small movings and revivals in some places on Long Island and in New Jersey. I there had the comfort of a short interview with Mr. [Samuel] Davies of Virginia. From the little opportunity I had, I was much pleased with him and his conversation. He seems to be very solid and discreet, and of a very civil, genteel behavior, as well as fervent and zealous in religion. He gave an account of the probability of the settlement of one Mr. [John] Todd, a young man of good learning and a pious disposition, in a part of Virginia near to him. Mr. Davies represented to the Synod the great necessities of the people in the back parts of Virginia, where multitudes were remarkably awakened and reformed several years ago, and ever since have been thirsting after the Word and ordinances of God. The people are chiefly from Ireland, of Scotch extraction. The Synod appointed two men to [go] down and preach among these people, viz. one Mr. [Robert] Henry, a Scotchman, who has lately taken a degree at New Jersey College; and Mr. [Nehemiah] Greenman, the young man who was educated at Mr. David Brainerd's charge.

The people of Northampton are in sorrowful circumstances, yet destitute of a minister, have met with a long series of disappointments in their attempts for a resettlement of the ministry among them. My opposers have had warm contentions among themselves. Of late they have been wholly destitute of anybody to preach steadily among them. Sometimes [they] meet to read and pray among themselves; and at other times set travelers, transient persons to preach, that are hardly fit to be so employed: not long since they set one such to preach, whom Maj. [Joseph] Hawley, a leading man, called down out of the pulpit in the midst of his sermon, as being unfit to be there.

My wife joins with me in most respectful salutations to you and yours, desiring your prayers, that God would be with us in all our wanderings through the wilderness of this world. I am, dear Sir,

> Your most affectionate brother in the labors of the gospel,
> Jonathan Edwards.

161. TO THE REVEREND THOMAS GILLESPIE

(Trask Library, ALS, two folio leaves; Dwight ms. transcript, four quarto leaves. Published in Dwight ed., *1*, 513–16.)

* * *

Stockbridge, November 24 N.S., 1752

Rev. and Dear Brother,

In letters and pamphlets lately received from some of my correspondents in Scotland, I have received the affecting and surprising account of your deposition, for not assisting in the settlement of Mr. [Andrew] Richardson at Inverkeithing.[1] The circumstances of which affair seem to be such as abundantly manifest your cause to be good, at the same time that they plainly show the persecuting spirit with which you have thus been proceeded against. 'Tis strange that a Protestant church should condemn and depose one of her ministers for conscientiously declining to act in a forced settlement of a minister over a congregation that have not chosen him as their pastor, but are utterly averse to his administrations, at least as to a stated attendance upon them. 'Tis to be wondered at that such a church, at this time of day, after the cause of liberty in matters of conscience has been so abundantly defended, should arrogate to herself such a kind of authority over the consciences of both ministers and people, and use it in such a manner, by such severity to establish that which is not only so contrary to that liberty of Christians wherewith Christ has made them free, but

---

1. In 1752 the General Assembly ordered the settlement of Andrew Richardson at Inverkeithing despite the congregation's opposition. Gillespie supported the people and was removed from his position at Carnock.

so directly contrary to her own professed principles, acts and resolutions entered on public record.

The several steps of this proceeding, and some singular measures taken, and the hastiness and vehemence of the proceeding, are such as savor very strongly of the very spirit of persecution; and must be greatly to the dishonor of the Church of Scotland; and are such as will naturally engage the minds of God's people abroad in the world in your favor, as suffering very injuriously. 'Tis wonderful that a church which has itself suffered so much by persecution, should be guilty of so much persecution. This proceeding gives reason to suspect that the Church of Scotland, which was once so famous, is not what it once was.

It appears probable to me at this distance, that there is something else at the bottom, besides a zeal to uphold the authority of the church. Perhaps many of the clergy of the Church of Scotland have their minds secretly infected with those lax principles of the new divinity, and have imbibed the generous doctrines (as they are accounted) which are so much in vogue at the present day, and so contrary to the strict, mysterious, spiritual, soul-humbling principles of our forefathers. I have observed that these modern, fashionable opinions, however called noble and generous, are commonly attended, not only with a haughty contempt, but an inward, malignant bitterness of heart towards all the zealous professors and defenders of the contrary spiritual principles, that do so nearly concern the vitals of religion, and the power of experimental godliness. This, be sure, has been the case in this land. I have known many gentlemen (especially in the ministry) tainted with these large principles, who, though none seem to be such great advocates for liberty and freedom of thought, and condemn a narrow and persecuting spirit, so much as they; yet in the course of things have made it manifest that they themselves had no small share of a persecuting spirit. They were indeed against anybody's restraining their liberties, or pretending to control them in their thinking and professing as they please; and that is what they mean truly, when they plead for liberty. But they have that inward enmity of spirit towards those others mentioned, that if they see an opportunity to persecute them under some good cloak, and with some fair pretext, will eagerly embrace it, and proceed with great severity and vehemence.

Thus Sir, perhaps, if the truth were known, it would appear that some of your most strenuous prosecutors hate you much more for something else than for your not obeying the orders of the General

Assembly. I don't pretend to know how the case is: I only speak from what I have seen and found here in America in cases something similar. However, 'tis beyond doubt that this proceeding will stand on the records of future time for the lasting reproach of your prosecutors; and your conduct, for which you have suffered, will be to your lasting honor in the church of God. And which is much more, that which has been condemned in you by man, and for which you have suffered from them, is doubtless approved of by God; and I trust you will have a glorious reward from him: for the cause you suffer in is plainly the cause of God. And if God be for us, who can be against us? [Rom. 8:31]. If he justifies, what need we care who condemns? [v. 33]. Not only is the mercy of God, dear brother, manifested in its being granted you to suffer for his sake, but in mercy it is to be taken notice of in many of the circumstances of this suffering. Particularly, that he has excited so many to appear for you; that you had the major part of the presbytery which you belong to, with you in this affair (though God has honored you above all the rest in calling you to suffer for his name); that the major part of the commission of the General Assembly did in effect approve of the conduct of the presbytery, judging it no censurable fault; that no greater part of the Assembly had a hand in your deposition; that so many of God's people in Scotland have on this occasion very boldly appeared to befriend you, as suffering in a righteous cause, openly condemning the conduct of your most bitter prosecutors and testifying an abhorrence of their conduct; and that many have appeared liberally to contribute for your outward support, so that by what I understand, you are like to be no loser in that respect; by which your enemies will be, perhaps, entirely disappointed: and above all, that you have been enabled through the whole of this affair, to conduct yourself with so much Christian meekness, decency, humility, proper deference to authority, and composure and fortitude of mind; which is an evident token that God will appear for you, and also that he will appear against your enemies.

When I received your kind letter, soon after my dismission from Northampton, so full of expressions of sympathy towards me under what I suffered, I little thought of your being brought so soon under sufferings so similar. But seeing God has so ordered it in his providence, my prayer and hope is that he would abundantly reward your sympathy in my case. "Blessed are the merciful: for they shall obtain mercy" [Matt. 5:7].

As to myself, I still meet with difficulties in my new station, which arise partly from private views (as is to be feared) of some particular persons of some note and distinction, who are concerned with the affairs of the Mohawks here; and partly from the same spirit, and the same persons (and others nearly related to them) that fomented the contention with me at Northampton. However, the people, all, both Indians and English, excepting a very few of the above-mentioned relation, are firmly united to me. And the Commissioners in Boston, who are my constituents, and from whom I have my support, are altogether on my side; and are endeavoring to their utmost to remove the difficulties that attend our affairs, by which the cause of religion here, especially among the Mohawks, suffers much more than I do, or am like to do, in my personal and temporal interest. These difficulties which have arisen have indeed almost brought the Mohawk affair to ruin, which the last year was attended with so glorious a prospect. It would be very tedious to relate the particulars of this unhappy affair, and undesirable as it would tend to hurt the reputation of particular persons. I think God by these things calls me to expect no other than to meet with difficulties and trials while in this world. And what am I better than my fathers, that I should expect to fare better in the world than the generality of Christ's followers in all past generations?

May all our trials be for our purification, and our being more and more meet for our Master's use, and prepared to enter into the joy of our Lord, in a world where all tears shall be wiped from the eyes of God's people. Let us, dear Sir, earnestly pray one for another, that it may be thus with us; and that, however [we] may be called to labor and to suffer, we may see peace on God's Israel, and hereafter eternally glory and triumph with his inheritance.

God has of late mercifully preserved my wife and my youngest daughter [Elizabeth], in time of very sore and dangerous sickness, and restored them again. My eldest daughter [Sarah] has also been sick and is restored in a considerable degree.

Northampton people remain in sorrowful circumstances, destitute of a settled minister, and without any prospect of a settlement, having met with many disappointments. But all don't as yet seem to be effectual to bring 'em to a suitable temper of mind.

I much desire to hear from you, and to be informed of your present circumstances. I am, dear Sir,

Your affectionate brother in the gospel ministry,
Jonathan Edwards.

P.S. I intend to send to Mr. [Thomas] Foxcroft of Boston, desiring him to put up for you one of my answers to Mr. [Solomon] Williams, which I suppose is now printed;[2] of which I ask your acceptance.

162. TO WILLIAM HOGG

In this last of four letters Edwards mailed to Scottish friends in November 1752, he again summarizes his Stockbridge difficulties and lists what he views as their causes. No names are disclosed, but the identities of Joseph Dwight and Abigail Sergeant, the Williams family and their relatives, and Capt. Martin Kellogg, are clear. He is heartened by the unswerving loyalty of the Boston Commissioners, the Indians, English townsfolk, and friends like Hogg.

(Beinecke Library, ALS, two quarto leaves.)

* * *

Stockbridge, November 25 N.S., 1752

Dear Sir,

I thank you for your kind letter of May 8, 1752, added to all the other testimonies of your unmerited respect and friendship. The pamphlet entitled *Private Judgment Defended*,[1] which you speak of as what you had sent to Mr. [Thomas] Prince for me, is not come to hand; probably through Mr. Prince's forgetfulness, which often has been the case with letters and pamphlets that have been sent to him for me from Scotland. For though he be an eminently worthy man, and one who has laid me under obligations, yet he is forgetful; and probably more so now, it being a time of affliction with him, by reason of the late death of his daughter. I intend at the first opportunity to send to Boston and inquire after this pamphlet, and another sent to him for me by Mr. [John] MacLaurin, which is not come to hand.

I have great reason always to remember with much gratitude your tender sympathy on occasion of the late great troubles I met with at Northampton, and the extraordinary respect testified since, not only by word but deed. I have great reason to remember the kindness of friends, and friends at a great distance and unknown; but have more special reason thankfully to take notice of and remember the kindness of a gracious God that has raised up these friends, and has made them his instruments to convey his bounty to us. God's dealings with me and

2. *Misrepresentations Corrected.*
1. *Private judgment defended; or, The lawfulness and duty of refusing obedience to the highest of Church Judicatures when their commands are judged unlawful* (Edinburgh, 1752).

my family have been mixed; affliction and mercy has been intermingled, formerly and lately, and is so still. God has mercifully opened
a door for usefulness here at Stockbridge; and has given us a settlement, in many respects comfortable, after we were turned out [of]
Northampton. But here with our mercies we have our difficulties;
which are indeed much greater calamities to the important affair of
the instruction of the Six Nations, than to me or my family, though we
suffer not a little by them.

Our calamities have arisen from three sources. The last year, after so
remarkable an appearance of forwardness in the Mohawks to come
and settle in New England, and submit to instruction, not only were
the Commissioners in Boston, of the Society in London for Propagating the Gospel in New England and Parts Adjacent, much animated by
it; but the General Court took much notice of it, and appointed a
committee of three gentlemen to take care of, and promote this affair.
The chief of these three gentlemen [Joseph Dwight], has since contracted an acquaintance with a gentlewoman in Stockbridge [Abigail
Dwight], and has married her; and makes this town the place of his
constant abode, having brought his family hither. He being a person of
a very sanguine and enterprising, and something of a sovereign temper, has taken the management of the Mohawk affair almost wholly
into his own hands; and claims the whole power of the management of
it to the General Court's Committee, exclusive of the Commissioners,
who maintain all the instructors here, out of the charitable fund committed to them. And this gentleman, having designs and views very
diverse from those of the Commissioners and those that are employed
by them, this has led him to measures quite contrary to theirs; which he
has pursued with great resolution. And the Commissioners having
principally entrusted me with the care of their affairs here, this has
occasioned first a misunderstanding and jealousy in him towards me,
and the two schoolmasters [Timothy Woodbridge and Gideon
Hawley] maintained by the Commissioners, and at length to an open
opposition.

Another source of difficulty is this. In the case of the late great
controversy at Northampton, there was a number of gentlemen belonging to other towns, of a certain family of considerable note in New
England, which had long manifested a jealous and unfriendly spirit
towards me, at least some of them ('tis needless for me to say what I
think were the first causes of this unfriendliness), who on occasion of
the foresaid controversy, sat in on the side of my opposers, were their

chief counselors during the whole continuance of the controversy. One or two of the inhabitants of Stockbridge were of the same family; who when my coming to settle here was first talked of, greatly opposed it. But when they saw the stream was too strong for them seemed to concur in it, and appeared very friendly. But since the forementioned gentleman of the General Court's Committee has married into the family, they have thrown off the appearance of friendship in a great measure, and act entirely in concert with him in his opposition, and are abetted and upheld in it by some gentlemen of note in other places, of the same family, the same that fomented the contention at Northampton.

A third source of difficulty is this. Mr. Isaac Hollis of High-Wycombe in Buckinghamshire, in England, in Mr. [John] Sergeant's time, made large remittances hither for the support of a boarding school in Stockbridge. Mr. Sergeant took much pains to find a suitable master, a man of learning. But being disappointed, he, the year before his death, improved an aged man [Martin Kellogg], that was lame and not able to follow husbandry, a man of pretty good abilities, but not a man of learning, as a present supply, till a suitable master could be found; but grew very uneasy at his conduct, convinced of his utter unfitness for the business, and resolved to dismiss him, and procure some fitter person. But he dying soon, this man was left in the school, and continues in it still, others being loath to inform Mr. Hollis of his unfitness. Means have been used to persuade him, but all to no effect. And by what he has perceived of a dislike of his conduct, he is very much out of temper, and sets himself very much against the other schoolmaster, whom the Commissioners have provided for the Mohawks; which keeps things in great confusion among them. Thus, Sir, you see something of the unhappiness of the situation of affairs here.

Endeavors have been used by my opposers to disaffect the inhabitants of the town, and also the Commissioners in Boston towards me; but hitherto all in vain. The people all, both Indians and English, excepting those forementioned, are firmly united to me. And the Commissioners seem to have their eyes wide open with regard to our affairs; and are exerting themselves to their utmost to extricate us out of these difficulties. And 'tis to be hoped God in his providence will appear for us. I desire, Sir, that you would be helping together by your prayers for us, and for the poor Indians, which suffer most by these contentions.

I have the more reason to hope in your fervent prayers from the experience I have had of your cordial friendship, and the account you gave me of your own experience of affliction. I pray God abundantly to reward your love and beneficence towards me, and bless you and your family, and make your blessings yet more and more. My wife joins with me in most cordial and grateful salutations to you, Mrs. Hogg, and your surviving children. God has lately raised from sore and dangerous sickness, my wife and youngest daughter [Elizabeth].

I intend to give orders that one of my answers to Mr. [Solomon] Williams,[2] should be put up for you, which when you have read I desire you would lend to Mr. [Thomas] Davidson. I have with this sent a letter to him; desire him to pardon my treating him with common civility, in giving him the title of Reverend, though he desires I would not. I am, dear Sir,

> Your most obliged and affectionate friend and servant,
> Jonathan Edwards.

163. TO SIR WILLIAM PEPPERRELL

Edwards makes an impassioned plea to Sir William that he not write to the London Society opposing Edwards. Joseph Dwight had visited Pepperrell, his old commander-in-chief, urging him to do so. Edwards feared that Dwight would be heeded as a veteran of the 1745 campaign: Dwight had been officer in charge of the artillery train, third in command of the land forces, and, later, judge of admiralty for the port of Louisburg.

In the year 1753, Edwards reached his lowest point. His discouragement did not prevent him from fighting back desperately to save his position, however. He describes events, quotes opponents, and offers references to substantiate his claims. He displays surprising knowledge of the actions and strategies of those pitted against him. One by one, he refutes the charges in Dwight's petition against him, which was presented to the Massachusetts General Court in November 1752.[1]

Basically, Edwards pleads for the right to know firsthand all charges against him, and for the opportunity to defend himself before any action is taken. His self-defense, presented here in print for the first time, must be deemed successful, as Pepperrell declined to condemn him to the Society.

(Trask Library, ALS draft, one folio leaf, envelope cover, addressed on recto to Edwards at Stockbridge, one broadside, *An Act more effectually to prevent profane Cursing and Swearing,* Feb. 13, 1746, and one large quarto leaf

2. *Misrepresentations Corrected.*

1. On the Dwight petition, see the headnote to Letter No. 164, JE to Speaker Thomas Hubbard, Mar. 19, 1753, below.

in five pieces, on envelope cover, addressed to Edwards at Stockbridge; Dwight ms. transcript, ten quarto leaves. See SIB, *8*, 58; Parsons, 253.)

* * *

Stockbridge, January 30, 1753

Sir,

Deacon [Timothy] Woodbridge informs me that Capt. Ephraim Williams [tells him] that the Colonel [Joseph Dwight] engaged you to write to England against me, and to use your interest with the Corporation in London, that I may be turned out of my business here in Stockbridge; and that you have promised him, that you would so do. If I have been misinformed, I hope you will pardon me for giving so much heed to the report, as to write to you upon it. I looked on the report the more to be regarded as coming from Colonel Dwight's brother-in-law [Capt. Ephraim Williams], who went to Boston with Colonel Dwight and professedly went on the same business, viz. to endeavor that I should be removed from Stockbridge, and was with him all the while he was in Boston.

Now Sir, I beseech you, before you proceed in this affair, with patience and candor to hear me a few words, in an affair that so nearly and greatly concerns me.

Though I don't know what Colonel Dwight has said to you to my prejudice—it being said, when I was at a great distance, having no opportunity to speak for myself—yet I may conclude, if this report be true, that what he has said has made a very great impression on your mind, to my prejudice. I am sensible, therefore, that, in speaking for myself so long after, I come under great disadvantage; but yet may well hope for something to counteract this disadvantage from Your Honor's candor, justice and Christian benevolence. Such must needs be the influence of these principles in the heart of one of your character, that, if you have resolved on this proceeding, as thinking yourself constrained for the public good to do that which tends to destroy the future usefulness of a minister of the gospel, though one of the least of Christ's servants, and to the ruin of his poor [family] that have already been great and distinguished sufferers through the opposition they have met with in the world, yet this resolution must be come into with no small degree of regret and operation of a spirit. And such a spirit will open your ear and make you glad to hear anything that can be said (if anything can be said truly) in my defense; so that you may be justified, without proceeding to such an ungrateful work.

Being encouraged from these considerations, I take leave to give Your Honor some brief rehearsal of some things past, which may tend to give some light in our affairs. And in what I shall say, I shall endeavor to give [it] in the fear of God.

There has for many years appeared a prejudice in the family of the Williamses against me and my family, especially ever since the great awakening in Northampton, about eighteen years ago. To inform you, Sir, of the first rise of this prejudice, and by what means and steps it was established, would be unnecessary, and would be a trespassing on your patience; only I would say, as I can say with truth, and before him who searches all hearts, that I have sought peace with them, and that their displeasure was not from any injury I offered them. It has been my care to avoid those things by which prejudices might be continued, and endeavor to live in friendship with them. However, there has been a most apparent and rooted misunderstanding, at least with some of the family, which was manifested by the frequent testimonies of their dislike and ill opinion, in what they said of me behind my back, reflecting on me and reproaching and avoiding my house. Col. Israel Williams of Hatfield, though my first cousin and lived within five miles of me and very often at Northampton riding by my house backwards and forwards continually, never set foot in my house above thrice in fourteen years before I left Northampton. Mr. [Jonathan] Ashley of Deerfield, who married into the family, though a neighboring minister, and related to me, and very often was in the town, generally shunned the house, and very rarely came to it on any occasion. I was rarely visited by any of the rest of the family, though I very often used to visit them, endeavoring, if possible, to wear away this prejudice and strangeness. But all never availed. I should tire you if I should go about to give you a particular account of the many ways in which this prejudice was manifested.

When the late great controversy began between me and my people concerning terms of communion, which issued in a separation between me and them, the family of the Williamses deeply engaged themselves in this controversy, on the side of my opposers, who were principally upheld, directed and animated by them in that controversy, greatly misrepresenting my opinion, exhibiting it in a very injurious light. The controversy had begun some time before Col. Elisha Williams went to England; and he was much resorted to for advice by my opposers, and was their chief advisor, till he set out for England, and had begun to write against me, and then, when about to embark, he committed his papers to his brother Solomon Williams of Lebanon, who finished what he had begun and published his book against me full of injurious misrepresentations and written with no small degree of bitterness and contempt. When Colonel Elisha was gone, our people resorted very much to his brother, Col. Israel Williams of Hatfield, as their advisor, who engaged in the quarrel with exceeding vehemence. They also made much use of his brother [Jonathan] Ashley of Deerfield, and Col. [Oliver] Partridge, who is one of the family, and Mr. [Chester] Williams of Hadley, who were all very active in that quarrel.

When my coming to Stockbridge was first talked of, Col. Ephraim Williams, uncle to Colonel Elisha, Colonel Israel, etc., opposed it with exceeding vehemence. And his daughter, Mrs. [Abigail] Sergeant, manifested her utmost dislike of it, and also Capt. [Martin] Kellogg, who has ever been a great familiar of Col. Elisha Williams. His son Ephraim also spoke very loudly, and in very hard and harsh expressions against [me], said that he should look on his estate at Stockbridge as good for nothing if I came here. Col. Israel Williams did also very much oppose it, and egged on his relations here at Stockbridge in their opposition.

However, when it was seen that there was a great union and universal engagedness in all the rest of the people, both English and Indians, for my settlement, and that there was no hope of preventing it, Colonel Williams and his daughter Sergeant and Captain Kellogg appeared as though their minds were changed. But yet I had certain information, from time to time, of things [said] by each of 'em privately, that plainly showed their hearts to be as they were before. As to Capt. Ephraim [Williams, Jr.], who had not then left Fort Massachusetts, he still went on with the most open vehement opposition.

Colonel Dwight for many years had been my great friend and was wont to express on all occasions the highest esteem of me. When the family of the Williamses opposed me in the time of the great contention at Northampton about terms of communion, he was my zealous friend, was wont to express esteem [of me], as Col. [Joseph] Pynchon informs me, beyond all other ministers in New England. And when my coming to Stockbridge was proposed, he favored it, and spoke much for it, spoke of me as a very suitable person for the business, as Mr. Speaker [Thomas] Hubbard of Boston can testify; and after I was settled at Stockbridge, used to express a strong desire of being under my ministry, spoke of it as a privilege, which he had long earnestly desired. And when he first came here to treat with the Mohawks, he used abundantly to consult me and made great use of it in almost every step he took.

And thus things continued, till he had entered into an acquaintance and close friendship with Mrs. Sergeant, when there began apparently to be more of a neglect and coldness, which however I took no great notice of. But that which at the beginning was neglect and coldness, soon came to secret opposition, and that to a very great degree indeed. Thus, before ever there was any open breach of friendship, or ever he had said one word to me, he once and again spoke to Mr. [Gideon] Hawley, the schoolmaster, employed here by the Commissioners to instruct the Mohawks, warning him to beware of me, representing me as one disposed to meddle in affairs that did not belong to me. He signified to him that he was sensible that he had an high opinion of me, but he might see cause to alter his opinion on further acquaintance with me, warning Mr. Hawley not to inform me what he had said. He once labored for hours with Mr. Hawley alone, representing me as a busybody, meddling with what was none of my business in coming to preach to the Mohawks and instruct their children. Though I had been most expressly advised so to do by the Commissioners, my con-stituents, he told Mr. Hawley that I invaded his province by so doing, and doubtless will get away money that belonged to him, no less than £150; evidently, through his whole discourse, industriously laboring to raise prejudices and beget an indignation in him towards [me], and all this even [before] I was sensible that ever I had done anything that he was affronted at—though since he represents me as having affronted him before, in that I charged a contradiction on him. I, in discourse with him once, indeed was very positive that he had forgotten some-thing that he had [said], but did not represent it in that light, as though he contradicted himself, nor did I use one disrespectful word. Nor did [he] in the least insist in the time of it that he looked upon it that I affronted him, or that I left him after that conversation under any disgust. No such thing was intended as an affront nor was there any appearance of his taking it as an affront at the time that I discoursed. And he owned to me afterwards that he did not suppose I meant to charge him with a willful contradiction.

After he had twice had such conversation with Mr. Hawley against me, as forementioned, I supposed he had heard that I had heard of it, and he came to me to talk with me about it. I had notice beforehand that he was coming, and considered the matter, and determined to treat him with all proper respect, but yet with plainness to let him know how things appeared to me, which I looked on as acting the most Christian part. When he first began the conversation, he told me that he was ready to think, by some things that he perceived, that I looked on him as not my friend. I told him it was true, I did not think he was, not from what I had lately heard, but supposed that he was become my enemy. He says I used the epithet "bitter," and said "bitter." I don't remember it, nor yet will I deny, for I am not sure I did not. He endeavored to satisfy me that it was no argument of want of friendship, and after long hearing him I gave my reasons why what he said did not clear up the matter to my satisfaction, but without the least manifestation of heat or any disrespectful language, and particularly asked him how it could consist with friendship for him, before ever he had said anything to me, to labor so much to possess Mr. Hawley's mind with an opinion that I was intermeddling and encroaching, only because I preached to the Mohawks; on which his countenance changed and he replied with much smartness and severity in his air, "To deal plainly with you, Mr. Edwards, I do think you have no business to preach to the Mohawks and that you do no good there. You have business enough among your own people and, if you must instruct children, you may instruct Deacon Woodbridge's school"; and went on [in] this manner with this castigating language for a considerable time. I don't know but my countenance might change under this discipline, for I was greatly surprised. But this I know: I was exceeding watchful and careful not to return one disrespectful word. And then I produced the note of the Commissioners, wherein they had very expressly desired me to preach to the Mohawks till a distinct missionary was appointed over 'em. The note was very plain and seemed for a minute to put him to a pause, but he soon recovered himself and replied with smartness, "Indeed Mr. Edwards, I don't understand this note as you do." I replied, "The note is very plain; however, I will pay so much regard to Your Honor's judgment as to write the Commissioners again, to have their further instructions." He replied with a menacing air, "Aye, and I will write too." He continued with his air of severity and resentment as long as he stayed in the room and, as he went away, he desired to know if I was satisfied by the account he had given of his conduct. I told him I was not, but added that I should always endeavor to treat him with [the] respect due to him in his place, and hoped I should be open to conviction that he was my friend if his conduct hereafter showed him to be so.

This is the only time that ever a word passed between him [and me] about any matter of misunderstanding between us or anything wherein he found fault with me, even to this day, from whence he can represent me as stiff, quarrelsome, inflexible, and implacable. After this, I perceived by what I heard of his talk abroad, there were great manifestations, many things said representing me in a very odious light.

Indeed, after the Court at Concord, and some of the Commissioners had talked with him there about his difference with me, he wrote a letter to Deacon Woodbridge desiring him to endeavor a reconciliation between him and me. I told Deacon Woodbridge that if by a reconciliation he meant a dismissing all personal resentment, I stood ready for it. If he meant that I shall manifest my approbation of all his measures, I thought I ought not to be obliged to act contrary to my own judgment in this. If he meant that I should declare that I thought him my cordial friend as he has insisted before, I could not be obliged to this if his conduct plainly showed the contrary.

However, soon after he came to town, that I might show a placable disposition, I went to pay my respects to him. But he began no conversation on these affairs and shunned my house and, as I perceived, went on abundantly in manifestation of great resentment in what he said of me behind my back, in which his friends here, the family of the Williamses, concurred, especially Captain Ephraim, who was open and without all respect or reserve declaring himself as determined to his utmost to oppose me and, as he expressed it, to *give my true character to the world*, which he represented as very black.

'Tis given as great reason of the resentment of these gentlemen that I have opposed Mrs. [Abigail] Dwight's being the mistress of the female school; but nothing that I have done in that affair could be condemned by any impartial person whatsoever if all that I have done were known just as it is.

It has not been my inclination to meddle in that affair, nor have I sought it, nor did I ever say anything about [it], till the Commissioners wrote to me expressly desiring my thoughts about the female school. And then, that I might proceed in the most Christian manner possible, I, on considering the matter, I determined in the first place to talk with her about it. Accordingly, [I] went [there] for this end. I mentioned the objection I had against it, and did it in Colonel Dwight's presence, and told her that, if she was like to make that change in her condition which was talked of, I did not see how she could attend the business of a schoolmistress.

She made but little reply to me then, but afterwards she took an opportunity alone and renewed the conversation. I told her more plainly my objection, how that if she married Colonel Dwight and was the mother of his numerous family, besides her own, and probably a third between, she could not attend to the school.[2] She gave me to understand she did not expect to have the immediate inspection of the children, but to act as an overseer. I told her I was persuaded it was the expectation of the Society that she should do the part of a school-mistress and instructor and that I supposed a committee would be sufficient for the superintendence and oversight, and much more talk I had upon the affair.

But the talk, though altogether friendly, and though I perceived no resentment then, yet I have reason to think from what followed, was an occasion of the deepest resentment. Abundance of reflections, I heard, were cast upon me after that, and carried amongst the Wil-liamses in distant places, that I was {intending to procure the school for} my own daughter.

Under these circumstances I conducted myself with as great a de-gree of care and watchfulness as I was capable of. I have kept as still as I could and endeavored in a quiet and silent manner to avoid meddling with their business as much as possible. What I have said at any time has been chiefly by way of vindication from the false reports and misrepresentations that were [circulated]. But this has been inter-preted as quarreling, and all that I have said or done has been beheld with an evil and jealous eye. I have been watched with the utmost vigilance, and my conduct, that has been innocent and have acted in the integrity of my heart, has been represented and interpreted in the most severe manner. As, for instance, in the Report of the Committee 'tis represented as though I, on the sabbath, warned a meeting of the Indians on purpose, to give opportunity to Deacon Woodbridge and others to persuade the Indians to take away their children from Cap-tain Kellogg, when I had no thought of it, [it] was no part of the business I intended, nor did I imagine when I warned that meeting that anybody else had any such thought. The meeting met especially to warn the Indians against wandering abroad, as they were wont to do in

2. In the MS, JE deleted the phrase "she could not attend to the school."

the spring and summer, greatly to their hurt, exposing them to many temptations.

And whereas I am complained of in Colonel Dwight's report as meddling with what did not belong to me in introducing Mr. Hawley— all that I did of that affair was in the simplicity of my heart, having no reason to imagine that anybody would find fault with it. The Commissioners had desired me to send for Mr. Hawley and introduce him into the school by a letter from Mr. [Andrew] Oliver, dated December 31, 1751. They desire me to *employ Mr. Hawley,* and desired me to do more than I cared to do. They desired me to agree with him as to the terms on which he should be employed, and Colonel Dwight himself had manifested himself in very great haste to have one introduced; and as to my expecting him that way, I remember nothing of it.

What Colonel Dwight calls my introducing him was only telling them that that was the person the Commissioners had provided and telling them in what manner their children must be governed, etc., and desired a manifestation of their consent, which they gave with great alacrity. And as to my introducing Mr. Ashley as an assistant, 'twas greatly misrepresented. Mr. Ashley and his wife [Rebecca Kellogg Ashley] had all along from the beginning been employed in assisting in teaching—because the Mohawks insisted upon it, and with the approbation of the Committee for aught appears—and now in particular, when they heard another master was coming, they were at first much alarmed, for Mr. Ashley and his wife would be turned out of the business; and therefore, to quiet their minds, I told 'em Mr. Ashley and his wife would still assist [and] were not to be turned out. And that they indeed insisted greatly upon it appears by a speech made by the sachem afterwards in my hearing.

I had no thoughts of this being an intermeddling in the business of the Committee, or of anybody's finding fault with it. It could not be thought that I did it in opposition to Colonel Dwight, or with any thought of doing what he should dislike, because it was before any known breach of friendship between him and me; and at that very time he had just before, and as he was going that journey, came to my house and expressly told me he should at all times be glad of my advice in the management of affairs, and manifested still the same confidence in me in a letter he sent me by his son at that time when Mr. Hawley was introduced.

It seems to be hinted in the Report that I, with other persons, have been wont, as 'tis expressed, to minimize, contradict, oppose and counteract the measures pursued by the Committee—which is exceeding injurious representation of things. What particular instances he has respect [to], or what he mentioned as a confirmation of this general accusation, I cannot learn, and so am under no advantages to vindicate myself. As I said before, I never had any conversation with him on any affair wherein he manifested any dislike of my conduct but once in my life, and of that conversation I have given as fair an account as I am able. I can truly say as in the presence of God, I have studied for the things that make for peace and, since I perceived that any giving my judgment in the Mohawk affairs was not well taken, I have sought to my utmost to let those matters alone and not to intermeddle with them.

What further Colonel Dwight has accused me of to Your Honor or predicated at Boston I cannot tell, and therefore know not what to answer. I would entreat you, Sir, to consider how unequal is my advantage, when he has had so great opportunity in Boston indefatigably to labor with all the most considerable gentlemen in New England for six weeks together, when I, the person suffering, was far out of the way and had no opportunity to say anything for myself, being at 150 miles distance. How easy is it for a gentleman of his abilities, when animated with great resentment, under such circumstances to make a man look very black.

I hear that he has abundantly represented me as a person of [an] exceeding stiff, inflexible temper. I knew that this was abundantly said of me by the family of the Williamses in the late controversy at Northampton and by my other opposers who were encouraged by them. And all my sufferings there, my losing the best salary of any country minister in New England, and casting myself and my numerous family on the wide world, which was from a fear of offending God, was all laid to stiffness and willfulness. And it has been represented that I had rather undo myself and my family than yield an ace. And in several former religious controversies about Arminian principles, controversies with Mr. [Robert] Breck, Mr. [John] Read, Mr. [Noah] Merrick, in the time of the late religious revival, I have been abundantly charged by my Arminian opposers as willful and inflexible, when, God knows, I have studied the things that might make for peace, and have earnestly sought it, and have yielded as far as I dared to do for that sake, and sometimes so far that I have been much troubled in conscience afterwards. And I can recollect no instance wherein that charge of stiffness has been made but on occasion of some religious affair.

You must, Sir, be so well acquainted with the history of the martyrs as to be sensible that this has ever been the cry against the sufferers for religion, that they were stiff, willful, perverse and inflexible; and thus, Sir, it most evidently [has] been in my case. I have had no credit for my conscientiousness, and this has been the name it has been called, and thus I came by this reproach, which Colonel Dwight has lately adopted, though in former controversies he earnestly stood in my vindication.

As to my not learning the Indian language, Colonel Dwight knew how the case was like to be before, when he recommended me for this business, as now. And as to this, I doubt not, Sir, but if I had opportunity fully to represent to you the state of the place and the Indians, it would be easy to satisfy you that it would not be worth the while for another missionary here to spend his time to learn the language, as this was Mr. [John] Sergeant's steady opinion, of which there are many witnesses. It would evidently be a waste of his time, that might be spent much more profitably for the Indians' good in labors to bring them to the English tongue, the knowledge of which has greatly increased among them within a few years.

And as to my fitness for the business in other respects, my communicative faculty, etc., 'tis not proper for me to give my judgment. I think it reasonable that the judgment of such should be regarded, who have experience, being the continual subjects of my instruction, particularly all my people, every man, woman and child, that has any understanding, both English and Indian, except the two families of Colonel Dwight and Colonel Williams.

But I fear I have tried your patience. I hope you will excuse my saying so much in my own defense, who am an instance of suffering wrongfully in my reputation through the reproaches of my enemies, perhaps beyond any that ever has been in New England.

Now, Sir, I humbly request, that if you had determined to endeavor my being turned out of my business here, you would once more take the matter into your impartial consideration. And I would pray you to consider, Sir, the disadvantage I am under, not knowing [what] has been said against me in conversation, not knowing what to answer to. The ruin of [my] usefulness and the ruin of my poor family (which has greatly suffered in times past for righteousness' sake) are not things of equal consideration with the public good. Yet, certainly, I should first have an equal, impartial, and candid hearing, before I am executed for the public good.

I must leave the matter, dear Sir, to your justice and Christian prudence, committing the affair to him who knows all the injuries I have suffered, and how wrongfully I now suffer, and is the great protector of the innocent and oppressed, beseeching him to guide you in your determinations and mercifully to order the end.

My duty to your excellent Lady [Mary Pepperrell],

Your obliged, most humble servant,

Jonathan Edwards.

164. TO SPEAKER THOMAS HUBBARD

This letter is a point-by-point refutation of Col. Joseph Dwight's Report to the Massachusetts House of Representatives of November 22, 1752.[1] Although addressed to the Speaker, the letter was also designed to be read to the assembly. The document is similar to those sent to Sir William Pepperrell and Andrew Oliver. Edwards reiterates that he was not personally apprised of the charges or given a chance to reply to them. He asks for a fair hearing and that no action be taken until he receives one.

Hubbard, as Speaker, had to agree to the assembly's favorable vote on the report, but he was most sympathetic to Edwards. In 1753, he became a Commissioner of the New England Company, whose Boston members were also supporters of Edwards'.

Time was running out, however, and because of lack of support for Gideon Hawley, more Mohawks were on the verge of leaving Stockbridge. Once they had left, few ever returned.

(Trask Library, AL draft, on two broadsides: one a Mass. fast day proclamation for Mar. 15, 1749, dated Feb. 16, 1749/50, with a duodecimo leaf attached, the other a Yale master's commencement announcement for 1751, listing candidates and theses titles; Dwight ms. transcript, ten quarto leaves. See William Kellaway, *The New England Company, 1649–1776* [London, 1961], p. 295.)

* * *

1. Report of the Committee appointed for managing the affairs of the Six Nations, submitted to the General Court, Nov. 22, 1752; acted on, Dec. 13 and afterwards. See MAR, vol. 32, pp. 299–309; and *JMHR*, 29 (1752–53), 32, 34, 87–88, 104–05. The rejoinder by Stockbridge residents, English and Indian, is in a memorial presented to the General Court. See MAR, vol. 32, pp. 365–74.

[Stockbridge,] March 19, 1753

Sir,

You are well acquainted with the things that were said and done privately and publicly in Boston the winter past in the time of the sitting of the General Assembly, with great industry [to] injure my character and to beget in the members of the Assembly an ill opinion of me and raise their indignation against me, not only as an useless, but a troublesome, mischievous person in this place, and very hurtful to the public interest, evidently endeavoring, if possible, to procure something to be done by the honorable Assembly that should tend to my being turned out of the ministry here.

You doubtless, Sir, are sensible what vast disadvantage a person lies under when one has a personal quarrel with him, and another, animated with the highest resentments and has long had his spirit greatly embittered towards him, has opportunity to accuse him as he thinks proper and make his own representations of him, his temper, and conduct, to set forth as he pleases the nature, circumstances, and tendency of his action, and puts his own gloss on his words and speech, and this not only in public speeches, but in a laborious manner and with indefatigable endeavors in private conversation, time after time, [for] six weeks together; he, the person accused, being not there at all to correct, interrupt, restrain, or answer him, or to say anything for himself, but being all the while 150 miles off, far enough out of the capacity of defending himself or detecting his adversary in any of his earnest and violent attempts to ruin his character, and so to ruin his interest and usefulness in the world, in consequence of it. How easy must it be for a gentleman of Col. [Joseph] Dwight's abilities, when animated with that high degree of resentment he has long expressed towards me, and the great resolution if possible to procure my removal from Stockbridge—I say, how easy must it be for such a gentleman, under these circumstances, to make another appear very odious, with the assistance of others united with him in his quarrel, and who for many years have manifested the deepest prejudice against him.

I am also under another great disadvantage: that much of that which has been said, which appears to have had great influence on the minds of many of the General Court, was said privately, so that 'tis impossible for me to have full and certain information [of] what they were, so that I know not what to answer to or wherein particularly my character needs vindication. The wounds have been secret, which renders them the more fatal as being hidden. The person wounded has no advantage to apply the necessary remedy. Indeed, I have had an opportunity to see a copy of the Report Colonel Dwight carried in to the Assembly, wherein what is alleged against me is either only his suspicion or general charges, but I am not there informed of the particulars by which these general accusations were supported.

In that Report I am treated with a great degree of injuriousness. He mentions it in me as an instance of an unaccountable and violent opposition, affront, and abuse of Capt. [Martin] Kellogg, that on the Lord's day, 19th of April last, after divine service, I publicly[2] warned a meeting of the Stockbridge Indians on purpose to give opportunity to Deacon [Timothy] Woodbridge and others to persuade the Indians to take away their children from Captain Kellogg, whereas I solemnly declare it was no part of the business that I aimed at, nor did any such thing enter into my heart, or any imagination that anyone else had any thought of improving that meeting for any such end, when I warned it. The spring was then coming on and so the time approaching when the Indians used to begin to wander about among the Dutch and elsewhere, greatly to their hurt. It was if possible to prevent this, and to warn them against some other things, that was my end in warning that meeting, without any respect to Captain Kellogg's school. If I was guilty of any crime, it was in my being present while the schoolmaster, which the Commissioners provided for the Mohawks, desired the Stockbridge Indians to take away some of their disorderly boys from among the Mohawks (supposing they had no business there), who greatly corrupted them and promoted these continual disorders in his school, which were very discouraging to the Mohawks, tending, as he supposed, to defeat the designs of the Commissioners and of the government with regard to the Mohawks.

Another great complaint against me in the Report was that I "introduced Mr. [Gideon] Hawley into the school, and placed Mr. [Ben-

2. JE deleted the following passage: "said to the Stockbridge Indians that I had something of consequence to say to 'em and desired they would meet me the next day at the school house, and then said that, if any of the English people desired to be present, they might. And that after my warning the Indians against going so much abroad into the way of temptation, to drunkenness, etc., then some others there present at the meeting advised the Stockbridge Indians to take away some of their children from Capt. Kellogg's school, their children not being well-governed, etc. And then says that he is humbly of [the] opinion, that those measures was premeditated and concocted by all the forenamed persons, with a design, so far as they thought proper, to break up the said Hollisian school. Here I am charged with having a main hand in this, which is mentioned as an instance of unaccountable opposition, affront and abuse of Capt. Kellogg, and with this very aggravating circumstance, that I had in the affair, by warning the meeting on the Lord's day after divine service for this end."

jamin] Ashley as an assistant instructor in the school." What I did in that affair was in the simplicity of my heart, having no imagination nor any reason to imagine that anybody would find fault with it. The Commissioners had desired me to send for Mr. Hawley and introduce him into the school, by a letter from their secretary. And whereas Colonel Dwight blames me for doing this business of introducing a master when I had reason speedily to expect him here who is one of the General Court's Committee, whose proper business he supposes it to be, to this I would say two things. One is, I knew nothing when to expect him here; and secondly, he himself, by a letter sent me by his son [Henry Dwight], at that very time had desired me to introduce a master into the school and, therefore, I must suppose that he desired not to wait for him to do it, which letter I have sent you a copy of.

And as to my "introducing Mr. [Benjamin] Ashley as an assistant instructor," this is greatly misrepresented. Mr. Ashley and his wife [Rebecca Kellogg Ashley] had all along from the beginning been employed in assisting in teaching the children (the Mohawks insisting upon it), and it had always been done with the approbation of the Committee for aught [that] appeared. When they (the Mohawks) heard that another master was coming, they were at first much alarmed for fear Mr. Ashley and his wife would be turned out of their business. And therefore, to quiet their minds, I told 'em that Mr. Ashley and his wife were not to be turned out, but would still assist, which they took particular notice of in their reply, as what they were very glad of. And that they indeed greatly insisted on it appeared afterward by what they very largely delivered on this subject in a public speech by their sachem in Colonel Dwight's presence. I had no thought of this being an intermeddling with the business of the Committee, or thing what would be disagreeable to them. It would not be thought that anything I did in this affair was done in opposition to Colonel Dwight, because it was all done "before there was any known breach of friendship between him and me," between whom there had long subsisted a great friendship, and it was also done while as yet the Colonel seemed to put the greatest confidence in me. When he was going that very journey in which he was then about, he called at my house and expressed his confidence in me, and did expressly tell me that he should, at all times, be glad of my advice in the management of the Mohawk affairs, and still manifested the same confidence just at that very time in the letter he sent me by his son, desiring me to introduce a master of the school, as you will see by the copy I send you.

It seems to [be] mentioned as a great aggravation of my thus "taking the business of the Committee out of their hands," to introduce Mr. Hawley, that he, viz. Colonel Dwight, was at the expense of a journey of his son of 260 miles out and home, to procure the said Hawley for a master for the boys, which is a great misrepresentation. When he sent his son on this journey, it was not to procure Mr. Hawley to be a master for the boys, but it was that he himself, viz. his son, might be a master for the boys, as appears by the letter he then sent to me by his son, of which I here send the copy. Indeed, after he came here and perceived that I had already orders from the Commissioners to send for and introduce Mr. Hawley, I persuaded him to go to Dover, about forty miles from hence, to carry a letter to Mr. Hawley from me. But all this Colonel Dwight was entirely ignorant of, and it was entirely beside his intention. His journey, on which his father sent him, was entirely for another end, viz. that he [the son] might be the master himself.

It is suggested in the Report that I have been wont, as 'tis expressed, "to criminize, contradict, oppose, and counteract the measures reasonably pursued by the Committee in conformity and obedience to the General Court's orders." Here I am altogether at a loss what words or actions of mine this part of the Report has respect to. Colonel Dwight has never given me to understand, and I am left to conjecture from what I hear of what he has charged me [with] from time to time by word of mouth, either openly or in private [to] the Commissioners behind my back. If he means that I have treated him unhandsomely in anything I have said to his face, as I have been informed that he has often charged me with it, I would now humbly but solemnly declare that I never spoke a disrespectful word to him in my life, but have used the greatest care at all times to treat him with respect. And [I] have heard that he had openly before the House of Representatives represented me as meddling, assuming, and contentious and said that, whoever should go to Stockbridge in the service of the General Court, must either quarrel with me or with their own consciences. With regard to so high a charge, I would now humbly declare that I never had any conversation [with or] said a word to Colonel Dwight against any of [the] measures he had taken or was pursuing in the Mohawk affair but once, and that was against his settling two independent masters to keep school, viz. Captain Kellogg and Mr. Hawley in one room. And this I know he did of his own head, without the concurrence of either of the rest of the Committee, because it was directly contrary to what he had fully declared to me to be the design but the day before—which was that Mr. Hawley should be the sole schoolmaster for Mohawk children. And none of the Committee had been here since. He has charged me with treating him unhandsomely in this discourse and by fastening a contradiction upon him, the whole foundation of which was this: that, in discourse with him, I was very positive that he had said something to me before, which then he did not remember and was positive he never had said. But [I] did not represent it in that light, as though he contradicted himself, nor did I use one disrespectful word to him, nor did I in the least imagine in the time of it that he looked upon it that I had affronted him. There was no appearance of his taking it as an affront when I left him, but, on the contrary, he appeared pleased and yieldable to what I had proposed concerning the school. And afterward, he owned to me that he did not suppose that I meant to charge him with a willful contradiction of himself, and I was far from having the least reason to imagine that the freedom I used on that occasion would be ill taken; I having had much to encourage me in using freedom with [him], there having subsisted a very great and peculiar friendship between him and me for many years, and there was at this time no appearance of any breach of friendship—and besides, I had been invited but a little before to give him my advice with respect to the Mohawk affair on all occasions.

This, as I said before, was the only time that ever I had any conversation with him wherein there was any appearance of my opposing his measures with respect to the Mohawk affairs. And I desire it may be further observed that, though I am charged abundantly with assuming and meddling with things which did not belong to me, even so that it was impossible for the agents of the government to do their duty without quarreling with me, yet he never in his life was so kind as to inform me of any one instance wherein he found fault with me, wherein he supposed I intermeddled with anything that did not belong to me, but only my preaching to the Mohawks, and instructing them in religion, which I was expressly ordered to do by a written note under the hand of the honorable Secretary, as the Commissioners themselves are witnesses. Colonel Dwight once talked with me about this, and told me with much warmth that I had no business to preach to the Mohawks, and did no good there, and that I had business enough among my own people, etc.

And I desire it may be further observed that this was the only time that ever a word passed between Colonel Dwight and me about any misunderstanding between us, or anything wherein he signified the least dislike of anything in me, or any part of my conduct, from the beginning of my life to this day. Though before this he had from time to time appeared, in what he had said and done against me behind my back, to be my enemy, with great industry from time to time laboring with [the] schoolmaster, employed by the Commissioners to instruct the Mohawks, to disaffect him toward me and alienate him from me, telling him he was sensible he had a high opinion of me, but he might see cause to alter his opinion of me on further acquaintance, advising him to beware of [me], and representing me as a busybody, and invading his province, and getting away the money that properly belonged to him in my coming to preach to the Mohawks—all this, as I said before, when he had [never] so much as hinted to me that he had disliked anything I had done, which was the first visible rise of all the controversy he has had with me, at the same time charging Mr. Hawley by no means to tell me what he had said.

And when I conversed with him at the time forementioned about this matter, though it has often been represented that I talked to him disrespectfully, and great misrepresentations have been made of that conversation, yet I solemnly declare I used not one disrespectful word to him, but with great care and strictness guarded [against] all disrespectful treatment, which I am ready to declare before Colonel Dwight and before the omniscient God.

I have heard that Colonel Dwight has objected it against me as a great instance of my assuming, intermeddling disposition that I have opposed his wife's being the mistress of the female school. With respect to that matter, I would humbly say that it has not been my intention to meddle at all in the affair, nor did I ever say anything about it till the Commissioners had written expressly to me desiring my thoughts about the female school. And then, that I might proceed in the most Christian manner possible, on consideration I determined in the first place to talk with her about it. Accordingly, I went to Mrs. [Abigail] Sergeant and began the conversation with her on that affair in Colonel Dwight's presence, and told her that, if she was like to make this change in her condition which was talked of, I did not see how it would be possible for her to attend the business of a schoolmistress as it ought to be done. She at first made little reply but, Colonel Dwight going out of the room, resumed the subject, and then I told her more plainly that if she married Colonel Dwight and was the mother of his numerous family besides her own and probably a third which might probably arise from this marriage, which she would have to breed and bear and bring up, she, being moreover of a weak constitution, [would not be able to discharge the duties of a school mistress.][3] She, in her reply, gave me to understand that she did not expect to have the immediate instruction of the children in reading and the like, but only to act [as] an overseer. I told her I was persuaded what the Society in London and the Commissioners in Boston aimed at was a school-mistress to have the principal instruction of the children. But this conversation, though altogether friendly, I have reason to think was highly resented by many things which followed, many reproaches continually uttered in the family of the Williamses.

Under these circumstances I have conducted myself with as great a degree of care and watchfulness as I have been capable of. I have studied to be quiet and to mind my own business and to let their affairs alone. What I have said at any time has been chiefly by way of vindication from the false reports which have been spread abroad of me, but this has been interpreted as quarreling and all that I have said or done has been beheld with an evil and jealous eye. I have been watched with the utmost vigilance, and my conduct, that has been innocent and wherein I have acted in the integrity of my heart, has been interpreted and misrepresented in the most severe manner. When I perceived that my giving my judgment in the Mohawk affairs was not well taken, I have to my utmost let those matters alone. And when I have gone to the Mohawks, I have only preached the gospel to 'em, and talked to 'em and counseled 'em concerning their souls' concerns, and have said nothing to 'em about other affairs. [I] never have said a word to 'em tending either directly or indirectly to impede any of the designs of the Committee with them, nor have I ever said a word to any one of the Stockbridge Indians about Mrs. Sergeant's, alias Dwight's, or Captain Kellogg's schools tending in any respect to prejudice them against either of those schools or against [any] thing that the Committee designed, and have endeavored to mind the proper business of a missionary and minister of Christ, and would have been glad thus to have gone on in silence if they would have let me alone. And if [at] any time I have not been silent, it has been when some of my opposers have come to me and put me upon speaking, urging me to give reasons, etc. And though on such occasions I have said as little as possible, yet what I have said has been the occasion of great accusations and outcries, which

3. Lacuna in MS; this lengthy editorial insertion emulates JE's language in related letters.

have been most extensively propagated to the very unrighteous injury of my reputation.

'Tis said in the Report of the Committee that endeavors had been used, with workmen employed by the Committee, to desist their labors, pretending that what they were employed about was not agreeable to the mind of the government, and that they would never be paid for it. To this I would say that, if this be intended as a charge against me, as seems by the connection, it is exceeding injurious and altogether groundless, there having nothing of that nature, with that which is here mentioned, more or less, either directly or indirectly, ever been said or done by me.

Colonel Dwight, in the Report, after the forementioned accusations of me and others as having been guilty of violently affronting and abusing Captain Kellogg and criminizing, contradicting, and opposing the Committee, he represents, from multiplied managements of this kind, the school, which appeared in the most fair, prosperous, and desirable circumstances, sensibly decayed, and that tens were reduced to units. This is an exceeding injurious representation. For here I would observe, in the first place, that that school never was in desirable circumstances but, on the contrary, in most lamentable circumstances till Mr. Hawley came and took it out of Captain Kellogg's hands— Colonel Dwight himself being judge, as this appears by this letter of his, which I send you a copy of. And secondly, as the school never was in prosperous circumstances till it was taken out of Captain Kellogg's hands into Mr. Hawley's, by the Colonel's own judgment, there, for a little while, was the school in very happy circumstances. The Mohawks many ways testified their great joy that now they had a schoolmaster, that now a regular school was set up after so long continued irregularity and confusion. So it never was in prosperous circumstances any longer than Mr. Hawley had the school. [But when,][4] through the high displeasure of these gentlemen with Mr. Hawley, endeavors were used to weaken [his] school and get away his scholars and set up another school in opposition to his under Captain Kellogg, under whom before the school had long been in such lamentable circumstances, then again the school immediately began to languish. And as they have gone on with great strife, getting away Mr. Hawley's boys and breaking up his school to establish Captain Kellogg's in opposition to his, then

4. MS damage; conjectural reading.

the Mohawks were exceedingly discouraged [and] disheartened, and the Mohawk affair almost came to nothing. These things are most notorious facts, so that the occasion of the great encouragement of the Mohawks, their alacrity in the affair of the school, was not Captain Kellogg's good management, as is represented, but their being delivered from his management and put under the care of another that took better care of them, as the Mohawks themselves loudly declared. Thirdly, 'tis evident that the discouragement of the Mohawks with respect to their continuance here, and so the departure of many of them from hence, has not been owing to any opposition to Captain Kellogg or any conduct of his opposers. And their [being] displeased with the conduct of the opposers is notoriously manifest by what has constantly appeared in the Mohawks themselves, if we will allow them to be interpreters of their own sense, and are able to tell what they have disliked and been uneasy at. For, in the first place, they never objected against the conduct of any of these persons—that Colonel Dwight represents as those who have so greatly discouraged—never manifested any uneasiness with them, but on the contrary, have generally continued in the manifestations of an uninterrupted friendship with their affection to 'em and good feeling of them, appearing zealously attached to 'em. But, on the other hand, they have been abundant in testifying their uneasiness with the conduct of their opposers that Colonel Dwight represents as the great supporters of the Mohawk affair.

There is no one Englishman in New England they have so often manifested their uneasiness with and dislike of as Captain Kellogg. They are very often expressing their uneasiness to him, and Hendrick in particular, as Captain Kellogg owned to me. I have been witness to their finding fault with him to his face once and again. They have often found great fault with his management in the school, and this, from time to time, in the most public manner. They have found great fault with his private conduct, his temper, and many said they have greatly found fault with Colonel Dwight from time to time. It was through uneasiness at the conduct of Colonel Dwight and Captain Kellogg that Hendrick, that was the first promoter of the affair, has long deserted it and went back once, when coming in, greatly displeasured, and declared he never would have any hand in it any more. He never manifested any displeasure with any others, but he, whose conduct the Mohawks have chiefly disliked and been discouraged with, may be judged by this: that, in case of open controversy, they have very openly taken part against Colonel Dwight and Captain Kellogg in favor of those that were opposed by 'em; as in a remarkable manner once, when Colonel Dwight openly and in their presence contended with Mr. Hawley, their spirits were greatly vexed on this occasion against the Colonel and in favor of Mr. Hawley. These facts are notorious and can be abundantly proved.

And now very lately the Mohawks have been abundant in expressing their uneasiness at the conduct of these persons and in favor of those that are opposed by 'em, and most of 'em talk much of going away even on that very account. That the Mohawk affair is come almost to nothing is very manifest through the discouragement of the Mohawks and their going away, and nothing is more evident than the great expense of the country is rendered almost wholly in vain, and that the Mohawks' uneasiness thus doubtless is the cause of their going away, after they had for a while appeared so well-pleased. But certainly, they must be allowed to know themselves what they are uneasy with, and their own sense is easily learned by what they have continually expressed from the beginning and are expressing every day. And the country might easily know, if they will believe those that see and know, unless they will reject the testimony of a multitude, yea, the voice of the inhabitants of the town in general, because one or two gentlemen, desperately engaged in private quarrels, say they must not be believed.

The discouragement of the Mohawks is apparently very much owing to the negligence they observe with respect [to] the care and instruction [of their children]. And whose negligence it is may easily be judged by notorious facts that may be easily made certain by a small degree [of attention], as particularly this: that although Captain Kellogg for his last year's service, beginning with the last end of the summer '51, drew £160 sterling from Mr. [Isaac] Hollis' for what he did for the Mohawks, yet he was gone to Newington more than one-third of the year; and, as to the time he was here, till February, he had not so much as the form of a school, as Colonel Dwight himself being witness in what he says in this letter of his, which I send you a copy of. And after this he resigned all his scholars to Mr. Hawley, who was the sole schoolmaster for a considerable time. After this, he took three or four of his scholars and taught 'em very unsteadily for two or three weeks, and then went away to Newington, and his brother, Joseph, came and were here in his room for more than two months, but never pretended at all to instruct the boys. When Captain Martin Kellogg returned, for a long time he pretended not to keep any school till, just at the end of the year, he took four or five scholars again and kept 'em for a few weeks, and thus this year was spent, for which he drew £160 sterling.

His negligence is what to my knowledge the Mohawks had been very uneasy with and greatly discouraged by. 'Tis represented in the Report of the Committee that, by Captain Kellogg's prudence, the minds of the Indians were reduced to that state that, with abundant pleasantness and seeming satisfaction, they gave up their children not only to the instruction, but correction and discipline, of the school. This representation is exceeding astonishing. This doubtless refers to their giving up their children to the instruction and correction of the school when Mr. Hawley was introduced by me in Colonel Dwight's absence, which I gave Colonel Dwight an account of when he came, when the satisfaction of the Indians, on that occasion, was indeed remarkable, manifesting great joy that now there was like to be an end of that long, continued, confused state of things that Captain Kellogg had kept things in, rejoicing that now some order and regularity was like to be expressed; which things they expressed in the plainest terms as what was the occasion of their joy, the former disorders having been long the occasion of their great grief. One of the sachems on that occasion, with his own hands, brought a rod into the school and delivered it into Mr. Hawley's hands to correct the children with. So that Captain Kellogg had brought their minds to that state as to occasion this satisfaction and joy no otherwise than by his great negligence and disorder. He had long grieved 'em and now they [were] delivered from him, their children were taken out of his hands. Of this there are sufficient witnesses [who] can be produced.

And indeed nothing is more manifest than that 'tis Captain Kellogg's and his supporters' management, and their great and constant opposition to those [to] whom the Mohawks are zealously attached, is the very thing that has brought this affair almost to nothing after the fairest prospects and wholly frustrated the expense of the government.

I have heard that Colonel Dwight has greatly insisted, in his conversation with many members of the Court, on my great unfitness for the place I am in, by reason of my not being like to learn the language of the Indians, and that, by reason of my age, I am not capable of learning it. On this I would observe that Colonel Dwight knew how the case was before, when he much recommended me as a proper person for the place I am in, as he does now. And my people, and the Commissioners, whose business it was to judge of these matters, all knew how the case was before they called me to this business and settled me in. But, if I were as young as Mr. [John] Sergeant was when he first came hither, I am persuaded there is no judicious and impartial person who, if they fully understood the state of the case—how many of the Indians already understood the English tongue, what progress the English tongue hath made amongst them of late, what a way we are now in of promoting the progress of it, and the great necessity there is of the English tongue being introduced, and how much a minister, preaching to 'em and conversing with them in Indian, would tend to hinder the progress of the English—I say, if those things were thoroughly known and considered, there is no judicious and impartial person but would be convinced that it would be great loss of time, and rather prejudicial than helpful to the cause I am engaged in, for me to spend seven years in endeavors to learn this difficult language, as Mr. Sergeant did, without ever being able to make a sermon without the help of an interpreter, at best, or ever praying in their tongue any otherwise than by a form. If I should spend so much time in learning the language, and should then be able to preach to 'em by that time, 'tis probable most of the congregation would be able to understand preaching in English. And, if I should then set up preaching to 'em and conversing with them in Indian, it would be a great interruption to the progress of the English tongue, as it would be taking away from 'em the principal means of learning them such words and phrases as are used in divinity, which is by delivering those words and phrases to 'em in English, in their hearing, and then having 'em interpreted to 'em in their own language. Mr. Sergeant was fully sensible of these things in his lifetime, and therefore he often said, as there is sufficient testimony, that it would never be worth the while for another missionary to trouble himself about learning the language.

The Indians themselves are sensible of the vanity of this objection, and cry out of the unreasonableness of it. I think nothing is more apparent than that I can spend my time much more profitably in laboring to bring in the English language among the Indians, and in other labors for their benefit, than in endeavors to learn their language.

'Tis very probable that my enemies, who seem to be irrepressibly engaged to have me removed and restless in their endeavors for it, will again bring on something before the General Court that they hope will have a tendency to my removal, by inducing the Commissioners to act something against me, or otherwise. If they should do so, I wish that this, my letter, which I have writ to Your Honor in my own defense, might be communicated to the Assembly.

I know not what are the things which Colonel Dwight has said against me that have chiefly impressed the minds of the members of the Court to my disadvantage, nor what further Colonel Dwight intends to say. But I trust in the justice of the honorable Assembly, that nothing will be hearkened to, so far as to be made the ground of any manner of proceeding in any respect to my disadvantage, till I have appeared, face to face, with my accusers before them, and have liberty to speak freely for myself, in answer to every allegation and suggestion against me. I hope that the Assembly, who have patiently heard so much said against me in the Committee's Report, will also be ready to hear this letter, which I write in my own defense, and that they will entertain no prejudices against me till they have given me opportunity to speak fully for myself, *viva voce*. Though it be not the General Court, but the Commissioners, that have the care of the Indian mission in this place, yet, as I have any regard to my character, it may well be supposed that I should not be willing that my reputation with so honorable and great an Assembly should be left to the mercy of my enemies, without my having any opportunity to confront them and speak for myself. [. . .]

[Jonathan Edwards.]

165. TO ESTHER EDWARDS BURR

Edwards takes a break from his Stockbridge struggles to concentrate on offering spiritual solace for his daughter's soul and physical remedies for her body. His approach to life and death is unabashedly biblical and Puritan. Following a long tradition that claims snakes have healing powers, Edwards joins ranks with those who take the caduceus not just symbolically but literally.

(BPL, ALS, two quarto leaves, addressed on verso to Mrs. Esther Burr at Newark.)

* * *

Stockbridge, March 28, 1753

Dear Child,

We are glad to hear that you are in any respect better, but concerned at your remaining great weakness. I am glad to see some of the contents of your letter to your mother; and particularly that you have been enabled to make a free-will offering of yourself to God's service, and that you have experienced some inward divine consolations under your affliction, by the extreme weakness and distressing pains, you have been the subject of. For these you ought to be thankful, and also for that unwearied kindness and tender care of your companion [Aaron Burr], which you speak of. I would not have you think that any strange thing has happened to you in this affliction: 'tis according to the course of things in this world, that after the world's smiles, some great affliction soon comes. God has now given you early and season-able warning, not at all to depend on worldly prosperity. Therefore I would advise, that if it pleases God to restore you, to let upon no happiness here. Labor while you live, to serve God and do what good you can, and endeavor to improve every dispensation to God's glory and your own spiritual good, and be content to do and bear all that God calls you to in this wilderness, and never expect to find this world anything better than a wilderness. Lay your account to travel through it in weariness, painfulness and trouble, and wait for your rest and your prosperity till hereafter, where they that die in the Lord rest from their labors, and enter into the joy of their Lord. You are like to spend the rest of your life (if you should get over this illness) at a great distance from your parents; but care not much for that. If you lived near us, yet our breath and yours would soon go forth, and we should return to our dust, whither we are all hastening. 'Tis of infinitely more importance to have the presence of an heavenly Father, and to make progress towards an heavenly home. Let us all take care that we may meet there at last.

As to means for your health, we have procured one rattlesnake, which is all we could get. It is a medicine that has been very serviceable to you heretofore, and I would have you try it still. If your stomach is very weak and will bear but little, you must take it in smaller quantities. We have sent you some ginseng. I should think it best for you to make trial of that various ways: try stewing it in water, and take it in strength and quantity as you find suits your stomach best. You may also try steeping it in wine, in good Madeira or claret; or if these wines are too harsh, then in some good white wine. And whether you stew or steep it, you had best to slice it very thin, or bruise it in an iron mortar. And for a cordial take some spices steeped in some generous wine that suits your taste, and stomach. And above all the rest, use riding in pleasant weather; and when you can bear it, riding on horseback; but never so as to fatigue you. And be very careful to avoid taking cold. And I should think it best pretty much to throw by doctors, and be your own physician, hearkening to them that are used to your constitution.

I desire that Mr. [Aaron] Burr and you would be frequent in counseling Timmy [Edwards] as to his soul-concerns.

Commending you to God, before whom we daily remember you in our prayers, I am

Your affectionate father,
Jonathan Edwards.

P.S. Your mother would have you use a conserve of raisins; a pound of good sugar to a pound of raisins, after they are stoned. Mix with it nutmegs, mace, cinnamon, cloves, ground in a spice mill, with some orange-pith; one nutmeg to half a pound of conserve, and the other spices in the same quantity. Take a little as suits your stomach, in the morning, and an hour before dinner, and in the afternoon, the same spices and orange-pith to be put into your spiced wine. But when you take this, you must omit taking the wine. The only danger we apprehend in these things is that possibly the heat of 'em may raise a fever; therefore you must observe the operation of them as to that. And when you drink your spiced wine, you may mix some water with it to abate the heat of it. Your mother has also an inclination that you should sometimes try a tea made of the leaves of Robin's plantain,[1] if it be known at Newark by that name; she says she has found it very strengthening and comfortable to her in her weakness.

The family all unites in their love to you.

166. TO TIMOTHY EDWARDS

Edwards' fourteen-year-old son Timothy is ill at Newark, where he has gone to begin studies at the College of New Jersey. Edwards, in this letter, exhorts his son to seek salvation as a first priority.

(Trask Library, Dwight ms. transcript, two quarto leaves. Published in Dwight ed., *1*, 525–27.)

*   *   *

Stockbridge, April 1, 1753

My Dear Child,

Before you will receive this letter, the matter will doubtless be determined, as to your having the smallpox. You will either be sick with that

---

1. Poor-Robin's-plantain (*Erigeron pulchellus*). Homer D. House, *Wild Flowers* (New York, MacMillan, 1934), p. 312, plate 239b.

distemper, or will be past danger of having it, from any infection taken in your voyage. But whether you are sick or well, like to die or like to live, I hope you are earnestly seeking your salvation. I am sure there is a great deal of reason it should be so, considering the warnings you have had in word and in providence.

That which you met with, in your passage from New York to Newark, which was the occasion of your fever, was indeed a remarkable warning, a dispensation full of instruction, and a very loud call of God to you, to make haste and not to delay in the great business of religion. If you now have that distemper, which you have been threatened with, you are separated from your earthly friends; none of them must come to see you; and if you should die of it, you have already taken a final and everlasting leave of them while you are yet alive, not to have the comfort of their presence and immediate care, and never to see them again in the land of the living. And if you have escaped that distemper, it is by a remarkable providence that you are preserved. And your having been so exposed to it, must certainly be a loud call of God, not to trust in earthly friends, or anything here below. Young persons are very apt to trust in parents and friends, when they are sick, or when they think of being on a deathbed. But this providence remarkably teaches you the need of a better friend, and a better parent, than earthly parents are; one who is everywhere present, and all-sufficient; that can't be kept off by infectious distempers; who is able to save from death or to make happy in death; to save from eternal misery and to bestow eternal life.

It is indeed comfortable, when one is in great pain, languishing under sore sickness, to have the presence and kind care of near and dear earthly friends; but this is a very small thing, in comparison of what it is, to have the presence of an heavenly Father and a compassionate and almighty Redeemer. In God's favor is life, and his lovingkindness is better than life. Whether you are in sickness or health, you infinitely need this. But you must know, however great need you stand in of it, you don't deserve it. Neither is God the more obliged to bestow it upon you, for your standing in necessity of it, your earnest desiring of it, your crying to him constantly for it, from fear of misery, and taking much pains. Till you have savingly believed in Christ, all your desires, and pains, and prayers lay God under no obligation; and if they were ten thousand times as great as they are, you must still know, that you would be in the hands of a sovereign God, who hath mercy on whom he will have mercy. Indeed, God often hears the poor, miserable cries of sinful, vile creatures, who have no manner of true regard to him in their hearts; for he is a God of infinite mercy, and he delights to show mercy for his Son's sake; who is worthy, though you are unworthy; who came to save the sinful and the miserable, yea, some of the chief of sinners.

Therefore, there is your only hope; and in him must be your refuge, who invites you to come to him, and says, "He that cometh to me, I will in no wise cast out" [John 6:37]. Whatever your circumstances are, it is your duty not to despair, but to hope in infinite mercy through a Redeemer. For God makes it your duty to pray to him for mercy; which would not be your duty, if it was allowable for you to despair. We are expressly commanded to call upon God in the day of trouble; and when we are afflicted, then to pray.

But, if I hear that you have escaped—either that you have not been sick, or are restored—though I shall rejoice, and have great cause of thankfulness, yet I shall be concerned for you. If your escape should be followed with carelessness and security, and forgetting the remarkable warning you have had, and God's great mercy in your deliverance, it would in some respects be more awful than sore sickness. It would be very provoking to God, and would probably issue in an increasing hardness of heart; and, it may be, divine vengeance may soon overtake you. I have known various instances of persons being remarkably warned, in providence, by being brought into very dangerous circumstances and escaping, and afterwards death has soon followed in another way.

I earnestly desire, that God would make you wise to salvation and that he would be merciful and gracious to you in every respect, according as he knows your circumstances require. And this is the daily prayer of

> Your affectionate and tender father,
> Jonathan Edwards.

P.S. Your mother and all the family send their love to you, as being tenderly concerned for you.

167. TO SEC. ANDREW OLIVER

Edwards' hopes that Stockbridge would become a center for Mohawk education were dashed when most of them left. As an alternative, Edwards proposes to the Commissioners that the mission become a base for outreach to the Indians. Two of his expectations were never fulfilled: John Brainerd did not bring his Indian village north, and Alexander Gordon did not become a career missionary. Gideon Hawley did devote his life to working with Indians, however. Edwards gives a statesmanlike review of the situation and tells why he considers the village of Onohquaga, New York, to offer the best options.

(Trask Library, AL draft, two octavo leaves on a letter cover addressed to Edwards at Northampton, and one folio leaf on a letter cover to Edwards at Stockbridge; Dwight ms. transcript, five quarto leaves.)

* * *

Stockbridge, April 12, 1753

Honorable Sir,

Mr. [Timothy] Woodbridge and I, having long since wrote to the Commissioners desiring their instructions relating to our conduct in the present state of the important affairs of Stockbridge, and having had no return, and concluding that our letters have failed, considering the opportunities there have been; and that I have lately received letters from some of the Commissioners which make no mention of these letters of ours; and new scenes appearing requiring the information to be given to the Commissioners and their speedy considering and proper instruction to be given to them; and not finding any good opportunity to send to Boston by any that are going on other business: these things are the occasion of Mr. [Gideon] Hawley's now coming to Boston to wait on the Commissioners.

The last Tuesday, Indians young and old went away from Stockbridge and are never like to return again. They have long manifested a great uneasiness at the management of affairs here and the conduct of those persons their affairs have almost wholly fallen [to], and have shown themselves very much grieved that others, that used to be concerned in their instruction, have been excluded.

As to the two families which remain of the Conneenchee tribe, they have likewise manifested great uneasiness, and 'tis not very probable that they will continue very long. One of the heads of these families lately told Col. [Joseph] Dwight that he had broke up the affair. 'Tis evident that at present nothing more is to be expected from the Mohawk affair in this place, so that, if anything further be done, it must be in their own country.

There are some other things also have lately opened that it is necessary the Commissioners should be informed [of], in order to their being under advantage to give the best directions when future measures [are] to be taken for the enlightening the Six Nations.

The Correspondents in New York and New Jersey of the Society in Scotland for Propagating Christian Knowledge have determined, if providence favors, to settle a mission among the Six Nations. To that end they have chosen Mr. [Alexander] Gordon, a pious young gentleman who has lately been a tutor at New Jersey College, to come to Stockbridge and be here with Mr. Hawley to learn the Mohawk language with him, in order to his being fitted for the business. Mr. Gordon is expected here to prosecute this design at the beginning of May.

And beside this, Mr. [John] Brainerd, the pastor of the Indian congregation at Bethel in New Jersey, who is supported by the Correspondents, having met with much trouble from the enemies of religion in those parts, and his Indians being greatly disturbed with regard to the possession and improvement of their lands, the Correspondents have of late had a disposition that he, with his schoolmaster and whole congregation, should remove (if a door might be opened) and take up a new settlement somewhere in the country of the Six Nations. Mr. Hawley has seen Mr. Brainerd and conversed with him on the subject this spring. He manifests an inclination to such a removal and says his Indians will be ready for it. If such a thing as this could be brought to pass, it would probably tend greatly to the introducing the gospel and promoting the interest of religion among the Six Nations, as his congregation I suppose are the most religious and virtuous company of Indians in America. And some of them have now been long established in religion and virtue.

According to the best understanding I can get of the country of the Six Nations, the most convenient place to be chosen as the chief seat of those affairs is the country about Onohquaga near the head of the Susquehanna River.

I apprehend from some things Deacon Woodbridge has informed me of, that the Commissioners have had very wrong information concerning the Onohquaga Indians, as though they were a very despicable company, a kind of renegades, scarcely to be reckoned as of the Six Nations, being out of the country of those nations.

There are indeed some here who have sometimes spoken very contemptibly of 'em, which seems to have been, not from any manner of ground in fact or so much as any color of reason, but mainly because those Indians appeared peculiarly attached to Mr. [Benjamin] Ashley and his wife [Rebecca Kellogg Ashley] and under their influence. But there are others in Stockbridge [who] have had as much opportunity to

know what is the true state of those people as they. The Onohquaga
Indians who have been here are properly of the Six Nations that are
the original united tribes of the Iroquois. All but one or two [are] of the
nation of the Oneidas, and they appear not to be looked upon [as]
contemptible by the rest of the Five Nations, by what was once openly
said of 'em at a public conference by the sachems of the Conneenchees,
who advised us to treat the Onohquagas with peculiar care and kindness, as excelling their own tribe in religion and virtue, giving many
instances of their virtue. And we have found the testimony they gave
of 'em to be true. They have appeared to be far the best disposed
Indians we have had to do with, and would be inclined to their utmost
to assist, encourage, and to strengthen the hands of missionaries and
instructors, should [any] be sent among [them], and do all they can to
forward their success among themselves and other Indians round
about.

There seems to be no room for a missionary in the country of the
Proper Mohawks. The Society for Propagating of the Gospel in Foreign Parts have long since taken them under their care, and pretend to
support a mission among them.[1] A mission from the Commissioners
in Boston would not be borne by them, nor by the Dutch, who are
always among them. And as to the country of the Cayugas, and the
original seat of the Oneidas, they seem not to be convenient places for
settling a mission, on two accounts. They are in the road to Oswego,
where the Dutch are incessantly passing and repassing with their rum,
with which they are continually making them drunk, and would be, in
many other respects, a continual hindering and afflicting a missionary
and embarrassing his affairs, for they are exceedingly opposed to the
New England people's having anything to do with them.

Besides, the nation of the Cayugas are mostly in the French interest,
and many of the Oneidas, so that a missionary would there be afflicted
and perhaps in danger by the French. And it is very evident that the
country of the Onondagas is no country for our missionaries; to go
about to settle a mission there would be like settling missionaries in
Canada, for that nation have entirely gone over into the French interest. They are in the road of the French, as they go up a-trading to

1. The SPG mission effort among the Mohawks actually had a long, honored tradition,
beginning in 1709 and continuing until after the death of Sir William Johnson in 1774. It
included such leaders as Thomas Barclay, William Andrews, John Miln, Henry Barclay, and
John Ogilvie. William W. Kemp, *The Support of Schools in Colonial New York by the Society for the
Propagation of the Gospel in Foreign Parts* (New York, 1913), pp. 197–98, 208–33.

Mississippi, and their distant settlements, and the nations on the Great Lakes; and they have of late built a fort in their country, and have in effect annexed it to Canada. And the country of the Senecas will not be much more convenient for the purpose, both by reason of its very great distance, and also because most of the nation are firmly united to the French, who constantly maintain their missionaries among them.

Onohquaga is within the territories of the Five Nations, and not so far from the other settlements, but that it may be convenient for making excursions to the several tribes, as convenient perhaps as any place that can be found. It is, I suppose, as near to the heart of their country as any place, unless Oneida and Cayuga. They are much out of the way of the French, and considerably out of the way of the Dutch, are in a pleasant, fruitful country, surrounded by many settlements of Indians on every side, and where the way is open by an easy passage down the river, which runs through one of the most pleasant, fruitful parts of America for four or five hundred miles, exceedingly peopled on both sides and on its several branches by Indians. Onohquaga is the road by which several of the nations pass as they go to war with the southern nations. And there will be this advantage which missionaries will have, that the Onohquaga Indians are great friends to the English, and though some of the Dutch have tried much to disaffect them to the English, their attempts have been in vain. They are very desirous of instruction, and to have the gospel settled in their country.

There are several towns of the Onohquagas, and several missionaries might probably find sufficient employ in those parts. If Mr. Brainerd should settle somewhere in that country, with his Christian Indians and one or two more missionaries not at a great distance, they might be under advantage to assist one another, as they will greatly need one another's company and assistance in so difficult a work, in such a strange, distant land. They might be under advantage to consult one another, and to act in concert and to help one another in any case of peculiar difficulty. Many English people would be found to go from New England and settle; the greatest difficulty would be that there would be danger of too many English settlers, and of such as are not fit for the place.

But in order to accomplish these things, especially in order to such a body of new Indians coming from the Jerseys and settling in the country of the Six Nations, the consent of those nations, or at least several of them, must be obtained. The method which Mr. Woodbridge, Mr. Hawley, and I have thought of, which we submit to the wisdom of the

Commissioners, is this: that Mr. Woodbridge and Mr. Ashley and his wife should go, as speedily as possible, into the country of the Proper Mohawks—they being the first tribe in honor (though not in numbers)—and should spend some weeks, perhaps a month, among them, to get acquaintance with them, and endeavoring to gain their approbation of measures, for settling the gospel in the country of the Six Nations. Mr. Hawley, in the meantime, keeps Mr. Woodbridge's school. Then, that Mr. Hawley and Mr. Gordon should go up to 'em there, and go with them from thence to Onohquaga; and when they have acquainted themselves well with the people and the state of the country, and find things agreeable, and see a hopeful prospect, then for Mr. Woodbridge to return and leave Mr. Hawley and Mr. Gordon there, and forthwith to send word to Mr. Brainerd and propose to him to come up with some of his chief Indians to see the country. And if, on the observations they make, and the acquaintance they get with the people and country, they think there is an encouraging prospect, then to endeavor to gain a conference with some of the chiefs of the Five Nations, at an appointed time, to know whether they will consent, etc., which will require some considerable time; so that, if they can obtain it, Mr. Brainerd must return home, and he and his chief Indians must come again to the treaty at the time and place appointed.

Your Honor will easily perceive that these things will require time and that, in order to finishing these affairs this year, there will be need of expedition, which may show the reason why we thought it necessary that Mr. Hawley should come to Boston; for, if these things are to be done this year, we had need speedily to know the minds of the Commissioners, and therefore that the case would not allow of waiting for and depending on uncertain, occasional opportunities of sending to 'em and hearing from 'em. 'Tis also proper that the Commissioners should have opportunity to agree with Mr. Hawley concerning the reward of his services.

Mr. Brainerd told Mr. Hawley, that if he removed with his Indians, he should choose to do it speedily, that the longer it was delayed, the more difficult it would be, by reason of his building, and the Indians increasing their buildings and improvements, at Bethel. Probably, if the removal can't be brought about the next year, it never will be. And if his Indians remove the next [year], it will be necessary that they remove so early as the spring, as to plant there that one year. And if so much needs to be done this summer, [it is] as much as it will be possible to find time for.

Though we project the measures mentioned above, we are sensible they will be attended with much uncertainty. "Man's heart deviseth his way, but the Lord directeth his steps" [Prov. 16:9]. Many are the desires of men's hearts, but the counsel of the Lord, that shall stand. Unthought-of difficulties may arise to confound all our projects, as unforeseen difficulties have dashed all the pleasing hopes we entertained and the fair prospects we had concerning the Mohawk affairs at Stockbridge the year before last. And I would humbly propose it to consideration whether it won't be necessary to leave these affairs in some measure to discretion, to be determined as the complicated, uncertain, changing state of things shall require, to save the trouble and charge of frequently going or sending to Boston for new instructions, and the disadvantages, which affairs may be laid under, through the lengthy, uncertain way of sending for and receiving new orders by occasional opportunities.

There will be a necessity of Mrs. Ashley's going as an interpreter, and of his going with her who will be willing to instruct the Indians in their husbandry, who has been well instructed in it himself. I believe he will not be very difficult as to his wages, though probably he expects to know what they will be. [. . .]

[Jonathan Edwards.]

168. TO SEC. ANDREW OLIVER

Edwards lists a number of reasons why Abigail Dwight is unfit to be mistress of the female school. Foremost is her alienation of the Indians; but he also cites her lack of time, uninterest, and marriage to Col. Joseph Dwight. Her marriage gives her a conflict of interest, for her husband is inspector of schools who wishes to be his own administrator. Moreover, Dwight derides and circumvents the Boston Commissioners.

The postscript is a confidential message to Oliver urging his discretionary use of the first. The letter of April 12 (No. 167) is intended for the regular meeting of the Commissioners.

(Trask Library, AL draft, on a Mass. fast day proclamation for Apr. 19, 1753, dated Mar. 7, 1753, and an irreg. part of one folio leaf; Dwight ms. transcript, six quarto leaves.)

* * *

Stockbridge, April 13, 1753

Honored Sir,

Since I have now so good an opportunity, it may be proper not only to write concerning a mission into the country of the Six [Nations], but also to write something particularly concerning the affairs which do more immediately concern us, the inhabitants of Stockbridge, and the welfare and success of the means of grace and instruction here.

Since affairs between me and the inhabitants of Stockbridge on one side, and Col. [Joseph] Dwight and the Williamses on the other, are come to so great extremities that these last have as it were engaged in open and proclaimed war with the former, [it] may be an excuse for me in using a greater freedom in opening myself concerning our affairs. And particularly, I humbly conceive I may be justified in exposing my mind more fully than ever I have yet done concerning Mrs. [Abigail] Dwight being the mistress of the school, as 'tis now most apparent that my own interest, the success of my ministry, and the peace of the town is to the utmost concerned in this affair. I would therefore now assert the following things may be considered with respect to her being established in that business:

1. I desire it may be considered whether there be the least probability of her devoting herself to the business of a school mistress in any steady manner. She is now the mother of Colonel Dwight's large family, besides her own, and is like to be the mother of a third family which she will have to breed and bear and take care of, as now appears. 'Tis the less likely that she will submit to so laborious a life for her having married into a family of such rank and estate, and 'tis known that both she and her husband are sufficiently inclined to grandeur, and besides her being a person of an infirm constitution. And more than all this, she has plainly signified to me that she did not expect any such thing as her having the immediate instruction of the children, but only to inspect and oversee the affairs of the school and direct another mistress that should be under her.

2. She is a person that the Indians have a general distaste for. She is of a family which they have the greatest aversion to of any whatsoever, and they have a personal dislike of her. This appears not only by what they say of her, but is very apparent by their conduct since she and her friends have endeavored to gain the consent of the Indians to her having the care of their children. There appears an universal aversion in the Stockbridge Indians to it. So that she appears evidently long

since to have despaired of getting any of their children, and left off trying, and has betaken herself wholly to the Mohawks, who also are far from manifesting any liking to her. She has obtained their children no otherwise than by leaving her own house and coming down to them and as it were forcing them to read to her. After Mr. [Gideon] Hawley left the school, she first used to go down to the boarding school into Capt. [Martin] Kellogg's room, and there by his help used to persuade the children to read to her. But they have, both the Conneenchees and Oneidas, manifested their dislike of her. They have ridiculed her pretending of setting up a female school. One of the Conneenchees or Proper Mohawks once ridiculed her pretense of keeping a female school. "She comes," said he, "and catches our children by the blankets and pulls 'em and forces 'em to come and read to her, and she pulls so hard that, if they would not comply, they did not know but she would pull their blanket off."

And since that of late Captain Kellogg has gone to Newington, she and her husband have left their house and have lived constantly at the new schoolhouse, to be in the way of the children, but still are unsuccessful in their attempts to gain their affections.

The children themselves have manifested a disgust. There is so great an intercourse and friendship between the Mohawks and Stockbridge Indians that there is no probability that the one will like those that the others have an aversion to.

3. If she be established the mistress of the school, the affairs of both the boarding schools and all affairs relating to the Mohawks, if any of them shall continue, would fall almost entirely into the hands of such persons as the Indians have a general, great aversion to, as into the hands of Colonel Dwight and his new friends. Colonel Dwight's continuance here has seemed to depend on his wife's being the mistress of the girls' school. This, therefore, is the point that he and the Williamses have drove at above all others. While he is here, he takes the affairs of the Mohawks and the male school entirely into his hands and manages all as he pleases. And if his wife be the mistress of the girls' school, 'tis apparent that then he will have the management of that school. But Colonel Dwight is a person very distasteful to the Indians of all sorts. His conduct in the whole series of it has been very disagreeable to 'em and their distaste has been long increasing and is now become rooted, not only with the Stockbridge Indians, but the Iroquois; as their behavior does openly manifest, there having lately gone off at once about two-thirds of these Indians in a declared dislike of him and his con-

duct. These Indians, the day before their departure, as they came to take their leave of some of us, told us that it was nothing that we had done that had discouraged them, that what we had been [and] done had been all straight, as they expressed [it], but that it was the conduct of Brigadier Dwight that had discouraged them. They mentioned many things that he had done and said which they judged to be very wrong and manifesting an ill spirit. And the Indians that are left, they also have testified the same disapprobation of their conduct and lay all the blame of the failing of the affair to them. Now I desire it may be considered, whether it can be expected that Indian affairs of Stockbridge should prosper under the care and management of such as are so very distasteful to 'em?

4. I desire it may be considered, whether it can tend to the prosperity of the affairs of the Commissioners at Stockbridge for them to wholly have the management of such as are evidently striving to their utmost to diminish the power and influence of the Commissioners in those affairs and, as much as in 'em lies, to wrest 'em out of their hands. This appears many ways with respect to Colonel Dwight and his new friends. He has found much fault with the Commissioners, as though they had taken more upon them than belonged to them, and in the direction that they have given concerning the schools, has insisted greatly that those affairs ought to be wholly in the hands of the General Assembly; which has been to say in effect that they ought to be wholly in his own hands. He always undertakes to manage all affairs as the agent of the Assembly. He has often declared the necessity of those affairs being wholly in the hands of the General Court. He has found great fault with the instructions that the Commissioners have given to their schoolmaster here, and has insisted upon it that it must come to that at last, that the General Court Committee, and not the Commissioners, must have the power of all affairs of the schools.

5. I humbly conceive it can't be for the health of our affairs that they should fall into [the] hands of such, to engross all power and establish in themselves a power that is independent and despotical. Such an inclination has been manifest many ways: it appears by their striving by the help of the General Assembly to carry their points with a strong hand, and as it were to oblige the Commissioners to comply with what they would have [done]; in removing such as they have employed as one obnoxious to 'em; and also by their applying directly to the Corporation in London, and in a neglect of their Commissioners here, if possible, to gain their point there, and by inducing them to force their

Commissioners to do what they would have 'em. It appears in their endeavors to have all such removed as don't yield to them in the exercise of such a degree of power as they claim, and comply with all their measures. It appears also by the vast resentment [with] which Colonel Dwight has treated Col. [Joseph] Pynchon for not complying with some of his measures, though he is one that has equal authority, as a Committeeman, with himself.

6. It may be considered whether it can be for the health of the affairs of the Commissioners that affairs should all be in the hands of such as are, in effect, avowed enemies to all that are employed here by the Commissioners, as their missionary and both their schoolmasters; whether it can tend to the good of the Indian souls to have affairs in the hands of such as are taking all opportunities to disaffect the minds of the Indians towards their ministers. 'Tis manifest such have been the continual endeavors of the Williamses, of which we have a very late instance. When Captain Kellogg lately went down to Wethersfield, he with promises of presents persuaded a couple of Indian schoolboys of the Stockbridge tribe to go thither with him. And in the account they give of what they met with there, they say that at Wethersfield, Col. [Elisha] Williams and others got round and told 'em they had not a good minister, that the people where he was before had thrown him away, and the poor Stockbridge Indians, they were willing to take him, but they had best let him go back again from whence he came and they would get a good minister for 'em; and that they brought a writing to 'em to have them sign it, but that they refused and told 'em that they were poor boys and it was not their business; that they urged them much and, on their continuing to refuse, they brought 'em some wine and gave it to 'em and, after they had been drinking that, they brought the paper again and asked 'em if they were willing now.

They are so open in manifestation of their dislike of me and ill opinion of me that, if Mrs. Dwight be the mistress of the school, it may be expected that the children themselves will be brought up in disaffection to their minister. And there seems to be no hope of any real reconciliation and coalescence with those people, such is Colonel Dwight's temper. And he has already gone such great length in his opposition to and injuries of me, by his great endeavors to his utmost to ruin my character in the most public manner, and by what is sent to England against me by him or his friends. And, 'tis evident by things which have appeared, he will take nothing as a reconciliation but my declaring that I look upon him as my hearty friend and my falling in with him in his measures.

I hear indeed that he makes the most solemn protestations of his desire of peace, appealing to heaven, etc. But at the same time it is manifest he is industriously carrying on his schemes in opposition. He encompasses himself with snares. He is constantly laying up materials for accusation, which has appeared by his sitting with his pen in his hand when one of my neighbors and friends has conversed with him on these heads, catching and writing down his words that he thought made for [his] purpose.

7. Colonel Dwight and his friends not only set themselves against your missionary and schoolmasters here, but they maintain an opposition and strife with the whole town. The inhabitants in general look on themselves nearly concerned while they [the opposers] are openly and professedly endeavoring to deprive them of their minister. The people have gone to talk with him on this affair, but he has treated them with roughness and contempt. Even Mr. [Josiah] Jones, Mrs. Dwight's own uncle, who at first was much against my coming hither, is now greatly against their measures. And I humbly conceive, it can't tend to the flourishing of our affairs that they should be in the hands of such persons who maintain a kind of open war with the inhabitants of Stockbridge in general, both English and Indians.

8. If Mrs. Dwight be the mistress of the school, the children will be under the care of such as will probably set them a very ill example and, particularly, by bringing them up in a neglect and contempt of the public worship {of God}. So it has been that Colonel Dwight himself, for a long time, has seldom attended the public worship, and his wife has been very negligent of it, as are most of the family of the Williamses. And even of late, Colonel Dwight has wholly absented himself for about six weeks, though he has attended Mr. Hawley's instruction of the Mohawks, they being given in the room where he has lived. She has of late almost wholly absented.

9. 'Tis sufficiently evident, by the trial Mrs. Dwight has already made, that the affair of the female school cannot prosper in her hands. The last year, both he and she laid out themselves very much to get scholars. They could get but four, three Stockbridge children and one Mohawk. The Mohawk girl soon left her house and went [away]. The Stockbridge girls were also, after some time, discouraged. Their parents exceedingly disliked her management of 'em. Now 'tis apparent she can get no Stockbridge children and seems wholly to have given up

the point as to them and, having betaken herself to the Mohawks by going to them when they won't come to her, yet nothing prospers under her hands. The Mohawks are rather driven away by the management of her and her husband and the whole affair is expiring under their hands.

'Tis probable that Colonel Dwight will come to Boston with new accusations against us and abundance of such representations, if possible to possess the minds of the General Assembly and Commissioners with an ill opinion of the state of things here and the conduct of the officers here employed by you, with many peremptory assertions and the most solemn protestations, as his manner is. But I humbly desire that no prejudice may be understood against us from anything he shall [say,] unless we are first heard face to face. They give out very threatening words. Colonel Dwight and his friends have expressed themselves with great assurance as to my being removed and his carrying all his designs, perhaps to terrify us and keep us in subjection.

And innumerable are the methods devised and measures taken to supplant, but [my] reliance, under God, is on the wisdom of the Commissioners. [. . .]

[Jonathan Edwards.]

Stockbridge, April 13, 1753

Sir,

I send the letter dated as a private letter to Your Honor, desiring you to use your own discretion with respect to communicating of it to the Commissioners. I use this caution especially on two accounts: Colonel Pynchon has lately hinted that there is a design of prosecuting me in the law for some letters I have wrote [to] Boston concerning Colonel Dwight, employing some gentleman in Boston to get copies or a sight of those letters; and secondly, not knowing but that Col. Ephraim Williams, who is a Commissioner, would demand a sight of letters sent about the female school. If Your Honor thinks there is no danger of any harm by use of these means, I should choose that these letters should be communicated to the Commissioners.

Sir, this I choose, that both the letters I have written should be shown to the Commissioners if you think best. I wrote this as a letter to Your Honor in particular, that you may dispose of it according to your discretion and either to present or communicate it when Your Honor chooses. I had rather trust your wisdom than my own as to the disposal of it.

169. TO THE REVEREND THOMAS FOXCROFT

Edwards had a solid base of support among the Stockbridge residents, English and Indian, and the Boston Commissioners. Thus shielded, he wrote fewer apologetic letters in 1753 and instead concentrated on completing *Freedom of the Will,* which he finished by summer. Here he begins promoting the book.

(Beinecke Library, ALS, one folio leaf, addressed on verso to the Reverend Thomas Foxcroft, minister of the gospel in Boston, overwritten with later sermon notes in Foxcroft's hand.)

* * *

Stockbridge, April 13, 1753

Rev. and Honored Sir,

I thank you for your favor of March 19 and for the particular informations you give me, tending to relieve my mind with regard to the bold and vaunting manner of those that seek my overthrow. You say gentlemen in Boston seem to think that I am apt to magnify things with respect to the attempts made for my overthrow. Perhaps they would not think so if they heard and saw all that is said and done here. Brig. [Joseph] Dwight has, from time to time, expressed to our people his assurance that he should be successful in his designs against me, and that I should undoubtedly be removed in a little time. To the like purpose, several of the Williamses have expressed themselves, though I now begin to think that these bold and great threats were designed only to terrify us, and thereby to bring us to their own terms.

I have herewith enclosed proposals for printing by subscription something I have been writing, with a letter to Mr. [Samuel] Kneeland. I am afraid you will be sorry at the sight of these proposals, as they may give you a prospect of a great addition to the trouble I have already put you to. I am indeed concerned about it, and ashamed to ask of you to continue that assistance with respect to this piece, which you have afforded in times past with respect to former publications. But I will venture at present to ask this of you, viz. to forward the letter to Mr. [John] MacLaurin, and about thirty of the proposals with it. It would also much oblige me if you use some endeavors to spread the proposals and to forward subscribing. This with my humble service to your family and request of a remembrance in your prayers is from, Sir,

Your most obliged son and servant,
Jonathan Edwards.

170. TO THE REVEREND JOHN ERSKINE

A respite after feverish correspondence with the Boston Commissioners provides an opportunity for Edwards to write to Erskine. He summarizes recent events both in the Indian mission and in his family. Under difficult conditions, Edwards is close to finishing his manuscript on *Freedom of the Will*. He requests subscriptions to facilitate its publication.

(Trask Library, ALS, two quarto leaves, addressed on verso to the Reverend John Erskine, Minister of the Gospel at Kirkintilloch; Dwight ms. transcript, two quarto leaves. Published in Dwight ed., *1*, 533–34.)

* * *

Stockbridge, April 14, 1753

Rev. and Dear Sir,

After many hindrances, delays, and interruptions, divine providence has so far favored me, and smiled on my design of writing on the Arminian controversy, that I have almost finished the first draft of what I first intended. And am now sending the proposals for subscription to Boston to be printed, with a letter to Mr. [Thomas] Foxcroft[1] to send thirty of those proposals to Mr. [John] MacLaurin with a letter to him; wherein I have desired him to deliver half of them to you, as you have manifested yourself ready to use endeavors to get subscriptions in Scotland. The printing will be delayed to wait for subscriptions from thence: I therefore request that you endeavor to promote and expedite the affair.

Stockbridge affairs relating to the Indians are in many respects under a very dark cloud. The affair of the Iroquois or Six Nations here is almost at an end, as I have given a more particular account to Mr. MacLaurin. The Commissioners in Boston, I believe, are discouraged about it, and have thought of sending and settling a missionary in their own country. The Correspondents of the Society in Scotland have also determined to send a missionary there, and have chosen Mr. [Alexander] Gordon, a tutor of the college at Newark, for that end. Mr. Gordon is expected here at the beginning of May, to live at my house with Mr. [Gideon] Hawley, in order to learn the Iroquois language with him. 'Tis probable that he and Mr. Hawley will go up and spend this

---

1. See Letter No. 169, JE to Foxcroft, Apr. 13, 1753, above.

summer in the Iroquois country. The Correspondents have also a disposition that Mr. [John] Brainerd should remove with his whole congregation of Indians to settle somewhere in the country of the Six Nations, and he himself and his Indians are ready for it. 'Tis probable something will be done to prepare the way for it, or at least to see whether the way can be prepared or any door opened for it, this summer.

Some of those Indians have a great desire that the gospel should be introduced and settled in their country. Some of the Stockbridge Indians have of late been under considerable awakenings, two or three elderly men, that used to be vicious persons.

My family is now in usual health. My daughter [Esther] Burr in New Jersey has been very ill all the winter past. We last heard from her about five weeks ago; when it was hoped there was some amendment.

My wife [Sarah] joins with me in respectful and affectionate salutations to you and Mrs. [Christian Mackay] Erskine. Desiring a remembrance in your prayers, I am dear, Sir,

> Your affectionate brother and obliged friend and servant,
> Jonathan Edwards.

171. TO THE REVEREND THOMAS FOXCROFT

(Beinecke Library, ALS, one folio leaf, addressed on verso to the Reverend Thomas Foxcroft, Minister of the Gospel in Boston, heavily overwritten in Foxcroft's hand. There is a notation on the back that it was received June 8, 1753, per Mr. Allen, and answered July 13. The reply is not extant.)

* * *

Stockbridge, May 24, 1753

Rev. and Honored Sir,

I thank you for your favor by Mr. [Gideon] Hawley. He, with Mr. [Timothy] Woodbridge, Mr. [Benjamin] Ashley, and his wife [Rebecca Kellogg Ashley], went away the last Tuesday in order to go into the country of the Six Nations. Mr. [Alexander] Gordon, that Mr. Hawley expected to go with him, fails. The Correspondents had at one meeting appointed him to go, but at a late meeting, wherein some members were present who were absent before, they determined that it was not best till they had sent to Scotland to know the minds of the Society.[1] Mr.

1. The Society in Scotland for Propagating Christian Knowledge.

[Ebenezer] Pemberton in particular was earnest in opposition to his going at present. This is some discouragement to Mr. Hawley.[2]

I humbly thank you for the readiness you manifest to assist in the publication of what I have written against Arminians, in promoting subscriptions, and in the care of the press. With respect to the character, I should be glad the book might be printed in the best character Mr. [Samuel] Kneeland has, and that it should be done every way in as handsome a manner as may be. I think the character in which my answer to Mr. [Solomon] Williams[3] is printed is better than that of my book on *Religious Affections,* but Mr. Hawley tells me that Mr. Kneeland has sent for new types; perhaps they will be better than any he now has.

I have had thoughts of writing to some gentlemen your way to take some of the proposals and endeavor to promote subscriptions; but I did not know but I should be thought too troublesome. I should be glad if I knew anybody that I could be so free with as to desire 'em a little to exert themselves in the time of the commencement at Cambridge: I had thought of writing to Col. [William] Brattle, who kept at my house at Northampton the biggest part of a week once, in the time of a treaty with Indians at Deerfield. But I have not acquaintance enough to know how it will do. I should be glad of a word of advice from you. With respect to the other two colleges, New Haven and Newark, I have no difficulty. I know who to improve.

My wife joins with me in respectful salutations. Desiring continued interest in your prayers, I am, Sir,

Your obliged son and servant,
Jonathan Edwards.

172. TO A SINGING TEACHER

Edwards was encouraged to sing from his youth and valued singing throughout his life as an integral part of worship. Here he calls for assistance in helping Stockbridge residents, Indian and English, achieve more effective expression of their praise in song.

(Sterling Library, Samuel Rossiter Betts Autograph Coll., ALS, two-thirds of a folio leaf. The recipient is unidentified.)

* * *

2. The Hawley biography in SIB, *12*, 395, states that Gordon did go, and mentions details concerning how Hawley and Gordon worked together. The decision to permit him apparently came after this letter was written.

3. *Misrepresentations Corrected.*

Windsor, June 4, 1753

Sir,

There is very great need of somebody at Stockbridge to teach the Indians to sing. They have good voices and many of them are apt to learn, and I should be glad if I could get you there the next fall or winter to that end, if you could be obtained on reasonable terms. I desire that you would inform me whether you would be willing to come, and on what terms. Your pay will be good and the English people there are a very agreeable sort of people. I suppose you would expect to be paid, not only for the time you should spend at Stockbridge, but for your journey at least in part, but perhaps you might afford to come if we should pay for your journey from Westfield. It might not be out of your way to come as far as Westfield or Springfield on your own business, it being in your way to Deerfield.

Please to send me a letter, and order it to be left either at my father's at Windsor, or Mr. [Samuel] Hopkins' of Springfield, or Capt. [Timothy] Dwight, [Jr.]'s of Northampton, and that as soon as may be, that if you can't come I may get somebody else. I am, Sir,

Your humble servant,
Jonathan Edwards.

173. TO COL. JOSEPH DWIGHT

With the exception of the Williams family, the congregation of the Stockbridge church sided with Edwards. Consequently, when the Williamses declined to participate in the Lord's Supper (Ephraim Williams contended they had been barred) and absented themselves from worship, they put themselves at odds with the rest of the congregation. Edwards repeatedly invited the Williamses to open meetings with the church in order to resolve differences. They demurred and held out as firmly for closed conferences. In the absence of agreement on arrangements, no meeting between the family and the church took place on this matter during Edwards' pastorate.

(RIHS, ms. 1133, ALS, one quarto leaf, slightly damaged near bottom, addressed on verso to the Honorable Joseph Dwight, Esq., in Stockbridge. Only three fragments [RIHS, ms. 1146], each a quarter of a folio leaf, are known to remain of the July 3, 1753 letter, to which this replies.)

*   *   *

Stockbridge, July 5, 1753

May It Please Your Honor,

A considerable part of the English members of the church, being together and having heard your letter of July 3, they desire me to inform you, that as they long ago sent one of their number to inform you that they were disposed to reconciliation, and stood ready fully to converse with Your Honor, with respect to the reasons of all parts of their conduct towards you, if you would appoint time and place, and give 'em opportunity; so what they did then is still in force, and their minds are not altered.

They also think it requisite that Mrs. [Abigail] Dwight should give the church the reasons of her openly turning her back on the sacrament of the Lord's Supper, she having united herself to this church in covenant, and so bound herself to join with the church in upholding and attending the ordinances of the gospel. We desire you to inform her that, when [sh]e can attend it, the pastor is ready to [appo]int a church meeting to that end. I am, Sir,

Your most humble servant,
Jonathan Edwards.

174. TO TIMOTHY EDWARDS

Edwards counsels his son to secure a thorough grounding in languages, which are essential for a proper education, even if it takes added time. The youth should revel in health and find joy in learning but always remember his mortality.

(Maine Historical Society, Fogg Coll., ALS, one folio leaf, addressed on verso to Timothy Edwards at Newark.)

* * *

Stockbridge, July 17, 1753

Dear Son,

I rejoice, and desire to do it with thankfulness and praise to God, that we have heard from time to time of your being in health, wherein you have been distinguished from many of your near relations of late; as particularly your brother [Timothy] Dwight, your brother [Elihu] and sister [Sarah] Parsons, your sister [Esther] Burr, and your sister Eunice. I hope you will improve life and health while God continues them to prepare for sickness and death, which you must expect: death will certainly come at the time which God has appointed, whether you are prepared or unprepared.

I rejoice to hear that you follow your studies and make good proficience. How great your proficience is I can't certainly tell, but I hardly think it will be best for you to enter the college the next commencement. One of the chief things that is the ruin of New England scholars is their going to college before they have a thorough acquaintance with the languages: 'tis a wound they never get over as long as they live. They never come to such a degree of learning in any measure, as they might otherwise do. This you will be sensible of hereafter, if your life is preserved.

If you don't enter college this year, we should be willing to see you here in the fall with Mr. [Aaron] Burr and his wife. You may possibly regret the putting off your freshmanship a year longer, and so serving some that now you are a companion to, but that is a little thing in comparison of the forementioned disadvantage, a thing not worth the regarding. If you are brought up to learning, I would fain have you have good learning and be a good scholar. A poor scholar is a poor creature. Above all, I desire that you may have grace to make a good improvement of learning, and all other talents, without which they will but aggravate your condemnation.

That God would give you that infinitely important blessing is the fervent prayer of your tender and affectionate father,

Jonathan Edwards.

P.S. Your mother, brothers, and sisters give their love to you.

P.P.S. Your mother desires you would send your old coat in Sir [Elijah] Williams' trunk, or any other old clothes you have that you have done with, which will be serviceable to your brothers. Give my service to Sir Williams and tell him I beg that favor of him to allow those clothes a place in his trunk.

175. TO THE REVEREND JOSEPH BELLAMY

(New York, Pierpont Morgan Library, ALS, one quarto leaf, addressed on verso to the Reverend Joseph Bellamy in Bethlehem.)

*   *   *

Stockbridge, August 6, 1753

Rev. and Dear Sir,

I have sent a couple of men for my sheep, Mr. [Samuel] Brown and
Hinds.[1] This is to desire that you would see to the delivery of 'em, and
see that justice is done about it. I have but a moment's time. You say the
sheep have been on charge. I suppose I shall see you before long and
then I will take care of that matter. Pray, come and see us.

I am, Sir, your loving brother,
Jonathan Edwards.

176. TO LIEUT. JOHN ELY

(Firestone Library, Jonathan Edwards Collection, ALS, one quarto leaf,
addressed on verso to Lieut. John Ely at Springfield.)

* * *

Stockbridge, August 27, 1753

Sir,

Please to send us by Deacon [Samuel] Brown five or six yards of tow-
cloth and also five or six yards of check, that which is good and serviceable and reasonable. And if you have any good paper, send me a
couple of quire. And take an account of these things. Herein you will
oblige your humble servant,

Jonathan Edwards.
P.S. Please also to send three sets of knitting needles of the common
size.

177. TO MAJ. EPHRAIM WILLIAMS, JR., ET AL.[1]

Following up on his letter of July 5 (No. 173), which was addressed specifically to Col. Joseph Dwight, and on subsequent correspondence sent to the
extended Williams family (no longer extant), Edwards reiterates the congregation's desire to meet publicly with its detractors. Although the colonel will

1. Apparently a resident of Northampton. Trumbull, 2, 622, lists a Phinehas Hinds as a
Revolutionary War soldier from Northampton.
1. This refers to Ephraim Williams the younger, who had been commissioned Major of
the Southern Militia of the County of Hampshire in Boston, June 7, 1753, and recommis-
sioned by Gov. Shirley on Aug. 10, assigned to the Foot Company in Stockbridge. Ephraim
Williams, Sr. had left Stockbridge for good prior to Aug. 14, to live in Deerfield. Wright,
pp. 70, 72.

be out of town on the date appointed, Edwards notes the meeting should take place. Colonel Dwight, after all, was not a member of the church.

(RIHS, ms. 1134, ALS, one folio sheet, addressed on verso to Maj. Ephraim Williams, Mr. Josiah Williams, Mrs. Abigail Dwight, Mrs. Judith Williams, in Stockbridge.)

* * *

Stockbridge, September 11, 1753

To Maj. Ephraim Williams, Mr. Josiah Williams, Mrs. Abigail Dwight, and Mrs. Judith Williams, members of the Church in Stockbridge:

What I lately wrote to you signifying the desire and expectation of the church of your meeting them the next Thursday, was not in my own name, but it was in fulfillment of a vote of the church which I have no power to alter. They have by their own vote appointed a meeting on purpose to hear you, and desired me to inform you that they expected you should then be present; and will doubtless then meet and expect that you should appear; not the less for Col. [Joseph] Dwight's not being at home at that time, if that is like to be the case, which the church knows nothing about. Colonel Dwight is not one of the complainers, nor one of the church, and the church are not sensible of any concern they have with him in this affair, and know not of any reasons why they should first inquire when he is like to be in town, before they venture to appoint a meeting to hear those of their own members who have exhibited so high a charge against their pastor and brethren. The church doubtless supposes that the complainers are, or should be, able to give the reasons of their own complaint.

It might be very hard for the church to accommodate all their meetings and proceedings to the convenience and leisure of every one of such a number of their disaffected members; and besides that to the convenience and pleasure of others that they are not concerned with. An end is put to all proceedings of the church for its own regulation and preservation, if this be reasonably expected. You have now an opportunity to offer your reasons and evidences to support your charge, if you have any to offer, and to lay before the church the reasons why you insist on a council, and to have 'em considered; which I hope you will embrace, rather than to cast contempt on the church (which you have obliged yourselves in covenant to submit to) by refusing to appear before 'em.

I am your pastor and servant for Jesus' sake,
Jonathan Edwards.

178. TO THE REVEREND AARON BURR

This is a letter of transfer of church membership for Esther Edwards Burr. (Firestone Library, Jonathan Edwards Collection, ALS, one quarto leaf, addressed on verso to the Reverend Mr. Aaron Burr at Newark).

* * *

Stockbridge, September 17, 1753

To the Reverend Aaron Burr, Pastor of the Church of Christ in Newark, to be communicated.

Reverend and Beloved,

By this I would inform you, that [at] a meeting of the church of Stockbridge on the 14th instant, it was unanimously voted, that whereas Mrs. Esther Burr, formerly Edwards, a member of this church, has in divine providence been removed from hence to dwell at Newark, she be recommended to your stated communion as a member in full standing; having heretofore been admitted in such standing in this church, by recommendation from the First Church of Northampton, and having so remained without offense during her continuance here.

Jonathan Edwards, Pastor of the Church in Stockbridge.

179. TO MAJ. EPHRAIM WILLIAMS, JR., ET AL.

Edwards informs Major Williams and his relatives, who are complaining of their treatment, of the unanimous vote of the Stockbridge church. He repeats that grievances against the church should properly be considered first by the church itself. The appeal should then go to the Boston Commissioners, who have jurisdiction over the church, not to a council of churches.

(RIHS, ms. 1175, ALS, two folio leaves, addressed on verso to same individuals as in the internal address.)

* * *

Stockbridge, September 18, 1753

To Maj. Ephraim Williams, Mr. Josiah Williams, Mr. Jonathan Devreux, Mrs. Abigail Williams, Mrs. Abigail Dwight, and Mrs. Judith Williams, members of the church in Stockbridge:

The following is a copy of the votes passed by this church at their meeting on the 14th instant; which as they concern you, I now send to you. I am your servant

For Jesus' sake,
Jonathan Edwards.

I. Whereas a charge of scandalous offenses has lately been exhibited against this church, and especially against the pastor and some of the members, and laid before the church in a writing signed by Maj. Ephraim Williams and others; and there being some reason to apprehend from the tenor of the said writing, together with the conduct of the subscribers, that their intention is, that the charges which they have exhibited in this writing should be directly carried to a council, and the evidences by which they would support them be laid before them in the first place; therefore voted, that whether ever their complaint be carried to a council, or any others besides the church themselves, or no, yet the nature of things manifestly requires that the reasons and evidences they have to justify their charge should first to be laid before the church, before whom they have laid the complaint. And the church has an undoubted right to insist on this, and authority to require it; and that whether it be supposed to be proper that the church should act as decisive judges in the affair or not.

II. As to what is (as we think unseasonably and preposterously) desired, in the forementioned writing, viz. that the things they allege therein should be referred to the judgment and final decision of a council; voted, that it appears to this church, that the peculiar state of this church, and also the circumstances of this case are such, that if the judgment of these things be referred to any other judges besides the church themselves, 'tis proper and necessary that the whole affair be first laid before the honorable Commissioners for Indian Affairs, that they, on a full hearing of it, may have opportunity to use their own wisdom in endeavors to put an end to the calamities which attend their affairs in this place. This appears to us to be what the nature of the case requires, for the following reasons:

1. The circumstances of this church and congregation are very peculiar, much differing from those of most other churches; the Commissioners having the chief care of the religious concerns of this town; the very being of the church being owing to them, under God: it being brought about through their care and expense, and

in pursuance of the important ends of their commission; and the settlement of the town being to accommodate an important religious affair which they are trustees of. For which reasons it must be supposed, that so far as the religious concerns of the church come under the care of any out of the church, they chiefly fall under their care, and must most properly in the first place come under their cognizance. And as the difficulties which now attend this church, to the highest degree concern the interest of the Commissioners here, threatening no less than the utter subversion of their affairs, therefore we think they can't fitly be referred to the determination of others, without their judgment and advice.

2. The foresaid complaint exhibited by Maj. Ephraim Williams, etc., is in the first place against the missionary, as behaving himself altogether unworthy of his ministerial character. And we think we can't in justice to the Commissioners, by any means, refer that matter to the decision of other judges, without their cognizance and advice; because that would be referring it to the judgment and final determination of other judges, whether the missionary the Commissioners have appointed is fit for the business they employ him in, and so in effect to take the affair of the appointment of a missionary out of their hands, and as much as in us lies, to give others power, without consulting them, to disannul and break up their establishment of a missionary here.

3. Not only is the pastor complained of, but the whole church, which partly consists of Indians, which must in a peculiar manner be looked upon as under the care of the Commissioners; the grand design of their commission being to take care of the spiritual concerns of the Indians.

4. Referring these things to an ecclesiastical council in the first place, we think would not be effectual to bring these difficulties to an issue.

Therefore voted by the church, that considering these things, and being willing to proceed in the fairest and most charitable manner with the complainers, the church make the said complainers this offer: that the affairs they desire should be referred to the judgment of a council, should first be laid before the Commissioners, either the whole body of the Commissioners, or their Committee, as they shall choose; and that opportunity be first given to them to use their wisdom in endeavors to put an end to our calamities, if they think fit; and that if they, after they have had full cognizance of the affair, judge it necessary or expedient that the affair be referred to an ecclesiastical council, we are ready to comply with it, and to refer ourselves to such a council in a manner agreeable to the usage and principles of Congregational churches: and we are willing to leave the affair of calling a council wholly to the advice of the Commissioners.

Voted unanimously,
Test.: Jonathan Edwards, Pastor.

180. TO EDWARD BROMFIELD

The London Society asked the Boston Commissioners for Indian Affairs to nominate candidates from three colonies to be future Commissioners. Of the nominees, they would select five or six to work with Elisha Williams and Ephraim Williams, Sr., in supervising the Stockbridge mission.

The whole idea was anathema to Bostonians, who had no intention of cooperating in such a project. Nevertheless, they informed Edwards and he submitted this evaluation. His Boston sponsors were receptive, not wanting their strength diluted or control lost.

For the benefit of the English, Edwards stresses distance and communication difficulties. For the Bostonians, he emphasizes that the province in general, and Boston in particular, would be logical centers of administration. The repeated mention of Wethersfield, Col. Elisha Williams' area, was designed to raise the Commissioners' ire, as a reminder of that gentleman's numerous attempts to bypass them. After heated opposition, the Londoners hastily canceled the proposal.

(Trask Library, AL draft, one octavo leaf, addressed on verso to Mr. Bromfield, Oct. 16, 1753, in Edwards' hand, and one quarto leaf, an envelope cover, addressed on verso to Edwards at Stockbridge; Dwight ms. transcript, four quarto leaves. See also Alderman Library, New England Company Letterbook, letters of Jasper Mauduit to Andrew Oliver, Apr. 27, 1753, and Mar. 7, 1754.)

*   *   *

Stockbridge, October [16], 1753

Honored and Dear Sir,

As you have been pleased to mention to me the proposal lately made to the Commissioners for Indian Affairs in Boston from the Society in London, in which they say they were confirmed (by something in my letter to Mr. [Jasper] Mauduit) in the expedience of nominating nine persons in the provinces of Massachusetts, New York, and colony of Connecticut, that the Society might choose six out of the members to be joined with the two Colonel Williamses as Commissioners for Stockbridge affairs, to act by correspondence with the Commissioners in Boston, and to inform me what persons the Commissioners have nominated, and to ask my thoughts of this: I have considered of the matter with much deliberation.

On being first informed that they speak of being partly led to this proposal by something I had wrote, I am very much at a loss what they could refer to. But in looking over my papers, by a rough draft of my letter to Mr. Mauduit which I have kept, I find I there referred to something I had said in letters I have before written to the Commissioners and another to the Speaker of the House of Representatives, in these words: "What renders it the more necessary {that things here should be under} the immediate care of trustees on the spot, is the misunderstanding and jealousy here subsisting between some of the chief of the present English inhabitants of the town, which is one of our greatest calamities. Things on this account do much more need careful inspection and, therefore, the gentlemen entrusted ought be such as [are] perfectly impartial—in no way interested in, or related to, these contending parties}."[1]

This I suppose must be what the Society must have referred to in their late letter to you. But my meaning seems to be quite mistaken. What I then had in my mind, which I then supposed might have taken effect, was in being moved to some gentlemen of the best character and wholly impartial and disinterested and disengaged in the contention that had subsisted here, to come and settle here. And they should be entrusted in some degree with the care of our affairs.

But the thing which is now proposed by the Corporation cannot answer in any measure the intention I had in view, and I supposed their making such a proposal must be owing to their unacquaintedness with the state of Stockbridge and the country around us. 'Tis probable that they supposed that Stockbridge was just in the corner of the Province of the Massachusetts, where it borders on the colonies of Connecticut and New York, and that each of these colonies were so peopled around us that a number of persons [of] ability and character might be found in each of these provinces that might be well qualified to have the inspection and care of the important affairs of this place,

---

1. JE made a dash in the MS draft, intending to fill in the quotation replicated here from Letter No. 133, his letter to Hubbard, Aug. 31, 1751, above.

who, by reason of their neighborhood, might have much greater advantage for a full and particular information in the state of things and the more frequent, easy, expeditious, and effectual interposition to direct and regulate them as the state [of] things requires on emergent occasions. But if they were as fully acquainted with our geography and the state of things here as we are, they would at once see that the appointing a kind of subordinate body of Commissioners out of those nominated to have the more immediate oversight and direction of our affairs, would have a contrary tendency to a very great degree, and that, instead of expediting and making more easy the management of our affairs, it would unspeakably clog and embarrass them. Most of these gentlemen live at such a distance from us and so much more out of the way of communication with us than Boston and are at such a distance one from another, that it must render their proper inquiries and sufficient informations of our affairs and united acting in them and management of them infinitely cumbersome, and rendered so impracticable that it never can be expected to take place.

Boston being our metropolis and the chief center of business for the whole country, we have more frequent opportunities of reciprocal communication with Boston than with most of the places where these gentlemen live, taken singly. But how much greater still is the difference if these places are taken collectively. New York is nearly as far from us as Boston. Albany at nearest is forty miles from us. Wethersfield is seventy miles. Hartford, the place of Mr. P. and L.,[2] is near as far. Mr. [Roger] Wolcott's habitation at Windsor is above sixty-five. Mr. Lyman at Suffield is more than fifty. Dr. [Israel] Ashley at Westfield, above forty. Mr. Porter of Hadley, about sixty. The communication of Stockbridge with Boston is more frequent and easy than even with Hartford and Wethersfield. And if the whole body of the Commissioners lived at Wethersfield, they would not be under so good advantage to look after our affairs as they are at Boston, unless they should travel and from time [to] time come on the spot and view our affairs themselves. And how much more difficult must [be] the meeting of these persons to consult on our affairs than of the Commissioners in Boston that live so near together. They often are called together in a few hours as occasions arise. But how otherwise will the case be with respect to the gentlemen nominated, who live at so great a distance one from another, Hartford and Wethersfield being about

2. These men are unidentified.

130 miles distant from New York, and 110 from Albany. Hadley is about 100 from Albany, about fifty from Wethersfield, and about 180 from New York. Albany is about 170 from New York, and there is nothing in the state of the country that gives occasion for any great communications from one of those places to another, unless from Albany to New York. As to Col. Ephraim Williams, who used to live at Stockbridge, his state of health is so exceedingly broken by many fits of the palsy that he has put all his estate out of his hands and is removed to live at Deerfield, which is about 200 miles from New York, about seventy from Wethersfield, about 120 miles from Albany on the usual road, and eighty from Stockbridge.

If we should take only the gentlemen in Connecticut alone, the Commissioners in Boston can meet and confer and act unitedly with ten times the ease as they can. But general meetings from these distant places to confer on our affairs will be so difficult that there will [be] no reason ever to expect 'em. And indeed, if any such thing should be expected that our affairs should first come under the inspection and determination of those corresponding Commissioners before they can properly fall under the cognizance of the Commissioners in Boston, it must issue in that which will be little if anything short of laying a fatal block in the way of all further management of affairs and putting a final stop to all further proceedings in those affairs, which are already sufficiently embarrassed.

There, Sir, I have here represented my thoughts of this affair as they appear to me, humbly asking your candid acceptance of what I have written and pardon of the freedom I have used. I remain, Sir,

Your most humble and obliged friend and servant,
Jonathan Edwards.

181. TO THE REVEREND THOMAS GILLESPIE

Edwards and Gillespie had much in common. Both promoted revival, both were dismissed from their pastorates by ecclesiastical bodies for matters of conscience, and both failed to be restored through church channels. In this letter, Edwards empathizes with his Scottish counterpart and offers encouragement. Despite persistent opposition, Edwards no longer feels threatened by his adversaries.

(Trask Library, ALS, two quarto leaves; Dwight ms. transcript, two quarto leaves. Published in Dwight ed., *1*, 535–37.)

* * *

Stockbridge, October 18, 1753

Rev. and Dear Sir,

The last November I wrote a letter to you, and desired Mr. [Thomas] Foxcroft to put up with it for you one of my answers to Mr. [Solomon] Williams.[1] After that, in the latter part of the winter, I received a letter from you, dated June 15, 1752, with Milton on *Hirelings,* and duplicates of a *Letter from a Gentleman in Town,* etc., and *Answers to the Reasons of Dissent,* etc.[2] I now return you my hearty thanks for these things. Since that, I have received letters from Mr. [John] MacLaurin and Mr. [John] Erskine, with various pamphlets and prints relating to your extraordinary affair.

I think, dear Sir, that although your sufferings are like to continue, the General Assembly having neglected to restore you to your former station and employment in the Church of Scotland,[3] yet your sufferings are attended with many manifestations of the gentleness and fatherly kindness and favor of the great Governor of the world, in the many alleviating, supporting circumstances of your persecution; in that so many of God's ministers and people have appeared to be so much concerned for you, and have so zealously and yet so properly exerted themselves in your behalf, and have so many ways given their testimony to the goodness of the cause wherein you suffer and the unrighteousness of those hardships which you have been subjected to; and that even so great a part of the General Assembly themselves have in effect given this testimony for you, there being but a very small majority, but what openly appeared for the taking off the censure of the former Assembly, without any recantation, or so much as application from you desiring them so to do.

You have some peculiar reasons to rejoice in your sufferings, and to glorify God on the account of them. They, having been so greatly taken notice of by so many of the people of God, and there being so much written concerning them, tends to render them, with their circumstances, and particularly the patience and meekness with which you have suffered, so much the more extensively and durably to the glory of the name of your blessed Lord, for whom you suffer. God is reward-

---

1. *Misrepresentations Corrected.*

2. John Milton, *Considerations Touching the Likeliest Means to Remove Hirelings Out of the Church* (London, 1659); *A Letter from a Gentleman in Town to His Friend in the Country* (Edinburgh, 1752); *Answers to the Reasons of Dissent from a Resolution of the General Assembly to Apply to Parliament for an Augmentation of Stipends* (Edinburgh, 1750).

3. See Letter No. 161, n. 1, of JE to Gillespie, Nov. 24, 1752, above.

ing you by laying a foundation, in what has been said and done and written concerning your sufferings, for glory to his own name and honor to you, in his church, in future generations. Your name will doubtless be mentioned hereafter with peculiar respect, on the account of these sufferings, in ecclesiastical history; as they are now the occasion of the exercise of a tender affection in multitudes of God's saints that otherwise would perhaps have never heard of you, and of their fervent prayers for you; as they are doubtless an occasion of a peculiar notice which saints and angels in heaven take of you, and of their praises to God on your account; and will be the occasion of a peculiar reward which God will hereafter bestow upon you, when you shall be united to their assembly.

As to my own circumstances, I am still meeting with trouble, and expect no other as long as I live in this world. Some great men have mightily opposed my continuing the missionary at Stockbridge, and have taken occasion abundantly to reproach me, and endeavor my removal. But I desire to bless God; he seems in some respects to set me out of their reach. He raises me up friends who are exerting themselves for me in opposition to my enemies; particularly the Commissioners for Indian Affairs in Boston, with whom innumerable artifices have been used, to disaffect them towards me, but altogether in vain. Gov. [Jonathan] Belcher also has seen cause much to exert himself in my behalf on occasion of the opposition made to me. My people, both English and Indians, steadfastly adhere to me, excepting the family with whom the opposition began and those related to that family, which family greatly opposed me while at Northampton. Most numerous, continual, and indefatigable endeavors have been used to undermine me, by alienating my people from me. Innumerable mean artifices have been used, with one and another, young and old, men and women, Indians and English; but hitherto they have been greatly disappointed. But yet they are not weary.

As we, dear Sir, have great reason to sympathize one with another, with peculiar tenderness, our circumstances being in so many respects similar, so I hope I shall partake of the benefit of your fervent prayers for me. Let us thus endeavor to help one another (though at a great distance) in traveling through this wide wilderness, that we may have the more joyful meeting in the land of rest, when we have finished our weary pilgrimage. I am, dear Sir,

> Your most affectionate brother and fellow-servant,
> Jonathan Edwards.

My wife [Sarah] joins in most affectionate regards to you and yours.

Jonathan Belcher,
anonymous mezzotint,
undated, Department of
Rare Books and Special
Collections, Princeton
University Libraries

182. TO MAJ. EPHRAIM WILLIAMS, JR., ET AL.

Continuing his efforts to deal with the dissenters within the Stockbridge church, Edwards reasserts the original jurisdiction of the local church on matters of dispute within it. He quotes objections made in response to his earlier letter and refutes each one individually. The new document was unanimously approved by the congregation.

(RIHS, ms. 1137, ALS, three folio leaves.)

* * *

[Stockbridge, c. November 19, 1753]

At a meeting of the church of Stockbridge, November 19, 1753, the church having considered a writing sent to the pastor to be communicated to them, dated October 26, 1753, signed *Ephraim Williams, Jr., Jonathan Devreux, Josiah Williams, Abigail Dwight, Judith Williams;* voted to send to the above-named persons the following message:

Brethren and Sisters,

As you are members of this church, who have subjected yourselves to our care and watch, and as we are obliged to watch over you, and seek your spiritual welfare; we would propose the following things to your serious consideration.

1. Whether you don't grossly abuse this church in saying, *The church intimates that they have a right to determine and issue the matters of your complaint themselves;* and whether it ben't with the most glaring absurdity that you say that *you think this is evidently hinted in our first vote,* in our saying these words: "WHETHER EVER THEIR COMPLAINT BE CARRIED TO A COUNCIL, OR ANY OTHER BESIDES THE CHURCH THEMSELVES, OR NO"; and again in the second vote in these words: "As to what is as we think unseasonably and *preposterously*" [i.e. as beginning at the wrong end][1] "desired in the forementioned writing, *viz.* that the things alleged therein should be referred to the judgment and final decision of a council; voted, that it appears to this church, that the peculiar state of the church, and also the circumstances of the case, are such that IF THE JUDGMENT OF THESE THINGS BE REFERRED TO ANY OTHER JUDGES BESIDES THE CHURCH THEMSELVES, {'tis proper and necessary that the whole affair be first laid before the honorable Commissioners for Indian Affairs}":[2] when nothing can be more manifest than that the church, in thus expressing themselves conditionally, avoid saying, or giving the least intimation, whether they think these things should be finally issued by themselves or no. Is it therefore proper or becoming on such a foundation, to go on in such a reflecting, reproachful manner, to tell us, *that this carries in it an air of unreasonable stiffness, selfwilledness, and also guilt?* and then, in such taunting language, to say, *now suppose the pastor and church should meet, and gravely determine the complaint to be groundless; and agree that for the future they will view themselves in a good light, and decree that all other churches should make the same judgment, and view them in the same light,* etc.?

2. Whether or no it becomes you, in this application you make to the church, to which you have, in solemn covenant, as in the presence of God, united yourselves, putting yourselves under their care and watch; to treat them in such an assuming manner, interspersing here and there, in invidious and supercilious language, such censorious suggestions and insinuations; and that, even before you give us any opportunity to confer with you about those things you find fault with us for; refusing to give us such an oppor-

1. JE's brackets.
2. In the MS, JE drew a dash. The interpolation is taken from Letter No. 179.

tunity, though it has been so much insisted on; suggesting that our votes carry in them *an air of unreasonable stiffness, self-willedness and guilt, in not daring to venture the affair on a proper issue; charging us with an unreasonable shyness, against bringing the matter of your grievance, to a fair and impartial trial;* and say, that our votes *appear manifestly calculated to relieve some particular private interests, rather than to serve a public cause, not withstanding the promoting the religious interest of this church is the thing so much pretended to in our votes;* and saying, *there is ground to suspect methods will be used to evade the force of reasons, and tamper with evidences;* and again, saying, *it appears to you that, under a pretense of our paying a venerable regard to the honorable Commissioners, we are indeed consulting private interest and artfully evading a proper and just examination and issuing the matters of your grievance;* adding *that you must needs think our conduct a dark symptom of a bad cause, and consciousness of the danger and consequences of a fair and impartial trial;* and again, suggesting that what we have voted is *a fetch and scheme to secure against a fair trial, and thereby lengthen out the controversy and protract things, until there may be an opening for employment to the destruction of the church's peace,* etc.

We beseech you to reflect on the temper you manifest in these things, and consider whether this be a conduct becoming Christians, and whether herein you han't given this church just and great cause of offense; and whether the tolerating such treatment of churches by their members, in their applications to 'em in ecclesiastical matters, would not tend utterly to subvert all peace and order in churches.

3. Whether or no your saying, you think it evident by the votes of the church that *the church claims a power of determining and issuing matters of complaint themselves,* does well agree with your afterwards charging the church with dishonesty and indifference in taking upon them to do *one ecclesiastical thing* themselves, without advice from others, even so much as suspending one of its members. Certainly if we pretend to a power to do all ourselves alone, without any advice from others, then we may, at the same time, claim a power to suspend one person without inconsistence with our pretenses.

4. Is your now denying it to be proper that you should lay the reasons and evidences of your complaint before the church, and of asserting that *the nature of things evidently requires* that you should not, well consist with your past pretenses, when you was cited by

this church to come and let them hear your reasons and evidences, and you utterly disclaimed a disobeying the church in this matter: not pretending to refuse ever to do it; and pleading that your affairs required one of you to be absent, that you could not be all present at that time; and desiring that this matter might be deferred till you could see Col. [Joseph] Dwight and the church together?

5. In your complaint you say, *you heartily desire, on your parts, to have the matters of offense removed, and that we offer you Christian satisfaction on these heads;* and say that *in case we decline this, you desire we would join with you in calling a council,* etc., pretending plainly not to desire a council, but on a refusal of satisfaction. Now we desire you to consider, whether if you are hearty in thus seeking satisfaction (and so to prevent occasion for a council) as you profess, you are consistent in refusing fully to lay before us the matters of offense, and plain evidences thereof for our conviction. Is not plainly setting before guilty persons the evidences of their guilt, a proper step to be taken for their conviction, that they may be brought to proper humiliation and repentance? And especially, is it not proper when public satisfaction is required, that the persons supposed to have offended, should be convinced, not only that they are guilty, but should be shown that their guilt is attended with that visibility and evidence, as properly to require public satisfaction?

6. Some of your charges are only general. Thus you charge the pastor with a *series of actions,* wherein he has behaved altogether unbecoming his character as a minister and his profession as a Christian. But you specify but one thing as an offense in him in particular, *viz.* his omitting to communicate a letter written to the church by Colonel Dwight; though your general charge implies a great number of very heinous offenses. We desire you to consider, whether it be reasonable to expect public satisfaction of him for such a number of crimes, when he is not so much as informed what they are, or that the church should refer their series of great offenses, to the final decision of a council, without his or their knowing what the things are that they refer, and are to [be] judged of.

7. Your complaint not only contains matters of charge against the pastor, and church in general, but against some particular members, particularly against two of them as guilty of forgery. Now we desire you to consider whether you act reasonably, in expecting that this matter, as well as others, should be carried directly to a

council, without giving the church any opportunity to hear what evidences there are of their being guilty of such a crime; or what they can say for themselves; or knowing but that these particular persons would be convinced of their fault, and would give you satisfaction, if you should fully lay before them the grounds and reasons of your being offended with them, and the evidences of their guilt. And have we any power to force these brethren, that we have solemnly taken under our care, to refer this matter, which you charge them with, to a council, which you and we should choose for them, without ever hearing them ourselves?

8. How can the church know whether there will be any occasion for a council, before they have heard particularly what the accused and the accusers will say, when they appear face to face? How can they know but that, when they come to confer together, the accused may offer that to the accusers, which may convince 'em that they have been misinformed and that at least some of the charges are grounded on plain mistakes of matters of fact, to their full satisfaction that they have taken up things very wrong, so that they themselves may be convinced that there is no occasion to trouble any council with these things, or to carry such groundless accusations anywhere abroad, to the injury of the good name of innocent persons?

9. And besides all that has been already mentioned, let it be considered, that before ever you sent in your complaint, most of you who are complainers having openly withdrawn from the communion of the church, the church had voted to call upon you to appear to give the reasons of this conduct. In which vote one of yourselves was concurring. The church then, when they first took this matter in hand, had doubtless power so to do. None, we presume, will say that this was not a matter that was proper for the church's inquiry and examination. And if they had power to take it in hand at all, they had power at least to cite you to appear before 'em, in order to hear you upon it. And if it could be properly taken out of their hands, to be carried before other judges, it must be in consequence of such an appearance, and the church's first hearing your reasons, and conferring with you upon them face to face, and not by you refusing to appear at all. And as by your own declaration, part of the design of your complaint is to give the reasons of your said withdrawing communion, therefore the church (as they have power to demand opportunity particularly to inquire of you,

and confer with you about these reasons, before they are carried to other judges) have power to require you to appear, more particularly to explain your complaint, and exhibit the evidences on which you ground the righteousness of that treatment of the church, and God's ordinances in it, viz. openly rejecting communion with them in these ordinances. We pray you to consider how strange and unexampled is the method of your proceeding. How many instances have there been in the country of persons absenting themselves from the communion in churches to which they belonged, from their being offended with the ministers or church? And when was ever any such thing advanced, that the churches that had the care of them, had no power to call 'em to an account before 'em in such cases? How unreasonable is that rule of proceeding which is now advanced by you! viz. that persons that are cited before any judicatory (in a case in which they have proper power and right to cite 'em to appear) may, without complying with the citation, throw in a complaint against that judicatory; and by that means, not only claim liberty of appeal, but also at once to divest that judicatory of all power; and so entirely to set 'em aside, as even to make void their citation. Let it be considered, whether according to such maxims as these, persons in all cases whatever, mayn't set aside and disable all judicatories on earth, and exempt themselves from even appearing before any judges, till the last day.

We entreat you seriously and thoroughly to consider these things. If you do so, we doubt not but you must be convinced that your conduct towards the church is very unreasonable and injurious.

And as to our joining with you in referring the matters of your complaint to other judges besides the church, 'tis time enough to talk further of that matter, when you have done your duty with respect to your appearing before this church, as you have been required, and which we still demand of you. You must first appear before this church, to exhibit your evidences, and give the church opportunity to interrogate you concerning the reasons of your withdrawing from their communion (those of you who have withdrawn), before any such step can be taken as you propose (if it ever be taken) without the plainest irregularity and absurdity. And since you have refused to obey the church, when cited to appear before 'em, and persisted in it against the repeated remonstrances of the pastor; insisting on that reason, that your affairs would not allow all the complainers to be present, we may well expect now, that you should find a time when all of you that have signed the complaint will be present; and inform us of it; that a church meeting may be appointed to hear you all together, which we will wait in expectation for the present.

As to the Commissioners first having an opportunity to use their wisdom, to see if they can't remove our difficulties, before their affairs here are put into the hands of others, that should have power, in effect, to break 'em up, without their having any such opportunity: when you come to give us the reasons and evidences of your complaint, and so the reasons of your withdrawment from our communion, we shall be willing more particularly to give our reasons why we insist on such a method, so natural and rational and evidently necessary; and shall be ready to hear your objections against anything the church has voted in that affair, if offered with decency. But you may assure yourselves, we shall never think ourselves obliged to hear you, if in discoursing on this subject, you persist in treating the church in the manner you have done, in your late written message, or ever admit any to speak on your behalf, that treats the church in such a manner.

As the church stands ready to meet you, and confer with you; so we would not have you expect that we should carry on a controversy with you by writing, or meet any more to hear your written messages, you yourselves refusing to be present.

Voted unanimously,

Test.: Jonathan Edwards, Pastor.

183. TO COL. TIMOTHY DWIGHT

By June 1753 Col. Timothy Dwight, the father-in-law of Edwards' daughter Mary, had had enough of Northampton. He had failed to find Edwards another church in the town, experienced persistent animosity from the townspeople, and come to feel that the church's situation was deteriorating. Consequently, he planned to move to Enfield or Suffield, Connecticut. Edwards tries to entice him to Stockbridge. In the end, Colonel Dwight remained at Northampton, and the situation there was gradually resolved.

(Sterling Library, Dwight Family Papers, AL fragment, one quarto leaf. Col. Timothy Dwight's intention is stated in a letter to Thomas Foxcroft, June 6, 1753, Trask Library.)

* * *

Stockbridge, December 10, 1753

Dear Sir,

This is to desire you renewedly to take into your consideration your removing and settling in this town. 'Tis probable that Brig. [Joseph] Dwight and the Williamses would be glad to exchange with you. And as to your great objection against coming here, that here you will not have sufficient business to keep you employed, I am willing to allow that there is something in it. But yet I cannot but be of opinion, that it has much more than its due weight with you, especially considering how much there is in the other scale to counterbalance it. On the one hand it is to be considered, that though you will be more distant from your business at Enfield and Suffield, yet there will be no necessity of relinquishing it; and perhaps not your probate business. But if you resign the latter, you will not be out of employ; you will probably find, one way or other, more business here than you expect, and full as much as will be for your comfort. 'Tis further to be considered, that you have all [. . .]

[Jonathan Edwards.]

184. TO THE REVEREND THOMAS FOXCROFT

Edwards manifests concern at not receiving a response to his regular letters, requests, and the recent submission of his manuscript of *Freedom of the Will.* He need not have worried. His friend at the other end of the province was upholding him in every way: dispatching his packets and guiding his work through the press. Edwards also shares his latest evaluation of Joseph Bellamy.

(Beinecke Library, ALS, two quarto leaves, addressed on verso to the Reverend Thomas Foxcroft in Boston.)

* * *

Stockbridge, February 5, 1754

Rev. and Honored Sir,

I humbly desire you to take the care of this packet to Mr. [John] MacLaurin of Scotland.

Since I returned from Boston, I have wrote often to you, and sent many letters and packets of great importance; but never have heard whether any one of them has arrived. I long since sent away my book against the Arminians, and want to know very much what is become of it.

I have here enclosed a number of subscriptions which Mr. [Joseph] Bellamy obtained. I have not counted them. Mr. Bellamy told me that there was about 170, and that he had obtained about thirty more, which he had in another paper, which he could not very readily find. Please to inform the printer of this. I was the week before last at Mr. Bellamy's, at Bethlehem; being sent for by him, to give advice, together with some other ministers, on occasion of his being applied to by the Presbyterian congregation in New York, to be their pastor. We did [not] advise Mr. Bellamy to leave his people at present, his people being greatly united to him, and it appearing doubtful whether there would be an happy union, and general satisfaction, in the congregation at New York, with respect to Mr. Bellamy's ministry, and principles concerning the admission of members. We thought that congregation had been too hasty in their proceeding, and had not so thoroughly considered the matter, and sufficiently ripened things, for the giving Mr. Bellamy a call. But I think it something probable that they will renew their call. If they should, and should be united in it, and take proper steps in their proceeding, I don't know but they may succeed. But it will depend much on the opinion of the Consociation of that county. For my part, I wish they might succeed. For although Mr. Bellamy is in some respects a little unpolished; yet he is a man of such gifts and grace, such activity, resolution, attended with sagacity and prudence, that I know of no man in any measure so likely to be a means of uniting that congregation, and maintaining its peace, of greatly increasing it and very much promoting the interest of religion in that flourishing town as he. He has the happiest talents of managing in the midst of difficulties, pleasing and influencing all sorts of people; and yet suppressing and bearing down those things that are bad; of any man I know of. He is of very good natural abilities, benevolent, agreeable, sprightly and sociable; as well as of extraordinary gifts for the pulpit, and has the greatest ability to command the attention of an auditory, and reach the hearts of his hearers, of any man I know of. And is yet an indefatigable student. I should greatly rejoice to hear of his being settled in that congregation, and should think, if it were brought about with general satisfaction, it was a token of great good to that city. I am, honored Sir,

Your obliged son and servant,
Jonathan Edwards.

185. TO BRIG. JOSEPH DWIGHT

At last, Edwards receives the welcome news that he will be in sole charge of the Indian schools at Stockbridge. The issue was settled by Rev. Isaac Hollis, preeminent patron of the project. Hollis may have been influenced by New Jersey governor Jonathan Belcher, the Boston Commissioners, or the letters of Edwards himself. The schools were diminished at this point by the departure of the Mohawks. Nevertheless, Edwards' leadership of the Indians was now vindicated.

(Trask Library, Dwight ms. transcript, one quarto leaf. No original Hollis ms. can be found, although its existence is confirmed by other sources. In his transcript, Dwight crossed out words that apparently were in the original; in such instances, the words are restored.)

* * *

Stockbridge, February 25, 1754

Honorable Sir,

I have enclosed, and send to you, a copy of what Mr. [Isaac] Hollis has sent to me, signifying his desire, that I should take the care of his school for the future. This is to ask the favor of you, that, when you think fit to resign the care of it, you would give me seasonable notice of it; and likewise that you would be pleased to inform me of the present state of the school, how many boys belong to it, and who they are, and what bedding and other household stuff, or utensils and tools for work, or books, paper, ink or other implements for writing, or other things, are now in being, which have been procured for the benefit of that school, at Mr. Hollis' expense; that I may take care of them. I also request, that you would give me a full account of the state of the school, in all its present circumstances; that I may the better know what needs to be done, in speedily taking care of it, and ordering matters relating to it; so that the great ends of it may be best promoted, and Mr. Hollis' noble and Christian desires and just expectations may be best answered. I would pray you to give me notice, when I may wait on you, in order to receive from you this information, so as best to suit your leisure and convenience. Herein you will oblige

Your most humble servant,
Jonathan Edwards.

Stockbridge, February 25, 1754

Honorable Sir,

It is now late in the evening, and the evenings are so shortened, that there can be no opportunity for the conference proposed this evening. I should be glad to wait on you tomorrow on this affair if you should be at home. But as you say that you are like to be from home, I will wait on you, God willing, the next day at or about nine o'clock in the morning. I suppose that Mr. Hollis does not expect that I should take the care of defraying the charge of his school, until I have taken the affairs of the school in general under my care. Probably the General Court expects to bear the charge of the school until some agent of Mr. Hollis has opportunity for this. But this must be left to Your Honor's judgment. I remain, Sir,

Your humble servant,
Jonathan Edwards.

186. TO THE REVEREND JOSEPH BELLAMY

The Presbyterian church of New York City is still interested in calling Bellamy as its minister (see No. 184). Edwards declares his readiness to assist, especially by writing, but needs pointers on how to be most helpful.

(Trask Library, ALS, two quarto leaves, addressed on verso to the Reverend Mr. Joseph Bellamy, Minister of the Gospel at Bethlehem; PCUSADH, ms. copy, Bellamy, *1*, 355–56. Published in part, Webster, pp. 633–34.)

* * *

Stockbridge, February 28, 1754

Rev. and Dear Sir,

'Tis wholly needless that I should come again on the affair of your going to New York, and altogether improper, as I suppose now the affair will properly be referred to the Association or Consociation. And besides, I think I can do more good by writing than by coming.

I wish you had been a little more particular in your information. I desire you would write to me again as soon as possible. I have a mind to write a letter to the moderator of your Association; but only I want to know much more about the matter, that I may know the better how to write. Please to inform me whether Lawyer [William] Smith has received my letter, and what he writes to you, and what has been done at New York, and at the Presbytery, and what and after what manner application has been made in this affair, and what is going to be done further. Probably I shall have a mind to write to some others besides ministers about this affair. Therefore, I desire you to be particular and full and speedy in your writing to me. Particularly inform me when the Association meets on this affair.

By the will of God, Mr. [Samuel] Hopkins and I are going a journey to Deerfield the last week in March about the installment of Mr. [Edward] Billing at Greenfield. I would also go to Windsor before I return; shall therefore be gone near three weeks.

If it should finally so come to pass that you should remove to New York, my wife desires to buy your Negro woman, as she supposes she will do better for the country than the city. She will probably come along through your place some time in April, when she will talk with you about it.

The last week, I received a letter from Mr. [Isaac] Hollis in England, in which he commits his school wholly to my care, and makes me sole trustee of all his affairs here. I am, Sir,

Your affectionate friend and brother,
Jonathan Edwards.

187. TO BRIG. JOSEPH DWIGHT

Edwards, newly authorized administrator of the Indian schools, moves rapidly to establish a basis of accountability for the boarding school. One of his initial acts will be to determine whether the Mohawks intend to stay at Stockbridge.

(Trask Library, Dwight ms. transcript, one quarto leaf.)

* * *

Stockbridge, February 28, 1754

Honored Sir,

To prevent mistakes and future controversies, I would inform you, that, when I came yesterday from your house, I went directly to the boarding school to inform Mr. [Cotton Mather] Smith of our conclusion, and get some more certain information concerning the state of the school; and that although Mr. Smith had before mentioned ten boys as belonging to the school, yet now he tells me that three of the largest had left the school, and I understanding that they were men grown told him that I would not have him take them any more. I also understand that another of the ten boys has been gone from the school for some time to his father's house where he is sick, viz. Unkatunk's son Abraham; and that I therefore shall not expect to be accountable for the boarding, for the time which I mentioned, of more than are actually in the school for that time. When I was at the boarding school, I observed several English children of Your Honor's family, that I suppose are there boarded and instructed. And as these share in the labors of the schoolmaster and eat with those of whom I have the care, I think there should be some consideration of it.

I will also signify that I have often been informed that the Mohawks have long had the resolution, all of them, both old and young, to leave Stockbridge as soon as [sugaring] time is over. I have appointed a conference with them tomorrow concerning the matter; and if I find that they stand to such a resolution, I shall then at the time of the conference suspend any farther expense upon them from that time on Mr. [Isaac] Hollis' account; and shall give you information accordingly. I am, Sir,

Your most humble servant,
Jonathan Edwards.

188. TO BRIG. JOSEPH DWIGHT

Edwards quickly completed his questioning of the Mohawks; he found them fixed in the decision to leave Stockbridge, a course of action that had been approved by their tribal leaders.

(RIHS, ms. 1139, ALS, one quarto leaf, addressed on verso to the Honorable Joseph Dwight, Esq. in Stockbridge; Trask Library, Dwight ms. transcript on one quarto leaf.)

*   *   *

Stockbridge, March 2, 1754

Honorable Sir,

Having conferred with the Mohawks, they inform me that they had all agreed and resolved the last fall, that they would all go away this spring, and that their doing so is agreeable to the determination of the Council of their nation, the sachems of the Conneenchee Tribe, and can't be altered unless it be by a new determination of their sachems.

Therefore, agreeable to what I signified before, I shall forbear to expend any of Mr. [Isaac] Hollis' money upon them so long as they appear to persist in this resolution. Agreeably to this, I informed Mr. [Cotton Mather] Smith the last night. I am, Sir,

> Your most humble servant,
> Jonathan Edwards.

189. TO THE REVEREND THOMAS FOXCROFT

Edwards sends additional instructions about printing *Freedom of the Will*, plus his plans for correspondence and news of Bellamy.

(Beinecke Library, ALS, one folio leaf overwritten with later notes by Foxcroft, addressed on verso to the Reverend Mr. Thomas Foxcroft, Minister of the Gospel in Boston; enclosure, same coll., ALS, one quarto leaf.)

* * *

> Stockbridge, March 6, 1754

Rev. and Honored Sir,

In my great fullness of care and business I have forgot whether I had received your favor of January 3 before I last wrote to you or since. However, I now thank you for that letter. With that I received a couple of letters from Scotland. I desire to be thankful to God who has restored you from your late illness.

I have here troubled you with another small addition to be made to my book that is in the press, with directions annexed where to insert it. I think you will be at no difficulty to find the place.

I am about to write to the Commissioners and Mr. [Thomas] Prince about Mr. [Isaac] Hollis' school, and what I have done and [am] about to do in pursuance of his desire that I should take the care of his school; which letters you will probably see.

This, with respectful salutations to your family and desire of your prayers, is from, honored Sir,

> Your greatly obliged son and servant,
> Jonathan Edwards.

P.S. I would propose whether it might not be best to put the papers containing the additions to be made to my book, into the ms. at the places where they are to be inserted, to prevent their being overlooked and forgotten.

Honored Sir, I just now (it being the 11th of March) received your letter of February 27, after I had folded up this and all my letters. I thank you for your favor. I should prefer such a page as that of my answer to Mr. [Solomon] Williams,[1] rather than such a small page as you mention, less than a psalter. But yet, I should insist on good white paper and the printer's best types.

New York congregation, though denied, have not given over seeking for Mr. [Joseph] Bellamy; they have sent up again after him. But now take a new method; they don't as yet make application to Mr. Bellamy, but to the Association to which he belongs. I am something inclined to think they will prevail.

I wish the printing of my book might be hastened. I am sorry Mr. [Samuel] Kneeland has not yet begun it. I am afraid the subscribers will be out of patience. I am, Sir,

> With [great] respect, and your obliged servant, etc.,
> Jonathan Edwards.

Enclosure

N.B. I desire that what is written on the opposite leaf[2] may be inserted, in the body of the discourse (not in the margin) in that section of the IInd part, entitled *Of Liberty of Will consisting in Indifference*, near the beginning, after these words or words like these: "But inasmuch as this [opinion] has been of such long standing [in the world], and has been so generally received, and so much insisted on by Pelagians, semi-Pelagians, Jesuits, Socinians, Arminians and others, it may deserve a [yet] more full consideration. And therefore I shall now proceed to a more particular and thorough inquiry into this notion."

In that section of the IVth part that treats of the objection about *Stoical* fate, I mention the *Epicureans* as maintaining a doctrine of contingence opposite to the fate and necessity of the *Stoics*. This is the notion I have had, but on thinking further on the matter I am a little diffident of the sufficiency of my evidence of the matter. I therefore would leave the judgment of this matter with you, who have greater opportunities to know, and if I am mistaken, please to make the necessary alterations.[3] I am, Sir,

> Your humble servant,
> Jonathan Edwards.

---

1. *Misrepresentations Corrected.*

2. The MS addition has not been located. Presumably, the text is either the third paragraph beginning on *Works, 1*, 203, or in the paragraphs immediately following.

3. Mention of the Epicureans holding a doctrine of contingence was dropped from this section by Foxcroft, as requested (*Works, 1*, 372–74).

190. TO SEC. JOSIAH WILLARD

Edwards writes Willard about a number of items: Hollis' decision to put him in complete charge of the Indian schools; his request to Brig. Joseph Dwight that he surrender the school to Edwards; and the hoped-for return of three Mohawk boys. He asks Willard's advice about the house designed for the boarding school. Thus, Edwards reestablishes the line of authority through official government channels.

(MAR, vol. 32, pp. 476–78a, ALS, two folio leaves, and envelope cover addressed to the Honorable Secretary for the Province of the Massachusetts Bay in Boston; in addition, p. 478 includes an extract of the Hollis letter; Trask Library, AL draft, on two envelope covers, both addressed on verso to Edwards at Stockbridge: one two-thirds of a folio leaf, the other, a quarto leaf.)

* * *

Stockbridge, March 8, 1754

Honorable Sir,

Having lately received a letter from the Reverend Mr. Isaac Hollis in England, concerning his school in this place, desiring me to take the care of it, I thought it proper and just, by the first opportunity, to give you information of it; as the affair of this school is what the General Court have interested themselves in, and have been waiting to know the mind of its pious and generous founder and patron concerning. And not knowing whether he has signified his mind in any letter to Your Honor, or any public committee, or any other way for the information of the honorable Assembly, I have with this sent an extract of Mr. Hollis' letter to me, for you either to communicate to the General Assembly, or otherwise to dispose of, according to your discretion.

After I received this letter from Mr. Hollis, I speedily informed Brig. [Joseph] Dwight of it: who manifested himself ready to resign the care of the school; but offered to continue things in their present situation for a week or fortnight, till I could be prepared to take the care of it; provided that I would engage to answer the expense from the day that I received Mr. Hollis' orders. I signified to him, that I supposed the General Court expressed no other than to be at the charge of the school till some agent for Mr. Hollis could possibly be in a capacity to take the care of it. But he insisting on the contrary, I did on advice accept his offer. The special reason of my desiring him to take care of the school, as he had done, for a little while, though it were at Mr. Hollis' expense, was this: the Mohawks had often informed me and others of a resolution they had taken of all going away this spring, to return no more; and I was willing to prevent their being broken up immediately, and all sent home, before I could have proper opportunity to inform them of Mr. Hollis' new orders, and thoroughly to inform myself whether they would all persist in their resolution of going home this spring.

The last Friday, I had a conference with them all, men, women and children, at my house, many of my neighbors being present; when I opened the affair fully to them, they appeared still to persist in their resolution of going away; and said they had come to an agreement the last fall all to go away this spring, in pursuance of a determination of the Council of their nation; and that they could not act otherwise, without applying renewedly to the said Council of the sachems of their tribe. I gave Colonel Dwight notice of what had passed; and informed him that I should forbear to expend anything more upon them, so long as they persisted in this resolution. But since that, I have had the offer of half the boys that belong to the school, who are of the Six Nations; viz. three of 'em; there being but six in all. Their parents came to me, earnestly desiring me to take their children, manifesting themselves willing to take care of their own maintenance, not expecting that the Province would maintain 'em any longer. I accordingly consented to them. They were just then going into the woods to make sugar, taking their children with them, as their manner is. And now I wait for nothing but their return in order to the taking them under my care. If any of the rest should in like manner change their minds, as to the taking their children away to their own country, I stand ready to provide for their maintenance and education; and with the leave of the honorable Commissioners, whose servant (under God) I am, shall take the care of Mr. Hollis' school according to his desire.

I shall need, Sir, your advice with respect to the house in which the school has lately been kept, whether I may still make use of it for the benefit of the boarding school; the house having been built at the charge of the Province, on land which our Indians have sequestered for the benefit of that school. I am, Honored Sir, with the greatest respect,

Your most humble servant,
Jonathan Edwards.

191. TO TREASURER ANDREW OLIVER

(Trask Library, ALS, in sermon on Luke 11:21–22, addressed to the Honorable Andrew Oliver, Esq., Treasurer of the Honorable Commissioners for Indian Affairs in Boston.)

* * *

Stockbridge, April 9, 1754

Sir,

Please to deliver to Mr. [. . .]¹ the twenty-four pounds, ten shillings, lawful money of the salary of Mr. Gideon Hawley, which he has desired you to advance to me in the order I have herewith sent to you, to be left with Capt. Timothy Dwight of Northampton, taking his receipt, viz. the receipt of him who takes the money at Boston.

> I am Your Honor's most humble servant,
> Jonathan Edwards.

I desire you to agree with the man that brings the money and pay him out of it.

192. TO COL. TIMOTHY DWIGHT

Edwards has just returned from three weeks' travel to Westfield, to Edward Billing's installation at Greenfield, and to his parents' home in East Windsor. He requests Dwight to forward the papers for the sale of his land in Winchester, Connecticut.

(Trask Library, ALS, one quarto leaf, addressed on verso to Col. Timothy Dwight at Northampton. See also Ballantine for Mar. 19, 1754; Edwards' letter to Joseph Bellamy, Feb. 28, 1754 [No. 186], above; Timothy Dwight's letter to Thomas Foxcroft, Feb. 22, 1754, Sterling Library, Manuscripts and Archives; and SIB, 9, 27.)

* * *

Stockbridge, April 15, 1754

[Dear Sir,]¹

[When] I came home from my late journey, I looked among my papers for the deed and plan of my land at Winchester, and could not

---

1. JE left a blank space to supply the name of bearer.
1. The salutation is torn off.

find them; and then I remembered that I had sent them to you a year or two ago, desiring you to sell the land for me. Therefore, I desire you would send them to me by my son, that I may draw and execute a deed, and send it down to you, pursuant to Col. [Ebenezer] Hinsdale's proposal. Possibly it may be in your way to come up to Stockbridge yourself, when my son returns.

Brig. [Joseph] Dwight is doubtless about to remove; and I hear that Elijah Williams is in a disposition to sell. Our difficulties with the Indians I think are all over. All was manifestly owing to the juggling tricks of the French, by which the Indians were filled with terrifying apprehension concerning the English. But we have had full discourse with the Indians, which seems to have dissipated their jealousies, and mightily to have eased their minds.

This, with love to sister [Experience King] Dwight, is from, Sir,

> Your affectionate brother and humble servant,
> Jonathan Edwards.

193. TO THE REVEREND THOMAS PRINCE

Brig. Joseph Dwight's letter to Gov. William Shirley of March 25, 1754, sent shock waves through official Boston and the Commissioners for Indian Affairs. Dwight implied that Edwards was responsible for the departure of Mohawks from Stockbridge. Even Prince, a staunch of Edwards', was moved to send two upbraiding missives.

Here Edwards replies, first calmly giving a review of events, which Prince, famed historian that he was, would savor. Then he proceeds to deny the charges; he puts forth reason after reason justifying his course of action. This epistle stands as Edwards' definitive summary of his Stockbridge stewardship up to that point.

(MHS, Ms. Large Coll., ALS, six folio leaves. Joseph Dwight's letter to Governor Shirley is in MAR, vol. 32, pp. 486–88, ALS, one folio leaf and one quarto leaf.)

* * *

Stockbridge, May 10, 1754

Rev. and Honored Sir,

I thank you for your favor of April 17, which came safe to hand the last week with Mr. [Isaac] Hollis' money; which was brought from Northampton by my son.

I find by the contents of your letter that there is need of your having laid before you a particular account of many things relating to the past and present state of Mr. Hollis' school, that you may have some tolerable idea of the circumstances of the affair.

Mr. Hollis has maintained a school in this place in all about nine years, three years before Capt. [Martin] Kellogg was improved and six years before one Mohawk was taken into the school on Mr. Hollis' account. After the school was set up and had been continued for some time, consisting only of Stockbridge boys, the Stockbridge Indians, excited by Mr. [John] Sergeant, gave of their own land, a farm of 200 acres of an excellent soil, within half a mile of the meetinghouse, for the use of the boarding school, with a special view to the benefit of their children; for the school had then always consisted of such only; and it was long before any of the Mohawks looked this way. The farm is very conveniently situated, being a peninsula, encompassed on three sides by the river; and is of great value. The Indians, besides giving this farm, helped to clear some of it, and were at the trouble and cost of building a bridge over the river to accommodate the school. Afterwards an house was built for the school on this farm; and about £500 laid out upon [it], which had been charitably contributed in Stockbridge and other places; besides £500 more given by the Commissioners; and all this before the Mohawks so much as talked of coming hither.

When the Mohawks first came down in the fall of the year, 1750, Captain Kellogg did not take any of 'em on Mr. Hollis' account. But not having heard from Mr. Hollis a long time, and not knowing but he was dead, he dismissed all Mr. Hollis' scholars (Stockbridge boys), and in their room took Mohawk boys to look after; not on Mr. Hollis' account, but on the account of the country, and was paid by the Province. When the Mohawks first came, Captain Kellogg was mightily taken, and was very full of his promises to them what great things should be done for them and their children; how well they should be fed and clothed and instructed, and looked after in all respects; raising their expectations very high. Which promises the Indians remembered, and often put us in mind of 'em afterwards.

Captain Kellogg went on with the Mohawks at the charge of the Province till the next summer, 1751; when, Mr. Hollis having been informed of the Mohawks' coming Captain Kellogg received a letter from him, wherein he writes as supposing his school still in being consisting of twelve boys, agreeable to his former orders which related only to Stockbridge boys; and he now ordered him to add twelve boys more to the number; far from ordering him to dismiss his twelve Stockbridge boys; but his letter plainly implying the contrary. On which Captain Kellogg, now having no boys at all on Mr. Hollis' account, goes about to get his twenty-four boys. And to make up the number, he took up some Mohawks and some Stockbridge boys, but the greater part Mohawks; for by this time the Stockbridge Indians were heartily sick of Captain Kellogg's managements, and but few of their boys could be obtained by him: so that he could not make up his full number of twenty-four as yet.

By this time, there began to appear an uneasiness among the Stockbridge Indians; that whereas they had given the farm, built the bridge, etc. to accommodate the school, with a special view to the benefit of their own children, their boys had the fall before been turned away and Mohawks taken into the house and upon the farm in their stead. And we had several meetings with 'em on this affair, before they could be quieted with respect to it. Finally, they were made easy with this, that there was no design of excluding their children, or taking away the land from them; but that special regard should be had to their children still, according to their intention in the sequestration of the farm; and that the Mohawks were like to improve their land but a little while, the design being that they should be removed to the Hoplands.

In the month of August of that summer, 1751, was here in Stockbridge a grand conference of the Committee of the General Court with the sachems of the Mohawks; who came down from their own country with a great train of about 100, young and old, being invited hither to confer about the affair of the Mohawks' settling in the country, and putting their children to school here. In the conference, the Mohawks objected that the promises of the English concerning their care for the instruction of their children in times past had not been fulfilled. They mentioned a treaty which they had had with this Province many years ago, wherein the English had promised to send them a missionary to preach to 'em, and a schoolmaster or masters to instruct their children; and produced a silver box with the Province seal in it, which they said was given 'em to confirm these promises: which yet had never been fulfilled. Moreover they said, that when some of their people came down hither the preceding fall, they were promised that their children should be handsomely clothed, and in other respects well looked after; whereas, they found their children naked, and nasty, and in a worse condition than they were in [in] their own country; and that they observed a great neglect and woeful confusion in the manner of their instruction, quite diverse from what they had observed in English schools.

In the reply, Col. [Joseph] Dwight acknowledged and lamented that their children had been neglected; but told 'em that if their children stayed, speedy and effectual care should be taken that there should be a thorough amendment, and they should soon see it with their own eyes. And finally, after much deliberation, the Indians consented to leave their children; but were careful to inform the Committee that it was in a dependence on these promises being fulfilled, and that they should be deceived no more with fair promises without performance.

Nevertheless, things still went on as they did before in the same negligence and confusion. Colonel Dwight was much in observing that Captain Kellogg was quite incorrigible, and that there was no hopes of any order or success in the school so long as he had the care of it; and that, therefore, there was a great necessity of a new master for the boys. Accordingly, the Commissioners were applied to with Brigadier Dwight's zealous concurrence. But it was a long time before another master could be obtained; and so, a long time before there was any happy alteration in the school, agreeable to the expectations of the Mohawks and the Committee's promises. So that many of the Mohawks were much discouraged, many that were coming from the Mohawk country turned back again; and Hendrick, the chief speaker of the Mohawks, declared he would never have anything more to do with the Stockbridge affair. But in February 1752, a master was obtained, viz. Mr. [Gideon] Hawley; whom I, by the Commissioners' order, introduced into the school, informing the Indians how he would now set up a regular school. At which they appeared highly pleased; said this was what they had waited and longed for. And when Mr. Hawley began his school, and the Mohawks observed the regularity of his managements, and the order of his school, there were the greatest testimonies of satisfaction and well-pleasedness that ever I saw in 'em on any occasion. But this fair weather lasted but a very little while. Colonel Dwight had by this time got far in his acquaintance and friendship with the family of the Williamses, who were greatly attached to Captain Kellogg, and against his being removed. So that now all at once the Brigadier seemed strangely changed, and was for continuing Captain Kellogg, and soon appeared openly against me and against Mr. Hawley; so that Captain Kellogg was continued, and claimed most of the boys as his own. In consequence of which, Mr. Hawley's regular school was soon broken all in pieces, and things reduced to as great and greater confusion than ever; and all the joy, and pleasing expectations which appeared in the Mohawks on Mr. Hawley's first coming, were dashed in pieces; so that the number of the Mohawks soon began to diminish. Many went home to return no more. Thus things continued in dreadful confusion, the affair languishing to the end of that year. And in the following April, 1753, above twenty of the Indians of the Five Nations, who came from Onohquage (who had appeared the best disposed of any of the Indians), went away at once, openly declaring before many witnesses that it was from no dissatisfaction with me, or any of my people, that they went away, but wholly from a dislike of the management of Colonel Dwight and Captain Kellogg. The Mohawks that removed expressed great dissatisfaction also at the same things and in the same manner.

The uneasiness of the Stockbridge Indians also now increased; insomuch that they had a meeting and sent their sachem to warn Captain Kellogg off from their land which they had sequestered for the use of the boarding school.

Then it was in the spring of the last year that a Stockbridge Indian was killed in the woods by a couple of Englishmen or Irishmen, which put our Indians into a very great ruffle.[1]

The summer following, the heads of the families of the Mohawks that were left were at my house; and in a long conversation, declared before several witnesses their great uneasiness here by reason of Colonel Dwight's and Captain Kellogg's managements, and their resolution of all going away, finally to leave Stockbridge ere long. After this, they were at my house again and declared the same thing before several of the people of the town who happened to be at my house at that time. And being then particularly inquired of, whether their design of going away was from any uneasiness with me or any of my people, they declared it was not, but wholly and only the managements of Colonel Dwight and those that joined with him. This they declared in a variety of expressions.

After this, the same summer, Hendrick, the chief speaker of the tribe, came down from the Mohawk country, and being at my house with some other Mohawks, declared the same thing again, concerning their resolution of all going away, finally to leave Stockbridge in a short time, mentioning the like grounds of their uneasiness; and among

1. See the following letter for more on this incident and its outcome.

other things which he mentioned as occasions of their dissatisfaction was Colonel Dwight's so much opposing me.

In the September following, came on the trial of the men that had killed the Indian; when they were acquitted of murder, and not executed. On which, by degrees, appeared more and more uneasiness among the Indians, both the Stockbridge Indians and Mohawks; who often were expressing their resentments in their conversation.

That fall, Captain Kellogg died at Newington, and Brigadier Dwight took the care of Mr. Hollis' school, undertaking to do the part of a schoolmaster himself, the school still consisting partly of Mohawks, and partly of Stockbridge Indians. But I could not perceive that the Indians were any better pleased than before.

After this, one and another of the Mohawks were at my house from time to time, and often spoke of their design of going all away in the spring, never to come again.

After Colonel Dwight had pretended to keep school himself for some time, he got a young gentleman, one Mr. [Cotton Mather] Smith, to come and keep the school; who kept it till Mr. Hollis' letter to me arrived. But still the Mohawks persisted in expressing the same resolution of all going away in the spring; and went away, a considerable part of 'em, just before Mr. Hollis' letter arrived, near half the scholars (by Mr. Smith's account), the rest intending to follow as soon as the time for making maple sugar was over.

Mr. Hollis' letter arrived just about the time that the Indians began to go into the woods to make sugar, and at a time when the uneasiness of the Indians, both Mohawks and Stockbridge Indians, and their disaffection towards the English on account of the men's being acquitted that killed the Indian, greatly increased, and in some was risen to an extreme height (though secretly), occasioned by some young Indians who had been abroad among some nations of Indians which have been lately been very much under the influence of the French; and had in their resentment and revenge entered into a conspiracy, with some other Indians abroad (who are much disaffected to the English), to destroy all the English in Stockbridge, and burn all their houses, and go away to Canada. And there are some things that make it look very probable that they had drawn some of the young Mohawks, who were reckoned as of Mr. Hollis' school, into the conspiracy.

When Mr. Hollis' letter came to hand, there were ten left in Stockbridge, who were accounted as belonging to the school, though not all Mohawks; some of them very unsuitable members of the school who were taken in, not agreeable to Mr. Hollis' orders to Captain Kellogg, when they were old, men-grown, two of them married men and had children. When I went to the school to inquire into the state of it, Mr. Smith told me that four out of the ten had declared they would never come to school any more. Some of these old ones had lately appeared very cross and surly. 'Tis probable that they had entered then into the bloody design before-mentioned with some of the Stockbridge young men.

When I received Mr. Hollis' letter, I proceeded with the greatest precaution and prudence I was capable of. I was here entrusted alone; but I took the best advice I could come at. When I informed Colonel Dwight of Mr. Hollis' orders, he offered to continue things along in the school, in the state they were then in (if I would be at the charge of it) till I could be ready to take the care of them myself. It being impossible I should be ready to take the immediate care of 'em in an instant, I accepted this offer, and especially that I might have time to inform myself whether the Mohawk scholars were to be obtained under a new regulation; it being now just the time when they were all going out a-sugaring, wives and children (as their manner is), when they would be wholly absent from the school, as they always are at such seasons. And then (if they persisted in their long-fixed and often-declared resolution), as soon as they had done sugaring, they would immediately leave the country; and so could not possibly at any time at all be in the school. It was therefore necessary to let things continue as they were till I could have opportunity to inquire into that matter, before I pretended to put the affair on a new footing.

But as soon as I could, I sent for the Mohawks, all, men, women, and children, to my house and desired the English people of the town that were my friends to be there, to be witnesses, and assisting in the conference. When all were met, I told the Indians the orders I had from Mr. Hollis; made 'em the offer of taking their children; discoursed the matter very largely, some of my friends assisting me. I told 'em as much of the care I would take of their children as I thought was best. Mr. [Timothy] Woodbridge discoursed very largely to them, and used many arguments with them to induce 'em to leave their children under my care; told 'em what a probability there was that the school would be under better regulation than it had been. But they replied, that they had heard such promises concerning the school so often, and had been so often disappointed that they were discouraged; and moreover said that the affair of their removal had been determined in a council of the sachems of their nation, which they could not depart from without carrying the affair to them again. It is a vanity (to the utmost degree) for any to pretend that I, or my interpreter, misunderstood them. It was not a transient saying only, that was suddenly taken up: the matter of their going away was very largely discoursed, and repeated, with reasons given very particularly in a long conversation on the subject; besides the same thing said over and over for three-quarters of a year before, as before observed. As to their, or their children's, weeping, or showing themselves grieved that I would not take care of their children,[2] 'tis a misrepresentation of the grossest sort. For not only was there nothing of that nature, but no such thing was hinted at as "that I would not take care of their children." Indeed, afterwards, I sent Colonel Dwight word that I should no longer desire him to take care of 'em on my account, or chose not to be at the charge of paying for what he should do, hiring the master he had provided, etc. so long as the Indians persisted in this resolution; for that would have been a perfect throwing away Mr. Hollis' money. The Indians were then going away, with all their children, into the woods, to be absent wholly from the school. And as soon as they returned, appeared fixed in their resolutions to leave the country, to be absent forever from the school. However it may have been the manner of those that had the care of those things, to draw pay from Mr. Hollis for masters for many months while they were not at all employed in the business, 'tis what I always have borne a testimony against; and therefore could not with a good face go into the same practice myself.

What stories some of my enemies might tell the Indians concerning my designs, to make 'em cry, I can't tell. I know it has been the manner of some to take almost an unbounded liberty in stories they have told the Indians to disaffect 'em to me. And I have good reason to think there are some in the town would do their utmost to alienate the Indians from me, and to discourage the Mohawks from letting their children come under my care.

Besides what I said to the Mohawks at the forementioned conference, I afterwards, at every opportunity, renewed my offers of taking their children; and offered for the present to take 'em to my own house, and look after 'em as my own children. Yea, and have actually taken one of them to live at my house before the others went away. And

---

2. These charges—that Hollis gave money for a Mohawk school, that members of that tribe were leaving as a result of JE misinterpreting their intention, and of the weeping episode—are all leveled in Dwight's letter to Shirley.

because the parents were none of 'em willing to leave their children unless they could live here themselves, I have laid out myself to get some land for 'em to improve; and also to get it plowed for 'em; and to this end have been at the trouble of a great deal of consultation with the English and the Stockbridge Indians.

The representation made in the letter you speak of is of a piece with what is daily done here. There are some here that industriously spread abroad such representations, and say that the school was in flourishing circumstances till it came into my hands, and that I immediately threw up the school after I had taken it. And that I had broken up the Mohawk affair, etc., etc.

They have been this several years murdering the Mohawk affair themselves with cruel hands; and now just as it is expiring, they lay to me the mischief which they have most apparently done themselves; and are indefatigably endeavoring to possess everybody with an agreeable opinion. And I have no reason to expect anything else of them, as long as they stay here, but that they will with all imaginable industry and craftiness, not to say guile and deceitfulness, seek by all means, [to] clog, embarrass, and ruin my affairs. And from the representations which are sent to Boston, we may easily conjecture what representations will be sent to Mr. Hollis. But I would entreat you, Sir, for the future, in justice to me, to pay no regard to the representations of my known and open enemies. And I desire, Sir, that you would show the person or persons to whom the letter you mention was written about my grieving the Mohawks, what I have here written concerning that matter, and the testimonies about it which I herewith send.[3]

But to resume my narrative. Though the Mohawks seemed to be so much fixed in their resolution of all leaving the place, yet some of 'em, on further consideration, came and offered to deliver their children to me, as soon as they should return from sugaring; which offer I readily accepted, and told 'em they should come and live at my house till I could get a good master to come and board 'em and look after 'em. After this, the mother of two of the children that were offered came to me again with her eldest son (one of those fellows I mentioned before as disaffected and probably joining in the horrid designs of some of the young Indians of the Stockbridge Tribe) and told me that this, her son, would not consent to her leaving any of her children.[4] I then renewedly used arguments to persuade her. The woman seemed to

3. The testimonies have not been located.
4. The Indians commonly are governed very much by their children—JE's note.

have a great mind her children should stay, and seemed to argue the matter much with her son; but he would by no means consent. But finally she promised she would return some time in the summer, and bring back her children, and put 'em under my care, and so left some of her things at my house as a pledge of it.

Now there was left but one Mohawk boy, whom I have taken to my own house. Besides the Mohawks, there were a number of Stockbridge boys which had belonged to Mr. Hollis' school; which therefore, if I tied myself exactly to Mr. Hollis' instructions, I should have collected together. But I knew most of 'em were wholly unfit to answer his design, never having been at all cultivated under Captain Kellogg's care, but rather had grown more rough and wild than when he first took them, and were now past their forming age, and would be likely to corrupt and spoil the rest of the scholars. There were two of 'em that were not past a capacity of cultivation. These, therefore, I took. And instead of those others (some of which had a mind to come in), I took three new ones that were young, such as I thought likely and promising. I thought if I pretended to keep the school in being, I could not take less than six. So that the school now consists of one Mohawk, and five Stockbridge boys. The Mohawk is at my house. The others live all at the house of Mr. Joseph Woodbridge; a very desirable family; the man one of the best sort of men that I am acquainted with, the most faithful and thorough in business, and of the most generous Christian and public spirit. The boys at present go to school to Mr. Timothy Woodbridge, whom I have desired to take extraordinary pains with them, till I can get another master for 'em.

This, Sir, is what I have done, and I will now give you the reasons of my conduct. It was apparent that it was absolutely necessary that the school should be kept in being. To let it sink for the present under a notion of reviving it again sometime hereafter would be the way to have it sink finally, especially as to the Mohawks. To have let fall the school wholly, because new Mohawk boys are not to be obtained, in hopes of getting half a dozen Mohawk boys hereafter to begin the school with them, would have been to have proceeded on a vain and unreasonable expectation. They have been so often disappointed with respect to the state of the school, and so continually and long deceived with fair promises of a better state of it, that 'tis now apparent that not the hearing of the ear, but the sight of the eye only, will convince 'em. There is not the least hope of ever regaining Mohawk children to the school any other way than this, viz. by giving them to see, not only that the school is upheld, but that 'tis well settled, and indeed in good circumstances, and established under a far more happy regulation than it used to be. And this they must see for some time, before their prejudices will be removed. If they see this indeed brought to effect, and that the school is established and continues in good circumstances, then perhaps, by Mr. Hawley's help, in length of time a number, yea, a considerable number of Mohawk boys might be obtained. But how should they see this if the school has no being? And when the Mohawks at present refuse to leave their children, how shall we give the school a being, that the Mohawks may see it, and see its flourishing state, in order to our gaining their children, otherwise than by our constituting the school at present of such children as can be had? And it was of vast importance that the school, now it is come into new hands, should be soon amended and settled under a happy regulation. For if the Indians, after they have seen it so long in such miserable, broken circumstances, and have had their patience and hopes so worn out by multiplied disappointments, should see it continuing in its broken state still, now it is got into quite other hands, it will tend to their utterly despairing of ever seeing it otherwise; and the not taking speedy care that it might be otherwise, would be to give the finishing stroke to that important affair that was before just expiring.

Therefore, that now the Indians might see the school happily settled under a good regulation, the school must be kept in being, and the first thing to be done must be to seek a good master to settle in the business, who should board 'em, and every way take care of 'em. Accordingly, this was the thing I immediately applied myself to. I went to Dr. [Israel] Ashley, and proposed the affair to him, conversed largely with him upon it, left it to his consideration and then visited him again at Westfield, and finally prevailed so far that he consented to come up to Stockbridge and bring his wife to see the place. And accordingly they came up, and were [here] the last week and spent the sabbath here. But when the Doctor came to see your letter to me, it seemed to discourage him and put an end to his entertaining any thoughts of coming, at least till the affairs of the school should be further settled by Mr. Hollis. And indeed I could not have the face to desire it of him. But I exceedingly regret, that the settling the school in proper form is thus hindered. 'Tis a thousand pities! 'Tis to be feared the consequences will be very unhappy. I take the Doctor to be the fittest man for the business that can be found in New England. I have long been acquainted with him, have had intimate conversation with him as to his soul's concerns;

I take him to be a man of real experimental piety. He is a gentleman of liberal education. He has a most established character, for a man of the greatest integrity and fidelity, a public-spirited, generous man; one of great concern for the interest of religion; of great skill and activity in the management of business; and having a singular talent at instructing and governing children; and one that thoroughly understands farming. He might probably have been a great blessing, not only to that school, but to the town in general with respect to all its important affairs.

With regard to the school's consisting at present chiefly of Stockbridge boys, it is further to be considered that Mr. Hollis' letter imports no such thing, as that his school should consist only of Mohawks, only in case I find his school wholly broke up; otherwise, he directs me to collect together all that used to be of his school; and his school has for the most part consisted wholly of Stockbridge boys; and in all its stages from the beginning, partly of them. And Mr. Hollis had no reason to think any other from his past instructions to Captain Kellogg but that there were twelve of his Stockbridge scholars to be found, to be collected by me. Indeed, there were more of his scholars of this sort than I have taken up (some of which would be glad to be accepted); but only instead of old, uncultivated ones, on whom Mr. Hollis' money would be thrown away, I have taken three young ones, of a proper age to have Mr. Hollis' ends influenced upon them. I found Mr. Hollis' school consisting of ten, when his letter arrived; and we may well suppose that he expects that I should carry on the school with as many as I find in it; and not only so, but also collect others that are scattered from it. But instead of that, I have not made it to consist of more than half so many; having taken up but six, besides the two Mohawk children that are promised to come in the summer (whose coming is uncertain); and if they come there will be eight.

If it had been so that I could immediately have got six Mohawk boys, yet to have filled the school only with Mohawks and wholly to have neglected the Stockbridge children, would have been of immediate, fatal consequence. You see, Sir, how much the Stockbridge Indians have done for the school with a special respect to the benefit of their own children in it; and how jealous they have been of the interest they claim, and indeed may well claim, and with what difficulty they have been made easy that the Mohawks should have so much of the benefits as they have had. And now on my taking the school, their jealousy immediately appeared. They manifested that they expected to be consulted in the affair. Accordingly, I called a meeting of them. At the meeting they put me in mind of their giving the land, with a special respect to their children. To have excluded their children would have been a fatal consequence, especially at this time when they have just been in so great a ruffle about the man that was killed. I would have by no means had anything to do with the school on these terms, as to be obliged to constitute it only of Mohawks. It would have been to expose myself to great trouble, and the ruin of my usefulness among the Indians.

I should not have thought, Sir, that I had run any venture in proceeding as I have done, had it not been for your letter. But I am here alone entrusted with this business, and could do no otherwise than according to my own best discretion, with the advice of my friends that are here, who see the state of things and have known Mr. Hollis' and Mr. Sergeant's manner from the beginning; who thought it no venture to do as I have done. They say Mr. Sergeant, who undoubtedly was a very honest, faithful man, ever went on those principles to attend Mr. Hollis' instructions as far as the state of things (which he knew and which it was impossible for Mr. Hollis to know) would allow, but to proceed so as not to defeat Mr. Hollis' main design, for fear of departing from his instructions in some punctilios; and that Mr. Sergeant took a far greater liberty than I have done in this respect, and was never blamed for it by Mr. Hollis.

But we in our great caution, lest we should not be punctual to Mr. Hollis' instructions, are knocking on the head the thing which he mainly has his heart upon, and taking a course to spend his money to little purpose, in comparison of what might be, if we acted as we see the state of things absolutely requires.

I know not what I shall do. I have been endeavoring to persuade the Mohawks to let me have their children with such arguments, that probably the school would soon be under much better regulations than it used to be. But if they see it long in an unsettled state, I shall soon be ranked with others that heretofore have deluded 'em with such promises, and shall have no more credit with them. But now I must wait for new instructions from Mr. Hollis; and you see, Sir, how long it has been in times past before we could have any new instructions from him. For five or six years past, his letters have not arrived but about once in two years. And we find it is commonly two or three months before we can have a return from Boston. I can't but think Mr. Hollis will be grieved when he comes to understand the state of things;

and will be ready to blame us for needless and excessive caution, when he comes to understand the bad consequences of it.

This affair comes into my hands under the most difficult, perplexed circumstance imaginable, just as all was falling into ruin, etc. You was pleased, Sir, in your former letter kindly to warn me against triumphing on the receipt of Mr. Hollis' letter. I took the caution well. But really at present I have much greater temptation to be heartily sorry, that I have any concern in a matter embarrassed with so many discouraging, perplexing circumstances, than to triumph in it.

I desire, Sir, that you would lay these things before some of my friends in Boston and take their thoughts. And I desire that as soon as possible, you would write to Mr. Hollis, giving him some account of these affairs, in such a manner as you shall think most prudent. I had rather trust your judgment than my own as to the manner of informing Mr. Hollis, in order to the best influence on his mind. But 'tis very necessary that he should make a return with the utmost possible expedition, and give me some more full and explicit instructions concerning the school. I wish, Sir, that you would urge that, if possible, we may have a letter before winter. Since Dr. Ashley's coming is put by, I have sent into the Jerseys for a young gentleman to come from thence to instruct the scholars this summer, while they are boarded at private houses as at present. But 'tis absolutely necessary that I should have new orders from Mr. Hollis. For since I have received your letter, I have determined to proceed no further with the school without new instructions, than only so as to spend the money which I have received; for to be at the charge of the school myself, will presently break my small estate and ruin my family. And please to desire Mr. Hollis, if he intends the affair shall go on, to make a new remittance, which may arrive, at furthest, the next spring, for much will be saved by having ready money to pay for the necessaries of the school. I shall give Mr. Hollis particular and exact accounts what I do with his money.

The sachem of the Stockbridge Tribe has a son that he has a great desire should be in the school. I am exceeding sorry I did not know it before I had completed my number of six. He, being the chief man of the whole tribe, it would be happy if his son might be in the school. Mr. Hollis in his letter to me says, "If any of the boys should appear capable, I would have them educated for the ministry, that they may be preachers to their countrymen." I want to know whether Mr. Hollis will allow to educate Stockbridge boys; for I know some such that would be likely and promising, whose parents would be glad they might have such an education.

'Tis absolutely necessary that Mr. Hollis should not so tie my hands, but that I may have some liberty to act as I see the necessity of affairs requires, otherwise I shall be often extremely perplexed and embarrassed, and his money will be lost. It has been grievous to me to see others throw away his money; but it will be more grievous to have a hand in doing so myself. I want to be able to tell a master, that I may agree with for a settlement in the business, what dependence he might have for a support in case Mr. Hollis should be removed by death. This question was put by Dr. Ashley, and I may expect the same inquiry will be made by any other that I shall endeavor to obtain to settle in the business.

'Tis needful that Mr. Hollis should be informed that Colonel Dwight refuses to deliver up the cattle and household furniture which belongs to the boarding school, which was purchased with his money. The reason he gives is "that Mr. Hollis is in debt to Captain Kellogg and to him, and it concerns him to look to himself."

Dr. Ashley talked of going to Boston at the end of this month. I wish you could see him, and would endeavor to prevent his giving over all thoughts of coming to Stockbridge, though our affairs are unsettled and under difficult circumstances at present.

And pray, Sir, let me have a letter from you speedily. If there is no opportunity sooner, there will be one by Capt. [John] Ashley of Sheffield or Dr. Ashley, who are both coming to Boston in the latter end of May. And there will be often opportunities to send to my son-[in-law], Capt. [Timothy] Dwight of Northampton, which may be known of by inquiring of Mr. [Edmund] Dwight of Boston. My wife is gone to New Jersey. Please to present my humble regards to Mrs. [Deborah Denny] Prince. My daughter, Lucy, joins with me in presenting respects to Mrs. Sally, if she be returned from New Jersey.

And pray for me, Sir, that I may have the divine assistance in the difficult affairs which lie so heavy on my feeble shoulders. I am, honored Sir,

> Your most respectful son and servant,
> Jonathan Edwards.

194. TO SEC. JOSIAH WILLARD

Edwards brings a troublesome Indian situation to the attention of the Secretary of the Province. The son of an honored Stockbridge Indian had been killed by two Englishmen the year before. When one of the perpetrators was acquitted and the other given a light sentence, the Indians were outraged and demanded restitution. Indemnity was authorized by the General Court and the Governor but never paid. Edwards' intervention helped break the bureaucratic logjam. Upon transmittal of the payment, the crisis was resolved.

(MAR, vol. 32, pp. 521–22, ALS, two folio leaves, one addressed on verso to the Honorable Josiah Willard, Esq., Secretary of the Province of the Massachusetts Bay in Boston. See also *JMHR* 30 [Jan. 23, 1754], 200. Timothy Woodbridge and Joseph Dwight had appealed earlier to Governor Shirley, MAR, vol. 32, pp. 482–85. See Patrick Frazier, *The Mohicans of Stockbridge* [Lincoln, Neb., 1992], pp. 105–06.)

*   *   *

Stockbridge, May 22, 1754

Honorable Sir,

This is to entreat you to use your influence that the money which the General Court has granted to [Solomon] Waunaupaugus, the uncle of the man that was killed here the last year,[1] may be speedily delivered, in order to its being conveyed to Stockbridge.

It is very manifest that it is a matter of great importance, not only to us in Stockbridge, but to New England, that the Indians be quieted with respect to that matter. Your Honor has doubtless been informed to what a height the uneasiness has risen with some, even to that degree that some of the young fellows belonging to this tribe, in confederacy with some other Indians of other tribes, had formed a design of a general massacre of the English inhabitants of this town (though I am far from supposing that the generality of the Indians were in the conspiracy). The ill influence of this affair is very extensive. It is evident it reaches other tribes to a great distance; and will be a handle which the French, at this juncture, will make the utmost improvement of; and probably have made much use of it already. It seems to affect the Mohawks no less than our Indians. There were many appearances as though some of them were in the forementioned conspiracy. The Indian that endeavored to draw the Negroes into the plot, informed one of them that the Mohawks were to come and strike the first stroke, and be leading in the destruction of the town.

I have been privately informed by an Indian who is very friendly to me (who desires that his name may not be known in the affair), that some of the Five Nations had talked with our Indians about this matter, and had suggested that the English were not friendly, but had an

1. He was actually the father of the victim.

inimical and murderous design upon the Indians; and mentioned the conduct of the English with relation to the Indian that was killed, as an evidence of it; and that their talk had filled our Indians with suspicions and resentment; and those young fellows who were chief in the foresaid bloody design, had lately been in the country of the Shawnees, where is a mixture of some of the Five Nations with other Indians; and that the French had then lately been among those Indians, and had endeavored to possess their minds with a persuasion, that the English were on a design of extirpating all Indians within their reach; and had so far persuaded the Indians that it was indeed so, that they kept a constant watch every night; and that these Indians, having heard of the affairs of Stockbridge, told our young men that were there that the English made fools of them, and that though they pretended to show 'em kindness and to instruct 'em, they did but deceive them, that they were only opening a wide mouth to swallow 'em up, when they should see a convenient time. And that this caused our young men to return to Stockbridge so full of resentment, which gave rise to their conspiracy.

Everything shows it to be very requisite that the matter be speedily made up. The Indians are like children in that respect as well as others, that they don't love delays. It don't satisfy 'em to tell 'em of something hereafter to be given 'em. Therefore I wish the matter was well finished with them; which I think should be done speedily, and with formality. I wish that instead of appointing some of our own inhabitants to treat with them, the General Court had sent a committee from Boston; which the Indians would have taken much more notice of; and it would have had a greater and better effect upon them. It would not have been beyond the importance of the affair for the General Court to have been at this trouble.

Please to excuse my using so much freedom in expressing my thoughts and desires. I do it in a confidence of that friendship to me, which you have often testified. This, with my most humble respects to your family, is from, honored Sir, with all dutiful respect,

Your most humble servant,
Jonathan Edwards.

195. TO MAJ. JOSEPH HAWLEY

Troubled by a guilty conscience, Hawley asks Edwards for a frank evaluation of his conduct during and after the dismissal proceedings at Northampton. Edwards does not mince words; he obliges with an indictment of the members' actions, especially Hawley's. He reveals the deep personal hurt he had previously minimized, and with the zeal of a prophet calls for repentance as a way to avert final judgment. Hawley received these strictures with humility and contrition. His apologies grew stronger with the passage of time.

(NYPL, Hawley Papers, ALS, four folio leaves, addressed on verso of the fourth to Maj. Joseph Hawley in Northampton; ms. fragment, Beinecke Library. Published in Faust and Johnson, pp. 392–401. Related letters in NYPL, loc. cit.: Hawley to Edwards, Jan. 21, 1755, ALS draft, two folio leaves; and Hawley to the Reverend David Hall, May 5, 1760, ALS, two folio leaves, fragments missing. Published in Hopkins, pp. 66–72; Dwight ed., *1*, 421–27.)

* * *

Stockbridge, November 18, 1754

Dear Sir,

I now, as soon as I am able, set myself about answering your letter of August 11, though I am still so weak that I can write but with a trembling hand, as you may easily perceive. I was taken ill about the middle of July, and my fits have now left me a little more than a fortnight. But I have been greatly reduced by so long continued an illness, and gain strength very slowly, and cannot be so particular in my answer to your letter as I might be if I had more strength.

I rejoice in the good temper and disposition of mind which seems to be manifested in your letter; and hope that whatever I may have suffered, and however greatly I may think myself injured in that affair which is the subject of your letter, wherein you was so much of a leader, I have a disposition, in my consideration of the affair and what I shall write upon it, to treat you with true candor and Christian charity. Nevertheless, I confess that the thing you desire of me is disagreeable to me, viz. very particularly giving my judgment concerning your conduct in that affair; and it is with no small reluctance that I go about answering such a request, upon two accounts: 1. As it obliges me renewedly to revolve in my mind, and particularly to look over, that most disagreeable and dreadful scene, the particulars of which I have long since very much dismissed from my mind, as having no pleasure in the thoughts of them; and 2. As 'tis (and will be looked upon by you, however serious and conscientious you may be in your desires and endeavors to know the truth) a giving a judgment in my own case, a case wherein I was concerned to a very high degree; and therefore will be much more likely to be a giving of it in vain.

Notwithstanding, seeing you desire it, and seem to desire it in so Christian a manner, I will give you my judgment plainly, such as it is, and as impartially as I am able, leaving the consequence with God.

You know very well that I looked on myself, in the time of the affair, as very greatly injured by the people in general, in the general conduct, management, and progress of it from the beginning to the end. That this was then my judgment was plain enough to be seen; and I suppose no man in the town was insensible of it. And what were the main things wherein I looked on myself injured, and what I supposed to be the aggravation of the injury was also manifest: as particularly that the church and Precinct had all imaginable reason to think that in my receiving that opinion which was the subject of the controversy, and in the steps I took upon it, the declaration I made of it, etc., I acted altogether conscientiously, and from tenderness of spirit, and because I greatly feared to offend God; without, yea, to the highest degree against, all influence of worldly interest, and all private and sinister views. I think it was hardly possible for the affair to be attended with circumstances exhibiting greater evidence of this. I think if my people, therefore, when the affair was first divulged, had been acted by a Christian spirit or indeed by humanity (though they might have been very sorry and full of concern about the affair), would, especially considering how long I had been their pastor, [and they] had always from the beginning, and from so long experience, acknowledged me to be their faithful pastor, and most of them esteemed [me] to be the chief instrument in the hand of God of the eternal salvation of their souls; I say they would have treated me, if influenced by Christianity or humanity, with the utmost tenderness, calmness, and moderation, not to say honor and reverence; and would have thought themselves obliged to have gone far in the exercise of patience. But instead of this, the town and church were at once put into the greatest flame. The town was soon filled with talk of dismissing and expelling me, and with contrivances how to do it speedily and effectually. And a most jealous eye, from that day forward, was kept upon me, lest I should do that slyly and craftily that should tend to hinder such a design. And almost every step that I took in the affair was, by their suspicious eyes, looked upon in such a view; and therefore everything served to renew and heighten the flame of their indignation. Even when I addressed myself to 'em in the language of moderation and entreaty, it was interpreted as a design to flatter the people, especially the more ignorant, to work upon their affections, and so to gain a party and prevent a vote for my dismission, or at least to prevent the people's being united in any such vote. And there was no way that I could turn myself, nothing that I could do or say but it would have some such uncharitable construction put upon it.

As I began the affair in the fear of God, after much and long-continued prayer to him, so I was very careful in the whole progress of it, and in every step to act uprightly and to avoid every unrighteous and underhanded measure. Nor had I ever once formed a design forever to establish myself at Northampton, and impose myself on the people, whether we should remain differing in our opinion in the point in controversy, or not; nor did I ever take one step with any such view. The things I aimed at were these two: 1. That the people should be brought to a calm temper before extremes were proceeded to; and 2. That they should, in such a temper, hear what I had to say for myself, and my opinion.

But nothing could be done. The people most manifestly continued in a constant flame of high resentment, and vehement opposition, for more than two years together; and this spirit, instead of subsiding, grew higher and higher, till they had obtained their end in my expulsion. Nor indeed did it cease then, but still they maintained their jealousy of me, as if I was secretly doing the part of an enemy to 'em, so long as I had a being in the town; yea, till they saw the town well cleared of all my family. So deep were their prejudices, that their heat was maintained; nothing would quiet 'em till they could see the town clear of root and branch, name and remnant.

I could mention many things that were said and done in a public manner, in meetings of the Precinct, church, and their committees, from time to time, from the beginning, fully to justify and support what I have said and supposed, till my dismission (besides the continual talk in all parts of the town, in private houses, and occasional companies). But I think this can't be expected, as it would be writing a history that would take up no less than a quire of paper. I would only observe that I was from [time] to time reprehended by one that commonly was chosen [moderator] of Precinct and church meetings, and chairman of their committees [Seth Pomeroy], in a very dogmatical and magisterial manner, for making so much mischief, putting the church to so much trouble. And once he told me he did it by the desire and vote of the whole Committee, which was very large, consisting of all or most of the chief men of the town. I was often charged with acting only from sinister views, from stiffness of spirit, and from pride, and an arbitrary and tyrannical spirit, and a design and vain expectation of forcing all to comply with my opinion. The above-mentioned person chiefly improved by the town and church, and set at their head in these affairs, once said expressly, in a church meeting in the meetinghouse, "That it was apparent that I regarded my own temporal interest more than the good of the church; that the church had reason to think I designedly laid a snare to ensnare the church; and that they had best by all means to beware and see to it that they were not ensnared." And said much more to the same purpose. And he was never frowned upon but smiled upon by the church; continuing in such a way of treatment of me, was still made much of, and set foremost in the management of the affair.

There were multitudes of Precinct and church meetings, many meetings of committees, and conferences with me about this affair. I am persuaded there was not one meeting, but that this unreasonable, violent spirit was apparent, and as governing and prevalent. It seemed from the very beginning to govern in all proceedings, and almost every step that was taken. The people were so far from seeking any composition, that it was often declared in the meetings that if I should retain my opinion, though I should be convinced that continuing in it, I might go on in Mr. [Solomon] Stoddard's way, they would by no means have me for their minister; and their Committee declared against any endeavors [to] bring me to this before the last Council. Yea, they seemed to have a dread of my consenting to this.

It being thus, I think the whole management of the affair was exceeding provoking and abominable to God; as most contrary to what ought to be in all public affairs, especially affairs of religion and the worship of Christian societies; and so contrary to the treatment due to me from that people; and especially in an affair so circumstanced, wherein they had such glaring evidences of my acting only from tenderness of conscience, and with regard to the account I had to give to my great Master; and wherein I so carefully avoided everything irritating, and never offered the people any provocation, unless yielding and condescending, as I did to them (in things which I supposed they insisted on merely from humor and prejudice) in many instances for peace's sake was a provocation; an affair wherein I with great constancy maintained a diligent watch over my own spirit; an affair wherein I sought peace and pursued it, and strove to my utmost to avoid occasions of strife, and to treat everyone in a Christian manner.

Such an affair being so managed, I think no one should have put their hand to it, unless it were to check and restrain, and if possible to bring the people to an exceeding different temper and manner of conduct, and convince and show 'em how far they were out of the way of their duty; and till this could be done, I think not a step should have been taken by any means, to promote and forward their designs. Instead of this, I am persuaded a judicious Christian, in a right temper of mind, being a bystander, would have beheld the scene with horror; especially considering the dreadful work that [it] was making with the credit and interest of religion, by such a town and church as that of Northampton, of such a profession and fame.

And therefore, Sir, I think you made yourself greatly guilty in the sight of God, in the part you acted in this affair; becoming, especially [towards the latter] part of it, very much their leader in it; and much from your own forwardness, putting yourself forward as it were, as though fond of intermeddling and helping; which was the less becoming, considering your youth, and considering your relation to me. Your forwardness especially appeared on this occasion, that after you was chosen as one of a committee to plead their cause before a council, you came to me, and desired me to stay the church on purpose, that you might have opportunity to excuse yourself from the business; which was accordingly done, and you did excuse yourself, and was excused. But yet, when the matter came to be pleaded before the Council, you (I think very inconsistently) thrust yourself forward, and pleaded the cause with much earnestness, notwithstanding. 'Tis manifest that what you did in the affair from time to time, not only helped the people to gain their end in dismissing me, but much encouraged and promoted the spirit with which it was done; your confident, magisterial, vehement manner had a natural and direct tendency to it.

As to your Remonstrance[1] to the last Council, it not only contained things that were uncharitable and censorious, by which facts were misinterpreted and overstrained, but it was full of direct, bold slanders asserted in strong terms, and delivered in very severe, opprobrious language, merely on suspicion and surmise. As particularly therein, if

---

1. The "Reflections on the Remonstrance sent to Mr. Clark and Mr. Edwards" (Beinecke Library, ALS, five quarto leaves, n.d. [June 1751–May 1752]) cites a document sent by members of the First Church of Northampton to Rev. Peter Clark, to be communicated to the Council of May 1751, considering the settlement of JE over a second church in Northampton, as the "Remonstrance." Specific quotations are given. The MS of the Remonstrance could not be located. The extant letter of Hawley to the Council does not contain the points quoted in the Retractions. See Hawley to the Council, NYPL, Hawley Papers, AL, two folio leaves, unsigned, n.d. [May 16, 1751], and incomplete.

I mistake not, was asserted that I had said after my dismission, that "I was de jure and de facto still the pastor of that church," which was a false charge. Again, I was charged with "having a desire to be settled over a few of the members of the church to the destruction of the whole; and that I set out on a journey with a certain gentleman to procure a council to install me at Northampton; and that I contrived to do it at such a time, because I knew the church was at that time about to send for a candidate, etc., that I might prevent their success therein; and that I was ready to settle in that place, and for the sake of it had refused an invitation to Stockbridge; that I had neglected this opportunity for the sake of settling over an handful; that I had a great inclination to continue at Northampton as a minister, at the expense of the peace and prosperity of the greater part of the town; yea, that I was greatly engaged for it." Here is a heap of direct slanders, positively asserted, all contrary to the truth of fact. I had not refused the invitation to Stockbridge, or neglected that opportunity. I had no inclination or desire to settle over these few at Northampton, but a very great opposition in my mind to it, abundantly manifested in what I continually said to them on occasion of their great and constant urgency. It was much more agreeable to my inclination to settle at Stockbridge, and though I complied to the calling of a council to advise in the affair, it was on these terms, that it should not be thought hard that I should fully and strongly lay before 'em all my objections against it. My discourse with particular ministers applied to in their own houses, was chiefly in opposition to Col. [Timothy] Dwight; and so was my discourse before the Council when met. I earnestly argued before them against their advising me to settle there, with hopes that what I said would prevail against it, and very much with that conclusion; and what I said against it was the thing that did prevail against it, and that only. I complied to the calling of the Council with a view to these two things: 1. To quiet the minds of those, who in so trying a time had appeared my steadfast friends, that they might not always think exceeding hardly of me; and 2. The country having been filled with gross misrepresentations of [the] controversy between me and my people, and the affair of my dismission, and the grounds of it, to the great wounding of my character at a distance, I was willing some ministers of chief note should come from distant parts of the country, and be upon the spot, and see the true state of things with their own eyes. It was very contrary to truth that I contrived to set out at that particular time, because just then the church were about to apply to a candidate, etc., that I might prevent their success; for I knew not of any such thing. I had then no notice of that design or determination of the church. Nor was that true that is suggested, that the procuring a council was the thing that occasioned our setting out on that journey. Each of us had other business, and should have gone had no such thing as a council been projected; and therefore we went far beyond all parts where any of those ministers dwelt, and spent much more time there than with any of them. As to my seeking to disappoint and ruin the town and destroy its peace, etc., I did not in all this affair take one step with any view at all to a disappointment of the town and church in any of their measures for the settling another minister. I might mention other things in the Remonstrance but I am weary.

These things, being so, I cannot think the church's Reflections[2] do in any wise answer their faults in this paper, and the injuries therein done to me. In their Reflections they grant that they used too strong terms, and language too harsh, that in some things they were too censorious, and had not sufficient grounds to go so far in their charges, that they should not have expressed themselves thus and thus; but had better have used other specified terms, which yet would have been for the hurt of my reputation. I confess, dear Sir, I have no imagination that such sort of reflections and retractions as these, will be accepted in the sight of God as sufficient, and all that is proper in such a case; and that it will be found that they that think so, do greatly deceive themselves. The church in their Remonstrance seemed to contrive for the strongest, most severe and opprobrious, aggravating kind of terms, to blacken my character, and wound my reputation in the most public manner possible. In their Reflections on themselves a contrary course is taken. There, instead of aggravating their own fault (which is the manner of true penitents) they most manifestly contrive for the softest, mildest terms, to touch their own faults in the most gentle manner possible, by the softest language.

On the whole, Sir (as you have asked my opinion), I think that town and church lies under great guilt in the sight of God. And they never more can reasonably expect God's favor and blessing till they have their eyes opened to be convinced of their great provocation of the Most High, and injuriousness to man, and have their temper greatly altered; till they are deeply humbled; and till they openly and in full terms confess themselves guilty, in the manner in which [they] are

2. Also known as Retractions; see preceding footnote.

guilty indeed (and what my opinion of that is, I have in some measure declared), and openly humble and take shame to themselves before the world, and particularly confess their faults and seek forgiveness where they have been peculiarly injurious. Such terms, I am persuaded, the righteous God will hold that people to; and that it will forever be in vain for 'em to think to go free and escape with impunity in any other way. Palliating and extenuating matters, and daubing themselves over with untempered mortar, and sewing fig leaves will be in vain before him whose pure and omniscient eye is as a flame of fire.

It has often been observed what a curse persons have lived under, and been pursued by, for their ill-treatment of their natural parents; but especially may this be expected to follow such abuses offered by a people to one which in their own esteem is their spiritual father. Expositors and divines often observe, that abuse of God's messengers has commonly been the last sin of an offending, backsliding people, which has filled up the measure of their sin, put an end to God's patience with them, and brought on them ruin. And 'tis also commonly observed that the heads and leaders of such a people have been remarkably distinguished in the fruits of God's vengeance in such cases. And as you, Sir, distinguished yourself as a head and leader to that people in these affairs, at least the main of them, so I think the guilt that lies on you in the sight of God is distinguishing; and that you may expect to be distinguished by God's frowns, unless there be true repentance, and properly expressed and manifested, with endeavors to be a leader of the people in the affair of repentance, as in their transgression. One thing which I think aggravated your fault, was that you yourself thought me in the right in that opinion wherein I differed from my people. As to the nature and essence of true religion, my people and I in general were agreed. The thing wherein we differed was that supposing that our common opinion of the nature of true godliness to be right, a profession of it, or of those things wherein we supposed the essence of it consisted, was necessary to church communion. In this you agreed with me and not with the people. So that in effect you owned my cause (in the thing which was the main foundation of controversy) to be good, and yet, in the manner before observed, set yourself at their head in their violent opposition to me.

You say that in all your disputes, you ever had a full persuasion of my sincerity and true sanctity. If so, then doubtless what Christ said to his disciples takes hold of you. "He that receiveth you receiveth me," and "he that despiseth you despiseth me, and he that despiseth [me] despiseth him that sent me" [Matt. 10:40, Luke 10:16]. And "take heed ye despise not one of these little ones"; he that offendeth one of them, "it were better for him that a millstone were hanged about his neck, and he drowned in the depths of the sea" [Matt. 18:10, 6].

Thus, Sir, I have done the thing you requested of me. I wish you may accept it in as Christian a manner as you asked it. You may possibly think that the plain way in which I have given my judgment shows that I am far from being impartial and that I show a disposition to aggravate and enhance things, and set 'em forth in the blackest colors; and that I plainly manifest ill will to you. All that I shall say to this is, that if you think so, I think you are mistaken. And having performed the disagreeable task you desired of me, I must leave you to judge for yourself concerning what I say. I have spoken my judgment with as great a degree of impartiality as I am master of, and that which is my steady and constant judgment of this awful affair; and I doubt not will be my judgment as long as I live. One thing I must desire of you, and that is, that if you dislike what I have written, you would not expect that I should carry on any paper or letter controversy with you on the subject. I have had enough of this controversy, and desire to have done with it. I have spent enough of the precious time of my life in it heretofore. I desire and pray that God may enable you to view things truly, and as he views them; and so to act in the affair as shall be best for you, and most for your peace, living and dying.

With respectful salutations to your spouse, I am, Sir, your kinsman and friend, that sincerely wishes your truest and greatest welfare and happiness, in this world and the world to come,

Jonathan Edwards.

196. TO THE REVEREND THOMAS FOXCROFT

Edwards sends instructions for the editing, publication, and distribution of *Freedom of the Will*.

(Beinecke Library, ALS, one large quarto leaf, addressed on verso to the Reverend Mr. Thomas Foxcroft, Minister of the Gospel, in Boston.)

* * *

Stockbridge, December 20, 1754

Rev. and Honored Sir,

I should have wrote to you long ago, if I had been able, but have been held under extreme weakness for five months by being followed with fits of the ague. And now must be excused in writing but a few words, having spent myself in writing to the Commissioners. I have sent an account of errata to Mr. [Samuel] Kneeland and would acknowledge my great obligations to you in the care you have taken about the impression. I have ordered Mr. Kneeland to present you with five books on my account, all in calf, and two neatly bound with giltlines and one of them lettered on the back. He binds the books poorly. The covers are so apt to warp that they will warp as they lie upon the table. I wish that he would take care that the books sent to Scotland may be handsomely bound. Mr. [Timothy] Woodbridge, who brings this, will give the Commissioners a full account of our present extraordinary state.

Desiring a constant remembrance in your prayers, and presenting cordial respects to your family, I am, Sir,

Your obliged son and servant,
Jonathan Edwards.

197. TO TREASURER ANDREW OLIVER

(Beinecke Library, ALS, in "History of Redemption" ms. notebook 1, pp. 111, 116; no outside address, but inside heading, "To the honorable Andrew Oliver Esq., Treasurer to the honorable Commissioners for Indian Affairs in Boston.")

* * *

Stockbridge, December 20, 1754

Sir,

Please to deliver to Capt. Timothy Woodbridge of this town my half-year's salary due on the 17th day of this month. Herein you will oblige Your Honor's

Most humble servant,
Jonathan Edwards.

198. TO THE REVEREND JOSEPH BELLAMY

Edwards compresses much information into this brief note to his follower. He hopes to see both him and the books he has borrowed (throughout his career, Edwards made a practice of lending books). Bellamy responded with a visit in the company of Samuel Hopkins for two nights and one day, February

11 to 13, 1755,¹ during which time Edwards read them a treatise he was preparing on "The Last End of God in the Creation of the World."²

Edwards' sojourn with his sisters at Windsor was carried out as scheduled. The Reverend John Ballantine records in his diary that Edwards and his son lodged with him on April 22 and 30, 1755, which means that Edwards stayed there both on his way to and his way back from Windsor. Ballantine further hosted his friend on May 1 and 8 of that year; the latter time Edwards came with two of his sons.

Bellamy had been called as pastor of the First Presbyterian Church in New York City in January 1754. After visits back and forth by committees and Bellamy, as well as extensive correspondence, Bellamy declined the call in July 1754. In a letter of January 22, 1755, to Nathaniel Hazard, a prime mover on the New York pulpit committee, Bellamy gave enthusiastic endorsement to the Reverend David McGregore of Derry, New Hampshire, who was then being considered. He promised that he would also seek Edwards' opinion; this is the terse reply of concurrence. Like Bellamy, McGregore declined.

The last item concerns the forwarding of mail, always a matter of chance in the days before an organized postal system. Stockbridge, on the main route between Boston and Albany, was a logical place for mail redistribution.

(Beinecke Library, ALS, one quarto leaf, addressed on verso to the Reverend Mr. Joseph Bellamy at Bethlehem. On the Stockbridge visit, see Samuel Hopkins, "Memoir," in Edwards A. Park, ed., *The Works of Samuel Hopkins, D.D.* [Boston, 1865], pp. 49–51. On Edwards' lending habits, see Beinecke Library, ms. "Account Book," pp. [67]–[68], which lists sixteen instances of lending in 1755, six to Hopkins, and two to Bellamy. See also Ballantine for dates listed. And on McGregore, see Bellamy, pp. 429–31; Sprague, *3,* 29; Webster, p. 649.)

* * *

1. In a letter dated Feb. 10, 1755, Hopkins tells Bellamy that he expected him every week, to join in a visit to JE. He has postponed going by himself until he could "have the favor of accompanying one of his [JE's] best friends." Hopkins hears that JE is bloated and concerned about dropsy. He adds, "It may be a kind visit from some of his friends might so raise his spirits as to be the means of altering the tone of his blood." The letter either was never sent, being obviated by Bellamy's actual appearance, or was the cause of his immediate action. Sterling Library, ALS, one quarto leaf, addressed on verso to Bellamy at Bethlehem.
2. See *Works, 8,* 399–536. This was first published as *Two Dissertations, I. Concerning the End for which God created the World. II. The Nature of True Virtue* (Boston, 1765).

Stockbridge, January 24, 1755

Rev. and Dear Sir,

I am sorry you have put by your journey hither, I want to see you very much, and to have you bring the books. I must, if providence allows, be at Windsor the week after the 20th of April to meet my sisters there from distant parts according to appointment. I would not fail of seeing you before that time by any means.

I am fully of your mind about Mr. [David] McGregore. I wonder I never thought of him before.

I have here sent along a number of letters for you which have come to my hand. One that came from Boston I guess has a piece of gold in it.

Kind respects to Mrs. Bellamy. I am Sir,

Yours most affectionately,
Jonathan Edwards.

199. TO BRIG. JOSEPH DWIGHT

From the late summer of 1754 into 1755, Stockbridge was gripped by panic, for an Indian attack seemed imminent. Soldiers were sent in for defense. Fortifications were hastily built around Edwards' home, making it the town's central garrison.

Edwards reports here that the demands on his hospitality have exceeded his ability to satisfy them. Supplies are diminished, and his physical strength is low; it is impossible for him to continue boarding a large number of troops.

(Trask Library, ALS, one quarto leaf, inscribed on verso to Brigadier Dwight, Feb. 26, '55; Dwight ms. transcript, one quarto leaf. Published in Dwight ed., *1*, 544–45; Arthur L. Perry, *Origins in Williamstown* [New York, 1894; rev. 1896, 1900], p. 253.)

* * *

Stockbridge, February 26, 1755

Honorable Sir,

We have not lodgings and provision so as to board and lodge more than four soldiers, and being in a low state as to my health and not able to go much abroad, and upon that and other accounts under much greater disadvantage than others to get provisions, it is for this reason, and not because I have a disposition to make difficulty, that I told the soldiers of this Province that had hitherto been provided for here that we could not board 'em any longer.

I have often been told that Your Honor has intimated that you expected other business for them in a short time. Capt. [Stephen] Hosmer has sent three of his men to lodge at my house, which I am willing to entertain, as I choose to board such as are like to be continued for our defense in times of danger. [Benjamin] Stebbins has manifested to us a desire to continue here. Him therefore I am willing still to entertain with your consent.

Beseeching Your Honor's candid construction of that, which [is] not intended in any inconsistence, with all proper honor and respects,

> Your most humble servant,
> Jonathan Edwards.

200. TO THE REVEREND THOMAS FOXCROFT

The dream of creating a Mohawk school collapsed with the departure of the Mohawks and Gideon Hawley. With the Williamses still undermining his efforts, and Stockbridge on military alert, Edwards pleads with the Commissioners for whatever help they can devise.

(Beinecke Library, ALS, one large quarto leaf, close and signature missing, endorsed on verso, "Rev. Mr. Edwards, Rec^d. Mar 25. 1755 [per] Mr. Woodbridge, Answd. [per] D^o"; overwritten by Foxcroft.)

* * *

Stockbridge, March 8, 1755

Rev. and Honored Sir,

I thank you for your favor of January 9, 1755. The Messrs. [Timothy and Joseph] Woodbridge, wait on you with this, who come to Boston to represent to the Commissioners the sorrowful state of our affairs. Our case is such as calls loudly for whatever the Commissioners can do to retrieve it, if there is anything that they can do. And it calls for the prayers of the true friends of the kingdom of Christ. At this time, when we are brought under great calamities by enemies from without, the savages of the wilderness, our difficulties from within don't diminish but increase, and all arise from the old source. I have wrote something particularly to Sec. [Josiah] Willard, Mr. [Andrew] Oliver, and Mr. [Thomas] Hubbard; which letter you will probably see; and will hear more from the messengers of the town. The Indians, in a full meeting, have chosen some of their company to go with the Woodbridges: but they have been so much tampered with, and have had so much done to corrupt them, that I don't know how they will conduct themselves.[1]

I hope, Sir, we shall have your prayers for us, with respect both to our difficulties from without and from within: and I desire your [. . .]
[Jonathan Edwards.]

201. TO THE REVEREND THOMAS PRINCE

This is a cover letter, asking Prince to convey an accompanying report to Thomas Hubbard. With the Mohawk exodus, the original intention for the Hollis school was not being fulfilled. Under the circumstances, Edwards sees no point in continuing the school without renewed instructions from the sponsor.

Lucy Edwards did not go to Boston during the summer of 1755. Instead, she escaped embattled Stockbridge by visiting the home of her aunt Abigail Noyes in New Haven, in August and September.

(AAS, Curwen Family Papers, box 3, f. 3, ALS, one quarto leaf, addressed on verso to the Reverend Mr. Thomas Prince in Boston. On Lucy Edwards, see Burr, pp. 130, 140, 153.)

* * *

Stockbridge, April 14, 1755

Rev. and Honored Sir,

I have no heart to propose to the Commissioners any such thing as their maintaining Mr. [Isaac] Hollis' school, while we wait to hear from him. I have observed an aversion in 'em to meddle in his affairs; and then I cannot say so much concerning the advantage that this school is like to be of, in this time of war and confusion, as I think will be likely to induce 'em to run the venture of being at such a charge: but unless I hear very speedily from Mr. Hollis shall throw up his school.

I would entreat you very speedily to deliver this letter to Mr. Speaker [Thomas] Hubbard.

1. The Indians went to Boston and were heard by a committee of the House of Representatives. Among other things, they expressed their great love for the minister and schoolmaster, but said that some English were trying to break the peace between the Indians and these leaders. Joseph Pynchon, the committee chairman, who was not about to cross his Brookfield neighbor, Joseph Dwight, concluded, "But as the Persons referred to as disturbers of the peace were not present, the Committee are not able to give any light as to the facts." MHS, Israel Williams Papers, pp. 62 f., read in Council, Apr. 26, 1755.

We have some thoughts of sending my daughter Lucy to Boston to live at your house this summer, according to a former invitation from you, and repeated pressing invitation from Miss Sally. Lucy is now at Northampton.[1]

My wife joins with me in respectful salutations to you, Mrs. Prince and Miss Sally.

Asking a remembrance in your prayers, I am, Sir,

> Your obliged, humble servant,
> Jonathan Edwards.

202. TO MAJ. JOSEPH HAWLEY

This note, without date or place of origin, was probably written after Hawley's favorable response of January 1, 1755, to Edwards' letter of November 18, 1754 (No. 195), and is proof of their mended friendship. Hawley was elected from Northampton and Southampton to the House of Representatives. Because of his frequent trips to Boston, he took on the job of mail carrier.

(NYPL, Hawley Papers, ALS, fragment.)

* * *

[Stockbridge, after January 1, 1775]

Sir,

I have sent a letter to Mr. [Thomas] Prince by the bearer, to be committed to your care. I request of you the favor of taking special care of it, and delivering it with your own hands, as soon as ever you get to Boston. Pray don't fail. Herein you will particularly oblige. Yours, etc.

> Jonathan Edwards.

203. TO THE REVEREND JOHN ERSKINE

Edwards acknowledges receipt of books and letters. For his correspondent in Scotland, he recapitulates events at Stockbridge, showing how minor occurrences in the town's dealing with the Indians often brought about larger repercussions. He correctly assesses the crucial significance of English-French tensions in America at this time. Amid dark clouds, he finds a "hopeful prospect" in the impending Indian mission of Gideon Hawley.

---

1. Lucy was at the home of her older sister, Mary, the wife of Timothy Dwight, Jr.

(Trask Library, ALS, two folio leaves; Dwight ms. transcript, four quarto leaves; another ms. transcript in unidentified hand, four quarto leaves. Published in Dwight ed., *1*, 545–48; Faust and Johnson, pp. 402–06.)

* * *

Stockbridge, April 15, 1755

Rev. and Dear Sir,

The last year in the spring I received, without a letter, a packet containing the following books: Casaubon on Enthusiasm, Warburton's *Principles of Natural and Revealed Religion*, Merrick on Christ the true Vine, Campbell's Apostles Enthusiasts, Discourse on the Prevailing Evils of the Present Time, Remarks on Apostles Enthusiasts, Moncrief's Review and Examination of Some Principles in Campbell's Apostles Enthusiasts, Gilbert of the Guilt and Pardon of Sin, Hervey on *The Cross of Christ*, An Account of the Orphan School, etc. at Edinburgh, *Memorial Concerning the Surgeon's Hospital*, Gairdner's *Account of the Old People's Hospital, State of the Society in Scotland for Propagating Christian Knowledge*, Abridgement of the Rules of Said Society, Regulations of the Town's Hospital at Glasgow, Annals of the Persecutions of the Protestants in France.[1]

1. Meric Casaubon, *A Treatise Concerning Enthusiasme* (London, 1655; 2nd ed., rev. and enl., London, 1656); William Warburton, *The Principles of Natural and Revealed Religion Occasionally Opened and Explained; in a Course of Sermons* (vols. 1–2, London, 1753–54; vol. 3, London, 1767); Marshal Merrick, *The Parable of the Vineyard and Christ, the True Vine* (London, 1753); Archibald Campbell, *A Discourse proving that the Apostles were no enthusiasts . . . With a preface containing some reflections on a late book, entitled, Christianity as Old as the Creation; and on what Mr. Woolston alledges with respect to the resurrection of Jesus Christ* (London, 1730). No information could be found on "Discourse on the prevailing Evils of the present Time." *A letter to Professor Campbell, whereto is subjoin'd remarks on his vindication of the Apostles from enthusiasm* (London, 1731); Alexander Moncrieff, *An Enquiry into the Principle, Rule, and End of Moral Actions, wherein the Scheme of Selfish-love, laid down by Mr. Archibald Campbell . . . Is Examined, and the Received Doctrine Is Vindicated* (Edinburgh, 1735); Thomas Gilbert, *A learned and accurate Discourse concerning the Guilt of Sin, pardon of that Guilt, and prayer for that pardon* (London, 1695; rep. Edinburgh, 1720); James Hervey, *The Cross of Christ the Christian's Glory* (London, 1753); *A brief account of the rise, progress, and management . . . of the Orphan-School, etc.* (Edinburgh, 1735); *Memorial concerning the Surgeons Hospital* (Edinburgh, 1737); Andrew Gairdner, *An historical account of the Old People's hospital, commonly called, the Trinity Hospital in Edinburgh; also, proposals how to raise a fund for the maintenance of widows and orphans, under the title of a Charity-Bank* (Edinburgh, 1728); Robert Walker, *A short account of the rise . . . and present state of the Society in Scotland for propagating Christian knowledge* (Edinburgh, 1748); *Abridgement of the Statutes and Rules of the Society in Scotland for Promoting Christian Knowledge* (Edinburgh, 1732); *A short account of the Town's Hospital in Glasgow; with the regulations and abstracts of the expenses for the first eight years* (3rd ed., Glasgow, 1742); *Annals of the rise, progress,*

In the beginning of last December, I received another packet without a letter, the wrapper superscribed with your hand. In this were the following pamphlets: A Sermon by a Lay Elder before the Commission, *A Letter to a Gentleman at Edinburgh,* Resolution of the General Assembly of May 22, 1736, Rutherford's *Power of Faith and Prayer, Inquiry into the Method of Settling Parishes, The Nature of the Government and Constitution of the Church of Scotland, Essay on Gospel and legal Preaching, Necessity of Zeal for the Truth,* A Vindication of the Protestant Doctrine of Justification against the Charge of Antinomianism.[2] The last week, I received a letter from you dated July 11, 1754, which was found at Mr. [Thomas] Prince's by one that went to Boston from hence, and had lain there Mr. Prince could not tell how long. In this letter, you make mention of these last-mentioned pamphlets received last December. I now return you my hearty thanks for this letter and these generous presents. I should have wrote to you long ago, had I not been prevented by the longest and most tedious sickness that ever I had in my life; I being followed with fits of the ague, which came upon me about the middle of last July, and were for a long time very severe and exceedingly wasted my flesh and strength, so that I became like a skeleton. I had several intermissions of the fits by the use of the Peruvian bark; but they never wholly left me till about the middle of last January. In the meantime, I several times attempted to write letters to some of my friends about affairs of importance; but found that I could bear but little of such writing. Once, in attempting to write a letter to Mr. [Aaron] Burr, a fit of the ague came upon me while I was writing; so that I was obliged to lay by my pen. When my fits left me, they left

---

and persecutions, of the famous reformed churches in France: which are at this day groaning under the cruel bondage of popish tyranny (2nd ed. London, 1753).

2. No information could be found for "A sermon by a Lay Elder before the Commission." John Bisset, *A Letter to a Gentleman at Edinburgh, containing remarks upon a late Apology for the Presbyterians in Scotland, who keep communion in the ordinances of the Gospel, with Mr. George Whitefield* (2nd ed. London, 1753); *Resolution of the General Assembly of the Church of Scotland, upon the Report of their Commissioners sent to London to Endeavour the repeal of the act 10ᵐᵒ Annae reimposing patronages* (Edinburgh, 1736); Samuel Rutherford, *The Power and Prevalency of Faith and Prayer Evidenced, in a practical discourse upon Matth. 9. 27–31* (London, 1731); Gordon Thomas, *An enquiry into the method of settling parishes, conform to the acts and practices of the Church of Scotland, through the different periods of her administration and government, from the Reformation to the present time* (Edinburgh, 1732); [John MacLaurin], *The Nature of Ecclesiastic Government and of the Constitution of the Church of Scotland illustrated* (Glasgow, 1754); [James Ballantyne], *An Essay upon Gospel and Legal Preaching . . By a Minister of the Church of Scotland* (Edinburgh, 1723); Allen Logan, *The necessity of zeal for the truth; and of restraining error by the exercise of church-discipline* (n.p., 1730); James Hog, *A Vindication of the doctrine of grace, from the charge of antinomianism; contained in a letter to a minister of the gospel* [Ralph Erskine] (Edinburgh, 1718).

me in a poor, weak state, all over bloated; so that I feared whether I was not going into a dropsy. I am still something swelled, and much overrun with scorbutic maladies. Nevertheless, I have of late gradually gained strength.

I lately received a letter from Mr. [John] MacLaurin, dated August 13, 1754, which Mr. Prince sent me with a letter from himself, wherein he informed that the captain of a ship from Glasgow, then lately arrived, brought an account of Mr. MacLaurin's death, that he died very suddenly with an apoplexy, a little before he left Glasgow. Since I received that letter, I sent to Mr. Prince desiring to know more of the certainty of the account. Mr. Prince writes back, that he sees no reason to doubt of it. This is an affecting piece of news; it is an instance of death which I have much cause to lament. He has long shown himself to be a very worthy, kind, and obliging friend and correspondent of mine. And doubtless the Church of Scotland has much cause to lament his death. There is reason to think that he was one of them that stood in the gap, to make up the hedge in these evil times. He was a wise, steady, and most faithful friend of gospel truth, and vital piety, in these days of great corruption. I wish that I may take warning by it, as well as by my own late sickness to prepare for my departure hence.

I have nothing very comfortable to write concerning my own success in this place. The business of the Indian mission, since I have been here, has been attended with strange embarrassments, such as I never could have expected or so much as once dreamed of; of such a nature, and arising from such a quarter, that I take no delight in being very particular and explicit upon it. But besides what I especially refer to, some things have lately happened that have occasioned great disturbance among the Indians, and have tended to alienate 'em from the English. As particularly the killing of one of them in the woods by a couple of travelers, white men, who met him and contended with him. And though the men were apprehended and imprisoned, yet, on their trial, they escaped without sentence of death; one of them only receiving a lighter punishment, as guilty of manslaughter: by which these Indians, and also the Indians of some other tribes, were greatly displeased and disaffected towards the English.[3] Since this, the last fall, some Indians from Canada (doubtless instigated by the French) broke

3. The Stockbridge Indians resented the killing of one of their leaders by two Englishmen, who received little or no punishment; delay of the indemnity payment; stereotyping of them, by reinforcing troops, as being like the Schagticoke and Canadian Indians; and desecration of an Indian grave by soldiers. See Letter No. 194, JE to Willard, May 22, 1754; and Sedgwick and Marquand, *Stockbridge,* pp. 72–76.

in upon us on the sabbath, between meetings, and fell upon an English family, and killed three of them, and about an hour after killed another man coming into the town from some distant houses; which occasioned a great alarm in the town and in the country. Multitudes came from various parts for our defense, that night and the next day; and many of these conducted very foolishly towards our Indians on this occasion, suspecting them to be guilty of doing the mischief, charging them with it, and threatening to kill them, and the like. After this, a reward being offered by some private gentleman, to some that came this way as soldiers, if they would bring them the scalp of a Canada Indian; two men were so extremely foolish and wicked that they, in the night, dug one of our Indians, that had then lately died, out of his grave, to take off his scalp; that by pretending that to be the scalp of a Canada Indian, whom they had met and killed in the woods, they might get the promised reward. When this was discovered, the men were punished. But this did not hinder, but that such an act greatly increased the Indians' jealously and disaffection towards the English.[4] Added to these things, we have many white people in the neighborhood, many Dutch and some English, that will at all times, without any restraint give them rum; which is constant temptation to their most predominate lust.

Though I have but little success and many discouragements here at Stockbridge, yet Mr. [Gideon] Hawley, missionary among the Six Nations (who went from New England to Onohquaga, a place more than 200 miles to the westward from hence), has of late had much encouragement. Religion seems to be a growing, spreading thing among the savages in that part of America, by his means; and there is an hopeful prospect of way being made for another missionary in those parts. Which may have happy consequences, unless the Six Nations should go over to the French; which there is the greatest reason to expect, unless the English should exert themselves vigorously and successfully against the French in America, this year. They seem to be waiting to see whether this will be or no, in order to determine whether entirely to desert the English, and cleave to the French. And if the Six Nations should forsake the English, it may be expected that the Stockbridge Indians, and almost all nations of Indians in North America, will follow 'em. It seems to be the most critical season with the British dominions in America, that ever was since the first settlement of these colo-

---

4. See the preceding note.

nies. And all probably will depend on the warlike transactions of the present year. What will be done, I can't tell. We are all in a commotion from one end of the British America to the other: and various expeditions are projected and preparing, for one to Ohio, another to the French forts in Nova Scotia, another to Crown Point. But these affairs are not free of embarrassments: great difficulties arise in our present, most important affairs, through the disunited state of the several governments. 'Tis hard for them to agree upon means and measures. And we have no reason to think the French are behind us in their activity and preparations. A dark cloud seems to hang over us; we need the prayers of all our friends, and all friends to the Protestant interest. Stockbridge is a place much exposed, and what will become of us in the struggles that are coming on, God only knows.

I have heard that Messrs. [Gilbert] Tennent and [Samuel] Davies are arrived in America, having had good success in the errand they went upon.[5]

Mr. [Joseph] Bellamy is not like to go to New York, principally by reason of the opposition of some of the congregation, and also of some of the neighboring ministers. I have heard they have lately unanimously agreed to apply themselves to Mr. [David] McGregore of New Londonderry, alias Westfield, in New England, to be their minister; who is a gentleman that I think, if they can obtain him, will be likely to suit 'em, and well to fill the place. And I have heard that there has been some difference in his own congregation, that has lately made his situation there uneasy. If so, he will be more likely to consent to the motion from New York.

My wife joins with me in respectful and affectionate salutations to you and Mrs. Erskine. I am, Sir,

> Your affectionate and obliged brother,
> Jonathan Edwards.

Sir,

In a journey I went to Northampton the last April, I carried the foregoing letter, with others for Scotland so far, seeking an opportunity to send 'em from thence to Boston. But there I met another letter from Mr. Prince, with a joyful contradiction of his former ac-

---

5. In Nov. 1753, Tennent and Davies had gone to England, Scotland, and Ireland for what turned out to be a successful fund-raising journey for the College of New Jersey. Alexander, pp. 48–50; Sprague, 3, 142; Webster, pp. 393–95; Maclean, pp. 149–54; and Pilcher, pp. 27–146.

count of Mr. MacLaurin's death,[6] which occasioned my bringing my packet home again. Nevertheless, after I had broke open and revised this letter, I thought best to send it along, enclosed in a wrapper to Mr. MacLaurin; who I hope is yet living, and will convey this to you. I am, dear Sir,

> Your affectionate brother,
> Jonathan Edwards.

Stockbridge, June 2, 1755.

204. TO JONATHAN EDWARDS, JR.

After mid-April 1755, Gideon Hawley returned to Onohquaga, the Indian settlement near modern Binghamton, New York, taking with him Edwards' son Jonathan, Jr. The lad was not quite ten but was already speaking Mahican with his friends at school and play. Later, Jonathan noted that he knew more Indian words than English at that time. His father encouraged him, probably thinking of future missionary service. The Indians welcomed him and were especially pleased at his proficiency with their language. Although the sojourn was planned to last a year, the deteriorating military situation and bitter weather forced Hawley to return young Jonathan home in January 1756.

This letter, written the day after his son's tenth birthday, is characteristic of Edwards' communications to his children. The primary emphasis is on religious commitment and the brevity of life.

(Beinecke Library, ALS, two quarto leaves, addressed on verso to Jonathan Edwards, Jr., at Onohquaga. Published in Robert Ferm, *Jonathan Edwards the Younger* [Grand Rapids, Mich., 1976], pp. 15–16. See also SIB, *12*, 396–97. By May 9, 1755, Hawley was in Onohquaga; Boyd and Taylor, *1*, 274–75.)

*   *   *

Stockbridge, May 27, 1755

Dear Child,

Though you are a great way off from us, yet you are not out of our minds: I am full of concern for you, often think of you, and often pray for you. Though you are at so great a distance from us, and from all your relations, yet this is a comfort to us, that the same God that is here, is also at Onohquaga; and that though you are out of our sight and out of our reach, you are always in God's hands, who is infinitely gracious; and we can go to him, and commit you to his care and mercy. Take heed that you

---

6. The death of MacLaurin did occur on Sept. 8, 1754.

don't forget or neglect him. Always set God before your eyes, and live in his fear, and seek him every day with all diligence: for 'tis he, and he only can make you happy or miserable, as he pleases; and your life and health, and the eternal salvation of your soul, and your all in this life and that which is to come, depends on his will and pleasure.

The week before last, on Thursday, David[1] died; whom you knew and used to play with, and who used to live at our house. His soul is gone into the eternal world. Whether he was prepared for death, we don't know. This is a loud call of God to you to prepare for death. You see that they that are young die, as well as those that are old: David was not very much older than you. Remember what Christ has said, that you must be born again, or you never can see the kingdom of God. Never give yourself any rest, unless you have good evidence that you are converted and become a new creature. We hope that God will preserve your life and health, and return you to Stockbridge again in safety; but always remember that life is uncertain: you know not how soon you must die, and therefore had need to be always ready.

We have very lately heard from your brothers and sisters at Northampton and at Newark, that they are well. Your aged grandfather and grandmother, when I was at Windsor, gave their love to you. We here all do the same. I am,

> Your tender and affectionate father,
> Jonathan Edwards.

205. TO THE REVEREND THOMAS FOXCROFT

Edwards writes as hostilities against the French are heating up on the frontier. Preparations are under way to capture the fort at Crown Point, on Lake Champlain. Timothy Woodbridge would have been a likely candidate to lead the troops from the Stockbridge area, but he was engaged as a negotiator and policy maker in the Susquehannah Company from 1754 to 1769. It was he who paid the Six Nations for the Pennsylvania land in 1754, an act that precipitated a half-century of conflict and litigation.

(Beinecke Library, ALS, one folio leaf, addressed on verso to the Reverend Thomas Foxcroft, Minister of the Gospel, in Boston. On Woodbridge, see Boyd and Taylor, *1*, 47–2, 98; and J. T. Adams, *Dictionary of American History* [6 vols. New York, 1940], *6*, 451–52.)

* * *

1. Not further identified; possibly the Mohawk boy who had been living with the Edwardses (see No. 193).

Stockbridge, June 3, 1755

Rev. and Honored Sir,

I thank for your letter of March 31 by Mr. [Timothy] Woodbridge, and for the kind concern at the difficulties I meet with in this place. The people who have made difficulty heretofore are far from being yet at rest. I have heard that they have lately conceived new hopes of accomplishing their designs. I imagine it to be from Col. [Israel] Williams of Hatfield, his being chosen representative.[1] I suppose they depend on his influence especially with Gov. [William] Shirley.

Mr. Woodbridge is not like to go to Crown Point. But the reason of it has been greatly misrepresented by his enemies, as though he was disliked by the Indians as their captain, and that they all refused to enlist under him. Whereas, on the contrary, he is I suppose the only person they would be willing to go under, and many of them showed a forwardness to go under him, and most of 'em would probably have insisted, if he would have gone. But the true reason of his not going was the earnest solicitations of the Susquehannah Company in Connecticut, further to assist them in their business.

I humbly desire you to take particular care of the enclosed packet to Mr. [John] MacLaurin;[2] and if anything be come from Scotland for me, to forward it to Stockbridge.

I am yet in a low state as to my health; and the lower by reason of a great hurt I received in a late journey to Windsor by a dangerous fall from my horse, the horse pitching heels over head with his whole weight upon me. But through mercy I am much better than I have been. I desire you to pray for me, that God would be with me under my various troubles, and sanctify mercies and afflictions. This, with humble respects to your family, is from, honored Sir,

Your obliged friend and humble servant,
Jonathan Edwards.

206. TO CAPT. TIMOTHY WOODBRIDGE

Because of his remote location in Stockbridge, Edwards had to rely on travelers to Boston or elsewhere for shipments of chocolate, which seems to

1. Col. Israel Williams was elected seventeen times from Hatfield to the Massachusetts House of Representatives. JE refers to the 1755 election. *JMHR*, 32 (1755), part 1, p. 4; SIB, *8*, 302.
2. JE had still not received official word of MacLaurin's death on Sept. 8, 1754.

have been a staple in the Edwards household. Here Edwards writes a note, covering a missing letter, regarding one such shipment and the financial arrangements involved.

(Beinecke Library, ALS, "History of Redemption" ms. notebook 1, pp. 108–09, 118–19).

* * *

[Stockbridge,] June 4, 1755

Sir,

I desire you to deliver this letter, which I have wrote to Col. [John Henry] Lydius about the chocolate, desiring him to deliver the whole of it to you. And here send the paper by which it appears under Mr. [Gideon] Hawley's own hand that the whole £12 was reckoned to me.

If you will bring what remains you will much oblige

Your humble servant,
Jonathan Edwards.

P.S. Please to send me those two dollars you had of me to go to Boston with.

207. TO COL. ISRAEL WILLIAMS

Only five days before the Battle of Lake George, in which the colonists fought against an invading force of French and Indians, Stockbridge received word that defensive Connecticut troops would soon withdraw from the area. This unexpected development has been attributed to Col. Israel Williams' ridicule of Edwards' move to secure the soldiers; Williams considered them unnecessary. Connecticut authorities took him seriously enough to recall their men. Brig. Joseph Dwight then made a direct appeal to Lieut. Gov. William Pitkin of Connecticut and secured the return of forces but not until the following year. On their return to western Massachusetts, Williams refused to command them, on the ground that he had not been consulted. Between the withdrawal and return of Connecticut troops, Edwards and his Stockbridge friends use this petition to entreat Williams to send in Massachusetts soldiers so that they will be protected.

(MAR, vol. 54, p. 96, ALS, one folio leaf, addressed on verso to Col. Israel Williams at Hatfield. See SIB, *8*, 307–08; and Joseph Dwight to William Pitkin, July 7, 1755, HSP, Gratz Colonial Wars, #17.)

* * *

Stockbridge, September 4, 1755

Sir,

Yesterday a message was sent to us from Connecticut, by the Committee of War there, informing us that they had ordered all their soldiers stationed here, and at Pantoosuck, to leave these places the next Monday. The messenger informs us that the Committee of War expressed it as their opinion that Stockbridge still needs defense; but that this is no longer to be expected from Connecticut, seeing they have very lately done so much for the defense of the country in general; and that therefore they continued their men till next Monday, that we might have a little time to apply for help elsewhere.

We think it manifest that, if the town be left wholly destitute of soldiers, we shall be greatly exposed. If this be understood by the enemy (as probably it will), it will invite them to us as their ready and easy prey. They would glory much in destroying this town, and taking so many forts; and would be fond of embracing such an opportunity of dislodging the English inhabitants, and so breaking the union between the English and Indians, and drawing off this tribe, among the many others that are forsaking the English interest and joining with the French since the Ohio defeat.[1]

We therefore desire, Sir, that our case may be considered, that a speedy supply of soldiers may be ordered, for this station, sufficient to keep our forts and in other respects to defend the people. We are, Sir, your most humble servants,

Jonathan Edwards
Josiah Jones
Samuel Brown
Joseph Woodbridge
Stephen West
Timothy Woodbridge
Elijah Williams
John Taylor
John Willard.

P.S. There are thirty of our Indians, or more, gone with Gov. [William] Shirley; being urged by him, they were very backward, making this objection, that the town, and their wives and children would be left very defenseless by the absence of so many. On which the Governor

1. On July 9, 1755, British forces under Maj. Gen. Edward Braddock were defeated, and Braddock himself was killed, in a battle along the Monongahela River near Fort Duquesne (Pittsburgh).

offered them, that a sufficient number of English soldiers should be kept here for the defense of the town. On this dependence our Indians left the town. Of this we have undoubted information from many of our Indians that were present.

Besides, we have just now word sent us by Mr. Van Schaack of Kinderhook,[2] that they have received late information, that two large parties of Indians are now come out against our frontiers; one designed for the Dutch settlements, the other for New England. 'Tis very likely that they would thus endeavor to cut out work for us at home, while our army is in distress, to prevent, if possible, our sending sufficient succors to our army. The army at Crown Point, doubtless, see that they shall have time enough to make excursions.

208. TO COL. ISRAEL WILLIAMS

Edwards reinforces the plea he and other Stockbridge residents had sent to Williams the day before. James Gray carried the town's request to Williams and added his own. The Battle of Lake George, which took place a few days later, proved the townspeople's fears were not unfounded.

(Trask Library, AL fragment, one quarto leaf; Dwight ms. transcript, one quarto leaf. See also James Gray to Israel Williams, MHS, Israel Williams Letters, I, ALS, Sept. 6, 1755.)

* * *

Stockbridge, September 5, 1755

Sir,

Yesterday the English inhabitants of this town sent away a letter directed to you, to be conveyed to Hatfield, representing the state of the town, as left very greatly exposed by the drawing off all the Connecticut soldiers, and Gov. [William] Shirley's (by his urgency) persuading away almost all the Indian inhabitants, fit for war; who objected much against going on this account, that the departure of so many would leave the town, and their wives and children too, defenseless; and that the Governor removed their objection, by promising that a sufficient number of English soldiers should be maintained here during their absence, for the defense of the town. And also that we had just now information sent us in writing from Mr. Van Schaack,[1] that

2. There were a number of members of the family there at the time, though JE may refer to Cornelius, since his son Henry was away at war. See Edward A. Collier, *A History of Old Kinderhook* (New York, G. P. Putnam's Sons, 1914), pp. 100–01.

1. See preceeding note.

two large parties of Indians are lately gone out from Crown Point against our frontiers; and so entreating that soldiers may speedily be sent. But being informed today that you are gone from Hatfield, and not knowing whether you will seasonably receive the forementioned letter, I now, on the desire of the people, give you this brief information of what was therein written; earnestly desiring that we may not be left so easy and open[2] prey to our enemies, who, we have reason to think,[3] have the means of learning our situation, and are certainly preparing to attack some of the most defenseless of the frontier villages. We hope that the troops may be forwarded immediately; for, having no adequate means of repelling an attack, we have no security for a single day. I am, respectfully,

> Your obedient servant,
> Jonathan Edwards.

209. TO THE REVEREND THOMAS FOXCROFT

(Beinecke Library, ALS, one quarto leaf, torn, irregular, partly overwritten in later hand, addressed on verso to the Reverend Thomas Foxcroft, Minister of the Gospel, in Boston.)

* * *

Stockbridge, September 15, 1755

Rev. and Honored Sir,

My son [Timothy] waits on you with this, and with a packet prepared and sent away long ago, in order to go to Boston, to be conveyed to Scotland; but was strangely neglected by the messenger who was to have carried it, and at last came back to me again.

I request your prayers and blessing for my son, who is now a member of New Jersey College; and ask your prayers for me, and my whole family, with respect to all the difficulties which attend [our] present circumstances; and for two of my children who are ill; of whose case my son, the bearer of this, can inform you. I am, honored Sir,

> Your most obliged friend and humble servant,
> Jonathan Edwards.

2. MS breaks off; Dwight's transcript is used for the remainder of the letter.
3. Dwight MS has "are not ignorant," which is crossed off.

210. TO THE REVEREND THOMAS PRINCE

Edwards furnishes Prince with a brief report on the Hollis school and some family news.

(Princeton University, Seeley Mudd Library, Gen. Mss., *Princeton University Memorial Book of the Sesquicentennial of 1876*, p. 366, Sesquicentennial Records Collection A141, ALS, one quarto leaf, addressed on verso to the Reverend Thomas Prince, Minister of the Gospel, in Boston.)

* * *

Stockbridge, September 15, 1755

Rev. and Honored Sir,

My son [Timothy], a member of New Jersey College, waits on you with this, if God permit, to pay his, and my duty to you. For him, I ask your prayers and blessing. I had dismissed Mr. [Isaac] Hollis' scholars (not having heard anything from him) about the middle of last July, agreeable to your advice. But soon after, I received a letter from him, dated the last April; wherein he desires me to increase the number of his boys to sixteen. On which, I restored his school, and increased it; so that it now, in the whole, consists of eleven. I have reserved room for four or five Mohawk boys; intending to try if I can obtain some, through Mr. [Gideon] Hawley's influence: though I have no great expectation of it, so long as the war continues. Mr. Hollis desires me to draw a bill upon him for what money I want. I have thoughts of going this week to New York and New Jersey, and propose to endeavor to sell my bill there. I have prepared a large packet for Mr. Hollis, giving him a very large and particular account of his affairs, and intend to send it with the bill. Two of my children are ill, which makes my setting out this week on my journey something uncertain. I desire your prayers for them, and for us all. My wife joins in most respectful salutes to you, Mrs. Prince and Miss Sally. I am, Sir,

Your most obliged son and servant,
Jonathan Edwards.

211. TO ELIZABETH SCOTT WILLIAMS

Edwards tries in this letter to mend his quarrel with Elizabeth Williams, the widow of Elisha Williams. He is prompted by reports that she has tarnished his reputation in letters to London and Norwich, England. No doubt this intel-

ligence was conveyed by Samuel Davies, recently returned from those places.[1]
Edwards reminds Williams that because they are human, they are both subject
to misunderstandings, but as Christians, they serve the same cause. He considers his motives in opposing her husband's efforts at Stockbridge to have
been proper and wonders whether she might see things in a different light if
she had a fuller understanding of his position. He concludes on a note of
condolence.

No reply from Elizabeth Williams is extant, but her notation on this letter
indicates that she took Edwards' appeal as an attack on her late husband's
veracity, and would have none of it.[2]

(HSP, Gratz Amer. Colonial Clergy Coll., ALS, two folio leaves; Trask Library, AL draft, three fragments: one c. 20 cm.; another, one folio sheet, on a
letter cover addressed to Edwards at Stockbridge; a third, one quarto leaf, also
on a letter cover to Edwards at Stockbridge; also a Dwight ms. transcript.)

* * *

Stockbridge, October 30, 1755

Madam,

I have very lately seen a gentleman, who has, not long since, been in
London and Norwich in England, and conversed with many persons
of note in each place, and with those of your particular acquaintance in
the latter. And from the informations he has given me, concerning
what he heard in both those places, especially in Norwich, I have
reason to think that you have wrote and sent thither, that which has
been much to the disadvantage of my reputation: which is the occasion
of my writing this letter to you, the design of which is not to demand
satisfaction, or to testify my resentment; but in calmness and charity to
say something for myself, and in meekness to plead my cause, with one
whom (however she has thought and spoke ill of me, and I have suffered much by her means, without cause) I can embrace in my charity,

1. Davies had travelled to England and Scotland in 1753 and 1754 on a fund-raising tour
for the College of New Jersey; he visited Norwich from Sept. 3 to 17, 1754, and was in the
company of a John Scott (Mrs. Williams was the daughter of Rev. Thomas Scott of that city).
Pilcher, *SD*, pp. 140, 149, 156; and Pilcher, pp. 42–87, 123–27, 131–33. Davies and JE both
participated in the meeting of the Presbyterian Synod of New York, held in Philadelphia,
beginning Oct. 1, 1755. Pilcher, *SD*, p. 159; *Records of the Presbyterian Church in the United
States of America* (Philadelphia, 1841), pp. 262–63.

2. At the end of the letter, Mrs. Williams inserted the following note: "Wrote as I have too
much reason to think, and as it has been judged by some of the most judicious, with a design
to have me acknowledge I had been under influence from my dear Col. and his brother, etc.
which was very far from being the case. With the answer."

as a true follower of the Blessed Lamb of God. I am so sensible of the exceeding infirmity, we are the subjects of in the present state, that what I have heard lately and formerly of what you have expressed with warmth of spirit, to the disadvantage of my character (as I think unjustly) don't make it difficult with me to make large allowance, for what I know of the circumstances you have been in, since you came into this part of the world, greatly tending to prejudice you; and to introduce, and fix in your mind the most disadvantageous ideas of my temper and conduct, in many respects. I suppose I am well sensible, what has been abundantly said of me, by some persons, concerning my natural temper; and the light in which my behavior, in many instances of it, has been continually represented. Nor am I insensible, what parts of my conduct, both before and since I have been at Stockbridge, but especially since, have been looked upon as chiefly obnoxious to censure, by those whose representations you have been most in the way of.

'Tis no part of my present aim, to detract in the least from the character of those persons, or to endeavor to restore and support my own character on the spoils of theirs; but only to entreat you, Madam, sedately to consider, what may come to pass, through the general great infirmity of mankind, in this present state of imperfection, darkness and confusion; what diverse, and even opposite opinions of persons and things, men, even of good character, often receive, and strongly and zealously maintain. And especially, how often this happens in their opinions of persons that have acted in a public capacity, and very important station; and in the passages and incidents of whose lives, have occurred things that have been extraordinary, and beside the common course of events, and which have made much noise in the world, unusually attracting the observation, and engaging the attention and conversation of a country; and that in this case, it will be hard to form a right judgment: especially if such a person's conduct is so much, and so long the subject of talk, that in the issue, there is a division into different parties, of opposite opinions concerning the matter, and the affair is clouded with the dust of controversy, managed with zeal and earnestness; as often is the case. And that also sometimes things fall out exceeding unhappily between persons and families, in the general of good character, so that misunderstandings arise, prejudices are strangely imbibed, and strongly fixed. And though there be no real, or at least no great foundation, still the prejudice subsists; and by some means or other, a kind of mist of darkness is maintained, causing things to be viewed on each side in very false colors: in which, probably, the grand enemy of the peace and welfare of mankind has a great hand.

It is not hard to conceive that in such case, it may be next to impossible for a stranger, that comes from a far country, and falls wholly among one of these opposing parties, or misunderstanding families, and at the very juncture when the controversy is at the greatest height; to view things in a true and clear light, or to avoid being greatly blinded, and strongly prejudiced, in the first forming and fixing a judgment of the affair; especially if it be fixed soon, without time for much circumspection, or any long deliberation. A person, Madam, of your discerning, and who has had your opportunities, must needs have observed much of this kind in the world. Therefore I would entreat you to consider whether this may not possibly be your case, with respect to me. So it has pleased God to order in his providence, that my life has been attended with a succession of such incidents of various kinds, as have, for more than twenty years past, been the subjects of much noise in the country; about which others have been divided in their sentiments, and men's spirits have been engaged, with no small warmth, especially in some families. And I would pray you, Madam, to consider that you are a stranger in the country; and therefore cannot judge of such affairs, as if you had always lived in the country, and had, from the beginning, been acquainted with its affairs; the rise of different parties, the tempers, views, interests and manners of different combinations and families; the first original of misunderstandings, which are subsisting between persons of various sorts and sets; and that your lot, from your first arrival hither, or rather before your arrival, was cast among (or rather in union with) those who have been on one side, with regard to my affairs; and that you never have properly had any opportunity to hear what I have to say for myself, or to know how things would appear to you, if I were to have opportunity of free and full conversation with you.

If this had been, and I had been heard with candor, and you had a view of the story of my life, from the beginning, with all the circumstances of those passages of it, about which so much has been said, and with relation to which I have been so much blamed by some; you might probably have had quite other thoughts; and many things which now appear very dark and mysterious, might have been explained, and have appeared very intelligible to you; and you might be convinced that you have truly misapprehended facts, and misconceived of the principles and spirit from which I have acted, in many instances. Not that I am so vain as to pretend that my conduct has been so pure, that I have had no cause of self-reflection and humiliation before God. But this he knows, who searches my heart; that I have long made it my great care to approve myself to him, and to act in such a manner, and from such principles, as have been prescribed in the excellent rules which have been given, and the amiable and perfect example which has been set by him who is the Lamb of God, and light of the world. And this I know, that if, in the important business I am employed in, I have acted, as some suppose, from private resentment, from implacableness of spirit, or stiffness and willfulness of temper, or an assuming disposition, and fondness of rule and authority, or any principle of a like kind; I must have acted very contrary to the spirit and nature of the Christian religion, and extremely unbecoming the character of a minister of Jesus Christ; and never can expect to be justified before my great Master and judge.

But I forbear; perhaps any expressions which may seem to denote a confidence of my own integrity, may be thought to arise from ignorance of my own heart. And I confess that experience teaches me, the need of constantly maintaining of a watchful and jealous eye over my own heart, with humble prayer to God for light to enable me to judge truly of myself. But this I will venture to affirm with confidence, that if I have acted from such unchristian principles, and without an hatred of all remains of 'em in myself and habitual, earnest hungerings and thirstings after that righteousness, and true Christian piety and virtue, which consists in the contrary amiable dispositions of heart; attended with earnest cries to God, with many tears, as the infinite fountain and sovereign bestower of such precious endowments; it must be because I have been extremely and totally blinded concerning myself. My desire is, and has long been, that God would search me and prove my heart, and see if there be any wicked way in me, and lead me in the way everlasting. I desire to speak and act at all times, as having in view the account which I have shortly to give to that omniscient and righteous judge, who is not liable to be blinded by vain pretenses and professions, nor mislead by prejudices and misinformations.

I doubt not, Madam, but that you thought you had sufficient grounds for the judgment you have formed of my temper and conduct, and the report you have made of them. But I would entreat that there may yet be room for reflection and consideration, whether it is not possible that you may have apprehended things much worse than they are. If you should still think it your duty to persist in the same representations, which you have heretofore made to my disadvantage; and it should happen hereafter by divine providence that you should, by some means, come to be convinced, that you had wounded and greatly wronged an innocent person, and a minister of Jesus Christ; who, notwithstanding all that had been judged and said by others concerning him, had indeed been acting in the fear of God, with tenderness of conscience, endeavoring in all things to acquit himself to the divine acceptance; and was influenced by quite other principles than you imagined; would not this deeply affect a mind endowed with a truly Christian humility, candor and benevolence of heart, such as I charitably believe you are possessed of? However, if you never should have this conviction in this world of darkness, as possibly you may not, I hope I shall always feel the same readiness to forgive you, which hitherto I have found; though I know myself to be much injured, and may perhaps greatly suffer through your report to my disadvantage. I shall comfort myself with hopes of the time when all God's people shall meet together in an unembarrassed, unalloyed charity, in a world of such clear and perfect light as shall abolish all misunderstandings, and even the strongest prejudices and dissipate the thickest clouds, through which many of them now view one another [under a] very false and disadvantageous light.

I know not, Madam, what construction you may put upon my writing as I now do. I know, when once persons have imbibed a deep prejudice against others, it has a tendency to cause them to look on everything they say or do in quite another light, than otherwise they would do. But I ask your candor; and I ask your prayers, that God would take away what he sees amiss in my heart. If I am so ill a person as you have conceived, I need your prayers the more.

I condole with you the loss you have sustained in the death of Col. [Elisha] Williams, your honorable consort; for whose sake you left your dear native land and crossed a vast ocean, to dwell in a strange land; and who doubtless, was under God, the greatest support and comfort of your life. That God would now appear as your mighty support and comforter, in your bereaved, desolate circumstances and sanctify the late death of this your nearest relation, and other relations, to you and me, is the sincere prayer of, Madam,

> Your most respectful and humble servant,
> Jonathan Edwards.

212. TO THE REVEREND JOHN ERSKINE

Edwards comments on books recently received and evaluates the progress of the war. Despite recent victories at Nova Scotia and Lake George, English forces have suffered setbacks at Niagara and Crown Point. Worst of all is Braddock's defeat on the Monongahela River. Reflecting growing colonial discontent with British interference, Edwards complains about the unwillingness of the "ministry at home" to allow American forces to fight for themselves.

(Trask Library, ALS, two folio leaves in pieces, one shorn, the second addressed on verso to the Reverend Mr. John Erskine, Minister of the Gospel, at Culross, in Scotland; Dwight ms. transcript, two quarto leaves. Published in Dwight ed., *1*, 550–52.)

* * *

Stockbridge, December 11, 1755

Rev. and Dear Sir,

I last wrote to you in July 24, 1755. Since that, in the latter part of last October, I received a letter from you, dated June 23, 1755, together with the *Essays on the Principles of Morality,* from Mr. [William] Hogg; and the *Analysis of the Moral and Religious Sentiments of Sopho,* from yourself.[1] I thank you for your letter and present: and shall write a letter of thanks to Mr. Hogg, for his present by your hands, added to former instances of his generosity. I had before read that book of essays; having borrowed Mr. [Joseph] Bellamy's; and also that book of Mr. David Hume's which you speak of.[2] I am glad of an opportunity to read such corrupt books; especially when written by men of considerable genius; that I may have an idea of the notions that prevail in our nation. You say that "some people say that Lord Kames' being made a Lord of Session would have been prevented, if Chancellor [Philip Yorke, Earl of] Hardwicke, and Archbishop [Thomas] Herring had seasonably seen his book." I should be glad to know who this Chancellor Hardwicke is, and what his character. By your mentioning him in such manner, I am ready to suppose he may be in some respects of good character. And it is a matter of thankfulness, if a man of good character, and a friend to religion be Lord Chancellor.

1. Henry Home, Lord Kames, *Esays on the Principles of Morality and Natural Religion* (Edinburgh, 1751); and John Bonar, *An Analysis of the Moral and Religious Sentiments of Sopho* [Lord Kames] *and David Hume, Esq.* (Edinburgh, 1755).

2. Titles by David Hume in JE's "Catalogue of Reading" (Beinecke Library) are *A Treatise of Human Nature* (2 vols. London, 1739–40), *Philosophical Essays Concerning Human Understanding* (London, 1748), and *An Enquiry Concerning the Principles of Morals* (London, 1751). See also *Works, 1,* 14, n. 1; and *8,* 604, n. 1.

As to our warlike concerns, I have not heretofore been very particular in writing about them, in my letters to Scotland, supposing it highly probable that you would have earlier accounts from Boston, New York and Philadelphia, than any I can send you, living at so great a distance from any of the seaports. Nevertheless, seeing you propose my sending some account of the present posture of affairs, I would say that it appears to me, that notwithstanding some remarkable favors of heaven, of which we are very unworthy, it has in the general been a year of great frowns of providence on the British America. Notwithstanding our success at Nova Scotia, and our having the better in the battle near Lake George, and taking the French General prisoner; yet, considering the advantages the enemy hath obtained against us, by Gen. [Edward] Braddock's defeat; especially in gaining over and confirming the Indians on their side, and disheartening and weakening our friends, and what we have suffered from our enemies, and how greatly we are weakened and almost sunk with our vast expenses, especially in New England, and the blood as well as money we have expended; I say, considering these things, and how little we have gained by all our cost and trouble, our case is no better, but far worse than it was in the beginning of the year. At least, I think it certain that we have obtained no advantages in any wise to balance our trouble and expense of blood and treasure. The expedition to the eastward has been remarkably succeeded; but the other three expeditions, that against the French forts on the Ohio, that against Niagara, and that against Crown Point, have all been unsuccessful as to their main design. And though the army under Gen. [William] Johnson had a kind of victory over the French and took the Baron Dieskeau, their General, prisoner; yet we suffered very greatly in the battle; and the taking of the French General, probably, was the saving of his army; for by telling a lie to our army, viz. that the French were in continual expectation of being greatly enforced by a large body that marched another way, and had appointed to meet them near that place, our army was prevented from pursuing the enemy after they had repelled them; which if they had done, they might have been under great advantages to have cut 'em off, and prevented the return of almost all of them to Crown Point; which could be no otherwise than through the water, in their bateaux. Our army never proceeded any further than the place of the engagement, but having built a fort there, near *Lake George,* alias *Lake St. Sacrament,* after they had built another near Hudson's River, about fourteen miles on this side, and left garrisons, lately returned. As also has the army under Gen. [William] Shirley, who went with a design against Niagara, after having built some vessels of force in the Lake Ontario, and strengthened the fortifications at Oswego and sent for the remains of General Braddock's army to Albany, there to go into winter quarters. The governors of the several provinces, in the latter part of the last month, had a meeting to confer together concerning our warlike affairs, and to agree on a plan of operations, to be recommended to the government at home, for the next year. But I have heard nothing of their determinations. The Indians have not done much mischief on the frontiers of New England, since our army have been above us; but have been dreadful in their ravages in the back settlements of Virginia and Pennsylvania.

It is apparent that the ministry at home miss it very much in sending over British forces to fight with Indians in America, and in sending British officers to have the command of our American forces. Let them send us arms, ammunition, money and shipping; and let New England men manage the business their own way; who alone understand it. And to appoint British officers over them is nothing but a hindrance and discouragement to 'em. Let 'em be well supplied and supported and defended by sea, and then let 'em go forth under their own officers, and manage in their own way, as they did in the expedition against Cape Breton. All the provinces in America seem to be fully sensible that New England men are the only men to be employed against Canada: as I had opportunity abundantly to observe in my late journey to New York, New Jersey and Philadelphia. However, we ought to remember that neither New England men nor any other, are anything unless God be with us. And when we have done all at finding fault with measures taken and instruments employed, we can't expect prosperity unless the accursed thing be removed from our camp [Josh. 7].

God has lately frowned on my family in taking away a faithful servant,[3] who was a great help to us. Two of my children have been under threatening infirmities, but are something better. I desire your prayers for us all. My wife joins with me in affectionate and respectful salutations to you and Mrs. Erskine. I am, reverend and dear Sir,

Your obliged brother and affectionate friend,
Jonathan Edwards.

3. This individual is not further identified.

213. TO SAMUEL BROWN

(MAR, vol. 32, p. 705, ALS, one quarto leaf.)

*   *   *

Stockbridge, January 30, 1756

Province of Massachusetts to Jonathan Edwards of Stockbridge	D[ebto]r
To timber for building of fort about the minister's house in Stockbridge, which cost me 20*s* L. M.	£1-0-0
To 180 meals to Indians that wrought at the fort, at 4*d*	£3-0-0

£4-0-0

Errors excepted.
Jonathan Edwards.[1]

To Mr. Samuel Brown of Stockbridge
Sir,
    Please on my behalf to exhibit the preceding account and get the same made payable to yourself. So you will oblige your

Friend and servant,
Jonathan Edwards.

214. TO PRES. AARON BURR

This letter is singular in being devoted almost entirely to family news. It reflects a sanguine mood, which doubtless encouraged Edwards' daughter Esther to visit Stockbridge shortly afterward. To her dismay, she found the town anything but peaceful, as her father had described.

(Firestone Library, Edwards Papers, ALS, facsimile of the original. Esther Burr's stay at Stockbridge was Aug. 30 to Sept 22, 1756; she gives a graphic account of it in Burr, pp. 219–25.)

*   *   *

Stockbridge, March 14, 1756

Rev. and Dear Sir,
    I received your letter of February 10 the day before yesterday; for which I thank you. We rejoice in the smiles of heaven on you and your

---

1. Here Justice of the Peace Joseph Dwight notarized the account, signed Feb. 5, 1756.

family, and particularly on the late addition[1] to your family and the comfortable circumstances of both mother and child. For these favors we would bless God.

I had before heard of the birth of your son two ways, one by a letter from daughter [Esther Edwards] Burr before your return from Philadelphia, another by Dr. [Samuel] Reynolds, whom I saw at Windsor with Mr. Henry Dwight (the Brigadier's son) in their return from their long journey for Mr. Dwight's health. They came through Newark a few days after your wife's delivery. This Mr. Dwight is since dead. He died a fortnight ago last Saturday morning at Springfield, the same week that I met him at Windsor, at Mr. [Joseph] Perry's, on Monday. I was then at Windsor on a visit to my father and was gone two sabbaths: one of which I spent at Windsor, the other at West Springfield. I found my father more broken than ever I saw him, but yet he knew me, and was capable of some degree of conversation, and was able to walk a little; my mother infirm, but holds the powers of her mind unbroken. Sister [Esther] Hopkins was very sorrowful, and in a low state of health. She hoped for a letter from you in her affliction.[2] Her son at Hadley was married about a month ago to Mrs. [Chester] Williams, the former minister's widow.[3] They have as yet no man on probation at Springfield.

We in this place have of late been free from alarms, through supposed appearances of Canada Indians, as I think have the people on all our frontiers in New England. Brig. [Joseph] Dwight and his wife have talked much about moving away, and seemed determined upon it, the winter past, but he has been long absent at Boston; possibly soliciting for a post in Gov. [William] Shirley's army. If he obtains one, he will probably leave his family here.

We are all through mercy in a tolerable state of health. I saw daughter [Mary] Dwight at Springfield. She gave an account that her family were well. I don't know but Mr. [Timothy] Dwight, [Jr.], your brother, may go into the war this year, though I have nothing to certify me of it.

I desire you would send word when you would have Timmy come down. If the vacancy is like to be early this year, perhaps it will be needless for him to come till that is past.

1. Aaron Burr, Jr., born Feb. 6, 1756, who later became vice president of the United States and participated in the infamous duel with Alexander Hamilton.

2. Rev. Samuel Hopkins of West Springfield had died on Oct. 5, 1755.

3. Samuel Hopkins (1729–1811). Marrying the widow of a deceased minister (in this case, Chester Williams) was a time-honored way to succeed him in the pulpit.

Please to convey the enclosed to Gov. [Jonathan] Belcher.[4]

Give our love to your wife, and to little Sally, and remember us in your prayers. I am, dear Sir,

Your affectionate friend and father,
Jonathan Edwards.

215. TO THE REVEREND WILLIAM McCULLOCH

Edwards discusses a recent publication on prophecy, developments with John Brainerd and Gideon Hawley, who are currently missionaries to the Indians, and the relative British and French strategic positions in North America.

(Trask Library, ALS, two folio leaves; Dwight ms. transcript, four quarto leaves. Published in Dwight ed., *1*, 553–55.)

*   *   *

Stockbridge, April 10, 1756

Rev. and Dear Sir,

I thank you for your favor of August 1755, with Mr. Imrie's *Letter*,[1] which came to hand in the latter part of the last month. It recommends a man, especially a minister of the gospel, to me, to see in him evidences of a disposition to be searching into the prophecies of Scripture, relating to the future advancement of Christ's kingdom on earth: it looks as though he were a man of concern for Christ's kingdom and interest in the world, and were one of those who took pleasure in the stones, and favored the dust of Zion. But it has proved by events, that many divines that have been of this character, have been over-forward to fix the times and seasons, which the Father hath put in his own power. However, I will not positively charge Mr. Imrie with this, before I see what he has to say in proof of those things which he has advanced. I think that neither I, nor any other person that knows no more than what is contained in his letter, of the reasons that he builds his opinions upon, have any opportunity to judge of those opinions. And therefore, I should think it a pity that his private letter to Mr. [William] Hogg was published to the world, before his reasons were prepared for the press. This letter has been reprinted in Boston, but coming

---

4. The enclosure has not been located.

1. See David Imrie, *A Letter from the Reverend Mr. David Imrie, Minister of the Gospel at St. Mungo, in Annandale. To a Gentleman* [William Hogg] *in the City of Edinburgh* (Edinburgh, 1755; rep. Boston, 1756).

abroad with so little mention of the grounds of his opinion, gives occasion to the profane to reproach and ridicule it, and its author.

With respect to Mr. [John] Brainerd and Mr. [Gideon] Hawley, and their Indians, concerning which you desire to be informed: the Correspondents have altered their determinations from time to time with respect to Mr. Brainerd and his Indians. They seemed inclined at first to their removal to Wawwomung, alias Wyoming; and then to Onohquaga; and then to Wyoming again. And finally, about a twelvemonth ago, they wholly dismissed him from his employ as a missionary to the Indians, and pastor to the Indian church at Bethel. I can't say I am fully satisfied in their conduct in doing this so hastily; nor do I pretend to know so much concerning the reasons of their conduct as to have sufficient grounds positively to condemn their proceeding. However, that congregation is not wholly left as sheep without a shepherd, but are in part committed to the care of Mr. William Tennent, [Jr.]; who lives not far off and is a faithful zealous minister; who visits them, and preaches to 'em once a week; but I think not often upon the sabbath. The last fall, I was in New Jersey and Philadelphia, and was present at a meeting of the Correspondents when Mr. Tennent gave an agreeable account of the then-present state of those Indians with respect to religion; and also of their being in better circumstances as to those lands than they had been. Mr. Brainerd was then at Newark with his family; where he had been preaching as a probationer for settlement, ever since Mr. [Aaron] Burr's dismission from that place on account of his business as President of the College. But whether Mr. Brainerd is settled, or like to settle there, I have not heard. At the forementioned meeting of the Correspondents, I used some arguments to induce them to reestablish Mr. Brainerd in his former employ with his Indians, and to send them to Onohquaga. But I soon found it would be fruitless to urge the matter. What was chiefly insisted on as an insuperable obstacle to Mr. Brainerd's going with his family so far into the wilderness, was Mrs. [Experience Lyon] Brainerd's very infirm state. Whether there was indeed any sufficient objection to such a removal at that time or no, divine providence has since that time so ordered the state and consequences of the war subsisting here in America, that insuperable obstacles are laid in the way of their removal, either to Onohquaga, Wyoming, or any other parts of America that way. The French by their indefatigable endeavor with the nation of the Delawares (so called from their ancient seat, about Delaware River, though now chiefly residing on Susquehanna River and its branches) have stirred them up to make war on the English; and dreadful have been the ravages and desolations they have made of late on the back parts of Pennsylvania and New Jersey. They are the principal nation inhabiting the parts about Susquehanna River, on which both Wyoming and Onohquaga stand. The latter indeed is above the bounds of their country; but yet not very far from them: and the Delaware Indians are frequently there, as they go to and fro. On which account, there is great danger that Mr. Hawley's mission and ministry there will be entirely broke up. Mr. Hawley came from thence about two months ago (with one of my sons [Jonathan, Jr.], about ten years old, who had been there with them near a twelvemonth, to learn the Mohawk language). He has since been to Boston to consult the Commissioners for Indian Affairs, that have employed him, and returned: and yesterday went from my house to meet some of his Indians at an appointed time and place in the Mohawk country, to determine with them whether it will be safe for him to return to abide with them. If not, yet he will be under the pay of the Commissioners till next fall, and the issue be seen of the two expeditions now in prosecution, one against Crown Point, the other against the French forts at Frontenac and Niagara near Lake Ontario; which may possibly make a great alteration as to the state of the war with the Indians. If Mr. Hawley determines not to return to Onohquaga this spring, he will probably go as chaplain to the Indians in Gen. [William] Shirley's army, in the expedition to Lake Ontario.[2]

You speak of the vast superiority of the numbers of the English in America to those of the French, and that some therefore think the settlements of the former are in no great danger from the latter. Though it be true that the French are twenty times less than we are in number; yet it may be a question, whether other things they exceed us in, when all jointly considered, won't more than countervail all our excess of numbers. They vastly exceed us in subtlety and intrigue, in vigilance and activity, in speed and secrecy; in acquaintance with the continent of North America, in all parts west of the British settlements, for many hundred leagues, the rivers, lakes, mountains, the avenues and passes; and also in the influence they have among the various tribes and nations of Indians; and in their constant care, skill and indefatigable diligence in managing them; to alienate 'em from

---

2. Hawley was ordered to report for duty as chaplain in June 1756, and took part in the campaign against Crown Point. After release, he set out again for his mission in December, but was forced to turn back because of severe weather. He reached Sheffield and spent the rest of the winter studying with Samuel Hopkins. SIB, 9, 398.

the English, attach 'em firmly to themselves, and employ them as their tools: besides the vast advantage they have in time of war, in being all united under the absolute command of one man, the Governor of Canada; while we are divided into a great many distinct governments, independent one of another; and in some respects of clashing interests: which unspeakably clogs and embarrasses our affairs, and makes us, though a great, yet an unwieldy, unmanageable body, and an easy prey to our vigilant, secret, subtle, swift and active (though comparatively small) enemy.

As to a description of the situation of those parts you mention, I can give you no better than you have in maps that abound in Great Britain. With respect to the situation of Stockbridge; it is not in the province of New York as you have been informed, but in the utmost border of the province of the Massachusetts on the west, next to the province of New York; about forty miles west of Connecticut River, about twenty-five miles east of Hudson's River, and about thirty-five miles southeast from Albany. A place exposed in this time of war. Four persons were killed here in the beginning of September 1754, by Canada Indians; which occasioned a great alarm to us and great part of New England.[3] Since this we have had many alarms; but God has preserved us. I desire your prayers that we may still be preserved, and that God would be with me and my family and people, and bless us in all respects.

My wife and family join with me in their respects to you and yours. I am, dear Sir,

Your affectionate brother and servant,
Jonathan Edwards.

216. TO ABIGAIL WILLIAMS SERGEANT DWIGHT

(John Rylands Univ. Library of Manchester, ALS, one quarto leaf, addressed on verso to Mrs. Abigail Dwight in Stockbridge.)

* * *

[Stockbridge,] May 16, 1756

Madam,

This is to pray you to send me word, whether you are about to send out a team to Claverack for goods; and if you are, whether it be prob-

---

3. The attack on Stockbridge occurred Sept. 1, 1754. See John Worthington to Josiah Willard, MAR, v. 54, pp. 323–26; JE's petition of Oct. 22, 1754, MAR, v. 13, pp. 581–82; and *JMHR*, *31*, 10, Nov. 9, 1754. The Indians were Schagticokes (Segwick and Marquand, *Stockbridge*, pp. 73–75).

able there would be room in the cart at its return for some goods of mine of perhaps about 200 weight, if I should bear a proportionable part of the charge.

Herein you will oblige,

> Your most humble servant,
> Jonathan Edwards.

217. TO THE REVEREND JOSEPH BELLAMY

Bellamy, who was used to having only divinity students in his spacious home, took in a contingent of Indian boys to teach. To be sure that he took the proper approach in this new venture, he wrote to his mentor for instructions. This is Edwards' reply, an abbreviated educational plan, giving particular attention to Bellamy's questions about arithmetic, the catechism, and the use of the Bible.

(Beinecke Library, ALS, one folio leaf, addressed on verso to the Reverend Mr. Joseph Bellamy at Bethlehem. Published in *NEQ* 1 [1928], 240–42; Faust and Johnson, pp. 408–09. See Bellamy's reply of May 31, 1756, Trask Library, Dwight ms. transcript, one quarto leaf; published in Dwight ed., *1*, 555–56.)

* * *

Stockbridge, [June 1756]

Rev. and Dear Sir,

I should be glad that you would use thorough endeavors with the boys to teach 'em arithmetic; let there be a thorough trial with them whether they can learn. If they can't, I shall think it is hardly worth the while to send 'em abroad under the notion of giving them an extraordinary education. I would also propose the following things, viz. that pains be taken with 'em to teach 'em the English tongue, to learn 'em the meaning of English words and what the name of everything is in English; and as far as may be, teach 'em the meaning of the English that they read, and make 'em turn it into Indian. And that they be taught to pray; that you write out for them various forms of prayer, and make 'em understand them, and turn them often into Indian. And to teach 'em the Assembly's Catechism,[1] and endeavor as far as may be to make 'em to understand it. To ask 'em questions of the Scripture history, not only the lessons they read, but of the main things in the general history of the Bible in their order. I wish you would send

1. Probably the Westminster Shorter Catechism, first published in London and Edinburgh, 1647.

to [New] York to Mr. [William] Smith, or somebody that understands, and get some plain maps of the land of Canaan, and places adjacent, and if you don't choose to have 'em for your own for the use of your children, I will be at the cost of 'em for the use of Mr. [Isaac] Hollis' school; and show them where the places are they read of in the Bible, or that you tell 'em of, from the Scripture history. And also teach 'em a little of the chronology of the Scripture: how long the flood was after the creation; how long the calling of Abraham was after the flood, etc.

Mr. Hollis expects that I should give him an account very particularly of the progress of his boys. And as I have given him an account of my putting these boys under your care, as giving them great advantage for learning, so I am concerned that I may be able to give him a good account, that shall be encouraging to him. I find there are some good folks here, that can inquire how much the boys have learned at your house in arithmetic, etc. and can make observations and reflections on the profit they obtain by going to you, and can put the question whether there be anything to answer the extraordinary expense and trouble, and ask whether they might not have profited as much here. But you must give no hints that I have told you of it. 'Tis with a vast deal of difficulty that I have at last got the boys away after manifold objecting, hiding, and skulking, to avoid going. I have sent one of my books to the library at New Haven: I would pray you to take care to convey it.

My love and service to Mrs. Bellamy. I am, Sir,

> Your cordial friend and brother,
> Jonathan Edwards.

P.S. I suppose Isaac[2] will bring down two coats, and that there will be no need to get him a new one this winter; and therefore I would not have a new one made for him, unless you see it absolutely necessary; as I suppose it will not be.

218. TO THE REVEREND GIDEON HAWLEY

Pessimism prevails in this letter, as Edwards cites one defeat after another, with none of his usual "signs of hope." The message could scarcely have been calculated to raise the spirits of the recipient, particularly since it contained the wild rumor that a large French army was headed his way. Gideon Hawley, now army chaplain on the Crown Point campaign, was already discouraged. Perhaps the letter was intended as commiseration or simply a confession of

---

2. Probably an Indian or slave; not further identified.

frustrations. At any rate, Edwards acknowledges his young friend's communication and keeps in touch.

(MHS, S. P. Savage Papers, ALS, two quarto leaves, addressed on verso to the Reverend Mr. Gideon Hawley, Chaplain to Col. Gridley's Regt. at Lake George. Published in part in *PMHS* 43 [1909–10], 651. On Hawley, see SIB, *12*, 392–411.)

*   *   *

Stockbridge, October 9, 1756

Rev. and Dear Sir,

I thank you for yours of September 20, which contains very affecting accounts. God indeed is remarkably frowning upon us everywhere: our enemies get up above us very high, and we are brought down very low; they are the head, and we are the tail. God is making us, with all our superiority in numbers, to become the object of our enemies' almost continual triumphs and insults. Many things that have happened doubtless make us very contemptible in their eyes, and in the eyes of almost all nations of Indians on the continent.

And in Europe things don't go much better, that I can understand. I think it is now put out of all doubt, after many contradictory accounts, that Minorca was surrendered to the French on the 29th day of last June; principally through the wretched cowardice or treachery of Admiral [John] Byng. This, with the taking of Oswego[1] with its circumstances, will tend mightily to animate and encourage the French nation, and give 'em vast advantages, and weaken and dishearten the English, and make 'em contemptible in the eyes of the nations of Europe. I see very little good effect of the awful frowns of heaven upon us.

I am just now returned from a journey to Windsor and Northampton; and by what I observed, instead of a spirit of a humiliation and penitent supplication to heaven, a spirit of discontent, murmuring and mutual jealousy prevails, finding fault with rulers, officers, etc. together with great degrees of discouragement.

This province, on a motion from Lord Loudon, have ordered 1,000 men to be ready to march on My Lord's call, from this county and the county of Worcester, to join the army. The last sabbath a post was sent

1. Forts Oswego and Ontario were captured and destroyed by the French under Montcalm, Aug. 13–14, 1755. See Edward P. Hamilton, *The French and Indian Wars* (New York, 1962), pp. 280–82.

from My Lord to the colonels in these counties, informing that he had received advice from Gen. [John] Winslow, that all the French regulars and the whole power of Canada were in motion to attack our camps; ordering them forthwith to send the 1,000 men; and I suppose they are now just ready to march. Some of our captives who escaped from Canada are very lately come into No. 4,[2] on Connecticut River, that say 13,000 are coming against you, to inform of which a post was sent to Lord Loudon this week.

What will become of us, God only knows. It looks as if something great, and perhaps almost decisive, were to happen before winter.

Let us unite in earnest, humble cries to the God of armies and the God of sovereign and infinite mercy, which alone can be our hope.

My family, through mercy are well and give their service to you. My daughter [Mary] Dwight of Northampton is lying in, and very weak, and we left the infant sick and like to die.[3]

I desire your prayers. I am, dear Sir,

Your obliged brother and servant,
Jonathan Edwards.

219. TO THE REVEREND THOMAS FOXCROFT

(Beinecke Library, ALS, one quarto leaf, addressed on verso to the Reverend Mr. Thomas Foxcroft, Minister of the Gospel, in Boston.)

* * *

Stockbridge, October 28, 1756

Rev. and Honored Sir,

In addition to all the innumerable favors with which you have obliged me, I ask this of you, that you would take the care of the conveyance of this packet to Mr. [John] Gillies. I should be glad if it might be sent as speedily and as safely as may be. I fear my last packet for Scotland miscarried. I have lately received a letter from Mr. [John] Erskine, in which he says nothing of receiving my last letter to him; and Mr. [Aaron] Burr informs me that Mr. [William] McCulloch complains he has had no letter from me in two years.

2. No. 4 was a post at the present Charlestown, New Hampshire, a focal defense point, illustrated by Gen. Amherst's order to cut a road through the wilderness of what is now Vermont, to it from Crown Point, New York, in 1759. Mary F. Charlton, "The Crown Point Road," *Vermont Historical Society Proceedings*, n.s., 2 (1931), 163–93.

3. Erastus Dwight, who lived until 1821. Solomon Clark, *Antiquities, Historicals and Graduates of Northampton* (Northampton, 1882), pp. 121–22.

Our affairs at Stockbridge have been attended with more quietness of late than in some times past. But yet the war is in many respects an occasion of unhappiness to our affairs; especially as most of our Indian men that are capable of it have been gone into the war, and are still many of them absent with our soldiers, where they are exposed to all manner of temptations. But this is but one among innumerable calamities which are the consequence of the present war, in which God is in a most awful manner frowning upon us, and greatly threatening us with general ruin.

I hope, Sir, you will remember us before God, [who] live in a place so much exposed. Present my respects to your family, and to Mrs. [Edward] Bromfield[1] and her family. I am, honored Sir,

> Your most obliged son and servant,
> Jonathan Edwards.

220. TO TIMOTHY EDWARDS

Edwards dispatches funds to help finance his son's senior year at the College of New Jersey.

(Beinecke Library, ALS, one quarto leaf; Trask Library, transcript in an unknown hand, two-thirds of one folio leaf.)

* * *

Stockbridge, November 4, 1756

Dear Son,

I have ordered Mr. [Abraham] Fonda to deliver to Mr. Peter Livingston of New York, the value of three doubloons full weight, i.e. seventeen pounds eight shillings [New] York money, for you, and have wrote to Mr. Livingston to convey it to you, together with a pair of stockings, which we send you.

We are all through mercy in comfortable state of health, and not so much afraid of the enemy of late. We left your sister [Mary] Dwight in a low state. She had had a very weak lying-in, and her new-born child, when we came away, was very like to die; but hope 'tis not dead, because we have heard nothing since.[1]

---

1. Edward Bromfield, her husband, friend of JE and a Commissioner for Indian Affairs, had died Apr. 10, 1756 (*Boston Gazette*, Apr. 19, 1756). The Edwardses often stayed at the Bromfield home when visiting Boston.

1. Erastus Dwight.

I would have you send a particular account of your state at Princeton, and concerning your studies, etc. Commending you to the care of a gracious God, I remain

> Your very affectionate father,
> Jonathan Edwards.

221. TO LIEUT. GOV. SPENCER PHIPS ET AL.

This letter is an urgent plea for soldiers to protect Stockbridge from attack by the French and hostile Indians. No action was taken, so another petition followed on April 18, 1757, requesting a minimum of thirty men. Existing forts were deemed understaffed and inadequate. To show that the dire conditions described in this petition were not exaggerated, a second was sent, written and signed by Joseph Dwight, Edwards, and two sons of Ephraim Williams, Sr., Josiah and Elijah. In a time of crisis, personal differences were put aside in the need to unite for common defense.

(MAR, Milit. vol. 76, p. 134, ALS, one folio leaf, inscribed on verso: "To Lye on the Table." Second petition, MAR, vol. 117, pp. 286–87. For action on petitions, see *JMHR* 32, II [1756], 353, 391, 400; 33, II [1757], 269, 405, 444. Boston's final allowance for Stockbridge was sixteen men "and no more," but Connecticut was asked to send thirty-two.)

* * *

Stockbridge, November 16, 1756

To the Honorable Spencer Phips, Esq., Lieutenant Governor and Commander-in-Chief in and over His Majesty's Province of the Massachusetts Bay, the Honorable Council and House of Representatives, in General Court assembled:

The petition of the English inhabitants of the town of Stockbridge humbly showeth: that there now subsisting an open war between the English and French, and our enemies in Canada having a so much greater force than ever before, and being (as we have reason to think) now so well furnished and provided, and so considerable a part of them being so near us; and being flushed with their late successes, and it appearing to us not probable that the whole of the forces of our active enemies with these circumstances will be wholly still till next summer: also apprehending that the enemy may be more likely to look towards Stockbridge for having been provoked by what they have suffered from the Stockbridge Indians this year; especially if the enemy, by any means, should understand that the town is destitute of soldiers; that our Indians have gone into the wars both on this and the last year on repeated encouragement and assurances given by Gen. [William] Shirley that effective care should be taken, that Stockbridge should be defended with English soldiers; our request therefore is (the time being near expired for which the billet of soldiers here has been allowed) that Your Honors and the Honorable Court, if in your wisdom you shall think fit, would allow that a number of soldiers should still be subsisted here for the defense of the place; [and your petitioners shall as in duty bound ever pray, etc.][1]

Jonathan Edwards
Timothy Woodbridge
Samuel Brown
Josiah Jones
Stephen Nash
John Willard
Elihu Parsons
Joseph Woodbridge.

222. TO THE REVEREND THOMAS FOXCROFT

This letter was accompanied by the following letter, of the same date, to Edward Wigglesworth. In both, Edwards deplores the doctrinal declension of the times. *Original Sin* is almost completed and *Concerning the End for Which God Created the World* and *The Nature of True Virtue* are already written. He again seeks Foxcroft's expert editorial assistance and oversight of publication for these works.

Gideon Hawley's Boston visit with this letter was to prove pivotal in his life. Instead of returning to New York, he was persuaded to become minister in Mashpee, Massachusetts, as well as supervisor of nearby Indian preachers, roles which would occupy him for the next fifty years.

(Beinecke Library, ALS, one folio leaf, addressed on verso to the Reverend Mr. Thomas Foxcroft. According to a notation, the letter was received per Mr. Hawley on Feb. 26, 1756, and answered per the same on Mar. 28.)

*   *   *

1. The final phrase in brackets is in Timothy Woodbridge's hand.

Stockbridge, February 11, 1757

Rev. and Honored Sir,

I thank you for your favor of January 10 and for your care in conveying the letter from Scotland, with the Serious Call to United Prayer to God at This Day.[1] I am glad such a thing is proposed, and wish that many may heartily comply with it. I have here enclosed a letter I have presumed to write to Dr. [Edward] Wigglesworth, and sent it open that you may see it; which I desire you would seal, and safely deliver or convey to him.

I cannot in the least doubt but that the guilt of the land (which already is great, and awfully testified against by heaven at this day) will be greatly increased by the neglect, if none should now appear to attempt a full vindication of the doctrine of Christ's divinity. I have heard that the ministers your way showed themselves much concerned, when Dr. Gill's book against infant baptism was published here, and got Mr. Clark to write an answer;[2] but how small a matter was that in comparison of the error now broached, and so boldly maintained, with an open challenge to the ministers of the country to maintain the contrary doctrine if they can? And what a mighty ado was made all over the country, in publishing testimonies from the press against Mr. [George] Whitefield's itinerant preaching? And will all be silent now, as though the most open denial of the divinity of our Savior, and endeavoring to root the doctrine out of the country, were a light matter in comparison of the other?

I wish that at this day, when every evangelical doctrine is run down, and such bold attempts are made to drive all out of doors, the press mayn't labor only with performances that are leveled against Christ, and the religion he taught. I should particularly be glad that Mr. [Joseph] Bellamy's late sermon, which I think is well done, to defend the great doctrine of justification by Christ's righteousness (which has been especially impugned by Dr. [Jonathan] Mayhew) might be reprinted in Boston.[3] I have sent one of 'em to Mr. [Samuel] Kneeland,

1. No information on this publication has been found.

2. John Gill, *The Argument from Apostolic Tradition, in Favour of Infant-Baptism . . . Consider'd* (London, 1751); Peter Clark, *A Defence of the Divine Right of Infant-Baptism* (Boston, 1752).

3. Joseph Bellamy, *The Law, Our Schoolmaster. A Sermon Preached at Litchfield, June 8, 1756, before the Association of Litchfield* (New Haven, 1756). The sermon was not reprinted. Jonathan Mayhew's critique of justification by faith alone is in *Sermons upon the Following Subjects, Viz. On Hearing the Word* (Boston, 1755).

with some corrections, proposing to him to reprint it, if he durst run the venture of having vent for the impression. What he will think of it, I can't tell; perhaps he may ask some of the ministers' advice.

I have lately been writing a defense of the doctrine of original sin; wherein I have largely handled the principal arguments I know of for that doctrine; and have particularly considered everything, of any consequence, in Dr. Taylor's book against that doctrine;[4] a book that has done more to root out the gospel, in all this western part of New England, than any other book. I have almost prepared this for the press. I have also written two other discourses, one on *God's End in Creating the World;* the other concerning *The Nature of True Virtue.* As it appeared to me, the modern opinions which prevail concerning these two things, stand very much as foundations of that fashionable scheme of divinity, which seems to have become almost universal. My discourse on virtue is principally designed against that notion of virtue maintained by My Lord Shaftesbury, [Francis] Hutcheson, and [George] Turnbull; which seems to be most in vogue at this day, so far as I can perceive; which notion is calculated to show that all mankind are naturally disposed to virtue, and are without any native depravity. My discourse on original sin will be about as large as my book on free will; and the other two discourses will make another volume something less.

I would pray you, Sir, to excuse me, in my proposing to you, and requesting of you to correct the press, if it would not be too great a burden in your advanced years and infirm state. I am sensible that my proposing any such thing to you needs an apology, especially after I have burdened you so much in this way in times past, and have received so many and great favors of this kind. I know I shall have no reason to be displeased if you decline what I propose and that you rather will have reason to be displeased with me for proposing it. My chief apology for asking you is, that I know not where else to go: I have not acquaintance or interest with the younger ministers sufficient to encourage me to apply to 'em. I am sensible my publications are not looked upon by all, with that candor which I have from you. Such as think me too forward, and too apt to think the world stands in need of my instructions, will not, with a very good will, put to their hand to assist me. If you, Sir, decline the inspection of the press, as what would be too great a burden, I desire that you would at least assist me by your

4. John Taylor, *The Scripture-Doctrine of Original Sin, Proposed to Free and Candid Examination* (London, 1740). For a discussion, see *Works, 3,* 16–20, 68–70.

advice where to go, and whom to apply to; and if another undertakes, that still you would have some care and inspection of the affair. I have thoughts, if God permit, of coming to Boston some time in the spring; when I may perhaps bring the copy of my defense of the doctrine of original sin.

We have had less drunkenness of late among the Indians than for many years.

I would desire you, Sir, to send me word by the bearer whether there is like to be an opportunity of conveyance to Scotland in a short time.

My respects to your family. Desiring an interest in your prayers, I am, Honored Sir,

Your respectful and obliged son and servant,
Jonathan Edwards.

P.S. (February 17.) Mr. [Gideon] Hawley proves unexpectedly to be the bearer of this letter. He has seemed of late to be at a great loss in his own mind as to his duty with respect to his mission to Onohquagas. His long absence from his Indians has been an unhappy thing; as in other respects, so I fear in that, that it has considerably disengaged and unhinged his mind with respect to that business. I have conversed with him very freely and fully about the matter. I believe he is concerned to know his duty. I wish that he may be directed, and that the Commissioners may be directed in what they shall say and do with regard to the affair.

223. TO DR. EDWARD WIGGLESWORTH

This letter presents Edwards as guardian of the faith. He was alarmed at a footnote in a published sermon by Jonathan Mayhew, pastor of the West Church, Boston, that cast aspersions on the traditional doctrine of the Trinity. His fears increased with the republication of Thomas Emlyn's *Humble Inquiry*, with a preface by a "layman," who challenged theologians to refute the Arian doctrine.

Edwards writes to Wigglesworth, pleading with him to defend orthodoxy against these attacks. Wigglesworth, the honored first Hollis Professor of Divinity at Harvard, had led the college's protest against Whitefield, but that had been more than ten years earlier. In 1757 he was regarded as a strong Calvinist; his respected voice would command public attention.

Wigglesworth declined in a courteous reply, stating that he had already upheld the doctrine of biblical inspiration, which he considered more basic, against criticism by Mayhew. Furthermore, in the Thursday lectures, Boston ministers had leaped to defend the deity of Christ. Controversy was counterproductive; the discussion would die down, if it was ignored. Edwards submitted this letter to Foxcroft for his information and to aid any action Foxcroft might take before forwarding it (see the preceding letter). Foxcroft reported that recent challenges to trinitarianism had been called to the attention of the Harvard Overseers, but no action had been taken. Edwards, however, was concerned that unrestrained rationalism applied to Christian doctrine would cause great damage if it were not counteracted. Thus, the Stockbridge seer anticipated consequences that affected New England churches for the next century.

(The mss., once in the CL, are now lost. The letter, with selections from Wigglesworth's reply, is published in Joseph S. Clark, *Historical Sketch of the Congregational Churches in Massachusetts, from 1620–1858* [Boston, 1858], pp. 180–85.)

* * *

Stockbridge, February 11, 1757

Rev. and Dear Sir:

I can't assign any particular acquaintance as my warrant for troubling you with these lines; not being one of them that have been favored with opportunities for such an advantage. I only write as a subject and friend of the same Lord, and a follower and fellow-disciple of the same Jesus. A regard to his interests has made me uneasy ever since I read Dr. [Jonathan] Mayhew's late book, sometime the last year, and saw that marginal note of his, wherein he ridicules the doctrine of the Trinity.[1]

And my uneasiness was increased after I had wrote to Mr. [Thomas] Foxcroft upon it, and fully expressed my sentiments to him concerning the call of God to ministers that way, or others whose business it was to teach the doctrines of Christianity, to appear publicly on this occasion in defense of this doctrine; and he, in reply, informed me that the same affair had been proposed and considered at the Board of Overseers; and in the issue nothing concluded to be done. Very lately Mr. Emlyn's book has fallen into my hands,[2] published in New England by one that calls himself a layman; who, in his dedication to the ministers

1. Mayhew, *Sermons upon the Following Subjects, Viz. On Hearing the Word*, pp. 268, 269n.
2. Thomas Emlyn, *An Humble Inquiry into the Scripture-account of Jesus Christ; or, A Short Argument concerning His Deity and Glory, according to the Gospel* (5th ed., Boston, 1756). For background, see Charles W. Akers, *Called unto Liberty: A Life of Jonathan Mayhew, 1720–1766* (Cambridge, Mass., Harvard Univ. Press, 1964), pp. 117–21, 258, n. 13.

of the country, gives them an open and bold (though a very subtle and artful) challenge to answer that book, and defend the proper deity of Christ, if they can. Since I have read this book I am abundantly confirmed that my opinion, signified to Mr. Foxcroft, was right; and that the call of God that some one should appear in open defense of this doctrine, is very loud and plain; and that an universal neglect of it in the churches of New England on this occasion, will be imputed by the head of the church, whose glory is so struck at, as a lukewarmness that will be very displeasing.

Though I live so much at a distance, yet I know so much of the state of the country, that I am persuaded it will be of very bad consequence. This piece, by many, will be looked upon as invincible. It will be concluded that those who maintain the divinity of Christ are afraid to engage, being conscious that they are unable to defend their cause; and the adversary will triumph, and that cause will more and more prevail.

Now, Sir, I humbly conceive that you, above all others in the land, are called to engage in this cause. You are set for the instruction of our youth in divinity in the principal seminary of learning; and it will be among them especially that these pernicious principles will be like to gain ground. Something from you will be more regarded and attended to than [from] any other person.

I have heard say that your health is not firm; which may possibly be an objection with you against engaging in a laborious controversy, which, if once begun, may possibly be drawn out to a great length; and probably spending your time in controversy may be much against your inclination. But yet you doubtless will allow that the case may be so, that Christians may be evidently called, in adverse providences, to engage in very irksome and laborious services, and to run considerable ventures in the cause of their Lord, trusting in him for strength and support; as men, in a just war for their king, in many cases doubt not of their being called to great fatigues, and to very great ventures even of life itself. And shall all stand by at such a day as this, under the testimonies of God's anger for our corruptions, which are already so great, and see the cause of Christ trampled on, and the chief dignity and glory of the King of Zion directly and boldly struck at, with a challenge to others to defend it if they can, and be silent, every one excusing himself from the difficulty and fatigue of a spiritual warfare?

I live one side, far out of the way; I know not what the view of the ministers of the country is; I can only judge what the case requires. I think Zion calls for help; I speak as one of her sons. If nothing be done, I dread the consequences. I entreat you, Sir, for Christ's sake, not lightly to refuse what I have proposed and requested, and forgive the freedom which has been used by, honored Sir, with great esteem and respect,

Your son and servant,
Jonathan Edwards.

224. TO THE REVEREND JOSEPH BELLAMY

Edwards thanks Bellamy for the books he has sent and offers suggestions for dealing with the Indian boys he has taken into his home.

(CL, ALS, one quarto leaf, addressed on verso to the Reverend Mr. Joseph Bellamy in Bethlehem.)

* * *

Stockbridge, February 12, 1757

Rev. Sir,

I heartily thank you for the books. What you have sent, both of Cudworth and Tindal, are spoken of in the title pages as being the first volume, as though there were another volume of each.[1] If you have the remaining volumes, I should be glad you would bring 'em when you come in the spring, and also bring Doddridge.[2] I have lately wrote largely to you, and sent you a "Catalogue of Books," which you say nothing of.[3] I suppose therefore you had not then received. I should have inserted in the "Catalogue" Dr. Leland's *Answer to Tindal* in two

1. Ralph Cudworth, *The True Intellectual System of the World* (London, 1678; rep. 1743); Matthew Tindal, *Christianity as Old as the Creation* (London, 1730). Each work comprised several parts, published in one volume, which perhaps accounts for JE's confusion.

2. Possibly Doddridge's *Family Expositor.*

3. The Catalog of Books JE mentions is not extant; however, an earlier list from 1751 for teaching Indian children, perhaps drawn up for William Pepperrell (Beinecke Library), includes the following titles and may have been similar to the one sent to Bellamy: "Samuel Johnsons English Dictionary/ The newest & best Abridgement of Boyles Lectures/ The last vol. of Lardners Credibility of the Gospel History being the 12 vol. of the 2d Part/ The 4th Vol. of Warburtons divine Legation of Moses/ The world in Miniature/ The present state of great Britain by John Chamberlaine Esq. the newest Edition/ Matho or Cosmotheoras, In which the first Principles of Philosophy & Astronomy are accommodated to the Capacity of young Persons or such as yet have no Tincture of the sciences. By the Author of the Nature of the human soul. The English Edition/ A spelling dictionary by the Rev. Mr. Thomas dycke."

volumes, octavo, but that I supposed you had it.[4] But I see the answer you had is another, and I suppose a far less famed and more inconsiderable thing. I should be glad you could come sometime about the latter end of April, for I have thought of going to Boston in May.

Concerning the Indian boys, I am at a loss what to do with them— whether it ben't best to let 'em be here in the summer, that there may be some contrivance for their being set to work under Mr. [Timothy] Woodbridge's care. However, I believe it would be best to say nothing to 'em positively about it for the present, but only to feel their dispositions something at a distance, by asking them some questions: as, what they should think of coming up in the spring, and making a visit to their friends, and then going back again? How long a visit they should insist upon, etc. And begin very low with them at first, asking whether a week would satisfy 'em, and if they can't be brought to that, then propose a fortnight, etc. And after you have satisfied yourself as to their dispositions, you may write to me again; and there may probably be an opportunity for you to receive a reply before you come up yourself. And finally, perhaps you may get some terms of 'em, that you may oblige them by firm promise to stand by, that if we will allow 'em to stay in Stockbridge so long, they will willingly, and without making an objection return again.

Unless my son, Timmy, or some man of learning be put in to be the master, they will have no advantage to get forward in their learning here at least as to many things, but rather will be likely to go back and lose some things they have learnt. I should be glad if you would write as particularly about 'em as you can in your next letter, that I may come to a full determination about them. I am, Sir,

Your affectionate friend and brother,
Jonathan Edwards.

P.S. I should be glad, if you have done with my books, you would bring 'em when you come. I want to look in Turretin.[5]

225. TO THE REVEREND TIMOTHY EDWARDS

(Trask Library, AL fragment, one leaf; Dwight ms. transcript, one quarto leaf. Published in Dwight ed., *1*, 557–58.)

* * *

4. John Leland, *An Answer to a Late Book Intituled Christianity As Old as the Creation* (2 vols. London, 1733).
5. Francis Turretin, *Institutio Theologiæ Elencticæ*.

Stockbridge, March 24, 1757

Honored Sir,

I take this opportunity just to inform you that, through the goodness of God, we are all in a comfortable state of health and that we have not long since heard of the welfare of our children in New Jersey and at Northampton.

I intend, God willing, to[1] be at Windsor some time near the beginning of June, purposing then to go a journey to Boston. I intended to have gone sooner, but I foresee such hindrances, as will probably prevent my going till that time. We rejoice much to hear, by Mr. Andrewson,[2] of your being so well, as to be able to baptize a child at your own house the sabbath before last. We all unite in duty to you and my honored mother and in affectionate and respectful salutations to sisters and cousins, and in a request of a constant remembrance in your prayers. I am, honored Sir,

Your dutiful son,
Jonathan Edwards.

226. TO THE REVEREND JOHN ERSKINE

In this letter, of which only an extract is available, Edwards reports to his Scottish friends on the first revival at the College of New Jersey. The letter illustrates one use made of such communications: quoting them in letters to others, thus multiplying their influence. These letters were also read from the pulpit, as Edwards frequently did, or published.

(Printed in John Gillies, *Historical Collections Relating to Remarkable Periods of the Success of the Gospel* [2 vols. Glasgow, 1754; rev. 1845], pp. 522–23. On the College revival, see Maclean, *1*, 155–56. Webster, p. 262, quotes Aaron Burr writing to Edwards on Feb. 12 and 22, and in Mar. 1757, but with a different wording from the present letter.)

* * *

Stockbridge, April 12, 1757

[. . .] Amidst the great darkness which attends the state of things in British America, God is causing some light to arise. We have news truly joyful concerning the college in New Jersey. I had a letter from Mr. [Aaron] Burr, dated February 14, 1757, wherein he says,

1. MS fragment breaks off; rest of text is from the Dwight MS transcript.
2. Possibly Ashbel Anderson, a resident of Scantic. Barbour Collection of Connecticut Vital Statistics to 1850, Connecticut State Library.

I have never had more constant hurry and fatigue with the College than this winter; and never so much comfort. There has been a growing concern about the things of religion among the students for some time past; some that have been very vain and careless have been remarkably reformed. One at present under as deep convictions as I have almost ever seen; and they seem to be of the right kind. There has been a religious society for prayer, etc. that meet once a week, ever since the College has been under my care, though attended but by few till this winter; but now I think above half the students join in it. I am acquainted by Mr. [Richard] Treat of some revival of religion at Faggs Manor,[1] under the preaching of Mr. [George] Duffield; as also in Philadelphia under Mr. Gilbert Tennent.

Mr. Burr adds, in a postscript, dated February 20:

The person I mentioned as under deep convictions has hopefully met with a saving change. Though much old experience has taught me to judge of these things more by the fruits than any account of experience for a short season. Some others seem deeply concerned. There don't appear at present any signs of such imprudence as have too often attended the revival of religion. Such as we look upon to be truly religious in the society I have endeavored to direct and caution in the best manner I could; and they seem to conduct with prudence, and are no small comfort and assistance to me on this occasion. I concluded with our pious governor [Jonathan Belcher] that, as soon as the season would admit of the Trustees meeting, we would keep a day of fasting and prayer, to implore the divine blessing on the College, and humbly to adore him that his providence has so remarkably appeared for it: have fixed on the first Tuesday in April for that purpose.

Afterwards, in a second postscript, dated February 22, he says, "I have now much more to add about the religious concern in College, but must refer to my wife's letter. I never saw anything in the late revival that more evidently discovered the hand of God."

His wife [Esther Edwards Burr] in her letter to her mother (Mrs. [Sarah] Edwards) of February 21, says,

---

1. Faggs Manor, at New Londonderry, Chester County, Pennsylvania, was the site of a famous school, founded by Rev. Samuel Blair. Alexander, pp. 147–77; Noble, pp. 7–15; Wesley M. Gewehr, *The Great Awakening in Virginia, 1740–1790* (Durham, N.C., Duke Univ. Press, 1930), pp. 223–24.

Although I have wrote one letter, I doubt not but another will be agreeable, when it brings such good news concerning Zion. A great and glorious work is going on in College. God is evidently here in a surprising manner. Mr. Burr mentioned the hopeful conversion of one. I can now add another, that has been the subject of a very remarkable and evident work of grace; and many under anguish of soul seem to be brought to the birth. Mr. [Elihu] Spencer says, he never saw anything more remarkable in the late revival than what he saw the last night. This morning a pious young man came to call Mr. Burr, said a number were met in one room in great distress. Certainly a glorious work of God is going on.

After this, I had another letter from Mr. Burr about the end of the same month of February, wherein he says,

For near a week past, a religious concern has been universal, not one student excepted. There is a surprising alteration in the Society. The minds of the students are taken off from their vanities and vicious courses, to which they were most addicted; their conversation seems naturally to turn on the things of religion, and it seems to be without affectation. The utmost harmony prevails, not the least appearances of censuring, judging, etc. Though a considerable number have received comfort, there is no public proclamation about it. Time must discover what genuine effects will remain. I can't but hope a number have been enabled sincerely to give themselves to Christ. It has been remarkably carried on by the still voice of the Spirit; no boisterous methods; no special pathetic addresses to the passions. I told you in my last, that above half the students joined in a religious society that had long been kept in College; I can now tell you, that last week the whole Society joined, not one excepted. It would do you good to see the solemnity and good order which everywhere appears. When the religious concern first began, I called such as were hopefully pious, laid before them what I thought had obstructed the work of God heretofore. Their conduct has been very prudent. I sent for Mr. William Tennent, [Jr.], who spent sundry days here, who perfectly agreed with me as to the method of conducting this important affair, and has been exceeding helpful by private applications.

I have also lately heard very credibly, that there has appeared the winter past, a very evident reformation in the College at New Haven in Connecticut; that many have changed their meetings for mirth and diversion into meetings for prayer, etc., and much more good order, sobriety, and diligence than common, has appeared through the whole Society. That college is now the largest, having the greatest number of students of any in America.

There is also at this time a very remarkable awakening and revival of religion at Bedford, a small town about thirty miles from hence, and under the pastoral care of Mr. [Jedediah] Smith, a pious young minister. [. . .]

[Jonathan Edwards.]

P.S. After I had finished the preceding letter, the same day I received a letter from Mr. [Joseph] Bellamy, in which he informs me of a pretty remarkable revival of religion lately in two parishes in Lebanon, viz. those under Mr. [Solomon] Williams and Mr. [Eleazar] Wheelock.

P.P.S. (April 13.) I this morning received another letter from Mr. Burr, wherein he says as follows:

> The behavior of the students has tended much to silence our enemies, who invented and spread the most false and malicious reports, upon which some sent for their children; but they are all like to return, excepting the two sons of one gentleman, who went so far that he did not know how to come back, but I am persuaded is heartily sorry for what he has done. It is matter of thankfulness, that I have not one scholar but speaks well of the reformation; so that their being called home has served to confute the false reports. The religious concern has had a good effect on all, and with many, I trust, issued in a saving conversion to God.

227. TO THE REVEREND JOHN ERSKINE

Edwards sent this letter to Scotland for publication in response to Erskine's plea that he clarify his views concerning freedom of the will. Followers of Henry Home, Lord Kames had distorted the meaning of Edwards' treatise in order to uphold Kames' *Essays*. This communication was to emphasize the differences between Kames and Edwards. A second letter to Erskine, sent the following week, replied to a more extreme, anonymous pamphlet, *Objections to the "Essays on the Principles of Morality and Natural Religion" Examined*. Edwards considered both letters so important that he sent duplicate copies by diverse routes.

(Trask Library, partial AL draft, two folio leaves. Published in *Remarks on the Essays on the Principles of Morality, and Natural Religion, by Lord Kames; in a Letter to a Minister of the Church of Scotland* [Edinburgh, 1758]; also in the third and subsequent editions of *Freedom of the Will* [London, 1768], including *Works, 1,* 453–65. Edwards' incomplete draft consists of rough, preliminary notes. The published text of 1758 is followed here; the footnotes are Edwards'. See *Works, 1,* 443–52.)

*   *   *

Stockbridge, July 25, 1757

Rev. Sir,

The intimations you have given me of the use which has, by some, been made of what I have written on the *Freedom of the Will,* etc. to vindicate what is said on the subject of liberty and necessity by the author of the *Essays on the Principles of Morality and Natural Religion,* has occasioned my reading this author's *Essay* on that subject, with particular care and attention. And I think it must be evident to everyone, that has read both his *Essay* and my *Inquiry,* that our schemes are exceeding reverse from each other. The wide difference appears particularly in the following things.

This author supposes, that such a necessity takes place with respect to all men's actions, as is inconsistent with liberty,[1] and plainly denies that men have any liberty in acting. Thus in p. 168, after he had been speaking of the necessity of our determinations, as connected with motives, he concludes with saying, "In short, if motives are not under our power or direction, which is confessedly the fact, we can at bottom have no liberty." Whereas I have abundantly expressed it as my mind, that man, in his moral actions, has true liberty; and that the moral necessity which universally takes place, is not in the least inconsistent with anything that is properly called liberty, and with the utmost liberty that can be desired, or that can possibly exist or be conceived of.[2]

I find that some are apt to think, that in that kind of moral necessity of men's volitions, which I suppose to be universal, at least some degree of liberty is denied; that though it be true I allow a sort of liberty, yet those who maintain a self-determining power in the will, and a liberty of contingence and indifference, hold an higher sort of freedom than I do: but I think this is certainly a great mistake.

1. Kames, *Essays on the Principles of Morality and Natural Religion* (hereafter *Essays*), pp. 160, 161, 164, 165, and many other places. (All of the notes to this letter are by JE; page references to the *Inquiry* [i.e. *Freedom of the Will*] in the notes to and text of this letter are to *Works, 1.*)
2. *Inquiry,* pp. 163–66, 272–73, 343–49, 358–59, 363, 377–83.

Liberty, as I have explained it, in p. 163 and other places, is "the power, opportunity, or advantage that anyone has to do as he pleases," or "conducting, *in any respect,* according to his pleasure"; without considering how his pleasure comes to be as it is. It is demonstrable, and I think has been demonstrated, that no necessity of men's volitions that I maintain, is inconsistent with this liberty; and I think it is impossible for anyone to rise higher in his conceptions of liberty than this: if any imagine they desire higher, and that they conceive of a higher and greater liberty than this, they are deceived, and delude themselves with confused ambiguous words, instead of ideas. If anyone should here say, "Yes, I conceive of a freedom above and beyond the liberty a man has of conducting in any respect as he pleases, viz. a liberty of choosing as he pleases." Such an one, if he reflected, would either blush or laugh at his own instance. For, is not choosing as he pleases, conducting, *in some respect,* according to his pleasure, and still without determining how he came by that pleasure? If he says, "Yes, I came by that pleasure by my own choice," if he be a man of common sense, by this time he will see his own absurdity: for he must needs see that his notion or conception, even of this liberty, don't contain any judgment or conception how he comes by that choice, which first determines his pleasure, or which originally chose his own will respecting the affair. Or if any shall say, that "a man exercises liberty in this, even in determining his own choice, but not as he pleases, or not in consequence of any choice, preference, or inclination of his own, but by a determination arising contingently out of a state of absolute indifference"; this is not rising higher in his conception of liberty: as such a determination of the will would not be a voluntary determination of it. Surely he that places liberty in a power of doing something not according to his own choice, or from his choice, has not a higher notion of it, than he that places it in doing as he pleases, or acting from his own election.

If there were a power in the mind to determine itself, but not by its choice or according to its pleasure, what advantage would it give? And what liberty, worth contending for, would be exercised in it? Therefore no Arminian, Pelagian, or Epicurean, can rise higher in his conceptions of liberty, than the notion of it which I have explained: which notion is, apparently, perfectly consistent with the whole of that necessity of men's actions, which I suppose takes place. And I scruple not to say, 'tis beyond all their wits to invent a higher notion, or form a higher imagination of liberty; let them talk of sovereignty of the will, self-determining power, self-motion, self-direction, arbitrary decision, liberty *ad utrumvis,* power of choosing differently in given cases, etc., etc., as long as they will. 'Tis apparent that these men, in their strenuous affirmation, and dispute about these things, aim at they know not what, fighting for something they have no conception of, substituting a number of confused, unmeaning words, instead of things, and instead of thoughts. They may be challenged clearly to explain what they would have: they never can answer the challenge.

The author of the *Essays,* through his whole "Essay on Liberty and Necessity," goes on that supposition, that, in order to the being of real liberty, a man must have a freedom that is opposed to moral necessity: and yet he supposes (p. 175) that such a liberty "must signify a power in the mind of acting without and against motives, a power of acting without any view, purpose or design, and even of acting in contradiction to our own desires and aversions, and to all our principles of action"; and is "an absurdity altogether inconsistent with a rational nature." Now whoever imagined such a liberty as this, a higher sort or degree of freedom, than a liberty of following one's own views and purposes, and acting agreeable to his own inclinations and passions? Who will ever reasonably suppose that liberty, which is an absurdity altogether inconsistent with a rational nature, to be a kind of liberty above that which is consistent with the nature of a rational intelligent designing agent.

The author of the *Essays* seems to suppose such a necessity to take place, as is inconsistent with some supposable "power of arbitrary choice";[3] or that there is some liberty conceivable, whereby men's own actions might be more "properly in their power,"[4] and by which events might be more "dependent on ourselves":[5] contrary to what I suppose to be evident in my *Inquiry.*[6] What way can be imagined, of our actions being more in our power, from ourselves, or dependent on ourselves, than their being from our power to fulfill our own choice, to act from our own inclination, pursue our own views, and execute our own designs? Certainly, to be able to act thus, is as properly having our actions in our power, and dependent on ourselves, as a being liable to be the subjects of acts and events, contingently and fortuitously, "without desire, view, purpose or design, or any principle of action" within ourselves; as we must be, according to this author's own declared sense,

3. *Essays,* p. 169.
4. Ibid., pp. 191, 185, 197, 296.
5. Ibid., p. 183.
6. *Inquiry,* pp. 426–28.

if our actions are performed with that liberty that is opposed to moral necessity.

This author seems everywhere to suppose, that necessity, most properly so-called, attends all men's actions; and that the terms "necessary," "unavoidable," "impossible," etc. are equally applicable to the case of moral and natural necessity. In p. 173, he says, "the idea of necessary and unavoidable equally agrees, both to moral and physical necessity." And in p. 184, "All things that fall out in the natural and moral world are alike necessary." P. 174: "This inclination and choice is unavoidably caused or occasioned by the prevailing motive. In this lies the necessity of our actions, that in such circumstances it was impossible we could act otherwise." He often expresses himself in like manner elsewhere, speaking in strong terms of men's actions as "unavoidable," what they "cannot" forbear, having "no power" over their own actions, the order of them being "unalterably" fixed, and "inseparably" linked together, etc.[7]

On the contrary, I have largely declared, that the connection between antecedent things and consequent ones, which takes place with regard to the acts of men's wills, which is called moral necessity, is called by the name of "necessity" improperly; and that all such terms as "must," "cannot," "impossible," "unable," "irresistible," "unavoidable," "invincible," etc., when applied here, are not applied in their proper signification, and are either used nonsensically, and with perfect insignificance, or in a sense quite diverse from their original and proper meaning, and their use in common speech:[8] and that such a necessity as attends the acts of men's wills, is more properly called "certainty," than "necessity"; it being no other than the certain connection between the subject and predicate of the proposition which affirms their existence.[9]

Agreeable to what is observed in my *Inquiry*,[1] I think it is evidently owing to a strong prejudice in persons' minds, arising from an insensible habitual perversion and misapplication of suchlike terms, as "necessary," "impossible," "unable," "unavoidable," "invincible," etc., that they are ready to think, that to suppose a certain connection of men's volitions without any foregoing motives or inclinations, or any preceding moral influence whatsoever, is truly and properly to suppose such

7. *Essays*, pp. 180, 188, 193, 194, 195, 197, 198, 199, 205, 206, 172.
8. *Inquiry*, pp. 149–55, 158–62, 308, 350–53, 355–56, 361–64, 428–29.
9. Ibid., pp. 151–53.
1. Ibid., pp. 351–53.

a strong irrefragable chain of causes and effects, as stands in the way of, and makes utterly vain, opposite desires and endeavors, like immovable and impenetrable mountains of brass; and impedes our liberty like walls of adamant, gates of brass, and bars of iron: whereas all such representations suggest ideas as far from the truth, as the east is from the west. Nothing that I maintain, supposes that men are at all hindered by any fatal necessity, from doing, and even willing and choosing as they please, with full freedom; yea, with the highest degree of liberty that ever was thought of, or that ever could possibly enter into the heart of any man to conceive. I know it is in vain to endeavor to make some persons believe this, or at least fully and steadily to believe it: for if it be demonstrated to them, still the old prejudice remains, which has been long fixed by the use of the terms "necessary," "must," "cannot," "impossible," etc.: the association with these terms of certain ideas inconsistent with liberty, is not broken; and the judgment is powerfully warped by it; as a thing that has been long bent and grown stiff, if it be straightened, will return to its former curvity again and again.

The author of the *Essays* most manifestly supposes, that if men had the truth concerning the real necessity of all their actions clearly in view, they would not appear to themselves, or one another, as at all praiseworthy or culpable, or under any moral obligation, or accountable for their actions:[2] which supposes, that men are not to be blamed or praised for any of their actions, and are not under any obligations, nor are truly accountable for anything they do, by reason of this necessity; which is very contrary to what I have endeavored to prove, throughout the third Part of my *Inquiry*. I humbly conceive it is there shown, that this is so far from the truth, that the moral necessity of men's actions, which truly take place, is requisite to the being of virtue and vice, or anything praiseworthy or culpable: that the liberty of indifference and contingence, which is advanced in opposition to that necessity, is inconsistent with the being of these; as it would suppose that men are not determined in what they do, by any virtuous or vicious principles, nor act from any motives, intentions or aims whatsoever; or have any end, either good or bad, in acting. And is it not remarkable, that this author should suppose, that, in order to men's actions truly having any desert, they must be performed "without any view, purpose, design, or desire," or "any principle of action," or any-

2. *Essays*, pp. 207, 209, and other places.

thing "agreeable to rational nature"? As it will appear that he does, if we compare, pp. 206, 207, with p. 175.

The author of the *Essays* supposes, that God has deeply implanted in man's nature, a strong and invincible apprehension, or feeling, as he calls it, of a liberty, and contingence of his own actions, opposite to that necessity which truly attends them; and which in truth don't agree with real fact,[3] is not agreeable to strict philosophic truth,[4] is contradictory to the truth of things;[5] and which truth contradicts,[6] not tallying with the real plan:[7] and that therefore such feelings are deceitful,[8] are in reality of the delusive kind.[9] He speaks of them as a wise delusion,[1] as nice artificial feelings, merely that conscience may have a commanding power:[2] meaning plainly, that these feelings are a cunning artifice of the Author of Nature, to make men believe they are free, when they are not.[3] He supposes that by these feelings the moral world has a disguised appearance.[4] And other things of this kind he says. He supposes that all self-approbation, and all remorse of conscience, all commendation or condemnation of ourselves or others, all sense of desert, and all that is connected with this way of thinking, all the ideas, which at present are suggested by the words "ought," "should," arise from this delusion, and would entirely vanish without it.[5]

All which is very contrary to what I have abundantly insisted on and endeavored to demonstrate in my *Inquiry;* where I have largely shown, that it is agreeable to the natural sense of mankind, that the moral necessity or certainty that attends men's actions, is consistent with praise and blame, reward and punishment;[6] and that it is agreeable to our natural notions, that moral evil, with its desert of dislike and abhorrence, and all its other ill-deservings, consists in a certain deformity in the nature of the dispositions and acts of the heart, and not in

3. Ibid., p. 200.
4. Ibid., p. 152.
5. Ibid., p. 183.
6. Ibid., p. 186.
7. Ibid., p. 205.
8. Ibid., pp. 203, 204, 211.
9. Ibid., p. 183.
1. Ibid., p. 209.
2. Ibid., p. 211.
3. Ibid., p. 153.
4. Ibid., p. 214.
5. Ibid., pp. 160, 194, 199, 205, 206, 207, 209.
6. *Inquiry*, Pt. IV, Sec. 4, throughout.

the evil of something else, diverse from these, supposed to be their cause or occasion.[7]

I might well ask here, whether anyone is to be found in the world of mankind, who is conscious to a sense or feeling, naturally and deeply rooted in his mind, that, in order to a man's performing any action that is praise or blameworthy, he must exercise a liberty that implies and signifies a power of acting without any motive, view, design, desire, or principle of action? For such a liberty this author supposes that must be which is opposed to moral necessity, as I have already observed once and again. Supposing a man should actually do good, independent of desire, aim, inducement, principle or end, is it a dictate of invincible natural sense, that his act is more meritorious or praiseworthy than if he had performed it for some good end, and had been governed in it by good principles and motives? And so I might ask, on the contrary, with respect to evil actions.[8]

The author of the *Essays* supposes that the liberty without necessity which we have a natural feeling of, implies contingence: and speaking of this contingence, he sometimes calls it by the name of "chance." And 'tis evident, that his notion of it, or rather what he says about it, implies things happening "loosely," "fortuitously," by "accident," and "without a cause."[9] Now I conceive the slightest reflection may be sufficient to satisfy anyone, that such a contingence of men's actions, according to our natural sense, is so far from being essential to the morality or merit of those actions, that it would destroy it; and that, on the contrary, the dependence of our actions on such causes, as inward inclinations, incitements and ends, is essential to the being of it. Natural sense teaches men, when they see anything done by others of a good or evil tendency, to inquire what their intention was; what principles and views they were moved by, in order to judge how far they are to be justified or condemned; and not to determine, that, in order to their being approved or blamed at all, the action must be performed altogether fortuitously, proceeding from nothing, arising from no cause. Concerning this matter, I have fully expressed my mind in the *Inquiry*.[1]

If the liberty which we have a natural sense of as necessary to desert,

7. Ibid., Pt. IV, Sec. 1, throughout, and pp. 426–28.
8. See this matter illustrated in ibid., Pt. IV, Sec. 4, esp. pp. 360–62.
9. *Essays*, pp. 156, 157, 158, 159, 177, 178, 181, 183, 184, 185. (The MS draft ends at this point.)
1. *Inquiry*, pp. 326–28, 332–33, 360–61, and other places.

consists in the mind's self-determination, without being determined by previous inclination or motive, then indifference is essential to it, yea, absolute indifference; as is observed in my *Inquiry*.[2] But men naturally have no notion of any such liberty as this, as essential to the morality or demerit of their actions; but, on the contrary, such a liberty, if it were possible, would be inconsistent with our natural notions of desert, as is largely shown in the *Inquiry*.[3] If it be agreeable to natural sense, that men must be indifferent in determining their own actions; then, according to the same, the more they are determined by inclination, either good or bad, the less they have of desert: the more good actions are performed from good dispositions, the less praiseworthy; and the more evil deeds are from evil dispositions, the less culpable; and in general, the more men's actions are from their hearts, the less they are to be commended or condemned: which all must know is very contrary to natural sense.

Moral necessity is owing to the power and government of the inclination of the heart, either habitual or occasional, excited by motive; but, according to natural and common sense, the more a man does anything with full inclination of the heart, the more is it to be charged to his account for his condemnation, if it be an ill action, and the more to be ascribed to him for his praise, if it be good.

If the mind were determined to evil actions by contingence, from a state of indifference, then either there would be no fault in them, or else the fault would be in being so perfectly indifferent, that the mind was equally liable to a bad or good determination. And if this indifference be liberty, then the very essence of the blame or fault would lie in the liberty itself, or the wickedness would, primarily and summarily, lie in being a free agent. If there were no fault in being indifferent, then there would be no fault in the determination's being agreeable to such a state of indifference: that is, there could no fault be reasonably found with this, viz. that opposite determinations actually happen to take place *indifferently*, sometimes good and sometimes bad, as contingence governs and decides. And if it be a fault to be indifferent to good and evil, then such indifference is no indifference to good and evil, but is a determination to evil, or to a fault; and such an indifferent disposition would be an evil, faulty disposition, tendency or determination of mind. So inconsistent are these notions of liberty, as essential to praise or blame.

2. Ibid., pp. 203–05.
3. Ibid., esp. in Pt. III, Sec. 6 and 7.

The author of the *Essays* supposes men's natural delusive sense of a liberty of contingence to be, in truth, the foundation of all the labor, care and industry of mankind;[4] and that if men's "practical ideas had been formed on the plan of universal necessity, the *ignava ratio*, the inactive doctrine of the Stoics, would have followed"; and that "there would have been no room for forethought about futurity, or any sort of industry and care":[5] plainly implying, that, in this case, men would see and know that all their industry and care signified nothing, was in vain, and to no purpose, or of no benefit; events being fixed in an irrefragable chain, and not at all *depending* on their care and endeavor; as he explains himself, particularly, in the instance of men's use of means to prolong life:[6] not only very contrary to what I largely maintain in my *Inquiry*,[7] but also very inconsistently with his own scheme, in what he supposes of the ends for which God has so deeply implanted this deceitful feeling in man's nature; in which he manifestly supposes men's care and industry not to be in vain and of no benefit, but of great use, yea, of absolute necessity, in order to the obtaining the most important ends and necessary purposes of human life, and to fulfill the ends of action to the "best advantage"; as he largely declares.[8] Now, how shall these things be reconciled? That, if men had "a clear view of real truth," they would see that there was "no *room*" for their care and industry, because they would see it to be in vain, and of no benefit; and yet that God, by having a clear view of real truth, sees that their being excited to care and industry, will be of excellent use to mankind, and greatly for the benefit of the world, yea, absolutely necessary in order to it; and that therefore the great wisdom and goodness of God to men appears, in artfully contriving to put them on care and industry for their good, which good could not be obtained without them; and yet both these things are maintained at once, and in the same sentences and words by this author. The very reason he gives, why God has put this deceitful feeling into men, contradicts and destroys itself; that God in his great goodness to men gave them such a deceitful feeling, because it was very useful and necessary for them, and greatly for their benefit, or excites them to care and industry for their own good, which care and industry is useful and necessary to that end: and yet the very

4. *Essays*, p. 184.
5. Ibid., p. 189.
6. Ibid., pp. 184, 185.
7. *Inquiry*, esp. Pt. IV, Sec. 5.
8. *Essays*, pp. 188–92, and in many other places.

thing that this great benefit of care and industry is given as a reason for, is God's deceiving men in this very point, in making them think their care and industry to be of great benefit to them, when indeed it is of none at all; and if they saw the real truth, they would see all their endeavors to be wholly useless, that there was "*no room*" for them, and that the event don't at all *depend* upon them.[9]

And besides, what this author says, plainly implies (as appears by what has been already observed) that it is necessary men should be deceived, by being made to believe that future events are contingent, and their own future actions free, and with such a freedom, as signifies that their actions are not the fruit of their own desires, or designs, but altogether contingent, fortuitous and without a cause. But how should a notion of liberty, consisting in accident or loose chance, encourage care and industry? I should think it would rather entirely discourage everything of this nature. For surely, if our actions don't depend on our desires and designs, then they don't depend on our endeavors, flowing from our desires and designs. This author himself seems to suppose, that if men had indeed such a liberty of contingence, it would render all endeavors to determine or move men's future volitions, in vain: he says, that, in this case, "to exhort, to instruct, to promise, or to threaten, would have no purpose."[1] Why? Because (as he himself gives the reason) then our will would be "capricious and arbitrary," and we should "be thrown loose altogether," and our arbitrary power could do us good or ill only "by accident." But if such a loose fortuitous state would render vain others' endeavors upon us, for the same reason would it make useless our endeavors on ourselves: for events that are truly contingent and accidental, and altogether loose from and independent of all foregoing causes, are independent on every foregoing cause within ourselves, as well as in others.

I suppose that it is so far from being true, that our minds are naturally possessed with a notion of such liberty as this, so strongly, that it is impossible to root it out, that indeed men have no such notion of liberty at all, and that it is utterly impossible, by any means whatsoever, to implant or introduce such a notion into the mind. As no such notions as imply self-contradiction and self-abolition can subsist in the mind, as I have shown in my *Inquiry*;[2] I think a mature sensible consideration of the matter, sufficient to satisfy anyone, that even the great-

9. Ibid., pp. 188, 189, etc.
1. Ibid., p. 178.
2. *Inquiry*, pp. 325–26. See also pp. 174, 179, 190–91, 196, 270–73, 345–46, 357–60.

est and most learned advocates themselves for liberty of indifference and self-determination, have no such notion; and that indeed they mean something wholly inconsistent with, and directly subversive of what they strenuously affirm, and earnestly contend for. By a man's having a power of determining his own will, they plainly mean a power of determining his will, as he pleases, or as he chooses; which supposes that the mind has a choice, prior to its going about to conform any action or determination to it. And if they mean that they determine even the original or prime choice, by their own pleasure or choice, as the thing that causes and directs it; I scruple not most boldly to affirm, that they speak they know not what, and that of which they have no manner of idea; because no such contradictory notion can come into, or have a moment's subsistence in the mind of any man living, as an original or first choice being caused, or brought into being, by choice. After all they say, they have no higher or other conception of liberty, than that vulgar notion of it, which I contend for, viz. a man's having power or opportunity to do as he chooses: or if they had a notion that every act of choice was determined by choice, yet it would destroy their notion of the contingence of choice; for then no one act of choice would arise contingently, or from a state of indifference, but every individual act, in all the series, would arise from foregoing bias or preference, and from a cause predetermining and fixing its existence, which introduces at once such a chain of causes and effects, each preceding link decisively fixing the following, as they would by all means avoid.

And such kind of delusion and self-contradiction as this don't arise in men's minds by nature: it is not owing to any natural feeling which God has strongly fixed in the mind and nature of man; but to false philosophy, and strong prejudice, from a deceitful abuse of words. It is "artificial"; not in the sense of the author of the *Essays*, supposing it to be a deceitful artifice of God; but artificial as opposed to natural, and as owing to an artificial deceitful management of terms, to darken and confound the mind. Men have no such thing when they first begin to exercise reason; but must have a great deal of time to blind themselves with metaphysical confusion, before they can embrace, and rest in such definitions of liberty as are given, and imagine they understand them.

On the whole, I humbly conceive, that whosoever will give himself the trouble of weighing, what I have offered to consideration in my *Inquiry*, must be sensible, that such a moral necessity of men's actions as

I maintain, is not at all inconsistent with any liberty that any creature has, or can have, as a free, accountable, moral agent, and subject of moral government; and that this moral necessity is so far from being inconsistent with praise and blame, and the benefit and use of men's own care and labor, that on the contrary it implies the very ground and reason, why men's actions are to be ascribed to them as their own, in that manner as to infer desert, praise and blame, approbation and remorse of conscience, reward and punishment; and that it establishes the moral system of the universe, and God's moral government, in every respect, with the proper use of motives, exhortations, commands, counsels, promises, and threatenings; and the use and benefit of endeavors, care and industry: and that therefore there is no need that the strict philosophic truth should be at all concealed from men; no danger in "contemplation" and "profound discovery" in these things. So far from this, that the truth in this matter is of vast importance, and extremely needful to be known; and that the more clearly and perfectly the real fact is known, and the more constantly it is in view, the better; and particularly, that the clear and full knowledge of that which is the true system of the universe, in these respects, would greatly establish the doctrines which teach the true Christian scheme of divine administration in the city of God, and the gospel of Jesus Christ, in its most important articles; and that these things never can be well established, and the opposite errors, so subversive of the whole gospel, which at this day so greatly and generally prevail, be well confuted, or the arguments by which they are maintained, answered, till these points are settled: while this is not done, it is, to me, beyond doubt, that the friends of those great gospel truths, will but poorly maintain their controversy with the adversaries of those truths: they will be obliged often to dodge, shuffle, hide, and turn their backs; and the latter will have a strong fort, from whence they never can be driven, and weapons to use, which those whom they oppose will find no shield to screen themselves from; and they will always puzzle, confound, and keep under the friends of sound doctrine; and glory, and vaunt themselves in their advantage over them; and carry their affairs with an high hand, as they have done already for a long time past.

I conclude, Sir, with asking your pardon for troubling you with so much said in vindication of myself from the imputation of advancing a scheme of necessity, of a like nature with that of the author of the *Essays on the Principles of Morality and Natural Religion.* Considering that what I have said is not only in vindication of myself, but, as I think, of the most

important articles of moral philosophy and religion; I trust in what I
know of your candor, that you will excuse,

Your obliged friend and brother,
Jonathan Edwards.

228. TO THE REVEREND JOHN ERSKINE

In a cover letter that was apparently sent with the foregoing treatment of
Lord Kames' views on the will, Edwards defends his views against attacks from
both Arminians and antinomians. Once more, he sounds the call of *Freedom of
the Will:* belief in self-determination is fatal to sound doctrine and antithetical
to a proper view of human nature; it fosters independence from the Deity,
leads to self-justification, deprives one of a sense of guilt, hardens the heart,
and glorifies the creature rather than the Creator. Only conviction, evangelical humiliation, and conversion will suffice, and they must be the work of God.

(Trask Library, AL fragment, probably writer's copy, four folio leaves; incomplete Dwight ms. transcript, four quarto leaves. Published in Wellwood,
pp. 516–23; Dwight, *1,* 558–63; *Works, 1,* 465–70. See also *Works, 1,* 69–75;
and Mary Ava Chamberlain, "Jonathan Edwards against the Antinomians
and Arminians" [Ph.D. diss., Columbia University, 1990], ch. 3–4.)

*   *   *

Stockbridge, August 3, 1757

Rev. and Dear Sir,

In June last I received a letter from you, dated January 22, 1757,
with *Mr. Anderson's Complaint Verified,* and *Objections to the Essays Examined.*[1] For these things I now return you hearty thanks.

The conduct of the vindicator of the *Essays* from objections made
against them seems to be very odd; many things are produced from
Calvin, and several Calvinistic writers to defend what is not objected
against: his book is almost wholly taken up about that which is nothing
to the purpose; perhaps only to amuse and blind the common people.
According to your proposal, I have drawn up something, stating the
difference between my hypothesis and that of the *Essays;* which I have
sent to you, to be printed in Scotland, if it be thought best; or to be
disposed of as you think proper. I have wrote it as a letter to you: and if
it be published it may be as a letter from me to a minister in Scotland.

---

1. No information could be found on "Mr. Anderson's Complaint Verified." [Henry
Home, Lord Kames], *Objections against the Essays on Morality and Natural Religion Examined*
(Edinburgh, 1756).

Lord Kames' notion of God's deceiving mankind by a kind of invincible natural instinct or feeling, leading them to suppose that they have a liberty of contingence, and self-determination of will, in order to make 'em believe themselves and others worthy to be blamed or praised for what they do, is a strange notion indeed; and it is hard for me to conjecture what his views could be in publishing such things to the world.

However, by what I have heard, some others seem to be so far of the same mind, that they think, that if it be really true that there is no self-determining power in the will, as opposed to any such moral necessity as I speak of, consisting in a certain connection between motive and volitions, 'tis of mischievous tendency to say anything of it, and that it is best the truth in this matter should not be known by any means. I cannot but be of an extremely different mind. On the contrary, I think the notion of liberty, consisting in a contingent self-determination of the will, as necessary to the morality of men's dispositions and actions, almost inconceivably pernicious; and that the contrary truth is one of the most important truths of moral philosophy that ever was discussed and most necessary to be known; and that for want of it those schemes of morality and religion, which are a kind of infidel schemes, entirely diverse from the virtue and religion of the Bible, and wholly inconsistent with and subversive of the main things belonging to the gospel scheme, have so vastly and so long prevailed and have stood in such strength. And I think whoever imagines that he, or anybody else shall ever see the doctrines of grace effectually maintained against their adversaries, till the truth in this matter be settled, imagines a vain thing. For allow these adversaries what they maintain in this point, and I think they have strict demonstration against us. And not only have these errors a most pernicious influence in the public religious controversies that are maintained in the world, but such a sort of notions have a most fatal influence, many ways, on the minds of men of all ranks in all transactions between God and their souls. The longer I live, and the more I have to do with the souls of men in the work of the ministry, the more I see of this. Notions of this sort are one of the main hindrances of the success of the preaching of the Word, and other means of grace, in the conversion of sinners. This especially appears when the minds of sinners are affected with some concern for their souls, and they are stirred up to seek their salvation. Nothing is more necessary for men in such circumstances than thorough conviction and humiliation, that their consciences should be properly convinced of their real guilt and sinfulness, in the sight of God, and their deserving of his wrath. But who is there, that has had experience of the work of a minister, in dealing with souls in such circumstances that don't find, that the thing that mainly prevents this, is men's excusing themselves with their own inability? and the moral necessity of those things, wherein their exceeding guilt and sinfulness in the sight of God, most fundamentally and mainly consists: such as living from day to day without one spark of true love to the God of infinite glory, and fountain of all good, their having greater complacence in the little vile things of this world than in him, their living in a rejection of Christ, with all his glorious benefits, and dying love; and after all the exhibitions of his glory and grace, having their hearts still as cold as a stone towards him; their living in such ingratitude for the infinite mercy of his laying down his life for sinners. They, it may be, think of some instances of lewd behavior, lying, dishonesty, intemperance, profaneness, etc. But the grand principles of iniquity, constantly abiding and reigning, from whence all proceeds are overlooked; conscience don't condemn 'em for these things because they can't love God of themselves; they can't believe of themselves, and the like. They rather lay the blame of these things, and their other reigning wicked dispositions of heart to God, and secretly charge him with all the blame. These things are very much for want of being thoroughly instructed in that great and important and certain truth, that a bad will, or an evil disposition of heart, itself is wickedness. 'Tis wickedness in its very being, nature and essence, and not only the occasion of it, or the determining influence, that it was at first owing to. Some it may be will say, they own 'tis their fault that they have so bad a heart, that they have no love to God, no true faith in Christ and gratitude to him, because they have been careless and slothful in times past, and have not used means to obtain a better heart, as they should have done. And it may be they are taught that they are to blame for their wickedness of heart, because they as it were brought it on themselves in Adam, by the sin he voluntarily committed, which sin is justly charged to their account; which perhaps they don't deny. But how far are these things from being a proper conviction of their wickedness *in their enmity* to God and Christ? To be convinced of the sin of something that long ago, was the occasion of their enmity to God; and to be convinced of the wickedness of the enmity itself; are quite two things.

And if sinners under some awakening find the exercise of corruption of heart, as it appears in a great many ways in their meditations, prayers and other religious duties, and on occasion of their fears of hell, etc., etc.; still this notion of their inability to help it, excusing them, keeps 'em from proper conviction of sin herein. Fears of hell tend to convince men of the hardness of their hearts. But then when they find how hard their hearts are, and how far from a proper sensibility and affection in things of religion; they are kept from properly condemning themselves for it, from the moral necessity, or inability that attends it. For the very notion of hardness of heart implies moral inability. The harder the heart is, the more dead in sin, and the more unable to exert good affections and acts. Thus, the strength of sin is made the excuse for sin. And thus I have known many under fears of hell justifying or excusing themselves, at least implicitly, in horrid workings of enmity against God in blasphemous thoughts, etc.

'Tis of great importance that they that are seeking their salvation, should be brought off from all dependence on their own righteousness: but these notions, above all things prevent it. They justify themselves in the *sincerity* of their endeavors. They say to themselves, they do what they can; they take great pains; and though there be great imperfection in what they do, and many evil workings of heart arise, yet those they can't help: here moral necessity comes in as an excuse. Things of this kind have visibly been the main hindrance of the true humiliation and conversion of sinners, in the times of awakening, that have been in this land, everywhere, in all parts, as I have had opportunity to observe in very many places. When the gospel is preached, and its offers and invitations and motives most powerfully urged, and sinners' hearts stand out, here is their stronghold, their sheet anchor. Were it not for this, they would either comply, or their hearts would condemn them for their horrid guilt, in not complying.

And if the law of God be preached in its strictness and spirituality, yet conscience is not properly convinced by it. They justify themselves with their inability; and the design and end of the law, as a schoolmaster to fit for Christ, is defeated. Thus both the law and the gospel are prevented from having their proper effect.

This doctrine of a self-determined will, as the ground of all moral good and evil, tends to prevent any proper exercise of faith in God and Christ, in the affair of our salvation, as it tends to prevent all dependence upon them. For instead of this, it teaches a kind of absolute independence in all these things that are of chief importance in this affair; our righteousness, depending originally on our own acts, as self-determined. Thus our own holiness is from ourselves as its determining cause, and its original and highest source. And as for imputed righteousness that should have any merit at all in it, to be sure, there can be no such thing. For self-determination is necessary to praise and merit. But what is imputed from another is not from our self-determination or action. And truly, in this scheme, man is not dependent on God; but God is rather dependent on man in this affair: for he only acts consequentially, in acts in which he depends on what he sees we determine and do first.

The nature of true faith implies a disposition to give all the glory of our salvation to God and Christ. But this notion is inconsistent with it: for it in effect gives the glory wholly to men. For this is the very doctrine that is taught, that the merit and praise is his, whose is the original and effectual determination of the praiseworthy deed. So that, on the whole, I think it must be a miracle indeed, if ever men are converted that have imbibed such notions as these, and are under their influence in their religious concerns.

Yea, these notions tend effectually to prevent men's ever seeking after conversion with any earnestness. 'Tis manifest that men never will be in earnest in this matter, till their consciences are awakened, and they are made sensible of God's anger, and their danger of suffering the terrible effects of it. But that stupidity, which is opposed to this awakening, is upheld chiefly by these two things: their insensibility of their guilt in what is past and present; and flattering themselves as to what is future. These notions of liberty of contingence, indifference and self-determination, as essential to guilt or merit, tend to preclude all sense of any great guilt for past and present wickedness. As has been observed already, all wickedness of heart is excused, as what, in itself considered, brings no guilt. And all that the conscience has to recur to, to find any guilt, is the first wrong determination of the will, in some bad conduct before that wickedness of heart existed, that was the occasion of introducing or continuing it. Which determination arose contingently, from a state of indifference. And how small a matter does this at once bring men's guilt to, when all main things, wherein their wickedness consists, are passed over? And indeed the more these principles are pursued, the more and more must guilt vanish, till at last it comes to nothing, as may easily be shown.

And with respect to self-flattery and presumption, as to what is future, nothing can possibly be conceived more directly tending to it, than a notion of a liberty, at all times possessed, consisting in a power to determine one's own will to good or evil; which implies a power to determine one's own will to good or evil; which implies a power men have, at all times, to determine them to repent and turn to God. And what can more effectually encourage the sinner, in present delays and neglects, and embolden him to go on in sin, in a presumption of having his own salvation at all times, at his own command? And this notion of self-dependence and self-determination, tends to prevent or enervate all prayer to God for converting grace; for why should men earnestly cry to God for his grace, to determine their hearts to that, which they must be determined to of themselves? And indeed it destroys the very notion of conversion itself. There can properly be no such thing, or anything akin to what the Scripture speaks of as conversion, renovation of the heart, regeneration, etc. if growing good by a number of successive self-determined acts, be all that is required, or to be expected.

Excuse me, Sir, for troubling you with so much on this head. I speak from the fullness of my heart. What I have long seen of the dreadful consequences of these prevalent notions everywhere, and what I am convinced will still be their consequences, so long as they continue to prevail, fills me with great concern. I therefore wish that the affair were more thoroughly looked into, and searched to the very bottom.

I have reserved a copy of this letter, and also of my other to you dated July 25, intending to send them to Mr. [Aaron] Burr, to be by him conveyed by the way of New York or Philadelphia. Looking on these letters as of special importance, I send duplicates, lest one copy should fail. The packet in which I enclose this, I cover to Mr. [John] Gillies, and send to Boston, to the care of Mr. [William] Hyslop to be conveyed to Mr. Gillies. But yet have desired him, if he has a more direct opportunity to convey the packet to Edinburgh by the way of London, then to put a wrapper over the whole inscribed to you; and to write to you, desiring you to break open the packet, and take out the letters which belong to you. I have left the other letters, as well as these to you open, excepting the wrapper to Mr. Gillies, that he that first receives the packet, either you or he, may read the letters to the rest, and then seal and convey them. And I should be glad if Mr. [William] McCulloch might also see all the letters as well as Mr. Gillies.

You will see, Sir, something of our sorrowful state, on this side of the water, by my letter to Mr. McCulloch. O Sir, pray for us; and pray in particular for

> Your affectionate and obliged friend and brother,
> Jonathan Edwards.

P.S. Please for the future to direct your letters for me, to be left with Mr. William Hyslop, merchant in Boston, a Scots gentleman, who married a kinswoman of mine, and who maintains a correspondence both to London and Scotland, and will be very faithful and friendly.

229. TO THE REVEREND JOSEPH BELLAMY

Edwards sends subscription forms for his latest book, *Original Sin.* He also insists that Bellamy come to Stockbridge, to pick up the Indian boys and escort them back to Bethlehem. Bellamy could not know that he had little time to resolve his differences with Aaron Burr; Burr died the following month, on September 24. Edwards alerts Bellamy that, in case of attack from the French and Indians, he may accept Bellamy's invitation to take refuge in his home.

(Beinecke Library, ALS, one quarto leaf. See Bellamy's letter to Edwards of May 31, 1756, Dwight ed., *1*, 555–56.)

*   *   *

Stockbridge, August 6, 1757

Sir,

I have yet found no opportunity to send to Boston. It is a very small matter to draw written copies of the proposals, so much at least of 'em as is necessary. I will get more printed copies as soon as I can. But in the mean-time, written ones may answer present exigence.

I suppose you must come up with the Indian boys in the fall; or rather they must be sent a fortnight before, and you must come after, and the affair of their return with you must be strongly secured, if it should be thought best that both should return.

I would propose whether it ben't best that all former misunderstandings between Mr. [Aaron] Burr and you should be buried:[1] and whether (on supposition you are not well satisfied about some things)

---

1. Bellamy's support of New Light extremists such as James Davenport had displeased Burr, and Bellamy felt that Burr, who did not approve of Bellamy's strict admission standards and unpolished manner, had not done enough to support his candidacy for the First Presbyterian Church of New York City. Burr to Bellamy, Jan. 13 and June 28, 1742, and May 14, 1754, in Bellamy. Mark Valeri of Union Theological Seminary in Virginia kindly provided this information.

it will answer any good end to keep them alive. I am forced in many instances so to bury old misunderstandings.

Respects to your family, and love to Indian boys, from Sir,

Your affectionate brother,
Jonathan Edwards.

P.S. I don't know but we must soon flee to Bethlehem.

230. TO THE TRUSTEES OF THE COLLEGE OF NEW JERSEY

Edwards' response to the invitation to become president of the College of New Jersey is equivocal. He leads off with a number of deficiencies, any one of which might disqualify him. First, the move would be difficult and expensive, perhaps beyond his means. Then he confesses his physical weaknesses and social limitations. Moreover, his teaching ability does not extend to the broad range of subjects mastered by the late president, Aaron Burr. Finally, he views his specialty as writing, rather than speaking. He reports the work in progress on the *History of Redemption,* the *Harmony of the Old and New Testament,* and other projects. Notwithstanding these factors, he is willing to seek advice of a council on whether he should accept, if the Commissioners consent. The Trustees, brushing these objections aside, pressed him to accept without delay.

(No ms. has been located. Text based on Hopkins, pp. 75–78. The letter is in reply to Richard Stockton to Edwards, Sept. 29, 1757, ALS; the Trustees follow up in Richard Stockton to Edwards, Nov. 4, 1757, ALS; both in the Beinecke Library.)

*   *   *

Stockbridge, October 19, 1757

Reverend and Honored Gentlemen,

I was not a little surprised, on receiving the unexpected notice of your having made choice of me to succeed the late President [Aaron] Burr, as the head of Nassau Hall.

I am much in doubt whether I am called to undertake the business, which you have done me the unmerited honor to choose me for. If some regard may be had to my outward comfort, I might mention the many inconveniences and great detriment, which may be sustained, by my removing with my numerous family, so far from all the estate I have in the world (without any prospect of disposing of it, under present circumstances, without losing it, in great part) now when we

have scarcely got over the trouble and damage sustained by our removal from Northampton, and have but just begun to have our affairs
in a comfortable situation for a subsistence in this place; and the expense I must immediately be at to put myself into circumstances toler-
ably comporting with the needful support of the honor of the office I
am invited to; which will not well consist with my ability. But this is not
my main objection.

The chief difficulty in my mind, in the way of accepting this important and arduous office, are these two: first my own defects, unfitting
me for such an undertaking, many of which are generally known;
besides other, which my own heart is conscious to. I have a constitution
in many respects peculiar unhappy, attended with flaccid solids, vapid,
sizy and scarce fluids, and a low tide of spirits; often occasioning a kind
of childish weakness and contemptibleness of speech, presence, and
demeanor; with a disagreeable dullness and stiffness, much unfitting
me for conversation, but more especially for the government of a
college. This poorness of constitution makes me shrink at the
thoughts of taking upon me, in the decline of life, such a new and great
business, attended with such a multiplicity of cares, and requiring such
a degree of activity, alertness and spirit of government; especially as
succeeding one, so remarkably well qualified in these respects, giving
occasion to everyone to remark the wide difference. I am also deficient
in some parts of learning, particularly in algebra, and the higher parts
of mathematics, and in the Greek classics; my Greek learning having
been chiefly in the New Testament.

The other thing is this; that my engaging in this business, will not
well consist, with those views, and that course of employ in my study,
which have long engaged, and swallowed up my mind, and been the
chief entertainment and delight of my life.

And here, honored Sirs (emboldened by the testimony, I have now
received of your unmerited esteem, to rely on your candor), I will with
freedom open myself to you.

My method of study, from my first beginning the work of the ministry, has been very much by writing; applying myself in this way, to
improve every important hint; pursuing the clue to my utmost, when
anything in reading, meditation or conversation, has been suggested
to my mind, that seemed to promise light in any weighty point. Thus
penning what appeared to me my best thoughts, on innumerable subjects for my own benefit. The longer I prosecuted my studies in this
method, the more habitual it became, and the more pleasant and

Richard Stockton, "The Signer," attributed to John Wollaston, undated, the Art Museum, Princeton University, bequest of Mrs. Alexander T. McGill

profitable I found it. The further I traveled in this way, the more and wider the field opened, which has occasioned my laying out many things, in my mind, to do in this manner, if God should spare my life, which my heart hath been much upon: particularly many things against most of the prevailing errors of the present day, which I cannot with any patience see maintained (to the utter subverting of the gospel of Christ) with so high a hand, and so long continued a triumph, with so little control, when it appears so evident to me, that there is truly no foundation for any of this glorying and insult. I have already published something on one of the main points in dispute between the Arminians and Calvinists: and have it in view, God willing (as I have already signified to the public), in like manner to consider all the other controverted points, and have done much towards a preparation for it.

But besides these, I have had on my mind and heart (which I long ago began, not with any view to publication) a great work, which I call *A History of the Work of Redemption,* a body of divinity in an entire new method, being thrown into the form of an history, considering the affair of Christian theology, as the whole of it, in each part, stands in reference to the great work of redemption by Jesus Christ; which I suppose is to be the grand design of all God's designs, and the *summum* and *ultimum* of all the divine operations and degrees; particularly considering all parts of the grand scheme in their historical order. The order of their existence, or their being brought forth to view, in the course of divine dispensations, or the wonderful series of successive acts and events; beginning from eternity and descending from thence to the great work and successive dispensations of the infinitely wise God in time, considering the chief events coming to pass in the church of God, and revolutions in the world of mankind, affecting the state of the church and the affair of redemption, which we have an account of in history or prophecy; till at last we come to the general resurrection, last judgment, and consummation of all things; when it shall be said, "It is done. I am Alpha and Omega, the Beginning and the End" [Rev. 22:13]. Concluding my work, with the consideration of that perfect state of things, which shall be finally settled, to last for eternity. This history will be carried on with regard to all three worlds, heaven, earth, and hell: considering the connected, successive events and alterations, in each so far as the Scriptures give any light; introducing all parts of divinity in that order which is most scriptural and most natural: which is a method which appears to me the most beautiful and entertaining, wherein every divine doctrine, will appear to greatest advantage in the brightest light, in the most striking manner, showing the admirable contexture and harmony of the whole.

I have also for my own profit and entertainment, done much towards another great work, which I call *The Harmony of the Old and New Testament,* in three parts. The first considering the prophecies of the Messiah, his redemption and kingdom; the evidences of their references to the Messiah, etc. comparing them all one with another, demonstrating their agreement and true scope and sense; also considering all the various particulars wherein these prophecies have their exact fulfillment; showing the universal, precise, and admirable correspondence between predictions and events. The second part: considering the types of the Old Testament, showing the evidence of their being intended as representations of the great things of the gospel of Christ: and the agreement of the type with the antitype. The third and great part, considering the harmony of the Old and New Testament, as to doctrine and precept. In the course of this work, I find there will be occasion for an explanation of a very great part of the holy Scripture; which may, in such a view be explained in a method, which to me seems the most entertaining and profitable, best tending to lead the mind to a view of the true spirit, design, life and soul of the Scriptures, as well as to their proper use and improvement.

I have also many other things in hand, in some of which I have made great progress, which I will not trouble you with an account of. Some of these things, if divine providence favor, I should be willing to attempt a publication of. So far as I myself am able to judge of what talents I have, for benefiting my fellow creatures by word, I think I can write better than I can speak.

My heart is so much in these studies, that I cannot find it in my heart to be willing to put myself into an incapacity to pursue them any more, in the future part of my life, to such a degree as I must, if I undertake to go through the same course of employ, in the office of a president, that Mr. Burr, did, instructing in all the languages, and taking the whole care of the instruction of one of the classes in all parts of learning, besides his other labors. If I should see light to determine me to accept the place offered me, I should be willing to take upon me the work of a president, so far as it consists in the general inspection of the whole society and subservient to the school, as to their order and methods of study and instruction, assisting myself in immediate instruction in the arts and sciences (as discretion should direct and occasion serve, and the state of things require), especially the senior class: and added to all, should be willing to do the whole work of a professor of divinity, in public and private lectures, proposing questions to be answered, and some to be discussed in writing and free conversation, in meetings of graduates and others, appointed in proper seasons for these ends. It would be now out of my way, to spend time, in a constant teaching of the languages; unless it be the Hebrew tongue, which I should be willing to improve myself in, by instructing others.

On the whole, I am much at a loss, with respect to the way of my duty in this important affair: I am in doubt, whether if I should engage in it, I should not do what both you and I should be sorry for afterwards. Nevertheless, I think the greatness of the affair, and the regard due to so worthy and venerable a body, as that of the Trustees of Nassau Hall, requires my taking the matter into serious consideration: and unless you should appear to be discouraged, by the things which I have now represented, as to any further expectation from me, shall proceed to ask advice, of such as I esteem most wise, friendly and faithful; if after the mind of the Commissioners in Boston is known, it appears that they consent to leave me at liberty, with respect to the business they have employed me in here.

[Jonathan Edwards.]

231. TO ESTHER EDWARDS BURR

Edwards wrote a letter of condolence to his daughter, Esther, on the death of her husband, Aaron Burr, president of the College of New Jersey. Her answer proved the buoyancy of her faith. She reported that she was sustained by Scripture and religious experience. In this rejoinder, Edwards expresses gratification at her response and gives news of the progress on the call from the College of New Jersey. He tells of his letter to the Trustees, his hopes for prompt resolution of details, and plans for a council. What the latter will advise is unknown, but their judgment will be decisive.

(CL, ALS, one folio leaf, addressed on verso to Mrs. Esther Burr at Princeton, New Jersey. Published in Faust and Johnson, pp. 414–15; Burr, pp. 297–99. The original of the letter of Esther Burr to Edwards, Nov. 2, 1757, and a Dwight ms. transcript, are in the Trask Library. The Burr letter is published in Dwight ed., *1*, 571–73, and Burr, pp. 295–97. A parallel letter of Esther Burr to her mother, Sarah Edwards, Oct. 7, 1757, is published in Hopkins, pp. 89–90; Dwight ed., *1*, 566–67; and Burr, pp. 293–94.)

*   *   *

Stockbridge, November 20, 1757

Dear Daughter,

I thank you for your most comfortable letter; but more especially would I thank God that has granted you such things to write. How good and kind is your heavenly Father! How do the bowels of his tender love and compassion appear, while he is correcting you by so great a shake of his head! Indeed, he is a faithful God; he will remember his covenant forever; and never will fail them that trust in him. But don't be surprised, or think some strange thing has happened to you, if after this light, clouds of darkness should return. Perpetual sunshine is not usual in this world, even to God's true saints. But I hope, if God should hide his face in some respect, even this will be in faithfulness to you, to purify you, and fit you for yet further and better light.

As to removing to Princeton, to take on me the office of president, I have agreed with the church here, to refer it to a council of ministers, to sit here December 21, to determine whether it be my duty. Mr.

[William] Tennent can inform you more of the matter. I with this, enclose a letter to him, which I desire may be delivered to him as soon as possible. I have wrote more particularly about the council, in my letter to the Trustees, directed to Mr. [Richard] Stockton, which Mr. Tennent will see.[1]

I know I can't live at Princeton, as a president must, on the salary they offer: yet I have left that matter to their generosity. I shall have no money wherewith to furnish the house. I hope Mr. Tennent will exert himself to get a full Trustees meeting, to settle College affairs. I shall not be willing to come thither, till that is well done. If the Trustees don't send me an account of their doings immediately by the post to Claverack, I wish you would do it, and direct your letter to be left with Capt. Jeremiah Hogeboom. I should be glad, on some accounts, to have the letter before the council.

What the council will do, I can't tell. I shall endeavor as fairly and justly as possible to lay the matter before 'em, with every material circumstance. Deacon [Timothy] Woodbridge is a cunning man, and an eloquent speaker; he will strive to his utmost to influence the council by his representations, and perhaps, by influencing the Indians, to make such representations before the council as will tend to persuade them that it's best for me to stay. And their judgment must determine the matter. Not only has Mr. Woodbridge and others a friendship for me and liking to my ministry, but it is greatly against their temporal interest for me to leave them.

As to Lucy's coming home, her mother will greatly need her, especially if we remove in the spring. But yet, whether your circumstances don't much more loudly call for her continuance there, must be left with you and her. She must judge whether she can come consistently with her health and comfort at such a season of the year. If she comes, let her buy me a staff, and ask advice, and get a good one or none. Mr. [William] Esselstein has promised a good horse and side saddle, and his son to wait on her to Stockbridge. And I suppose Mr. [Abraham] Fonda can let her have a horse and side saddle to Mr. Esselstein's.

If you think of selling Harry,[2] your mother desires you not to sell him, without letting her know it.

Timmy is considerably better, though yet very weak. We all unite in

1. See Letter No. 230, JE to the Princeton Trustees, Oct. 19, 1757, above. Richard Stockton was Clerk of the Trustees of the College, and William Tennent II was President pro tem of the Board (Maclean, pp. 109–10, 171–72).

2. A slave owned by Aaron Burr. Further biographical data unavailable. Burr, p. 99, n. 11.

love to you, Lucy, and your children. Your mother is very willing to leave Lucy's coming away wholly to you and her. I am

> Your most tender and affectionate Father,
> Jonathan Edwards.

232. TO THE REVEREND MARK LEAVENWORTH

In colonial Congregational churches it was considered mandatory to have a council to advise on important decisions like ordination or dismissal of a minister. Edwards had already received permission from the Commissioners to be released from his duties as missionary and go to Princeton as president of the College of New Jersey. Now, the council had to obtain the local church's permission. Edwards, with carte blanche on the choice of members, packed it with his staunch supporters. This is the sole invitation to the council known to exist. Of those whom he invited, four were Harvard graduates and five were Yale graduates. Six resided in Connecticut, only three in Massachusetts. The college representatives from New Jersey were both Yale alumni. Bad weather and poor attendance prevented the council from meeting on the original date. Instead, it convened on January 4, 1758, and approved Edwards' move.

(HSP, Gratz Univ. and College Presidents Coll., ALS, one quarto leaf, addressed on verso to the Reverend Mr. Mark Leavenworth, Pastor of the First Church in Waterbury.)

* * *

Stockbridge November 21, 1757

Rev. and Dear Sir,

The pastor of this church being desired by the Trustees of New Jersey College, to remove from hence to Princeton, in order to the taking upon him the office of President of that College; they having gained the consent of the Commissioners in Boston hereto; it is determined by the unanimous agreement of both pastor and brethren of the Church of Stockbridge, wholly to refer it to the judgment of a number of ministers, whether it be his duty to comply with this proposal; who are desired to meet here on Wednesday the 21st of the approaching December, fully to consider and give their judgment in this affair. And 'tis desired that you among others would be present and assisting at that time.

The other ministers chosen are the Reverend Messrs. [Anthony] Stoddard of Woodbury, [Timothy] Pitkin of Farmington, [Daniel] Brinsmade of Judea, [Daniel] Farrand of Canaan, [Samuel] Hopkins of Sheffield, [Peter] Reynolds of Enfield, and [Edward] Billings of Greenfield, and [John] Ballantine of Westfield: all chosen by the joint and unanimous consent of pastor and brethren.

I now write by the consent, and at the desire of the church, and hope, Sir, you will not fail. So you will oblige, Sir,

Your respectful friend and brother,
Jonathan Edwards.

233. TO THE REVEREND JOSEPH BELLAMY

Edwards writes his final recorded Scripture exegesis to his faithful disciple, as from one theologian to another.

(Trask Library, ALS, two folio leaves, addressed on verso to the Reverend Mr. Joseph Bellamy at Bethlehem; Dwight ms. transcript, four quarto leaves.)

*   *   *

Stockbridge, December 1, 1757

Rev. and Dear Sir,

Yesterday I received your two letters of the 12th and 17th of November, but I saw nor heard nothing of Mr. Hill.[1] I thank you for your concern that I may be useful in the world.

I lately wrote you a letter informing you of our choice of a council to sit here on the 21st of this month; and enclosed in it a letter missive to Mr. [Daniel] Brinsmade, who is one of the council. I hope before this time you have received it. Don't fail of letting me see you here; for I never wanted to see you more.

As to the question you ask about Christ's argument in John 10:34–36, I observe:

First, that it is not all princes of the earth that are called "gods" in the Old Testament, but only the princes of Israel that ruled over God's people. The princes that are called "gods" in the 82nd Psalm are, in the same sentence, distinguished from the princes of the nations of the world. "I have said, Ye are GODS; . . . But ye shall die like men, and fall like one of the PRINCES."

Secondly, the reason why those princes of Israel were called "gods," was that they, the rulers and judges of God's Israel, were figures of him, who is the true King of the Jews and Prince of God's people, who

---

1. Possibly Abraham Hill of Woodbury, who died in 1776, or Isaac Hill of Woodbury and Bethlehem, who died in 1775. William Cothren, *History of Ancient Woodbury, Connecticut* (Waterbury, 1854), p. 567.

is to rule over the house of Jacob forever, the Prince and Savior of God's church or spiritual Israel, gathered from all nations of the earth; who is God indeed. The throne of Israel, or of God's people, properly belonged to Christ; he only was the proper heir to that crown: and therefore the princes of Israel are said to *sit upon the throne of the Lord* (I Chron. 29:23). And the kingdom of Israel under kings of the house of David is called the "kingdom of the Lord" (II Chron. 13:8). And because Christ took the throne as the antitype of those kings, therefore he is said to sit upon their throne (Luke 1:32). Thus, the princes of Israel are called "gods," in that 82nd Psalm, and "sons of God" or all of them "children of the Most High," being appointed types and remarkable representations of the true Son of God, and in him of the true God. They were called "gods," and "sons of God," in the same manner as the Levitical sacrifices were called "an atonement for sin," and in the same manner as the manna was called the "bread of heaven" and "angels' food." These things represented, and by special divine designation, were figures of the true atonement, and of him who truly was angels' food; and in the same sense as soul, the person especially pointed at in the 82nd Psalm, is called "the Lord's anointed," or "Messiah" (as it is in the original) or "Christ," which are the same. And it is to be observed, that these typical gods and judges of Israel are distinguished from the true God and true judge of God's people who was to come as their antitype, in the next sentence, Ps. 82:8, "Arise, O GOD, thou JUDGE of the earth; for thou shalt inherit all nations." This is a wish for the coming of Christ, that king that should reign in righteousness and judge uprightly, who was to inherit the Gentiles as well as the Jews. And the words as they stand in connection with the two preceding verses, import thus much: "As to you, the temporal princes and judges of Israel, you are called gods and sons of God, being exalted to the place or seat of kings, judges and saviors of God's people, the kingdom and heritage of Christ. But you shall die like men, and fall like other princes. Whereby it appears that you are truly no gods, nor any one of you the true Son of God, which your injustice and oppression also shows. But oh, that he who is truly God, the true and just Judge and Savior (who is to be King over Gentiles as well as Jews), would come and reign." It is to be observed that when it is said in this verse, "Arise, O GOD," the word GOD is *Elohim*, the same that is used, v. 6, "I have said ye are gods. I have said ye are *elohim*."

Thirdly, as to those words of Christ, John 10: 35, "If he called them gods, UNTO WHOM THE WORD OF THE LORD CAME," I suppose that by the word of God, its coming to these princes of Israel, is meant their being set forth by special and express divine designation to be types or figurative significations of God's mind. Those things which God had appointed to be types to signify God's mind, were a visible word. Types are called "the word of the Lord," as in Zech. 11:10–11, and ch. 4:4–6. The word of the Lord came to the princes of Israel, both as they by God's ordering became subjects of a typical representation of a divine thing, which was a visible word of God; and also as this was done by express, divine designation, as they were marked out to this end by an express, audible and legible word: as in Ex. 22:28 and Ps. 82:1; and besides these, the thing they were appointed types of was Christ, who is called the Word of God. Thus, the word of God came to Jacob as a type of Christ, I Kgs. 18:31, "And Elijah took twelve stones according to the number of the tribes of Jacob UNTO WHOM THE WORD OF THE LORD CAME, saying, Israel shall be thy name." The word Israel is "Prince of God," Jacob being by that express, divine designation appointed as a type of Christ (who is called by that name, "Israel," Is. 49:3), the true prince of God in his prevailing in his wrestling with God, to save himself and his family from destruction by Esau, that was then coming against him, and obtaining the blessing for himself and his seed. Now,

Fourthly, Christ's argument lies in these words, "the Scripture cannot be broken." That word of God by which they are called "gods," as types of him that is truly God, must be verified, which they can't be unless the antitype be truly God. They are so-called as types of the Messiah, or of the Anointed One (which is the same) or the Sanctified or Holy One, or him that was to be sent, which were all known names among the Jews for the Messiah. (See Dan. 9:24–25; Ps. 89:19–20; Ps. 16:10; John 9:7.[2]) But it was on this account that the types or images of the Messiah were called gods, because he that they represented was God indeed. If he were not God, the word by which they were called, gods, could not be verified. As the word by which the legal sacrifices were called an atonement, and are said to atone for sin, was true, in no other sense, than as they had relation to the sacrifice of Christ, a true atonement. If Christ's sacrifice had not truly atoned for sin, the word that called the representations of it an atonement, could not be verified. So if Jesus Christ had not been the true bread from heaven, and angels'

2. The intended reference is possibly John 9:22.

food indeed, the Scripture that called the type of him the bread of
heaven, and angels' food, would not have been verified, but would have
been broken. These, Sir, are my thoughts on John 10:34, etc.

> I am yours most affectionately,
> Jonathan Edwards.

P.S. December 5.

Sir,

The opportunity for conveyance of my letters to ministers chosen to
be of the council your way, not being very good, I here send other
letters, desiring you to take the care of conveying them with all possible
care and speed.

234. TO CAPT. NATHANIEL DWIGHT

Edwards does not explain when or how he acquired joint title with his aunt
Rebecca Hawley to land near Pelham, Massachusetts. It is evident, however,
that he is trying to liquidate assets and get his affairs in order for the expected
transition to Princeton. In this letter Edwards appoints Nathaniel Dwight to
survey and subdivide the tract.

(Firestone Library, Jonathan Edwards Coll., ALS, two quarto leaves, addressed on verso to Capt. Nathaniel Dwight at Cold Spring.)

* * *

Stockbridge, December 5, 1757

Sir,

I have now wrote to Maj. [Joseph] Hawley, urging that the land that
is owned by his mother and me south of Pelham, which hitherto has
lien in common betwixt us, should be surveyed and divided as soon as
possible; and have proposed that you should be the surveyor, and
should act for me in the division. The method of division which I have
proposed, is that the whole, which is near 2,000 acres, should be divided into twenty equal parts, and each part marked in the plan according to its quality, *good, bad,* or *indifferent,* and the parts of each
quality drawn for by themselves or if any other method be thought
more convenient, I am willing to consent to it; and shall leave it with my
son [Timothy] Dwight, [Jr.,] to act for me, in agreeing on the method
of division, with you and Major Hawley.

I would pray you at the first opportunity, to confer with Major
Hawley and your kinsmen about the matter, and undertake in the
affair, and proceed in it as soon as the weather and other circum-

stances will possibly admit of it: and I will see you satisfied for your trouble. In thus doing you will oblige, Sir,

> Your cordial friend and humble servant,
> Jonathan Edwards.

235. TO THE REVEREND GIDEON HAWLEY

Edwards summarizes what happened at the council meeting to approve the call from the College of New Jersey. In a few days, he will leave to assume his duties there. Meanwhile, Hawley was in eastern Massachusetts on a trial mission with Indians, which eventually led to a lifetime commitment. Edwards authorizes Hawley to collect the closing payments for Edwards' ministry at Stockbridge to repay money owed him.

(HSF, A. C. Thompson Papers, ALS, two quarto leaves, addressed on verso to the Reverend Mr. Gideon Hawley, Minister of the Gospel at Mashpey, near Sandwich.)

* * *

Stockbridge, January 14, 1758

Rev. and Dear Sir,

I thank you for yours of December 6 from Barnstable.

My church unanimously agreed with me to refer this question, viz. whether it was my duty to comply with the motion of the Trustees, etc., to the final decision of a council of these gentlemen, viz. Messrs. [Anthony] Stoddard of Woodbury, [Timothy] Pitkin of Farmington, [Daniel] Brinsmade of Judea, [Mark] Leavenworth of Waterbury, [Daniel] Farrand of Canaan, [Samuel] Hopkins of Sheffield, [Peter] Reynolds of Enfield, [John] Ballantine of Westfield, and [Edward] Billings of Greenfield, to meet here December 21, at which time, by reason of the difficulty of the weather, but three came; therefore they adjourned to January 4, and wrote to the rest to come at that time without fail. Which time proved yet more difficult: nevertheless five came, though one of 'em not seasonably. But they proceeded to hear and judge of the matter and unanimously determined that my call was clear to go, etc. I am therefore by the will of God about to set out on my journey in a few days, being greatly pressed to go speedily by letters after letters from the Trustees, and by two of their number, viz. Messrs. [Caleb] Smith and [John] Brainerd, whom they sent to Stockbridge. I shall leave my family here till spring. I hope to come and assist in their removal next May.

I desire, Sir, your fervent prayer to God that I may have his favor and assistance in this great and arduous [task], for which I am so insufficient of myself.

Stockbridge people, both English and Indians, have agreed to try for Mr. John Brainerd to be the missionary here, and accordingly have wrote to him and to the Commissioners.[1]

I have here enclosed an order on Mr. [Andrew] Oliver to pay you for the five last sabbaths of my preaching here, which have passed since my last half-year expired, which I desire you to give me credit for.

My family joins in cordial respects to you. I am, dear Sir,

Your affectionate friend and brother,
Jonathan Edwards.

236. TO COLLEGE TREASURER JONATHAN SERGEANT

Edwards arrived in Princeton in late January 1758. He promptly entered upon his presidential responsibilities and made the initial class assignments. On February 23, he was inoculated for smallpox; he died on March 22 from an adverse reaction. Even in the midst of fatal illness, he musters the strength to remind the College Treasurer that his salary is due to be paid soon. Thus the correspondence of the great theologian ends on a financial note.

(Firestone Library, Jonathan Edwards Collection, ALS, one quarto leaf, addressed on verso to Mr. Jonathan Sergeant, College Treasurer, at Newark.)

* * *

Princeton, February 28, 1758

Sir,

This is to desire that when you come next to this place, you would come prepared to pay me an £100, for so much will be due to me from the College Treasury, in the month of March approaching. I also shall desire to borrow an £100 of the College the next May, which the Trustees have consented to.

This with humble service to Mrs. Sergeant is from, Sir,

Your humble servant,
Jonathan Edwards.

1. No action was taken and Brainerd remained in New Jersey for the balance of his career.

PERSONAL WRITINGS

INTRODUCTION

Edwards' "Resolutions," "Diary," "On Sarah Pierpont," and "Personal Narrative" have all become classics of American literature. In addition to offering rare glimpses into the private thoughts of one of America's most intriguing and influential figures, they attest to his talents as a writer. These four works have frequently been published together, not only because they are among the few pieces of an auto-biographical nature by Edwards that we have but because they have much in common. At points, they intersect and supplement one another. In addition, they cover nearly the entirety of Edwards' life, from his early spiritual travails and self-discipline in the "Resolutions" and "Diary" to his search for a fellow godly soul in "On Sarah Pierpont" to his retrospective summary of his religious awakening experiences in the "Personal Narrative."

"Resolutions" and "Diary"

Resolutions are defined as "firm determinations." For Edwards, they were neither pious hopes, romantic dreams, nor legalistic rules. They were instructions for life, maxims to be followed in all respects. Edwards depended on the sustaining strength of his omnipotent Deity to enable him to live up to them.[1]

The "Resolutions" were Edwards' guidelines for self-examination. Puritans set great store by biblical injunctions to submit themselves to divine searching and to monitor their motives and actions. On a community level, congregations were exhorted to practice introspection as a duty of great consequence.

---

1. On the "Resolutions," see John Dewey, *Human Nature and Conduct* (New York, 1922), pp. 14–88; Conrad Cherry, *The Theology of Jonathan Edwards: A Reappraisal* (Garden City, N.Y., Doubleday, 1966; rep. Bloomington, Ind., Indiana Univ. Press, 1990), pp. 34–43, 126–58; Sang H. Lee, *The Philosophical Theology of Jonathan Edwards* (Princeton, Princeton Univ. Press, 1989); Stephen J. Stein, "'Like Apples of Gold in Pictures of Silver': The Portrait of Wisdom in Jonathan Edwards's Commentary on the Book of Proverbs," *Church History* 54 (1985), 324–37; *Works, 10*, 52, 55–56, 263–264, 352; *Works, 13*, 163–64, 242–43.

Edwards lays out his "Resolutions" in a matter-of-fact style, treating them much like scientific principles. Of the seventy resolutions, the first dated one, No. 35, was written on December 18, 1722, when the "Diary" begins. The last, No. 70, was composed on August 17, 1723. Thus, at least half were devised during Edwards' New York pastorate and subsequent stay in East Windsor, before he received his Master's degree in September 1723. The date and place of composition of the early, undated resolutions are unknown.

Drawing up resolutions was a standard practice for educated people in the eighteenth century. Scholars have long compared Edwards' and Benjamin Franklin's resolutions.[2] In addition to arguing about Edwards' and Franklin's respective skills and significance as autobiographers, scholars have discussed the two men as philosophers, scientists, and religious commentators.[3] They have seen in these representative figures two sides of the Enlightenment, as well as the different patterns of the American character.[4]

Franklin's resolutions in his *Autobiography* stand in interesting comparison with Edwards'.[5] Both men agreed on the value of making resolutions, evaluating their effectiveness, and following them life-long. And the resolutions show that the two were united on the importance of speaking the truth, living in moderation, helping others, and doing one's duty. Each counseled himself (and others) to avoid sloth, make good use of time, cultivate an even temper, and pray for divine assistance; and each offers an energetic, thoughtful approach to life.

Beyond these similarities, however, the two differ greatly, and the resolutions reflect this. Franklin was satisfied with only thirteen resolutions, while the earnest Edwards drew out his list to seventy. They also differed in spirit and purpose. Franklin represents the Age of

2. Van Wyck Brooks, *America's Coming-of-Age* (New York, Huebsch, 1915); Carl Van Doren, *Benjamin Franklin and Jonathan Edwards: Selections from Their Writings* (New York, Charles Scribner's Sons, 1920).

3. Alfred O. Aldridge, "Benjamin Franklin and Jonathan Edwards on Lightning and Earthquakes," *Isis* 41 (1950), 162–64; David Levin, *The Puritan in the Enlightenment: Franklin and Edwards* (Chicago, Rand McNally, 1963).

4. Perry Miller, "Benjamin Franklin—Jonathan Edwards," in *Major Writers in America*, ed. by Perry Miller et al. (New York, Harcourt, Brace & World, 1962), *1*, 83–98; David Seed, "Exemplary Selves: Jonathan Edwards and Benjamin Franklin," in *First Person Singular: Studies in American Autobiography*, ed. A. Robert Lee (New York, St. Martin's Press, 1988), pp. 37–56; Barbara B. Oberg and Harry S. Stout, eds., *Benjamin Franklin, Jonathan Edwards, and the Representation of American Culture* (New York, Oxford Univ. Press, 1993).

5. Benjamin Franklin, *Autobiography*, ed. Leonard Labaree et al. (New Haven, Yale Univ. Press, 1964), pp. 148–64.

Reason. His emphasis is on this world and the preparation of a good citizen. His "Resolutions" were brief, epigrammatic, and eclectic. Jesus and Socrates equally merited imitation. Prayers were an afterthought in Franklin's daily practice. In contrast, Edwards remained the exemplar of Puritanism, depicting himself, along with all humans, as weak and sinful, helpless without divine intervention. Because the ultimate intention of the "Resolutions" was to produce a soul fit for eternity with God, they served as a set of practical day-to-day guidelines for achieving that end. Edwards adjured himself to study the Scriptures above all other books and to pray steadfastly; Jesus was to be trusted as Lord; God was present, personal, and primary.

The "Resolutions" are straightforward statements of purpose; the "Diary" records Edwards' efforts to follow them. As such, the "Diary" may tell us the most about Edwards as a person—at least as a young man. In the 148 entries he bares his soul about his struggles to establish ideals for living. The work is unique, a revelation of his feelings and efforts from the time he lived in New York through his tutorship at Yale, one of the most formative periods of his life.[6]

Diaries were kept by many colonial New Englanders, clergy and laity alike. Sometimes they merely recorded the weather or passing events; at other times they contained sermons; but in their fullest development, they logged their authors' spiritual progress. In the case of Edwards, this enterprise took on Pauline proportions. His youthful ambition was to be the most "complete Christian" of his age.[7] He accepted the strenuous effort involved and dedicated every thought, every action, to the promotion of that goal. His sole ambition was to realize his greatest potential and maximum usefulness for the glory of God.

Several themes run through the entries. One of them is the danger of temptation. Edwards felt the allure of riches and luxury. He had to train himself to resist a life of ease and procrastination, which was most attractive, especially when compared with the demands of study and the weariness of physical labor. Another source of peril was the body's

6. See Perry Miller, "Jonathan Edwards on the Sense of the Heart," *Harvard Theological Review* 41 (April 1948), 123–45, and "The Rhetoric of Sensation," in *Errand Into the Wilderness* (Cambridge, Belknap Press, 1956), 167–83; Roland A. DeLattre, *Beauty and Sensibility in the Thought of Jonathan Edwards* (New Haven, Yale Univ. Press, 1968); Stein, "'Like Apples of Gold'"; Wilson H. Kimnach, "Jonathan Edwards's Pursuit of Reality," in *Jonathan Edwards and the American Experience,* ed. Nathan O. Hatch and Harry S. Stout (New York, Oxford Univ. Press, 1988), pp. 103–17.

7. See "Resolutions" No. 63 and "Diary" for Jan. 14 and July 13, 1723.

need for sustenance and rest. If the dinner call came while Edwards was in the middle of a project, the meal would be forfeited. He viewed sleeping as a potential waste of time, to be cut to a minimum; consequently, he attempted to push the limits of his constitution. A further snare for the socially awkward Edwards was silence. His natural reticence often restrained him from speaking to people about spiritual matters, even when he felt the need to do so.

Time management was a major concern to Edwards. His aim was to rise early, work late, and fill every moment with constructive activity. At first, he even begrudged time for recreation, although he came to realize the need for exercise and the profit of sociability. Eventually, he followed the custom of giving a half-hour a day to chopping wood.

In contrast to the public image we have of Edwards the stoic, the "Diary" displays a man of surprising volatility and a wide range of emotions. Edwards often found himself in the Slough of Despond. Early on, he admits to being "exceedingly, dull, dry, and dead," and later he is "overwhelmed with melancholy." Some causes of the depressed states may have been loneliness or "evangelical humiliation," but undoubtedly his melancholy also stemmed from the almost impossible standards he set for himself and his despair at not being able to meet them. Yet at other times, his sense of the majesty and holiness of God filled him with awe, wonder, and thankfulness.

A recurring concern was personal relationships. Jonathan's father, Timothy, had a reputation as an excellent teacher but a strict disciplinarian; his mother, Esther, who was known for her "native intelligence," was demanding as well. Entries from May 1723 until May 1724 exhibit strain between son and parents. Young Edwards returned home from New York brimming with enthusiasm and eager to try novel approaches to ministry and theology, only to find a cool, resistant reception, evident in the "Diary" from his first day back. Repeatedly, Jonathan resolves to suppress his discontent with his parents.[8] He keeps reminding himself of his duty toward them and his indebtedness to them. But he also promises that when he is old, he will be reasonable and receptive to new ideas.

Edwards looked back on his youth with misgivings about the self-righteousness he exhibited in his strict performance of the "duties" of religion. However, his attending to the "means of grace" established patterns that held throughout his life. Ethicists from Plato to John

---

8. See "Resolutions" Nos. 44, 46, 47, 58, 59, 60, 62; and the following "Diary" entries for 1723: May 18 and 27, July 23, Aug. 13, Sept. 23, Dec. 9 and 31.

Dewey have recognized the central role of habit in the formation of character—and indeed, Edwards himself incorporated the concept into his view of the will. He recognized at an early age how individual actions create those patterns. The study of Scripture was for him particularly important. The Word of God, Edwards was convinced, provided him with enlightenment beyond human reason. He recorded his delight at certain biblical passages and his exhilaration at the implications of even single words. The "Diary" also tells much about his attitude toward prayer. Personal communion with the Almighty, which was to be a hallmark of his theology, was an experience Edwards sought on a daily basis. As in the "Personal Narrative," he mentions singing during devotion a number of times. Several brief prayers are included in the "Diary," with reminders of the need for prayer, along with instructions on the proper method of praying.

Finally, Edwards finds solace and renewal in nature. He often walked alone—in the grove by the Hudson in New York, in fields of flowers—gazing at trees and clouds. Even his dreams were of mountain vistas and vernal grandeur. In later years, his daily rides to the woods and meditations there were a direct outgrowth of these refreshing moments in his youth. Eventually, they contributed to a philosophical theology that included the "book of nature" as well as the "book of grace" as a source of divine truth.

"On Sarah Pierpont"

"On Sarah Pierpont" is an excellent example of the Puritan plain style. Its lyric qualities invite oral recitation. Originally untitled, its subject is traditionally considered to be Sarah Pierpont, who became Edwards' wife in 1727. Although the original is no longer extant, Edwards is thought to have written the tribute on the blank endpaper of a book that he probably presented to her. If the assumed date of writing—sometime in 1723—is correct, she was thirteen years old and he was twenty. He had known her since taking up his residence at Yale College in 1719.

The nineteenth century was famous for its emphasis on the "great man"; in the eighteenth century, the prime interest lay in the "godly person." When Edwards penned his meditation, the young minister was contemplating not Sarah Pierpont's appearance but her religious dedication and way of life. The account is austerely beautiful, describing her artless faith and radiant spirit. The tone is one of admiration.

On one level, the text amply confirms the most obvious interpretation. Edwards has heard reports of a maiden with sterling spiritual qualities. Enraptured by her idealistic way of life, he longs to achieve the same intimacy with God that she enjoys. Yet scholars have also noted the symbolic possibilities in the text. The woman can be interpreted as an expression of Edwards' own vision of holiness, and the piece as a whole can be seen as an important early example of the aesthetic foundations of Edwards' thought.[9]

"On Sarah Pierpont" has been the subject of both popular and scholarly literature. Popular writers have used the piece to create a romantic, idealized picture of the relationship between Jonathan and Sarah, often picking up on his description of their marriage as an "uncommon union." Yet the importance of his relationship to Sarah was always its spiritual nature. Nevertheless, romantics have occasionally used the little historical knowledge we have about Sarah Pierpont to create largely fictitious narratives of the Edwards' domestic lives. Most notable in this vein is Elisabeth Dodds' *Marriage to a Difficult Man* (1971).[1] Some writers have even invented memoirs and letters by Sarah in the interest of creating an idyll of domestic bliss in the Edwards parsonage.[2]

Within the evangelical religious cultures of the nineteenth and twentieth centuries, these romanticized accounts had a definite didactic aim. They were written to set forth the Edwardses as a model for Christian marriage and family life. As such, these accounts may more accurately be said to reflect the authors' assumptions than the actual lives of Jonathan Edwards and Sarah Pierpont.

Scholars, too, have viewed "On Sarah Pierpont" in two main ways. Literary historians consider it, along with the "Personal Narrative," to be an example of Edwards' artistry. In their estimation, the composi-

---

9. *Works, 10,* 279–81; Terrence Erdt, *Jonathan Edwards: Art and the Sense of the Heart* (Amherst, Univ. of Mass. Press, 1980), pp. 80–82; Norman S. Grabo, "The Veiled Vision: The Role of Aesthetics in Early American Intellectual History," *William and Mary Quarterly* 19 (1962), 493–510.

1. Elisabeth D. Dodds, *Marriage to a Difficult Man: The "Uncommon Union" of Jonathan and Sarah Edwards* (Philadelphia, Westminster Press, 1971). See also William M. Shea, "Jonathan Edwards and Sarah Pierpont: An Uncommon Union," in *Foundations of Religious Literacy,* ed. John V. Apczynski (Chico, Cal., Scholars Press, 1983), pp. 107–26; Perry Beam, "'Sarah Pierpont' and the Gentle Side of Jonathan Edwards," *Pleiades* 10 (1990), 38–42; Edna Gerstner, *Jonathan and Sarah: An Uncommon Union* (Morgan, Penn., Soli Deo Gloria Pub., 1995).

2. A. D. Gridley, "Diary and Letters of Sarah Pierpont," *Hours at Home* 5 (1867), 295–303, 417–25; and see the undoubtedly spurious letter attributed to Sarah Pierpont Edwards in J. B. Wakeley, *Anecdotes of George Whitefield* (New York, 1879), p. 278.

tion deserves to be classified as poetry. Religious historians interested in the evolution of Edwards' views of religious affections and the nature of true sainthood refer to the tribute to Sarah Pierpont in conjunction with her own narrative of 1742, which depicts a lengthy and traumatic religious episode. For these scholars, Sarah emerges as Jonathan's paradigm of experimental piety, as evidenced by the gender-neutral version of Sarah's narrative that he offered in *Some Thoughts*.[3] More recently, Jonathan and Sarah's relationship has been examined for what it tells us about the changing nature of gender roles in early America.[4]

"Personal Narrative"

The "Personal Narrative," Edwards' extended historical account of his own spiritual journey, may have been written in response to a request from his future son-in-law Aaron Burr. In a letter to Edwards in March 1741, Burr thanks him for his of December 14, 1740, adding: "I desire to bless God that he inclined you to write and especially to write so freely of your own experiences; I think it has been much blessed to my spiritual good. Though I have often heard and read of others' experiences, I never [met] with'm anything that had the like effect upon me. It came in a most seasonable time, and was the means of clearing up several things that I was in the dark about."[5] Although the December 14 letter has not been found, Hopkins states that the "Personal Narrative" was written nearly twenty years after the "Resolutions" and "Diary,"[6] which would coincide with the date of the correspondence with Burr.

The "Narrative," first published by Hopkins in 1765, has a buoyancy and optimism that are absent from the "Diary." Here Edwards relates the significant points of his experience rather than the mechanics. The "Diary" has an immediacy because it records daily struggles, but the "Narrative" has the sweep and continuity of retrospection. Whereas

3. Sarah Pierpont Edwards' own version is published in Dwight ed., *1*, 171–86, and JE's edition of it is in *Works, 4*, 331–41. See Julie Ellison, "The Sociology of 'Holy Indifference': Sarah Edwards's Narrative," *American Quarterly* 56 (1984), 479–95; Amanda Porterfield, *Feminine Spirituality in America: From Sarah Edwards to Martha Graham* (Philadelphia, Temple Univ. Press, 1980), pp. 39–48.

4. Ruth H. Bloch, "Women, Love and Virtue in the Writings of Edwards and Franklin," in *Benjamin Franklin, Jonathan Edwards, and the Representation of American Culture*, ed. Oberg and Stout, pp. 134–51.

5. Burr's letter is in Trask Library, ALS, two oversize folio leaves.

6. Hopkins, *Life*, p. 23.

the former was often written in the middle of youthful crises, the latter is the product of a mature soul.

The "Narrative" resolves questions raised in the "Diary." Edwards was concerned that he did not fit the usual Puritan paradigm of conversion. He confided as much to his "Diary," saying, "I cannot speak so fully to my experience of that preparatory work, of which divines speak."[7] Consequently, he decided to look "nicely and diligently" into the nature of conversion. Later, composing his own narrative gave him the opportunity to summarize what he had learned. Having been the pastor of Northampton for more than a decade and seen two awakenings, he had learned much. The order or structure of experience, he had come to realize, was not as important as the "indwelling principle" and the "nature," or guiding disposition, of the soul. Descriptions of conversion relations—ironically, such as the one Edwards himself was writing—were not as reliable as the fruits of faith.

In the same manner as the *Confessions* of Augustine or Rousseau, Edwards' "Personal Narrative" is a literary reconstruction. Edwards probably did not intend his account to be published, and without knowing what restrictions he put on the distribution of the manuscript, we cannot say whether anyone beyond Edwards' closest acquaintances read it before his death. But such scholars as Daniel Shea have pointed out that Edwards carefully composed the "Narrative," mindful of its instructive component within the context of revivals.[8] Selectively choosing from his "Diary" and private notebooks, Edwards avoided anything that hinted of enthusiasm on the one hand or works-righteousness on the other. The "Personal Narrative" worked toward a balanced description of the true saint that blended a conviction of personal inability, a new sense of the heart, and the idea of being swallowed up in the beauty and holiness of God. Edwards edited his own experience to fit his prescription of the model saint. Experimenting with his own narrative, he laid the groundwork for publishing similarly edited accounts later, first that of his wife and then, most ambitious of all, that of David Brainerd. In both these compositions, Edwards presents his subject to fit a preconceived standard.

As in his depictions of his wife and David Brainerd, Edwards in his

7. "Diary" for Dec. 18, 1722.

8. Daniel B. Shea, Jr., "The Art and Instruction of Jonathan Edwards's *Personal Narrative*," *American Literature* 37 (1965), 17–32. See also Norman S. Grabo, "Jonathan Edwards' *Personal Narrative*: Dynamic Stasis," *Literatur in Wissenschaft und Unterricht* 2 (1969), 141–48.

"Personal Narrative" is attempting to describe the personal "sense of divine things" that the saint possesses. Painfully aware of the insufficiency of words for such a task, he frequently resorts to paradoxical language.[9] Nowhere is this better illustrated than in his description of his feelings following a discussion with his father in the spring of 1721: "There came into my mind, a sweet sense of the glorious majesty and grace of God, that I know not how to express. I seemed to see them both in a sweet conjunction: majesty and meekness joined together: it was a sweet and gentle, and holy majesty; and also a majestic meekness; an awful sweetness; a high, and great, and holy gentleness." Elsewhere, the majesty and glory of God is symbolized by thunder and lightning, formerly feared but now welcomed as an incentive to worship.[1] An image for God's benign qualities is the sun. Edwards sees the individual believer as a little flower, able to share the rays of the great source of light and to have beauty and fragrance, a sublimity of its own, as a result.

Edwards is one of a long line of colonial writers, including William Bradford, Anne Bradstreet, and Edward Taylor, for whom nature plays a significant part. In the "Narrative," nature has a positive inspirational role. For Edwards, contemplation of nature took on a sacramental perspective. Sitting alone beneath a tree or walking in the woods, he would have extraordinarily intense interactions with the divine. On one occasion, in 1737, while walking in the woods, he had such a "view" of God's glory that for an hour he was "in a flood of tears, and weeping aloud." Such times of solitude and meditation were for Edwards occasions of renewal.

The "Personal Narrative" has attracted wide attention among literary scholars, many of whom see it as perhaps the best example of Edwards' artistry, with the exception of *Sinners in the Hands of an Angry God*. Some consider the document a new and quintessentially American form of self-discovery that builds on the traditional Puritan conversion narrative.[2] Others have found in it a psychological profile that shows Edwards struggling to subdue his will and overcome personal and societal insecurities. Richard Bushman, in particular, has ex-

9. Paul David Johnson, "Jonathan Edwards's 'Sweet Conjunction,'" *Early American Literature* 16 (1981), 270–81.

1. See "Images of Divine Things," no. 28, in *Works*, *11*, 58.

2. Robert F. Sayre, *The Examined Self: Benjamin Franklin, Henry Adams, Henry James* (Princeton, Princeton Univ. Press, 1964), pp. 34–39; David L. Minter, *The Interpreted Design as a Structural Principle in American Prose* (New Haven, Yale Univ. Press, 1969), 72–77.

plored how Edwards epitomizes Puritan consciousness and identity.[3] However we view it, the "Personal Narrative" is an incomparably rich source for understanding Edwards.

Editing the Texts

None of Edwards' original manuscripts exists for any of the four personal writings printed here. Rather, we must rely solely on the work of later editors and copyists. Two documents even combine separate printed versions.

Selections from the "Resolutions" were first printed by Hopkins, in his *Life* (pp. 6–9). Dwight then published the entire list of seventy in his "Memoir" (*1*, 68–73). The cover of "Resolutions and Private Diary," with Edwards' autograph title, is at the Beinecke Rare Book and Manuscript Library of Yale University. The basic text comes from Hopkins because it is the earliest version and because, on examination of other texts he published for which the manuscripts exist, I believe that his is more accurate than Dwight's published version. Passages in double square brackets indicate words available only in Dwight.

The "Resolutions" were distributed throughout the nineteenth century to supply models of Christian living. They were printed, along with articles of faith and church covenants, in Leicester, Massachusetts (1805); Beverly, Massachusetts (1807); Vermont (1808); Pembroke, New Hampshire (1823); in *The Christian's Scripture Directory* (1841), pp. 57–72; as a tract (n.d.); and in the *American Journal of Education* 27 (Hartford, 1877), 724–27.[4]

The "Diary" presents the same sort of problems as the "Resolutions." Hopkins printed portions of it (*Life*, pp. 10–21), and Dwight published it in its fullest form (*1*, 76–94, 99–106). As with the "Resolutions," Hopkins' selections from the "Diary" are used; and text within double brackets indicates material available only in Dwight's edition. Dwight also left behind a copy of a portion of the "Diary" (Trask

---

3. Richard L. Bushman, "Jonathan Edwards and Puritan Consciousness," *Journal for the Scientific Study of Religion* 5 (1966), 383–96, and "Jonathan Edwards as Great Man: Identity, Conversion, and Leadership in the Great Awakening," *Soundings* 52 (1969), 15–46. See also David Leverenz, *The Language of Puritan Feeling: An Exploration in Literature, Psychology, and Social History* (New Brunswick, Rutgers Univ. Press, 1980), pp. 225–57.

4. Johnson, *Printed Writings*, pp. 101–03.

Library, four quarto leaves). The beginning and end points of this fragment, as well as textual variances, are indicated in the notes.⁵

Several days and dates in the "Diary" do not appear to coincide with either the calendar or other dates. In some cases, this may be attributed to Edwards' habit of dating the beginning of days, in the old Hebrew and Puritan style, at sundown. This is particularly noticeable on Saturday nights, a frequent time for his self-evaluation, when he would begin the sabbath at sunset, and sometimes give to Saturday night the date for Sunday (see Mar. 24, Apr. 7, and Apr. 14, 1723). Other discrepancies may be due to Edwards' incorrect dating or to transcribal or typographical errors (see Friday, June 1; Saturday, June 25; all of October; and Thursday, Nov. 26, 1723).

The only text among the four based wholly on a manuscript copy transcribed by Dwight is that of "On Sarah Pierpont." It is in the Trask Library and contains miscellaneous dates and notes on the verso relating to Dwight's memoir of Edwards' life. Thomas A. Schafer has determined that Dwight amended the text as he copied it out, crossing out words and phrases and supplying his preferred readings in interlineations. An attempt has been made here to restore Edwards' original text according to Schafer's analysis. "On Sarah Pierpont" was first printed in Dwight ed., *1*, 114–15, and reprinted in Stoughton, *Windsor Farmes*, pp. 82–83. On analysis, I judge Stoughton's version to be an adaptation of Dwight, although Wilson H. Kimnach argues that Stoughton may have had access to the original (*Works, 10*, 280). The original, which is not believed to be still extant, was described by Stoughton (p. 82) as being written on a blank leaf of a book.

Modern anthologies of Edwards' writings have made "On Sarah Pierpont" a standard. C. C. Goen includes it (*Works, 4*, 68) without attempting a critical approach. However, Kimnach presents a literary analysis of it and lists the printed variations (*Works, 10*, 8–9, 276–81). He also suggests that the sermon *True Love to God* has overtones of the meditation (ibid., 632–43). "On Sarah Pierpont" has appeared in various collected works and anthologies of Edwards but was never printed as a broadside.⁶

Hopkins was the first to print the piece that has become known as the

5. I am indebted to Thomas A. Schafer for editorial advice on the "Diary" and for permitting me to use his transcription and study of the "Diary" cover. See *Works, 10*, 52–55, 262–75, 465, 507; *Works, 13*, 11, 43–44, 77–81, 114.

6. Johnson, *Printed Writings*, p. x.

"Personal Narrative" (*Life,* pp. 23–39), and his text is used here. He entitled it "An Account of His Conversion, Experiences, and Religious Exercises, Given by [Edwards] Himself." As with the "Resolutions," the "Personal Narrative" was frequently reissued during the nineteenth century. Dwight reprinted it (*1*, 58–62, 64–67, 98–99, 131–36). Other early editions, too numerous to list here, include *An Account of the Conversion and Religious Experience of . . . Jonathan Edwards* (London, 1780) and *Conversion of President Edwards* (New York, 1827).[7]

Thomas A. Schafer has demonstrated that Edwards used his "Diary" and early "Miscellanies" in composing the section of the "Personal Narrative" relating to the New York period. Edwards even says as much within the text, referring to entries for January 12, 1723, on his "solemn dedication," and for May 1, 1723. Edwards also borrowed freely from "Miscellanies" no. a, a meditation on holiness, in preparing his narrative.[8] The paragraph beginning "I remember the thoughts I used then to have of holiness" opens a passage that paraphrases his first, formative thoughts on the topic.

7. Ibid., pp. 94–95.
8. *Works, 13*, 77–78.

RESOLUTIONS

Being sensible that I am unable to do anything without God's help, I do humbly entreat him by his grace to enable me to keep these Resolutions, so far as they are agreeable to his will, for Christ's sake.

Remember to read over these Resolutions once a week.

1. Resolved, that I will do whatsoever I think to be most to God's glory, and my own good, profit and pleasure, in the whole of my duration, without any consideration of the time, whether now, or never so many myriads of ages hence. Resolved to do whatever I think to be my duty, and most for the good and advantage of mankind in general. Resolved to do this, whatever difficulties I meet with, how many and how great soever.

2. Resolved, to be continually endeavoring to find out some new invention and contrivance to promote the forementioned things.

[[3. Resolved, if ever I shall fall and grow dull, so as to neglect to keep any part of these Resolutions, to repent of all I can remember, when I come to myself again.]]

4. Resolved, never to do any manner of thing, whether in soul or body, less or more, but what tends to the glory of God; nor be, nor suffer it, if I can avoid it.

5. Resolved, never to lose one moment of time; but improve it the most profitable way I possibly can.

6. Resolved, to live with all my might, while I do live.

7. Resolved, never to do anything, which I should be afraid to do, if it were the last hour of my life.

[[8. Resolved, to act, in all respects, both speaking and doing, as if nobody had been so vile as I, and as if I had committed the same sins, or had the same infirmities or failings as others; and that I will let the knowledge of their failings promote nothing but shame in myself, and prove only an occasion of my confessing my own sins and misery to God. Vid. July 30, [1723].]]

9. Resolved, to think much on all occasions of my own dying, and of the common circumstances which attend death.

[[10. Resolved, when I feel pain, to think of the pains of martyrdom, and of hell.]]

11. Resolved, when I think of any[1] theorem in divinity to be solved, immediately to do what I can towards solving it, if circumstances don't hinder.

[[12. Resolved, if I take delight in it as a gratification of pride, or vanity, or on any such account, immediately to throw it by.]]

13. Resolved, to be endeavoring to find out fit objects of charity and liberality.

14. Resolved, never to do anything out of revenge.

15. Resolved, never to suffer the least motions of anger to irrational beings.

[[16. Resolved, never to speak evil of anyone, so that it shall tend to his dishonor, more or less, upon no account except for some real good.]]

17. Resolved, that I will live so as I shall wish I had done when I come to die.

18. Resolved, to live so at all times, as I think is best in my devout frames, and when I have clearest notions of things of the gospel, and another world.

[[19. Resolved, never to do anything, which I should be afraid to do, if I expected it would not be above an hour, before I should hear the last trump.]]

20. Resolved, to maintain the strictest temperance in eating and drinking.

21. Resolved, never to do anything, which if I should see in another, I should count a just occasion to despise him for, or to think any way the more meanly of him.

[[22. Resolved, to endeavor to obtain for myself (as much happiness, in the other world,) as I possibly can, with all the power, might, vigor, and vehemence, yea violence, I am capable of, or can bring myself to exert, in any way that can be thought of.

23. Resolved, frequently to take some deliberate action, which seems most unlikely to be done, for the glory of God, and trace it back to the original intention, designs and ends of it; and if I find it not to be for God's glory, to repute it as a breach of the 4th Resolution.]]

24. Resolved, whenever I do any conspicuously evil action, to trace it back, till I come to the original cause; and then both carefully endeavor

1. "Any" is from Dwight (*1*, 69); Hopkins (p. 6) reads "my."

to do so no more, and to fight and pray with all my might against the original of it.

[[25. Resolved, to examine carefully, and constantly, what that one thing in me is, which causes me in the least to doubt of the love of God; and to direct all my forces against it.

26. Resolved, to cast away such things, as I find do abate my assurance.

27. Resolved, never willfully to omit anything, except the omission be for the glory of God; and frequently to examine my omissions.]]

28. Resolved, to study the Scriptures so steadily, constantly and frequently, as that I may find, and plainly perceive myself to grow in the knowledge of the same.

[[29. Resolved, never to count that a prayer, nor to let that pass as a prayer, nor that as a petition of a prayer, which is so made, that I cannot hope that God will answer it; nor that as a confession, which I cannot hope God will accept.]]

30. Resolved, to strive to my utmost every week to be brought higher in religion, and to a higher exercise of grace, than I was the week before.

[[31. Resolved, never to say anything at all against anybody, but when it is perfectly agreeable to the highest degree of Christian honor, and of love to mankind, agreeable to the lowest humility, and sense of my own faults and failings, and agreeable to the Golden Rule; often, when I have said anything against anyone, to bring it to, and try it strictly by the test of this Resolution.]]

32. Resolved, to be strictly and firmly faithful to my trust, that that in Prov. 20:6, "A faithful man who can find?" may not be partly fulfilled in me.

33. Resolved, always to do what I can towards making, maintaining and establishing[2] peace, when it can be without over-balancing detriment in other respects. [[Dec. 26, 1722.]]

34. Resolved, in narrations never to speak anything but the pure and simple verity.

[[35. Resolved, whenever I so much question whether I have done my duty, as that my quiet and calm is thereby disturbed, to set it down, and also how the question was resolved. Dec. 18, 1722.]]

36. Resolved, never to speak evil of any, except I have some particular good call for it. [[Dec. 19, 1722.]]

2. Dwight (*1*, 70): "preserving."

37. Resolved, to inquire every night, as I am going to bed, wherein I have been negligent, what sin I have committed, and wherein I have denied myself: also at the end of every week, month and year. [[Dec. 22 and 26, 1722.]]

38. Resolved, never to speak anything that is ridiculous,[3] or matter of laughter on the Lord's day. [[Sabbath evening, Dec. 23, 1722.]]

39. Resolved, never to do anything that I so much question the lawfulness of, as that I intend, at the same time, to consider and examine afterwards, whether it be lawful or no: except I as much question the lawfulness of the omission.

[[40. Resolved, to inquire every night, before I go to bed, whether I have acted in the best way I possibly could, with respect to eating and drinking. Jan. 7, 1723.]]

41. Resolved, to ask myself at the end of every day, week, month and year, wherein I could possibly in any respect have done better. [[Jan. 11, 1723.]]

42. Resolved, frequently to renew the dedication of myself to God, which was made at my baptism; which I solemnly renewed, when I was received into the communion of the church; and which I have solemnly re-made this 12th day of January, 1722–23.

43. Resolved, never henceforward, till I die, to act as if I were anyway my own, but entirely and altogether God's, agreeable to what is to be found in Saturday, Jan. 12. [[Jan. 12th, 1723.

44. Resolved, that no other end but religion, shall have any influence at all on any of my actions; and that no action shall be, in the least circumstance, any otherwise than the religious end will carry it. Jan. 12, 1723.

45. Resolved, never to allow any pleasure or grief, joy or sorrow, nor any affection at all, nor any degree of affection, nor any circumstance relating to it, but what helps religion. Jan. 12 and 13, 1723.]]

46. Resolved, never to allow the least measure of any fretting uneasiness at my father or mother. Resolved to suffer no effects of it, so much as in the least alteration of speech, or motion of my eye: and to be especially careful of it, with respect to any of our family.

47. Resolved, to endeavor to my utmost to deny whatever is not most agreeable to a good, and universally sweet and benevolent, quiet, peaceable, contented, easy, compassionate, generous, humble, meek, modest, submissive, obliging, diligent and industrious, charitable,

3. Ibid., "sportive."

even, patient, moderate, forgiving, sincere temper; and to do at all times what such a temper would lead me to. Examine strictly every week, whether I have done so. [[Sabbath morning, May 5, 1723.]]

48. Resolved, constantly, with the utmost niceness and diligence, and the strictest scrutiny, to be looking into the state of my soul, that I may know whether I have truly an interest in Christ or no; that when I come to die, I may not have any negligence respecting this to repent of. [[May 26, 1723.

49. Resolved, that this never shall be, if I can help it.]]

50. Resolved, I will act so as I think I shall judge would have been best, and most prudent, when I come into the future world. [[July 5, 1723.

51. Resolved, that I will act so, in every respect, as I think I shall wish I had done, if I should at last be damned. July 8, 1723.]]

52. I frequently hear persons in old age say how they would live, if they were to live their lives over again: resolved, that I will live just so as I can think I shall wish I had done, supposing I live to old age. [[July 8, 1723.

53. Resolved, to improve every opportunity, when I am in the best and happiest frame of mind, to cast and venture my soul on the Lord Jesus Christ, to trust and confide in him, and consecrate myself wholly to him; that from this I may have assurance of my safety, knowing that I confide in my Redeemer. July 8, 1723.]]

54. Whenever I hear anything spoken in commendation[4] of any person, if I think it would be praiseworthy in me, resolved to endeavor to imitate it. [[July 8, 1723.]]

55. Resolved, to endeavor to my utmost to act as I can think I should do, if I had already seen the happiness of heaven, and hell torments. [[July 8, 1723.]]

56. Resolved, never to give over, nor in the least to slacken my fight with my corruptions, however unsuccessful I may be.

57. Resolved, when I fear misfortunes and adversities, to examine whether I have done my duty, and resolve to do it; and let it be just as providence orders it, I will as far as I can, be concerned about nothing but my duty and my sin. [[June 9 and July 13, 1723.

58. Resolved, not only to refrain from an air of dislike, fretfulness, and anger in conversation, but to exhibit an air of love, cheerfulness and benignity. May 27 and July 13, 1723.

4. "Commendation" is from Dwight (*1*, 72); Hopkins (p. 9) reads "conversation."

59. Resolved, when I am most conscious of provocations to ill-nature and anger, that I will strive most to feel and act good-naturedly; yea, at such times, to manifest good nature, though I think that in other respects it would be disadvantageous, and so as would be imprudent at other times. May 12, July 11, and July 13.

60. Resolved, whenever my feelings begin to appear in the least out of order, when I am conscious of the least uneasiness within, or the least irregularity without, I will then subject myself to the strictest examination. July 4 and 13, 1723.

61. Resolved, that I will not give way to that listlessness which I find unbends and relaxes my mind from being fully and fixedly set on religion, whatever excuse I may have for it—that what my listlessness inclines me to do, is best to be done, etc. May 21 and July 13, 1723.]]

62. Resolved, never to do anything but duty; and then according to Eph. 6:6–8, do it willingly and cheerfully "as unto the Lord, and not to man; knowing that whatever good thing any man doth, the same shall he receive of the Lord." [[June 25 and July 13, 1723.

63. On the supposition, that there never was to be but one individual in the world, at any one time, who was properly a complete Christian, in all respects of a right stamp, having Christianity always shining in its true luster, and appearing excellent and lovely, from whatever part and under whatever character viewed: resolved, to act just as I would do, if I strove with all my might to be that one, who should live in my time. Jan. 14 and July 13, 1723.

64. Resolved, when I find those "groanings which cannot be uttered," of which the Apostle speaks [Rom. 8:26], and those "breakings of soul for the longing it hath," of which the Psalmist speaks, Ps. 119:20, that I will promote them to the utmost of my power, and that I will not be weary of earnestly endeavoring to vent my desires, nor of the repetitions of such earnestness. July 23 and Aug. 10, 1723.]]

65. Resolved, very much to exercise myself in this all my life long, viz. with the greatest openness I am capable of, to declare my ways to God, and lay open my soul to him: all my sins, temptations, difficulties, sorrows, fears, hopes, desires, and everything, and every circumstance; according to Dr. Manton's 27th sermon on the 119th Psalm.[5] [[July 26 and Aug. 10, 1723.

66. Resolved, that I will endeavor always to keep a benign aspect,

5. Thomas Manton, *One Hundred and Ninety Sermons on the Hundred and Nineteenth Psalm* (London, 1681). The doctrine of Sermon XXVII, on Ps. 119:26 (pp. 162–70), reads: "They that would speed with God, should learn this point of Christian ingenuity, unfeignedly to lay open their whole case to him." See also the "Diary" for July 26, 1723, below.

and air of acting and speaking in all places, and in all companies, except it should so happen that duty requires otherwise.]]

67. Resolved, after afflictions, to inquire, what I am the better for them, what good I have got by them, and what I might have got by them.

[[68. Resolved, to confess frankly to myself all that which I find in myself, either infirmity or sin; and, if it be what concerns religion, also to confess the whole case to God, and implore needed help. July 23 and Aug. 10, 1723.

69. Resolved, always to do that, which I shall wish I had done when I see others do it. Aug. 11, 1723.

70. Let there be something of benevolence, in all that I speak. Aug. 17, 1723.]]

DIARY

[[Dec. 18, [1722]. This day made the 35th Resolution. The reason why I, in the least, question my interest in God's love and favor, is, 1. Because I cannot speak so fully to my experience of that preparatory work, of which divines speak; 2. I do not remember that I experienced regeneration, exactly in those steps, in which divines say it is generally wrought; 3. I do not feel the Christian graces sensibly enough, particularly faith. I fear they are only such hypocritical outside affections, which wicked men may feel, as well as others. They do not seem to be sufficiently inward, full, sincere, entire and hearty. They do not seem so substantial, and so wrought into my very nature, as I could wish. 4. Because I am sometimes guilty of sins of omission and commission. Lately I have doubted, whether I do not transgress in evil speaking. This day, resolved, No.

Dec. 19. This day made the 36th Resolution. Lately, I have been very much perplexed, by seeing the doctrine of different degrees in glory questioned; but now have almost got over the difficulty.

Dec. 20. This day somewhat question, whether I had not been guilty of negligence yesterday, and this morning; but resolved, No.

Dec. 21, Friday. This day, and yesterday, I was exceedingly dull, dry and dead.]]

Saturday, Dec. 22, 1722. This day revived by God's Spirit. Affected with the sense of the excellency of holiness. Felt more exercise of love to Christ than usual. Have also felt sensible repentance of sin, because it was committed against so merciful and good a God. This night made the 37th Resolution.

Sabbath-day night, Dec. 23. Made the 38th Resolution.

Monday, Dec. 24. Higher thoughts than usual of the excellency of Jesus Christ and his kingdom. [[Concluded to observe, at the end of every month, the number of breaches of resolutions, to see whether they increase or diminish, to begin from this day, and to compute from that the weekly account, my monthly increase, and, out of the whole, my yearly increase, beginning from new year days.

Wednesday, Dec. 26. Early in the morning yesterday, was hindered by the headache all day; though I hope I did not lose much. Made an addition to the 37th Resolution, concerning weeks, months and years. At night; made the 33rd Resolution.

Saturday, Dec. 29. About sunset this day, dull and lifeless.

1722–23. Tuesday, Jan. 1. Have been dull for several days. Examined whether I have not been guilty of negligence today; and resolved, No.]]

Wednesday, Jan. 2, 1722–23. Dull. I find by experience, that let me make resolutions, and do what I will, with never so many inventions, it is all nothing, and to no purpose at all, without the motions of the Spirit of God: for if the Spirit of God should be as much withdrawn from me always, as for the week past, notwithstanding all I do, I should not grow; but should languish, and miserably fade away. [[I perceive, if God should withdraw his Spirit a little more, I should not hesitate to break my resolutions, and should soon arrive at my old state.]] There is no dependence upon myself. [[Our resolutions may be at the highest one day, and yet, the next day, we may be in a miserable dead condition, not at all like the same person who resolved.]] It is to no purpose to resolve, except we depend on the grace of God; for if it were not for his mere grace, one might be a very good man one day, and a very wicked one the next. [[I find also by experience, that there is no guessing out the ends of providence, in particular dispensations towards me—any otherwise than as afflictions come as corrections for sin, and God intends when we meet with them, to desire us to look back on our ways, and see wherein we have done amiss, and lament that particular sin, and all our sins, before him—knowing this, also, that all things shall work together for our good; not knowing in what way, indeed, but trusting in God.

Saturday evening, Jan. 5. A little redeemed from a long dreadful dullness, about reading the Scriptures. This week, have been unhappily low in the weekly account; and what are the reasons of it? abundance of listlessness and sloth; and, if this should continue much longer, I perceive that other sins will begin to discover themselves. It used to appear to me, that I had not much sin remaining; but now, I perceive that there are great remainders of sin. Where may it not bring me to, if God should leave me? Sin is not enough mortified. Without the influences of the Spirit of God, the old serpent would begin to rouse up himself from his frozen state, and would come to life again. Resolved, that I have been negligent in two things: in not striving enough in duty; and in not forcing myself upon religious thoughts.]]

Sabbath day, Jan. 6, at night. Much concerned about the improvement of precious time. Intend to live in continual mortification, without ceasing, [[and even to weary myself thereby,]] as long as [[I am]] in this world, [[and never to expect or desire any worldly ease or pleasure.

Monday, Jan. 7, at night, made the 40th Resolution.]]

Tuesday, Jan. 8, in the morning. Higher thoughts than usual of the excellency of Christ, and felt an unusual repentance of sin therefrom.

Wednesday, Jan. 9, at night. Decayed. I am sometimes apt to think, I have a great deal more of holiness than I have. I find now and then, that abominable corruption which is directly contrary to what I read of eminent Christians. [[I do not seem to be half so careful to improve time, to do everything quick, and in as short a time as I possibly can, nor to be perpetually engaged to think about religion, as I was yesterday and the day before, nor indeed as I have been at certain times, perhaps a twelvemonth ago. If my resolutions of that nature, from that time, had always been kept alive and awake, how much better might I have been, than I now am.]] How deceitful is my heart! I take up a strong resolution, but how soon does it weaken!

Thursday, Jan. 10, about noon. Reviving. 'Tis a great dishonor to Christ, in whom I hope I have an interest, to be uneasy at my worldly state and condition. When I see the prosperity of others, and that all things go easy with them—the world is smooth to them, and they are happy in many respects, and very prosperous, or are advanced to much honor etc.—to grudge and envy them, or be the least uneasy at it; to wish or long for the same prosperity, and that it would ever be so with me. Wherefore concluded always to rejoice in everyone's prosperity, and to expect for myself no happiness of that nature as long as I live; but depend upon afflictions, and betake myself entirely to another happiness.

I think I find myself much more sprightly and healthy, both in body and mind, for my self-denial in eating, drinking, and sleeping.

I think it would be advantageous every morning to consider my business and temptations; and what sins I shall be exposed to that day: and to make a resolution how to improve the day, and to avoid those sins. And so at the beginning of every week, month and year.

I never knew before what was meant by not setting our hearts upon these things. 'Tis, not to care about them, to depend upon them, to afflict ourselves much with fears of losing them, nor please ourselves with expectation of obtaining them, or hope of the continuance of them. At night made the 41st Resolution.

Saturday, Jan. 12, in the morning. I have this day solemnly renewed my baptismal covenant and self-dedication, which I renewed when I was received into communion of the church. I have been before God; and have given myself, all that I am and have to God, so that I am not in any respect my own: I can challenge no right in myself, I can challenge no right in this understanding, this will, these affections that are in me; neither have I any right to this body, or any of its members: no right to this tongue, these hands, nor feet; no right to these senses, these eyes, these ears, this smell or taste. I have given myself clear away, and have not retained anything as my own. I have been to God this morning, and told him that I gave myself *wholly* to him. I have given every power to him; so that for the future I will challenge no right in myself, in any respect. I have expressly promised him, and do now promise almighty God, that by his grace I will not. I have this morning told him, that I did take him for my whole portion and felicity, looking on nothing else as any part of my happiness, nor acting as if it were; and his law for the constant rule of my obedience; and would fight with all my might against the world, the flesh, and the devil, to the end of my life. And did believe in Jesus Christ, and receive him as a prince and a Savior; and would adhere to the faith and obedience of the gospel, how hazardous and difficult soever the profession and practice of it may be. That I did receive the blessed Spirit as my teacher, sanctifier and only comforter; and cherish all his motions to enlighten, purify, confirm, comfort and assist me. This I have done. And I pray God, for the sake of Christ, to look upon it as a self-dedication; and to receive me now as entirely his own, and deal with me in all respects as such; whether he afflicts me or prospers me, or whatever he pleases to do with me, who am his. Now, henceforth I am not to act in any respect as my own. I shall act as my own, if I ever make use of any of my powers to anything that is not to the glory of God, and don't make the glorifying him my whole and entire business; if I murmur in the least at afflictions; if I grieve at the prosperity of others; if I am anyway uncharitable; if I am angry because of injuries; if I revenge; if I do anything, purely to please myself, or if I avoid anything for the sake of my ease; if I omit anything because it is great self-denial; if I trust to myself: if I take any of the praise of any good that I do, or rather God does by me; or if I am any way proud.

This day made the 42nd and 43rd Resolutions. [[Whether or no, any other end ought to have any influence at all, on any of my actions or, whether]] any[1] action ought to be any otherwise, in any respect, than if nothing else but religion had the least influence on my mind. Answer, No. Wherefore, I make the 44th Resolution.

Query: whether any delight, or satisfaction, ought to be allowed, because any other end is obtained, besides a religious one? In the afternoon, I answer, Yes; because, if [we] should never suffer ourselves to rejoice, but because we have obtained a religious end, we should never rejoice at the sight of friends, we should not allow ourselves any pleasure in our food, whereby the animal spirits would be withdrawn, and good digestion hindered. But the query is to be answered thus: we never ought to allow any joy or sorrow, but what helps religion. Wherefore, I make the 45th Resolution.

The reason why I so soon grow lifeless, and unfit for the business I am about, I have found out, is only because I have been used to suffer myself soon to leave off, for the sake of ease, and so, I have got a habit of expecting ease; and therefore, when I think I have exercised myself a good while, I cannot keep myself to it any longer, because I expect to be released, as my due and right. And then, I am deceived, as if I were really tired and weary. Whereas, if I did not expect ease, and was resolved to afflict myself by business, as much as I could, I should continue with as much[2] vigor to my business, without vacation time to rest. Thus, I have found it in reading the Scriptures; and thus, I have found it in prayer; and thus, I believe it to be in getting sermons by heart, and other things.

At night. This week, the weekly account rose higher than ordinary. It is suggested to me, that too constant a mortification, and too vigorous application to religion, may be prejudicial to health. But nevertheless, I will plainly feel it and experience it, before I cease, on this account. It is no matter how much tired and weary I am, if my health is not impaired.

1. Beginning of text from the Dwight MS transcript fragment.
2. Dwight originally wrote "as much," crossed it off, and interlineated "the same." JE probably wrote "as much."

Jan. 13, sabbath day. I plainly feel, that if I should continue to go on, as from the beginning of the last week hitherto, I should continually grow and increase in grace. After the afternoon meeting, made an addition to the 45th Resolution. At noon; I remember I thought I loved to be a member of Christ, nor anything distinct, but only a part, so as to have no separate interest, or pleasure of my own. At night, resolved to endeavor fully to understand I Cor. 7:29–32, and to act according to it.

Monday, Jan. 14. About ten o'clock in the morning, made this book, and put these papers in it.[3] The dedication I made of myself to my God, on Saturday last, has been exceeding useful to me. I thought I had a more spiritual insight into the Scriptures, when reading the 8th [chapter] of Romans, than ever before.

At night. Great instances of mortification are deep wounds given to the body of sin, hard blows that make him stagger and reel: we thereby get great ground and footing against him, and he is the weaker ever after. And we have easier work with him the next time. He grows cowardly; and we can easily cause him to give way, until at length, we find it easy work with him, and can kill him at pleasure. While we live without great instances of mortification and self-denial, the old man keeps whereabouts he was; for he is sturdy and obstinate, and will not stir for small blows. And this, without doubt, is one great reason why many Christians do not sensibly increase in grace. After the greatest mortifications, I always find the greatest comfort. Wrote the 63rd Resolution. Such little things as Christians commonly do, will not show increase of grace much. We must do great things for God. It will be best, when I find I have lost any former, ancient, good motions or actions, to take notice of it, if I can remember them.

Supposing there was never but one complete Christian, in all respects of a right stamp, having Christianity shining in its true luster, at a time in the world; resolved to act just as I would do, if I strove with all my might to be that one, that should be in my time.[4]

Jan. 15, Tuesday, about two or three of clock. I have been all this day decaying. It seemed yesterday, the day before and Saturday, that I should always retain the same resolution to the same height. But alas! how soon do I decay. O how weak, how infirm, how unable to do anything of myself. What a poor, inconsistent being! What a miserable

3. Dwight (*1*, 80*n*) notes: "He refers to slips of paper on which the first part of the Diary is written; as far as Jan. 15, at night."
4. The preceding paragraph appears only in Hopkins, pp. 12–13.

wretch, without the assistance of God's Spirit. While I stand, I am ready to think I stand by my own strength, and upon my own legs; and I am ready to triumph over my (spiritual) enemies, as if it were I myself that caused them to flee. When alas, I am but a poor infant, upheld by Jesus Christ; who holds me up, and gives me liberty to smile to see my enemies flee, when he drives them before me; and so I laugh, as if I myself did it, when it is only Jesus Christ leads me along, and fights himself against my enemies. And now, the Lord has a little left me; how weak do I find myself. O let it teach me to depend less on myself, to be more humble, and to give more of the praise of my ability to Jesus Christ. The heart of man is deceitful above all things, and desperately wicked, who can know it? [Jer. 17:9].

The occasion of my decaying, is a little melancholy. My spirits are down, and I am concerned because I fear I lost some friendship the last night. And my spirits being low, my resolutions have lost their strength. I differ today from yesterday, in these things. I do not resolve anything today, half so strongly. I am not so perpetually thinking on and renewing my resolutions, as I was then. I am not half so vigorous as I was then; nor am I half so careful to do everything with vigor. Then, I kept continually acting; but now, I do things slowly, and satisfy myself by thinking of religion in the meantime. I am not so careful to go quick from one business to another. I felt humiliation, about sunset. What shall I do frequently, with a good grace, to fall into Christian discourse and conference? [[At night.]] The next time I am in such a lifeless frame, I will force myself to go quick from one thing to another, and do those things with vigor, in which vigor would ever be useful. The things, which take off my mind, when bent on religion, are commonly some remarkable change and alteration: journeys, change of place, change of business, change of studies, and change of other circumstances; or something that makes me melancholy; or some sin.

Jan. 17, Thursday. About three o'clock, overwhelmed with melancholy.

Jan. 18, Friday. At night. Beginning to endeavor to recover out of the death I have been in for these several days.

Jan. 20, sabbath day. At night. The last week I was sunk so low, that I fear it will be a long time, 'ere I shall be recovered. I fell exceedingly low in the weekly account. I find my heart so deceitful, that I am almost discouraged from making any more resolutions. Wherein have I been negligent in the week past; and how could I have done better, to help the dreadful, low estate in which I am sunk?

Jan. 21, Monday. Before sunrise, answered (the preceding questions): I ought to have spent the time in bewailing my sins, and in singing psalms, especially psalms or hymns of repentance; these duties being most suited to the frame I was in. I do not spend time enough in endeavoring to affect myself with the glories of Christianity. Fell short in the monthly account. It seems to me, that I am fallen from my former and ancient sense of the pleasantness of religion.

Feb. 5, Tuesday. At night. I have thought, that this being so exceedingly careful, and so particularly anxious, to force myself to think of religion, at all leisure moments, has exceedingly distracted my mind, and made me altogether unfit for that, and everything else. I have thought, that this caused the dreadful, low condition I was in on the 15th of January. I think I stretched myself farther than I could bear, and so broke. For now, it seems to me, though I know not why, that I do not do enough to prepare for another world. I do not seem to press forward,[5] [[to fight and wrestle, as the apostles used to speak. I do not seem so greatly and constantly to mortify and deny myself, as the mortification of which they speak represents. Therefore, wherein ought I to do more in this way? I answer: I am again grown too careless about eating, drinking and sleeping—not careful enough about evil speaking.]]

Saturday, Feb. 16. I do certainly know that I love holiness, such as the gospel requires.

At night. [[For the time past of my life, I have been negligent, in that I have not sufficiently kept up that part of divine worship, singing the praise of God in secret, and with company.]] I have been negligent for the month past in these three things; I have not been watchful enough over my appetite in eating and drinking; in rising too late a-mornings; and in not applying myself with application enough to the duty of secret prayer.

Sabbath day, Feb. 17, near sunset. Renewedly promised, that I will accept of God, for my whole portion; and that I will be contented, whatever else I am denied. I will not murmur, nor be grieved, whatever prosperity, upon any account, I see others enjoy, and I am denied. [[To this I have lately acted contrary.

Thursday, Feb. 21. I perceive that I never yet have adequately known, what was meant by being weaned from the world, by not laying up treasure on earth, but in heaven, by not having our portion in this

5. End of text from Dwight MS transcript fragment.

life, by making the concerns of another life our whole business, by taking God for our whole portion. I find my heart, in great part, yet adheres to the earth. O that it might be quite separated from thence. I find when I have power and reputation as others, I am uneasy, and it does not satisfy me to tell me, that I have chosen God for my whole portion, and that I have promised to rest entirely contented with him.

Saturday, Feb. 23. I find myself miserably negligent, and that I might do twice the business that I do, if I were set upon it. See how soon my thoughts of this matter, will be differing from what they are now. I have been indulging a horrid laziness a good while, and did not know it. I can do seven times as much in the same time now, as I can at other times, not because my faculties are in better tune; but because of the fire of diligence that I feel burning within me. If I could but always continue so, I should not meet with one quarter of the trouble. I should run the Christian race much better, and should go out of the world a much better man.]]

Saturday, Mar. 2. [[O how much more base and vile am I, when I feel pride working in me, than when I am in a more humble disposition of mind! How much, how exceedingly much, more lovely is an humble, than a proud, disposition! I now plainly perceive it, and am really sensible of it. How immensely more pleasant is an humble delight, than a high thought of myself! How much better do I feel, when I am truly humbling myself, than when I am pleasing myself with my own perfections.]] O, how much pleasanter is humility than pride! O, that God would fill me with exceeding great humility, and that he would evermore keep me from all pride! The pleasures of humility are really the most refined, inward and exquisite delights in the world. How hateful is a proud man! How hateful is a worm that lifts up itself with pride! What a foolish, silly, miserable, blind, deceived, poor worm am I, when pride works! [[At night. I have lately been negligent as to reading the Scriptures. Notwithstanding my resolutions on Saturday was se'night,[6] I have not been sedulous and diligent enough.]]

Wednesday, Mar. 6, near sunset. Felt the doctrines of election, free grace, and of our not being able to do anything without the grace of God; and that holiness is entirely, throughout, the work of God's Spirit, with more pleasure than before.

[[Thursday, Mar. 7. I think I now suffer from not forcing myself enough on religious thoughts.

6. "Seventh night," i.e. end of the week, or time to do an accounting on the "Resolutions."

Saturday night, Mar. 24. I intend, if I am ever settled, to concert measures, and study methods, of doing good in the world, and to draw up rules of acting in this matter, in writing, of all the methods I can possibly devise, by which I can in any respect do good.

Saturday night, Mar. 31. This week I have been too careless about eating.]]

Monday morning, Apr. 1. I think it best not to allow myself to laugh at the faults, follies and infirmities of others.

Saturday night, Apr. 7. This week I found myself so far gone, that it seemed to me, that I should never recover more. Let God of his mercy return unto me, and no more leave me thus to sink and decay! I know, O Lord, that without thy help, I shall fall innumerable times, notwithstanding all my resolutions, how often so ever repeated.

Saturday night, Apr. 14.[7] I could pray more heartily this night for the forgiveness of my enemies, than ever before. [[I am somewhat apt, after having asked one petition over many times, to be weary of it; but I am now resolved not to give way to such a disposition.]]

Wednesday, May 1. Forenoon. Last night I came home, after my melancholy parting from New York.[8]

I have always, in every different state of life, I have hitherto been in, thought the troubles and difficulties of that state, to be greater than those of any other, that I proposed to be in; and when I have altered with assurance of mending myself, I have still thought the same; yea, that the difficulties of that state, are greater than those of that I left last. Lord, grant that from hence I may learn to withdraw my thoughts, affections, desires and expectations, entirely from the world, and may fix them upon the heavenly state; where there is fullness of joy; where reigns heavenly, sweet, calm and delightful love without alloy; where there are continually the dearest expressions of their love: where there is the enjoyment of the persons loved, without ever parting: where those persons, who appear so lovely in this world, will really be inexpressibly more lovely, and full of love to us. How sweetly will the mutual lovers join together to sing the praises of God and the Lamb! How full will it fill us with joy to think, this enjoyment, these sweet exercises, will never cease or come to an end, but will last to all eternity.

7. Dwight (*1*, 84): "13."
8. Marking the end of his pastorate at a Presbyterian church in New York City, begun in Aug. 1722. JE spent most of the spring and summer of 1723 at East Windsor. See *Works, 10*, 261–93.

Remember, after journeys, removes, overturnings and alterations in the state of my life, to reflect and consider, whether therein I have managed the best way possible, respecting my soul? And before such alterations, if foreseen, to resolve how to act.

Thursday, May 2. [[Afternoon. I observe this, that when I was at New York, when I meditated on things of a religious nature, I used to conceive of myself as walking in the fields at home; but now I am at home, I conceive of myself as walking in the fields, which I used to frequent at New York.]] I think it a very good way to examine dreams every morning when I awake, what are the nature, circumstances, principles and ends of my imaginary actions and passions in them, to discern what are my chief inclinations, etc.

Saturday night, May 4. Although I have in some measure subdued a disposition to chide and fret, yet I find a certain inclination, which is not agreeable to Christian sweetness of temper and conversation: either by too much dogmaticalness, too much of the egotism; a disposition to be telling of my own dislike and scorn; and freedom from those that are innocent, yea, common infirmities of men; and many other such like things. O that God would help me to discern all the flaws and defects of my temper and conversation, and help me in the difficult work of amending them: and that he would fill me so full of Christianity, that the foundation of all these disagreeable irregularities may be destroyed, and the contrary sweetnesses and beauties may of themselves naturally follow.

Sabbath day, May 5, in the morning. This day made the 47th Resolution.

[[Monday morning, May 6. I think it best commonly to come before God three times in a day, except I find a great inaptitude to that duty.

Saturday night, May 11. I have been to blame, the month past, in not laying violence enough to my inclination, to force myself to a better improvement of time. Have been tardy with respect to the 47th Resolution. Have also been negligent about keeping my thoughts, when joining with others in prayer.]]

Sabbath-day [[morning]], May 12. [[I have lost that relish of the Scriptures and other good books, which I had five or six months ago. Resolved, when I find in myself the least disposition to exercise good nature, that I will then strive most to feel good naturedly. At noon. Observe to remember the meditations which I had at Westchester, as I was coming from New York; and those which I had in the orchard; and those under the oak tree. This day, and the last night, I read over and reviewed those reflections and remarks, which I find to be a very beneficial thing to me. After the afternoon meeting.]] I think I find in my heart to be glad from the hopes I have that my eternity is to be spent in spiritual and holy joys, arising from the manifestation of God's love, and the exercise of holiness and a burning love to him.

Saturday night, May 18. [[This week past, spent in journeying to Norwich, and the towns thereabouts. This day returned, and received a letter, from my dear friend, Mr. John Smith. The last Wednesday, took up a resolution, to refrain from all manner of evil speaking, for one week, to try it, and see the effect of it: hoping, if that evil speaking, which I used to allow myself in, and to account lawful, agreeably to the resolutions I have formed concerning it, were not lawful, or best, I should hereby discover it, and get the advantage of temptations to it, and so deceive myself, into a strict adherence to my duty, respecting that matter; that corruption, which I cannot conquer by main strength, I may get the victory of by stratagem. I find the effect of it already to be, to make me apt to take it for granted, that what I have resolved on this week, is a duty to be observed forever.]]

I now plainly perceive what great obligations I am under to love and honor my parents. I have great reason to believe, that their counsel and education have been my making; notwithstanding, in the time of it, it seemed to do me so little good. I have good reason to hope that their prayers for me, have been in many things very powerful and prevalent; that God has in many things, taken me under his care and guidance, provision and direction, in answer to their prayers for me. I was never made so sensible of it as now.

[[I think it the best way, in general, not to seek for honor, in any other way, than by seeking to be good, and to do good. I may pursue knowledge, religion, the glory of God, and the good of mankind, with the utmost vigor; but, am to leave the honor of it, entirely at God's disposal, as a thing with which I have no immediate concern; no, not although, by possessing that honor, I have the greater opportunity to do good.

Memorandum. To be particularly careful, lest I should be tardy in any point, wherein I have been negligent, or have erred, in days, weeks, months, or years past.

Sabbath-day morning, May 19. With respect to my journey last week, I was not careful enough, to watch opportunities of solemnly approaching to God, three times a day. The last week, when I was about to take up the Wednesday Resolution,[9] it was proposed to me, in my thoughts, to omit it until I got home again, because there would be a more convenient opportunity. Thus am I ready to look at anything as an excuse, to grow slack in my Christian course. At night. Concluded to add to my inquiries, as to the spending of time—at the beginning of the day, or the period, what can I do for the good of men? and, at the end, what have I done for their good?

Tuesday morning, May 21. My conscience is, undoubtedly, more calm, since my last Wednesday Resolution,[1] than it was before.

Wednesday, May 22. In the morning. *Memorandum.* To take special care of these following things: evil speaking, fretting, eating, drinking and sleeping, speaking simple verity, joining in prayer, slightiness in secret prayer, listlessness and negligence, and thoughts that cherish sin.

Saturday, May 25. In the morning. As I was this morning reading the 17th Resolution, it was suggested to me, that if I was now to die, I should wish that I had prayed more that God would make me know my state, whether it be good or bad; and that I had taken more pains to see and narrowly search into this matter. Wherefore, *Memorandum,* for the future, most nicely and diligently to look into our old divines' opinions concerning conversion. Made the 48th Resolution.

Monday afternoon, May 27. *Memorandum.* Not only to keep from an air of dislike, anger and fretfulness, in discourse or conversation; but, let me also have as much of an appearance of love, cheerfulness, and benignity, as may be, with a good grace. These following things, especially, to beware of, in order to the better observation of the 47th Resolution: diffidence,[2] discontent, uneasiness, and a complaining temper, self-opinion, self-confidence, melancholy, moroseness, slight,[3] antipathy, privacy, indolence, and want of resolution—to beware of anything, in discourse or conversation, that savors of these.]]

Friday, June 1. Afternoon. I have abundant cause, O my merciful Father, to love thee ardently, and greatly to bless and praise thee, that thou hast heard me in my earnest request, and hast so answered my prayer for mercy to keep from decay and sinking. O, graciously, of thy

9. As described in the entry for May 18, 1723, above.

1. Ibid.

2. Dwight prints "distrust," but "diffidence" was probably JE's word, being listed first between the horizontal lines on the inside of the "Diary" front cover, where this list is reproduced.

3. The comma is inserted on the basis of the inside cover of the "Diary," where "slight" is listed as an item separate from "antipathy." It is possibly an abbreviation for "slightiness."

mere goodness, still continue to pity my misery, by reason of my sinfulness. O my dear Redeemer, I commit myself, together with my prayer and thanksgiving into thine hand.

[[Saturday night, June 8, at Boston. When I find myself listless and dull, and not easily affected by reading religious books, then to read my resolutions, remarks, reflections, etc. One thing, that would be of great advantage to me, in reading to my profit, would be, the endeavoring, with all my might, to keep the image and picture of the thing in my mind, and be careful that I do not lose it, in the chain of the discourse.

Sabbath day, June 9, after the afternoon meeting. *Memorandum.* When I fear misfortunes, to examine whether I have done my duty; and at the same time, to resolve to do it, and let it go, and be concerned about nothing, but my duty and my sin.

Saturday morning, June 15, at Windsor. Have been to blame, this journey, with respect to strict temperance, in eating, drinking and sleeping, and in suffering too small matters to give interruption to my wonted chain of religious exercises. Concluded to protract the Wednesday Resolution,[4] to the end of my life.

Tuesday morning, June 18. *Memorandum.* To do that part, which I conveniently can, of my stated exercise, while about other business, such as self-examination, resolutions, etc. that I may do the remainder in less time.

Friday afternoon, June 21. I have abundant cause, O my merciful Father, to love thee ardently, and greatly, to bless and praise thee, that thou hast heard me, in my earnest request, and so hast answered my prayer, for mercy, to keep me from decay and sinking. O, graciously, of thy mere goodness, still continue to pity my misery, by reason of my sinfulness. O, my dear Redeemer, I commit myself, together with my prayer and thanksgiving, into thine hand!

Saturday morning, June 22. Altered the 36th Resolution, to make it the same with the Wednesday Resolution.[5] If I should take special care, every day, to rise above, or not to fall below, or to fall as little as I possibly could, below what I was the day before, it would be of great advantage to me. I take notice, that most of these determinations, when I first resolve them, seem as if they would be much more beneficial, than I find them.

4. As described in the entry for May 18, 1723, above.
5. Ibid.

Tuesday morning, June 25. Last sabbath, at Boston, reading the 6th, 7th, and 8th verses of the 6th to the Ephesians, concluded that it would be much to my advantage, to take the greatest care, never to do anything but my duty, and then to do it willingly, cheerfully, and gladly, whatever danger or unpleasant circumstances it may be attended with; with goodwill doing it, as to the Lord, not as pleasing man, or myself, knowing that whatsoever good thing any man doth, the same shall he receive of the Lord.

Saturday morning, June 29.[6] It is best to be careful in prayer, not to put up those petitions, of which I do not feel a sincere desire: thereby, my prayer is rendered less sincere, less acceptable to God, and less useful to myself.]]

Monday [[noon]], July 1. Again confirmed by experience of the happy effects of strict temperance, with respect both to body and mind. Resolved for the future to observe rather more of meekness, moderation and temper in disputes. [[I find I am not careful enough, to keep out all thoughts, but religious ones, on the sabbath. When I find the least uneasiness, in doing my duty, to fly to the 43rd Resolution.

Wednesday night, July 3. I am too negligent, with respect to improving petty opportunities of doing good; thinking, that the good will be very small, and unextended, and not worth the pains. Resolved, to regulate this, as that which is wrong, and what ought not to be. Again confirmed, by experience, of the happy effects of a strict temperance, with respect both to body and mind.

Thursday morning, July 4. The last night, in bed, when thinking of death, I thought, if I was then to die, that, which would make me die, in the least degree fearfully, would be, the want of a trusting and relying on Jesus Christ, so distinctly and plainly, as has been described by divines; my not having experienced so particular a venturing, and entirely trusting my soul on Christ, after the fears of hell, and terrors of the Lord, encouraged by the mercy, faithfulness and promises, of God, and the gracious invitations of Christ. Then, I thought I could go out of the world, as much assured of my salvation, as I was of Christ's faithfulness, knowing that, if Christ did not fail me, he would save me, who had trusted in him, on his word. At night. Whenever things begin to seem in the least out of order, when things begin to feel uneasy

6. Dwight ed. (*1*, 88): "25."

within, or irregular without, then to examine myself, by the strictest examination. Resolved, for the future, to observe rather more of meekness, moderation and temper, in disputes.

Friday morning, July 5. Last night, when thinking what I should wish I had done, that I had not done, if I was then to die; I thought I should wish, that I had been more importunate with God, to fit me for death, and lead me into all truth, and that I might not be deceived, about the state of my soul. In the forenoon, made the 50th Resolution.

Thursday night, July 11. This day, too impatient, at the church meeting. Snares and briars have been in my way, this afternoon. It is good, at such times, for one to manifest good nature, even to one's disadvantage, and so as would be imprudent, at other times.

Saturday morning, July 13. Transferred the conclusion of June 9, to the Resolution, No. 57; and the conclusion of May 27, to No. 58; and May 12, and July 11, to No. 59; and of July 4, at night, to No. 60; and of May 24, to No. 61; and of June 25, to No. 62; and, about noon, the Resolution of January 14, to No. 63. In times past, I have been too free, in judging of the hearts of men, from their actions.]]

Thursday, July 18, near sunset. Resolved to endeavor to make sure of that sign the apostle James gives of a perfect man, Jas. 3:2, "If any man offend not in word, the same is a perfect man, and able also to bridle the whole body."

[[Friday afternoon, July 19. I Pet. 2:18, "Servants, be subject to your masters, with all fear; not only to the good and gentle, but also to the froward." How then, ought children to honor their parents. This verse, together with the two following, viz. "For this is thankworthy, if a man, for conscience toward God, endure grief, suffering wrongfully; for what glory is it, if, when ye be buffeted for your faults, ye shall take it patiently; but if, when ye do well and suffer for it, ye take it patiently, this is acceptable with God."

Saturday noon, July 20. Dr. Manton's sermon, on the 119th Psalm, pp. 140–41, of evil-speaking:[7]

> Use 2nd. To them that either devise or receive reproaches; both are very sinful. . . . Hypocrites, and men that put themselves into a garb of religion, are all for censuring, take a mighty freedom that way; these men bewray the rottenness of their hearts. . . . Alas, in our own sight we should be the worst of men; the children of God

7. Thomas Manton, *One Hundred and Ninety Sermons.* JE is excerpting the second Use of Sermon XXIII, on Ps. 119:22 (pp. 135–42), with the doctrine, "That reproaches are an usual, but yet a great and grievous afflictions to the children of God."

do ever thus speak of themselves, *as the least of saints, the greatest of sinners, more brutish than any man, of sinners, whereof I am the chief.* . . . You rob them of the most precious treasure. He that robs thee of thy name, is the worst kind of thief, Prov. 22:1, "A good name is rather to be chosen, than great riches." . .

Objection. But must we in no case speak evil of another? or may we not speak of another's sin in any case?

Solution 1. It is a very hard matter to speak evil of another without sin. . . . In one way or another we shall dash upon the command; better let it alone. . . .

[3.] If you speak of the failings of another, it should be with tenderness and grief; as when they are incorrigible, and likely to infect others, or when it is for the manifest glory of God. . . .

[Secondly,] to them that receive the slander. He is a slanderer who wrongs his neighbor's credit by upholding an ill report against him.]]

Monday [[afternoon]], July 22. [[I find, it would be desirable, on many accounts, always to endeavor, to wear a benign aspect, and air of acting and speaking, in all companies, except it should so happen, that duty requires it otherwise. I am afraid, I am now defective, in not doing whatever my hand finds to do, with my might, with respect to my particular affairs. Remember to watch, see and know how it is. Vid. August 31.]] I see there is danger of my being drawn into transgression by the power of such temptations as a fear of seeming uncivil, and of offending friends. Watch against it. [[I might still help myself, and yet not hurt myself, by going, with greater expedition, from one thing to another, without being quite so nice.]]

Tuesday [[afternoon]], July 23. When I find those "groanings which cannot be uttered" [Rom. 8:26], the Apostle speaks of; and those "soul-breakings, for the longing it hath," the Psalmist speaks of (Ps. 119:20), to humor and promote them to the utmost of my power, and be not weary of earnestly endeavoring to vent my desires, [[and not to be weary of the repetitions of such earnestness.]]

To count it all joy when I have occasion of great self-denial, because then I have a glorious opportunity of giving deadly wounds to the body of sin, and greatly confirming and establishing the new nature: I seek to mortify sin, and increase in holiness; these are the best opportunities, according to January 14.

To improve afflictions of all kinds as blessed opportunities of forcibly bearing on in my Christian course, notwithstanding that which is so very apt to discourage me, and to damp the vigor of my mind, and to make me lifeless: also as opportunities of trusting and confiding in God, and getting a habit of that, according to the 57th Resolution. And as an opportunity of rending my heart off from the world, and setting it upon heaven alone. [[According to January 10, and the 43rd and 45th Resolutions; and according to January 12, February 17, and 21, and May 1.]] To improve them as opportunities to repent of, and bewail my sin, and abhor myself. And as a blessed opportunity to exercise patience; to trust in God, and divert my mind from the affliction, by fixing myself in religious exercises. Also, let me comfort myself, that 'tis the very nature of afflictions to make the heart better; and if I am made better by them, what need I be concerned, however grievous they seem for the present?

[[Wednesday night, July 24. I begin to find the success of my striving, in joining with others, in the worship of God; insomuch, that there is a prospect, of making it easy and delightful, and very profitable, in time. Wherefore, resolved, not to cease striving, but to continue it, and redouble it.

Thursday morning, July 25. Altered, and anew established, the 8th Resolution. Also, established my determination of April 1. *Memorandum.* At a convenient time, to make an alphabet of these resolutions and remarks, that I may be able to educe them, on proper occasions, suitable to the condition I am in, and the duty I am engaged in.]]

Friday afternoon, July 26. To be particularly careful to keep up inviolable a trust and reliance, ease and entire rest in God in all conditions, according to 57th Resolution; for this I have found to be wonderfully advantageous to me. [[At night. Resolved, very much to exercise myself in this, all my life long: viz. with the greatest openness, of which I am capable, to declare my ways to God, and lay open my soul to him: all my sins, temptations, difficulties, sorrows, fears, hopes, desires, and everything, and every circumstance—according to Dr. Manton's 27th sermon, on the 119th Psalm.[8]

Saturday forenoon, July 27. When I am violently beset with temptation, or cannot rid myself of evil thoughts, to do some sum in arithmetic, or geometry, or some other study, which necessarily engages all my thoughts, and unavoidably keeps them from wandering.]]

---

8. Manton, *One Hundred and Ninety Sermons*, pp. 162–70. See also "Resolutions" No. 65, above.

Monday [[afternoon]], July 29. When I am concerned how I shall perform anything to public acceptance, to be very careful that I have it very clear to me, that I do what is duty and prudence in the matter.[9] [[I sometimes find myself able to trust God, and to be pretty easy when the event is uncertain; but I find it difficult, when I am convinced beforehand, that the event will be adverse. I find that this arises, 1. From my want of faith, to believe that that particular advantage will be more to my advantage, than disadvantage; 2. From the want of a due sense of the real preferableness of that good, which will be obtained, to that which is lost; 3. From the want of a spirit of adoption.

Tuesday night, July 30. Have concluded to endeavor to work myself into duties by searching and tracing back all the real reasons why I do them not, and narrowly searching out all the subtle subterfuges of my thoughts, and answering them to the utmost of my power, that I may know what are the very first originals of my defect, as with respect to want of repentance, love to God, loathing of myself—to do this sometimes in sermons. Vid. Resolution 8. Especially, to take occasion therefrom, to bewail those sins of which I have been guilty, that are akin to them; as for instance, from pride in others, to take occasion to bewail my pride; from their malice, to take occasion to bewail the same in myself; when I am evil-spoken of, to take occasion to bewail my evil speaking; and so of other sins. *Memorandum.* To receive slanders and reproaches, as glorious opportunities of doing this.]]

Wednesday [[afternoon]], July 31. [[After afflictions, to inquire, what I am the better for them; what good I have got by them; and what I might have got by them.]] Never in the least to seek to hear sarcastical relations of others' faults. Never to give credit to anything said against others, except there is very plain reason for it; nor to behave in any respect the otherwise for it.

[[Sabbath morning, Aug. 4. Concluded at last, at those times when I am in the best frames, to set down the aspirations of my heart, as soon as I can get time.

Tuesday afternoon, Aug. 6. Very much convinced of the extraordinary deceitfulness of the heart, and how exceedingly affection or appetite blinds the mind, and brings it into entire subjection. There are many things which I should really think to be my duty, if I had the same affections, as when I first came from New York; which now I

---

9. During the summer of 1723, JE was preparing his Master's *Quæstio* for commencement exercises in September. See *Works, 14,* 47–66.

think not so to be. How doth appetite stretch the reason, to bring both ends together.]]

Wednesday [[forenoon]], Aug. 7. To esteem as some advantage that the duties of religion are difficult, and that many difficulties are sometimes to be gone through in the way of duty. Religion is the sweeter, and what is gained by labor, is abundantly more precious: as a woman loves her child the better for having brought it forth with travail. And even to Christ Jesus himself, his mediatorial glory, his victory and triumph, his kingdom which he hath obtained; how much more glorious is it, how much more excellent and precious, for his having wrought it out by such agonies!

Friday [[afternoon]], Aug. 9. [[With respect to the important business which I have now on hand,[1] resolved, to do whatever I think to be duty, prudence and diligence in the matter, and to avoid ostentation; and if I succeed not, and how many disappointments soever I meet with, to be entirely easy; only to take occasion to acknowledge my unworthiness; and if it should actually not succeed, and should not find acceptance, as I expected, yet not to afflict myself about it, according to the 57th Resolution. At night.]] One thing that may be a good help towards thinking profitably in time of vacation is, when I light on a profitable thought, that I can fix my mind on, to follow it as far as possibly I can to advantage. [[I missed it, when a graduate at college, both in point of duty and prudence, in going against a universal benevolence and good nature.

Saturday morning, Aug. 10. Transferred my determination of July 23, to the 64th Resolution, and that of July 26, to the 65th. About sunset. As a help against that inward shameful hypocrisy, to confess frankly to myself all that which I find in myself, either infirmity or sin; also to confess to God, and open the whole case to him, when it is what concerns religion, and humbly and earnestly implore of him the help that is needed; not in the least to endeavor to smother over what is in my heart, but to bring it all out to God and my conscience. By this means, I may arrive at a greater knowledge of my own heart. When I find difficulty in finding a subject of religious meditation, in vacancies, to pitch at random on what alights to my thoughts, and to go from that to other things which that shall bring into my mind, and follow this progression as a clue, till I come to what I can meditate on with profit

---

1. Dwight notes, 1, 92*n:* "Perhaps the preparation of a public exercise for the college commencement, when he received his Master's Degree." See *Works, 14,* 47–66.

and attention, and then to follow that, according to last Thursday's determination.]]²

Sabbath day, after meeting, Aug. 11. Resolved always to do that which I shall wish I had done, when I see others do it. As for instance, sometimes I argue with myself, that such an act of good nature, kindness, forbearance, or forgiveness, etc. is not my duty, because it will have such and such consequences: yet, when I see others do it, then it appears amiable to me, and I wish I had done it; and I see that none of those feared inconveniencies follow.

[[Monday morning, Aug. 12. The chief thing, that now makes me in any measure to question my good estate, is my not having experienced conversion in those particular steps, wherein the people of New England, and anciently the Dissenters of Old England, used to experience it. Wherefore, now resolved, never to leave searching, till I have satisfyingly found out the very bottom and foundation, the real reason, why they used to be converted in those steps.]]

Tuesday³ [[morning]], Aug. 13. [[Have sinned, in not being careful enough to please my parents. Afternoon.]] I find it would be very much to advantage, to be thoroughly acquainted with the Scriptures. When I am reading doctrinal books or books of controversy, I can proceed with abundantly more confidence; can see upon what footing and foundation I stand.

[[Saturday noon, Aug. 17. Let there, in the general, be something of benevolence in all that I speak.

Tuesday night, Aug. 20. Not careful enough in watching opportunities of bringing in Christian discourse with a good grace. Do not exercise myself half enough in this holy art; neither have I courage enough to carry it on with a good grace. Vid. September 2.

Saturday morning, Aug. 24. Have not practiced quite right about revenge; though I have not done anything directly out of revenge, yet, I have perhaps, omitted some things, that I should otherwise have done; or have altered the circumstances and manner of my actions, hoping for a secret sort of revenge thereby. I have felt a little sort of satisfaction, when I thought that such an evil would happen to them by my actions, as would make them repent what they have done. To be satisfied for their repenting, when they repent from a sense of their error, is right. But a satisfaction in their repentance, because of the evil that is brought upon them, is revenge. This is in some measure, a

2. Possibly JE means the entry for Friday, Aug. 9, "At night."
3. Hopkins, p. 18: "Thursday."

taking the matter out of God's hands when he was about to manage it, who is better able to plead it for me. Well, therefore, may he leave me to boggle at it. Near sunset. I yet find a want of dependence on God, to look unto him for success, and to have my eyes unto him for his gracious disposal of the matter: for want of a sense of God's particular influence, in ordering and directing all affairs and businesses, of whatever nature, however naturally, or fortuitously, they may seem to succeed; and for want of a sense of those great advantages, that would follow therefrom: not considering that God will grant success, or make the contrary more to my advantage; or will make the advantage accruing from the unsuccessfulness, more sensible and apparent; or will make it of less present and outward disadvantage; or will some way, so order the circumstances, as to make the unsuccessfulness more easy to bear; or several, or all of these. This want of dependence, is likewise for want of the things mentioned, July 29. Remember to examine all narrations, I can call to mind; whether they are exactly according to verity.

Wednesday night, Aug. 28. When I want books to read; yea, when I have not very good books, not to spend time in reading them, but in reading the Scriptures, in perusing Resolutions, Reflections,[4] etc., in writing on types of the Scripture, and other things, in studying the languages, and in spending more time in private duties. To do this, when there is a prospect of wanting time for the purpose. Remember as soon as I can, to get a piece of slate, or something, whereon I can make short memorandums while traveling.]]

Thursday, Aug. 29. The objection my corruptions make against doing whatever my hand finds to do with my might is, that it is a constant mortification. Let this objection by no means ever prevail. [[Two great *quærenda* with me now are: How shall I make advantage of all the time I spend in journeys? And how shall I make a glorious improvement of afflictions?

Saturday night, Aug. 31. The objection, which my corruptions make against doing whatever my hands find to do with my might, is, that it is a constant mortification. Let this objection by no means ever prevail.

Sabbath morning, Sept. 1. When I am violently beset with worldly thoughts, for a relief, to think of death, and the doleful circumstances of it.]]

Monday [[afternoon]], Sept. 2. [[To help me to enter with a good

---

4. "Reflections" was JE's early title for the "Miscellanies."

grace, into religious conversation; when I am conversing on morality, to turn it over by application, exemplification or otherwise, to Christianity. Vid. August 28 and January 15. At night.]] There is much folly, when I am quite sure I am in the right, and others are positive in contradicting me, to enter into a vehement or long debate upon it.

[[Saturday, Sept. 7. Concluded no more to suffer myself to be interrupted, or diverted from important business, by those things, from which I expect, though some, yet but little profit.

Sabbath morning, Sept. 8. I have been much to blame, for expressing so much impatience for delays in journeys, and the like.

Sabbath evening, Sept. 22. To praise God, by singing psalms in prose, and by singing forth the meditations of my heart in prose.]]

Monday, Sept. 23. I observe that old men seldom have any advantage of new discoveries, because they are beside a way of thinking, they have been so long used to. Resolved, if ever I live to years, that I will be impartial to hear the reasons of all pretended discoveries, and receive them if rational, how long so ever I have been used to another way of thinking. [[My time is so short, that I have not time to perfect myself in all studies: wherefore resolved, to omit and put off, all but the most important and needful studies.

Thursday forenoon, Oct. 4, 1723. Have this day fixed and established it, that Christ Jesus has promised me faithfully, that, if I will do what is my duty, and according to the best of my prudence in the matter, that my condition in this world, shall be better for me than any other condition whatever, and more to my welfare, to all eternity. And, therefore, whatever my condition shall be, I will esteem it to be such; and if I find need of faith in the matter, that I will confess it as impiety before God. Vid. Resolution 57, and June 9.

Sabbath night, Oct. 7. Have lately erred, in not allowing time enough for conversation.

Friday night, Oct. 12. I see there are some things quite contrary to the soundness and perfection of Christianity, in which almost all good men do allow themselves, and where innate corruption has an unrestrained secret vent, which they never take notice of, or think to be no hurt, or cloak under the name of virtue; which things exceedingly darken the brightness, and hide the loveliness, of Christianity. Who can understand his errors? O that I might be kept from secret faults!

Sabbath morning, Oct. 14. Narrowly to observe after what manner I act, when I am in a hurry, and to act as much so, at other times, as I can, without prejudice to the business.

Monday morning, Oct. 15. I seem to be afraid, after errors and decays, to give myself the full exercise of spiritual meditation: not to give way to such fears.]]

Thursday, Oct. 18. To follow the example of Mr. B—— who, though he meets with great difficulties, yet undertakes them with a smiling countenance, as though he thought them but little; and speaks of them as if they were very small.

[[Friday night, Nov. 1. When I am unfit for other business, to perfect myself in writing characters.[5]

Friday afternoon, Nov. 22. For the time to come, when I am in a lifeless frame in secret prayer, to force myself to expatiate, as if I were praying before others more than I used to do.]]

[[Tuesday forenoon,]] Nov. 26.[6] 'Tis a most evil and pernicious practice in meditations on afflictions, to sit ruminating on the aggravations of the affliction, and reckoning up the evil, dark circumstances thereof, and dwelling long on the dark side; it doubles and trebles the affliction. And so when speaking of them to others, to make them as bad as we can, and use our eloquence to set forth our own troubles, and are all the while making new trouble, and feeding and pampering the old; whereas the contrary practice would starve our afflictions. If we dwelt on the light side of things in our thoughts, and extenuated them all that possibly we could, when speaking of them, we should think little of them ourselves; and the affliction would really, in a great measure, vanish away.

[[Friday night, Nov. 29. As a help to attention in social prayer, to take special care to make a particular remark, at the beginning of every petition, confession, etc.

Monday morning, Dec. 9. To observe, whether I express any kind of fretting emotion, for the next three weeks.]]

Thursday night, Dec. 12. If at any time I am forced to tell others of that wherein I think they are something to blame; for the avoiding the important evil, that would otherwise ensue, not to tell it to them, so that there shall be a probability of their taking it as the effect of little, fretting, angry emotions of mind. [[Vid. August 28. When I do want, or am likely to want, good books, to spend time in studying mathematics, and in reviewing other kinds of old learning; to spend more time in visiting friends, in the more private duties of a pastor, in taking care of worldly business, in going abroad and other things that I may contrive.

5. Dwight notes, 1, 100*n.:* "He probably refers to short-hand characters."
6. Hopkins, p. 18: "Thursday."

Friday morning, Dec. 27. At the end of every month, to examine my behavior, strictly, by some chapter in the New Testament, more especially made up of rules of life. At the end of the year, to examine my behavior by the rules of the New Testament in general, reading many chapters. It would also be convenient, sometime at the end of the year, to read, for this purpose, in the book of Proverbs.

Tuesday,]] Dec. 31. At night. Concluded never to suffer nor express any angry emotions of mind more or less, except the honor of God calls for it, in zeal for him, or to preserve myself from being trampled on.

Wednesday, Jan. 1, 1723–24. Not to spend too much time in thinking even of important and necessary worldly business. To allow everything its proportion of thought, according to its urgency and importance.

[[Thursday night, Jan. 2. These things established—That time gained in things of lesser importance, is as much gained in things of greater; that a minute, gained in times of confusion, conversation, or in a journey, is as good as a minute gained in my study, at my most retired times; and so in general that a minute gained at one time, is as good as at another.

Friday night, Jan. 3. The time and pains laid out in seeking the world, is to be proportioned to the necessity, usefulness, and importance of it, with respect to another world, together with the uncertainty of succeeding, the uncertainty of living, and of retaining; provided, that nothing that our duty enjoins, or that is amiable, be omitted, and nothing sinful or unbecoming be done for the sake of it.]]

Friday, Jan. 10. [. . .][7] Remember to act according to Prov. 12:23, "A prudent man concealeth knowledge."

[[Monday, Jan. 20. I have been very much to blame, in that I have not been as full, and plain and downright, in my standing up for virtue and religion, when I have had fair occasion, before those who seemed to take no delight in such things. If such conversation would not be agreeable to them, I have in some degree minced the matter, that I might not displease, and might not speak right against the grain, more than I should have loved to have done with others, to whom it would be agreeable to speak directly for religion. I ought to be exceedingly bold with such persons, not talking in a melancholy strain, but in one confident and fearless, assured of the truth and excellence of the cause.]]

7. Hopkins (p. 19) interpolates at this point: "After having wrote considerable in a shorthand, which he used when he would have what he wrote effectually concealed from everybody but himself, he notes the following words in round hand."

Monday, Feb. 3. Let everything have the value now, that it will have on a sickbed: and frequently in my pursuits of whatever kind, let this come into my mind; "How much shall I value this on my deathbed?"

Wednesday, Feb. 5. Have not in time past in my prayers, enough insisted upon the glorifying God in the world, and the advancement of the kingdom of Christ, the prosperity of the church, and the good of men. Determined that this objection is without weight, viz. that 'tis not likely that God will make great alterations in the whole world, and overturnings in kingdoms and nations, only for the prayers of one obscure person, seeing such things used to be done in answer to the united, earnest prayers of the whole church: and if my prayers should have some influence, it would be but imperceptible and small.

Thursday, Feb. 6. More convinced than ever of the usefulness of a free religious conversation. I find by conversing on natural philosophy, I gain knowledge abundantly[8] faster, and see the reasons of things much clearer, than in private study. Wherefore earnestly to seek at all times for religious conversation; for those that I can with profit and delight and freedom so converse with.

[[Friday, Feb. 7. Resolved, if God will assist me to it, that I will not care about things, when, upon any account, I have prospect of ill success or adversity; and that I will not think about it, any further than just to do what prudence directs to for prevention, according to Phil. 4:6, "Be careful for nothing"; to I Pet. 5:7, "Cast all your care upon God, for he careth for you"; and again, "Take no thought for the morrow" [Matt. 6:34]; and again, "Take no thought, saying, What shall I eat, and what shall I drink, and wherewithal shall I be clothed?" [Matt. 7:31]. "Seek ye first the kingdom of God, and all these things shall be added unto you" [Matt. 5:31, 33–34].

Saturday night, Feb. 15. I find that when eating, I cannot be convinced in the time of it, that if I should eat more, I should exceed the bounds of strict temperance, though I have had the experience of two years of the like; and yet, as soon as I have done, in three minutes I am convinced of it. But yet, when I eat again, and remember it, still, while eating, I am fully convinced that I have not eaten what is but for nature, nor can I be convinced that my appetite and feeling is as it was before. It seems to me that I shall be somewhat faint if I leave off then; but when I have finished, I am convinced again, and so it is from time

8. Dwight ed. (*1*, 102) used here; Hopkins (*Life*, p. 20) reads "abundance." In reference to "Natural Philosophy," the latter entries of LS, nos. 51–65, were probably being written at this time (*Works, 6*, 187–88).

to time. I have observed that more really seems to be truth, when it makes for my interest, or is, in other respects, according to my inclination, than it seems, if it be otherwise; and it seems to me, that the words in which I express it are more than the thing will properly bear. But if the thing be against my interest, the words of different import seem as much as the thing will properly bear. Though there is some little seeming, indecorum, as if it looked like affectation, in religious conversation, as there is also in acts of kindness; yet this is to be broke through.

Tuesday, Feb. 18. Resolved, to act with sweetness and benevolence, and according to the 47th Resolution, in all bodily dispositions, sick or well, at ease or in pain, sleepy or watchful, and not to suffer discomposure of body to discompose my mind.

Saturday, Feb. 22. I observe that there are some evil habits, which do increase and grow stronger, even in some good people, as they grow older; habits that much obscure the beauty of Christianity: some things which are according to their natural tempers, which, in some measure, prevails when they are young in Christ, and the evil disposition, having an unobserved control, the habit at last grows very strong, and commonly regulates the practice until death. By this means, old Christians are very commonly, in some respects, more unreasonable than those who are young. I am afraid of contracting such habits, particularly of grudging to give, and to do, and of procrastinating.]]

Sabbath day, Feb. 23 [[I must be contented, where I have anything strange or remarkable to tell, not to make it appear so remarkable as it is indeed; lest through the fear of this, and the desire of making a thing appear very remarkable, I should exceed the bounds of simple verity. When I am at a feast, or a meal, that very well pleases my appetite, I must not merely take care to leave off with as much of an appetite as at ordinary meals; for when there is a great variety of dishes, I may do that, after I have eaten twice as much as at other meals, is sufficient.]] If I act according to my resolution, I shall desire riches no otherwise than as they are helpful to religion. But this I determine, as what is really evident from many parts of Scripture, that to fallen man they have a greater tendency to hurt religion.

[[Monday, Mar. 16. To practice this sort of self-denial, when at sometimes on fair days, I find myself more particularly disposed to regard the glories of the world, than to betake myself to the study of serious religion.]]

Saturday, May 23. How it comes about I know not; but I have remarked it hitherto, that at those times when I have read the Scripture most, I have evermore been most lively, and in the best frames.

At Yale College[9]

Saturday night, June 6. This week has been a remarkable week with me with respect to despondencies, fears, perplexities, multitudes of cares and distraction of mind; being the week I came hither to New Haven, in order to entrance upon the office of Tutor of the College. I have now abundant reason to be convinced of the troublesomeness and vexation of the world, and that it never will be another kind of world.

Tuesday, July 7. When I am giving the relation of a thing, to abstain from altering either in the matter or manner of speaking, so much, as that if everyone afterward should alter as much, it would at last come to be properly false.

Tuesday, Sept. 2. By a sparingness in diet, and eating, as much as may be, what is light and easy of digestion, I shall doubtless be able to think clearer, and shall gain time. 1st, by lengthening out my life. 2dly, shall need less time for digestion after meals. 3dly, shall be able to study closer without wrong to my health. 4thly, shall need less time to sleep. 5thly, shall seldomer be troubled with the headache.

[[Saturday night, Sept. 12. Crosses of the nature of that, which I met with this week, thrust me quite below all comforts in religion. They appear no more than vanity and stubble, especially when I meet with them so unprepared for them. I shall not be fit to encounter them, except I have a far stronger, and more permanent faith, hope and love.

Wednesday, Sept. 30. It has been a prevailing thought with me, to which I have given place in practice, that it is best, sometimes, to eat or drink, when it will do me no good, because the hurt, that it will do me, will not be equal, to the trouble of denying myself. But I have determined, to suffer that thought to prevail no longer. The hurries of commencement, and diversion of the vacancy,[1] has been the occasion of my sinking so exceedingly, as in the three last weeks.

Monday, Oct. 5. I believe it is a good way, when prone to unprofitable thoughts, to deny myself and break off my thoughts, by keeping diligently to my study, that they may not have time to operate to work

9. Only Dwight ed. (*1*, 103) has this heading.
1. "The vacancy" was the customary two-week break at the close of each college quarter.

me to such a listless frame. I am apt to think it a good way, when I am indisposed to reading and study, to read of my own remarks, the fruit of my study in divinity, etc., to set me a-going again.

Friday, Nov. 6. Felt sensibly, somewhat of that trust and affiance in Christ, and with delight committing of my soul to him, of which our divines used to speak, and about which, I have been somewhat in doubt.

Tuesday, Nov. 10. To mark all that I say in conversation, merely to beget in others, a good opinion of myself, and examine it.

Sabbath, Nov. 15. Determined, when I am indisposed to prayer, always to premeditate what to pray for; and that it is better, that the prayer should be of almost any shortness, than that my mind should be almost continually off from what I say.]]

Sabbath day, Nov. 22. Considering that bystanders always espy some faults which we don't see ourselves, or at least are not so fully sensible of; there are many secret workings of corruption which escape our sight, and others only are sensible of: resolved therefore, that I will, if I can by any convenient means, learn what faults others find in me, or what things they see in me, that appear any way blameworthy, unlovely or unbecoming.[2]

[[Friday, Feb. 12, 1725. The very thing I now want, to give me a clearer and more immediate view of the perfections and glory of God, is as clear a knowledge of the manner of God's exerting himself, with respect to spirits and mind, as I have, of his operations concerning matter and bodies.

Tuesday, Feb. 16. A virtue, which I need in a higher degree, to give a beauty and luster to my behavior, is gentleness. If I had more of an air of gentleness, I should be much mended.

Friday, May 21. If ever I am inclined to turn to the opinion of any other sect: resolved, beside the most deliberate consideration, earnest prayer, etc., privately to desire all the help that can possibly be afforded me, from some of the most judicious men in the country, together with the prayers of wise and holy men, however strongly persuaded I may seem to be, that I am in the right.

Saturday, May 22. When I reprove for faults, whereby I am in any way injured, to defer, till the thing is quite over and done with; for that is the way, both to reprove aright, and without the least mixture of spirit, or passion, and to have reproofs effectual, and not suspected.

2. End of Hopkins' text of "Diary."

Friday, May 28. It seems to me, that whether I am now converted or not, I am so settled in the state I am in, that I shall go on in it all my life. But, however settled I may be, yet I will continue to pray to God, not to suffer me to be deceived about it, nor to sleep in an unsafe condition; and ever and anon, will call all into question and try myself, using for helps, some of our old divines, that God may have opportunities to answer my prayers, and the spirit of God to show me my error, if I am in one.

Saturday night, June 6. I am sometimes in a frame so listless, that there is no other way of profitably improving time, but conversation, visiting, or recreation, or some bodily exercise. However it may be best in the first place, before resorting to either of these, to try the whole circle of my mental employments.

Nov. 16. When confined at Mr. Stiles'.[3] I think it would be of special advantage to me, with respect to my truer interest, as near as I can in my studies, to observe this rule: To let half a day's, or at most, a day's study in other things, be succeeded, by half a day's, or a day's study in divinity.

One thing wherein I have erred, as I would be complete in all social duties, is, in neglecting to write letters to friends. And I would be forewarned of the danger of neglecting to visit my friends and relations, when we are parted.

When one suppresses thoughts that tend to divert the run of the mind's operations from religion, whether they are melancholy, or anxious, or passionate, or any others; there is this good effect of it, that it keeps the mind in its freedom. Those thoughts are stopped in the beginning, that would have set the mind a-going in that stream.

There are a great many exercises, that for the present, seem not to help, but rather impede, religious meditation and affections, the fruit of which is reaped afterwards, and is of far greater worth than what is lost; for thereby the mind is only for the present diverted; but what is attained is, upon occasion, of use for the whole lifetime.

Sept. 26, 1726. 'Tis just about three years, that I have been for the most part in a low, sunk estate and condition, miserably senseless to what I used to be, about spiritual things. 'Twas three years ago, the week before commencement; just about the same time this year, I began to be somewhat as I used to be.

---

3. JE was taken ill at North Haven, en route home from Yale, the latter part of Sept. 1725. He convalesced at the home of his friend, Rev. Isaac Stiles, for three months.

January 1728. I think Christ has recommended rising early in the morning, by his rising from the grave very early.

Jan. 22, 1734. I judge that it is best, when I am in a good frame for divine contemplation, or engaged in reading the Scriptures, or any study of divine subjects, that ordinarily, I will not be interrupted by going to dinner, but will forego my dinner, rather than be broke off.

Apr. 4, 1735. When at any time, I have a sense of any divine thing, then to turn it in my thoughts, to a practical improvement. As for instance, when I am in my mind, on some argument for the truth of religion, the reality of a future state, and the like, then to think with myself, how safely I may venture to sell all, for a future good. So when, at any time, I have a more than ordinary sense of the glory of the saints, in another world; to think how well it is worth my while, to deny myself, and to sell all that I have for this glory, etc.

May 18. My mind at present is, never to suffer my thoughts and meditations, at all to ruminate.

June 11. To set apart days of meditation on particular subjects; as sometimes, to set apart a day for the consideration of the greatness of my sins; at another, to consider the dreadfulness and certainty, of the future misery of ungodly men; at another, the truth and certainty of religion; and so, of the great future things promised and threatened in the Scriptures.]]

ON SARAH PIERPONT

They say there is a young lady in [New Haven][1] who is beloved of that almighty Being, who made and rules the world, and that there are certain seasons in which this great Being, in some way or other invisible, comes to her and fills her mind with exceeding sweet delight, and that she hardly cares for anything, except to meditate on him—that she expects after a while to be received up where he is,[2] to be raised out of the world and caught[3] up into heaven; being assured that he loves her too well to let her remain at a distance from him always. There she

1. Both the transcript and Dwight's published version include this interpolation. Stoughton, *Windsor Farmes*, p. 82, has a dash, with no location designated. The following footnotes, 2–9, relate to the Dwight transcript.

2. Dwight originally wrote "to dwell with him" here. He then crossed this phrase out, however, and wrote "where he is" instead. Cf. n. 4, below.

3. Dwight originally wrote "caught" here, crossed it out and wrote "ravished," and then rewrote the word "caught" above the word "ravished."

is to dwell with him, and to[4] be ravished with his love, favor[5] and delight, forever. Therefore, if you present all the world before her, with the richest of its treasures, she disregards it and cares not for it, and is unmindful of any pain or affliction. She has a strange sweetness in her mind, and sweetness of temper, uncommon[6] purity in her affections; is most just and praiseworthy[7] in all her actions; and you could not persuade her to do anything thought[8] wrong or sinful, if you would give her all the world, lest she should offend this great Being. She is of a wonderful sweetness, calmness and universal benevolence of mind; especially after those times[9] in which this great God has manifested himself to her mind. She will sometimes go about, singing sweetly, from place to [place]; and seems to be always full of joy and pleasure; and no one knows for what. She loves to be alone, and to wander in the fields and on the mountains, and seems to have someone invisible always conversing with her.

PERSONAL NARRATIVE

I had a variety of concerns and exercises about my soul from my childhood; but had two more remarkable seasons of awakening, before I met with that change, by which I was brought to those new dispositions, and that new sense of things, that I have since had. The first time was when I was a boy, some years before I went to college, at a time of remarkable awakening in my father's congregation. I was then very much affected for many months, and concerned about the things of religion, and my soul's salvation; and was abundant in duties. I used to pray five times a day in secret, and to spend much time in religious talk with other boys; and used to meet with them to pray together. I experienced I know not what kind of delight in religion. My mind was

4. Though Dwight includes the words "to dwell with him" here, the cross-out indicated by n. 2, above, may suggest that he moved them from an earlier place (i.e. at n. 2) in JE's original.

5. Though crossed out and not included in his published version, Dwight originally included the word "favor" here.

6. Though crossed out in favor of the word "singular" (which is interlineated in the transcript) in both the transcript and his published version, Dwight originally wrote the words "sweetness of temper uncommon" here. The word "uncommon" was repeated by JE on his deathbed, in relation to Sarah.

7. Though crossed out in favor of the word "conscientious" (which is interlineated in the transcript) in the transcript, Dwight originally wrote the word "praiseworthy" here.

8. Though crossed out and not included in his published version, Dwight originally included the word "thot" (thought) here.

9. Though crossed out in favor of the word "seasons" in both the transcript and his published version, Dwight originally wrote the word "times" here.

much engaged in it, and had much self-righteous pleasure; and it was my delight to abound in religious duties. I, with some of my school-mates joined together, and built a booth in a swamp, in a very secret and retired place, for a place of prayer. And besides, I had particular secret places of my own in the woods, where I used to retire by myself; and used to be from time to time much affected. My affections seemed to be lively and easily moved, and I seemed to be in my element, when engaged in religious duties. And I am ready to think, many are de-ceived with such affections, and such a kind of delight, as I then had in religion, and mistake it for grace.

But in process of time, my convictions and affections wore off; and I entirely lost all those affections and delights, and left off secret prayer, at least as to any constant performance of it; and returned like a dog to his vomit, and went on in ways of sin.

Indeed, I was at some times very uneasy, especially towards the latter part of the time of my being at college. Till it pleased God, in my last year at college, at a time when I was in the midst of many uneasy thoughts about the state of my soul, to seize me with a pleurisy; in which he brought me nigh to the grave, and shook me over the pit of hell.

But yet, it was not long after my recovery, before I fell again into my old ways of sin. But God would not suffer me to go on with any quietness; but I had great and violent inward struggles: till after many conflicts with wicked inclinations, and repeated resolutions, and bonds that I laid myself under by a kind of vows to God, I was brought wholly to break off all former wicked ways, and all ways of known outward sin; and to apply myself to seek my salvation, and practice the duties of religion: but without that kind of affection and delight, that I had formerly experienced. My concern now wrought more by inward struggles and conflicts, and self-reflections. I made seeking my salva-tion the main business of my life. But yet it seems to me, I sought after a miserable manner: which has made me sometimes since to question, whether ever it issued in that which was saving; being ready to doubt, whether such miserable seeking was ever succeeded. But yet I was brought to seek salvation, in a manner that I never was before. I felt a spirit to part with all things in the world, for an interest in Christ. My concern continued and prevailed, with many exercising things and inward struggles; but yet it never seemed to be proper to express my concern that I had, by the name of terror.

From my childhood up, my mind had been wont to be full of objections against the doctrine of God's sovereignty, in choosing whom he would to eternal life, and rejecting whom he pleased; leaving them eternally to perish, and be everlastingly tormented in hell. It used to appear like a horrible doctrine to me. But I remember the time very well, when I seemed to be convinced, and fully satisfied, as to this sovereignty of God, and his justice in thus eternally disposing of men, according to his sovereign pleasure. But never could give an account, how, or by what means, I was thus convinced; not in the least imagining, in the time of it, nor a long time after, that there was any extraordinary influence of God's Spirit in it: but only that now I saw further, and my reason apprehended the justice and reasonableness of it. However, my mind rested in it; and it put an end to all those cavils and objections, that had till then abode with me, all the preceding part of my life. And there has been a wonderful alteration in my mind, with respect to the doctrine of God's sovereignty, from that day to this; so that I scarce ever have found so much as the rising of an objection against God's sovereignty, in the most absolute sense, in showing mercy on whom he will show mercy, and hardening and eternally damning whom he will. God's absolute sovereignty, and justice, with respect to salvation and damnation, is what my mind seems to rest assured of, as much as of anything that I see with my eyes; at least it is so at times. But I have oftentimes since that first conviction, had quite another kind of sense of God's sovereignty, than I had then. I have often since, not only had a conviction, but a *delightful* conviction. The doctrine of God's sovereignty has very often appeared, an exceeding pleasant, bright and sweet doctrine to me: and absolute sovereignty is what I love to ascribe to God. But my first conviction was not with this.

The first that I remember that ever I found anything of that sort of inward, sweet delight in God and divine things, that I have lived much in since, was on reading those words, I Tim. 1:17, "Now unto the King eternal, immortal, invisible, the only wise God, be honor and glory forever and ever, Amen." As I read the words, there came into my soul, and was as it were diffused through it, a sense of the glory of the divine being; a new sense, quite different from anything I ever experienced before. Never any words of Scripture seemed to me as these words did. I thought with myself, how excellent a Being that was; and how happy I should be, if I might enjoy that God, and be wrapt up to God in heaven, and be as it were swallowed up in him. I kept saying, and as it were singing over these words of Scripture to myself; and went to prayer, to pray to God that I might enjoy him; and prayed in a manner quite different from what I used to do; with a new sort of affection. But it never came into my thought, that there was anything spiritual, or of a saving nature in this.

From about that time, I began to have a new kind of apprehensions and ideas of Christ, and the work of redemption, and the glorious way of salvation by him. I had an inward, sweet sense of these things, that at times came into my heart; and my soul was led away in pleasant views and contemplations of them. And my mind was greatly engaged, to spend my time in reading and meditating on Christ; and the beauty and excellency of his person, and the lovely way of salvation, by free grace in him. I found no books so delightful to me, as those that treated of these subjects. Those words (Cant. 2:1) used to be abundantly with me: "I am the rose of Sharon, the lily of the valleys." The words seemed to me, sweetly to represent, the loveliness and beauty of Jesus Christ. And the whole book of Canticles used to be pleasant to me; and I used to be much in reading it, about that time. And found, from time to time, an inward sweetness, that used, as it were, to carry me away in my contemplations; in what I know not how to express otherwise, than by a calm, sweet abstraction of soul from all the concerns o[f] this world; and a kind of vision, or fixed ideas and imaginations, of being alone in the mountains, or some solitary wilderness, far from all mankind, sweetly conversing with Christ, and wrapt and swallowed up in God. The sense I had of divine things, would often of a sudden as it were, kindle up a sweet burning in my heart; an ardor of my soul, that I know not how to express.

Not long after I first began to experience these things, I gave an account to my father, of some things that had passed in my mind. I was pretty much affected by the discourse we had together. And when the discourse was ended, I walked abroad alone, in a solitary place in my father's pasture, for contemplation. And as I was walking there, and looked up on the sky and clouds; there came into my mind, a sweet sense of the glorious majesty and grace of God, that I know not how to express. I seemed to see them both in a sweet conjunction: majesty and meekness joined together: it was a sweet and gentle, and holy majesty; and also a majestic meekness; an awful sweetness; a high, and great, and holy gentleness.

After this my sense of divine things gradually increased, and became more and more lively, and had more of that inward sweetness. The appearance of everything was altered: there seemed to be, as it were, a calm, sweet cast, or appearance of divine glory, in almost everything. God's excellency, his wisdom, his purity and love, seemed to appear in everything; in the sun, moon and stars; in the clouds, and blue sky; in the grass, flowers, trees; in the water, and all nature; which used greatly to fix my mind. I often used to sit and view the moon, for a long time; and so in the daytime, spent much time in viewing the clouds and sky, to behold the sweet glory of God in these things: in the meantime, singing forth with a low voice, my contemplations of the Creator and Redeemer. And scarce anything, among all the works of nature, was so sweet to me as thunder and lightning. Formerly, nothing had been so terrible to me. I used to be a person uncommonly terrified with thunder: and it used to strike me with terror, when I saw a thunderstorm rising. But now, on the contrary, it rejoiced me. I felt God at the first appearance of a thunderstorm. And used to take the opportunity at such times, to fix myself to view the clouds, and see the lightnings play, and hear the majestic and awful voice of God's thunder: which often times was exceeding entertaining, leading me to sweet contemplations of my great and glorious God. And while I viewed, used to spend my time, as it always seemed natural to me, to sing or chant forth my meditations; to speak my thoughts in soliloquies, and speak with a singing voice.

I felt then a great satisfaction as to my good estate. But that did not content me. I had vehement longings of soul after God and Christ, and after more holiness; wherewith my heart seemed to be full, and ready to break: which often brought to my mind, the words of the Psalmist, Ps. 119:28, "My soul breaketh for the longing it hath." I often felt a mourning and lamenting in my heart, that I had not turned to God sooner, that I might have had more time to grow in grace. My mind was greatly fixed on divine things; I was almost perpetually in the contemplation of them. Spent most of my time in thinking of divine things, year after year. And used to spend abundance of my time, in walking alone in the woods, and solitary places, for meditation, soliloquy and prayer, and converse with God. And it was always my manner, at such times, to sing forth my contemplations. And was almost constantly in ejaculatory prayer, wherever I was. Prayer seemed to be natural to me; as the breath, by which the inward burnings of my heart had vent.

The delights which I now felt in things of religion, were of an exceeding different kind, from those forementioned, that I had when I was a boy. They were totally of another kind; and what I then had no more notion or idea of, than one born blind has of pleasant and beautiful colors. They were of a more inward, pure, soul-animating and refreshing nature. Those former delights, never reached the heart; and did not arise from any sight of the divine excellency of the things of God; or any taste of the soul-satisfying, and life-giving good, there is in them.

My sense of divine things seemed gradually to increase, till I went to preach at New York; which was about a year and a half after they began. While I was there, I felt them, very sensibly, in a much higher degree, than I had done before. My longings after God and holiness, were much increased. Pure and humble, holy and heavenly Christianity, appeared exceeding amiable to me. I felt in me a burning desire to be in everything a complete Christian; and conformed to the blessed image of Christ: and that I might live in all things, according to the pure, sweet and blessed rules of the gospel. I had an eager thirsting after progress in these things. My longings after it, put me upon pursuing and pressing after them. It was my continual strife day and night, and constant inquiry, how I should be more holy, and live more holily, and more becoming a child of God, and disciple of Christ. I sought an increase of grace and holiness, and that I might live an holy life, with vastly more earnestness, than ever I sought grace, before I had it. I used to be continually examining myself, and studying and contriving for likely ways and means, how I should live holily, with far greater diligence and earnestness, than ever I pursued anything in my life: but with too great a dependence on my own strength; which afterwards proved a great damage to me. My experience had not then taught me, as it has done since, my extreme feebleness and impotence, every manner of way; and the innumerable and bottomless depths of secret corruption and deceit, that there was in my heart. However, I went on with my eager pursuit after more holiness; and sweet conformity to Christ.

The heaven I desired was a heaven of holiness; to be with God, and to spend my eternity in divine love, and holy communion with Christ. My mind was very much taken up with contemplations on heaven, and the enjoyments of those there; and living there in perfect holiness, humility and love. And it used at that time to appear a great part of the happiness of heaven, that there the saints could express their love to Christ. It appeared to me a great clog and hindrance and burden to me, that what I felt within, I could not express to God, and give vent to, as I desired. The inward ardor of my soul, seemed to be hindered and pent up, and could not freely flame out as it would. I used often to think, how in heaven, this sweet principle should freely and fully vent and express itself. Heaven appeared to me exceeding delightful as a world of love. It appeared to me, that all happiness consisted in living in pure, humble, heavenly, divine love.

I remember the thoughts I used then to have of holiness. I remember I then said sometimes to myself, I do certainly know that I love holiness, such as the gospel prescribes. It appeared to me, there was nothing in it but what was ravishingly lovely. It appeared to me, to be the highest beauty and amiableness, above all other beauties: that it was a divine beauty; far purer than anything here upon earth; and that everything else, was like mire, filth and defilement, in comparison of it.

Holiness, as I then wrote down some of my contemplations on it, appeared to me to be of a sweet, pleasant, charming, serene, calm nature. It seemed to me, it brought an inexpressible purity, brightness, peacefulness and ravishment to the soul: and that it made the soul like a field or garden of God, with all manner of pleasant flowers; that is all pleasant, delightful and undisturbed; enjoying a sweet calm, and the gently vivifying beams of the sun. The soul of a true Christian, as I then wrote my meditations, appeared like such a little white flower, as we see in the spring of the year; low and humble on the ground, opening its bosom, to receive the pleasant beams of the sun's glory; rejoicing as it were, in a calm rapture; diffusing around a sweet fragrancy; standing peacefully and lovingly, in the midst of other flowers round about; all in like manner opening their bosoms, to drink in the light of the sun.

There was no part of creature-holiness, that I then, and at other times, had so great a sense of the loveliness of, as humility, brokenness of heart and poverty of spirit: and there was nothing that I had such a spirit to long for. My heart as it were panted after this, to lie low before GOD, and in the dust; that I might be nothing, and that God might be all; that I might become as a little child.

While I was there at New York, I sometimes was much affected with reflections on my past life, considering how late it was, before I began to be truly religious; and how wickedly I had lived till then: and once so as to weep abundantly, and for a considerable time together.

On January 12, 1722/3, I made a solemn dedication of myself to God, and wrote it down; giving up myself, and all that I had to God; to be for the future in no respect my own; to act as one that had no right to himself, in any respect. And solemnly vowed to take God for my whole portion and felicity; looking on nothing else as any part of my happiness, nor acting as if it were: and his law for the constant rule of my obedience; engaging to fight with all my might, against the world, the flesh and the devil, to the end of my life. But have reason to be infinitely humbled, when I consider, how much I have failed of answering my obligation.

I had then abundance of sweet religious conversation in the family where I lived, with Mr. John Smith, and his pious mother. My heart was knit in affection to those, in whom were appearances of true piety; and I could bear the thoughts of no other companions, but such as were holy, and the disciples of the blessed Jesus.

I had great longings for the advancement of Christ's kingdom in the world. My secret prayer used to be in great part taken up in praying for it. If I heard the least hint of anything that happened in any part of the world, that appeared to me, in some respect or other, to have a favorable aspect on the interest of Christ's kingdom, my soul eagerly catched at it; and it would much animate and refresh me. I used to be earnest to read public news-letters, mainly for that end; to see if I could not find some news favorable to the interest of religion in the world.

I very frequently used to retire into a solitary place, on the banks of Hudson's River, at some distance from the city, for contemplation on divine things, and secret converse with God; and had many sweet hours there. Sometimes Mr. Smith and I walked there together, to converse of the things of God; and our conversation used much to turn on the advancement of Christ's kingdom in the world, and the glorious things that God would accomplish for his church in the latter days.

I had then, and at other times, the greatest delight in the holy Scriptures, of any book whatsoever. Oftentimes in reading it, every word seemed to touch my heart. I felt an harmony between something in my heart, and those sweet and powerful words. I seemed often to see so much light, exhibited by every sentence, and such a refreshing ravishing food communicated, that I could not get along in reading. Used oftentimes to dwell long on one sentence, to see the wonders contained in it; and yet almost every sentence seemed to be full of wonders.

I came away from New York in the month of April 1723, and had a most bitter parting with Madam Smith and her son. My heart seemed to sink within me, at leaving the family and city, where I had enjoyed so many sweet and pleasant days. I went from New York to Wethersfield by water. As I sailed away, I kept sight of the city as long as I could; and when I was out of sight of it, it would affect me much to look that way, with a kind of melancholy mixed with sweetness. However, that night after this sorrowful parting, I was greatly comforted in God at West-chester, where we went ashore to lodge: and had a pleasant time of it all the voyage to Saybrook. It was sweet to me to think of meeting dear Christians in heaven, where we should never part more. At Saybrook we went ashore to lodge on Saturday, and there kept sabbath; where I had a sweet and refreshing season, walking alone in the fields.

After I came home to Windsor, remained much in a like frame of my mind, as I had been in at New York; but only sometimes felt my heart ready to sink, with the thoughts of my friends at New York. And my refuge and support was in contemplations on the heavenly state; as I find in my diary of May 1, 1723. It was my comfort to think of that state, where there is fullness of joy; where reigns heavenly, sweet, calm and delightful love, without alloy; where there are continually the dearest expressions of this love; where is the enjoyment of the persons loved, without ever parting; where these persons that appear so lovely in this world, will really be inexpressibly more lovely, and full of love to us. And how sweetly will the mutual lovers join together to sing the praises of God and the Lamb! How full will it fill us with joy, to think, that this enjoyment, these sweet exercises will never cease or come to an end; but will last to all eternity!

Continued much in the same frame in the general, that I had been in at New York, till I went to New Haven, to live there as Tutor of the College; having one special season of uncommon sweetness: partic-ularly once at Bolton, in a journey from Boston, walking out alone in the fields. After I went to New Haven, I sunk in religion; my mind being diverted from my eager and violent pursuits after holiness, by some affairs that greatly perplexed and distracted my mind.

In September 1725, was taken ill at New Haven; and endeavoring to go home to Windsor, was so ill at the North Village, that I could go no further: where I lay sick for about a quarter of a year. And in this sickness, God was pleased to visit me again with the sweet influences of his spirit. My mind was greatly engaged there on divine, pleasant contemplations, and longings of soul. I observed that those who watched with me, would often be looking out for the morning, and seemed to wish for it. Which brought to my mind those words of the Psalmist, which my soul with sweetness made its own language, "My soul waiteth for the Lord more than they that watch for the morning: I say, more than they that watch for the morning" [Ps. 130:6]. And when the light of the morning came, and the beams of the sun came in at the windows, it refreshed my soul from one morning to another. It seemed to me to be some image of the sweet light of God's glory.

I remember, about that time, I used greatly to long for the conversion of some that I was concerned with. It seemed to me, I could gladly honor them, and with delight be a servant to them, and lie at their feet, if they were but truly holy.

But sometime after this, I was again greatly diverted in my mind, with some temporal concerns,[1] that exceedingly took up my thoughts, greatly to the wounding of my soul: and went on through various exercises, that it would be tedious to relate, that gave me much more experience of my own heart, than ever I had before.

Since I came to this town,[2] I have often had sweet complacency in God in views of his glorious perfections, and the excellency of Jesus Christ. God has appeared to me, a glorious and lovely being, chiefly on the account of his holiness. The holiness of God has always appeared to me the most lovely of all his attributes. The doctrines of God's absolute sovereignty, and free grace, in showing mercy to whom he would show mercy; and man's absolute dependence on the operations of God's Holy Spirit, have very often appeared to me as sweet and glorious doctrines. These doctrines have been much my delight. God's sovereignty has ever appeared to me, as great part of his glory. It has often been sweet to me to go to God, and adore him as a sovereign God, and ask sovereign mercy of him.

I have loved the doctrines of the gospel: they have been to my soul like green pastures. The gospel has seemed to me to be the richest treasure; the treasure that I have most desired, and longed that it might dwell richly in me. The way of salvation by Christ, has appeared in a general way, glorious and excellent, and most pleasant and beautiful. It has often seemed to me, that it would in a great measure spoil heaven, to receive it in any other way. That text has often been affecting and delightful to me, Is.. 32:2, "A man shall be an hiding place from the wind, and a covert from the tempest," etc.

It has often appeared sweet to me, to be united to Christ; to have him for my head, and to be a member of his body: and also to have Christ for my teacher and prophet. I very often think with sweetness and longings and pantings of soul, of being a little child, taking hold of

1. After a long convalescence at East Windsor, JE returned in the early summer, 1726, to the tutorship at New Haven, and remained until the end of the session in September.
2. "Northampton" (Hopkins, p. 33*n;* Dwight ed., *1*, 131).

Christ, to be led by him through the wilderness of this world. That text, Matt. 18 at the beginning, has often been sweet to me, "Except ye be converted, and become as little children" etc. I love to think of coming to Christ, to receive salvation of him, poor in spirit, and quite empty of self; humbly exalting him alone; cut entirely off from my own root, and to grow into, and out of Christ: to have God in Christ to be all in all; and to live by faith on the Son of God, a life of humble, unfeigned confidence in him. That Scripture has often been sweet to me, Ps. 115:1, "Not unto us, O Lord, not unto us, but unto thy name give glory, for thy mercy, and for thy truth's sake." And those words of Christ, Luke 10:21, "In that hour Jesus rejoiced in spirit, and said, I thank thee, O Father, Lord of heaven and earth, that thou hast hid these things from the wise and prudent, and hast revealed them unto babes: even so Father, for so it seemed good in thy sight." That sovereignty of God that Christ rejoiced in, seemed to me to be worthy to be rejoiced in; and that rejoicing of Christ, seemed to me to show the excellency of Christ, and the spirit that he was of.

Sometimes only mentioning a single word, causes my heart to burn within me: or only seeing the name of Christ, or the name of some attribute of God. And God has appeared glorious to me, on account of the Trinity. It has made me have exalting thoughts of God, that he subsists in three persons; Father, Son, and Holy Ghost.

The sweetest joys and delights I have experienced, have not been those that have arisen from a hope of my own good estate; but in a direct view of the glorious things of the gospel. When I enjoy this sweetness, it seems to carry me above the thoughts of my own safe estate. It seems at such times a loss that I cannot bear, to take off my eye from the glorious, pleasant object I behold without me, to turn my eye in upon myself, and my own good estate.

My heart has been much on the advancement of Christ's kingdom in the world. The histories of the past advancement of Christ's kingdom, have been sweet to me. When I have read histories of past ages, the pleasantest thing in all my reading has been, to read of the kingdom of Christ being promoted. And when I have expected in my reading, to come to any such thing, I have lotted upon it[3] all the way as I read. And my mind has been much entertained and delighted, with the Scripture promises and prophecies, of the future glorious advancement of Christ's kingdom on earth.

---

3. I.e. "relied on it" or "looked for it."

I have sometimes had a sense of the excellent fullness of Christ, and his meetness and suitableness as a savior; whereby he has appeared to me, far above all, the chief of ten thousands. And his blood and atonement has appeared sweet, and his righteousness sweet; which is always accompanied with an ardency of spirit, and inward strugglings and breathings and groanings, that cannot be uttered, to be emptied of myself, and swallowed up in Christ.

Once, as I rid out into the woods for my health, *anno* 1737; and having lit from my horse in a retired place, as my manner commonly has been, to walk for divine contemplation and prayer; I had a view, that for me was extraordinary, of the glory of the Son of God; as mediator between God and man; and his wonderful, great, full, pure and sweet grace and love, and meek and gentle condescension. This grace, that appeared to me so calm and sweet, appeared great above the heavens. The person of Christ appeared ineffably excellent, with an excellency great enough to swallow up all thought and conception. Which continued, as near as I can judge, about an hour; which kept me, the bigger part of the time, in a flood of tears, and weeping aloud. I felt withal, an ardency of soul to be, what I know not otherwise how to express, than to be emptied and annihilated; to lie in the dust, and to be full of Christ alone; to love him with a holy and pure love; to trust in him; to live upon him; to serve and follow him, and to be totally wrapt up in the fullness of Christ; and to be perfectly sanctified and made pure, with a divine and heavenly purity. I have several other times, had views very much of the same nature, and that have had the same effects.

I have many times had a sense of the glory of the third person in the Trinity, in his office of Sanctifier; in his holy operations communicating divine light and life to the soul. God in the communications of his Holy Spirit, has appeared as an infinite fountain of divine glory and sweetness; being full and sufficient to fill and satisfy the soul: pouring forth itself in sweet communications, like the sun in its glory, sweetly and pleasantly diffusing light and life.

I have sometimes had an affecting sense of the excellency of the word of God, as a word of life; as the light of life; a sweet, excellent, life-giving word: accompanied with a thirsting after that word, that it might dwell richly in my heart.

I have often since I lived in this town,[4] had very affecting views of my

4. Northampton.

own sinfulness and vileness; very frequently so as to hold me in a kind of loud weeping, sometimes for a considerable time together: so that I have often been forced to shut myself up. I have had a vastly greater sense of my own wickedness, and the badness of my heart, since my conversion, than ever I had before. It has often appeared to me, that if God should mark iniquity against me, I should appear the very worst of all mankind; of all that have been since the beginning of the world to this time: and that I should have by far the lowest place in hell. When others that have come to talk with me about their soul concerns, have expressed the sense they have had of their own wickedness, by saying that it seemed to them, that they were as bad as the devil himself; I thought their expressions seemed exceeding faint and feeble, to represent my wickedness. I thought I should wonder, that they should content themselves with such expressions as these, if I had any reason to imagine, that their sin bore any proportion to mine. It seemed to me, I should wonder at myself, if I should express my wickedness in such feeble terms as they did.

My wickedness, as I am in myself, has long appeared to me perfectly ineffable, and infinitely swallowing up all thought and imagination; like an infinite deluge, or infinite mountains over my head. I know not how to express better, what my sins appear to me to be, than by heaping infinite upon infinite, and multiplying infinite by infinite. I go about very often, for this many years, with these expressions in my mind, and in my mouth, "Infinite upon infinite. Infinite upon infinite!" When I look into my heart, and take a view of my wickedness, it looks like an abyss infinitely deeper than hell. And it appears to me, that were it not for free grace, exalted and raised up to the infinite height of all the fullness and glory of the great Jehovah, and the arm of his power and grace stretched forth, in all the majesty of his power, and in all the glory of his sovereignty; I should appear sunk down in my sins infinitely below hell itself, far beyond sight of everything, but the piercing eye of God's grace, that can pierce even down to such a depth, and to the bottom of such an abyss.

And yet, I ben't in the least inclined to think, that I have a greater conviction of sin than ordinary. It seems to me, my conviction of sin is exceeding small, and faint. It appears to me enough to amaze me, that I have no more sense of my sin. I know certainly, that I have very little sense of my sinfulness. That my sins appear to me so great, don't seem to me to be, because I have so much more conviction of sin than other Christians, but because I am so much worse, and have so much more wickedness to be convinced of. When I have had these turns of weeping and crying for my sins, I thought I knew in the time of it, that my repentance was nothing to my sin.

I have greatly longed of late, for a broken heart, and to lie low before God. And when I ask for humility of God, I can't bear the thoughts of being no more humble, than other Christians. It seems to me, that though their degrees of humility may be suitable for them; yet it would be a vile self-exaltation in me, not to be the lowest in humility of all mankind. Others speak of their longing to be humbled to the dust. Though that may be a proper expression for them, I always think for myself, that I ought to be humbled down below hell. 'Tis an expression that it has long been natural for me to use in prayer to God. I ought to lie infinitely low before God.

It is affecting to me to think, how ignorant I was, when I was a young Christian, of the bottomless, infinite depths of wickedness, pride, hypocrisy and deceit left in my heart.

I have vastly a greater sense, of my universal, exceeding dependence on God's grace and strength, and mere good pleasure, of late, than I used formerly to have; and have experienced more of an abhorrence of my own righteousness. The thought of any comfort or joy, arising in me, on any consideration, or reflection on my own amiableness, or any of my performances or experiences, or any goodness of heart or life, is nauseous and detestable to me. And yet I am greatly afflicted with a proud and self-righteous spirit; much more sensibly, than I used to be formerly. I see that serpent rising and putting forth its head, continually, everywhere, all around me.

Though it seems to me, that in some respects I was a far better Christian, for two or three years after my first conversion, than I am now; and lived in a more constant delight and pleasure: yet of late years, I have had a more full and constant sense of the absolute sovereignty of God, and a delight in that sovereignty; and have had more of a sense of the glory of Christ, as a mediator, as revealed in the gospel. On one Saturday night in particular, had a particular discovery of the excellency of the gospel of Christ, above all other doctrines; so that I could not but say to myself; "This is my chosen light, my chosen doctrine": and of Christ, "This is my chosen prophet." It appeared to me to be sweet beyond all expression, to follow Christ, and to be taught and enlightened and instructed by him; to learn of him, and live to him.

Another Saturday night, January 1738/9, had such a sense, how sweet and blessed a thing it was, to walk in the way of duty, to do that which was right and meet to be done, and agreeable to the holy mind of God; that it caused me to break forth into a kind of a loud weeping, which held me some time; so that I was forced to shut myself up, and fasten the doors. I could not but as it were cry out, "How happy are they which do that which is right in the sight of God! They are blessed indeed, they are the happy ones!" I had at the same time, a very affecting sense, how meet and suitable it was that God should govern the world, and order all things according to his own pleasure; and I rejoiced in it, that God reigned, and that his will was done.

APPENDIXES

APPENDIX A

BIOGRAPHICAL GLOSSARY

Abercrombie, Robert, Rev. (1712–1780), b. Scotland; settled Pelham, Massachusetts, 1744–55; sat on councils of 1750 and 1751.

Alvord, Benjamin (1695–1772), Northampton weaver, express rider, soldier.

Andrew, Samuel, Jr., Pres. (1656–1738), Harvard, 1675; settled Milford, Connecticut, 1685–1738, Yale rector pro tem, 1707–19.

Anville, Nicholas de la Rochefoucauld, duc d' (1700–1745), commander of French fleet against Louisburg.

Appleton, Nathaniel, Rev. (1693–1784), Harvard, 1712; settled Cambridge, Massachusetts, 1717–84.

Archbishop of Canterbury (see Herring, Thomas; Potter, John; Secker, Thomas).

Ashley, Benjamin (1715–c. 1758), schoolmaster of Indians at Stockbridge.

Ashley, Israel, Dr. (1710–1758), Yale, 1730; Westfield, Massachusetts, physician; d. during expedition to Ticonderoga.

Ashley, John, Capt., original proprietor of Sheffield, Massachusetts, 1733.

Ashley, Jonathan, Rev. (1712–1780), Yale, 1730; settled Deerfield, Massachusetts, 1729–80; sat on 1750 council.

Ashley, Rebecca Kellogg (1695–1757), Deerfield captive, 1704; wife of Benjamin Kellogg; interpreter for Gideon Hawley at Stockbridge; d. Onohquaga, New York

Backus, Eunice Edwards, (1705–1788), JE's sister; wife of Simon Backus; assisted as widow by JE.

Backus, Simon, Rev. (1701–1746), Yale, 1724; settled Newington, Connecticut, 1726–45; d. while chaplain on Louisburg campaign; JE's brother-in-law.

Ballantine, John, Rev. (1716–1776), Harvard, 1735; settled Westfield, Massachusetts, 1741–76; frequent host of JE and family.

Barber, Jonathan, Rev. (1713–1783), Yale, 1730; settled Orient, New York, 1740–57; visited JE with Whitefield.

Barnett, Curtis, Commodore (d. 1746), British naval officer.

Baxter, Richard (1615–1691), English Presbyterian minister and religious writer.

Beach, John, Rev. (1700–1782); Yale, 1721; settled Newtown, Connecticut, Congregational, 1724–32; Episcopal, 1732–82.

Beale, George, singing teacher for Timothy Edwards' church.

Belcher, Jonathan, Governor (1682–1757), Harvard, 1699; governor of Massachusetts and New Jersey

Bellamy, Joseph, Dr. (1719–1790), Yale, 1735; D.D., Aberdeen; settled Bethlehem, Connecticut, 1740–90; disciple of JE; New Divinity theologian.

Billing, Edward, Rev. (1707–1760), Harvard, 1731; settled Belchertown (Cold Spring), Massachusetts, 1740–52, Greenfield, 1753–60; sat on 1750 council; defender of JE.

Blair, Samuel, Rev. (1712–1751); ed. Log College; settled Faggs Manor, Pennsylvania, 1739–51; established academy; revivalist.

Braddock, Edward, Gen. (1695–1755), appointed major general in 1754 to head royal forces in North America; d. at battle of Fort Duquesne.

Brainerd, David (1718–1747), expelled from Yale, 1742; missionary to Indians; brother of John Brainerd.

Brainerd, Experience Lyon, wife of John Brainerd.

Brainerd, John (1720–1781), Yale, 1746; missionary to Indians; trustee, College of New Jersey, 1754–80; brother of David.

Brattle, William, Gen. (1706–1776), Harvard, 1722; Boston lawyer, politician and military commander; house guest of JE at Northampton for a week, August 1735.

Breck, Robert, Rev. (1713–1784), Harvard, 1730; settled Springfield, Massachusetts, 1734–84; ordination opposed by JE and Hampshire County Association; sat on 1750 council.

Brinsmade, Daniel, Rev. (1718–1793), Yale, 1745; settled Judea (Washington), Connecticut, 1748–93.

Bromfield, Abigail Conley, wife of Edward Bromfield.

Bromfield, Edward (1695–1756), Boston merchant, selectman, Overseer of the Poor; Massachusetts House of Representatives; frequent host of JE and family; forwarded JE's books and letters.

Brooks, Mercy (1670–1734), maid for JE's family at East Windsor, Connecticut.

Brown, James, Rev. (1721–1788), Yale, 1747; settled Bridgehampton, New York, 1748–75.

Brown, Samuel, Deac. (c. 1704–1784), Stockbridge resident.

Browne, Daniel (1698–1723), Yale, 1714; tutor, 1718–22; converted to Episcopalianism.

Buck, Daniel, Rev. (1695–1726), Yale, 1718; settled Southington (Farmington), Connecticut, 1724–26.

Buell, Samuel, Rev. (1716–1798), Yale, 1741; S.T.D., Dartmouth; settled East Hampton, New York, 1746–98; supplied Northampton pulpit in 1742; student of JE.

Bull, Nehemiah, Rev. (1700–1740), Yale, 1723; settled Westfield, Massachusetts, 1725–1740; founder of Stockbridge mission.

Burr, Aaron, Pres. (1716–1757), Yale, 1735; Presbyterian; settled Newark, New Jersey, 1736–55; president, College of New Jersey, 1748–57.

Burr, Esther Edwards (1732–1758), daughter of JE; wife of Aaron Burr; diarist.

Burr, Isaac, Dr. (d. 1759), Yale, 1753; physician, Hartford, Connecticut

Burr, Sarah [Sally] (1754–1797); daughter of Aaron and Esther Burr; m. Tapping Reeve.

Burt, Jonathan, Jr. (1697–1786), Northampton constable and schoolmaster.

Bush, Japheth, Stockbridge-area carpenter who built structure for female school.

Byng, John, Admiral (1704–1757), British navy, 1718–56; defeated at Minorca, 1756; court-martialled and executed.

Campbell, John, Lord Loudon (1705–1782), commander-in-chief of British forces in North America, 1756–57.

Carter, Ebenezer, appointed captain of Norwalk, Connecticut, militia, 1733.

Caughnawaugas, Mohawk Indians at Quebec; spoke same languages as the Oneidas.

Cauneebyenkees, alternate name for Proper Mohawks (see Coneenchee).

Cayuga (Quinqus, Quiquuhs), one of the five nations of the Iroquois, located at Lake Cayuga, New York.

Chamnloowanee (see Seneca).

Chandler, Samuel, Dr. (1693–1766), English Presbyterian minister of Old Jewry, who assumed support of Stockbridge mission after the death of Thomas Coram.

Chauncy, Charles, Rev. (1705–1787), Harvard, 1721; D.D., Edinburgh, 1741; settled First Church, Boston, 1727–87; leading Old Light; critic of JE on revivals.

Chauncy, Isaac, Rev. (1670–1745), Harvard, 1693; settled Hadley, Massachusetts, 1696–1741.

Chubb, Thomas (1679–1747), English deist; author of theological works; criticized by JE in *Freedom of the Will*.

Church, Benjamin, Capt. (1704–1781), venue master of Boston; subscriber to JE's books.

Clap, Mary Saltonstall Hanes (d. 1769), wife of Thomas Clap, 1740.

Clap, Thomas, Pres. (1703–1767), Harvard, 1722; settled Windham, Connecticut, 1725–39; president, Yale, 1740–64; engaged in pamphlet exchange with JE over Whitefield, 1744–45.

Clark, Caleb, Col. (1724–1792), Northampton resident; moved to Belchertown, c. 1756; justice of the peace; Massachusetts House of Representatives.

Clark, Noah (1694–1776), Northampton resident; messenger for JE.

Clark, Peter, Rev. (1694–1768), Harvard, 1712; settled Salem Village (Danvers), Massachusetts, 1716–68; supported JE, 1750; sat on 1751 council.

Collings, Nathaniel, Rev. (1677–1756), Harvard, 1697; settled Enfield, Massachusetts, 1699–1724.

Colman, Benjamin, Dr. (1673–1747), Harvard, 1692; D.D., Glasgow, 1731; settled Brattle Street, Boston, 1699–1747; published *Faithful Narrative*.

Colman, Sarah Crisp Clark (d. 1744), m. Benjamin Colman, 1732.

Conaughstansey, Abraham, elder brother of Hendrick; made a reader in Church of England, but advised Indians to come to Stockbridge; praised by JE.

Conneenchee (Proper Mohawks), principle tribe of Mohawks, located around Tiononderoge (Ft. Hunter) and Canajoharie, New York (see Mohawks).

Cook, Noah, Jr. (1688–1773), Northampton resident, deacon of church.

Cooper, Anthony A., third Earl of Shaftesbury (1671–1713), English philosopher; JE opposed his views in *Nature of True Virtue*.

Cooper, William, Rev. (1694–1743), Harvard, 1712; settled Brattle Street, Boston, 1716–1743; friend of JE, but opposed in Breck affair.

Coram, Thomas, Capt. (c. 1668–1751), English philanthropist; established London foundling hospital; raised funds for Stockbridge mission.

Cumming, Alexander, Rev. (1726–1763), College of New Jersey, 1760; A.M., Harvard, 1761; Presbyterian; settled New York, New York, 1750–53, New Brunswick, New Jersey, 1753–61.

Cutler, Timothy, Rev. (1684–1765), Harvard, 1701; D.D., Oxford, Cambridge, 1723; settled Stratford, Connecticut, 1709–19; Yale rector, 1719–22; converted to Episcopalianism; settled Christ Church, Boston, 1723–65.

D'Anville (see Anville).

Davenport, James, Rev. (1716-1757), Yale, 1732; itinerant, 1737–38, 1741–43; pastor of churches in Connecticut, New York, New Jersey; recanted Separatism and extreme revivalism.

Davidson, Thomas, Rev., dissenting minister, Braintree, England.

Davies, Samuel, Pres. (1723–1761), ed. Faggs Manor, Pennsylvania; settled Hanover County, Virginia, 1747–59; president, College of New Jersey, 1759–61; famed orator.

Demming, Timothy, youthful servant of JE's family at East Windsor, Connecticut, 1711–16; by 1723, a member of the church.

Dennie, Abigail Colman, Mrs. Albert (1715–1745), daughter of Benjamin Colman.

Dickinson, Jonathan, Pres. (1688–1747), Yale, 1706; Presbyterian; settled Elizabeth, New Jersey, 1709–47; president, College of New Jersey, 1746–47.

Dieskau, Ludwig August, Baron (1701–1767), commander of French forces; defeated and captured, battle of Lake George, Sept. 8, 1755.

Dinwiddie, Robert (1693–1770), b. Scotland; appointed Governor of Virginia, July 20, 1751.

Doddridge, Philip, Rev. (1702–1751), D.D., Aberdeen, 1736; English dissenting minister, Northamptonshire; author of religious works.

Draper, John (1702–1762), Boston printer and publisher.

Dudley, Paul, Judge (1675–1751), Harvard, 1690, classmate of Timothy Edwards; Massachusetts Superior Court Judge; member, Royal Society.

Dwight, Abigail Williams Sergeant (1721–1791), daughter of Col. Ephraim; m. (1) Rev. John Sergeant, (2) Col. Joseph Dwight.

Dwight, Edmund (1717–1755), Boston resident; moved to Halifax, Nova Scotia, in 1749.

Dwight, Experience King (1693–1763), of Northampton, wife of Col. Timothy Dwight, Sr.; mother-in-law of JE's daughter, Mary.

Dwight, Henry (1733–1756), Harvard, 1754; son of Gen. Joseph Dwight.

Dwight, Joseph, Brig. Gen. (1703–1765), Harvard, 1722; Massachusetts militia commander; legislator; judge; turned against JE after second marriage.

Dwight, Mary Edwards (1734–1807), daughter of JE; wife of Timothy Dwight, Jr.

Dwight, Sereno E., Rev. (1786–1850), Yale, 1803; D.D., 1833; settled Park Street, Boston, 1817–26; president, Hamilton College, 1833–35; transcribed and published JE's works.

Dwight, Timothy, Col. (1694–1771), Northampton lawyer and Hampshire County judge; strong supporter of JE.

Dwight, Timothy, Jr., Maj. (1726–1777), Yale, 1744; Northampton merchant; judge; JE's son-in-law.

Eaton, Joshua, Rev. (1714–1772), Harvard, 1735; lawyer, 1737–42; settled Spencer, Massachusetts, 1744–72; sat on 1751 council.

Ebenezer (see Manumaseet or Poohpoonuk)

Edwards, Esther Stoddard (1672-1771), daughter of Solomon Stoddard; wife of Timothy Ewards; mother of JE.

Edwards, Esther (see Burr or Hopkins).

Edwards, Eunice (see Backus, Eunice Edwards).

Edwards, Jerusha (1710–1729), sister of JE.

Edwards, Jerusha (1730–1748), daughter of JE; nursed David Brainerd in final illness.

Edwards, Jonathan, Jr., Pres. (1745–1801), Princeton, 1765; M.A., Yale, 1769; D.D., Glasgow, 1785; settled New Haven (White Haven), Connecticut, 1769–95; Colbrook, Connecticut, 1796–99; president, Union College, 1799–1801.

Edwards, Lucy (1715–1736), sister of JE.

Edwards, Lucy (see Woodbridge, Lucy Edwards).

Edwards, Mary (1701–1776), sister of JE; cared for parents in their old age.

Edwards, Mary (see Dwight, Mary Edwards).

Edwards, Mary Porter (1748–1782), first wife of Jonathan Edwards, Jr.

Edwards, Mercy Sabin (d. 1801), second wife of Jonathan Edwards, Jr., 1783.

Edwards, Pierpont, Hon. (1750–1826), College of New Jersey, 1768; son and youngest child of JE; lawyer, politician, jurist, New Haven and Bridgeport, Connecticut.

Edwards, Richard, Esq. (1647–1718), grandfather of JE; Hartford, Connecticut, merchant, lawyer, constable, selectman.

Edwards, Sarah Pierpont (1710–1758), daughter of Rev. James Pierpont of New Haven, Connecticut; married JE, 1727.

Edwards, Timothy, Rev. (1669–1758), Harvard, 1691; settled Windsor Farms (East Windsor), Connecticut, 1694–1758; father of JE.

Edwards, Timothy (1738–1813), College of New Jersey, 1757; merchant, Elizabeth, New Jersey, and Stockbridge, Massachusetts; justice of the peace, Essex County, New Jersey; member, Massachusetts Council.

Ellsworth, Ann Edwards (1699–1790), sister of JE; m. John Ellsworth; lived at East Windsor, Connecticut.

Ellsworth, John, Capt. (1697–1784), officer in Indian wars; JE's brother-in-law; possessed Edwards family manuscripts.

Ely, John, Lieut. (1707–1754), West Springfield, Massachusetts, resident; militia officer.

Erskine, Christian Mackay (d. 1810), daughter of George Mackay, third Baron Reay; wife of John Erskine.

Erskine, John, Dr. (1721–1803), D.D., Glasgow; settled Kirkintilloch, Scotland, 1744–53; Culross, 1753–58; New Greyfriars, Edinburgh, 1758–67; Old Greyfriars, 1767–1803; leader of evangelical party in General Assembly; published JE's works in Scotland.

Esselstein, William, of Kinderhook, New York; promised a horse and son to escort JE's daughter, Lucy, to Stockbridge, 1757.

Farrand, Daniel, Rev. (1722–1803), College of New Jersey, 1750; M.A., Yale, 1777; settled South Canaan, Connecticut, 1752–1803.

Five Nations (see Iroquois).

Fonda, Abraham, Dutch trader, Claverack, New York; lent newspapers to JE; promised to provide horse for JE's daughter, Lucy, 1757.

Forbush (Forbes), Eli, Dr. (1726–1804), Harvard, 1751; D.D., 1804; son-in-law of Rev. Ebenezer Parkman; expected as schoolmaster of Stockbridge, 1751, but settled North Brookfield, 1752–75; Gloucester, 1776–1804; lifelong interest in Indian education.

Foxcroft, Thomas, Rev. (1697–1769), Harvard, 1714; settled First Church, Boston, 1717–69; pro-revivalist; supervised publication of JE's works.

Francke, Auguste-Hermann, Dr. (1665–1727), Hamburg, 1685; German pietistic theologian, educator, philanthropist; founded orphan school at Halle.

Fraser, James, Rev. (1700–1769), Scottish divine.

Frederick, Prince of Wales (1707–1751); m. April 26, 1736, to Princess Augusta of Saxe-Gothe.

Frelinghuysen, Theodorus Jacobus, Rev. (1691–c.1748), Dutch Reformed pastor of churches in New Jersey and Pennsylvania, 1720–47; revivalist.

Frelinghuysen, John, Rev. (1727–1754), Dutch Reformed minister; settled Somerset County, New Jersey, 1750–54; conveyed revival news from Holland.

Frelinghuysen, Theodore, Jr., Rev. (1723–1761), Dutch Reformed minister; settled Albany, Catskill, and Schagticoke, New York, 1749–59.

Gay, Ebenezer, Rev. (1718–1796), Harvard, 1737; S.T.D., 1792; settled Suffield, Connecticut, 1742–1796.

Gay, Hannah Angier (1742–1762), wife of Ebenezer Gay.

Gee, Joshua, Rev. (1698–1748), Harvard, 1717; settled Second Church, Boston, 1723–48; defender of Whitefield and revivalism.

George II, King of England (1683–1760).

Gibbons, Thomas, Dr. (1720–1785), M.A., College of New Jersey, 1760; D.D., Aberdeen, 1764; English independent minister and writer.

Gibson, Edmund, Bishop (1669–1748), Oxford, 1691; Bishop of London, 1720–48; authority on church law; opposed Whitefield.

Gillespie, Thomas, Rev. (1708–1774), ed. Edinburgh; settled Carnock, Scotland, 1741–52, Dunfermline, 1752–73; theological writer; founder, Relief Church; revivalist; correspondent of JE.

Gillies, John, Rev. (1712–1796), privately ed.; L.L.D., Edinburgh, 1778; settled Glasgow, 1742–96; theological writer; son-in-law of Rev. John MacLaurin; reported on revivals.

Glas, John, Rev. (1695–1773), St. Andrews, 1713; Scottish preacher and theological writer; suspended by Synods of Angus and Mearns; founder of the "Glassites"; JE used his biblical commentaries.

Goddard, David, Rev. (1706–1754), Harvard, 1731; settled Leicester, Massachusetts, 1736–54; sat on 1751 council.

Gordon, Alexander (d. 1754), College of New Jersey, 1751; tutor, 1752–54; expected as missionary at Stockbridge, May 1753; went with G. Hawley, but did not remain.

Gould, Ebenezer, Rev. (d. c. 1778) Yale, 1721; Presbyterian; settled Greenwich, New Jersey, 1728–39; Cutchogue, Southold, New York, 1740–47; Middlefield and Middletown, Connecticut, 1747–56.

Graham, John, Jr., Rev. (1722–1796), Yale, 1740; settled West Suffield,

Connecticut (Second Parish), 1746–96.

Graves, Nathan, Northampton resident, admitted to church during JE's pastorate.

Green, Timothy (1703–1763), Boston printer; partner of Samuel Kneeland until 1753.

Greenman, Nehemiah, Rev. (c.1724–1779), Yale, 1748; settled Brookhaven and Westhampton, New York, 1748–49, Madison, New Jersey, 1750–52, Pilesgrove, New Jersey, 1753–79.

Grosart, Alexander B., Rev. (1827–1899), ed. Edinburgh; Scottish pastor, theologian, editor; published some of JE's writings, 1865.

Guyse, John, Rev. (1680–1761), D.D., Aberdeen, 1733; English Independent; settled Hertford, 1705–27, London, 1728–61; opponent of Arianism; co-sponsor of London publication of *Faithful Narrative*.

Hall, David, Rev. (1704–1789), Harvard, 1724; D.D., Dartmouth, 1777; settled Sutton, Massachusetts, 1729–89; pro-revival; sat on councils of 1750 and 1751.

Hannam, Dorothy Danks, m. Eleazar Hannam of Northampton, 1743; queried by JE in Bad Book affair.

Hatheway, Deborah (1722–1753), Suffield, Connecticut, resident; young convert.

Hawley, Gideon, Rev. (1727–1807), Yale, 1749; M.A., Harvard, 1763; missionary to Indians at Stockbridge and Onohquaga; settled Mashpee, Massachusetts, 1758–1807; protégé of JE.

Hawley, Joseph, Maj. (1723–1788), Yale, 1742; Northampton lawyer and deacon; deputy, General Court; led effort to dismiss JE; later apologized.

Hazard, Nathaniel (d. c. 1765), Newtown, Long Island, New York, merchant; official of First Presbyterian Church of New York City, serving on its pulpit committee; subscriber to JE's books.

Henchman, Daniel, Maj. (1725–1775), Boston printer, friend of JE.

Hendrick (Tiyanoga or Aromateka, c. 1680–1755); spokesman for Mohawks; sympathetic to English; met with JE in Stockbridge on education of Mohawks; member, Albany Conference, 1754; d. at battle of Lake George, Sept. 8, 1755.

Herring, Thomas, Archbishop of Canterbury (1693–1757), Cambridge, 1713; D.D., 1724; Abp., 1747–57; religiously tolerant.

Henry, Robert, Rev., Presbyterian; settled Charlotte, Virginia, 1755–66; Mecklenburg, North Carolina, 1766–67.

Hervey, James, Rev. (1714–1758), Oxford, 1776; English curate; popular devotional writer.

Hinds, Phinehas, Stockbridge resident; assisted JE in buying sheep.

Hinsdale, Ebenezer, Col. (1706–1763), Harvard, 1727; ordained as Indian missionary, 1733; Massachusetts House of Representatives, 1740; Deerfield, Massachusetts, deputy to General Court, 1750–52; commissioned, 1749.

Hobby, William, Rev. (1707–1765), Harvard, 1728; settled Reading (Wakefield), Massachusetts, 1733–64; defender of JE, Whitefield, and revival; sat on councils of 1750 and 1751.

Hogg, William, Mr. (d. 1766), Scottish merchant; Edinburgh town councilman, treasurer, and burgess; board member, SSPCK; patron of JE.

Hollis, Isaac, Rev. (1700–1774), resident of High-Wycombe, England; wealthy dissenter and philanthropist; chief patron of Stockbridge mission.

Holyoke, Edward, Pres. (1689–1769), Harvard, 1705; settled Marblehead, Massachusetts, 1716–37; president, Harvard College, 1737–69.

Hooker, John, Rev. (1729–1777), Yale, 1751; settled Northampton, Massachusetts, 1753–77.

Hopkins, Esther Edwards (1695–1766), eldest sister of JE, wife of Samuel Hopkins of West Springfield, Massachusetts; critical of JE's views on revival.

Hopkins, Samuel, Rev. (1693–1755), Yale, 1718; settled West Springfield, Massachusetts, 1720–55; co-founder of Stockbridge mission; moderate on revivals; co-wrote *Letter* with JE on Breck affair.

Hopkins, Samuel, Dr. (1721–1803), Yale, 1741; D.D., Brown, 1790; settled Great Barrington, Massachusetts, 1743–69, Newport, Rhode Island, 1770–76, 1780–1803; student of JE; New Divinity theologian; sat on 1758 council.

Hopkins, Samuel, Rev. (1729–1811), Yale, 1749; D.D., 1802; settled Hadley, Massachusetts, 1754–1809; son of Samuel and Esther Hopkins of West Springfield.

Horton, Azariah, Rev. (1715–1777), Yale, 1735; Indian missionary; settled Madison, New Jersey, 1741–52, Hanover, New Jersey, 1752–76.

Hosmer, Stephen, Capt. (1709–1782), Stockbridge militia officer.

Housatonic Indians (see Stockbridge Indians).

Hubbard, Jonathan, Rev. (1703–1765), Yale, 1724; settled Eastbury, Connecticut, 1731–33; Sheffield, Massachusetts, 1735–65; moderator of 1750 council.

Hubbard, Thomas, Speaker (1702–1773), Harvard, 1721; Boston merchant, land invester; Massachusetts House of Representatives; Speaker, 1750–59.

Hutcheson, Frances (1694–1746), Scottish philosopher and minister; professor, Glasgow Univ.; JE opposed his views in *Nature of True Virtue*.

Hyslop, William (b. 1714), Boston merchant, friend of JE; m. Mehitable Stoddard.

Ingersoll, Thomas, Capt., original proprietor of Sheffield, Connecticut, 1733.

Iroquois (Five Nations or Six Nations), Amerindian confederacy centered in New York, consisting of Cayuga, Mohawk, Oneida, Onondaga, Seneca, and later, Tuscarora.

John (see Wauwaumpequunnaunt).

Johnson, Samuel, Pres. (1696–1772), Yale, 1714; D.D., Oxford, 1743; tutor, 1716–19; settled West Haven (Orange), Connecticut, 1719–22; Episcopalian missionary, Stratford, Connecticut, 1724–54, 1764–72; president, King's College, 1754–63.

Johnson, William, Sir (1715–1774), superintendent of Indian affairs for Six Nations; regimental commander; defeated French at the battle of Lake George; advised JE on Indians at Albany, 1751.

Jones, Elisha, Weston, Massachusetts, resident.

Jones, Josiah (1701–1769); head of one of original Stockbridge English families; uncle of Abigail Williams Sergeant Dwight; at first opposed JE; later supported him.

Judd, Jonathan, Rev. (1719–1803), Yale, 1741; settled Southampton, Massachusetts, 1743–1803; ordination sermon by JE.

Kames, Henry Home, Lord (1696–1782), Scottish judge and philosopher; opposed by JE on view of will.

Kellogg, Joseph, Capt. (1691–1755), Indian interpreter; arranged treaty with Indians.

Kellogg, Martin, Capt. (1686–1753), Deerfield captive, 1704; Indian interpreter; schoolmaster of Indian school at time of JE's appointment.

Kennedy, Samuel (1720–1787), b. Scotland; College of New Jersey, 1754; Presbyterian; settled Basking Ridge (Somerset), New Jersey, 1751–87.

Kennedy, Hugh K., Rev. (1698–1764), D.D., Aberdeen, 1763; co-pastor of Scottish church in Rotterdam, Netherlands; revivalist.

King of England (see George II).

King of France (see Louis XV).

Kneeland, Samuel (1697–1769), Boston printer and publisher.

Konkapot, John, Capt. (Concopet, Popnehonuhwoh, c. 1700–c.1775), spokesman for Stockbridge Indians; supporter of mission and schools; given honorary title of "Captain" by English.

Leavenworth, Mark, Rev. (c. 1711–1797), Yale, 1737; settled Waterbury, Connecticut, 1740–97; pro-revival; invited to 1758 council.

Leavitt, Joshua, Capt., Suffield, Connecticut, resident; subscribed to JE's books.

Lewis, Thomas, Rev. (1716–1777), Yale, 1741; settled Bethlehem (Hunterdon County), New Jersey, 1747–54; also Kingswood, Oxford, and Hopewell, New Jersey; JE reported revivals at his churches.

London, Bishop of (see Gibson, Edmund; Sherlock, Thomas).

Louis XV (1710–1774), King of France.

Lowman, Moses, Rev. (1680–1752), ed. Holland; English non-conforming minister and theologian; JE commented on his views on apocalypse.

Lydius, John Henry, Capt. (1693–1791), trader with Indians, agent for Massachusetts in dealings with Mohawks.

Lyman, Isaac, Rev. (1725–1810), Yale, 1727; settled York, Maine, 1749–1810; student of JE.

Lyman, Moses, Deac. (1713–1768), b. Northampton, moved to Goshen, Connecticut, 1739; magistrate; Connecticut General Court.

Lyman, Phinehas (1716–1774), Suffield, Connecticut, resident; General Assembly; commander-in-chief of Connecticut forces in Crown Point campaign.

Lyman, Simeon, resident of Salisbury, Connecticut.

Lyttelton, George (1709–1773), M.P., Commons, 1735–54; Lords, 1756–73; politician and author; strong religious convictions.

Mackay, George, third Baron Reay (d. 1748), father-in-law of Rev. John Erskine.

MacLaurin, John, Rev. (1693–1754), Glasgow, 1712; settled Luss, Scotland, 1719–23; St. David's, Glasgow, 1723–54; theologian; correspondent of JE; initiated Concert for Prayer.

McCulloch, William, Rev. (1691–1771), Glasgow, 1712; settled Cambuslang, Scotland, 1731–71; oversaw revival, 1742; correspondent of JE.

McGregore, David, Rev. (1710–1777), M.A., College of New Jersey, 1764; Presbyerian; settled Londonderry (West or Second Church), New Hampshire, 1736–77; pro-revival.

Macklin, Elizabeth (d. 1760), Northampton resident; mother of John Macklin, who was implicated in Bad Book affair.

Mahican (River Indians), originally extended from Lake Champlain to Dutchess County, New York; Stockbridge became later center.

Manumaseet, Ebenezer, one of JE's Indian interpreters at Stockbridge.

Mather, Eleazar, Rev. (1637–1669), Harvard, 1656; settled Northampton, Massachusetts, 1658–69.

Mather, Samuel, Dr. (1706–1779), Yale, 1726; moved to Northampton, 1729; physician; justice of the peace; town clerk.

Mather, Samuel, Dr. (1706–1785), Harvard, 1723; S.T.D., 1773; M.A., Yale, 1725; settled Second Church, Boston, 1732–41; Tenth Cong. Society, Boston, 1742–85.

Mauduit, Jasper, Mr. (d. 1772), London draper; chair, Comm. of Deputies for Dissenters; governor, NEC, 1741–72; treasurer, 1748–65; London provincial agent for Massachusetts, 1762–65.

Miami Indians (Tooweehtoowees, Twightwees), mid-western Indian nation; important for access to Ohio and Mississippi river valleys.

Mills, Jedediah, Rev. (1697–1776), Yale, 1722; settled Stratford, Connecticut, 1753–76; New Light; friend of David Brainerd.

Mix, Elisha, Rev. (1705–1739), Yale, 1724; son of Stephen; cousin of JE and roommate at Yale.

Mix, Stephen, Rev. (1672–1738), Harvard, 1690; settled Wethersfield, Connecticut, 1694–1738; uncle of JE.

Mohawks, the easternmost nation of Iroquois, located from Canada south along Hudson and Mohawk rivers; first brought to Stockbridge by John Sergeant.

Moody, Joseph, Rev. (1700–1753), Harvard, 1718; schoolmaster, county treasurer, justice of the peace, judge; settled York, Maine, 1732–41.

Moody, Samuel, Rev. (1676–1747), Harvard, 1697; settled York, Maine, 1698–1747; moderate on revivals; welcomed Whitefield.

Morris, Robert Hunter, Justice (c. 1700–1764); Chief Justice for the Province of New Jersey, 1738–54, 1756–64; Governor of Pennsylvania, 1754–56.

Munson, Amos (1719–1748), Yale, 1738; licensed to preach, 1740; Washington, Connecticut, resident; JE consulted on candidacy for West Suffield, Connecticut, pulpit.

Nelson, John, Dr., Suffield, Connecticut, resident.

Nicholas (Etaw Oh Koam), Mahican chief; visited London, 1710;

resided in Stockbridge at times; sympathetic to Indian mission and JE.

Noyes, Joseph, Rev. (1688–1761), Yale, 1709; tutor, 1710–15; settled New Haven, Connecticut, 1715–61; Old Light; m. Abigail Pierpont (d. 1768), half-sister of JE's wife; hosted JE's daughters.

Oliver, Andrew, Lieut. Governor (1706–1774), Harvard, 1723; M.A., College of New Jersey, 1772; merchant, importer; sec.-treasurer, Commissioners for Indian Affairs (Massachusetts), 1741–74; justice of the peace; Massachusetts Council; Sec. of Province, 1756–71; Lieut. Governor, 1771–74; friend of JE.

Oneida (Oneiyuta), one of the original five Iroquois nations; located from Lake Oneida to upper Susquehannah River valley.

Onohquaga (Oquaga, Onohohoquauge, Aughquagas), a Mohawk tribe located on Susquehannah River; visited by Gideon Hawley and the Benjamin Ashleys; friendly to English and JE; brought children to Stockbridge for schooling.

Onondaga (Onoontagaes), one of the Five Nations; located between Lake Cazenovia and Lake Skaneatles, New York, from Ontario on north to the upper Susquehannah River on south.

Osborn, Joseph, Deac. (1705–1786), member of the East Hampton, New York, Presbyterian church, where Rev. Samuel Buell was minister.

Osborn, Hannah Hedges (1708–1775), wife of Joseph Osborn.

Paice, Joseph (c. 1728–1810), English merchant; director, South Sea Company.

Parkman, Ebenezer, Rev. (1703–1782), Harvard, 1721; settled Westborough, Massachusetts, 1724–82; diarist; frequently hosted JE and family members.

Parkman, Hannah Breck (1716–1801), second wife of Ebenezer Parkman, m. 1737.

Parsons, Sarah (Sally) Edwards (1728–1805), eldest daughter of JE; she and husband, Elihu Spencer, moved to Stockbridge in 1752; later, to Goshen, Connecticut.

Partridge, Oliver, Col. (1712–1792), Yale, 1730; Hatfield, Massachusetts, lawyer; judge; House of Representatives, 1741–47, 1761, 1765–67; attended Albany Conference, 1754; commander of western Massachusetts militia, 1757; sat on 1750 council.

Pearsall, Richard, Rev. (1698–1762), English Independent minister (Taunton) and writer.

Pemberton, Ebenezer, Rev. (1705–1777), Harvard, 1721; D.D., College of New Jersey, 1770; Presbyterian; settled New York, New York, 1727–53; New Brick, Boston, 1754–77; American Commissioners of SSPCK, 1756–77; and president.

Pepperrell, Mary Hirst, Lady (b. 1689), wife of Sir William Pepperrell; friend of JE.

Pepperrell, William, Sir (1696–1759), merchant; Massachusetts House of Representatives, 1726; Council, 1727; commander of Maine militia; Massachusetts chief justice, 1730; commander, Louisburg campaign, 1744–45; JE visited and corresponded with him.

Phelps, Charles, Esq., b. Northampton; mason; self-educated lawyer; moved to Hadley, Massachusetts, between 1743 and 1746; justice of the peace; subscriber to *Life of David Brainerd* and *Original Sin.*

Phelps, Miriam Austen (c. 1711–1787), wife of Ebenezer Phelps, neighbor of JE in Northampton.

Phips, Spencer (1685–1757), Harvard, 1703; Lieut. Governor of Massachusetts, 1732–57; Commissioner, 1733–57.

Pierpont, James, Rev. (1660–1714), Harvard, 1681; settled New Haven, Connecticut, 1684–1714; founder of Yale College; father-in-law of JE.

Pierpont, James, Jr. (1699–1776), Yale, 1718; tutor, 1722–24; Boston apothecary, 1724–c. 1736, then resided in New Haven, Connecticut; JE's brother-in-law; New Light; hosted Whitefield on first visit; led establishment of Separate Church of New Haven, 1742.

Pitkin, Timothy, Rev. (1727–1812), Yale, 1747; tutor, 1750–51; settled Farmington, Connecticut, 1752–1812; invited to 1758 council.

Pitkin, William, Lieut. Governor of Connecticut, 1754–66.

Pollock, Eunice Edwards (1743–1822), daughter of JE; m. (1) Thomas Pollock of North Carolina; (2) Robert Hunt of Elizabeth, New Jersey.

Pomeroy, Benjamin, Rev. (1704–1784), Yale, 1733; D.D., Dartmouth, 1774; m. sister of Eleazar Wheelock; settled Hebron, Connecticut, 1735–84.

Pomeroy, Ebenezer, Maj. (1669–1754), Northampton sheriff; leader of movement to have JE dismissed.

Pomeroy, Ebenezer, Jr. (1697–1774), Northampton deacon, 1739–74.

Pomeroy, John (1719–1760), Northampton artisan, asked to assist at Stockbridge.

Pomeroy, Seth, Maj. (1706–1777), Northampton blacksmith; leader of Louisburg campaign; moderator of meetings leading to JE's dismissal; instrumental in Crown Point campaign; died in Revolution.

Poohpoonuk, Ebenezer (Paupaumnuk), Stockbridge Indian, first convert baptized at mission; John Sergeant's interpreter.

Porter, Eleazar (b. c. 1698–1757), Hadley, Massachusetts, resident; Hampshire County magistrate.

Porter, Eleazar, Jr. (1728–1797), Yale, 1748; Hadley, Massachusetts, lawyer; judge; m. JE's daughter Susanna.

Porter, Susanna Edwards (1740–1803), youngest daughter of JE, wife of Eleazar Porter of Hadley, Massachusetts.

Potter, Francis, Rev. (1594–1678), English writer on Revelation; commented on by JE.

Potter, John (c. 1674–1747), Archbishop of Canterbury, 1737–47.

Potwine, John (1728–1785), East Hartford, Connecticut, resident; moved to East Windsor in 1770.

Pretender (see Stuart, Charles, Prince).

Prince, Deborah Denny (1699–1766), wife of Thomas Prince.

Prince, Deborah (1723–1744), daughter of Thomas Prince; friend of JE's family.

Prince, Mercy (1726–1752), daughter of Thomas Prince.

Prince, Sarah (Sally; 1728–1771), daughter of Thomas Prince; correspondent of Esther Edwards Burr.

Prince, Thomas, Sr., Rev. (1687–1758), Harvard, 1707; settled Old South, Boston, 1717–58; noted antiquarian; supported Whitefield and revival; friend and correspondent of JE; sat on 1751 council.

Prince, Thomas, Jr. (1722–1748), Harvard, 1740; publisher of *Christian History*, 1743–44; defender of revivals.

Prince & Princess of Wales (see Frederick, Prince).

Prince of Orange (see William IV).

Princess Amelia (1711–1786), daughter of George II.

Princess Caroline (1713–1757), daughter of George II.

Proper Mohawks (see Conneenchees).

Prudden, Esther Sherman (1713–1775), friend and correspondent of David Brainerd; wife of Job Prudden; sister-in-law of Joseph Bellamy.

Prudden, Job, Rev. (1715–1774), Yale, 1743; M.A., 1763; settled Milford, Connecticut (Separate), 1747–74.

Pynchon, John, Col. (1674–1742), clerk of court; county register; member, Springfield, Massachusetts, church opposed to settlement of Breck, 1735.

Pynchon, Joseph, Dr., Col. (1705–1765), Harvard, 1726; resident of Longmeadow, Brookfield, and Boston, Massachusetts; physician;

justice of the peace; judge; House of Representatives, 1744–47; Council, 1747–60; General Court committee for Stockbridge mission, but seldom visited.

Pynchon, William, Jr., Col. (m. 1721, d. 1741), resident, Springfield, Massachusetts; apprentice brazier; judge; commander of Hampshire County militia regiment; member, Springfield, Massachusetts, church opposed to settlement of Breck, 1735.

Quincy, Edmund, Judge (1681–1738), Harvard, 1699; resident, Braintree (Quincy), Massachusetts; selectman; member, House of Representatives, 1713–15; Massachusetts Council, 1715–30, 1731–38; superior court justice.

Quincy, Edmund, Squire (1703–1788), Harvard, 1722; Boston merchant; imported books for JE.

Rand, William, Rev. (1700–1779), Harvard, 1721; settled Sunderland, Massachusetts, 1722–45, Kingston, Rhode Island, 1746–79; Old Light; favored settlement of Breck, 1735; opposed Whitefield.

Randall, Thomas, Rev. (1711–1780), M.A., Edinburgh, 1720; Scottish minister; settled Inchture and Rossie, 1739–70; Stirling, 1770–90.

Rawson, Grindall, Rev. (1707–1777), Harvard, 1728; settled South Hadley, Massachusetts, 1733–41; Old Light; two councils of ministers, 1737 and 1741 (JE scribe at both), voted to approve him, but church still dismissed; settled Haddam and Lyme, Connecticut, 1745–77.

Read, John, Rev. (1680–1749), Harvard, 1697; settled Waterbury, Connecticut, 1698–99; East Hartford, Connecticut, 1699–1702; Windsor, Connecticut, 1703–1706; Boston lawyer; Massachusetts of Representatives, 1738; Council, 1741–42.

Read, Israel, Rev. (1718–1793), College of New Jersey, 1748; trustee, 1750–93; Presbyterian; settled Bound Brook (Somerset), New Jersey, 1750–93.

Reeve, Tapping, Hon. (1744–1823), Princeton, 1763; L.L.D., Middlebury, 1808, College of New Jersey, 1813; founded law school, Litchfield, Connecticut; Chief Justice of Connecticut; m. Sarah Burr, granddaughter of JE.

Reynolds, Peter, Rev. (1700–1768), Harvard, 1719; settled Enfield, Connecticut; pro-revival; sat on councils of 1750 and 1758.

Richardson, Andrew, Rev. (d. 1790), Scottish minister; settled Inverkeithing and Rosyth, 1735–49.

River Indians (see Mahicans).

Robbins, Philemon, Rev. (1709–1781), Harvard, 1729; settled Branford, Connecticut, 1733–81; teacher, 1729–30; New Light.

Robe, James, Rev. (1688–1753), ed. Glasgow; Scottish Presbyterian; settled Kilsyth, 1713–53; revivalist.

Robinson, William, Rev. (c. 1700–1746), ed. Log College; teacher, Hopewell, New Jersey, 1729–39; itinerant in middle colonies, 1740–46.

Rodgers, John, Rev. (1727–1811), ed. Faggs Manor, with Samuel Blair and Gilbert Tennent; worked with William Robinson in Maryland and Samuel Davies in Virginia.

Rogers, John, Sr., Rev. (1666–1745), Harvard, 1684; settled Ipswich, Massachusetts, 1688–1745; pro-revival.

Rogers, John, Jr., Rev. (1692–1773), Harvard, 1711; librarian, 1714–18; settled Kittery (Eliot), Maine, 1721–73; New Light.

Rogers, John, Rev. (1719–1782), Harvard, 1739; settled Gloucester (Fourth Parish), Massachusetts; New Light.

Root, Hannah (b. c. 1731), Northampton resident; assisted Edwards family, possibly as servant.

Root, Simeon (1718–1752), cited in Bad Book episode, brother of Hannah Root.

Root, Timothy (b. 1718), cousin of Simeon Root; cited in Bad Book episode.

Rose, slave of JE at Stockbridge; m. Joab, 1756.

Russell, Samuel, Rev. (1660–1731), Harvard, 1681; settled Branford, Connecticut, 1687–1731; founder and trustee of Yale College.

Russell, William, Rev. (1690–1761), Yale, 1709; tutor, 1713–14; settled Middletown, Connecticut, 1715–61; Old Light; m. sister-in-law of JE.

Sackett, Samuel, Rev. (d. 1784), Presbyterian; served various churches in New York; in 1751, at Bedford (Westchester), New York.

Searle, John, Rev. (1721–1787), Yale, 1745; settled Stoneham, Massachusetts, 1759–76; Royalton, Vermont, 1783–87; student of JE.

Secker, Thomas, Archbishop (1693–1768), Archbishop of Canterbury, 1758–68.

Seneca (Chamnloowanee), one of the original Five Nations of the Iroquois; largest, most powerful, and westernmost of the tribes.

Sergeant, Abigail (see Dwight, Abigail Williams Sergeant).

Sergeant, John, Rev. (1710–1749), Yale, 1729; tutor, 1731–35; missionary, Great Barrington and Stockbridge, 1735–49.

Sergeant, Jonathan (b. c. 1712), resident of Newark, New Jersey; treasurer, College of New Jersey, 1750–77.

Sewall, Joseph, Rev. (1688–1769), Harvard, 1707; S.T.D., Glasgow, 1731; settled Old South, Boston, 1713–69; New Light; commissioner, NEC.

Seward, William (1702–1740), English business manager for George Whitefield.

Shaftesbury, Lord (see Cooper, Anthony A.).

Sheldon, Benjamin, Captain of Northampton third militia company during French and Indian War; supporter of JE.

Sheldon, Jonathan, Capt. (1687–1769), Northampton resident, removed to Suffield, Connecticut, c. 1723; relayed mail for JE.

Sherlock, Thomas, Bishop (1678–1761), Bishop of London, 1748–61.

Shirley, William, Governor (1694–1771), b. England; Cambridge, 1715; arrived Boston, Massachusetts, 1731; judge, admiralty, 1733; advocate general; Governor of Massachusetts, 1741–56.

Singing teacher (see Beale, George and Wilson, Mr.).

Six Nations (see Iroquois).

Smith, Caleb, Rev. (1723–1762), Yale, 1743; settled Newark Mountain, New Jersey, 1748–62; trustee, College of New Jersey, 1750–62; president pro tem, 1758; sat on 1758 council.

Smith, Cotton Mather, Rev. (1731–1806), Yale, 1751; teacher, Stockbridge, 1753; settled Sharon, Connecticut, 1755–1806.

Smith, Jedediah, Rev. (1727–1776), Yale, 1750; settled Granville, Massachusetts, 1756–76; praised by JE but dismissed by Edwardseans in church.

Smith, John, Rev. (1702–1771), Yale, 1727; Presbyterian; met JE during New York pastorate, 1722–23; life-long friend; practiced medicine; settled Rye, New York, 1742–71.

Smith, Susanna Odell, wife of John Smith.

Smith, William, Hon. (1697–1769), b. England; Yale, 1719; tutor, 1722–24; lawyer, New York; Attorney General, Province of New York, 1751–69; judge, Superior Court of New York; trustee, College of New Jersey, 1746–69.

Spencer, Elihu, Rev. (1721–1784), Yale, 1746; D.D., U. Pennsylvania, 1782; missionary, 1748–49; settled Elizabeth, New Jersey, 1750–56; ministered at various churches in middle colonies and North Carolina, 1759–84; trustee, College of New Jersey, 1752–84.

Stadtholder (see William IV).

Stebbins, Benjamin, Cpl., served at Stockbridge, quartered at JE's house.

Stebbins, Thomas (1687–1758), prominent leader of Springfield, Massachusetts; sat on 1750 council.

Stiles, Ezra, Pres. (1727–1795), Yale, 1746; D.D., Edinburgh, 1765; declined position of Stockbridge missionary, 1749; Yale tutor, 1749–55; settled Newport, Rhode Island, 1755–76; Portsmouth, New Hampshire, 1777–78; president, Yale, 1778–95.

Stiles, Isaac, Rev. (1697–1760), Yale, 1722; prepared for college by Timothy Edwards; settled New Haven (North Haven), Connecticut, 1725–60; Old Light; JE convalesced at his home, Sept.-Dec., 1725.

Stockbridge Indians (Housatonic Indians), Mahicans centered at Stockbridge.

Stockton, Richard, Esq. (1730–1781), Princeton, 1748; lawyer; trustee, College of New Jersey, 1757–81; clerk, 1757–65; signer of Declaration of Independence.

Stoddard, Anthony (1678–1760), Harvard, 1697; settled Woodbury, Connecticut, 1700–60; judge; uncle of JE; invited to 1758 council.

Stoddard, Anthony II (1678–1748), Harvard, 1697; Boston merchant, constable, justice of the peace; judge; Secretary of Commissioners, NEC, 1733–48; frequently hosted JE and family members.

Stoddard, Esther Warham Mather (1644–1736), wife of Solomon Stoddard, grandmother of JE.

Stoddard, John, Col. (1682–1748), Harvard, 1701; M.A., 1715; Northampton merchant, leading figure in town and church; judge; Massachusetts House of Representatives; Council, 1727–39; uncle and supporter of JE.

Stoddard, Madam, prob. Prudence Chester Stoddard (1699–1780), widow of Col. John Stoddard.

Stoddard, Solomon, Rev. (1643–1729), Harvard, 1662; tutor, librarian, 1666–72; settled Northampton, 1672–1729; leading minister in Connecticut Valley; influential writer; revivalist; grandfather of JE.

Strong, Job, Rev. (1721–1751), Yale, 1747; Indian missionary, New Jersey, New York, 1747–49; settled Portsmouth, New Hampshire, 1749–51; ordination sermon by JE.

Strong, Thomas, Rev. (1715–1777), Yale, 1740; settled New Marlborough, Massachusetts, 1744–77.

Stuart, Charles, Prince (1720–1788), "The Young Pretender," elder son of "The Old Pretender" (James III, 1688–1766); led unsuccessful campaign in Great Britain to regain throne, 1744–45; fled to France.

Taylor, John (1694–1761), D.D., Glasgow, 1756; English theological writer; JE replied to his views in *Original Sin.*

Taylor, John (b. 1717), head of one of the original English families of Stockbridge; active in Berkshire County affairs.

Tennent, Gilbert, Rev. (1703–1764), b. Ireland; M.A., Yale, 1725; Presbyterian; settled New Brunswick, New Jersey, 1726–43; Philadelphia, 1743–64; trustee, College of New Jersey, 1746–64; famous revivalist.

Tennent, William, Sr., Rev. (1673–1746), b. Ireland; Presbyterian; settled Bensalem, Pennsylvania, 1721–26; Neshaminy, Pennsylvania, 1726–45; revivalist; founder of Log College.

Tennent, William, Jr., Rev. (1705–1777), ed. Log College; Presbyterian; settled Freehold, New Jersey, 1732–77; Kingston (Franklin), New Jersey, 1750; pro-revival.

Todd, John, Rev. (1719–1793), b. Ireland; College of New Jersey, 1750; Presbyterian; ministered to churches in Virginia, 1750–92, mainly Providence (Louisa), Virginia, 1752–93; interviewed by JE.

Tonaughquunnaugus, Jonah, an Onohquaga Indian.

Treat, Richard, Rev. (1708–1778), Yale, 1725; D.D., College of New Jersey, 1776; trustee, 1746–78; settled Abington, Pennsylvania, 1731–76; revivalist.

Turnbull, George, Prof. (c. 1562–1633), Scottish Jesuit; theological author; works read by JE.

Turretin, Francis (1623–1687), Protestant academic, based in Geneva; theological author; greatly admired by JE.

Tuscarora or Tuscaroras, Amerindian nation, originally of North Carolina, later of New York and Ontario; accepted as the sixth Iroquois nation.

Umpachanee, Chief (Aupauchinau), Stockbridge Indian; received military commission from English; his son visited John Sergeant at Yale College; friendly to English.

Van Valkenburgh, Jehoiakim (1692–c.1768), Dutch trader with the Indians at Stockbridge.

Verbryck, Samuel, Rev. (1721–1784), Dutch Reformed; settled Tappan and Clarkstown (Rockland), New York, 1750–84.

Wait, Thomas (d. 1755), Northampton resident; appealed fornication charges against him to council of churches, 1746.

Walley, John, Rev. (1716–1784), Harvard, 1734; settled Ipswich, Massachusetts, 1747–64; Bolton, Massachusetts, 1773–83; invited to 1751 council.

Warner, Oliver (b. 1723), apprentice hatmaker; accused in Bad Book episode, 1744.

Warren, Peter, Sir (1703–1752), English Vice-Admiral; gave large sum towards Indian education at Stockbridge.

Watts, Isaac, Rev. (1674–1748), English dissenting theologian, hymn-writer; sponsored London publication of *Faithful Narrative*.

Waumpanngeauss (Waumpongkoss, Waumpaucorse), Indian murdered at Stockbridge, 1753; exoneration of white suspects caused resentment among Indians.

Waunaubauquus (Waunaupaugus), uncle of Waumpanngeauss, killed in Stockbridge, 1753; granted indemnity by Massachusetts General Court.

Wauwaumpequunnaunt, John (Wonwanonpequunnonnt), a Stockbridge Indian, instructed in English by Stephen Williams and John Sergeant; interpreter for David Brainerd and JE.

Webb, John, Rev. (1687–1750), settled North Church, Boston, 1714–50; New Light; signed prefaces to *Faithful Narrative* and *Humble Inquiry*.

Wendell, Jacob (1715–1753), Harvard, 1733; Boston merchant; member, Brattle Street Church; friend and correspondent of JE.

Wesley, John (1703–1791), Oxford, 1724; English founder of Methodism; thought highly of JE; reprinted some of his works.

West, Gilbert (1703–1756), Oxford, 1725; D.C.L., 1748; English author, converted from deism; became Clerk of Privy Council, 1752.

West, Stephen, Rev. (1735–1819), Yale, 1755; D.D., Dartmouth, 1792; m. Elizabeth, daughter of Ephraim Williams, Sr.; settled Stockbridge missionary, 1758–75; New Divinity theologian, teacher; author; defender of JE; trustee, vice president, Williams College, 1793–1812.

Wetmore, Hannah Edwards (1713–1773), sister of JE; courted by John Sergeant; m. Seth Wetmore, 1746.

Wetmore, Seth, Judge (1700–1778), Middletown, Connecticut, lawyer; General Court of Connecticut, 1738–71; m. Hannah Edwards, sister of JE.

Wheelock, Eleazar, Pres. (1711–1779), Yale, 1733; D.D., Edinburgh, 1767; settled Lebanon (The Crank), Connecticut, 1735–70; founder, Indian Charity School; and Dartmouth College, 1769; New Light revivalist; friend and correspondent of JE.

Whitby, Daniel, Dr. (1638–1726), Oxford, 1657; theological writer, critical of Calvinism; JE opposed his views in *Freedom of the Will*.

White, Thomas, Rev. (1701–1763), Yale, 1720; Northampton teacher, 1721–24; settled Bolton, Connecticut, 1725–63; reported revival news to JE.

Whitefield, George, Rev. (1714–1770), Oxford, 1736; ordained, Church of England, 1739; internationally renowned itinerant evangelist; made two visits to Northampton.

Whitman, Elnathan, Rev. (1709–1777), Yale, 1726; tutor, 1728–32; settled Hartford, Connecticut, 1732–77; cousin of JE.

Whittelsey, Samuel, Sr., Rev. (1686–1752), Yale, 1705; settled Wallingford, Connecticut, 1710–52; Old Light.

Whittelsey, Samuel, Jr. (1713–1768), Yale, 1729; tutor, 1734–37; settled Milford, Connecticut, 1738–68; Old Light.

Wigglesworth, Edward, Dr. (c. 1693–1765), Harvard, 1710; D.D., Edinburgh, 1730; Hollis Professor of Theology, Harvard, 1722–65; opposed Whitefield; commissioner, NEC, 1725–55.

Wigglesworth, Samuel, Rev. (1689–1768), Harvard, 1707; physician; settled Ipswich (Hamilton), Massachusetts, 1714–68; New Light.

Willard, Josiah, Sec. (1681–1756), Harvard, 1698; tutor, 1703–06; mariner, 1706–15; Sec., Province of Massachusetts, 1717–56; judge, 1728–45; Council, 1734–56; supporter of Whitefield and JE; commissioner, NEC, 1745–56.

William IV, (Prince of Orange; d. 1751), Stadtholder, 1747–51; son-in-law of George II; failed to restore strength and unity of Netherlands under the house of Orange.

Williams, Abigail (see Dwight, Abigail Williams Sergeant).

Williams, Abigail Jones (1694–1784), resident of Stockbridge, second wife of Col. Ephraim Williams, Sr.; step-mother of Col. Ephraim Williams, Jr.; mother of Abigail Williams Sergeant Dwight.

Williams, Chester, Rev. (1718–1753), Yale, 1735; tutor, 1738–40; settled Hadley, Massachusetts, 1740–53; sat on 1750 council.

Williams, Ebenezer, Rev. (1690–1753), Harvard, 1709; settled Pomfret, Connecticut, 1750–53; involved in controversy between Thomas Clap and JE over Whitefield, 1744–45.

Williams, Elijah, Col. (1732–1815), College of New Jersey, 1753; M.A., 1760; son of Ephraim Williams, Sr.; Stockbridge iron manufacturer, merchant, public officer.

Williams, Elisha, Rector (1694–1755), Harvard, 1711; tutor, 1716–19; Connecticut House of Representatives, 1717–20; settled Newington, Connecticut, 1720–26; Yale rector, 1726–39; initially for revival, later against; merchant; appointed colonel, 1746; cousin and Wethersfield tutor of JE; his opponent at Northampton and Stockbridge; assisted Solomon Williams in responding to *Humble Inquiry;* in London, 1749–52.

Williams, Elizabeth Scott (d. 1776), b. England; m. (1) Col. Elisha Williams, 1751; (2) Judge William Smith, 1761.

Williams, Ephraim, Sr., Col. (1691–1754), one of original English settlers of Stockbridge; merchant, land invester; opponent of JE.

Williams, Ephraim, Jr., Capt. (1715–1755), commander, northern boundary of Massachusetts; prominent in Indian affairs; died in the battle of Lake George; legacy established Williams College.

Williams, Israel, Col. (1709–1789), Harvard, 1727; trader, judge; land invester; 17 terms, Massachusetts House of Representatives; active in militia; commanded defense of western New England; cousin and opponent of JE.

Williams, Judith (1728–1801), daughter of Ephraim Williams, Sr..

Williams, Solomon, Rev. (1700–1776), Harvard, 1719; D.D., Yale, 1773; settled Lebanon, Connecticut, 1722–76; responded to *Humble Inquiry;* cousin of JE.

Williams, Stephen, Rev. (1693–1782), Harvard, 1713; D.D., Dartmouth, 1773; Deerfield captive, 1704; settled Longmeadow, Massachusetts, 1714–82; a founder of Stockbridge mission, 1734; chaplain, Louisburg campaign, 1745; diarist; cousin of JE.

Williams, William, Rev. (1665–1741), Harvard, 1683; settled Hatfield, Massachusetts, 1685–1741; opposed settlement of Breck, 1735; opposed Whitefield; most influential minister in Hampshire County after death of Solomon Stoddard; uncle of JE.

Willison, John, Rev. (1680–1750), ed. Glasgow; settled Brechin, Scotland, 1703–16; Dundee, 1716–50; interested in revivals; church invaded in Jacobite Rebellion.

Wilson, Mr., singing teacher.

Winslow, John, Gen. (1703–1774), British military commander.

Wolcott, Roger, Major (1679–1767), East Windsor, Connecticut, resident; lawyer; justice of the peace; Chief Justice; militia commander, Louisburg campaign, 1745; Governor of Connecticut, 1751–54.

Woodbridge, Jahleel, Esq. (c. 1738–1796), College of New Jersey, 1761; Stockbridge resident; militia captain; judge; Massachusetts Council, 1780–84; m. Lucy Edwards, daughter of JE.

Woodbridge, Lucy Edwards, (1736–1786), wife of Jahleel Wood-bridge, daughter of JE.

Woodbridge, Timothy, Rev. (1656–1732), b. England; Harvard, 1675; settled Kittery, Maine, 1680–82, Hartford, Connecticut, 1683–1732; founder and trustee, Yale College, 1700–32.

Woodbridge, Timothy, Deac. (1709–1774), first English resident of Stockbridge; schoolmaster; magistrate; judge; land investor; agent and member of Susquehannah Company; staunch friend of JE.

Woodbridge, Timothy, Rev. (1713–1770), Yale, 1732; tutor, 1737–39; settled Hatfield, Massachusetts, 1739–70; sat on 1750 council.

Wooster, David, m. Mary Clap, daughter of Thomas Clap, 1746; war hero.

Worthington, John, Col. (1679–1744), member of the Springfield, Massachusetts, church; opposed settlement of Breck.

Wright, Asa (1710–1760), member of Northampton church; hosted ministers, 1747.

Wright, John, Rev. (d. after 1763), b. Scotland; College of New Jersey, 1752; with JE at Stockbridge, 1752; introduced to Erskine; worked with Samuel Davies in Virginia; settled Farmville, Virginia, 1754–61.

Yorke, Philip, Earl of Hardwicke (1690–1764), English politician; Lord Chancellor.

APPENDIX B

FRAGMENTARY LETTERS BY JONATHAN EDWARDS

Several letters by Edwards are so fragmentary as to render them unpublishable within the guidelines set forth by this edition. The following list itemizes these fragments for those who may wish to consult them.

Jonathan Edwards Collection, Beinecke Library:

Date	*Recipient*	*Location*
Aug. 29, 1749	Bromfield, Edward	Box 3, f. 204
Oct. 28, 1745	Woodbridge, Timothy, of Hatfield	Box 12, f. 901
No date	Foxcroft, Thomas	Box 22, f. 1305

No date   Foxcroft, Thomas   Box 22, f. 1306
(c.1754–55)

Jonathan Edwards Papers, Trask Library:

Date	*Recipient*	*Location*
No date	Edwards, Esther	ND f. 1, 3
No date	Unknown (Stockbridge era)	ND f. 1, 12.2, 12.3
No date	Unknown (Stockbridge era)	ND f. 2, 5
No date	Unknown	ND f. 2, 13.2
No date	Unknown (Stockbridge era)	ND f. 5, 1

APPENDIX C

LETTERS RECEIVED BY JONATHAN EDWARDS

The following is a list of all extant letters known to have been received by Edwards. As is evident in much of the correspondence written by Edwards himself, many other letters were sent to him. Only those listed below have been located.

Date	*Author*	*Location*
No date	Mather, Samuel	Beinecke Library
June 7, 1731	Perkins, Richard	Beinecke Library
Mar. 11, 1733	Parsons, Jr., David	Beinecke Library
Nov. 4, 1734	Bull, Nehemiah	Beinecke Library
Mar. 1741	Burr, Aaron	Trask Library
Dec. 1741	Parkman, Ebenezer	MHS
Feb. 15, 1742	Williams, Chester	Beinecke Library
Mar. 29, 1742	Woodbridge, Timothy	Trask Library
May 5, 1742	Edwards, Timothy	Extract only; *Some Thoughts* (*Works, 4,* 311)
May 6, 1742	Russell, William	Beinecke Library
Aug. 26, 1742	Bliss, Daniel[?]	Beinecke Library
Sept. 10, 1742	Hopkins, Samuel	Beinecke Library
[Oct.] 13, 1742	The "Covenanting Brethren" of Deerfield	Beinecke Library
Oct. 18, 1742	Stoddard, John	Beinecke Library
[Dec. 1742?]	Judd, Jonathan	Beinecke Library
Dec. 15, 1742	Judd, Jonathan	Beinecke Library

Mar. 17, 1743	Edwards, Sarah	Beinecke Library
Apr. 12, 1743	Lyman, Isaac	Beinecke Library
Apr. 19, 1743	Gay, Ebenezer	Beinecke Library
May 5, 1743	Hopkins, Samuel	Beinecke Library
July 2, 1743	Judd, Jonathan	Beinecke Library
Aug. 6, 1743	Parsons, David	Beinecke Library
Aug. 10, 1743	MacLaurin, John	Extract only; *Christian History* 1 (1743), 352–53
Aug. 13, 1743	McCulloch, William	*Christian History* 1 (1743), 361–63
Aug. 16, 1743	Robe, James	*Christian History* 1 (1743), 358–60; Dwight ed., *1*, 200–02
Oct. 26, 1743	Cooper, William	Trask Library
Nov. 15, 1743	Parsons, David	Beinecke Library
Jan. 1744	Williams, Chester (2 letters)	Beinecke Library
Feb. 8, 1744	Parsons, David	Trask Library
Feb. 28, 1744	Gray, William	Beinecke Library
May 2, 1744	Russell, William	Beinecke Library
June 25, 1744	Gray, William	Beinecke Library
Dec. 10, 1744	Clap, Thomas	Extract only; Thomas Clap, *Letter . . . to a Friend in Boston* (Boston, 1745)
Mar. 20, [1745?]	Williams, Stephen	Beinecke Library
Apr. 1, 1745	Clap, Thomas	Thomas Clap, *A Letter from the Rev. Mr. Clap . . . to the Rev. Mr. Edwards* (Boston, 1745)
Apr. 8, 1745	Doolittle, Benjamin	Beinecke Library
May 2, 1745	Williams, Chester	Beinecke Library
June 12, 1745	Strong, Thomas	Beinecke Library
Sept. 2, 1745	Judd, Jonathan	Beinecke Library
Sept. 25, 1745	Stevens, Thomas	Beinecke Library
Mar. 9, 1746	Wait, Thomas	Beinecke Library
Apr. 1, 1746	Pynchon, Joseph	Beinecke Library

May 6, 1746	Wadsworth, Daniel	Beinecke Library
June 23, 1746	Dwight, [Joseph]	Beinecke Library
Oct. 6, 1746	Woodbridge, John	Beinecke Library
Nov. 24, 1746	Gillespie, Thomas	Trask Library; Dwight ed., *1*, 224–30; *Edinburgh Quarterly Magazine* 1 (1798), 29–41; *Works*, 2, 470–77
Feb. 10, 1747	Unknown [Farmington, Connecticut]	Beinecke Library
Mar. 26, 1747	Williams, Chester	Beinecke Library
Apr. 5, 1747	Bellamy, Joseph	Beinecke Library
Oct. 5, 1747	Williams, Chester	Beinecke Library
Oct. 14, 1747	Williams, Chester	Beinecke Library
Oct. 30, 1747	Russell, William	Beinecke Library
Feb. 5, 1748	Belcher, Jonathan	Extract only; JE to the Rev. John Erskine, Oct. 14, 1748
Mar. 4, 1748	Brainerd, John	Extract only; JE to the Rev. William McCulloch, May 23, 1749
May 18, 1748	Hopkins, Samuel [of Springfield]	Beinecke Library
May 31, 1748	Belcher, Jonathan	Extract only; JE to the Rev. John Erskine, Oct. 14, 1748
June 29, 1748	Chapin, Thomas	Beinecke Library
Sept. 19, 1748	Gillespie, Thomas	Trask Library; Dwight ed., *1*, 252–61; *Edinburgh Quarterly Magazine* 1 (1798), 181–95; *Works*, 2, 490–500
[1749?]	Searle, John[?]	Beinecke Library
1749 [early?]	Rogers, John	Extract only; JE to the Rev. William Mc-

		Culloch, May 23, 1749
Mar. 17, 1749	Willison, John	Trask Library; Dwight ed., *1*, 270–73
Apr. 1, 1749	Davenport, James	Extract only; JE to the Rev. William McCulloch, May 23, 1749; and JE to the Rev. James Robe, May 23, 1749
June 26, 1749	Foxcroft, Thomas	Appendix to *Humble Inquiry*, in *Works*, *12*, 326–48
1750	Judd, Jonathan	Beinecke Library
Feb. 21, 1749/50	Parsons, David	Beinecke Library
Apr. 5, 1750	Williams, Stephen	Beinecke Library
May 21, 1750	Clark, Peter	Beinecke Library
June 2, 1750	Owen, John	Beinecke Library
June 4, 1750	Searle, John	HSF
June 11, 1750	Billing, Edward	Beinecke Library
Aug. 20, 1750	Williams, Solomon	Beinecke Library
Aug. 26, 1750	Davies, Samuel	Beinecke Library
Mar. 22, 1751	Ashley, Israel	Beinecke Library
Mar. 22, 1750/1	Ballantine, John	Beinecke Library
Apr. 26, 1751	Davenport, James	Extract only; JE to the Rev. John Erskine, June 28, 1751
May 17, 1751	Northampton Church Committee	Beinecke Library
July 10, 1751	Dwight, Timothy	Trask Library
Aug. 7, 1751	Pynchon, Joseph	Trask Library
Oct. 19, 1751	Willard, Josiah	MAR
Dec. 24, 1751	Williams, Ephraim	Beinecke Library
Mar. 11, 1752	Hopkins, Samuel	Trask Library
Apr. 27, 1752	Clap, Jonathan	Beinecke Library
May 8, 1752	Hopkins, Samuel	Trask Library
July 13, 1752	Burr, Aaron	Trask Library
Aug. 19, 1752	Williams, Elisha	RIHS

Apr. 19, 1753	Mauduit, Jasper	Alderman Library
May 2, 1753	Williams, Ephraim	RIHS
July 3, 1753	Dwight, Joseph[?]	RIHS
1753 [early fall]	Burr, Aaron	Trask Library
Sept. 23, 1753	Hollis, Isaac	MAR (extract only)
Dec. 19, 1753	Hazard, Nathaniel	MHS
Jan. 21, 1755	Hawley, Joseph	NYPL
Oct. 29, 1755	Wheelock, Eleazar	Baker Library
Mar. 30, 1756	Grant, Ebenezer	Beinecke Library
May 31, 1756	Bellamy, Joseph	Trask Library; Dwight ed., *1*, 555–56
Dec. 8, 1756	Belcher, Jonathan	New Jersey Historical Society
Dec. 27, 1756	Hawley, Gideon	Beinecke Library
Dec. 28, 1756	Hawley, Gideon	Beinecke Library
Feb. 12, 1757	Burr, Aaron	Extract only; Webster, p. 262
Sept. 29, 1757	Stockton, Richard	Beinecke Library
Nov. 2, 1757	Burr, Esther	Trask Library; Burr, pp. 295–97
Nov. 4, 1757	Stockton, Richard	Beinecke Library

GENERAL INDEX

In the following index, the abbreviation JE has been used for Jonathan Edwards. All works are by Edwards unless otherwise indicated.

Abercrombie, Robert, 224, 368; ordination of, 148; JE's letter to, 215–16
Abraham, 141, 330, 409–10
Adams, John, 490, 490*n*
Advice to Young Converts, 91
Affections, 117–18; natural, 97; religious, 126
Affliction, 147, 173–74, 245, 265, 337, 415, 418–20, 488, 550, 577, 609–10, 668, 675, 782
Africa, 73
African American school, 81*n*
Age of Reason, 742–43
Alexander the Great, 410
Allis, Samuel, 112
Alvord, Benjamin, 267
Andrew, Samuel, 37
Andrews, William, 583*n*
Angels, 183, 209, 610
Antichrist, 137–40, 219–20, 258. *See also* Satan
Apostles, acts of, 409
Appleton, Nathaniel, 78
Armageddon, 138
Arminianism, 50, 249, 266, 312, 312*n*, 348, 353, 357, 387, 484, 561, 625, 707, 727; JE's writings against, 265, 355, 591, 594, 596
Arnauld, Antoine, 33, 33*n*, 489*n*
Ashley, Benjamin, 396, 421–22, 468–69, 471, 473–74, 496, 498, 560, 565–66, 585, 595
Ashley, Israel, 403, 607
Ashley, John, 423, 506, 525, 530, 533
Ashley, Jonathan, 52, 112–13, 222, 301, 505, 554–55
Ashley, Joseph, 312*n*, 370
Ashley, Rebecca Kellogg, 474, 560, 566, 586, 595
Assembly of Pastors of Churches in New England, JE's letter to, 111–12
Associations, ministerial, 276–81, 324, 339–41

Assurance, God's, 109, 201, 330, 333–34
Astronomy (Gassendi), 33, 33*n*
Atonement, 735
Augustine, confessions of, 748
Authority, divine, 53, 225; civil and ecclesiastical, 114
Awakening, 116, 178, 225, 356, 377–78, 705. *See also* Revivals

Babel, 377
Babylon, 139, 410
Backsliding, 116, 135, 220, 227–29, 276, 335–36, 357, 381, 653
Backus, Eunice, 419–21, 421*n*
Backus, Simon, 205
"Bad Book" Affair, 14–15, 143
Ballantine, John, 100
Ballantyne, James, 662*n*
Baptism, 132–33, 283–84, 286, 342, 695, 756. *See also* Sacraments
Barclay, Henry, 583*n*
Barclay, Thomas, 583*n*
Baxter, Richard, 282, 301, 301*n*; on opposition to Cotton Mather, 286–87
Beach, John, 223, 223*n*
Beast (Revelations), 136–38, 140
Beauty, 180, 202; divine, 319
Behavior, 783
Belcher, Jonathan, 273, 365–66, 610, 656*n*, 703; on dedication of Brainerd described by JE, 242–44; disposition of, 261–63, 478; as president of Trustees of the College of New Jersey, 540
Bellamy, Joseph, 98, 210–11, 212, 216–17, 222–23, 235–36, 318, 320, 348, 348*n*, 349, 362–63, 366–68, 695, 695*n*, 700–701; and David Brainerd, 245–46, 266–67; on promoting *True Religion Delineated*, 287, 288, 288*n*; JE writes on his likely termination, 307–8; on discontinuing sacraments, 309; on JE's salary, 374–75; on education of Indians, 374–75, 541, 599–601; JE on attributes of,

INDEX OF BIBILICAL PASSAGES

851

NEW TESTAMENT